THE AGONY OF MODERNIZATION

BOOKS IN THE CORNELL INTERNATIONAL INDUSTRIAL AND LABOR RELATIONS SERIES

Cornell International Industrial and Labor Relations Report Number 16

THE AGONY OF MODERNIZATION

Labor and Industrialization in Spain

BENJAMIN MARTIN

ILR Press
School of Industrial and Labor Relations
Cornell University

Cover design by Kat Dalton
Cover photograph courtesy of the Library of Congress

Library of Congress Cataloging-in-Publication Data

Martin, Benjamin, 1917–
      The agony of modernization : labor and industrialization in Spain
  / Benjamin Martin.
          p.   cm.—(Cornell international industrial and labor
  relations report ; no. 16)
      Includes bibliographical references.
      ISBN 0-87546-165-4 (alk. paper)
      1. Labor movement—Spain—History—20th century.   2. Trade-unions—
  Spain—History—20th century.   3. Spain—Industries—History—20th
  century.   4. Labor policy—Spain—History—20th century.   I. Title.
  II. Series: Cornell international industrial and labor relations
  reports ; no. 16.
  HD8584.M28   1990
  331'.0946—dc20   89-77909
                                                                              CIP

Copies may be ordered through bookstores or from
ILR Press
School of Industrial and Labor Relations
Cornell University
Ithaca, NY   14851-0952

Printed in the United States of America
5 4 3 2 1

To the memory of my mother, Sophie

Publication of this book was supported in part by a grant from the Program for Cultural Cooperation between Spain's Ministry of Culture and United States Universities.

CONTENTS

TABLES AND FIGURES

ABBREVIATIONS

AIT	International Workingmen's Association
ASP	Popular Social Action
BOC	Workers and Peasants Bloc
CADCI	Autonomous Center of Commercial and Industrial Employees
CCOO	Workers Commissions
CEDA	Spanish Confederation of the Autonomous Right
CESO	Spanish Confederation of Workers Unions
CGT	French General Confederation of Labor
CGTU	Unitary General Confederation of Labor
CNCA	National Catholic Agrarian Confederation
CNS	National Syndical Centers
CNSL	National Confederation of Free Unions
CNT	National Confederation of Labor
CPE	Spanish Employers Federation
CRS	Social Reforms Commission
CRT	Catalonian Regional Labor Confederation
ERC	Catalonian Republican Left
FAI	Iberian Anarchist Federation
FCCB	Catalonian-Balearic Communist Federation
FJS	Socialist Youth Federation
FLE	Madrid Building Trades Labor Federation
FNA	National Agriculturists Federation
FNTT	National Federation of Land Workers
FORA	Argentine Regional Labor Federation
FOUS	Labor Federation for Trade Union Unity
FRE	Spanish Regional Federation of the First International
FSL	Libertarian Syndicalist Federation
FTRE	Workers Federation of the Spanish Region

FUE   University Students Federation
HOAC   Catholic Action Workers Brotherhood
IFTU   International Federation of Trade Unions
ILO   International Labor Organization
INP   National Institute of Social Security
IRS   Institute for Social Reforms
JAP   Popular Action Youth Federation
JOC   Young Christian Workers
ONC   National Corporative Organization
OSE   Spanish Syndical Organization
PCE   Spanish Communist party
PCOE   Spanish Communist Workers party
PNV   Basque Nationalist party
POUM   Workers Marxist Unification party
PSOE   Spanish Socialist Workers party
PSUC   Catalonian Unified Socialist party
SMA   Asturian Miners Union
SO   Workers Solidarity
SOV-STV   Basque Workers Solidarity
SUC   Building Construction Workers Industrial Union of Madrid
UFNR   Federal Nationalist Republican Union
UGT   General Workers Union
UP   Patriotic Union
USC   Catalonian Socialist Union

PREFACE

Nothing more graphically illustrates the consequences of Spain's belated modernization than the evolution of its labor relations. Incidents of worker protest and urban and rural conflict, many reminiscent of preindustrial jacqueries, occurred with regularity throughout the late nineteenth and early twentieth centuries. Yet it was not until World War I that the "labor problem" truly became a matter of national concern.

From that point on, labor unrest occurred in Spain on a large scale. The war and immediate postwar years saw the country convulsed by a major breakdown in labor relations. The pronunciamiento of 1923, which inaugurated the seven-year dictatorship headed by General Primo de Rivera, had as its primary purpose bringing an end to the bloody labor strife and terrorism that gripped the city of Barcelona. Throughout the 1930s steadily mounting polarization in labor relations and radicalization in trade unions placed the Second Republic in mortal peril. In few western European countries did proletarian discontent and labor action have so profound an effect on national life.

In western Europe sustained economic growth and the improving status of wage earners made trade unions a more integral part of the institutional, social, and economic fabric and had a moderating effect on their outlooks and policies. Such was not the case in Spain, where capitalist development had been only partial and highly uneven. Labor organizations thus continued to draw their force primarily from their roles as vehicles for popular protest amid frustration over the vestiges of preindustrialism that condemned the country to an excrutiatingly slow economic expansion.

The socioeconomic lag greatly enhanced the inflow of the new political credos—socialism, anarchism, anarcho-syndicalism—that were part and parcel of the Industrial Revolution but shaped and attenuated by Iberian underdevelopment. Spanish socialism sought to emulate the social dem-

ocratic practices of its western European counterparts but found it necessary periodically to resort to quasi-insurrectionary actions. The inherent
instabilities of the Catalonian textile economy ruled out any durable labor
peace in Barcelona, thus contributing to the remarkable influence of the
most insurrection-prone anarchist movement in western Europe and to
the pervasive spread of anarcho-syndicalism. The inability of the Second
Republic to meet the expectations of aroused rural and urban wage earners
was pivotal in plunging the country into the harrowing ordeal of civil
war. Modernization in labor relations has only come with the recent post-
Franco transition to democracy.

Despite the formidable role that labor developments and working-class
organization have played in contemporary Spanish affairs, Iberian and
European social and labor historiography have long suffered from the
absence of a general account and analysis incorporating the substantial
monographic research of recent date. It is the intent of this study to fill
that need.

A special debt of gratitude is owed to American and Spanish friends
and colleagues whose counsel and critical readings of parts of the man-
uscript have been of inestimable value. Edward Malefakis of Columbia
University was especially unstinting in providing guidance and editorial
assistance; Joan Connelly Ullman of the University of Washington and
Gabriel Jackson were also most helpful. Among the numerous Spanish
scholars, mention should be made of Pere Gabriel, Miguel Izard, Albert
Balcells, Casamiro Martí, Victor Alba, Manuel Pérez Ledesma, Santos
Juliá, and Ignacio Olábarri.

The preparation and publication of this book would not have been
possible without the fellowship provided by the U.S.-Spain Joint Committee for Cultural and Educational Cooperation, which made possible
an extended stay in Spain and a subsequent shorter visit, and a financial
grant from the Spanish Ministry of Culture.

I also give profuse thanks to the staffs of the Institut Municipal d'His-
tória, the Biblioteca del Fomento de Trabajo, the Fundación Figueras,
the Biblioteca de Catalunya in Barcelona, the Biblioteca Nacional, the
Archivo Historico Nacional, the Fundación Pablo Iglesias, the Servicio
Historico Militar, and the Biblioteca del Ministerio de Trabajo in Madrid;
as well as to the Library of Congress in Washington, D.C.

Special acknowledgment is due ILR Press editors Erica Fox and Trudie
Calvert for their unremitting efforts in weeding out stylistic inelegancies

and assuring bibliographic accuracy. They are, to be sure, not responsible for interpretations, judgments, and deficiencies in the text. Last but by no means least, my deepest gratitude to my wife, Liz, and my son, Eric, for their encouragement and forbearance toward my numerous absences in Spain.

THE AGONY OF MODERNIZATION

1

THE SOCIOECONOMIC SETTING

Spain and the European
Industrial Revolution

Spain's military supremacy in the Western world ended in the seventeenth century. Over the following two centuries the country was reduced to a humiliating second-rate status. Much of Spain's resources had been squandered on war, and the bullion gleaned from the Americas had gone largely to repay foreign bankers and military provisioners. Spain's decline took place as Europe entered the modern age and formed new social, economic, and political structures. As Paul Kennedy has written, "The horrendous costs of 140 years of war were . . . imposed upon a society which was economically ill-equipped to carry them."[1] The enormous debts contracted in waging wars had left Spain's finances in chaos, while the national ethos and culture remained those of a semifeudal, military society. The economic infrastructure suffered from long neglect as the spirit of commerce and enterprise atrophied.

Spain's debilitated condition was the result largely of an inherent incapacity to devise a relatively self-sufficient economy when imperial conquest and colonial exploitation no longer served as a basis for material sustenance. Many of those engaged in commercial and banking activities, the Jews and Moriscos, had been expelled from the country, and much of the lucrative trade with the South American colonies was in the hands of foreign entrepreneurs. Moreover, Spain, the citadel of the Counter-Reformation, had not experienced the great spiritual, political, and economic awakening that ushered in the new era. By the nineteenth century the country struggled painfully to come to terms with modernity. Powerful elites, whose wealth and station were linked with the status quo, resisted entry into the machine age and the world of bourgeois entrepreneurship.

3

In countries that experienced the industrial revolution, social and political modernization almost invariably preceded economic transformations. The intensity and duration of the stresses accompanying such changes were generally determined by the extent to which traditional practices and institutions remained embedded in the socioeconomic fabric. According to David Landes, "It was Europe's good fortune that technological change and industrialisation preceded or accompanied pari passu the other components of modernisation, so that she was spared the material and psychic penalties of unbalanced maturation." But "the urbanisation of Mediterranean Europe in the context of a preindustrial economy yielded a harvest of death, misery and enduring resentment."[2] Spain was distinctive in that economic modernization occurred not only at a comparatively late date but in an exceedingly slow and discontinuous fashion. In Italy industrial development began to take off in 1896. Spain did not experience comparable development until two decades later, at the time of World War I.

Residual archaisms were so great that although Spanish social and political mores outwardly appeared to resemble those of western Europe, they were actually often a thin veneer. "The reality was," observes Javier Tussell Gómez, "that although the theoretical similarity between Spain and England in the practice of political life was great, the two systems differed radically. The principal feature of the Spaniard was the survival of numerous characteristics that seemed to link him with the world of the ancien régime."[3]

In Spain the ancien régime had been gradually replaced by more or less modern political institutions, yet the underlying economic and social structure remained anchored to its preindustrial past or, as Stanley Payne has put it, "a 19th century oligarchy confronted with 20th century problems."[4] Far-reaching disequilibriums resulted with the rise of a dual economy, a traditional sector and one with capitalist features, that made it extremely difficult to govern the country and to establish a national consensus on fundamental problems. The resulting comingling of the archaic and the modern in the economic and social fabric nurtured a buildup of explosive dimensions.

An inefficient and semifeudalistic system of agriculture was an insurmountable encumbrance. As Nicolas Sánchez Albornoz explains, "One hundred years ago agriculture of an ancient sort presided over the Spanish economy with the same stringency that had been in effect for centuries and centuries. Some countries which suffered from similar fetters commenced to change. But Spain was far from having attained such an advantage."[5]

Agricultural retardation impeded the formation of a national industrial bourgeoisie, thus preventing them from acquiring sufficient cohesion and strength to influence the country's power centers. The single most important concentration of industrialists was in the small, peripheral area of Catalonia. "It is the misfortune of the Spanish bourgeoisie," Franz Borkenau has noted, "that its strongest section belongs to the disaffected border region, and not to the center of the country. No other factor contributed so much to the weakness of the Spanish bourgeoisie; here lies the tragical importance of the Catalan problem. . . . The one region whose leading classes were thoroughly in favor of Europeanizing the country has always been an outlying and suspected district."[6]

At a time when other nations were engrossed in socioeconomic transformation, Spaniards had yet to solve the problems of an empire in dissolution and a society held in thrall by its archaic undergrowth, a situation that prompted Karl Marx in the early 1870s to declare that "there are more priests in Spain than workers." The new production modes were absorbed slowly, and assimilation of the accompanying intellectual-scientific innovations lagged even further behind. One Spanish historian described it as a "thwarted" industrial revolution.[7]

The resulting near immobility generated a host of difficulties throughout much of the nineteenth century that made Spain "the most unruly and divided nation in Europe." Following a long, bitter, and bloody guerrilla war at the century's outset against Napoleonic France, the occupier imposed modernizing reforms but left the country in ruins. Vain and costly attempts were made to regain the South American colonies, whose loss deprived the economy of its most essential financial and commercial supports. Until the restoration of the monarchy in 1876 finally brought a period of political tranquillity, the country was ravaged by more than four decades of almost constant turbulence: the savage Carlist Wars that pitted urban liberals against rural clerical traditionalists, military pronunciamientos, a failed liberal revolution and its aftermath, among others.[8] Much of the turmoil arose from cleavages within the ruling elite, "the bicephalous oligarchy," that placed into separate warring camps those who sought to preserve traditional values and the liberalizers who attempted to introduce reforms. The inconclusive battle for power and the resultant institutional and political disarray prompted Antonio Maura to lament the "shapelessness of Spanish society."[9]

The imposition of a political power-sharing formula devised by the Conservative leader Antonio Cánovas del Castillo finally consolidated the monarchy and brought political peace. The political system of the Restoration appeared to be based on Western-style popular sovereignty, but in reality, the constitution that was adopted had been drafted, in Salvador de Madariaga's words, "with the clear intention of governing under, over, around, and even through it, but never honestly with it."[10] It consisted of a negotiated agreement with the leader of the Liberals, Práxedes Sagasta, that provided for the Conservatives and Liberals, "Los Partidos Turnantes," to alternate in running the country. Nothing was left to popular decision. Elections were carefully managed by the minister of the interior and the local political bosses (*caciques*), who brought out the vote for the government's candidates.

The Spanish-American War of 1898 deprived Spain of the remnants of empire, Cuba, Puerto Rico, Guam, and the Philippines, as well as its entire naval fleet; it was truly a "defeat without palliatives." The urgent need for economic and political modernization was epitomized by the Portuguese poet Guerra Junqueiro, who declared that Lagartijo (a famous bullfighter of the period) had been beaten by Thomas Edison. Bruised national pride notwithstanding, the colonies had cost more than they yielded. The 1898 debacle ultimately forced the government to embrace policies leading to greater economic self-sufficiency, import substitutions, and the erection of extremely high tariff barriers to shield incipient industrial development.

Industrial growth during the latter half of the nineteenth century proceeded at a very modest pace, uneven and sporadic, falling substantially short of domestic requirements and consequently incapable of providing a basis for economic takeoff.[11] Spain's failure to "catch the train of the industrial revolution" was mainly attributable to the disinterest of the ruling landed oligarchy, the absence of a modern spirit of entrepreneurship, and the dead weight of an inefficient and archaic agricultural system.

The economic growth lag widened existing disparities with other western European countries so that by the century's end Spain was in the category of underdeveloped nations together with Hungary, Poland, and Russia. Except for Italy and Portugal, Spain was last among western European nations to industrialize. The peninsula lagged at least half a century behind the more industrially advanced European countries.

Spain's nineteenth-century industrial development mainly involved the expansion of textile manufacturing in Catalonia, the construction of railway lines beginning at midcentury, and a great increase in minerals mining. Though industrialization was modest and affected only limited parts of the country, by the end of the century Spain had become an incipient industrial society. An industrial revolution had not taken place, but neither had the economy remained stationary. In the Basque region the foundations were in place as the century drew to a close for the future erection of an iron and steel heavy industry complex. A banking system was developing, textile making was concentrated in Catalonia, and urbanization was on the increase.

No substantive changes in the makeup of the economy had yet occurred, however. In the early twentieth century Spain could still be described as an agricultural and mining country. Industrialization was concentrated in isolated mining sites or enclaves on the geographical periphery of the country. Only in Catalonia, the Basque country, and to some extent Asturias did industrialization attain significant proportions at the turn of the century. Except for a few urban centers, the rest of the country maintained its rural character and social backwardness.

The combination of lagging industrial progress and a depressed agriculture imposed an abysmally low standard of living on Spain's wage earners. Miguel Izard describes the situation: "Meager economic growth made it difficult to obtain large profits in the secondary sector since demand elasticity was weak, with few possibilities for expansion. Under such conditions it was practically impossible to content oneself with modest profits extracted from considerable numbers of workers. Each 'manufacturer' had to squeeze his few workers to the maximum, to coerce to the limit."[12]

An industrialization pattern in which the modern factory system long remained confined to the outlying regions is a distinguishing hallmark of peninsular economic development. Thus the dynamic industrial-commercial metropolis of Barcelona (later to be joined by Bilbao) contrasted sharply with most of the rest of the country. This enormous disparity not only became the source of political and social tensions but largely shaped the trade union movement and the course taken by labor relations and social legislation, especially during the first four decades of the twentieth century.

At the dawn of the twentieth century Spanish society therefore displayed many of the features of its traditional way of life. There are no accurate statistics for this period on which to base a social profile, but its overall contours can be discerned. One recent estimate covering the reign of

Alfonso XIII (1902–29) places the titled nobility ("Los Grandes") at less than two thousand. Also included in the upper class were the latifundists and big farmers, senior military officers, the industrial and commercial bourgeoisie, high government officials, and the political elite, many of whom held titles. The middle class, embracing the liberal professions and medium-sized urban and rural proprietors, amounted to some twenty thousand persons. The clergy numbered eighty-eight thousand, and there were some twenty-seven thousand military officers. When the lower middle classes, primarily white-collar employees, small artisans, and shopkeepers, are added, these groups made up 25 to 30 percent of the actively engaged population. The remaining 70 to 75 percent of the active population, those at the lower end of the social pyramid, consisted of small farmers, agricultural laborers, and industrial and service workers.[13] The great predominance of agriculture in the economic life of the country is reflected in the fact that there were three times as many agricultural laborers as industrial workers.

"The entirety of the industrial bourgeoisie," observes Manuel Tuñon de Lara, "(if we go by figures derived from industrial taxation) was less than 63,000 enterprises. What can in fact be considered the big bourgeoisie was of an infinitely lesser number since close to 25,000 flour millers are to be excluded, 1,364 bakers, and more than 1,500 small soap manufacturers, as well as several thousand small semiartisanal industries, including part of the woolens industry. Basic industries, mines, public services, maritime transport, naval shipbuilding, and the like, which were structured along the lines of joint stock companies, were concentrated among a relatively limited number of persons."[14]

It was a quintessential oligarchical society whose select membership also constituted the ruling political elite. Antonio Maura estimated that the ruling group that monopolized power during the Restoration Era (1876–1923) consisted of some two thousand persons. As Raymond Carr notes, "The distinguishing feature of Spanish society was that the aristocracy and non-noble proprietors combined into a single class. Industrialists, politicians, military leaders, financiers, etc. were given noble titles so that many among the factory tycoons became more imbued with the mores of the landed oligarchy than the new bourgeois outlook."[15]

Demographic patterns also showed the effects of economic retardation. Despite relatively modest population increases during the late nineteenth and early twentieth centuries (a 3 million increase from 1873 to 1900, for a population in 1900 of 18.5 million), the lack of adequate land distribution, the waning of epidemics and famines, a drop in infant mortality, and a failure to expand agricultural output sufficiently meant that during the second half of the nineteenth century the country was once again unable to provide for its most basic needs.[16]

A slow growth economy could not keep pace with even moderate population increases. Because limited industrial expansion could ingest only a small fraction of the growing army of job seekers, a large number of immigrants, "driven by hunger and misery," moved to South America and North Africa. By 1900, for example, the total population of Asturias, approximately 627,000, was only slightly larger than that of "Overseas Asturias" (a local expression to describe Asturian emigrants, most of whom went to South America). Though a gradual improvement commenced that year, at least 10 percent of the population is estimated to have left the country between 1901 and 1911 in quest of economic opportunity, more than from any other European country. A depopulation of the country-side took place from 1875 to 1900 as an estimated 23 percent departed, many to seek their fortunes in the country's burgeoning industrial centers of Catalonia and the Basque country, where industrialization had created an expanding labor market and spurred increased demographic vitality.[17]

The Agricultural Albatross

Only in recent years has Spain become a predominantly urban country. Until the 1950s the economy was primarily agricultural with a preponderance of subsistence farming.[18] "Rudimentary methods that required little capital investment and the extensive use of manpower subsisted intact from time immemorial," observes Nicolas Sánchez Albornoz, "and kept output locked into a pair of hands and the earth. A large part of agrarian production was destined for the consumption of the rural mass, hence only a small part entered the market."[19] Agricultural retardation was thus a leading if not the most important cause for the slow pace of economic modernization.

Well into contemporary times the number of people engaged in farming occupations remained at about the same level as prevailed in the more advanced European countries on the eve of the industrial revolution or during its preliminary phases. According to Edward Malefakis, in 1900 the agricultural population constituted more than half the population in forty-six of the fifty Spanish provinces, more than 70 percent in thirty-six provinces, and more than 80 percent in twelve. Fifty years later, little had changed.[20]

The distinctive features of Spanish agriculture were its land tenure structures and extreme regional disparities. Tiny landholdings were by far the most characteristic, with those of medium size the exception.[21] Both are widespread in central and northern Spain but are also frequently encountered in the south as well. Until recently a large number of farmers in the Castilian provinces eked out a subsistence existence. Land fragmentation exists almost everywhere but nowhere so acutely as in Galicia, where the owners of minifundia make up 98 percent of the farm holdings. Raymond Carr emphasizes that "there was only a small middle sector of substantial farmers; a crude estimate in 1930 counts 96 per cent of all cultivators as small farmers and 3.1 as middle-sized farmers."[22]

Farms of medium size, those between ten and one hundred hectares, are particularly numerous in Catalonia and the northeastern provinces of Navarre and Alava. Spanish farmers in these areas resemble the independent peasants of France and other European countries. In general, however, the disproportionately great number of both very large estates and minifundia, as well as their concentration in certain regions, ultimately led to the crucial imbalance in the land tenure structure that traditionally has been the source of the twin problems that long bedeviled Spanish agriculture: low productivity and social unrest.

Landholding patterns in Andalusia, Extremadura, and La Mancha were distinguished from those in the rest of the country by the prevalence of large estates, the latifundia. "Because large estates controlled some two and one half to three times as much of the *cultivated* surface in the south as elsewhere (40.6 percent to 15.5 percent according to the Agricultural Census of 1962)," explains Edward Malefakis, "their importance in the social and economic life of Andalusia, Extremadura, and La Mancha was until recently comparable to that of the latifundia of the ancient Roman world."[23] For the regional distribution of property and employment in agriculture see table 1.1.

The agricultural population of Andalusia in 1900, for example, included a huge mass of landless, impoverished peasants and an equally large number of owners of tiny plots; 6 million possessed less than one hectare, grossly insufficient to sustain themselves and their families. Some ten thousand families owned 50 percent of the assessed lands, and 1 percent of the landowners possessed 42 percent of the capital value of farm holdings.[24]

Table 1.1.   Property and Rural Social Class Structure in Spain[a]

Region	Total Area (in thousands of hectares)	Males employed in agriculture (thousands of persons)	Index of property concentration (percentage)	Percentage of males by occupation	
				Peasant proprietors	Day laborers
Atlantic littoral	6,296	913	13.7	53.2	7.3
Galicia	2,944	613	9.9	55.9	6.6
Biscay provinces	3,352	300	20.8	47.3	9.1
Mediterranean litorral	7,533	986	23.0	28.1	26.0
Catalonia	3,193	279	22.2	30.1	11.9
Levante	4,340	706	23.2	27.3	31.5
North Central Spain	17,176	873	27.4	41.3	16.1
Old Castile	8,181	447	24.8	45.5	13.0
New Castile	3,725	165	29.5	33.9	23.6
Aragon-Ebro	5,270	261	30.2	38.9	16.8
Subtotals: small and intermediate property regions	31,005	2,772	23.8	39.6	16.6
Southwestern Spain	18,241	1,557	46.2	14.3	43.3
La Mancha	4,998	314	39.5	15.8	34.1
Estremadura	5,394	369	51.4	15.9	37.2
Andalusia	7,850	874	45.6	13.1	49.1
Spain as a whole (including islands)	50,747	4,545	33.4	31.0	25.7

Source: Edward Malefakis, "Peasants, Politics, and Civil War in Spain, 1931–1939," in Robert Bezuka, ed., *Modern European Social History* (Lexington, Mass.: D.C. Heath, 1972), p. 195.

[a]Population figures are for 1956, and land tenure figures partly for 1959, but both are indicative of pre–civil war conditions because Spanish agriculture changed very little before the 1960s. The proportion of the population in secondary occupational groups not listed above was as follows for Spain as a whole: labor-employing farm entrepreneurs, 19.2 percent; small tenants and sharecroppers, 15.1 percent; permanent hired hands, 9.0 percent.

The landholding patterns in the south, which differ from those in the rest of the country, originated in the redistribution of land following the defeat and expulsion of the Moors, a process that extended over several hundred years and was finally completed in the fifteenth century. Huge tracts of lands seized from their Moorish owners were given in grants by the royal house to the church, the nobility, and the various military orders that had participated in the Reconquest. The church and the nobility thereby secured a dominant role not only in landownership but also in the political control of the region. The enduring quality of these land tenure patterns is evident in that of the nine provinces that were conquered in the thirteenth century and now account for 26.8 percent of the country's total land surface, the old nobility in 1930 still possessed 53.6 percent of the land in eight of these provinces.

It is therefore largely for historical reasons that many of the rural inhabitants of Andalusia to this day reside in agro-towns rather than on farms. The term *pueblo,* which is normally applied in Spain to small villages, in Andalusia means good-sized towns as well. Many of these agro-towns encompass populations ranging from five to fifty thousand. Most of the *braceros,* the landless rural laborers who are hired by the day or for a harvesting season to work on nearby farms, reside in these towns. Earlier in this century they made up more than half of the employed population. The greatest concentration of *braceros* was to be found in the *pueblos* of Guadalquivir valley and the *campiñas* (flat expanses of cultivable land) of Córdoba, Seville, and Jérez.[25]

The personnel structure of a large estate consisted of a pyramidal arrangement in which a clear division existed between those who were part of the hierarchical ordering and those who were its subjects. The owner, *el amo,* usually of upper-class lineage (*señorito*) or of recently acquired wealth, was the ultimate authority. The actual running of the estate was usually in the hands of a manager, *el administrator,* who received a percentage of the profits. The foremen, *los capataz,* who were provided with their own houses and land plots cultivated and tended by the hired help, carried out the instructions of the manager. Under the foremen were the *manijeros,* group leaders, who for two reals more than the daily wage rate supervised the work of the *braceros.*

Generally three types of contractual arrangements existed for the employment of temporary labor. Laborers were hired on a daily basis from among those who congregated in the town squares. "Temporaries" or semipermanent work hands (*mayorales, caseros, manijeros,* and others) were contracted for a specific number of months, for a season, or for another period. Pieceworkers, *los distajeros,* were paid according to their output in olive picking, grain reaping, and the like. The distinctions between these three forms of employment were not always adhered to, and a *bracero* might be shifted from one contractual arrangement to another.[26]

The permanent work force (*los fijos*), employed on a regular basis, even today represents a very small part of the entire labor input. Of the current 460,000 farm laborers in Andalusia, only 9 percent can count on steady employment. The ratio between day laborers and permanent workers in 1931 ran about ten to one. Day laborers and minifundia owners seeking to supplement the income derived from their tiny plots are hired on a temporary, casual basis to perform most of the basic farm chores.[27] Farm labor traditionally has provided a highly insecure, meager livelihood because work is available for an average of about two hundred workdays annually. "The *bracero*," observes an agricultural historian, "spends one hundred to one hundred thirty days a year doing farm work in which he usually specialized (reapers, olive pickers, vineyard work, and so on); then to his dislike he performed road building and maintenance labor, emigrated to the mines of Linares, Peñarroya, or Rio Tinto, or joined the ranks of common laborers in the cities when he did not own a plot of land to care for during the rest of the year."[28]

Since most Andalusian latifundos were monocultivations of cereal grains or olives, labor requirements were seasonal and sporadic. Until the first decades of this century, years of poor harvests or economic depression meant for many *jornaleros* and their families the grim prospect of destitution and near starvation. Rural laborers and their families begging on the streets of Spain's towns and cities were a common sight in poor harvest years.

The general condition of Castilian farm laborers was not much different from those of southern Spain, but some of them had the recourse of employment in the mines during farm off-seasons. José Varela Ortega describes the farm labor situation in Castile:

The relation between labor supply and demand reversed with the seasons. It was this that produced a two-way emigration [*emigración de golondrinas*] between the Cantabrian and Castilian provinces. In the summer, when labor demand in Castile exceeded supply and the wage rates of the north, . . . people went to reap in the fields of the south. The appearance of Galicians especially, but also of Basques, arriving by train or on foot along the byways of the Meseta, was typical of the Castilian summer. During the rest of the year, when the situation was reversed, it was the Castilians who departed for the mines of Leon, Asturias, and especially those of Vizcaya. . . . When the day laborers worked they did so from sunup to sundown with time out for lunch and dinner. Their wages barely covered the rental of a miserable hovel lacking in "the most elemental hygienic conditions" and which permitted insufficient nourishment that made them victims of anemia and vulnerable to infectious diseases.[29]

At the conclusion of the nineteenth century gainful employment was not available for the 2 million *braceros,* and as a consequence wages paid to rural laborers, especially in the south, were abysmally low, greatly inferior to those received by miners and industrial workers.[30] A survey conducted in 1884, one year after the formation of the Social Reforms Commission, indicated that farm laborers received a daily maximum of 1.25 pesetas. A 1902 survey by the Institute for Social Reforms disclosed that despite regional and local variations, wages were uniformly low. The average wage for male adults outside harvest time hardly ever exceeded half a peseta and often was lower. The top rate almost invariably was less than 2 pesetas, and the maximum during harvests of 3 pesetas was rarely exceeded. Wages were lowest in Extremadura. One estimate places the earnings in 1902 of agricultural day laborers at one-third of the national average; another calculates annual earnings at less than those received by an unskilled industrial laborer (*peon*). The wage around 1910 was between slightly less than 1.75 pesetas and 2 pesetas for the latifundio provinces of the south and center and for the Levant. In areas with fewer agricultural proletarians, the rates were from 2 to 2.50 pesetas. By 1919 wages had risen from 30 to 60 percent compared with 1910.[31] Yet this increase in nominal wages masks a standstill or erosion in real wages because the price of bread increased by 45 percent, garbanzo beans by 90 percent, and clothing and shoes by 80 percent. These wage rates also were subject to fluctuations.[32]

An important element in the stagnation of farm labor wages was the farm crisis that lasted from 1880 to 1905. The massive influx of much cheaper grains from the United States, Canada, Argentina, and Australia spelled long-term disaster and destabilization for European agriculture—including Spanish agriculture.

Favored by a protectionist policy that shielded the domestic market, in which demand was on the rise because of population growth, Andalusian landowners compensated for lower profits by drastic wage cuts. Antonio Bernal explains the roots of the agrarian conflict: "Spanish farmers persisted in maintaining a wage cost similar to that which prevailed at the beginning of the nineteenth century. Wages scarcely amounted to 40 percent of overall costs and barely 20 percent of the gross product. Under such circumstances, transform and modernize? For what? Through domestic prices—protectionism and a high price differential—and with the maintenance of low wages—the abundance of manpower and the lack of alternative options—the burden of the crisis was transferred to the laboring class."[33]

With such extremely low labor costs there was little incentive for owners to operate their farms more efficiently or productively. Compared with the rest of Europe, productivity in 1913 was abysmally low.[34] Besides acting as a disincentive to mechanize, it fostered innumerable marginal farming plots (minifundos) that otherwise would not have been viable.

Pathetically low earnings were by no means exclusive to southern Spain's rural proletariat. Labor costs rose slightly during the 1880s in the Castilian Meseta, for example, leading to a slight increase in mechanization, "but it remained on a modest scale," observes a leading historian of the period, "because manpower even after the crisis continued to be abundant and cheap."[35]

The sorry plight of Spain's southern rural proletariat had been exacerbated by the massive public sales of church-owned land during the nineteenth century. Mounting deficits in the public debt induced Liberal governments to emulate this practice of resolving financial problems, initiated by Charles IV. Disentailment occurred in many parts of the country, but church landholdings were especially concentrated in the south. Communal lands were sold off at a later date. The first sales took place during 1836–49 and the second in the period 1859–67, involving approximately 60 percent of the land in the south.

Liberal reformers Juan Alvarez Mendizábal and Pascual Madoz, who headed governments during the two periods of disentailment, had intended that the land sales would lead to the creation of independent, medium-sized farm units in the south, similar to those that predominated in Navarre, Alava, and Catalonia. In the absence of government loans and credit at low interest rates, however, the less fortunate were unable to purchase land. The *poderosos* of the region—the local merchants, middle-class professionals, wealthy farmers, politicians, urban financiers, and aristocracy—took full advantage of the opportunity. Within a relatively short time the new purchasers, many of them absentee landlords especially in Andalusia and Extremadura, were able to accumulate huge estates at ridiculously low prices. As a result, the overall geographic pattern of landholding underwent little if any change; merely the owners changed.[36]

Deprived of the use of communal lands that had made life a bit more bearable and the imposition of harsher conditions of employment by the more rapacious parvenu landowners, the southern rural laborer fared badly during the latter half of the century. Southern Spain's rural proletariat became the most wretched and impoverished of the peninsula and probably of Europe, as reflected in living conditions and mortality rates. The 1877 census reported that 62.7 percent of all Spanish males and 81 percent of females were illiterate. The highest illiteracy rates were in Andalusia and Extremadura and in the south, the areas with the largest numbers of *jornaleros*.[37] Mortality rates there were also the highest in the country.

In times of distress the plight of these rural laborers was truly heart-rending. Joaquín Costa has written that at such times their nourishment consisted of "competing with the cattle for the grass, roaming the countryside in search of wheat, asparagus, green figs; the children naked and without shoes, and the adults covered with rags."[38]

This miserable situation affected large numbers of people. In Andalusia 78 percent of rural laborers were engaged in agricultural work in 1800 compared to a national average of 65 percent. The farming provinces of Córdoba, Jaen, and Seville contained the highest percentages, 80, 82, and 85 respectively. "Almost a century later," relates Eduardo Sevilla Guzman, "the situation was unchanged. The 1877 census indicates 80 percent, 82 percent, and 85 percent for day laborers with the total for Andalusia superior to that of 1800."[39] These figures support the contention that disentailment strengthened traditional land tenure patterns and further proletarianized much of southern Spanish rural society.

Disentailment disfranchised numerous tenant farmers and sharecroppers, who joined the already swollen ranks of the rural proletariat. The increased labor surplus further depressed wage standards and provided even less incentive for landowners to improve output by introducing mechanization and modern farming techniques. Casamiro Martí described the result as a vicious circle: "The difficult condition of agricultural laborers victimized by unemployment resulted in a considerable social pressure group supporting retarded farming methods that would enable greater employment."[40] In a 1906 parliamentary address Rafael Gasset estimated that between ninety and a hundred thousand Andalusian rural laborers were unemployed.[41]

In Asturias disentailment led to the creation of a large number of small and medium-sized farms. But only a poverty-stricken existence was possible on many of these small farms, and the peasants supplemented their earnings by working in the nearby coal mines.

Disentailment not only reinforced traditional structures but concentrated land in even fewer hands. Approximately 11,000 persons in southern Spain possessed 6.9 million hectares in 1900 while another 35,000 owned 3.5 million hectares. The remaining 9.3 million hectares were distributed among 7.8 million peasants of whom 6 million laid claim to less than one hectare. These statistics help explain the development of protest in New Castile, Extremadura, Murcia, and Andalusia.[42] As poverty and overpopulation grew worse, the desperation and simmering discontent endemic in the rural south increasingly erupted in explosive and violent outbursts.

This popular protest assumed various forms. The number of impoverished rural folk who normally engaged in begging in nearby towns and cities increased notably. Attacks on stores, bakeries, and the homes of the well-to-do as well as on farms increased substantially. Large numbers of peasants departed permanently for provincial capitals or emigrated overseas. Demonstrators gathered in front of government buildings demanding assistance, work, food, and moratoriums on taxes and tenant farm payments. Such expressions of distress were common throughout the Spanish countryside, but they were most frequent and intense in Andalusia.

Throughout the past and well into this century peasant unrest was pandemic. More than a century ago, August Blanqui considered Andalusia the most revolutionary region of Spain. From the final third of the nineteenth century to the civil war of the 1930s, it was probably the most restive agricultural zone in Europe. Unrest was first expressed in brigandage, banditry, crop burnings, destruction of machines, land seizures, and the organization of secret societies.[43]

Public authorities and landowners sought to cope through a series of stopgap measures. Well-to-do local farmers would house jobless farm laborers and their families, providing them with small daily sums in exchange for performing occasional chores. Municipalities and church groups established soup kitchens (Antonio Maria Calero claims that such forms of assistance almost always were in short supply), and government and local authorities sponsored public works programs. "Then," according to Calero, "if such remedies were exhausted and those in charge of administering them could not or did not wish to do so, complements of Civil Guards were augmented to repress disturbances. It should not be forgotten that the latter was constituted in 1844 by a moderate government 'to maintain order, public security and the protection of persons and properties both within and without the towns.' "[44]

Climatic conditions also caused distress among farm workers. Much of Andalusia consists of semiarid land that normally receives little rainfall. A year of extremely sparse or no rainfall spelled disaster for much of the population. Under normal climatic conditions the average farm laborer could amass enough earnings during harvest seasons to exist through the months of enforced joblessness. But when the dry spells became unusually prolonged, a chain process would take place. The lack of rain reduced the need for field labor, and the ensuing economic distress was exacerbated by increases in the prices of basic necessities occasioned by shortages.

Such economic distress generated social conflicts that enveloped the sectors of the community that were hardest hit by bad harvests—sharecroppers, small farmers, artisans, shopkeepers, and day laborers. Calero describes them as "normally spontaneous and unorganized, igniting during junctures of the greatest deterioration in living standards, of high unemployment, shortages, high prices for living essentials, and excessive governmental or military pressures. In most instances there was no specific political or ideological orientation; they were protest actions with concrete, immediate, daily objectives. At times they were promoted or exploited by leaders of the political opposition."[45]

During the closing decades of the nineteenth century numbers of rural laborers and minifundistas became increasingly drawn to the ideas of anarchism, and thenceforward social protest gradually assumed more organized forms. Unable to fulfill its aspirations either through the juridical process or by direct action, the Andalusian peasantry became tacitly allied with the most radical groups.[46]

The Primacy of Textile Manufacturing

Spanish industrialization began as it had in other countries with textile manufacturing. But the comparison stops there. Elsewhere it led to a diversification of the industrial base, but in Spain, because of disjointed and extremely slow economic development, textile making remained the principal industrial activity throughout the nineteenth century and well into the twentieth.

By the second half of the nineteenth century, textile manufacturing was concentrated in the region of Catalonia, made possible by a distinctive marriage of circumstance and tradition. Drawing on Barcelona's centuries-old mercantile, trading, and artisanal past, cotton textile making was initiated during the late eighteenth century. An entrepreneurial legacy and a relatively prosperous agriculture sustained an industrializing effort that was both indigenous and self-promoted. Its success was all the more remarkable because elsewhere in the country most industrial development and the construction of railway lines before World War I remained heavily dependent on foreign capital and technology.[47] Even railway construction in Catalonia was locally financed.

Catalonian enterprisers, according to Jaime Vicens Vives, benefited at a crucial point in the industry's development from favorable conditions during the 1850s that provided an impetus to economic growth and made possible the erection "of a platform on which Spain's industrialization was to be structured until 1914."[48] Europe at that time was in the throes of a large-scale economic and industrial expansion. The boom brought on by the advancing industrial revolution increased Spain's agricultural and commercial business and in turn boosted existing industries such as textile manufacturing.

Until the second decade of this century Catalonia was the only region whose economy was primarily based on manufacturing. At the turn of the century, 59 percent of taxes paid to the government for all types of production emanated from the principality that possessed only a tenth of the national population and, like Lancashire in England, accounted for 90 percent of the country's textile output. Industrial concentration provided Barcelona and other factory towns with high ratios of workers in their populations. Half of all inhabitants in Catalonia came to reside in Barcelona province as a result of the urbanization brought on by industrialization. By Spanish standards, the number of workers was exceedingly high, 117,000, or more than one-fifth of the city's half million residents, more than half of whom were employed in textile manufacturing.[49] In neighboring communities a similar proportion engaged in textile manufacturing, and the nearby towns of Sabadell and Tarrassa became the country's centers for wool and wool products.[50] The region was also a major producer of linen, silk, hemp, and jute.

An additional thirteen thousand workers were employed in factories and shops along the Costa Brava in the semiartisanal manufacture of bottle corks. Not for three decades would the rest of the country attain the industry/agriculture manpower ratios that Catalonia possessed in 1900. Barcelona, moreover, served as the country's principal port of entry and exit; half the peninsula's trade passed through the Ciudad Condal, which also ranked as the fourth cotton port in Europe after Liverpool, Bremen, and Le Havre. Understandably, therefore, the "social question" in the nineteenth century was primarily associated with the labor and social problems of Catalonia's textile work force.

Because it does not require massive capital outlays and is labor-intensive, using mostly unskilled workers and small numbers of skilled operatives, textile manufacturing has been regarded as the classic vehicle for inaugurating industrial development. It also can be made to yield surplus capital accumulations that can be employed in expanding into other industrial areas.

In Spain's early industrial development textiles performed a comparable function, but its generative effects were for a long period limited mainly to Catalonia. Gabriel Tortella observes, "We know as with England, it was the textile industry and later iron and steel that were the first to develop. But in contrast to what took place in England, cotton textiles did not carry the rest of the country with it because of the lack of a supportive backdrop: agricultural prosperity, a transportation network, an efficacious government, a high educational level, and so on."[51]

Uneven development begat more unevenness, leading to greater industrial concentration on the periphery of the peninsula. The preeminence of textiles gradually gave way with the emergence during World War I of metalworking industries such as machinery, railroad equipment, and automobiles. Nonetheless, textiles remained the nation's foremost manufacturing sector until the 1930s, and its employees continued to constitute the single largest element in the industrial work force. Furthermore, because textile manufacturing had succeeded amid persistent socioeconomic underdevelopment in much of the rest of the country, a fateful blemish was affixed on the nature and scope of Catalonian industrialization.

The principality's economy became heavily dependent on the cotton textile industry's good health. In 1898 it accounted for 70 percent of the region's gross national product and a comparable portion of its capital investments. By the mid-nineteenth century a quasi-monopoly in silks and woolens emerged, and toward its conclusion, Catalonian woolens had elevated Spain to third among the woolens manufacturing nations.

Endowed with an ideal humid, mild climate and excellent port facilities, Barcelona rapidly became the Manchester and Liverpool of Spanish textile manufacturing. Raw cotton was imported from the United States and coal from England to serve the cluster of textile factories and mills along the coast near Barcelona or in adjacent parts of Gerona and Tarragona provinces. To lessen fuel overhead costs and to recruit a work force accustomed to low wages, some cotton mills established operations in the *montaña* of Barcelona province, along the Ter, Fresser, Llobregat, and Cardoner rivers, where hydraulic power could be employed.[52]

Workers in the Ter-Fresser valleys, many of them recruited from nearby farming districts, generally resided in the factory towns of Manlleu, Rodo, and Torelló and consequently developed a sense of shared interests and labor organization. Textile mills in the Llobregat valley, in contrast, were located in isolated sites and within self-enclosed company towns (*colonias*) so that workers in this area for a long time remained outside the orbit of trade union organization. In 1930, when the number of *colonias* reached their highest point, there were some sixty along the Llobregat river valley and more than forty along the Ter.

With the introduction of electric power and the lessened attractiveness of hydraulic power, concentration in the Barcelona area increased even further. By 1901, 1,325 of the 1,563 cotton spinning mills and weaving sheds legally registered in Spain were in Catalonia, 1,237 of them in Barcelona province.[53] By that time only a scattering of textile-making establishments was to be found in the Catalonian hinterland. Beyond Barcelona province, parts of Gerona, Tarragona, and Lérida, as well as the bottle cork–producing towns of the Costa Brava, the remainder of the region continued to be largely devoted to agricultural pursuits.

Because of uneven economic development and the consequent retardation in the formation of a national market, textile factory owners became imprisoned in a vicious circle. Because they were hobbled by a mostly subsistence agriculture that gave the bulk of the population only minimal purchasing power, their fortunes were ineluctably tied to the successes or failures of a semifeudal, inefficient farming system. As Lucás Beltrán Flórez explains, "Good harvest and higher prices for wheat, olive oil, and wine meant a greater demand for cotton fabrics. Bad harvests or low prices resulted in small consumption of cotton goods and depression for our industry."[54]

Fully modern production technology could not be sustained in the absence of an adequate domestic market so quality remained inferior and costs high. Nor could exports offer a viable alternative despite the industry's low labor costs. With low productivity and unable to keep abreast of the latest technological developments, Spain could not compete in the world market.[55] Among the leading nations engaged in textile manufacturing in 1911, Spain ranked next to last as an exporter of cotton goods. Instead of a full-fledged manufacturing sector, it was relegated to the infelicitous status of an import-substitution industry.[56] In a study published in 1920 dealing with Spain's export problems, Francesc Bernis lamented that "during these past twenty years when Spanish industry has enjoyed unprecedented tariff protection, the cotton textile industries of Japan and Italy came into existence practically and have developed well beyond our own."[57]

Under ordinary circumstances modern industrial growth and progress lead to increasing concentration and larger production units. In the case of Catalonian textiles, however, a lack of investment capital, a shortage of credit facilities, and excessive protectionism led to the creation of an extremely fragmented industry, as described by Albert Balcells: "There were few enterprises in the Catalonian textile industry that covered the entire production process. Enterprise dispersion was a characteristic of Catalonian industry. In 1908 the Frenchman Eduard Escarra noted that examples of large capitalist enterprises were to be found only in the chemical, electric power, and automobile sectors."[58] It has been estimated that the region possessed thirteen thousand manufacturing enterprises in 1900 of which seven thousand were located in the city of Barcelona.

The bulk of the textile industry consisted of small units. Production functions (and labor organizational jurisdictions as well) were divided into three broad divisions: *arte fabril*, which encompassed firms specializing in the spinning of cotton thread and yarn and the weaving of fabrics as well as the grinding or regeneration of cloth or residuals, carding, combing, and the preparation of warps and weaves; *ramo de agua*, which covered a number of textile fibers, wool washing, burling, dressing, bleaching, dyeing, and portions of the printing process that were not performed by *arte fabril;* and *generos de punto,* or the production of knitted products and jersey. Each of these manufacturing categories involved distinctive technical and working conditions.

Though spinning and yarn-making installations were the most technologically sophisticated sector of the industry, when compared with leading foreign industries they were extremely modest. In England such installations generally had more than one hundred thousand spindles, but Spain's largest, and it was the exception, possessed sixty-seven thousand. Others ranged from five to twenty thousand, and quite a few operated with fewer spindles. The average was less than five thousand.[59]

Yarn and thread production was almost exclusively concentrated in the *montaña* of Barcelona province, among the numerous spinning mills in the Ter and Fresser valleys. Weaving sheds tended to cluster in the cities of Barcelona, Manresa, Vilanova, Sabadell, Tarrassa, Reus, and Salt de Gerona, and towns such as Mataró and Calella were the centers for the manufacture of knitted products and jersey.

The wide fluctuations in market requirements induced some of the larger enterprises to engage in a two-tier operation not unlike that employed by the Japanese. Larger firms would own small shops and mills or sub-contract to fill parts of the orders received. Many of them were interrelated in a complex maze of fragmented production specialties. Some served as auxiliaries to others, while still others were semidomestic or family operations. These arrangements permitted them to respond to increased demand during prosperous times without investing in machinery and personnel that would have to be scaled back when business decreased. Having part of the work performed by small shops reduced operating and labor costs.[60]

Jordi Maluquer argues that this industry configuration did not represent a disorderly production system but rather a practical response to the vagaries of market fluctuations: "The Catalonian textile industry was not, as has been said, an aggregate of liliputian enterprises submerged in a sterilizing marasmus against which it would have been easy to compete but rather a well-integrated, hierarchical structure adapted to the exigencies of market size and character. Medium and small enterprises and domestic workers—the putting-out system—formed well-articulated entities through which the large enterprisers disposed of a much greater operational decision-making capacity and were more resistant to abrupt market fluctuations than one imagined."[61]

Ralph Odell, a commercial agent for the U.S. Department of Commerce and Labor, who conducted a survey in 1911 of the Spanish cotton textile industry, provided the following description of working conditions:

There are three characteristics of the cotton industry that impress the American upon entering a Spanish cotton mill: First, the large number of operatives required; second, the predominance of female employees (only about 15% are males); third, the wide range of fabrics produced in each factory. . . . As the mills are all small as regards individual units, this method necessitates many details in management, separate mixings of cotton, and the production of a wide range of yarns.

Wages paid in the Spanish cotton mills are considerably lower than those prevailing in the United States, ranging from 8 pesetas ($1.43) per week, paid to doffers, to 28 pesetas ($5.02) paid to the most skillful weavers. The average wage is about 20 pesetas ($3.58) per week. . . . Operatives are less efficient than American workers and do not tend so many machines. . . . The variation in wages . . . depends on the location of the mill, the highest being paid in Barcelona and the lowest in the colonias or mill villages.

The hours of work are 66 per week for the day and 48 for the night run. Three fourths of the cotton mills in Spain are now being operated night and day.

Eleven hours constitute a working day according to the law but several of the mills that I visited were running 12 hours. Work usually begins at 5:30 A.M. and ends at 6:30 P.M. with a half hour stop at 8:30 A.M. for breakfast and an hour and a half at noon for lunch.[62]

A royal decree in August 1913 established the sixty-hour week for textile workers, but the sixty-six-hour week continued to be the general rule. Textile workers in Reus, for example, went on strike in 1915 to force employers to comply with the 1913 decree and the law limiting work for women and children.

The effects of meager modernization were evident in the mentality and practices of the Catalonian industrial elite. The tradition of family ownership remained strongly entrenched until very recently. Only a handful of the textile companies were incorporated. Francesc Cambó, the region's most prominent industrialist-politician, "believed that Catalonians remained a nation of shopkeepers whose horror of the limited liability company, whose fear of combination in order to win large markets, stemmed from the artisan's desire to be master in his own house."[63]

One industry authority has attributed this entrepreneurial parochialism to the social origins of most factory owners: "Almost all of our enterprises represent an industrial tradition that has carried on through various generations and expanded an industry that was originally small and, by such expansions, in some instances have become very important. Almost all big industrialists are sons of medium-sized manufacturers who, early in the past century, established small industrial firms of a family character."[64] Family ownership meant that capitalization had to be secured almost exclusively from profits rather than through the floating of joint stock issues.[65]

Albert Balcells places great emphasis on the conditions under which industrialization took place in Catalonia with its lack of raw materials and energy supplies, an inadequate and deficient transportation network, chronic political instability, and Madrid's indifference to national industrial development: "This has to be taken into account in comprehending the individualism and limited horizons of the Catalonian bourgeoisie as well as its relative political and social conservatism. The fact that an industrial revolution took place within the territory of a national minority that did not possess its own political power and that throughout the nineteenth century the politically dominant group remained in a preindustrial socioeconomic condition constantly created tensions."[66] Unable to act as representatives of an ascendant class, they functioned instead as a pressure lobby, a role that little endeared them to the governing authorities of Madrid.

Over the course of the nineteenth century, wealth and economic power became concentrated in the hands of the thirty families who amassed great fortunes through the control of yarn production. Five families owned more than 50 percent of the spindles, and much of the remainder was in the hands of an additional fifty. By the century's end the five leading families had extended their domain to encompass an estimated three-quarters of production facilities. In chemicals and metal manufacturing, industries closely related to textile making, half a dozen families occupied a similarly dominant position.

This apparent contradiction between extreme concentration of wealth and the plethora of small companies resulted from the acute shortages of investment capital, difficulties in obtaining credit, and protectionist strategies. Jaime Vicens Vives summed up the situation: "The Catalan economy depended on the prosperity of the cotton textile industry and ultimately, therefore, on policies set by a small group of entrepreneurs: the twenty to thirty families tightly knit through intermarriage that controlled the production of cotton yarn, through which they accumulated much capital during the nineteenth century. Their policies were seconded by the textile manufacturers, who made up a much larger group, for, in contrast to the concentration in yarn, cotton textile manufacturing was characterized by small-scale, individually or family-owned factories."[67]

Social conservatism of industrial elites is a common characteristic throughout Western economic development. In Catalonia it was reinforced by the marginal role accorded the business class in national economic policy making and the difficulties it encountered in dealing with an increasingly restive labor force.

Making a profit in textile manufacturing, especially for a great number of small and medium-sized enterprises, presented special problems. High-cost items such as imported raw cotton and coal as well as transportation were unalterable. To be sure, the high tariff barriers that were established in 1906 not only assured a captive domestic market but reduced competition and assured a level of profitability. An estimated 19.7 to 35 percent of the prices of textile products was attributable to high tariffs.[68] But inelasticity of domestic demand and the vagaries of agricultural prosperity limited the extent to which greater productive efficiency could be achieved through technological modernization.

Jordi Nadal places annual average industry growth until 1880 at 5.4 percent; as the industry increasingly encountered structural and conjunctural problems from 1880 to 1913, growth declined to an average 2.28 percent: "Manufacturing development during the 1880s began to decelerate, ending up in retrogression between 1909 and 1913. In 1888 probably the two most representative Catalonian companies—Güell and La España Industrial—both located in Sants, had to carry out drastic cutbacks of personnel and organization to reduce costs and maintain competitiveness. An official source in 1890 acknowledged that capital invested in manufacturing was yielding ever smaller returns." The main obstacle to the industry's good health and expansion was "agricultural immobility," which prevented any growth in domestic demand. "Periods of expansion (after 1904) would be exceptional depending upon extraordinary conjunctures. The 1914–18 conflict, for example, offered an opportunity for supplying the belligerent countries. A Barcelona industrialist in later years put it in candidly apt terms, illustrative of bourgeois morality, of a Hegelian deistic concept: 'When the crisis recurred on a truly alarming scale, Providence appeared in the horrible form of the world war and the industry was once again enabled to remain afloat.' "[69]

This period of intermittent crises occurred during the years in which a modern labor movement emerged in Catalonia. A prolonged industry recession commenced in 1885 following the onset of depression in the country's grain-raising regions caused by the entry of cheap foreign wheat. During 1886–87 it became especially severe. The Barcelona Universal Exposition of 1888 and an urban renovation program were partly intended to relieve high unemployment.

The turn of the century was a particularly trying time. Colonial markets were lost when reduced domestic consumer demand resulting from the agricultural depression had not yet been overcome, and, at the same time, the price of raw imported cotton rose sharply. But there also were positive developments. The repatriation of capital after 1898 from the colonies and the government's deflationary stabilization policies of 1899 to 1908 permitted much of the industry to undertake technological improvements. On balance, however, one economic historian asserts that "the loss of the crucial markets of Cuba, Puerto Rico, and the Philippines prefaced a lengthy depression from which the textile sector was never to recover."[70]

With the loss of overseas protected markets and the ensuing national recession, textile owners found themselves with bulging warehouses full of unsold cotton goods in 1900, in 1901, and again in 1908–9. Similar difficulties were encountered in the years immediately before World War I, though the industry's fortunes took a turn for the better starting in 1910 as agricultural conditions improved.

In an industry in which labor was a major cost and most other cost factors were beyond the control of the manufacturers, the reduction of labor overhead became vitally important. A universal remedy was the increased use of female labor. In 1857 only 35.7 percent of the Barcelona textile labor force consisted of women, but by 1906 their proportion had increased to 96 percent.[71] Layoffs were frequent, wages were often subject to reductions, work loads increased, and working hours extended without corresponding increases in pay. Real wage earnings often declined at times when inflation increased the cost of living, creating social tensions. An inflationary spiral occurred during the second half of the nineteenth century.

Crisis in the industry during the 1880s and the resulting labor cost-cutting measures led to a violent confrontation in 1890 with the moderate Tres Clases de Vapor Federación and its ultimate demise. An impressive number of people showed up for a May Day parade in 1890 staged by the beleaguered Barcelona working class. At the turn of the century, economic difficulties and retrogressive labor policies led to a prolonged period of militant, violent labor conflicts at the same time as Catalonian businessmen vigorously opposed passage of a law limiting the working hours and conditions for women and minors. Nor was it coincidence that the 1902 general strike in Barcelona and the Tragic Week of 1909 both took place during recessions in the textile industry.

Employers' opposition to unions, as Joan Ullman explains, was exacerbated because "the postwar depression . . . made it impossible for Catalan industry to absorb a majority of the labor force except for certain months of peak production or for certain prosperous years (such as 1905). Desperate for work, able to perform the simple tasks of a relatively primitive industry, these men and women constituted a constant source of scab labor that led to the failure of collective bargaining and peaceful strike action. Concurrently an alarming number of more skilled workers, the backbone of any labor movement, left for South America, France and Algeria."[72]

The constraints of a limited market and a laggard technology had by the century's conclusion converted demands for increased protectionist trade policies into the centerpiece of Catalonia's uneasy and abrasive relations with Madrid. Cánovas del Castillo, then prime minister, in a change of heart, modified his long-standing free trade convictions in 1890 and provided some customs relief to Catalonian textile interests, but it was not sufficient to overcome the industry's vulnerabilities or stem bourgeois Catalonia's political disaffection with the Madrid ruling elite. Hence the fateful decision early in this century by the Catalan business community to break with the dynastic ruling parties, the Conservatives in particular, arose less from feelings of ethnocultural repression than from the difficulties in persuading the authorities in Madrid, whose main clientele were agricultural and financial free traders, to erect customs barriers that would shield Catalonian textiles. Partly in response to the industry's doldrums following a period of disastrous agricultural harvests and partly to deflect the growing strength of Catalonian political regionalism, the desired protectionist walls were finally erected in 1906.

Despite the tonic effect of protectionist measures, market inconstancies led to continued repression of the work force, especially by employers intent on reaping a quick profit. In a report on the industrywide strike of 1913, a government labor inspector observed that "the industry's economic condition . . . is neither ruinous nor prosperous. Many looms lie idle; there is a lack of markets to reduce stockpiles and orders are few in comparison with other times. . . . Without necessarily incurring deficits a diminution in profits can be surmised even though employers in their projections had anticipated as much or larger profits than subsequently has been the case. The protective margin provided by the tariffs, the low wages of women and children, and the excessive number of work hours many obtain are the factors, having otherwise obtained ample profits in proportion to the capital that this industry represents, that generally explain the rapid enrichment of many factory owners."[73] These problems help explain, in part at least, the high union consciousness in a low-wage industry suffering from deformations imposed by a retarded national economy, and it served as the seedbed for a particularly virulent form of anarcho-syndicalism.

The radicalization of organized labor in Catalonia has been the subject of much speculation and conjecture. A host of reasons have been marshaled to explain why the most industrialized part of the country became the irrepressible fortress of anarcho-syndicalism. Market deficiencies, structural vulnerabilities, and the mill owners' response to the flowering of labor extremism were important. For a time workers' organized resistance to measures that cut the cost of labor were quelled, but ultimately the owners achieved only a Pyrrhic victory. A residue of resistance and class hostility had been permanently instilled in the workers. Furthermore, the suppression of trade unionism led the working poor of Barcelona to express their dissatisfaction through unchanneled, visceral outbursts exemplified by the Tragic Week of 1909. No other western European country except Italy had experienced such a popular urban uprising in this century.

Catalonian industrialists were not the only ones who resorted to poor working conditions and antiunionism. Almost everywhere these measures had been the practically universal recourse in early developing capitalism, but the extent to which they were used in the Catalonian textile industry was exceptional. Moreover, in the profoundly changed socioeconomic-political ambience of turn-of-the-century western Europe, it was incendiary to employ measures more appropriate to the early nineteenth century.

Nineteenth-Century Industrial Development

A liberalization in government policy during the 1860s permitted increasing amounts of foreign capital to enter Spain. Initially much of it was funneled into railroad construction. Further inducements led to the influx of even larger amounts that were invested in the exploitation of the peninsula's mineral deposits, which hitherto had been only marginally developed. Booming European industrial expansion had greatly increased the demand for a large variety of minerals and ores, and mining expanded rapidly in the century's closing decades to join agriculture as the leading sources of national income. Together they provided employment for 75 percent of the working population.

Industrial development throughout the nineteenth century became heavily dependent on foreign capital and technology largely because of the chronic shortage of domestic investment capital. Imbued with a preindustrial rentier mentality, many in business and finance continued to channel local capital into real estate and land transactions that yielded quick speculative returns or invested in foreign bond issues. Unlike its European counterparts, the Spanish government did little until the end of the century to stimulate or encourage industrial development through the use of public funds or subsidies.

By the latter part of the nineteenth century Spain's role in the European industrial revolution was to provide ores and minerals. Foreign capital, primarily British, came to dominate a much expanded mining industry and to enjoy extraterritorial rights, prompting Francesc Cambó to call the great mines of Peñarroya and Rio Tinto "economic Gibraltars."

At first, mining ventures concentrated on the extraction of silver, zinc, copper, pyrites, lead, and mercury. Most were located in the south, in the provinces of Murcia, Almeria, Jaen, Córdoba, Badajoz, Ciudad Real, and Huelva, where farming was the predominant economic pursuit. They also tended to be situated in isolated zones. By Spanish standards some of the foreign mining concerns paid relatively high wages, but the munificent returns they realized on their investments were made possible in part by the extremely modest labor costs they incurred by employing a work force accustomed to abysmally low wages.

The most extraordinary among the foreign mining enterprises was the huge Rio Tinto mine in Huelva province, which possessed one of the world's richest deposits of copper ore and pyrites. Following its purchase by a British company in the 1870s, operations were greatly expanded. Copper extraction rose from a million tons in 1885 to 2.71 million tons in 1900. By the 1880s Rio Tinto was the world's largest single mining operation.

The development of this enormous enterprise necessitated the recruitment of a labor force much larger than the neighboring rural communities could provide. The work force in 1873 numbered slightly less than a

Table 1.2.   Workers Employed in Mines, Quarries, and Smelting Plants,
1887–1931

Year	Mineworkers	Those engaged in processing	Total
1887	76,180	–[a]	–[a]
1901	87,382	22,167	109,549
1907	131,951	20,844	152,795
1918	132,220	30,114	162,334
1920	125,040	31,599	156,639
1926	103,704	55,692	159,396
1930	92,894	76,813	169,707
1931	93,984	68,534	162,518

Source: National Statistical Institute (INE); Miguel Martínez Cuadrado, La burgesía conservadora (1874–1931) (Madrid: Alianza Universidad, 1973), p. 189.
[a]Figures not available.

thousand, but by 1883 it had risen to roughly ten thousand and in 1909 had reached almost seventeen thousand. Large numbers of immigrants streamed in, mostly young men from rural areas throughout the country and from Portugal, as well as unemployed miners from Asturias, some of whom had been blacklisted following the defeat of a strike in 1906. Local inhabitants dubbed this diverse work force "Los Mohinos" (mohino is a cross between a stallion and a female ass). For statistics on the mine labor force, see table 1.2.

The miners were housed in company-owned billets and received considerably higher wages than southern agricultural laborers did. In 1888 the farm daily wage averaged the equivalent of one shilling six pence while an unskilled laborer at Rio Tinto earned an average of three shillings four pence. The presence of foreign companies and the sizable disparity in earnings between mineworkers and the neighboring impoverished farm populations of the Sierra led to the creation in southern Spain of enclaves with highly distinct social structures, shaped by the rigors and rhythms of an industrial regimen. The miners of southern Spain constituted a working-class elite.

The assimilation of the mine's rapidly expanded work force and the creation of social cohesion proved to be a lengthy and turbulent process. According to David Avery, "Right down until the time of the world war the mine's population bore the marks of an immigrant people, with its appearance, its speech and its customs testifying to the fact that its individual members were as much strangers to Rio Tinto as the British

in Bella Vista. The lack of social cohesiveness passed only gradually. . . .
The violence that was rife in the Spanish community in the last quarter
of the nineteenth century owed much to the poverty of the surroundings
and the rootlessness of the people."[74]

Iron ore deposits in the Basque province of Vizcaya (along with smaller
iron mines in the neighboring province of Santander) by the century's
end replaced the products extracted from the southern mines as the country's principal mineral export. Coal mining also began to expand in
Asturias.

For a time the mining boom helped reduce the huge deficits in the
national budget and improve the general economic situation. But it did
little to advance the development of the metal fabricating industry or
industry in general. As Sánchez Albornoz concludes, "For one reason or
another the mines ended up converted into foreign enclaves linked ter-
ritorially to Spain but without articulation to the rest of the economy."[75]
Most of the mined ores were shipped to European countries, where they
furnished the basic ingredients for burgeoning industrial establishments.
At the end of the century only 1 percent of Spain's exports consisted of
finished industrial goods, whereas minerals accounted for 23 percent and
agricultural products for the remainder.[76] During the early years of this
century, 9 million tons of iron ore were extracted, but only half a million
was retained for domestic processing or fabrication. Domestic production
of elaborated copper and processed sulfur was insufficient to meet the
country's needs and had to be made up by imports from Great Britain
and other countries to which most of the mined copper had been shipped,
underscoring Spain's role in the European industrial revolution as merely
a supplier of raw materials.

Spain's belated economic development amid highly sustained industrialization in the leading western European countries made Spain vulnerable to both conjunctural fluctuations and external pressures. Key areas
of economic activity consequently came under direct and indirect pressures
and were manipulated by foreign entrepreneurs who sought to shape
economic policies to conform to their interests. Because of this foreign
pressure and the government's urgency in making up the formidable
deficits in the national budget, Spain's mineral wealth was largely exhausted early in this century but not to support domestic industrial
development. Fiscal solvency was maintained but at a fearfully high price,
part of which was the large profits foreign capitalists took out of the
country.

The outcome was different in Vizcaya. Basque entrepreneurs joined with foreign investors in forming companies that mined the iron ore, and when exports reached their peak between 1880 and 1900, they employed the handsome profits to establish the foundations for their future predominance in heavy industry. An industrial complex, which included iron and steelmaking, structural steel, railroad equipment, shipyards, and heavy machinery, was built in Bilbao and its environs with the aid of British know-how. At the outset, however, the protection of high tariffs was necessary to assure its survival. Throughout the first half of the twentieth century high tariffs were maintained to assist Spanish industry, but at a cost because protectionism discouraged the entry of foreign technology and capital.

The formation of heavy industry consequently came as a late development in Spain's economic modernization. Earlier attempts to create such industrial ventures miscarried for a variety of reasons. All uniformly suffered from the inability of an underdeveloped, predominantly agricultural society to sustain them. The extraction of the abundant coal deposits in Asturias, for example, could be undertaken with modest financial resources, but the large capital outlays that were indispensable to launch an iron and steel complex were not available. Consequently, the railway system that was begun in the 1850s was almost entirely a foreign undertaking. Virtually everything, including steel rails, had to be imported from the more advanced industrial European countries. Spain was incapable of simultaneously creating a railway network and a heavy industry.[77]

A breakthrough, albeit gradual, occurred at the century's end with the industrial development of the Basque province of Vizcaya. Greatly increased demand from the industrializing nations of Europe and technological innovations in the making of iron and steel such as the Bessemer converter process, which made the province's hematite iron ore deposits highly sought after because of their low phosphorous content, furnished a basis for industrial takeoff. The proximity of the iron ore pits to the port city of Bilbao (Somorrostro, the largest of the mines, was only ten kilometers from the city) made them attractive to foreign investors and clients.

Iron ore exports as a source of capital accumulation and industrial diversification proved more successful in stimulating industrialization for Basque entrepreneurs than textile making had been for the Catalonians. High-grade ore was the most crucial raw material in the development of a heavy metalworking industry. Ore was extracted almost exclusively from open pits, a process that required relatively few skilled workers or expensive, complicated machinery. Thus productive efficiency could be rapidly attained using an untutored work force with no previous industrial tradition or experience. The proximity of the mine pits to the docks of Bilbao spared entrepreneurs major capital outlays for transportation facilities and equipment. Overhead cable cars carried the mined ore from the pits to the docks for loading. A further advantage was that with England as the principal export market, the freighters that hauled away the ore would return filled with British coking coal for the iron and steel mills of the Bilbao area. Coking coal from the nearby mines of Asturias could not equal the British either in quality or price.

Basque industrialists, unlike the Catalans, collaborated with British, Belgians, and Germans in setting up jointly owned firms. More corporate enterprises were founded in Vizcaya than in any other mining area of Spain. Basque enterprisers amassed considerable sums from their mining ventures and uncharacteristically invested these funds in the creation of an industrial complex. Many of the new ventures were set up as joint stock and limited liability firms, a departure from the family-controlled enterprises that previously characterized so much of Spanish business. This structure was unavoidable because, in contrast with the Catalonian textile-making industry's modest capital needs, heavy industry required large capital investment. Nowhere in the peninsula did the spirit of modern managerial enterprise take hold as it did in the Basque region, as was attested by the emergence of the banks of Bilbao as the country's most powerful and influential financial institutions, assuming a leading role in the financing of many of the newly created factories and in the expansion and modernization of the city's port facilities. Basque bankers and industrialists became the most influential and powerful of Spanish capitalists. Some of the capitalization of Asturian mining and industrial development came from Basque investors, and the ready acceptance by Asturian businessmen of the joint stock company financial structure, in addition to local capital deficiencies, undoubtedly derived from the Basque example.

Industrial growth and the mining boom generated considerable population growth. The first wave of immigrants, known as *los ambulantes,* came from the neighboring provinces of Logroño, Alava, Navarre, and Santander; those who followed hailed from the more distant provinces of Galicia, Burgos, León, and Palencia. Lucas Mallado, the inspector general of mines, estimated in 1910 that "out of a total of thirteen thousand workers in the mines of Vizcaya, barely three thousand are native of the Dominion (Señorio), some six thousand are from Galicia and the remaining four thousand from other parts of Spain."[78] The bulk of the work force was made up of farmers who worked in the mines when not needed for farm chores.

Vizcaya's population grew during the final decades of the century at twice the rate of Barcelona's or Madrid's. Employment in the metal industry increased from 2,245 in 1884 to 22,000 by 1900. Bilbao was transformed from a secondary port and trading center to a major maritime shipping port rivaling Barcelona. The number of the city's inhabitants soared from 32,734 in 1876 to more than 83,000 in 1900, making it one of Spain's leading urban industrial centers.

Rapid population growth and accelerated industrial expansion were also accompanied by horrors that had not been seen since Europe's early industrializing days. Bilbao suffered from a humid, generally inhospitable climate, and extreme overcrowding, an acute shortage of housing, poor hygienic conditions, frequent epidemics of cholera and smallpox, sanitation problems, and a high infant mortality made it a most unhealthy place.

For the local bourgeoisie, however, industrialization brought a cosmopolitanism to their lifestyles and to their business methods that had not been seen elsewhere in Spain. Collaborative ownerships with British entrepreneurs in iron mining and other ventures and the heavy shipping traffic between England and Bilbao shaped the outlooks of Basque enterprisers. José Luis Comellas notes, "Without losing its distinctiveness, Bilbao was transformed into a 'very English city.' . . . Because of the incessant traffic of iron ore and coal, relations with Great Britain were very close and British ways and customs were introduced. It was virtually obligatory for good Bilbao families to send their children to be educated at Eton, Oxford, or Cambridge."[79] Their British educations may have aided in persuading Basque factory magnates to deal with their labor problems in a somewhat less destructive manner than their Catalonian confreres.

In its developmental stages Vizcayan industry, largely concentrated in and around Bilbao, suffered from inefficient management and high unit production costs and was, therefore, not able to compete with the products of the more advanced industrial nations. The protectionist tariffs that were first introduced in 1891, among the highest in the world, provided badly needed insulation. Government orders for the construction of naval vessels to replace those lost in the Spanish-American War also protected nascent industrial development from the damaging effects of foreign competition.

Though industrial expansion proceeded at a fairly rapid pace, technological proficiency was not so easily achieved, partly because of the difficulties encountered in importing needed equipment under tariff restrictions and partly because of the limited scope of the domestic market. During the century's last decades the new mills could produce only iron ingots and tinplate; the production of steel was undertaken only in 1903. Several more decades passed before the metallurgical industries of Bilbao had attained a reasonable degree of productivity and technical proficiency.

At the turn of the century, Vizcayan metalworking consisted of one hundred factories with a work force of approximately eighteen thousand. Most were concentrated on a strip of land ten kilometers in length on the left bank of the Nervión estuary in the towns of Baracaldo and Sestao that adjoin Bilbao. This zone became the hub of the Spanish metal industry.[80]

Industrialization then spread to the neighboring province of Guipúzcoa but with certain differences. Except for its coastal areas, Guipúzcoa largely consists of hilly, mountainous terrain with towns and villages clustered in the valleys and along riverbanks. Because of this geographical characteristic and the prevailing pastoral social and economic patterns, industrial development around the end of the nineteenth century took the form of widely dispersed small and medium-sized manufacturing establishments distributed among the various towns and villages.

A French visitor in 1907 observed that "the tourist who travels through Guipúzcoa is struck by the fact that even the smallest village possesses factories; electrical wires on all sides, conveyors of power and light, descend to the river basins, rising gradually in indefinite series along the slopes of gorges. The noise of the machines in animated movement like an interior vibration, the tranquility of the village streets. The presence of chimneys announces that electrical energy is not the only one employed."[81]

According to Juan Pablo Fusi, in 1915, there were 285 "industrial centers," located in 45 towns, but only Tolosa, Eibar, Rentería, and Vergara possessed more than 20 factories. Most were small-sized, averaging, in 1907, only 19 workers.[82] A large variety of products were manufactured, including paper products, hunting shotguns, revolvers, ammunition, jewelry, shoes, metals, cement, and textiles. As in the past, traditional home work and domestic industry dominated Guipúzcoan economic life.

The work force of Guipúzcoa differed markedly from that of Bilbao. Before World War I few workers came from outside localities, and because these towns were situated in the heart of farming districts, most industrial work hands also performed farming chores, and many lived in farmhouses. Henri Lorin observed, "Life is confined to extremely limited horizons, cultivable land is parsimoniously distributed, and, moreover, one does not devote himself to agriculture with much inclination; indeed the land leaves them with spare time. It counsels peasants to vary their occupation, to manage without leaving the areas, so they become industrial workers."[83]

Thus for a long time the Guipúzcoan worker incorporated a blend of proletarian and peasant traits. "Industrialization," Fusi tells us, "had not destroyed the traditional forms of life. The labor tradition of Basque society, based on a strict sense of discipline and loyalty in work, was transmitted for a certain time at least to the manufacturing centers; the strong influence of Catholicism prevented the diffusion of radical ideas and contributed to the maintenance of harmonious and stable social relations."[84]

Toward the end of the century coal was mined at several locations in the country, including Aragon, Catalonia, Andalusia, and the Castilian province of León. But the most extensive deposits were in Asturias. Approximately 60 percent of national output during the period 1861 to 1913 came from that region.

During the greater part of the nineteenth century economic backwardness and the lack of roads and transportation facilities inhibited coal production. With the expansion of the railway network after the 1860s, however, and with the inauguration of the iron and steel industry of Vizcaya during the 1880s, demand for coal increased steadily. Also during the 1860s and 1870s, spurred by the easy accessibility of coal, various Spanish and foreign entrepreneurs erected ironmaking mills and metalworking factories in the Asturian urban centers of Gijón and Mieres.

The promotors of these industrial ventures had revived long-standing hopes of converting Asturias into the principal center for heavy industry, but these aspirations were nullified by the emergence of Bilbao and the Basque region as its hegemonic capital. For not only did the Basques employ their profits from the sales of their rich red hematite iron ore deposits to establish new factories, they also seriously undercut their rivals by obtaining coal, especially coke, not from the nearby Asturian mines but from England. Almost as much British coal was exported to Spain in 1900 as was produced domestically. Exports to the Basque region continued until World War I began. By that time Basque industry had become established, and Asturias had been permanently relegated to the status of a significant but secondary metallurgical manufacturing zone. Basque industrial growth had also increased that region's share of Spain's merchant marine commerce to 45 percent and accounted for 30 percent of the country's banking operations.

Available statistics on the size and distribution of the Asturian work force at the turn of the century are not very reliable. Mining employed roughly 11,000 persons, slightly less than a fifth of whom were children. An additional 5,000 worked in the iron mills and metalworking plants. Francisco Erice provides statistics: "In 1902 Barcelona possessed 117,000 wage earners, rising to 205,600 by 1919. The Vizcayan manufacturing population numerically exceeded that of Asturias. A census of Vizcayan industry in 1900 indicated a total of 42,738 employed, while Rafael Fuertes Arias estimated the number of Asturian mining and manufacturing workers at slightly more than 35,000. It should be kept in mind that the total population of Vizcaya was much smaller than that of Asturias."[85] The number employed in mining and manufacturing increased gradually before the world war. The war's advent halted British coal exports and thus greatly increased the demand for domestic coal, with the result that the work force more than doubled during the war years.

Most Asturian coal mines are located in rural valleys adjoining agricultural districts. From the outset, therefore, the bulk of the work force was recruited from nearby farming communities. The great majority of mine employees throughout the nineteenth century were rural folk who retained their peasant ways, alternating between working in the mines and pursuing their farm chores. Accounts of the period mention the frequent complaints of mine managers over the excessive rate of absenteeism, for, as David Ruiz says, "the fact of working in an Asturian mine and receiving a daily wage did not signify a direct dependence upon the enterprise nor absolute independence for the worker."[86] The admixture of proletarian and peasant traits, which is a frequent feature of early industrialization, characterized mine labor in Asturias and that of many similar extractive enterprises in the rest of the country until well into the present century.

There are no conclusive statistics on the number of mixed workers in

Asturian mines, but, as Adrian Shubert notes, "in 1896, José Suarez, chief government mining engineer for the region, estimated that 60 percent of the miners lived in *caserías* (farmhouses), which indicated that they were small farmers; however, this did not include those who worked the land but lived in the villages. When the Frenchman Paul Nicou visited the mining zones of Oviedo and Langreo it was unusual to encounter workers who did not combine industrial with agricultural work, unless they were outsiders."[87]

Gradually immigrants from the neighboring regions of Castile and Galicia joined the work force. The great expansion of coal production stimulated by wartime demand attracted even larger numbers of workers from outside the region. Modern factory proletarians first made their appearance during the concluding decades of the nineteenth century in the burgeoning industrial districts of Oviedo and Gijón.

In its early phases industrialization had had little visible effect on traditional urban centers such as Paris and London. In like fashion, the growth of manufacturing in Catalonia and the Basque country had only a marginal effect on Madrid's traditional patterns of economic and commercial life. Madrid remained outwardly unchanged until the years immediately preceding World War I. It was the Spanish city with the most traditional services, especially artisanal crafts. Economic and social activities derived from its position as the country's administrative, financial, and political capital. Its inhabitants included government functionaries, administrative personnel, service employees, middle-class professionals, and members of the aristocracy. Madrid remained the favored residence for much of the country's elite, the well-to-do, and the politicians.

The city's work force reflected this configuration. Building construction at the century's beginning was the single largest employer of labor, followed by the various service occupations. The popular saying under Louis Napoleon, "as the construction trades go, so goes Paris,"[88] could be equally applied to Madrid. Light manufacturing, including the production of luxury products and handicrafts, also was important. Women employed in manufacturing and "arts and crafts" (*artes y oficios*) represented 30 percent of the industrial labor force, and children below the age of eighteen made up an additional 27 percent. Though accurate figures do not exist, a considerable number of women must have been employed as domestics. Immigration during the early years of this century assumed substantial proportions, but in contrast to those who had migrated to the industrial centers, those who came to Madrid usually became construction laborers or entered one of the service trades. Industry consisted almost exclusively of small establishments with work forces consisting either of the owner and members of his family or a handful of employees. Many retained the atmosphere and personal relations of preindustrial enterprises. Until the 1930s much clothing manufacture and shoemaking was performed by home workers paid on a piecework basis.

Foreign capital throughout the early years of this century was instrumental in the inauguration of new industries such as chemicals, electric power, urban transport, and gas illumination, although they did not substantively alter the existing economic configuration. Cotton textile manufacturing in 1913, on the eve of the world war, retained its primacy over iron and steel production, a condition that bespoke the "profoundly disequilibrated, disharmonic, and unintegrated character of the Spanish industrialization process, replete with its asynchronisms and discontinuities."[89]

2

A MODERN LABOR FORCE AND SOCIAL LEGISLATION

Size and Distribution of the Labor Force

In the early twentieth century Spain's working population, with its substantial preindustrial residual, presented a mirror image of a society barely embarked on economic modernization. Of those actively employed, 68 percent were still in agriculture (over 80 percent in twelve provinces), 16 percent in industry, mining, transport, and commerce, and 16 percent in services (see table 2.1). Roughly 5 million in a total population of 19 million depended on farm work for their livelihoods compared with 2 million who derived their sustenance from nonagricultural employment. Little change had taken place between 1860 and 1900, and a good deal more time would elapse before this ratio would be substantively altered. The number in agriculture three decades later had declined ever so slightly, while the number of wage earners in industry had risen from 1 million to 1.8 million (see table 2.2). Jaime Vicens Vives's estimate of 1 million in the industrial sector is regarded by labor historian Pere Gabriel as excessively high; he considers six to eight hundred thousand a more realistic approximation after subtracting those engaged in traditional artisanal pursuits.[1]

Catalonia was the exception. Although it lagged appreciably behind Europe in technological development and entrepreneurial spirit, the region's social composition came closest to that of fin-de-siècle industrial Europe, with a working class estimated to number 250,000 to 300,000, roughly half in the modern sector. The number of gainfully employed grew between 1908 and 1910 to some 300,000 to 350,000 and, with the expansion that occurred in World War I, rose to around 460,000 and to half a million by 1920. The proportion of the working population

Table 2.1.   Distribution of the Employed Population in 1900

Sector	Number (in millions)	Percentage
Agriculture	4.5	68
Industry	1.0	16
Services	1.0	16

Source: Jaime Vicens Vives, *Historia económica de España* (Barcelona: Editorial Vicens, 1967), p. 567.

engaged in nonfarming pursuits experienced a corresponding increase, rising from an estimated 15 percent of the total population during the last third of the nineteenth century to 21 percent (a more accurate estimate) by 1930.

Precisely what portion of the estimated million employed in industry can be truly regarded as modern proletarians is extremely difficult to determine, partly because of the great numbers of employed and self-employed in the many thousands of small artisan and semiartisan shops—metal manufacturing in Madrid, for example, was conducted almost exclusively in small enterprises—whose traditional work methods and social relations between worker and owner (*amo*) had changed little over the years. If, then, this determination is limited to the more modern industrial sectors such as mining, metalworking, construction, transportation, and communications, about half a million can possibly be included.[2] Building construction was the single largest category employing large numbers of unskilled laborers (*peones*) on a semicasual seasonal basis. Industrial development and the quickening pace of urbanization spurred a building boom in many of the country's leading urban agglomerations. For the distribution of laborers by industry in the country and in Vizcaya see tables 2.3 and 2.4.

In the Iberian context half a million industrial workers may have seemed a large number, but they were a very small minority of the general population, far less than the one-third representation of workers in the gainfully employed populations of the advanced industrial nations of Europe.

The rural farm labor force has been estimated at between 700,000 and over 2 million. The smaller estimate does not include the great numbers of women and children who joined the rural labor force at harvest times. Juan Pablo Fusi has concluded that the number in Andalusia alone of those engaged in farm work was almost equal to the entire national

Table 2.2.   Distribution of the Employed Population (Males), 1900 and 1930 (in millions)

Year	Agriculture	Industry
1900	4.5	1.0
1930	4.4	1.8

Source: Luis Sánchez Agesta, *Historia del constitucionalismo español* (Madrid: Instituto de Estudios Políticas, 1955), p. 474.

industrial work force. Another sizable group that has eluded an accurate count is domestic servants, whose numbers in the early twentieth century were estimated at between 265,000 and 300,000. Female wage earners were most likely to be employed in domestic service.

The historian Manuel Tuñon de Lara has been a leading source for labor force estimates, and his most recent appraisal includes the following observations for 1910: "With respect to the working population . . . of the cities and countryside, the first sector in importance is the agricultural laborers with almost two million. Then comes the 283,000 employed in building construction, followed by clothing manufacture (276,000 persons of which 101,000 are women). Besides the 90,000 in mining (that number 119,000 according to the Institute for Social Reforms), the distinctly industrial sectors provided figures of 133,000 workers in textiles, 67,500 for metallurgy (probably more if one takes into account, according to the Institute for Social Reforms, that steelmaking alone employed almost 27,000 workers), the 110,000 employed in the food industries and the 39,000 in woodworking should be included."[3]

The growth of industry led to the formation of working-class barrios, some located in the center of cities, which expanded to create *ensanches* or suburban zones. This growth is described by José Sánchez Jiménez: "Remaining in the center of cities where industrialization had developed, the industrial zones produced a crowding together of manufacturing and living quarters. In a somber setting, factory buildings stood, colorless, mostly black and gray and malodorous, while worker districts, growing human concentrations with their hovels, shacks, and caves lacking in essential services, fostered a correlation between mortality and squalid habitat. By the end of the nineteenth century suburbs began to proliferate. The suburb was where the recently emigrated populace usually settled to seek wage security and regularity in the city through unskilled labor [*peonaje*] in building construction and other unspecialized types of employment."[4]

Table 2.3.   Distribution of the Employed Population by Industry, 1900 and 1910

Industry	1900	1910
Mining	81,000	99,000
Metallurgy	57,000	67,500
Building construction	271,000	283,000
Textiles	126,500	133,000
Transport and communications	138,400	158,000
Commerce[a]	295,000	333,800
Domestics	264,900	279,600
Total employed	1,233,800	1,353,900
Total population	18,594,405	19,927,150

Source: Manuel Tuñon de Lara, El movimiento obrero en la historia de España, 1900–1923, 3 vols. (Barcelona: Laia, 1972), 2:11–14.

[a]It cannot be ascertained how many in this category were salaried employees, self-employed, or small and medium-sized shopkeepers.

Barcelona, according to Jaime Vicens Vives, possessed half a million inhabitants with a laboring population numbering 160,000 in the period 1900 to 1910. The primary sector, peasants and truck gardeners of the plain, numbered 2,000, with 90,000 in the secondary and 34,000 in the tertiary. The secondary sector included 18,200 casual laborers employed in industry and commerce and 14,000 domestics in the tertiary. The industrial labor force contained 55,000 employed in textile manufacturing, 14,000 in building construction, and 5,000 in the metalworking industry. "White-collar workers (dependents—18,000) made up an important bloc, though not socially (to which for reasons of social similitude could be added an additional 7,000 employed in clothing manufacture). Those in transport numbered some 4,000."[5]

It would probably not be an exaggeration to surmise that half of Spain's 500,000 industrial proletarians, if not more, consisted of recent recruits from the countryside, peasants and farm laborers attracted to mine labor at Rio Tinto, to Murcia-Cartagena, Linares, Vizcaya, and Asturias-León, or those drawn to the burgeoning urban centers such as Barcelona, Bilbao, Zaragossa, Madrid, and others. Boasting worker populations in 1905 of almost 145,000 and 97,000 respectively, Barcelona and Madrid together made up a third of the national total (see table 2.5). Bilbao was then girding for a major expansion in basic metals fabrication and heavy ma-

Table 2.4.   Distribution of the Employed Population in the Province of
Vizcaya, 1900 and 1920

	1900		1920	
Industry	Number	Percentage	Number	Percentage
Agriculture	48,879	37.13	33,133	20.72
Fishing	5,966	4.55	4,483	2.80
Mines and quarries	14,281	10.89	7,686	4.81
Industry	28,457	21.70	61,328	38.35
Transportation	5,673	4.33	8,999	5.63
Commerce[a]	8,744	6.67	22,460[b]	14.04
Domestic service	11,785	8.98	11,505	7.19
Police force	1,682	1.28	2,027	1.27
Religion	2,587	1.97	3,233	2.02
Administration[c]	869	0.66	1,732	1.08
Liberal professions	2,185	1.67	3,332	2.08

Source: Ignacio Olábarri Gortazar, *Relaciones laborales en Vizcaya, 1890–1936* (Durango: L. Zugaza, 1978), p. 448.

[a]Commerce includes those working in taverns, cafés, ·hostels, liquor stores, and spectacles.

[b]The inordinate increase for 1920 is probably attributable to the inclusion of commercial establishments. Owners of enterprises are similarly included in other categories but nowhere else does it cause such a bulge in the overall breakdown.

[c]Administration includes employees of postal, telegraph, telephone, and radio.

chinery manufacture that would ultimately more than double the number employed in Vizcayan industry, from 28,000 in 1900 to 61,000 by 1920.

Such developments, however modest, nonetheless point to a gradually changing pattern in occupational employment. Small and medium-sized industrial establishments, and in some instances large enterprises, were becoming an increasingly prominent feature in the industrial life of Barcelona, Bilbao, Valencia, Oviedo, Gijón, and Málaga; elsewhere in the country, however, in the provincial capitals, towns, and villages, the production and distribution of innumerable manufactured articles continued to be turned out in the time-honored fashion. Much of the labor was performed by women. In Granada, for example, cottage industry still flourished, with local factories contracting women in a putting-out system to convert raw wool into yarn. Others knitted shawls and headgear on a piecework basis. And women using old-fashioned manually operated

Table 2.5.   Employment by Industry in Barcelona and Madrid, 1905

Barcelona[a]		Madrid	
Cotton textiles	18,251	Transportation	11,816
Metallurgy	8,943	Metallurgy	4,602
Construction	15,229	Construction	15,478
Printing	7,945	Printing	6,012
Total	50,378		37,908
Total working population	144,788[b]		97,140

Source: Manuel Tuñon de Lara, El movimiento obrero en la historia de España, 1900–1923, 3 vols. (Barcelona: Laia, 1972), 2:12–13. Tuñon de Lara states that figures for both cities are taken from "local statistics."

[a] The first employment census was undertaken by the municipality of Barcelona in 1905, but it does not include those employed in municipal services or commercial employees.

[b] Includes 34,333 women.

looms in private homes performed a great variety of weaving tasks mainly for local consumption.

Nor did the rise of modern textile mills in Catalonia put an end to traditional forms of production. According to Miguel Martínez Cuadrado, "Catalonian textile hegemony did not destroy artisanry or other industries such as linen, hemp cloth, jute, esparto grass, agave fibers, and others. The traditional family looms and primitive artisanry persisted in the most isolated corners of the country. But its economic influence had begun to decline during the second half of the nineteenth century."[6]

As in other European countries, urban wage earners tended to assume a style of dress peculiar to their occupations: "When in the past century country folk migrated to the cities they tended to retain their rural dress. Towards the end of the century, however, urban workers, including rural immigrants, sported the distinctive 'gorra y blusa' (cap and smock). In the Sunday promenades in the cities one could still recognize the members of the different trades by their dress—masons by their fresh white jackets, butchers by their striped aprons."[7] A Barcelona labor leader has left us a description of modes of dress:

At the beginning of the century an observer of Barcelona streets would have been able to tell the various social classes by the manner of dress that characterized the group they belonged to. The well-to-do bourgeois with cultivated beard was nattily attired in a wool suit and hat. A gold watch dangled conspicuously from his vest. The worker dressed according to his occupation, a striped blouse if he were a warehouse laborer, a blue cotton jacket if a mechanic or metalworker, and a white smock with a kerchief around his neck if he were in building construction. Teamsters and stevedores dressed in corduroy. Workers always went about wearing sandals and various types of caps. Upon reaching adulthood they sported mustaches. Only at their marriages did men wear suits. The suit was thereafter taken out of the closet only to attend other marriages and for burials.[8]

Spanish proletarians changed to blue overalls and black berets (*monos* and *boinas*) after World War I. "Cheaper and more practical, the new costume was to become the trademark of the urban working class in the next decade." In Barcelona and in other cities, writes Enric Ucelay da Cal, "The changeover from the beret, blouse, and sandals in the twenties and thirties gave way as a proletarian uniform to coveralls, a garment—now that it could be worn over other clothes—that implied the manual worker no longer sought to be a worker once he left his place of employment. . . . By the thirties it was not unthinkable for a worker in Barcelona to sport a tie while in agrarian Spain it would be looked upon as an intolerable provocation by the *señoritos* and by his proletarian comrades as well."[9]

The French journalist Jacques Valdour, who spent a year traveling and working in various parts of Spain, tells of encountering during his stay in Bilbao "recently arrived Aragonians still wearing their corduroy suits. Almost all Bilbao workers are dressed in a blue or black blouse, black sandals, and sporting small blue berets that are similarly worn by merchants and bourgeois."[10]

Reflecting the strong ethnic and regional attachments—the enduring bond with *patria chica*—so often displayed by Spaniards, many of the rural immigrants who steadily swelled Madrid's labor force tended to enter occupations according to their places of origin. Those who made bread and pastries were almost exclusively Galicians. Andalusians predominated among the employees of the area's two sugar factories located in Aranjuez and La Poveda, and Aragonese were especially numerous in the manufacture of cooking oil. Immigrants from the Levant at the height of the building construction season make bricks and roof and floor tiles, whereas those from Alicante specialized in mat making.[11]

Miners in southern Spain were obvious by their distinctive dress. The

Andalusian miner described by S. G. Checkland "wore a manta (a cloak of many colors), a handkerchief round his head or a tufted hat, canvas shoes with esparto rope soles, wide cloth breeches ending at the knee, a belt or cummerbund holding his knife, tobacco, and money. On Sundays he might wear a bright embroidered jacket."[12] Most of the administrative personnel at the foreign-owned Tharsis mine were Scotsmen, and the sight of them resplendent in their pith helmets and white jackets, mounted on horses, evoked an image of the Raj in the Andalusian countryside similar to that of India.

Wages and Living Conditions for Industrial Workers

Upon completing his study on poverty in turn-of-the-century England, B. S. Rowntree concluded that "no civilisation can be healthy or stable that is built on such a mass of stunted human lives."[13] If such an admonition could be leveled at Europe's most prosperous and dynamic society, it surely applied all the more to Spain, with its legacy of mass deprivation, then barely entering the initial phases of industrialization.

Though only fragmentary information exists, clearly the toll exacted on urban wage earners by malnutrition, disease, overwork, deficient housing, and unhealthy working conditions was nothing short of appalling. "The documentation," observes Vicens Vives, "leaves little doubt. The situation of the worker in Catalonia during the initial phases of industrial development was truly calamitous."[14] Life expectancy was largely a matter of social and economic status; the poor generally lived half as long as the well-to-do.

The great nineteenth-century expansion of Europe's urban centers prodigiously increased the spread of infectious diseases. In early twentieth-century Spain, where public health facilities and medical care were notoriously lacking and badly administered and where most cities lacked adequate sewage disposal services, the situation reached alarming proportions. Compared to the European average mortality rate of 18 per thousand, it was 29 per thousand. In Bilbao the death rate was especially high, with estimates ranging from 33.5 to 45 per thousand. Not only was it the worst in Spain, but at least one specialist contended that it was the highest in Europe.[15] In 1890 the city of Cádiz experienced a mortality rate of 44.6 per thousand, and the director of sanitation in 1900 attributed Seville's high death rate (40.7 per thousand), higher than those of Alexandria or Cairo and close to that of Madras, to the high incidence of typhoid fever.[16]

Angel Marvaud quotes an annual mortality rate for nonindustrial Madrid of 27 per thousand in 1910, comparing it with 17 per thousand for Paris and 16 for Brussels.[17] Joaquín Romero Maura tells us that "a population of sickly, undernourished appearance was responsible for the fact that the mortality rate of Barcelona (24.1 per thousand) was much higher than that of London, Paris, New York, and Tokyo, even higher than that of Rio de Janeiro, Marseilles, and Venice, and only slightly less than that of Naples . . . although, of course, much lower, starting with Madrid, than those of other Spanish cities."[18]

Infant mortality was horrendous. In 1900 Dr. Amalio Gimeno, a medical specialist and member of the Senate, estimated that 40 percent of all children died before the age of five. The extremely high proportion of women employed in textiles and clothing manufacturing and the exploitive nature of their work had a fearsome effect on infant mortality. According to Balcells, "A fourth of the children born in the city of Barcelona between 1905 and 1909 died before reaching two years of age—15 percent before reaching one year—and the mortality of minors less than two years also represented a fourth of all annual deaths in the city. Infant mortality was much higher in the industrial workers' districts."[19] It was equally high if not higher in the other Catalonian factory towns.

The extent of disease and occupational disorders must have been equally forbidding. The urban poor were extremely vulnerable to epidemics of typhus, cholera, and smallpox, which occurred with grim regularity. Madrid in the first years of this century was considered "the most overcrowded and disease-ridden capital city in Europe."[20]

The situation was even worse in the provinces. José Varela Ortega depicts conditions in the Castilian Meseta in particularly somber terms: "In general the conditions of health were lamentable. Smallpox had been eradicated at the beginning of the century; but in winter respiratory illnesses and in summer gastric, typhoidal, and malarial ones were common. In some barrios of Valladolid deaths from infectious diseases were greater than those from common ailments, and though it did not reach the proportions of some villages, the general mortality rate was approximately double that of Paris or Edinburgh."[21] José Sánchez Jiménez cites a mortality rate for Zamora of 51.6 per thousand, followed by Gerona, Jaen, and Salamanca. With an infant mortality of 280 per thousand, Madrid was referred to by a leading medical authority as "the city of death."[22] "During the first third of the twentieth century," concludes Nadal, "tuberculosis and, by extension, the other infectious diseases, exercised an implacable dominion over the peninsular city and countryside."[23]

The great shortage of housing and extremely cramped living quarters in the teeming tenement districts of most cities were largely responsible for this deplorable situation. One estimate concluded that the 124,000 families resident in Barcelona during 1910 occupied fewer than 32,000 lodgings, or one lodging for each four families, without taking into account the not inconsiderable part of the population that lacked housing.[24]

In the absence of data, one can only surmise that the incidence of industrial accidents must have been very high.[25] We do know, for example, that the accident rate among building construction day laborers in Barcelona was particularly high. Some inkling of the situation can be obtained from the findings of General José Marvá in a study of working conditions in the mining industry that he conducted for the Institute for Social Reforms (IRS): "Of a work force in 1908 of 54,143 men working inside the mines, 63,155 men and 2,574 women engaged in outside tasks, 26,320 men and 291 women in processing, the number of accidents was 275 deaths, 453 seriously injured, and 14,078 with minor injuries."[26] Since surveys of this type were not based on comprehensive figures for the entire industry, these findings undoubtedly err on the low side. Maximiano García Venero concluded that between 1904 and 1909, thousands of minors ten to eighteen years of age were injured in labor accidents.[27] Joaquín Romero Maura's description of the physical hazards confronting workers in Catalonia at the turn of the century bears out Vicens Vives's grim judgment.[28]

Emili Salut, who had lived and worked in Barcelona's fifth district, an area of factories and shops whose labyrinthine passageways contained unhealthy working-class tenements, tells of a woodworking factory that had come to be dubbed the "slaughterhouse" among local workers: "Every week an accident took place among the unskilled laborers (peons) and apprentices who totally lacked any mutual benefit coverage or insurance. The inordinate number of accidents arose from the desire to pay unskilled labor wages to peons to do the work of more qualified workers. Apprentices were also forced to operate machines for which they lacked sufficient technical training in their installation and operations. In general this was the hapless, brutal work organization in many industries at that time.

Brutal working conditions fermented as a natural consequence the primitive anarchism of those years."[29]

Abuses at the turn of the century were reminiscent of those of an earlier date in other countries, including the United States. Notable among them was the creation of "company towns," where workers were forced to make their purchases of daily necessities in company-owned stores and to take lodgings at exorbitant rates in company-owned or designated barracks that were often operated by unscrupulous subcontractors (the truck system). Such malpractices were particularly widespread in the mining towns of Vizcaya, where workers' resentments led to major labor conflicts during the 1890s.

But the overall situation in Spain was worse than in other countries because the rural areas from which industrial labor was mainly recruited furnished peasants whose impoverishment and living standards were generally inferior to those of western European countries at comparable stages of development. The Spanish diet was more frugal than that of any other place in Europe except the Balkans and southern Italy.[30]

Factory owners were consequently able to pay workers relatively low wages. Yet Spanish urban wage earners had to contend with inordinately high prices for essentials. It has been estimated that workers in Madrid during this century's first decade had to expend on the average two-thirds to three-quarters of their earnings on food compared to 34 percent in Brussels and 30 percent in Paris. Meat in 1909 was more expensive in Barcelona than in London. Spanish wages were the lowest in Europe, and the cost of living was among the highest.[31] The reasons for this situation derived from a combination of high tariffs, a deficient agricultural production, and a fiscal structure that levied disproportionately high taxes on basic necessities. For large numbers of workers who managed to eke out a quasi-subsistence standard of living, even the slightest downward trend in purchasing power had the most grievous consequences.[32] Even under normal conditions the inordinately high cost of living obliged many workers to include large amounts of bread in their daily diet, and the resulting nutritional deficiencies made them more vulnerable to infection. A recurring theme in Spanish labor conflicts and social protest is the periodic "subsistence crises" that arose when the gap between the cost of bread and other essentials and real wage earnings reached intolerable proportions.

A leading spokesman for the employers' point of view, the *Revista minera, metalurgica y ingeniería,* sought to deflect workers' dissatisfaction over the rising cost of living in 1890 by placing the blame on the government: "Spanish workers should not make difficulties for their employers but should press the government to do whatever necessary to make food cheaper, which would be the equivalent of a wage increase."[33]

Extremely low wages and rudimentary working conditions were thus the shared lot of most industrial laborers. The reasons go beyond the fact that Spain was in the formative stages of industrialization. Economic, technological, and social retardation often led factory and mine owners, especially in Catalonia, to maximize profits through a combination of low wages and high prices rather than by promoting technological innovation and creating greater demand for their products. The erection of steep tariff walls that were instituted at the end of the nineteenth century was accompanied by price fixing, fostering the creation of veritable domestic monopolies in some sectors that reinforced the tendency to pay low wages because it provided one of the few available means for enhancing competitiveness and increasing profits.

One consequence was that Spain suffered abuses and injustices reminiscent of the early phases of western Europe's industrial revolution. In the nature of social abuses, the forms of labor exploitation, and the bleakness and oppressiveness of urban proletarian existence, Spanish labor conditions replicated to a remarkable degree those that had prevailed in early nineteenth-century Europe.

Peter Stearns calls the terrible exploitation of women and children "the great moral scandal of the Industrial Revolution."[34] After more than half a century, the appearance of such exploitation in Spain was equally abhorrent. It highlighted yet another incongruity of Spanish retardation amid growing western European industrial prosperity and the advance of social legislation. To be sure, women in other European countries in the early twentieth century continued to be subjected to extreme forms of discrimination, but the more reprehensible abuses had been eliminated or were being moderated. Child labor was on the decline, but women continued to receive inferior wages.[35] Thus the repetition of some of the more offensive practices of the industrial revolution at a time when social reforms and trade union action were registering substantial progress elsewhere surely contributed to the widely held image of Spain as irretrievably backward and medieval.

Outside of agriculture the largest number of women and children workers were to be found in the textile industry. In 1905 the Barcelona textile mills employed 5,111 men, 16,466 women, 2,197 boys, and 1,195 girls.

Table 2.6. Distribution of Workers in the Cotton Textile Industry in
Barcelona, by Sex, 1906

Type of work	Men	Women	Total
Preparation	120	4,000	4,120
Spinning	100	80	180
Weaving	120	6,000	6,120
Totals	340	10,080	10,420

Source: Miguel Izard, *Industrialización y obrerismo* (Barcelona: Ariel, 1973), p. 75.

In cotton textiles, by far the city's most important industry, out of a total of 18,251 employed, some 3,412 were men, 11,732 women, 1,780 boys, and 1,327 girls. Large numbers of women and children were also employed in clothing manufacture, bottle cork making, linens, and papermaking.[36] A total of 22,245 minors were gainfully employed. For the distribution of employment by sex, see table 2.6.

The disproportionately large numbers of women and minors employed in the textile industry as well as wage differentials between male adult workers and women and children were generally comparable to those in France half a century before and in Lancashire and Manchester even earlier. The highest percentages of working women and children in the provinces of Valencia and Alicante were in papermaking and textiles, which together absorbed 80 percent of all children employed by industry.[37] Female labor was also used in a variety of other occupations including mining, food processing, building construction, chemicals, and port loading and unloading. In 1902 women constituted an estimated 21 percent of the country's industrial work force.

The highly discriminatory status of women was also expressed in their lack of literacy or rudimentary levels of education. Práxedes Zancada observed that "there are 6,806,834 women [in 1904] who completely lack any basic education while only 2,395,839 know how to read and write. Since it is reasonable to presume that the women with education belong to the upper and middle classes, it can be affirmed, as a consequence, that 98 percent of women workers find themselves in the deepest ignorance, totally without the most rudimentary principles of learning."[38] At that time approximately two-thirds of the population could neither read nor write.

Women normally received half the wages paid to men, and children were paid half again the wage of women. The large-scale employment of women in textile manufacturing was almost universal, but the emphasis given to their employment as well as to exploitation of children by Catalonian factory owners to minimize labor costs and maximize profits went well beyond customary practices (in 1901 women received two pesetas a day, half the wage of a male worker). Percentages of women and minors employed in Barcelona and Catalonia, consequently, were notably higher than in other Spanish industrial centers. A survey conducted by the Labor Inspection Service of the Institute for Social Reforms in 1913 confirms this wage differential: "The protective margin provided by the tariffs, the low wages of women and children, and the excessive hours worked that many manage violate the law in ingenious ways that are difficult to uncover; having otherwise obtained adequate profits in proportion to the capital this industry represents, these are the factors that generally explain the rapid enrichment of many factory owners."[39]

The attitude of male workers toward the employment of their wives and children tended to be highly ambivalent. Although it elicited deep resentments because of the resultant erosion of general wage standards, male workers did not earn enough to provide basic family needs. Barcelona's Institute for Statistics and Social Policy estimated in 1913 that the average daily wage of an individual worker ranged from 3.85 to 4 pesetas whereas the budget for a worker's family composed of husband, wife, and two children required approximately 5.75 pesetas daily (a peseta in 1912 equaled 19.3 cents). In 1901 Juan José Morato wrote, "There is really no possibility of living in Madrid under average conditions without a daily income of 5 to 5.50 pesetas. Is this the standard wage? No. The average daily wage of an adult male barely reaches 2.25 pesetas."[40] In 1914 the minimum daily wage for a manual worker in Granada was 2.50 pesetas whereas daily family requirements called for 5.47 pesetas.[41] A study of wages and prices for the region of Valencia, which includes the provinces of Valencia, Castellón, and Alicante, found that from 1880 to 1921 nominal wages consistently lagged well behind the cost of living.[42]

Male workers shared the then-current belief in the inherent inferiority of women and children.[43] Salut testified to the need for children to work: "The pressing needs of worker families in those days [turn of the century] caused the establishment of that lamentable custom of having their children commence working when they reached ten years of age, and, moreover, the parents could no longer pay the monthly school fee of one peseta. . . . Children were thus left in a permanent state of illiteracy and ignorance.

It was a normal occurrence to observe small apprentices asking passersby the names of streets they had arrived at, loaded down with wood planks on their heads, boxes, or crates."[44] The earnings of women and children thus became a permanent and necessary part of the family budget, prompting Stanley Payne to conclude that the real wages of women and children employed in Catalonian textile manufacture "were probably lower than those of similar workers at Manchester and Lyons even in the blackest phases of British and French industrialization."[45]

Wages in the new industrial centers of Bilbao, Oviedo, and Gijón, however, were generally the highest in the country, with those of Barcelona and Madrid somewhat lower. A French visitor to Bilbao in 1903 wrote, "Wages are generally higher than in other industrial regions of Spain, higher than those of Catalonia, for example. The lowliest laborers receive a minimum of 3 pesetas and an average of approximately 4 pesetas for ten hours of work; workers' children are employed at thirteen years of age. Women are the ones who perform most of the transport, constantly racing with a basket on their heads. They are remarkably strong and courageous, often more than the men, expressing themselves loudly in a highly savorous language. Their pay is 2.75 to 3 pesetas. It is only fair to observe that these wages are barely sufficient in a worker city where food and housing are very costly."[46] The daily struggle to make ends meet was obviously extremely hard for the working poor, yet the conditions of life for industrial workers were on the whole better than for peasants and agricultural laborers.[47]

Wages varied considerably by region or locality as well as in response to supply and demand in the job marketplace. Romero Maura has provided the following description of wage standards in Barcelona during the early years of this century:

Wages varied enormously from one industry to another according to the work performed and the age and sex of the worker. The aristocrats of labor were paid 40 to 80 pesetas weekly. It was an astronomic salary, one that was limited to a highly restricted number of workers: foremen in certain industries, textile painters in cotton print mills, managers of printing establishments. An office worker earned 4 to 5 pesetas a day according to the nature of the business and its location. A peon earned from 2 to 2.50 pesetas. Day laborers and children in the textile industry would earn as little as less than 1 peseta per day and only in extremely rare instances did it exceed 2.50 pesetas. Apprentices received even less. Workers were not paid for holidays and apparently often had difficulties in getting paid for overtime work. An office worker with a small family could subsist if he did not miss a single day and did not encounter unexpected outlays because of family illness or deaths. All contemporary estimates coincide in setting a minimum of 1.25 to 1.50 pesetas daily per person for a reasonable diet. To this must be added 15 to 25 pesetas for monthly rental. For the immense mass of peons the choice was clear: to live single and to sublet or to fall below the subsistence level. Surely the writer was right who said that 60 percent of the workers earned less than a transport horse.[48]

Juan Pablo Fusi's assertion that Vizcayan skilled workers in the years before World War I generally constituted a comparatively well-remunerated, modest elite is also true for workers in similar categories in other major urban centers. Unskilled male and female workers at the lowest ends of the wage scale found life virtually unsustainable on their earnings, and living conditions for the semiskilled, barring major disruptions, generally ranged from barely scraping by to a modestly tolerable livelihood. In numerous industries, textiles, mining, and metalworking most notably, many of the jobs were performed on a piecework basis.

The greatest misfortune that could befall a Spanish worker was to become ill or to be laid off or discharged. Some could benefit temporarily from assistance funds (*montepíos*) or the mutual aid societies, but in most instances being without work was catastrophic for the person who had no savings or government assistance. Most lived in rented lodgings so that if joblessness continued beyond a few weeks or if illness struck, they and their families faced the prospect not only of near starvation but of being homeless as well. In times of economic downturn and widespread layoffs in Barcelona, for example, the municipality and local churches joined in setting up soup kitchens and provided lodging in public buildings. In the rural areas a dole was provided through the creation of emergency public works programs for unemployed farm laborers. Thousands of unemployed as well as large numbers of casual laborers whose wages were a pittance, *los miserables* as they were called in Barcelona, regularly relied on public and church charitable assistance programs to avert destitution.

Working in a factory or shop usually amounted to spending ten to fifteen hours a day in an environment that was crowded, unhealthy, and lacking in the most elemental safety measures. A French observer described a Barcelona workday:

The length of the workday varies: workers generally arrive at the factory early and leave relatively late, but aside from times off, which are usually under relaxed control, their days are broken by fairly frequent rest breaks. Overall it is estimated that on the average they work ten to eleven hours. There are, however, exceptions and numerous abuses, especially concerning women and children. Without taking into account female domestic workers, one can easily find in Barcelona and elsewhere establishments where women work fourteen, fifteen hours and longer and for children the law of March 13, 1900, prohibits their entrance into the factory before ten to fourteen years of age and the length of their workday to six hours, but seems not to be very seriously adhered to because of the lack of controls by public authorities.[49]

The workweek for turn-of-the-century cotton textile workers ranged from sixty-four hours in the Barcelona area to seventy in the smaller textile towns of the region. The Madrid workday in 1905 varied according to season and occupation, ranging from eight hours for stonemasons, nine for street-paving workers, twelve for gas works employees, and sixteen for bakers. The ten-hour day prevailed in most other trades.[50]

José Marva in his 1909 study conducted for the Institute for Social Reforms on labor conditions in the mining industry recounts a typical working day in a coal mine: "Let us take, for example, underground work in the coal mines of the Cistierno area (León province). . . . You show up at the mine entrance at 6:00 in the morning, arriving at the worksite (a subterranean journey) at 6:30. Work ceases inside the mine thirty minutes to eat lunch. You halt work at 11:30, arrive at the entrance at 12:00 (midday). A rest period outside the mine from 12:00 to 1:00 P.M. Back at the mine entrance at 1:00 P.M. Return to the worksite at 1:30 P.M. Cease work at 5:30 P.M. Arrive at the open air by 6:00 P.M."[51]

Bilbao and Asturias experienced labor shortages, but Barcelona, Madrid, Valencia, and other cities attracted unskilled, untutored rural migrants in numbers well above the ability of local industries to absorb them. Catalonia and especially the Barcelona area, which attracted the greatest number, absorbed almost six hundred thousand from 1900 to 1930. The formidable problems of assimilation contributed appreciably to the city's long history of violence and unrest. As Vicens Vives notes, "Hardly had the industrial world digested one generation of immigrants, incorporating the latest techniques and gradually benefiting from wages that were not so low, when still another mass of the displaced was unloaded on it whose social and human condition was despairing. Because of this process, social tensions mounted persistently and seemed virtually unresolvable, especially at the beginning of the twentieth century."[52]

Peter Stearns's depiction of the social effects of the industrial revolution in western Europe is equally relevant for turn-of-the-century Spain: "Industry did not then eliminate the dangerous class. It did absorb a portion of it. But in early industrialization the class continued to grow in absolute numbers as the cities themselves expanded. They were the people who lived in the most crowded and filthy slums, whose food and clothing were still barely sufficient for survival. Segregated still within the city's populace, the urban poor seldom actively protested their mean lot . . . they represented a large and degraded element of the rising cities."[53] The anarchist Anselmo Lorenzo's despairing characterization of late nineteenth-century Madrid workers—"most of them pub crawlers [*tabernios*] and nattily dressed rogues [*chulos*] in their youth and always addicted to the vices"—sustains Stearns's description.[54]

Mediterranean port cities have traditionally attracted large floating populations of drifters and criminal elements. The addition of this element to the subproletariat of the working-class slums produced a highly combustible mixture that must have worked to convert Barcelona into one of Europe's most restive cities during the initial decades of this century.[55] Angel Ossorio y Gallardo, a perceptive conservative who served as civil governor of Barcelona province at the time of the Tragic Week of 1909, observed that "a revolution does not have to be prepared for the simple reason that it is always prepared."[56]

Social Reform and the Enactment of Protective Legislation

As the nineteenth century neared conclusion some of the more blatant abuses of industrial labor began to attract attention. Previously social reform had been an exotic plant nurtured by small groups of well-intentioned humanitarians and enlightened public figures whose efforts had had little effect. Protective legislation for factory workers had been enacted in many countries, but few enforced it. The rise of increasingly influential working-class movements finally bestirred most western European governments to take social reform seriously to retain the loyalty of the masses.[57]

The clear need for some checks on the unbridled expansion of industrial society led to a progressive abandonment of laissez-faire attitudes and the gradual assumption by the state of a regulatory and mediational role in industrial and labor affairs. Privileged groups were beginning to realize that reforms were essential to forestall more radical challenges to the existing order. Hence the social legislation that was promulgated in this period was largely inspired by a fear of the breakdown of the entire social system, as Robert O. Paxton writes: "For many liberals as well as conservatives the rapid growth of Marxist parties lit up the political sky with the lightning flashes of a coming storm."[58]

An analogous evolution was occurring in the church prompted by the massive dechristianization that was under way among the new industrial proletariat and the growing support for socialist movements. Pope Leo XIII's encyclical, *Rerum Novarum,* issued in 1891, deplored the abuses of unlicensed private enterprise and the plight of the worker. State, church, and employers, exhorted the pope, all had the obligation of improving the worker's lot. Thus both increased government intervention in social affairs and the new-found concern of the church in the condition of wage earners represented a response to the growing power of socialist and anarcho-syndicalist movements.

Most modern labor legislation in western Europe came into existence during the period 1890 to 1910. Provisions covering working conditions for women and children either were strengthened or newly adopted, and for the first time coverage was instituted for accident prevention, workers' compensation, industrial hygiene, minimum wages, the regulation of work contracts, maximum working hours, and government-sponsored insurance programs for illness, unemployment, and old age.

By 1900 most European countries, with the exception of Russia and the Balkan states, had adopted or were in the process of enacting legislation governing various aspects of industrial and commercial employment. Passage of protective regulations and a public airing of the "social question" commenced in Spain at the same time, probably at least partially spurred by overall European trends and by the new approach to church social policy inaugurated by Pope Leo XIII. But because working-class movements were relatively late to emerge in Spain as a significant social and political force, the role of middle-class reformers proved to be more important and enduring in the promotion of protective legislation.

Before 1900 Spain tried to repress insurrectionary uprisings in its colonial possessions that ultimately led to the Spanish-American War of 1898. The economic effect of these events was seriously to erode the purchasing power of wage earners and to lead to widespread social unrest and unprecedented strike activity. Rising discontent among workers thus led to the enactment of protective legislation.

During the First Republic (1873–74), enlightened elements had sought to promote ameliorative social legislation, but their sole success had been the passage of the Benot Law of July 24, 1873, that barred minors between the ages of thirteen and seventeen from working more than a ten-hour day and all juveniles below the age of seventeen from night work. With the fall of the First Republic in 1874, all labor protective laws were abrogated. But lack of enforcement and noncompliance among employers even before then had reduced the law to a dead letter, even in government-owned enterprises.

The first efforts in the 1880s to introduce modern protective measures were undertaken by social reformers who were almost exclusively middle- and upper-class intellectuals and politicians. An organized socialist movement barely existed and modern trade unionism was only incipiently present. The reformers were a small band of enlightened modernizers in both of the two principal Restoration parties, the Conservatives and Liberals.[59] The Conservative Eduardo Dato and Liberals Segismundo Moret and José Canalejas, who were among the leading proponents of reform, served in key government posts and as prime ministers. Adherents to the ideas of Krausism and supporters of the Free Institute of Education were also extremely important in promoting labor legislation; its leading proponent in this field was the Republican Gumersindo Azcárate, who later was to serve as the founding chairman of the Institute for Social Reforms.[60] Echoing the view then current in western Europe, all of them concurred with Azcarate that the enactment of social legislation signified a desire "to embark on the slow road of reform in order to avoid the violent one of revolution."[61]

This remarkable consensus on social reform occurred among people of diverse philosophical and political points of view because of converging changes in attitude on how to deal with social problems. The frequent collaboration in Great Britain and various Continental countries between conservatives and liberals in the passage of labor legislation probably also exerted some influence. But for Spanish Conservatives, strongly imbued with orthodox Catholic doctrine, Pope Leo XIII's encyclical, *Rerum Novarum,* had a pivotal effect in moderating their attitudes. Among these Conservatives were Cánovas del Castillo, architect of the Restoration bipartite rotational political structure and Conservatism's principal spokesman during the final quarter of the nineteenth century. He was also influenced by the example of Bismarckian Germany, which was then undertaking paternalistic social legislation and welfare measures in an effort to counter the socialist upsurge.[62] Cánovas was persuaded to acquiesce in if not actively support certain social reform initiatives promoted by his more enlightened colleagues. The abandonment by the Liberals of their traditional laissez-faire outlook in favor of a more interventionist role by government resulted in some of them becoming strong advocates of social reforms.[63]

Moret, Azcárate, and Canalejas, moreover, shared an admiration for things British, especially that country's system of social legislation and collective bargaining. Moret, the grandson of a British general (his matronymic is Prendergast) and a leading advocate of Krausist social policies, had written a doctoral dissertation with the title "Capital and Labor, Harmonious or Antagonistic Elements?" and for many years was a leading advocate in Spanish government circles for a more enlightened approach to labor problems.

The Liberal government headed by Sagasta, which took office in 1881, had a more tolerant attitude toward labor organization. Moret was named minister of the interior and charged with formulating a more progressive labor policy. Initial attempts to secure passage of protective legislation almost invariably went down to defeat because of employers' hostility and the indifference of political conservatives. The more permissive official policies, however, caused numerous worker societies to engage in attempts at collective bargaining. The moderate Tres Clases de Vapor Federación of Catalonia had become a significant influence in the textile industry's labor relations, the anarchist-led Workers Federation of the Spanish Region (FTRE) underwent a rapid expansion, and the public furor over the Mano Negra (Black Hand) labor terrorism in Cádiz province and unprecedented strikes in various parts of the country, including textile workers in Málaga and typographic workers in Barcelona and Madrid, gave impetus to social reforms.

Finding the avenue of legislative action closed to them, reformers pressed the Cortes and the government to convoke a congress to which a broad spectrum of influential figures and interested groups would be invited to propose reforms and legislation. In the end, however, Moret and others had to settle for the creation of a Social Reforms Commission (CRS) charged with collecting information on existing conditions and with only a consultative role in formulating policy recommendations in the fashioning of a more coherent approach to labor problems.

The CRS was bogged down by long delays and snaillike progress in completing its work—it lasted from 1883 to 1894—and was hampered by the general disinterest of the ruling elite, a lack of funds, and the suspicion and hostility of worker organizations. Though the hopes placed in it by social reformers and labor moderates were not fulfilled, it did serve in the longer run to promote a broader acceptance of government's mediational role in labor relations and prepare public opinion for the subsequent promulgation of social legislation. The actual passage of protective legislation commenced in 1900, and two years later José Canalejas, serving as minister of agriculture, industry, commerce, and public works, sought to promote social reform through the creation of a labor institute (*Instituto de Trabajo*), but it failed to win the approval of the Senate. During the following year, however, in the wake of the general strike in Barcelona, the Conservative government of Francisco Silvela, which included social reformers Antonio Maura as minister of the interior and Eduardo Dato in justice, established the renamed Institute for Social Reforms by decree.[64] Its formation and subsequent accomplishments moved Spain closer to acceptance of modern norms in both social legislation and industrial relations, a positive forward step in an otherwise depressing sociopolitical landscape.

According to Salvador de Madariaga,

> The guiding principle of the IRS, i.e., that the men chosen to control them should be selected on grounds of competence and not of political allegiance, was brilliantly vindicated in this case. A Conservative government chose as chairman of the institute Don Gumersindo Azcárate, one of the Republican leaders, a man universally respected in Spain for his integrity and for the simplicity of his life and trusted for his moderate views. As members of the organizing committee two specialists from the University of Oviedo, Professors Buylla and Posada, were selected despite their radical views, in collaboration with a retired military man, General Marvá, who made a reputation for himself in industrial affairs. The institute consisted of a collegiate body and a technical secretariat. The collegiate body was composed of eighteen government nominees and six employer and six labor representatives, chosen in each case by big industry, small industry, and agriculture, in equal parts so that

each category would be represented by two employers and two men. The government appointed its eighteen nominees with a statesmanlike regard for all shades of opinion. The very fact that the industrial members were to be elected acted as a powerful stimulus to association both on the employers' and on the men's side. The mandate of the institute was to study social and industrial conditions (what is known in America as a fact-finding agency), to study and prepare legislation and inspect industrial life. In all these fields the institute was eminently successful and, until its character and independence were destroyed by the dictatorship, it acted as a powerful element of industrial peace even when thwarted in its intelligent endeavors by the army, the reactionary employers, and the anarchist and syndicalist hotheads.[65]

Indeed, the achievements of the IRS were especially impressive considering the appalling conditions under which it operated. Grossly underfunded, with a ridiculously inadequate number of labor inspectors who could accomplish only a small fraction of their mandated functions,[66] with local bodies that were often either defunct or whose functions were misused by local politicians, the refusal of anarcho-syndicalist labor to participate in IRS activities, and its legislative recommendations more often than not rejected because of the opposition of powerful hostile elements, the institute, nevertheless, managed to leave an enduring imprint on Spain's labor relations and legal processes. For the first time, the concept of a tripartite consultative machinery was introduced in the formulation of labor policies and the mediation of labor disputes. Its research studies and field reports on social and labor problems were of excellent quality and represented substantive efforts to approach these issues in a scholarly, systematic manner; its gathering of statistics on social affairs and labor problems also was innovative. Furthermore, for the first time, labor organizations such as the prosocialist General Workers Union (UGT) were given access to a public advisory and regulatory agency.

During the years when Gumersindo Azcárate presided, the IRS was most influential. Following his death in 1917, he was succeeded first by the Viscount of Eza and then by Eduardo Sanz y Escartin, and the institute became steadily less effective. The post-Azcarate years, of course, saw the final breakdown of the Restoration political system and a towering crisis in the country's labor relations. The establishment in 1920 of a labor ministry reduced the IRS to a consultative body, and the advent in 1923 of the dictatorship headed by General Miguel Primo de Rivera, which charted an entirely new course in labor policies, brought to an end the IRS's two decades of productive activities.

Adolfo Posada calls this period "the first real stage" of modern protective legislation, and Alfredo Montoya Melgar characterizes it as "a succession and, of course, unsystematic series of dispositions that reveal the limited intentions of the legislators."[67] A more coherent ordering of legal provisions was to commence later, during the years 1917 to 1923.

Among the more notable laws that for the first time established norms were those covering industrial accidents, safety and hygiene, individual workers' employment contracts, collective bargaining, mediation, and arbitration. Both the January 30, 1900, Industrial Accident Law and the law of March 13, 1900, governing conditions of employment for women and children were sponsored by Eduardo Dato.[68]

The lengthy and torturous process of obtaining passage of the law prohibiting women's night work provides an insight into the temper of the times. Efforts to regulate night work were first made in 1891 by the Conservative government headed by Cánovas but were abandoned when the government fell that year. Another try in 1894 proved abortive. By 1900 Dato succeeded in having a law adopted covering the industrial employment of women and children but was not successful in including the provisions governing night work that he had sought. Such a law was passed in 1910 at long last, and Spain then became a signatory to the international convention prohibiting female night labor. But the law was not formally promulgated until July 11, 1912, because of obstructive actions in the Senate. It had taken two decades to obtain passage of this basic regulatory measure, and it was not fully enforced until 1920.[69]

The Industrial Accident Law, one of the most advanced in Europe at that time, contained innovative approaches to a number of problems in this area. Though less thoroughgoing, the law covering working conditions of women and children in industry still represented notable progress over the original measure that was adopted in 1873, and the standards it set were to enjoy a remarkably long life. Sunday became a legal day of rest in 1904. But no legislation adopted before 1907 was enforced until the formation that year of the Labor Inspection Service of the Institute for Social Reforms.

Laws forming industrial tribunals and industrial conciliation and arbitration councils were adopted in 1908 and 1909. A "chair law" passed in 1912 required employers to provide chairs for nonindustrial workers at times when sitting did not interfere with normal work requirements.

Taking inspiration from the Institute for Social Reforms, an analogous body, the National Institute of Social Security (Instituto Nacional de Previsión), was created in 1908, aided by the efforts of two Catholic social reformers, Jordi Maluquer and Severino Aznar. Like the IRS, it was conceived as a semiautonomous institution for the purpose of conducting research and producing studies on social welfare problems and pension systems and making recommendations to the government concerning proposed decrees and legislation. Its initial decade of existence has been described as functionally innocuous, and only eleven years later, in 1919, was the first obligatory workers' pension system installed.

The return to power in 1910 of the Liberals with José Canalejas as prime minister led to a further advance of social legislation. In the ensuing three years before Canalejas fell victim to an anarchist assassin, the nine-hour day was established for minors, the seventy-two-hour maximum workweek was instituted for textile employees, and night work was prohibited for women working in industry.

Despite the substantial broadening of government intervention in social affairs that this legislation and regulatory measures represented, its overall effect was marginal, for most of it was merely "theoretical legislation."[70] "The results," observes Raymond Carr, "in terms of modern labor legislation (which began with Dato's Workers' Compensation Act in 1900 and culminated in Romanones' eight hour day in 1918) were meager. The majority of what had been known as Sagasta's flock and of the Conservative deputies had neither interest nor faith in social amelioration as a branch of political science. Moreover, the poverty of the Institute, the indifference of the employers and the persistence of large pockets of artisan and domestic industry made enforcement of labour legislation by a handful of inspectors aided by local committees almost impossible. As in all countries it was factory labour which first enjoyed protection; the sweated trades of Madrid, like those of London, escaped control."[71] Angel Marvaud is even more caustic: "As so often happens south of the Pyrennees, many laws of a clarity and almost perfect harmonious construction exist only on paper. . . . Most of the reforms we have studied have remained dead letters for lack of application."[72]

Most employers were able to evade compliance with the laws both because of the shortage of labor inspectors and because the laws generally contained little enforcement authority. André Voyard provided a telling analysis of the failure to enforce the laws:

The law according to [the Labor Inspection] that is best observed is the one concerning industrial accidents. . . .

One should not be surprised for laws which have obligations and sanctions of a pecuniary nature are rarely ignored. The least observed law is that which establishes Sunday as a day of rest. Large industrial firms comply, commerce generally, and small shops constantly violate it. The clothing industry provides a large share of the violations of the law on women's work, especially at the beginning of each season, Saturday, and just before holidays. In the textile industries, food, forestry, agriculture, in transportation, in hauling with small hand trucks, legislative dispositions concerning child labor are overlooked. Employers oppose the reduction of children's workdays because they serve as helpers to adult workers. Families too often do not fulfill their obligations to their children so as not to deprive themselves of their small earnings. Infractions concerning child labor are rare in large factories and big industry. . . .

In certain milieux one is given to believe that all the resistance to labor laws is imputable to employer egoism; but numerous inspectors have observed that, for various reasons, many workers—discomfort caused by their work, fear of being taken as cowardly, negligence, and so on—refuse to abide by legal prescriptions that are intended to protect them in the conduct of their work.[73]

The Labor Inspection report for 1907 on compliance with the law governing working standards for women and children makes depressing reading: "The Law of March 13, 1900, cannot be said to have entered into effect [1907] in some areas of the peninsula where it is badly complied with or in almost all instances not observed at all. . . . If this law is infringed upon in all Spanish regions, this occurs in Catalonia in such a manner as to oblige the Inspection Service to propose correcting these scandalous infractions with severity."[74] A report on Andalusia observed, "The number of establishments that fully comply with the law of March 13, 1900, are so few that it is possible to declare that it is totally unobserved in some industries and almost not at all in the rest."[75] Maximiano García Venero noted that the 1904 law establishing Sunday as a day of rest was totally ignored and the 1908 law constituting conciliation and arbitration councils remained a dead letter; the law requiring the creation of local councils was often ignored.[76] Most of the enacted legislation generally had little or no effect until World War I.

The effect of noncompliance was particularly serious because the ratio of women and children in the national labor force remained stable during this century's first three decades and the length of the working day diminished very gradually until the 1930s. In the 1913 Catalonian industrywide textile strike the union demanded that employers outside Barcelona be forced to comply with legal provisions limiting the workday for women to eleven hours.

The almost universal disregard for the law in the labor field matches the general indifference toward legal controls in many spheres of daily life. Joaquín Costa once bitterly lamented, "In our country laws are passed to provide us the pleasure of ignoring them." Noncompliance was particularly distressing, however, because the social and political forces favoring protective enforcement proved to be so ineffectual. Before the war organized labor was weak and too inconsequential to influence the passage of legislation, not to speak of enforcement. What little influence it possessed was sapped by the disinterest of the anarcho-syndicalists, who represented at least half of all organized workers, in obtaining relief through legal means. The National Confederation of Labor (CNT) also barred its members from participating in any of the tripartite bodies established by the IRS and other agencies.

It was, in addition, very difficult to overcome the ingrained legacy of class injustice and government partiality. Social legislation during the early years of the twentieth century was generally received by many workers with cold indifference and contempt and by employers with unconcealed hostility. The UGT and the Socialist party that participated in the work of the Institute for Social Reforms and the National Institute of Social Security "maintained an unpleasant doctrinal but correct attitude in their personal dealings."[77]

The absence of an organized constituency in support of these reforms and a largely indifferent public consequently permitted the government authorities to ignore or merely offer lip service to the entreaties of social reformers and labor leaders and to be swayed by the hostility of employers to protective or regulatory measures. In times of social tensions or widespread labor unrest, a palliative would be proffered in the form of added labor legislation but with little or no provisions to assure compliance. The result was that adherence to the labor laws was generally viewed by employers with a disdain comparable only to the almost universal custom of tax evasion. The few that conformed almost invariably did so because they were forced to by labor organizations that represented their employees. A consequence of this mass noncompliance was that in contrast to France, where, as James Joll has noted, the introduction of laws for the improvement of working conditions and the establishment of workers' pensions "weakened the appeal of a purely revolutionary syndicalism," in Spain it had the totally opposite effect.[78]

Legal measures limiting the hours of work almost without exception were limited to industries that were unionized. Examples are the royal decree of December 27, 1910, establishing a maximum nine-hour day in the mines, another of January 12, 1920, that reduced the miners' workday to seven hours, and the decree of August 24, 1913, that limited work in the textile industry to ten hours per day. In two industries whose workers were particularly militant and well organized, building construction and bakeries, the eight-hour day was formally decreed in 1919, and employees were also granted a statutory right to a rest period during night shift work. Last but not least, the formal establishment of an eight-hour day by royal decree in 1919 and 1920 came on the crest of an unparalleled wave of social unrest and strikes.

These various laws and decrees covered only those employed in commerce and industry. Peasants and landless laborers were ignored, as is documented by Antonio Ramos Oliveira: "Incredible as it may appear, it is, nevertheless, a fact that from the time the oligarchy took over the helm of the Spanish ship and until the overthrow of the institutions in 1931, not a single law was passed to check the power of the great landowners. No restraint was placed on the freedom of the arrogant throng to fix wages as they pleased, no measure was taken to compel them to treat the braceros better than draught animals, nor was a single word said on the subject of leases."[79] The year 1931, which marks the advent of the Second Republic, also inaugurates the commencement of truly serious efforts by government authorities to enforce existing labor laws.

3

THE EMERGENCE OF MODERN
LABOR ORGANIZATION

Beginnings of Labor Organization
in Catalonia

Catalonia, the forerunner in Iberian industrialization, was also the cradle and vanguard of the Spanish labor movement, home to the first and largest agglomeration of factory workers. Balcells relates that "a reliable census in 1840 registered 26,540 workers employed in cotton spinning, weaving, and printing. Around 1850 they were at least 80,000 to which are to be added 9,000 who worked indirectly for this industry in the construction of factories, transport, machinery repair, and the like."[1] Spain's initial manifestations of worker organization and trade union consciousness emerged among these workers. The genesis of labor organization proceeded along more or less classic lines. The introduction of labor-saving machinery during the early decades of the nineteenth century produced a Catalonian version of Luddism, replete with destruction of machines and torching of newly mechanized mills.[2]

The cotton textile industry suffered from market instability throughout much of the century. The loss of the South American colonies was a severe blow, and the industry required a long period to recover. In conjunction with the impact of a changing technology, a general deterioration of working conditions took place.

A rising sense of disaffection and resistance became manifest by the mid- and late 1830s. Workers in Barcelona sought legal permission to organize. A royal circular in 1839 sanctioned the formation of mutual benefit societies for the first time.[3] As before, however, anything resembling association for purposes of collective bargaining remained rigorously prohibited. Nevertheless, a year later a group of skilled craftsmen formed the Cotton Weavers Mutual Protective Association, which is generally credited with inaugurating contemporary labor organization in Spain.

The organization soon enrolled three thousand members, and its initial success inspired craftsmen and operatives in other industries to organize. In early 1841 the various worker societies formed the Central Executive Junta in Barcelona, the first of its kind in Spain. Seven thousand of the approximately thirty thousand employed in the city's factories and workshops joined the worker societies.[4]

The Cotton Weavers Association was formed primarily in reaction to the steady erosion of earnings and other benefits as well as the intensified exploitation resulting from increased mechanization. Ostensibly organized as a mutual benefit society, it sought also to defend workers' standards by organizing and leading work stoppages. Employers refused to recognize the organization or to negotiate collective bargaining accords, but its presence was sufficient to induce the authorities in 1840 to create the first joint employer-employee commission (*comisión mixta*) in an effort to compromise differences between the two parties. Spain's first consumer cooperative was also established in that year.

It is one of those extraordinary incongruencies that despite Spain's retarded socioeconomic development, a nascent Catalonian trade unionism in the 1840s and 1850s experienced a degree of organization and support that make it an early landmark labor development in continental Europe. The precocity of organization among the workers employed in the cotton textile mills and shops derived from the concentration of the textile industry in a few nearby localities, which greatly facilitated contacts among workers; the extended crisis in the industry and the painful adjustment following the loss of the South American market; and the strong tradition of solidarity and mutual support that was a legacy from the old artisan guilds (*cofradías* and *gremios*).[5]

Worker organization before 1868 was precarious, frequently subjected to bans, and, more often than not, obliged to carry on in clandestine or semiclandestine fashion. Nonetheless, despite proscriptions and harassments by the authorities and employers, these groups developed steadily after 1840 to become an element of some consequence in regional labor, economic, and social affairs. During the early 1850s the musician Josep Anselm Clavé, a former lathe operator who participated in the political activities of moderate leftist groups, organized and directed worker choral societies throughout Catalonia to provide an alternative to the widespread habit of spending nonworking hours in the local tavern. These musical groups attained popular renown and also functioned as mutual benefit societies, often providing legal cover for the activities of clandestine labor organizations.

With a more liberal government in power and the advent of the Crimean War, which greatly increased the demand for textile products, employers became somewhat more willing to deal with worker organizations so as to avoid any interruption in production. Workers' organizational success consequently reached a zenith during the 1850s. The Unión de Clases (*clases* denotes the various crafts and trades), begun in 1854, enrolled a substantial part of the textile work force, and on January 25, 1855, a Central Junta of Leaders of the Working Class was formed with the objective of coordinating the various worker societies, representing them in dealings with the authorities, and mediating disputes between employers and workers.[6]

This success came to an abrupt halt when Captain General Juan Zapatero opposed the civil governor's conciliatory labor policies. Martial law was declared, the popular textile labor leader Josep Barceló was executed on trumped-up charges, union treasuries were seized, and dispositions were issued with the intent of annulling existing bargaining agreements. In protest, the junta called a general strike on July 2 that affected over half the industrial working population and paralyzed the industrial life of Barcelona and neighboring localities for eight days.

Despite official promises to legalize the right to organize and to reduce the workday for children, a wave of repression followed the conclusion of the strike, and numerous labor leaders were deported. Organized labor was not totally silenced, but the loss of so many of its leaders reduced it to relative ineffectiveness.

The prohibition of workers' organization was finally ended by the indulgence of a captain general, and between 1864 and 1868 these groups were again permitted to function. Many consumer and producer cooperatives were formed in this period, and both mutual benefit associations and resistance societies grew in numbers and influence. During December 1865 the labor periodical *El Obrero* sponsored the first conference of Catalonian worker groups, which was attended by representatives of forty societies.

It was the revolution of 1868, La Gloriosa, that in many parts of the country provided the impetus for the birth and development of more modern forms of labor organization. Though essentially a political revolution, totally without a social program, it evoked considerable social protest.[7] Thus for a time following the recognition of the right to associate and the institution of male universal suffrage, some of the more blatant obstacles to organization were removed. Despite the persistence of various prohibitions, the more permissive climate ushered in by the revolution enabled labor groups to flourish. Worker casinos, atheneums, and cultural centers in urban areas, some sponsored by Republicans and other progressive political groups, also served as centers for the rise of labor leaders.

At the time of the 1868 revolution workers had not yet organized in Madrid and much of the north.[8] In Catalonia, however, the Central Directorate of Worker Societies, claiming 5,345 adherents, was formed within a month following the revolution. A Catalonian workers' congress was convened several months later and attended by 100 delegates representing 61 organizations. Roughly 9 percent of the region's workers belonged to labor societies. Nationally, an estimated 195 societies were in existence with a total membership of around 25,000, 38 of them with 7,000 supporters in the Barcelona area (that figure rose to 10,000 by the following year). The main currents within Catalonian organized labor at that time were federal republicanism, mutualism, and cooperativism.[9]

A mere recital of these developments makes it abundantly clear why Barcelona and the Catalonians could henceforth lay claim to a leading role in national trade union affairs. It was a role that with the passage of time would loom ever larger. By the early twentieth century, Joaquín Maurín, the Catalonian Marxist writer, could claim that the "specific weight" of Barcelona province's proletariat equalled that of the entire rest of the country.

A distinctive feature of Catalonian labor organization from its earliest days was the inclusion not only of skilled and semiskilled craftsmen but of a significant portion of the textile industry's work force as well, in which unskilled labor and female employees predominated. The Unión de Clases, which had served as the leading textile workers' organization during the 1850s, was succeeded by the Tres Clases de Vapor Federación (the three *clases* being spinners, weavers, and dyers), which soon emerged as the country's most important trade union.[10] At its inception in 1869 it boasted a membership of eighty-five hundred. Unión Manufacturera (its full name was Unión de Obreros Manufactureras de la Region Española) was constituted in 1870 to serve as a national federation embracing all of the country's manufacturing employees. In reality, however, it functioned as an umbrella movement for thirty thousand Catalonian textile mill operatives, including the Tres Clases de Vapor, the Dyers Federation, and a number of craft unions. In the euphoria accompanying the establishment of the republic in 1873 it succeeded in forcing employers to raise wages and in reducing the workday from twelve to eleven hours. In subsequent years Unión Manufacturera went into a decline, practically disappearing by 1885.

A shift away from the mutual benefit form of organization to one more distinctly favoring collective bargaining began in 1868. Symptomatic of this change was the growing number of organizations influenced by anarchist and socialist ideas, which distinguished their laboristic class character by referring to themselves as "workers resistance societies against capital." The term *resistencia* during the formative period became synonymous with militant trade unionism.

Because of the great importance of textile manufacturing, labor organization in Catalonia included skilled and unskilled workers, whereas elsewhere in Spain, in the larger urban agglomerations where unionization first appeared, it usually consisted of small craft unions, mostly composed of preindustrial artisanal trades: typographers, bakers, barrel makers, tramway employees, carpenters, brick masons, cabinetmakers, ironworkers, and the like. In the 1880s, for example, the barrel makers (*toneleros*), a preindustrial skilled journeymen's craft, formed a national federation that constituted the country's most highly organized trade. Organization toward the end of the century also commenced at various coal and metal mining localities. Mining in that period was the country's most dynamic economic sector, a development that gave rise to massive labor recruitment and accompanying labor problems that led to the establishment of trade unions at a number of mining sites.

Worker organization (*societarismo*) during the latter half of the nineteenth century almost everywhere occurred largely under the influence of Republicanism. Most of the sixty-nine Republicans elected to the Constituent Cortes in 1869 came from the large cities where worker associations were concentrated, from Barcelona, Valencia, Zaragossa, Málaga, and Cádiz. Republicanism was primarily a political movement led and directed by middle-class elements supported by urban skilled and semi-skilled workers and artisans. Its appeal to workers, couched in paternalistic terms, included the advocacy of social reforms and the enactment of universal suffrage.

The Federal Republican party, led by Francesc Pi y Margall, the son of a Barcelona weaver, emerged as the dominant element in the political life of Barcelona and other cities during the 1860s and 1870s. Fundamental to the party's success was its support from organized workers, which was enhanced by the politicization of economic concerns during a period of chronic political instability. According to Casamiro Martí, "Workers who desired to maintain their class activity in the bargaining area perceived the necessity for politicizing their struggle to assure the legal right of association and to give weight to legal recognition of their organized efforts."[11]

The September 1868 revolution that ended the reign of the Bourbons came about through a pronunciamiento that led to the naming of General Francisco Serrano as acting regent and General Juan Prim as prime minister of the provisional government. The Constituent Cortes of the following year approved a constitution establishing a constitutional monarchy, a solution that represented a compromise between the two leading political groups, the Liberal Unionist and the Progressive Democratic parties. To the ardently Republican plebes of Catalonia, who had invested high expectations in the revolution, this formula appeared as a betrayal. Widespread indignation and disillusionment ensued. Josep Termes Ardevol recounts the events that followed:

> During September–October 1869 the Federal Republicans of Catalonia, Valencia, and Aragon rebelled in protest against the adoption of the constitution establishing the monarchy as Spain's form of government. The failure of the uprising and, above all, the incapacity shown by the Federals were leading factors in the break between Federal Republicanism and Revolutionary Laborism, causing the latter to initiate a campaign in favor of apoliticism. Other reasons for the spread of apoliticism included the provisional government's failure to carry out its pledges to abolish indirect taxation (food and port duties) and the abolition of obligatory military service [*las quintas*], failings that gave the popular classes the impression that politics was a fraud.[12]

The failure of the 1869 insurrection and the consequent discrediting of the Federal Republicans, preceded by a prolonged period of economic crisis and mounting social discontent, generated an increasingly radical mood among many wage earners. Thus an organized workers' movement that had started out as predominantly moderate and cooperativist now became increasingly receptive to libertarian antipolitics. An analogous disenchantment took place among Andalusian urban wage earners.

Formation of the Spanish Regional Organization of the First International

The arrival of Giuseppe Fanelli, Mikhail Bakunin's proselytizing emissary, shortly following the 1868 revolution, proved to be extraordinarily well timed.[13] A group, mostly of middle-class origin, influenced by Pierre-Joseph Proudhon and other anarchist thinkers, was already in existence at the Catalonian Atheneum of the Working Class, an educational and cultural center that was to furnish key (mostly middle-class) figures in the subsequent launching of an anarchist-oriented labor movement.[14] Federalist labor leaders' acceptance of anarchist postulates was considerably abetted by a shift away from the notion that the interests of the working class were best served through the reformism of the bourgeois left to the idea that the working class should take primacy in its struggle for liberation. Cotton textile workers, hitherto collaborators with progressive-minded employers and Republicans, thus increasingly joined the ranks of the First International.

Such a move on the part of the working classes had been under way for some time in many industrializing countries. "All systems of ideas," wrote Fernand Pelloutier, a seminal figure in the development of French syndicalism, "all the utopias for which workers have been blamed, have never come from them at all. They have come from middle-class people (bourgeois), well-intentioned, no doubt, who have sought remedies for our ills in their own ideas, burning the midnight oil instead of looking at our needs and at reality."[15]

The basic articles of anarchist faith, according to Mikhail Bakunin, were "atheism, the complete negation of all authority and power, the abolition of juridical law, the negation of the concept of the individual as citizen of the state replaced by the concept of free man, collective property, work as the basis for social organization, and that such an organization be a free federation from top to bottom."[16]

Its primary appeal derived from the anarchist objective of structuring industry and agriculture for public advantage. Capitalism and a highly centralized Spanish state were to be replaced by an economic system based on a decentralized, egalitarian society supported by the voluntary cooperation of free men. The worker would regain the lost joy of his labor in a society without government or property and the dignity of being his own master. Collectivism was the name given the Bakunin-ist recipe for the economic reorganization of society. Collectivism is the common ownership of the instruments of labor, their use by work-ers' production collectives, and the individual ownership of the integral product of each person's labor. Anarchism signifies the abolition of gov-ernments and their conversion into simple organs of administration of collective interests.[17]

The revolution would come about through a combination of spontaneity and conspiracy. The most wretched among the masses were the ones with the greatest penchant for rebelliousness: landless peasants, bandits, and especially the lumpenproletariat. But the overthrow of society required a concerted shove, and for this purpose a secret revolutionary vanguard had to be created to infiltrate and capture control of popular movements and to direct the revolution and maintain it on a proper course.

The formation of a political party serving as the instrument of prole-tarian emancipation, predicated by Marx, was denounced as "authoritar-ian." Two methods were possible, argued Bakunin: "The communists believe that they must organize the working-class forces to seize political power in states. Revolutionary socialists organize in order to destroy or, if you want a more polite word, liquidate states."[18]

Fanelli's visit, the first substantive contact between Spaniards and the First International (many of those contacted by Fanelli, who spoke no Spanish, thought he represented the International rather than merely its Bakuninist faction), at a moment of growing disillusionment with politics, placed the anarchists in an extremely favorable position. The absence of any counterefforts by Marxian socialists greatly facilitated the anarchist inroads.

The general climate between September 1868 and the fall of the Paris Commune in 1871 was conducive for labor organization and thus a pro-pitious time for the launching of a national labor body. A national labor congress sponsored by the Barcelona local federation was held in the city on June 18, 1870, at which the Spanish Regional Federation (FRE) of the First International (International Workingmens Association—IWMA) was formed. Of the eighty-nine delegates in attendance seventy-four rep-resented Catalonian unions, including thirty-three from the textile industry.

Three major currents were in evidence, the Bakuninists (antistate, antipolitical, and collectivist); the laborists, who were divided between those who were apolitical (though not antipolitical) and supporters of the

Federal Republican party; and those favoring cooperativism and trade union moderation. Most were nonpolitical *sindicalistas* (trade unionists).

The deliberations centered on whether to accept a political option, namely Federal Republicanism or apoliticism. Albert Balcells describes the debate: "The Bakuninists did not obtain a rejection of political action, and the final accord fixed the apolitical character of worker societies in the sense of preserving their independence from political parties and guaranteeing pluralism within the unions yet tolerating political action. Even this modified proposal was approved by only fifty-five votes in favor, twenty-four against, and eight abstentions. It triumphed thanks to the votes of delegates from outside Barcelona who mostly represented small organizations from artisan trades as well as from two-thirds of the Barcelona delegates, while the remaining third and a large majority of representatives from the Catalonian districts [*comarcas*] inclined more toward political and less to maximalist attitudes."[19]

Despite lack of support from the large and more representative participating organizations mostly led by moderates, the Bakuninists succeeded in dominating the proceedings and placing their supporters, mostly intellectuals, in key leadership posts. Their success, even though they numbered only several hundreds, was attributable to the ideological and factional cohesiveness of their semisecret organization in the Spanish section of Bakunin's Alliance for Social Democracy, which had been constituted five months earlier. Aliancistas caucused secretly before each congress or important gathering to establish the political and tactical line to follow. They were largely responsible for drafting policy documents and resolutions, and their disciplined cohesiveness enabled them to dominate the mass of delegates, who lacked any clear notion concerning many of the issues under discussion. Though the anarchists gained control of the organization's upper echelons, the FRE was essentially a tacit alliance between them and the moderate trade unionists.[20]

In spite of the Aliancistas' success in imposing a revolutionary collectivist orientation, the majority of the delegates were most immediately concerned with their jobs and not with effecting a radical, revolutionary transformation of society. Even the revolutionaries were in the initial period of the International's existence willing to give first priority to the immediate struggle against employer injustices, thereby sacrificing the purity of the revolutionary ideal.[21]

The growth of the International, as the FRE was commonly called, was rapid and intense. So long as it was free from official harassment it continued to expand. It began in 1871 with 1,700 supporters, and the number rose by 1872 to 11,500, more than half of them in Barcelona. By spring of that year it had attained an estimated 15,000 with 150 affiliated local federations. By late 1872 more than half of the FRE membership was concentrated in La Unión Manufacturera with the remainder mostly consisting of preindustrial artisanal craft societies; only a small number of agricultural laborers had been enrolled. Membership in early 1873 rose to 25,000 to 30,000, of which two-thirds were Catalonian affiliates. It had grown to 30,000 to 40,000 later that year, before the Alcoy uprising, "a figure that, nonetheless, was modest in comparison with the actual size of the working class."[22]

The main source of recruitment in most parts of the country came from the ranks of Federal Republicanism. It was no coincidence, as Josep Fontana concludes, that the areas where the influence of Federal Republicanism was greatest—Catalonia, Andalusia, Valencia, and Aragon—ultimately became the principal zones of anarchist strength: "This labor movement, disillusioned by its actions, separated itself from the hegemony of Republicanism, declared itself 'apolitical,' that is to say, hostile to the type of politics that was practiced in Spain at that time. Only in this sense is it proper to qualify Spanish anarchism as apolitical. In reality it was an alternative political formulation, the first specifically labor one."[23]

The Bakuninist-led FRE's introduction of militant autonomous forms of working-class action, including the establishment of a strike defense fund to provide financial assistance to striking workers, was instrumental in weaning large numbers of workers away from Republican allegiances. The Federalists, by contrast, never recommended strike action or encouraged resistance as a means of increasing wages.[24] In 1869, for example, Republican leaders in Catalonia displayed a marked indifference to the efforts of organized textile workers to obtain wage increases.

The ideas of Spanish anarchism were sufficiently diffuse and the organizational structure (federalist-local autonomy) flexible enough to permit adaptation to the highly varied conditions of Iberian political and economic life. As a consequence, the movement tended to absorb and reflect regional temperaments and outlooks. As early as the 1870s two distinct currents emerged, the peasant anarchism of Andalusia and the proletarian variant of industrial Catalonia.

The Internationalists' doctrines found ready acceptance in Andalusian labor circles, and the region ranked second in importance in the FRE. Its membership in 1872–73 of four thousand, of which 40 percent consisted of *braceros* and small farmers, represented a fifth of the federation's adherents.[25]

Andalusia was receptive to anarchist-oriented labor organization for several reasons that are made clear by an examination of its social and political history. The movement arrived at a time of growing radicalization not only of disfranchised rural casual laborers and urban workers but also of artisans, professionals, small farmers, and shopkeepers. Andalusia's radicalized petty bourgeoisie in the 1850s and 1860s has been described as one of the most prone to insurrection in Europe. Furthermore, Andalusia during the late nineteenth century had experienced a succession of social upheavals, and much of the ensuing discontent among the lower middle class and rural poor had been channeled into support for the Federal Republican party. Utopian socialist and libertarian ideas in vogue in mid-nineteenth-century western Europe had numerous devotees among the Federalists, especially in southern Spain.

Furthermore, in a society with intense local ethnic and regional loyalties (*la patria chica*), the emphasis of Bakunin's anarchism on political decentralization, reserving the greatest autonomy for provinces within the nation and municipalities within provinces, gave it an enormous advantage over Marxism. This advantage was enhanced because federalism, the cornerstone of the Federal Republican credo, had borrowed heavily from the ideas of Proudhon, whose writings had been widely popularized in Spain by Francesc Pi y Margall, one of Iberia's most distinguished public figures of the late nineteenth century and the patron saint of left Republicanism (and of anarchism as well), who served briefly as prime minister in 1873 (his translation of Proudhon's *Du principe federatif* appeared in 1868 on the eve of the September revolution).[26] Because Spanish anarchism was an amalgam of ideas taken from Bakunin and Proudhon, the ideological boundaries separating Federal Republicanism from anarchism were hazy and overlapping.

"Oligarchical power that supported the central state," according to Federalist doctrine as explained by Enric Ucelay da Cal, "would be destroyed, creating a direct local power in which all took part. The federal idea then would be the free municipality as the basis for society (thus linking federalist tradition and the anarchists), the historical regions composed of free municipalities forming 'pacts among equals' at all levels and creating a new Iberian union on the ruins of arbitrary bourgeois dominance. Such ideas, expressed in many different ways, flourished among the artisans and factory workers of Barcelona and industrial towns such as

Manresa, Tarrassa, Sabadell, and Mataró" and in the towns and cities of southern Spain as well.[27]

When the region's rich tradition of conspiratorial, insurrectionary politics is also taken into account, writes Antonio Maria Calero, "it is not surprising that the Internationalists' ideology and tactics responded rather closely to the exigencies of the region's proletariat. Moreover, the geography of anarchism and federalism practically coincided; the political radicalism and the anticentralist autonomous outlooks of both movements consequently are additional factors explaining this coincidence."[28]

Nor did the anarchists' propensity for violence detract from their appeal. To the contrary, in the hurly-burly of nineteenth-century Spanish politics a recourse to violent remedies had become endemic in political and social life. Violence was so integral a part of political discourse that it imbued Spanish anarchism with a distinctive character. James Joll observes, "Kropotkin's faith in human goodness and progress and his confidence in the possibilities of education seemed to be finding practical expression in the educational ideals of Ferrer and Anselmo Lorenzo. At the same time, these ideals and the fanatical devotion they inspired had their sinister side; nowhere more than in Spain was violent destruction an inherent part of the anarchist creed."[29] Leading thinkers such as Gregorio Marañon regarded anarchism and anarcho-syndicalism to be authentic manifestations of Spanish revolutionary psychology.

Possibly its strongest appeal derived from the widespread popular distaste for the sordidness and corruption of politics and political parties, which until the turn of the century remained the exclusive province of the well-to-do elite (*caciquismo*); the effect was to generate massive political indifference and apathy. Pi y Margall, after vainly seeking to rally working-class support for his party, ruefully concluded in the 1870s that the Spanish worker had become hopelessly apolitical. Even after the enactment in 1890 of the universal male suffrage law, the electoral process continued for many years to be discredited by the "tyranny of the *caciques*," vote-buying, intimidation (especially in the rural districts), and ballot stuffing. The antipolitics of the anarchists, therefore, provided an antidote of sorts.[30]

Contrary to some accounts, Andalusian anarchism was not in its initial phase a predominantly peasant movement. FRE membership in the region during the 1870s was primarily skilled artisans and journeymen—hat makers, stonemasons, shoemakers, carpenters, bakers, coopers, and the like—who were mostly concentrated in the urban areas. Farm laborers and small peasant proprietors constituted a minor part of the enrollment. The legendary *obreros conscientes,* those abnegated, ideologically committed idealists who made up the core of unquenchable anarchist faith and strength, were largely drawn from the ranks of the middle class, artisans, teachers, shopkeepers, skilled workers, and small farmers, an entirely comprehensible phenomenon in view of the extremely high illiteracy among workers, *jornaleros,* and *peons.* Tensions inevitably arose even at this early period between urban craftsmen, who sought to function along relatively pragmatic, laboristic lines, and those of a more extreme outlook who conceived of the organization as a revolutionary battering ram. The conflict would ultimately be resolved in the latter's favor.

The movement operated mostly as a semiconspiratorial elitist phenomenon. Four thousand within a labor force of 1 million could function only as a tiny vanguard group, though they at times demonstrated a mobilizational capacity that greatly belied their small numbers. In many localities they consisted of small nuclei; only in parts of Cádiz, Málaga, Seville, and a few other localities did the movement attain a following of truly mass popular dimensions.

The harsh suppression of the Paris Commune in 1871 dealt a grievous blow to the First International. Throughout Europe governments hastened to apply severe repressive measures against its associated organizations and supporters. In Spain and Italy (the latter to a lesser extent), however, national affiliates continued to flourish for a time. At long last in 1872 the Spanish government joined the repressive trend, but despite the government's directive to civil governors ordering the dissolution of FRE branches, the repression was relatively mild and the organization outside of Andalusia continued operating.

Following the abdication of King Amadeo and the proclamation by the Cortes in February 1873 establishing the Federal Republic, the government became more tolerant of the FRE, and the number of its supporters rose to a new high of fifty thousand. But this was merely a brief respite, for the naming of Pi y Margall as prime minister in June almost immediately led to a fatal splintering of the Federal Republican party, pitting Pi's supporters, the Benevolents, against the Intransigents, the latter adamantly refusing to settle for anything less than the immediate carving up of Spain into independent, self-governing cantons. Numerous Internationalists participated in Cantonalist uprisings during the summer of 1873 in Cartagena, Valencia, and the principal cities of Andalusia, though many labor leaders in Barcelona maintained their support for Pi y Margall's

Federalist faction. The FRE officially did not support the Cantonalist rebellions, but throughout lower Andalusia and those parts of the region where the Cantonalist uprisings received their broadest support, the uprisings "clearly took on an Internationalist character."[31]

In at least two instances Internationalists sought to take advantage of the confusion to promote insurrection. In the town of Alcoy, a paper manufacturing center in Alicante province that was an FRE stronghold and the home of the organization's Federal Commission, a labor dispute turned into a general strike and then degenerated into an insurrectionary takeover of the city hall, resulting in the murder of the mayor (a Republican) and others. In Sanlucar de Barrameda, a farming center in the province of Cádiz, where the Internationalists were strong, the Cantonalist uprisings provided a pretext for the insurrectionary seizure of the city. The republic took strong measures against these insurrections, imprisoning 120 at Alcoy and 150 at Sanlucar de Barrameda. Employers took advantage of the situation by reducing wages, cutting them at Sanlucar to half their former levels.[32]

The hapless Pi y Margall could not have become prime minister at a worse time. With his party rent asunder by the Intransigents' insurrectionary actions, the renewal of the Carlist Wars, and the country in a severe economic crisis, he confronted an all but hopeless situation. After less than four months in office he was forced to step down in favor of the more moderate Republican Salmerón, and by the following January the prostrate Republican government fell victim to a military coup headed by General Manuel Pavía. Both the Republicans and the Internationalists were banned, and all worker centers, including the Working Class Atheneum in Barcelona, were shut down. Some two hundred workers, anarchists among them, were deported to the Philippine island of Corregidor. Thus the coup ended efforts by urban middle-class elements to end political dominance by the agrarian oligarchy and deprived the Federalists of much of their popular following. For some time thereafter, they remained on the margin of political life.

Physical suppression was the FRE's lot. Local headquarters and publications were sequestered throughout the country, and numerous activists and supporters were imprisoned or forced into exile. But the organization had been accustomed since 1872 to operating in semilegality and easily adapted to the restrictions. To be sure, illegality led to a substantial loss in influence and membership. Most of the FRE's affiliated craft federations were gradually disorganized, and the Madrid federation disappeared in

1876. But the major impetus for the movement's rapid decline was a shift in outlook and mode of operations. Well before it became illegal, many within the Federal Commission developed anti-mass-movement, conspiratorial, insurrectionary notions, and the repression gave free reign to put these ideas into practice. Their goal was greatly facilitated by the disarray in Catalonia as a result of the republic's demise. In addition, anarchist militants in the Alliance for Social Democracy found themselves hopelessly divided and demoralized over ideological differences.

Extremists were therefore free to proceed with their sought-after doctrinal and organizational face-lifting. For a movement based on workers' societies engaged in open mass activity, the Quixotes of spontaneous revolutionary emancipation substituted a doctrine of armed struggle conducted under the aegis of a network of small, autonomous, ideologically committed groups. Both local and general strikes were discouraged as detracting from the revolutionary goal. The fomenting of revolution by insurrectionary means and individual initiatives ("propaganda by the deed") became the new bases for strategy and action. Anarchist militants, above all those of southern Spain, who were accustomed to operating clandestinely and under brutal police harassment, were the most receptive to the new approach.

Though the shift to ideological and operational maximalism was mostly characterized by verbal pyrotechnics, it induced the departure of more moderate elements, severely depleting the organization's ranks. Numerous affiliates in Barcelona withdrew and in 1877 formed the Federative Center of Barcelona Worker Societies. The plummeting of FRE influence encouraged Pablo Iglesias and his tiny band of Marxists in Madrid to attempt once more to launch a viable movement. At its peak the FRE laid claim to 270 local federations, but by 1881 it had been reduced to 48 federations with three thousand adherents. Many of the surviving branches operated merely as small underground nuclei of ideologues. By the late 1870s the conversion of what remained of the organization had been accomplished. Termes explains, "On the theoretical level the Regional Federation adopted a platform of espousal and solidarity with nihilism while various terrorist incidents took place unplanned and in isolation, unsuccessful attacks upon Alfonso XII in 1878 and 1879 (the first was carried out by a Catalonian worker of the International and the second by a Galician worker), and setting fire to farms and harvests in the Andalusian countryside."[33]

The rising incidence of terrorist acts in Spain paralleled and to some extent was probably inspired by those taking place in other European countries. "Propaganda by the deed" had become increasingly accepted among anarchists by 1878, and assaults were made on several leading European figures and heads of state. Vera Zasulitch in Russia sought to kill the chief of the St. Petersburg police, two attempts were made to assassinate the German emperor, and an attack was made on King Umberto of Italy.[34] The international anarchist congress of 1881 upheld the use of dynamite in the workers' struggle.

The Workers Federation of the Spanish Region

In 1880 the Conservative regime headed by Cánovas del Castillo was replaced with a Liberal one with Práxedes Sagasta as the new prime minister. The Conservatives' harsh antilabor policy gave way to a somewhat more tolerant attitude. Heartened by the prospect of resuming open legal activity, and acting in concert with local Aliancistas who had succeeded in purging their ranks of more extreme elements, in February 1881 the leaders of the reconstituted Barcelona labor federation engineered the ouster of the insurrectionist faction, which had maintained control of the FRE's practically defunct Federal Commission, and returned the organization to a policy favoring Bakuninist anarcho-collectivist trade unionism. The Workers Federation of the Spanish Region (FTRE) was constituted at a conference convened in Barcelona during September 1881. The congress adopted a resolution affirming the continuity of Bakuninist anarcho-collectivist tenets: "Our purely economic organization is distinct from and opposed to all bourgeois and workers political parties since they are organized for the conquest of power. We are organized to reduce existing political and juridical states to merely economic functions, establishing in their place a free federation of free associations of free producers. It is consequently abundantly clear that we are adversaries of parliamentary politics and decided champions of the economic struggle, of a policy demolishing all privileges and monopolies in the unjust structure of present-day society."[35]

Within a year of its formation the FTRE claimed a membership of fifty-eight thousand and 218 local federations; it had surpassed the FRE's achievements. Though referring to themselves as anarchists, many of the members were not. Nonetheless, as before, the federation's leadership and the formulation of its ideological identity were firmly in anarchist hands.

And as heretofore, organizational strength remained concentrated in Catalonia and Andalusia. But this time the relative standing of the two regions was reversed—there were thirty thousand Andalusians and thirteen thousand Catalonians. One reason for this shift was that the FTRE was unable to attract an important part of moderate Catalonian trade unionism, which, though apolitical, was anti-Bakuninist.[36]

Two-thirds of the membership and more than half the affiliated branches and local federations were now located in southern Spain, and the composition of the Andalusian movement had undergone major changes. The former predominance of urban workers and craftsmen had given way to a massive influx of rural *jornaleros* and small farmers, converting it into an essentially rural peasant movement.[37] The southerners nonetheless remained wedded to an extreme radical outlook with a penchant for insurrectionary actions.

Some chroniclers and labor historians have tended to dwell inordinately on the more romantic, exotic aspect of rural anarchism, on its semimystical millenarianism, its unalterable faith in the revolutionary spontaneity of the masses espoused by the ideologues. Reminiscent of itinerant medieval monks, the *obreros conscientes* trudged from hamlet to hamlet spreading the new religion (*la idea*) of the simple peasant faith in the miraculous powers of the revolution that would bring instant *reparto* (division of the land), a mystique capable of purifying the world.[38] The consequence of this romanticism has been to obscure the more practical side of the peasant struggle, the unremitting effort to eliminate *destajo* (piecework), to prevent wage cuts, and to force landowners to pay higher wages to casual labor, especially as harvest season approached. "The commonplace depiction of social conflicts at the end of the nineteenth century in Andalusia," observes Josep Fontana,

> is often depicted in only two shadings: the utopianism of anarchist campesinos and the no less irrational intransigence of the proprietors (emphasis on one or the other depending on the writer's convictions). But when we draw closer to the concrete reality of events, the image dissolves. Let us take, for example, the assault on Jerez in January 1892, when a group of some five hundred peasants invaded the town with the intention of initiating the "social revolution." If we are to believe a man who received firsthand testimony from the leading actors, especially of Fermin Salvochea, the organized labor movement had little to do with these events but suffered its consequences with the closing

down of unions and resistance societies. In Andalusian history of those years most sinister conspiracies were meticulously taken advantage of to repress the progress of labor organization. We find something more than the fear of "social revolution," a fear of wage increases that a deficiently structured agriculture was unable to tolerate. Irrationality thus evaporates. It was neither utopianism of the exploited nor gratuitous evil of the exploiters, rather a confrontation over real, concrete objectives.[39]

A direct relationship existed, to be sure, between the conversion of the Andalusian movement into a largely peasant organization and its adherence to a violent, insurrectionary creed. It was a phenomenon more in keeping with the mentality of a poverty-stricken, landless peasantry, subsisting in the intimidating, repressive atmosphere of rural Andalusia, that traditionally gave vent to its privations and rage either in secret or through explosive outbursts. It was therefore an easy distance from the brigandage and jacqueries of yesteryear to anarchist insurrectionism. In the words of Angel Marvaud, "Andalusian anarchism is an anarchism of sharp, brief crises; revolts in this part of the peninsula make one think not of reflective actions, lengthily prepared in advance, but of a series of extremely grave incidents, lacking cohesion, without direction, without any impulse but that of hunger and rage."[40]

The burgeoning of labor organization in the zone of Cádiz during 1881 and 1882 following the relaxation of official restraints also had the effect of substantially increasing acts of violence. Underlying this development were the ultraradical policies of the local FTRE leadership (the Jerez area and Seville province have been described as strongholds of "extreme force anarchism") and the coincidence of the labor revival with the onset of a severe drought and economic crisis that brought many farm laborers and their families to the brink of starvation.[41] Hunger stalked the streets of innumerable farming communities. The early 1880s had seen increased tensions between the rich and poor and daily violence against landowners and the well-to-do.[42] The writer "Clarin" (Leopoldo Alas) toured southern Spain during the month of December 1882 as a correspondent of the Madrid *El Dia*. He reported that hunger in Jerez had driven many of the unfortunates to beg in the streets because the municipality had done nothing to alleviate the suffering.

Alarmed by the rising social unrest, the authorities took precautionary measures by increasing surveillance of workers' societies and jailing numerous activists. The FTRE's national officers cautioned local leaders in Andalusia to avoid provocative actions that would invite a police crackdown and force a return to illegality, but their warnings fell on deaf ears and the situation inexorably moved toward a denouement.[43]

The result of the simmering unrest was the sensational "Black Hand" affair. A number of murders in the Cádiz area during 1882 and 1883 were attributed by police to adherents of Mano Negra, a secret society allegedly linked with the FTRE. Uncertainty persists to this day concerning the existence of such an organization or whether it was merely a police invention to justify dismantling the increasingly sizable and recalcitrant labor movement of southern Spain. Much to the dismay of many Andalusian militants, the FTRE Federal Commission denounced the violence and denied any connection with such a body. The affair nevertheless provided a pretext for a massive persecution that virtually destroyed the movement. A series of show trials was mounted in 1883 and 1884 attended by much sensationalism. Hundreds of activists and their supporters were imprisoned, many of them physically mistreated and tortured. Contemporary accounts estimated that within a month following the airing of the affair the number of those resident in jail rose from three hundred in Jerez and Cádiz to more than two thousand and three thousand respectively.

As a consequence, in the wake of the Black Hand scandal, the Internationalist revival declined as rapidly as it had risen. Workers deserted in droves as the organization became a casualty of doctrinal contradictions and police persecutions. The trial ended in the garroting of several anarchists and long prison terms for others. It also triggered a police witch-hunt throughout the country against libertarians and FTRE supporters.

Harsh and unremitting as the government's persecution was, the movement might have survived clandestinely. But the irreconcilable divisions over strategy and tactics could not be overcome. The Catalonian interest in maintaining and preserving a legal, functioning proletarian mass movement simply could not be accommodated with that of a desperate, landless peasantry that perceived salvation only through conspiratorial, insurrectionary means. The basic issue, as Romero Maura succinctly puts it, was "whether anarchist organizations should consist solely of convinced anarchists or should include all workers who were ready to join." But the Cádiz militants opposed any action to improve the immediate lot of the workers on the ground that it would dilute the revolutionary ardor of the masses.[44]

The anger aroused by the repression and their extreme radical convictions persuaded young militants of Cádiz and Seville, who considered themselves heirs to the FRE insurrectionary view, to adopt even more violent methods. The organization they formed, Los Desheredados (the Disinherited), differed little in outlook and function from the purported Black Hand society.[45] It was a largely secret terrorist group that organized commandos to mete out justice to abusive landlords, public officials, and informers, as well as to Barcelona "reformist" labor activists, who were regarded as traitors. Supporters were dispatched to Barcelona to aid in sabotaging and destroying the despised workers' organizations. The FTRE was formally disbanded in 1888, and anarchists began to organize in small cells, the *grupos de afinidad.*

The Rise of Anarchist and Anarcho-Syndicalist Activity

The FTRE's disintegration coincided with a rising tide of individual terrorist acts in Europe to which Spanish libertarianism eventually succumbed. "The anarchism imported into Spain in 1868 had been Bakuninist and anarcho-collectivist," observes Romero Maura; "thirty years later almost all anarchists were anarcho-communists."[46] Juan Díaz del Moral, a sympathetic observer, comments, "With delirious logic these men dismantled the combat cadres and committed themselves to the diffuse and spontaneous actions of isolated individuals. . . . And then began the terrorist attacks, which reached a climax during the final decade of the nineteenth century. . . . Uncontrolled groups replaced associations, as did public life by clandestine action. . . . Utopian doctrines, though permeated with humanism, highly educative and moralizing among some anarchist cadres at least, were negated or obscured by the furor and the fanatical exaltations, the insanity and the criminality of its lower social depths."[47]

With anarcho-collectivism in Barcelona relegated to a minority status and with the departure of many proletarian militants, intellectual groups and bohemians came to the fore, more attracted by the idea of action than by any desire to achieve an egalitarian society.[48] It coincided with a vogue for philosophical anarchism among numerous leading intellectuals and artists.

The abortive rising at Jérez on January 8, 1892, came in the midst of this philosophical change.[49] Some five hundred rural laborers and peasants, armed mostly with pitchforks and scythes, invaded the city. It is still unclear whether they intended to try to liberate imprisoned comrades or to seize the city in a pronunciamiento anarchist style to spark a revolutionary uprising. Jerez of Black Hand fame was the center of the Disinheriteds' influence, and that the group was led by anarchist militants suggests that what may have started out as a traditional protest against the jailing of some supporters was converted into a jacquerie, albeit with an anarchist gloss.

After occupying the town for several hours, during which some innocent passersby were killed, the mob was dispersed by police. Although the incident was relatively minor, it provided a pretext for the launching of still another harsh wave of repression. This time four anarchist militants were garroted and eighteen others sentenced to long terms at hard labor. Embittered by police persecution, anarchist terrorists plotted their revenge. The original purposes of propaganda by the deed were soon forgotten as the cycle of violence and counterviolence drove anarchists to seek retribution.

Pauli Pallàs, a young anarchist, unsuccessfully tried to assassinate General Arsenio Martínez Campos in Barcelona and was tried by court-martial and executed. A friend, Santiago Salvador, decided to avenge the execution by bombing the crowded Liceo theater, which resulted in the deaths of twenty persons and the wounding of many others. Twenty-nine incidents occurred in Catalonia between 1892 and 1893, nineteen in the Barcelona area.[50]

To counter the rash of terrorist attacks, the authorities sponsored a harsh antiterrorist law in 1894 and unleashed a repression that was undiscriminating in scope and brutal in application. Hundreds were rounded up in 1896, including many nonanarchists, after a bomb was thrown into a religious procession on Corpus Christi day (eight persons died), and thrown into the Montjuich prison, where they were subjected to terrible mistreatment in which some died under torture. More than fifty were exiled to the forbidding wastes of Spanish Sahara.[51]

Scandalized protests against the police atrocities were heard throughout Europe. A military court-martial meted out the death penalty to twenty-eight from diverse political quarters and life imprisonment for fifty-nine others. Not only leading anarchists but intellectual sympathizers were put on trial. Only one of the condemned actually belonged to a terrorist group. Because of the mounting outcry outside Spain, only five were eventually executed. Those responsible for the Corpus Christi bombing were never apprehended. The repression had a devastating effect on what remained of anarchist organization. Many leading figures fled to South America, where at the turn of the century they took leading roles in the formation and development of anarchist-influenced labor movements. Labor organization was severely weakened, and many Barcelona workers began to view the government as inherently antiworker. Anarchists began to seem more acceptable as collaborators.[52]

As anarcho-communism both in its more benign guise and its terrorist version became the dominant credo of Spanish anarchism, the way seemed open for a reassertion of moderate trade unionism by the late 1880s. The Liberal government of Práxedes Sagasta in 1887 pushed through the Jurisdictions Law (Ley de Jurisdicciónes) that gave labor organizations a legal status. The passage of this law, the generally tolerant climate, and the disarray that was overtaking anarchist-oriented labor organizations induced the Socialist Workers party (PSOE) in 1888 for the third time to attempt to constitute its labor arm, which led to the formation that year of the General Workers Union (Union General de Trabajadores—UGT).

The socialists' hope for success rested primarily on the UGT's prospects for growth in Catalonia, especially among textile workers. Several leaders of the Tres Clases de Vapor Federación, the region's largest and most formidable worker organization, had joined the PSOE, and since the early 1880s the federation's organ, *El Obrero,* had served as the principal diffuser in Spain of socialist ideas. UGT branches sprung up in several textile towns, largely composed of textile labor activists.

But the socialists' rosy prospects were soon undone by a disastrous labor conflict and estrangement between the PSOE and the Tres Clases de Vapor leadership. The 1890s, moreover, were a time of crisis and turbulence as the country was gripped by economic slump and the shattering effects of the defeat in the Spanish-American War of 1898. Many workers, who in normal times subsisted in a state of constant economic siege, suffered harsh privation; wages between 1873 and 1903 rose 30 percent, but the cost of living increased by 70 percent.

Violent strikes swept Barcelona and other Catalonian factory towns between 1890 and 1897 as the increasingly intransigent attitude of textile and other employers toward unions and collective bargaining impelled labor leaders to resort to violent tactics, bringing them closer to the anarchists. The propaganda by the deed mystique took root as terrorism reached its zenith between 1893 and 1897.

The general economic recession caused the textile industry to suffer from overproduction, and employers instituted retrenchment measures between 1887 and 1889 that included mass layoffs, wage cuts, and the lengthening of the workday. The adoption of protectionist policies by the government a few years later resulted in an upturn for the textile industry. Tres Clases de Vapor then sought the restoration of former wage scales, and despite the conciliatory efforts by the federation's leaders, employers invoked a lockout in Manresa and Alt Llobregat that forced the union to respond with an industrywide shutdown.

The textile spinning mills of the Ter-Fresser valleys constituted a stronghold of support for Tres Clases de Vapor. Much of the work force had been recruited from nearby farm areas, and when strikes or lockouts occurred, many of the striking workers were able to weather the periods of shutdown by returning to their farm households. The striking or locked-out workers, being of local origin—factory owners resided in Barcelona—often received community support in towns such as Manlleu and Torelló.

The union scored a partial victory largely because the textile factory owners delayed a decisive showdown until late in 1890, when a Conservative government under Cánovas del Castillo was due to replace the more tolerant Sagasta regime. The lockout was resumed shortly after the new government took office, and with the connivance of the authorities (they had refused to enforce the terms of the accord entered into earlier that year that had been arranged by the Sagasta administration) the employers succeeded in routing the union. Many union supporters were discharged and blacklisted. In many instances male workers were replaced by women and children, who were paid much lower wages. Thus the region's once powerful cotton textile workers' labor organization, which had achieved a membership of twenty-one thousand before the lockout, was reduced to a shattered force. Tres Clases de Vapor continued to exist for some years, but it never again was an element of consequence among cotton textile mill hands.

On the heels of this defeat, the impressive turnouts for the May Day processions in 1890 (fifteen thousand in Barcelona) and 1891 represented a belated attempt at unity by a divided and weakened labor movement. The destruction of labor organization in the cotton textile industry, the pacesetter for regional collective bargaining and employer of a third of the Barcelona work force, and the chilling effect it had on workers' militancy represented a grievous setback for the entire movement. The campaign for the eight-hour day, of which the May Day rally was an expression, had a special relevancy because it coincided with the efforts of textile workers to force the employers to shorten the lengthened workweek that had been instituted during the 1887–89 industrial downturn.

The dismantling of the region's most important organ of moderate trade unionism was an important contributing factor to the rash of terrorist incidents that convulsed the region from 1893 to 1896, for the debilitation of organized labor provided a powerful rationale for anarchist activists to abandon the quest for social revolution through mass struggle and to catalyze latent impulses of revolt through propaganda by the deed.

The setback for moderate trade unionism also contained a political dimension. What appeared at the outset as a golden opportunity for a socialist breakthrough in Catalonia soon came to naught. Within a year following the UGT's establishment, most of the leaders of Tres Clases de Vapor broke with the PSOE/UGT. Conflicting interests and outlooks could not be overcome. As Balcells analyzes the situation, "There was considerable tension in the socialism of the time between revolutionary theory and moderate gradualist practice, and the Barcelona revisionists sought to elevate practical possibilism to a theoretical or strategic possibilism. In view of the importance of Federal Republicanism in Catalonia and the social reformism that it embodied, the socialist possibilists were proponents, upon the establishment of universal suffrage, of an electoral alliance with the Federals."[53] Such an alliance was totally unacceptable to the PSOE's leaders in Madrid; not for several more decades would the party become reconciled to such a political collaboration. It was also impossible to forge an effective trade union strategy to respond to the harsh realities of the Catalonian labor struggle. Balcells continues, "Actually the UGT did not represent a left alternative to the 'trade unionism' of Tres Clases de Vapor. When the severity of the class struggle made moderate unionism unviable, it was not socialism that was called upon to replace it but anarcho-syndicalism, though anarchist contradictions caused a twenty-year delay, until the second decade of the twentieth century, for the majority of organized workers to adhere to an anarcho-syndicalist federation."[54]

After the Montjuich repression the scale of terrorism declined but did not entirely cease. An Italian named Angolillo, intent upon avenging the Montjuich horrors, came to Spain in 1897 from London and shot Prime Minister Cánovas del Castillo. In the years following, numerous other public dignitaries, including two prime ministers and a cardinal, fell victim to anarchist assassins. By the late 1890s anarchist terrorism gradually subsided, largely as a result of repressive measures, though it was not until the second decade of the twentieth century that Spanish anarchism succeeded in freeing itself from the destructive thrall of the terrorist creed and became reestablished as a proletarian mass movement. A residual had been deposited, however, that was to remain embedded in the libertarian mentality and would periodically reassert itself.

4

EARLY DEVELOPMENT OF THE GENERAL WORKERS UNION (UGT)

Socialist Trade Unionism and the General Workers Union

Following their expulsion from the FRE, a small group of Marxian socialists in 1872 formed La Nueva Federación Madrileña (New Madrid Federation).[1] Failing to gain much support, it disbanded the following year, leaving the Printing Arts General Society (Sociedad General del Arte de Imprimir) as the principal rallying center for local socialists until 1879.[2] The successful launching of a Marxist-oriented movement in the prevailing sociopolitical climate would have been no easy task even under normal conditions. It was made all the more difficult by the almost complete absence of any concerted effort on the part of Marxists, who controlled the International Workingmen's Association, to counter anarchist inroads during the crucial formative period of the late 1860s and early 1870s, a neglect that gave Bakunin and his supporters an inestimable advantage. By the time they bestirred themselves (Friedrich Engels and Paul Lafargue handled Spanish affairs in the International Secretariat), the task had assumed Sisyphean proportions.

Anarchist doctrine by then had become widely disseminated within radical and labor circles, although progressive and liberal quarters tended to favor socialism, and its supporters had gained an ascendancy of sorts within the nascent labor movement. As Antoni Jutglar observes, "Many affiliated worker societies that did not possess anarchist activists in their midst came to accept the basic postulates of apoliticism and collectivism."[3]

The repression of radical movements in France and other countries following the crushing of the Paris Commune brought socialist and anarchist agitators to Spain. Numerous Communards and Italian anarchists flocked to Barcelona, and the small, struggling socialist group received an assist with the arrival of Paul Lafargue, Marx's son-in-law, who remained for six months. Lafargue, a close friend and political associate of Jules Guesde, provided the Spanish acolytes with a more ordered, coherent, albeit doctrinaire ideological outlook.

Seven years later, on May 2, 1887, the Spanish Socialist Workers party (Partido Obrero Socialista Español) was formed, and the General Workers Union was founded in 1888.[4] The formation of the UGT as a socialist-oriented trade union center had been timed to profit from the disarray and decline of the anarchist-controlled FTRE, but this proved to be of little help.[5] The fledgling UGT was incapable of attracting enough former supporters of the FTRE, and for more than three decades the two movements remained as tiny socialist outposts outside the mainstream of social and political life amid an emerging labor movement mainly dominated by laborist and anarchist influences.

Throughout its formative years the socialist movement was dominated by skilled and artisanal workers, particularly the typographers. Worker organization in Madrid had been initiated in 1868 under the aegis of the FRE but with no lasting results. The establishment in 1874 of the Printing Arts General Society (Sociedad General del Arte de Imprimir) marked the real launching of the city's labor movement.[6] From its ranks came most of the *obreros conscientes,* who founded the PSOE and UGT. The party's initial Madrid membership included sixteen typographers, two jewelry makers, a marble mason, and five "intellectuals" (most of whom dropped out shortly thereafter).[7] The large majority of the two organizations' key figures, men such as Pablo Iglesias, García Quejido, Gómez Latorre, and Toribio Reoyo, started out as leaders of the typographers union.[8]

Consequently, for a very long time it retained the mentality and general outlook of the late nineteenth-century Madrid labor aristocrat. Juan José Morato, a socialist chronicler who had also worked as a Madrid typographer, recounts that "subjectively the typographers were to the working masses what the proletariat is to the so-called middle classes, the frock-coated workers, those who, with some exceptions, are commercial employees and certain types of railroad workers."[9]

They were also the products of a nonindustrial city whose economy consisted of light industry, manufacture of luxury items, artisanry, and services catering to the bureaucratic needs and lifestyles peculiar to the national capital. Understandably, therefore, both worker organization and class consciousness were virtually nonexistent. Only eight worker societies were in existence in 1885. Labor disputes were engaged in cautiously; the main interest seemed to be in organization building rather than leading or promoting labor conflict. Reflecting the dour, incorruptible abnegation embodied in the person of Pablo Iglesias, the movement's socialist beliefs tended to be refracted through the prism of the lifestyle and moral outlook of the politically committed Madrid labor aristocrat.

Iglesias, for example, opposed calling strikes before most of the workers in a given establishment had joined the union and assembled adequate strike defense funds—at a time when most labor organizations consisted of small minorities within enterprises—and insisted on engaging in work stoppages only when success was almost totally assured. His formula for a successful strike was to hold it "when work abounds and is not scarce, and consequently no extra work hands are available, when this makes it impossible or difficult to replace strikers with nonmember workers, when one can count beforehand on sufficient means to care for the former over a maximum period for the duration of the work stoppage that has been rationally calculated."[10] Not only were strikes to be well prepared and undertaken with prudence, but bargaining was to be conducted so as to facilitate peaceful, negotiated outcomes and not to take on a personal character. This bargaining approach was shaped by the great preponderance of small workshops in which owners and artisans (*maestros*) worked together.

Restoration Spain, a society possessed of an overpowering sociopolitical lethargy and lack of mobilization, could not have provided a more inhospitable climate for the introduction of a movement inspired by European socialism. A party that accorded a central role to political and parliamentary action was bound to encounter great difficulties in securing social reforms in a country where election results were usually rigged and parliamentarianism aroused widespread contempt, especially among workers.[11] Anarcho-syndicalist ideas were accepted because that philosophy rejected any participation in a corrupt parliamentary system and called upon the workers to rely only on their own strength through direct action. Its fervent advocacy of local rule, of Federalism, provided an equally powerful appeal. In a society in which much of the population felt no national identity and local and regional ties were paramount, a movement that stressed local autonomy rather than a disciplined, centralized structure enjoyed a great advantage. The early socialist movement was also hindered by its insensitivity to the ethnic-regional aspirations of the Basques and

Catalans. Hence, despite a certain benevolence shown toward the socialists by both Conservative and Liberal governments, especially the latter, though not to the extent of assuring fair elections, not until 1910, three decades after the party's foundation, did Pablo Iglesias finally succeed, at age sixty, in becoming the first socialist to enter parliament, and even then an electoral alliance with the Republicans was required to make it possible.

The British historian David Thomson has perceptively observed that "wherever universal suffrage remained for a long time impeded . . . or wherever its operation was severely limited by strong central authority. . . . socialists went on using the language and preaching the ideas of revolutionary doctrinaire Marxism even when their practice and their achievements were more moderate."[12] Surely this was the case with Spain.

Socialist progress was further hindered by the rudimentary level of political thought among the blue-collar exponents of Marxism and the consequent difficulty encountered by the leadership in adapting socialist doctrines to the peculiar conditions of Spanish underdevelopment. The Spanish labor movement, according to Gerald H. Meaker, "lagged perhaps half a century behind the rest of Europe, suffering (as Marx said of the German movement in the eighteen sixties) as much from the development of capitalism as from the incompleteness of that development."[13]

With few modifications Iglesias and his followers transplanted the French socialist leader Jules Guesde's primitive and doctrinaire version of Marxism, which was "totally unrelated to the economic and social conditions of the Restoration."[14] Its rigid sectarianism appealed to Iglesias. The subordination of the UGT to party control and direction—the same men who led the PSOE also headed the UGT—and its role as a party "transmission belt" closely adhered in practice if not in theory to Guesdian precepts.[15] During the party's first three decades, any suggestion of electoral or political cooperation with the Republicans, many of whom were sympathetic to socialist ideas, was rigorously rejected on the ground that collaboration with bourgeois parties was doctrinal apostasy, a rejection that contributed heavily to the party's long confinement to the political ghetto. Iglesias held that for the party to preserve its political standing and identity its most hostile attacks must be reserved for political parties whose ideas stood closest to its own, in his words, "to combat all bourgeois parties, most particularly the doctrines of the most advanced ones." "He consequently argued," notes Enrique del Moral Sandoval, "that for the party not to adhere to this criterion, especially with respect to circumstantial alliances, the identity of socialism might be diluted and could even be absorbed by the more progressive liberal parties."[16]

The imprint of Pablo Iglesias, who headed the movement for close to half a century, was a powerful factor in the shaping of Spanish socialism. A man of strong views and domineering spirit, he left an enduring mark on the evolution and configuration of the party long after his passing. As he grew older, he was affectionately called *el abuelo* (the grandfather) and in Catholic Spain, appropriately, *el santo laico* (the secular saint).

His harrowing, impoverished childhood reads like something from a Dickens novel. This man, self-educated with little formal schooling, of dour mien and ailing health inherited from years of privation, the epitome of *el obrero consciente,* demonstrated outstanding gifts of leadership, pedagogy, and tenacity at an early age. Few in political life have so consumingly dedicated their lives to a movement.[17]

Discipline, orderliness, and organization are axiomatic in Marxist political thinking, but in Spain such notions under the tutelage of Iglesias became the overriding preoccupations.[18] Partly as a reaction to the undisciplined exuberance of the anarchists with their great concern for individual initiative and spontaneity and partly because of his personality, "this austere and ascetic invalid stamped the party with his concern for morality in political life, his rigidity and his exclusive proletarian brand of calvinism."[19] Madrid, as Gerald Brenan points out, "as the seat of the court and the government, had at this time a very loose standard of conduct and the working classes were infected with the vices of the bourgeoisie. . . . This moral regeneration was of course essential if the Socialists were to hold their own in those corrupt times."[20] Despite Iglesias's intolerance for those who did not share his point of view, the movement's survival for many years was in no small measure owing to his tenacity.

Thus though the sluggish progress of the party and its trade union adjunct was largely the result of self-imposed infirmities of outlook and mentality, it also mirrored the profound social and political lethargy that enveloped the great mass of urban workers and the rural poor virtually until World War I. Outside of a few urban centers, there was no popular participation in the political life of the country. Mass parties did not exist, and trade unions tended to consist mostly of small groups of activists who could only episodically enlist the support of their fellow workers.

Organized labor at the century's dawning still involved only a tiny proportion of the work force.

At its formation the PSOE possessed a membership of forty, and the
1888 congress that founded the UGT reported a membership in excess
of three thousand, a third of them typographers. By 1890 the UGT
numbered close to four thousand, and five years later it had risen to only
sixty-five hundred. The early and mid-1890s were a time of acute frustration. Efforts to secure the affiliation of the barrel makers' and metalworkers' federations proved unsuccessful. Following the break with the
Catalonian Tres Clases de Vapor leadership, a Cotton Manufacturing
Workers Union was formed in an effort to maintain a foothold in the
industry. But the new venture gained little support in Catalonia, and the
UGT's remaining base in textiles, the local at La Industria Málagueña of
Málaga with nine hundred to a thousand members, vanished after an
unsuccessful strike in 1894 that resulted in a four-month prison sentence
for Pablo Iglesias.

Even after the UGT finally emerged from its vegetative existence,
the nurturing of solid trade union organization often proved elusive. It
was not uncommon in this period for workers to join unions during
times of heightened tensions or campaigns to secure improvements and
then to abandon them once the desired objective had been achieved.
When the union failed to gain its announced objectives and the inevitable employers' reprisals descended, workers would quickly lose heart,
and it would be years before a renewed effort at organization became
feasible.

The UGT's sectarian and localistic views made the acquisition of
doctrinal realism and the elaboration of adequate strike tactics and
trade union action torturous and painfully drawn out. Madrid, with its
artisanal traditions and craft organization, ultimately provided a relatively amenable venue for Iglesias's prudently cautious approach, but
his methods were wholly inappropriate not only for Barcelona but for
Vizcaya-Bilbao and Asturias as well, where the work force was concentrated in large industrial plants and mining communities. A protracted
process of trial and error consequently ensued before the organization
achieved a sufficient degree of tactical flexibility and an organizational
blend of craft and industrial unionism, often by ignoring official
strictures.

A major impediment was Iglesias's almost visceral hostility to the
employment of the general strike, whose utility in certain situations was

practically ruled out because of its exploitation for insurrectionary ends by the anarchists.[21] No other European socialist party expressed such adamant opposition. Iglesias insisted that the general strike be reserved for the seizure of power and the overthrow of capitalist society. To employ it for anything short of the ultimate assault on bourgeois power was unwarranted and adventuristic. Nonetheless, in 1905 the UGT launched an abortive attempt at a general strike—not labeled as such—to protest the rising cost of living.

Their undiscriminating opposition to the general strike sometimes placed the socialists in an untenable position. Stripped of its insurrectionary potential, the general strike could be a useful collective bargaining tool when employed judiciously in difficult labor disputes. The small size of most Spanish manufacturing establishments and their concentration in factory districts often contiguous to working-class neighborhoods made citywide or areawide work stoppages practical bargaining tactics for the unions. For this reason as well as strong employer resistance to their demands, workers in Barcelona, for example, often responded in mass to such strike calls despite the attempts by anarchists to convert them into revolutionary exercises. Hence it was difficult for the UGT/PSOE to oppose such ventures, as they did in the 1902 Barcelona general strike in support of the metalworkers because of anarchist participation, without doing violence to the growing popular tradition of working-class solidarity.[22]

In preparation for the celebration of May Day in Barcelona in 1890, the socialists advocated a one-day work stoppage with a parade ending in the presentation of petitions to the authorities demanding the eight-hour day. The anarchists, however, insisted on a general strike to last until the eight-hour day was won. With the support of numerous skilled worker societies, the Tres Clases de Vapor, and the Federal Republicans, the socialists won approval for their plan but only over the objections of a large minority who supported the anarchist proposal. Despite the earlier disagreement, the one-day work stoppage was generally supported and a huge crowd turned out for the socialist-directed celebration. A rival anarchist rally failed to assemble more than several hundred participants, but they voted by acclamation to continue the strike until the eight-hour day was won. Most factories and public transportation facilities were shut down the following day, and martial law was declared. Despite the socialist failure to support it, the strike remained in force for several more days. The military authorities and employers felt forced to enter into negotiations to end the shutdown, and it was finally concluded with the granting of several concessions: the tramway employees won shift work, each shift lasting eight or nine hours, and the port workers were granted an eight-hour day, as were some factory workers engaged in textile dyeing, shoe manufacturing, and masonry. Others also won wage increases. Manuel Pérez Ledesma sums up the results of the strike: "The Barcelona events in general clearly demonstrated the tactical differences between the socialist and anarchist sectors and their consequences. The triumph of the latter, though merely affecting a limited number of trades, and the purely symbolic character of the socialist action, as well as the lack of solidarity with the workers who decided to continue the strike, were factors that were decisively to influence the little echo during the years following that socialism and the UGT received within the Barcelona working class."[23]

Throughout its long and eventful pre–civil war history, the Spanish socialist movement often adopted contradictory attitudes toward the general strike. Though operating primarily as a moderate reformist, parliamentary political force and vociferously berating the anarchists for their irresponsible insurrectionist proclivities, it would regularly deviate from moderate norms, launching national and regional general strikes, some of them of an economic–trade union character and others with political intent and semirevolutionary objectives.[24]

The oligarchical monopolization of political power and the extremely slow reform of the electoral process tended to legitimize recourse to revolutionary coups d'état so frequent in the nineteenth century and regarded until the civil war as a perfectly acceptable means for gaining power or accomplishing basic reforms. Though of an essentially European social democratic cast, the Spanish movement consequently found its outlook and behavior shaped by the peninsula's political and social realities and thus became the most spasmodically "revolutionary" party in western Europe.

Nor was Spanish socialism totally immune to characteristics peculiar to a minority unionism, especially those of an anarchist or syndicalist strain. As Val Lorwin notes, "A small and fluctuating membership and the difficulties of many local strikes encouraged the vision of sudden victory through the general strike. That would depend less on organization and funds than on one vast 'surge of class consciousness' led by a militant elite."[25] This outlook motivated Facundo Perezagua, the architect and leader of the Vizcayan socialist movement.

Disaster in Catalonia and Success in Vizcaya and Asturias

During the first ten years of its existence UGT membership increased by no more than three thousand. From 1886 to 1906 organizational prospects were dimmed by the persistence of economic slump. Nonetheless, the basis for future expansion in the burgeoning industrial province of Vizcaya had been established, and initial penetrations in the factory towns of Asturias had begun. These two areas subsequently were to join with Madrid as the principal bastions of Iberian socialist trade union and political strength. By the turn of the century, the UGT's fortunes took a turn for the better as inflation and widespread privation resulting from the Spanish-American War gave rise to a modest upsurge in recruitment.

In 1898 the Workers Societies Center was formed in Madrid; most of its unions were affiliated with the UGT. New locals sprung up among plasterers, glaziers, bookbinders, leather tannery workers, pattern makers, molders, and others. With the affiliation of the railroad workers (Sindicato General de Ferrocarriles de España) the following year, UGT membership swelled to fifteen thousand. But Morato cautions that this figure merely reflected the number of adherents "on the books," not actual dues-paying members. "In reality," he observes "the Union consisted of 48 sections and 6,437 members."[26]

Life continued to be extremely precarious for most labor organizations as they were frequently harassed by the authorities and employers and possessed precious little financial resources and dues payers. Those that managed to survive were usually able to do so through the efforts of small bands of anarchists or socialist activists.

Within the Castilian heartland, Madrid functioned for a long time as a veritable enclave. "Prosper Merimee wrote at mid-century to the Countess of Montijo that to hear talk of socialism in Old Castile was like hearing that the emperor of China had become a monk." Three decades later this caricature still had roots in reality, as José Varela Ortega explains:

Only a handful of resistance societies managed to eke out a precarious existence during the Restoration. The only labor organization of note was the Valladolid railroad workers. The socialists at this century's dawning gained control of the Valladolid Workers Center to which all of the province's resistance societies were affiliated. Burgos and Guadalajara also possessed small groups of socialist worker activists. Strikes until the Great War numbered several tens involving a few hundred strikers. In the mining centers of Palencia, for example, Civil Guards were not concentrated simply because they were not necessary . . . Castilian farm laborers until 1903–4 proved incapable of organizing a strike worthy of the name. . . . Not till the 1920s were the first successes registered in the unionization of the working masses of the Castilian countryside. Consequently the number of Castilian workers of all types in 1904 associated to improve working conditions hardly amounted to 9,000 and in Valladolid they did not reach 1,500.[27]

Hopes ran high at the time of its formation that the UGT would be successful in erecting a solid base among the textile hands and skilled workers of Barcelona and other Catalonian industrial centers. Most of the delegates at the Barcelona founding congress represented local labor groups and other communities of the region; two-thirds of its membership at that time was concentrated in Catalonia. National headquarters was located in Barcelona, and promising bridgeheads were established in Mataró and Villanueva y Geltru. Yet efforts to put down roots in Catalonia ended in dismal failure and UGT membership in Barcelona and Catalonia remained inconsequential until the civil war.

The reasons for this failure have not yet been fully clarified, but several salient factors seem evident.[28] Most notable among them was the rigid, doctrinaire approach of Iglesias and others and their inexperience in dealing with the problems of industrial workers, which prevented them from formulating a trade union outlook and strategy attuned to the realities of the Catalonian labor scene; the UGT's refusal to support a 1902 local general strike called in solidarity with the metalworkers of Barcelona; the almost total subordination of UGT actions to the PSOE's directives, which was anathema to the apolitical unionists of Catalonia; an inability to retain the adhesion of key figures in the Tres Clases de Vapor, who ended up deserting the PSOE/UGT to form a rival regional socialist organization; and the paucity and general mediocrity of local socialist cadres, who were no match for their anarchist rivals. Surely the almost total suppression by the authorities of trade union activities during the 1890s in response to the spread of anarchist atrocities must have also figured prominently in the decision to move UGT headquarters. Furthermore, it was inconceivable for Catalonian unionists with their richer trade union tradition to renounce primacy in Spanish labor affairs to nonindustrial Madrid. And last but surely not least, domination of the PSOE and UGT from

Madrid caused many activists and workers to extend their Catalonian antipathy for anything emanating from the Castilian capital to include the unions as well. These feelings also prompted Catalonian labor unions to shun any possible linkage with the UGT in 1907 and to establish instead the unaffiliated, politically neutral regional labor body Solidaridad Obrera, which became the forerunner of the CNT.

As prospects for organizational growth in Catalonia grew progressively dim, new opportunities opened up in the industrializing zones of the Basque provinces and in the adjoining areas of Santander and Asturias. José Ortega y Gasset once observed that until the turn of the century the north had not really been incorporated into the life of the country. Surely a major factor in this assimilation was the labor and political mobilization of the area's wage earners under socialist influence. Labor organization in the Basque country and Asturias was practically nonexistent before their arrival. Previous attempts to establish resistance societies or even mutual benefit associations had been sporadic and usually short-lived. Neither the FRE nor its successor, the FTRE, had been successful in these areas.[29]

The first efforts at penetration in the Basque province of Vizcaya came amid large-scale expansion in the extraction of iron ores and with the commencement of the Bilbao estuary's transformation into Spain's principal center for iron- and steelmaking, shipbuilding, and the construction of heavy machinery. At the turn of the century Vizcaya possessed a larger mine work force than Asturias. A foothold was established among the various skilled and semiskilled craftsmen of Bilbao, who were assisted by the socialist nucleus in the formation of trade unions, collective bargaining, and strike actions.

Much of the early work of penetration was conducted by socialists who had been blacklisted in Madrid and then sent north (an analogous process took place in Barcelona periodically with anarchists who then emigrated not only to the Levant and southern Spain but also to South America, most notably to Argentina, Chile, Uruguay, and Brazil). One such person was Facundo Perezagua, a boilermaker, who went to Bilbao in the mid-1880s to organize for the PSOE/UGT and became one of the most gifted organizers in the Spanish labor movement.

"Those who have written about him," recounts Juan Pablo Fusi, "have observed his dry corpulence and the markedly semitic features of his physiognomy. His incorruptibility and honesty were acknowledged even by his opponents, his arrogance, a veritable malady, by his supporters. Incapable of accepting criticism of his conduct, he harbored a deep hostility toward those who did so. He would not permit leaders in his proximity who might diminish his prestige." As Iglesias came to personify Madrid, Perezagua, a sort of Spanish equivalent of Big Bill Haywood, filled a similar role for Vizcayan socialism. "This man of rhetorical violence, rudimentary education, authoritarian, inflexible, and austere, and like Iglesias, energetic and intransigent, created and led the socialist organization of Bilbao almost dictatorially for thirty years, deeply imprinted with his personal characteristics, at a time when parties and unions in Spain were most precariously institutionalized."[30]

The big opportunity came in the wake of successful rallies held to celebrate May Day in 1890 that were attended by numerous iron miners. A smoldering resentment had been gathering among the more than ten thousand miners over flagrant abuses in their working conditions and their general treatment.[31] Only a pretext was needed to set it off, and that was provided when five socialist employees were discharged from one of the mines and several hundred fellow workers walked out in sympathy. The strike then spread like wildfire throughout the mining zone and spilled over into the nearby industrial districts of Bilbao, affecting close to thirty thousand workers. Overwhelmed, the local police were powerless to control the situation.

The shutdown had been completely spontaneous, taking both the local authorities and the socialists unawares. Martial law was declared and the area placed under military control. General José Maria Loma, the military commandant, then invited the workers to submit their demands through legal channels. Once this avenue was opened, the striking miners turned to the socialists for assistance in framing their demands and conducting negotiations with the authorities and the employers. But the presence of the military and the rigorous application of martial law gave the advantage to the employers. Lacking either organization or strike defense funds, the strikers could not hold out for very long. Sensing victory, the employers refused any concessions until the workers returned to work. General Loma threatened to withdraw his troops if the miners' demands were not given proper consideration. Juan Pablo Fusi describes what happened next:

That very day [May 18] Loma, together with Generals Aguilar and Cappa, the Civil Governor Fernando Blanco, and local authorities traversed the mining zone. They met with worker committees in various localities, offering to use their influence in support of their demands. At Gallarta they spoke to more than five thousand miners, publicly committing themselves to the elimination of work barracks if they went back to work. Many workers, "deeply moved," gave vivas for Loma, the governor, and the army. At their passage "the workers removed their berets as a sign of respect." Later in Ortuella the acclamations were repeated. After that day nobody was in doubt that the strike could be considered as over. Work was resumed the next day in all the mines, and the representatives of the mining companies signed an agreement known as the Loma Pact in which the obligatory barrack housing was abolished and the ten-hour day established.[32]

It was the first time that Civil Guards had been charged with assuring compliance with a labor agreement.

Though the employers eventually reneged on their promises, the strike victory represented a major landmark for organized labor and Spanish socialism. Many more years would elapse, however, before the miners were able to secure an effective institutional role in labor relations. As late as 1904, fourteen years after the historic breakthrough, the miners' union still could claim only 723 members out of some 10,000.[33] Yet it had succeeded in instilling a spirit of solidarity among the miners and had given them a sense of economic and political power in spite of the inability of the UGT to establish a stable corps of activists and a mass dues-paying membership. In 1891, for example, four PSOE candidates won election to the Bilbao municipal council. Socialism in Vizcaya, like anarcho-syndicalism in Catalonia, served as the socializing vehicle for worker immigrants. A capacity for mobilization and militancy had been introduced that proved to be enduring and formidable. It was to serve as the basis for the conversion of Vizcaya into a socialist bastion second only to Asturias and Madrid.

Several decades of sharp, violent confrontations with employers followed, reminiscent of the bloody battles that scarred American coal fields and steel mills during the early part of this century before industrialists agreed to enter into a regularized bargaining relationship. By the end of the nineteenth century, however, the UGT had penetrated one of Spain's major industrial zones, thus taking a crucial step toward becoming a credible force among the industrial proletariat. Fusi concludes, "The events of 1890–92 attested to the fact that the Socialist party in Vizcaya was an emotional force capable of influencing thousands of workers. To be sure, it was the only Spanish region where this had occurred. Vizcayan socialism paradoxically had arrived at this status by means that were entirely opposed to those which the national socialist leadership considered appropriate to the party's electoral strategy."[34] In 1903, for example, Perezagua called a sympathy general strike in support of the iron miners' walkout, demanding wage increases and improvements in working conditions. After three days of near total industrial paralysis, the miners won their demands. During the early part of this century the Vizcayan labor movement became the vanguard of Spanish trade unionism.

With the establishment of a socialist base in Vizcaya efforts were undertaken to extend the zone of influence westward to Asturias. Socialist missionaries were dispatched, and the few existing worker societies in the industrial centers of Gijón and Oviedo were soon brought into the socialist fold, serving as stepping-stones in the penetration of the Asturian hinterland. The initial party *agrupaciónes* that were founded in December 1891 were composed largely of metalworkers, stevedores, and a variety of skilled craftsmen. Penetration of the coal mining zones proved to be more arduous and did not occur for five years.

Most coal mines adjoined isolated valley towns and villages, and their work forces consisted mostly of local peasants and farmers who worked part time in the mines. Persuading them of the benefits of unionization proved to be a protracted process. But the advent of the socialists coincided with major changes under way in the structure and operations of the coal mining industry, which was emerging from the doldrums of the century's final decade. Increases in the price of coal that made investment and expansion more attractive together with improved transportation facilities fostered technical modernization as output increased in response to the growth of industry and transportation. This led to the formation of an increasing number of larger, more modern enterprises that became dominant in an industry previously characterized by small, often semimanually operated mines.[35] Expanded operations required greater attention to productivity and labor discipline. But the character of the work force, the virtually endemic labor shortages, and the excessive absenteeism of those employed conspired against the mine owners. As Adrian Shubert notes, "In the years following the commencement of exploitation of the Asturian mines on a large scale, the capitalist managers were forced to resolve a fundamental problem: the chronic manpower shortages. Despite efforts to resolve them, be it by seeking to recruit large numbers of workers from outside the valleys in addition to incentives in the form of various social services or be it through mechanization of the mines to reduce the number of workers required, all of these efforts proved fruitless until World

War I. The available manpower came from the mine valleys and their immediate surroundings and neither was it in sufficient numbers nor appropriately disciplined to meet the exigencies of the large companies."[36]

Shubert also argues that the resistance of workers, who retained their rural farm mentality, represented a formidable stumbling block: "It is in the collision of these two antagonistic worlds that the roots of social protest in Asturias are to be sought. In resisting the owners' intentions, the miners found that a fundamental contradiction existed between their interests and those of an incipient industrial order. This experience which all shared provided the raw material with which union organizers could shape the unions and political parties that would in time form the Asturian labor movement."[37] Indeed, it is a telling insight into the nature of peninsular labor development that until well into this century one of the country's most highly vaunted proletarian phalanxes was composed of only partially assimilated industrial workers.

Socialist organization in a mining zone (Mieres) first took place in 1897, with others following shortly thereafter in Sama and Turon. By the century's conclusion there were twelve local sections with a total membership of six thousand, of which five thousand were dues payers. The party weekly organ, *La Aurora Social* (social dawn), published in Gijón, steadily expanded its readership.

The main center for the diffusion of socialist ideas during the initial phase was the city of Gijón, where a substantial labor and political base had been established among the city's industrial and port workers. By the turn of the century, however, the anarchists gained a foothold and in the years following emerged as the primary force among the city's wage earners, relegating the socialists to a minority status. The anarchist enclave that endured until the civil war was eventually extended to include part of the industrial complex of Duro-Felguera and some miners at Sama de Langreo.

During the ensuing decade, the organizational base remained fragile, reflecting the still nascent character of working-class consciousness that caused the movement to experience a succession of small advances and painful reverses. Possibly to a greater extent than anywhere else in the country with the exception of Andalusia, the functional lines dividing the party and the trade union often became indistinguishable. Many more people joined the party than the UGT.[38] Party branches often acted in both political and trade union capacities. Political organization initially took precedence, and the party branches then formed labor unions.

Expansion in the coal valleys was set back for a time because of a costly strike defeat in 1906 ("La Huelgona") that forced many activists, including Manuel Llaneza, a prominent mine worker leader, following their blacklisting, to seek employment outside the region. Several years later, the unionization campaign resumed. By 1910 the organizational base was sufficiently expanded to envisage the creation of a regional miners union.

With the establishment that year of the Asturian Miners Union (Sindicato Minero Asturiano—SMA) the foundations were laid for the union that was to become the most powerful and best organized in Spain. Boasting fifty-five affiliated branches at its inception, the SMA eventually embraced most of the region's mine labor force. Structured along industrial union lines, it included in its jurisdiction the various mine occupations and the employees of related railroad facilities and metalworking enterprises that were owned by the large mining firms. Centralized leadership control and the pooling of financial resources to create a large strike defense fund gave it formidable cohesion and force.[39]

The mine union's formation fortuitously coincided with the constitution of the Republican-Socialist electoral alliance, augmenting the political and labor influence of the Asturian socialists and permitting a number of their supporters to win office in municipal councils and generally weakening the hold of the political bosses (*caciques*) and the big mining and industrial companies on regional political affairs.

Almost from the outset the new union succeeded in winning substantial wage increases and improvements in working conditions, which encouraged rapid membership expansion. Collective bargaining power in 1912 was much enhanced because a long coal miners' strike in England cut off the supply of British coal. Increased demand for Asturian coal and higher prices made mine owners anxious to avoid labor trouble, and they acceded to union demands and even recognized the SMA as the bargaining representative. Thus before World War I the union had emerged as a redoubtable force and Asturias was one of the very few places in the country where a labor organization had established itself as an institutionalized participant in a labor relations structure.

By 1912 over half the coal mine labor force had been unionized, and at the outbreak of the war in 1914 some 80 percent of the thirty thousand employed in the industry were union members.[40] By 1916 the Asturian mine workers and the national railroad workers federation had become the two most powerful industrial affiliates of the UGT. During the war industrywide collective bargaining between the mine owners association and the union was initiated. A strike in 1919 in which thirty thousand participated ended in the winning of portal-to-portal pay and the seven-hour day, which Manuel Llaneza proudly hailed as a first among mine unions of the world.

Application of the industrial union structure to the Asturian metal industry, however, foundered on the practical impossibility of integrating the unions of two important companies in Gijón and La Felguera that were under anarchist control and the absence of competent leadership.

A notable contribution by the socialist movement to the general cultural and social welfare of workers came through the creation of a string of *casas del pueblo* (people's houses) throughout the country.[41] Inspired by Belgian socialists, these centers, usually built by local building construction tradesmen and financed by union members, housed meeting halls and the offices of local unions and labor federations. They often included a consumers cooperative nearby and provided a cultural program in the form of libraries, canteens, adult education programs (especially literacy courses), and choral and theatrical groups. Thus as socialist influence grew "Casas del Pueblo, with their primitive libraries and lecture courses, replaced the Republican casino as a centre of cultural diffusion."[42]

Casas del pueblo were particularly numerous and well developed in Asturias, where the socialist movement took a large role in working-class educational and cultural advancement. It was a tribute to the socialists' effectiveness that Father Maximiliano Arboleya, when seeking to create a Catholic-oriented trade union organization early in this century, began by setting up a *casa del pueblo* in the city of Oviedo. These centers served as important elements in the lives of many workers and their families in the isolated mining communities and in industrial towns. They were assisted by an innovative extension program devised by a group of enlightened liberal professors at the University of Oviedo, most of them Krausist social reformers and left Republicans, who sympathized with the UGT and its organizing efforts. Courses and lectures in cooperation with the unions were given in the *casas del pueblo* by university professors on a variety of topics ranging from primary school subjects to physiology, music, and literary readings.[43]

Industrial concentration in only a few areas of the country, regional cultural and ethnic particularities, and the generally unintegrated character of the national economy and transportation tended to confer a strong local stamp on labor market development, wage standards, collective bargaining, and the general climate of labor relations. This environment also shaped the evolution of the PSOE/UGT. The party's formal lines of authority and Iglesias's firm control over the central committee gave the impression of a tightly directed movement whose policy pronouncements emanated almost exclusively from a single central source. In practice, however, in the day-to-day operations and in the choice of organizational and trade union tactics and strategies, local leaders often had considerable latitude.

In the triangular zone that became the socialist heartland, Madrid, the Basque country, and Asturias, local figures emerged with leadership qualities and well-tuned political intuitions and whose temperaments and outlooks reflected their distinctive surroundings, the developing patterns of labor relations and economic development in their respective regions, local political realities, and employers' attitudes. Pablo Iglesias, the Madrid labor aristocrat, disliked taking risks and generally proceeded along moderate, reformist lines. In Vizcaya, Facundo Perezagua, confronting a plentitude of potential strikebreakers, a seasonally employed mine labor force, and extremely hostile employers, frequently resorted to militant trade union tactics, including the general strike. He felt constrained to employ mass violence and to take risks, as did many of his counterparts in comparable stages of trade union development in other industrial countries. The intransigence of employers led to many bitter confrontations over a period of several decades before a degree of mutual accommodation was reached.

Asturias produced Manuel Llaneza, a coal miner who combined the qualities of militant trade unionist and canny labor negotiator. Among the leaders of the Spanish labor movement he most closely resembled the early twentieth-century western European social democratic trade union leader. Before the war, when the SMA had not yet achieved hegemony among the miners and industrywide bargaining had not yet been introduced, he forcefully demonstrated his credentials as a tough, militant labor leader. But once the halcyon days of full production, big profits, and relatively high wages came to an end at the war's conclusion and cheaper, better-quality British coal again became available, he realized the vulnerability of the Asturian coal economy and sought (not always successfully) to exercise restraint and caution in collective bargaining, something Perezagua found impossible.[44]

Llaneza's evolution into a labor moderate was shaped in part by the distinctive sociopolitical setting (manpower shortages and a prospering industry) in which the Asturian labor movement operated and the years he spent (after being blacklisted following the failed strike in Mieres of 1906) in France and Belgium. For three years in France he was employed as a miner in the Pas de Calais area, a socialist reformist stronghold, and he also visited Belgium as a guest of the Socialist party, which was then led by Social Democrat Emile Vandervelde. Many of his subsequent ideas on collective bargaining strategy and the notion of forming a miners' industrial union derived from his experiences in those countries.[45]

Once the initial breakthrough had been accomplished, the peculiar nature of the Asturian situation made it much more feasible than in other industrial zones to build a strong and powerful trade union movement and to secure recognition from employers. Asturian coal mining, unlike other industries, did not have a large pool of surplus manpower in the years of early union development, which would have enabled employers to starve out workers who went on strike and to recruit strikebreakers as was the usual pattern in the rest of the country. As industry prospered, the impetus for mine owners to reach mutual accommodation was impelling. Labor conflict in the formative period was as acrimonious and violent in Asturias as it was in Vizcaya, yet not as severe as in Catalonia. A mitigating factor was the weight of liberal, progressive opinion in the political life of the region. Men such as Melquiades Alvarez exerted a moderating influence on Asturian public affairs, which made labor organization easier.[46]

The crucial factor in the final analysis was the differing economic prospects of the two regions. Heavy industry in Vizcaya underwent an expansion and consolidation while a similar process was under way among the UGT unions of the iron mine zones and the metalworking plants and mills of the Ria. Asturias, on the other hand, underwent a serious decline in the postwar demand for coal that led to a debilitation of this "almost mythical center of worker militancy,"[47] generating a retreat into apathy by some miners and inducing others to support radical extremist dissident labor groups.

Industrial Conflict and the Ascendancy of the UGT

Industrialization in Spain lacked sufficient scope and depth at the turn of the century to alter the country's economic configuration. But it had passed from underdevelopment to an incipient industrialization. The agricultural sector still employed 60 to 70 percent of the working population, and the industrial growth that had taken place was concentrated in peripheral regional zones. Textile manufacturing in Catalonia remained Spain's principal industrial pursuit and would hold primacy well into the 1920s.

Yet the gradual introduction of a modern economic infrastructure would ultimately provide the underpinnings for a substantial industrial expansion. The concentration of textile making in Catalonia, for example, had prompted the establishment of related industries such as dyemaking and manufacture of textile machinery. Eventually new industries would be created, including automobile assembly, machinery, chemicals, cement, the expansion of Barcelona's port and maritime facilities, and the introduction of hydroelectrical power installations. From 1876 to 1890, important quasi-monopolies concentrated in the region in such areas as maritime transport, banking, and the production and export of wine and bottle corks.

In Vizcaya the heavy dependence on iron mining lessened with the commencement of what would eventually develop into a formidable heavy industry complex made up of iron- and steelmaking (production, though modest, quadrupled between 1875 and 1900), heavy machinery, shipbuilding, and metal fabrication. The adjoining province of Guipúzcoa was emerging as a major center for the manufacture of paper and cement. And the impetus provided by the extension of the national rail network— it expanded from 7,478 kilometers of track in 1880 to 12,121 in 1899— spurred the development of commercial agriculture.

The increase in the country's industrial activity created a rising demand for Asturian coal, which led to the industry's expansion and modernization. Yet this progress did not signify a qualitative change. Spain, in the words of José Luis García Delgado, remained "a fragile economic system in which a solid industrial structure had not yet been consolidated and in which the weight of a retarded and inefficient agriculture continued to be decisive."[48]

Nonetheless, urbanization continued at a steady pace. By 1900 22 percent of the population lived in cities of over twenty thousand residents, a fourfold increase over the preceding four decades. Expansion of the rail system led to the peninsula's first major internal migration, mainly to the urban centers of Catalonia, Vizcaya, and Madrid.

The working population of Barcelona doubled between 1887 and 1900, from 79,000 to 145,000; in Madrid it swelled to more than 90,000.[49] Thousands more were employed in the big metal plants and shipyards of Bilbao and on a smaller scale in the steel mills and metal fabricating plants of Asturian industrial towns. Despite this modest yet marked growth in the number of industrial wage earners, by 1910 probably no more than 5 percent were unionized, most of them in Catalonia, Madrid, Asturias, and the Basque provinces.[50]

A noteworthy change in the national industrial complex was the gradual appearance of large industrial, transport, and commercial establishments among the great mass of mini-industrial shops that abounded in Spanish manufacture. Manpower distribution, however, was that of an incipient industrialized country: the single largest group of workers was engaged in building construction (25 percent), followed by transport (15 percent) and textile making (13 percent). Approximately two-thirds of Barcelona's wage earners were in textiles.

Most of the roughly half million workers in the modern industrial sector at the turn of the century were in Catalonia, Vizcaya-Guipúzcoa, and Asturias.[51] Others were located at the scattered, isolated mining operations, at the huge copper mine of Rio Tinto in Huelva province, and at Linares, León, Jaen, and Cartagena.

Since industrial expansion had only just occurred, the bulk of the work force was of peasant stock, freshly arrived at the urban and mining centers, disoriented and little assimilated to the rigors and rhythms of a proletarian regimen. Even in greater Barcelona, which boasted the country's most sizable and assimilated industrial proletariat, a large portion of the wage earners and the ever-present army of job seekers consisted of rural folk who had flocked to the area in numbers that well surpassed industry's capacity to absorb them. Anarchism found its greatest mass appeal among these impoverished, unlettered, and disoriented newcomers.

Although the country's socioeconomic transformation began in the 1890s, it was also a time of ruinous colonial wars, economic malaise, mounting social tensions, and growing institutional crisis that reached a denouement in the debacle of 1898. The colonial possessions of an intermediate-sized nation such as Spain were fair game in an era of great power imperialism, especially since a succession of governments lacked a coherent colonial policy or a national consensus on how to proceed. The country consequently was drawn into a series of costly, indecisive military actions in a vain and exhausting effort to retain its remaining overseas possessions. First, there was the war of Melilla in 1890, then the suppression of an uprising in Puerto Rico, an insurrection in Cuba, and soon thereafter still another in the Philippines. Thus the Spanish-American War of 1898 came as the crowning blow.

The extremely high cost in treasure and human lives of these military undertakings, the depreciation of the peseta, augmented French protectionist tariffs that seriously affected Spanish wine exports, as well as disastrous floods in La Mancha and Andalusia and excessive rainfall in the Levant dealt severe blows to a fragile economic structure. In Catalonia phylloxera devastated the region's prosperous vineyards. The accompanying sharp rise in the cost of living created widespread distress and discontent.

Exorbitant increases in the prices of basic commodities, especially bread, the imposition of added taxation on consumer articles as part of the government's postwar economic stabilization programs, and a sharp rise in the number of unemployed combined to plunge many working-class families into destitution and to raise social tensions throughout the country. Street demonstrations and riots erupted in many localities; martial law had to be declared in most of the Andalusian provinces. In Asturias, as Adrian Shubert has written, "the weakness of the labor movement's ideological and organizational penetration in the nineteenth century was underscored by a series of food riots that took place in Oviedo, Gijón, and Mieres during 1897 and 1898. . . . Descriptions of these occurrences suggest more eighteenth-century riots than organized modern labor protests."[52]

Labor conflict that previously hardly had caused a ripple in the national consciousness began to assume sizable proportions. Pitched battles took place in 1890 in the cotton textile industry of Catalonia between united employers and the Tres Clases de Vapor Federación as company lockouts were countered by the union's industrywide shutdowns affecting more than twenty thousand workers. The outcome of this confrontation was crucial to the survival of the region's entire labor movement, and rising tensions contributed to the large turnouts for the celebration of May Day in Barcelona and other industrial towns. Throughout the country these impressive demonstrations, some of which were followed by strikes, attested to workers' assertion of their right to protest that was increasingly making itself felt in the life of the country. The social unrest that burst forth in response to the intolerable strains placed on wage earners' livelihoods by the disaster of 1898 occurred, in the words of Vicens Vives, because of "the tenacious opposition of constituted society to give the slightest attention to their grievances."[53]

This manifestation, moreover, attested to the industrial proletariat's emerging trade union and political consciousness in response to urbanization and industrial development. But the appearance of industrial strife in a still traditional society, together with the gathering effects of universal manhood suffrage that was introduced in 1890, placed the Restoration political system and the new social forces on a collision course.

The forces of change and opposition were too weak and fragmented to pose a serious challenge following the trauma of 1898, but the responses to that situation can be regarded as the first in a succession of tremors leading to the full-scale sociopolitical breakdown that rocked the country from 1917 to 1923. It found expression at this early stage in the widening scope of labor unrest, the expanding role of organized labor, a new-found concern for the "social question," an attempt to defuse workers' protest through the belated enactment of additional protective labor legislation, and the emergence of important regional political movements in the two main industrial peripheries of Catalonia and the Basque country. And finally, the Socialist party was beginning to emerge from its chrysalis, still a marginal force but steadily developing into a movement of substance and influence.

In this context, the 1890 Vizcayan iron miners' strike was a landmark event, indicating that a major segment of the country's new industrial proletariat had become a potentially powerful force. Only 10 percent of the miners were formally organized, but the union could often count on the massed support of virtually the entire work force. The UGT/PSOE of Madrid had only a tiny handful of supporters, but, much to their astonishment, twenty thousand responded to the call for the 1890 May Day rally. The fifteen to twenty thousand who turned out in Barcelona gave added evidence of a growing capacity to mobilize workers.

Rising discontent among workers and the resulting labor disputes were mostly of spontaneous origin with socialists and anarchists seeking to catch up with and direct them. Most wage earners at this stage were capable of episodic displays of united action but constitutionally incapable of sustained organizational and financial support. "Resistance societies," Tuñon de Lara recounts,

were placing themselves under the influence of anarchists and socialists though formally maintaining their independence. Most of their memberships had joined out of an elemental awareness for socio-professional defense, but the leadership cores increasingly were made up of militants close to anarcho-syndicalism or socialism. . . . The evident fact was that labor organization at the beginning of the century constituted a mul-titudinous phenomenon. That in Madrid 30 percent of the workers were organized, in Barcelona close to 15 percent, in Asturias and Vizcaya more than 20 percent are highly significant indications. The percentages with respect to rural organization are more difficult to establish, for the number of adherents in the south can be qualified as "conjunctural," a majority of farm laborers being unionized or not depending on the occasion.[54]

Even the staid, conservative, church-sponsored Catholic worker circles attracted an increased number of adherents.

Labor unrest assumed widening proportions, its forms mirroring the distinctive and often highly disparate regional levels of socioeconomic development. Throughout the 1890s it occurred primarily in Catalonia and Vizcaya. Despite the surprisingly large May Day turnout, the socialist movement in Madrid failed to register any perceptible organizational progress, in large measure because of the onset of economic recession and job insecurity. Elsewhere prospects were not very encouraging either. The stunning breakthrough in Vizcaya in 1890 may have given promise of development of an important socialist base, but it still remained a distant hope that would reach fruition over the course of the next two decades. In a keenly felt setback the UGT lost its remaining foothold in the textile industry in 1894 following a bitterly contested strike of four thousand workers at the Málaga textile firm of La Industria Málagueña, notorious for its extremely low wages, that lasted almost three months and ended in total defeat. That defeat also represented a serious loss of socialist influence in an area that had been regarded as one of the party's most promising.

After prospects for growth and expansion in industrial Catalonia proved unrealizable and UGT headquarters moved from Barcelona to Madrid in 1899, the national capital became the preeminent bastion of Spanish socialism until the end of the civil war. Madrid from the earliest days had served as the primary source for leaders and influence so that the loss of UGT strength in Catalonia gave the city greater status in the movement. The UGT then possessed 4,774 members in the city, but the year fol-lowing that number rose to 13,318. By 1902 31 percent of the national membership was in Madrid, though the number of party militants—one estimate places it at several hundred—remained small.[55] The organizational surge of 1902–5 swelled membership rolls by an additional twenty thousand nationally with Madrid retaining its 31 percent ratio. The UGT advance had taken place amid a general expansion of labor organization during which, from the early 1890s to 1910, the number of unionized workers in Madrid went from less than a thousand to thirty thousand, thus placing it alongside Barcelona as one of Spain's principal "labor" cities. The ensuing dark years had a devastating effect on labor organization in the provinces but only a slight one on UGT-Madrid, with the result that the city's relative standing rose to 58 percent by 1908 and to two-thirds the next year and the number of party militants increased to a thousand.

In 1899 Pablo Iglesias made his dominance in the movement even more explicit by assuming the presidency of the UGT; he occupied that post until his death in 1925. The personnel of the national executive committee and posts in the PSOE other than that of chairman were designated by the Madrid *agrupación* (section). The situation in the UGT was roughly comparable because many of the party leaders held parallel responsibilities in the trade union organization. An imposing *casa del pueblo* in a former ducal mansion was established in 1908 to house the offices of local UGT and unaffiliated unions, their various welfare and recreational services, and the socialist labor center's national headquarters.

Toward the end of the decade 1900 to 1910, as economic conditions improved, labor organization in Madrid began to grow, spurred by workers' rising resentment over postwar inflation and eroded real earnings. Only four worker societies existed in 1890, with few members; by 1894 their number had increased to twenty but by 1904 had mushroomed to ninety. In Asturias footholds were being established among the journeymen and factory hands of the main urban centers to be followed by later incursions in the coal mining valleys. Enclaves were also constituted at mining localities in southern Spain. Much of the UGT's growth at the beginning of the century came from the railroad and mining sectors; about 30 percent of the railroad union membership was in Madrid.

In those days, however, workers supported trade unions mostly on an episodic and circumstantial basis. Juan José Morato had stated that the figure of 15,000 did not represent actual dues-paying membership, which was 6,437. He also observed that membership figures given by official sources and UGT congresses did not reflect the true situation: "The congresses did not truly reflect the actual state of the organization, first because established sections, even within their debility, were purely artificial contrivances, maintained by the will of a handful of firm, tenacious men. . . . Furthermore, there was the unending struggle with the lack of resources. Only by incurring serious risks could one institute higher dues— even the lower ones were not regularly paid, providing executive committees consequently with sparse funds, and this unimaginably reduced the paltry strike defense funds."[56]

Finally, by 1902, the UGT could count 32,778 effective members; it added 5,000 the next year and reached close to 57,000 in 1904. A notable breakthrough was achieved in the Valencia region, which had been considered an anarchist preserve. A strike victory by the sandal makers of Elche in 1903 in which UGT assistance proved decisive resulted in 6,642 members in Alicante province by 1906. In the political sphere also, modest advances were achieved. Eight municipal council seats were won in 1901 out of a total of twenty throughout the country. Iglesias became a councillor of the Madrid *ayuntamiento* in 1905. But these victories did not signify any effective breakthrough in winning the political loyalties of the workers. In the first decade of this century wage earners steadily enlisted in UGT unions, but they continued to vote Republican. Only after the election of Pablo Iglesias to parliament in 1910 did a shift commence in voting patterns from the Republicans to the PSOE.[57]

A major failing of the UGT during its formative period was its lack of influence in rural Spain and disinterest in the problems of farm laborers and small farmers. Membership in this sector for a long time remained inconsequential. Before 1900 peasant unions constituted only 3 or 4 percent of the entire membership, and it was not until 1918 that serious consideration was given to rural organization. Even in Andalusia greater importance was placed on party organization and activities than on the spread of UGT influence. In 1902 only 19 percent of UGT membership came from the farming sector, but by 1908 it had risen to 28 percent. During 1902 to 1915, in spite of this neglect, the number of industrial workers and miners in the union rose by 51 percent but those from the rural areas grew by 303 percent. Thus by World War I the UGT had acquired significant nuclei in southern and Castilian farming zones.

The UGT tended to neglect its outposts at mining sites in southern Spain before 1908. Among the more notable ones were the La Carolina mine, with nine UGT sections composed of 1,315 members in 1905, and Linares, with twenty-two locals and 1,946 adherents. Both were situated in the Sierra Morena mountain range of Jaen province and were to serve as the base from which the province, otherwise agricultural in nature, was subsequently converted into a socialist stronghold. At mines such as Peñarroya, previously Republican worker groups sought affiliation with the UGT. As the union's fortunes took a turn for the better, a more systematic proselytizing effort got under way. A potent base was established at the huge Rio Tinto copper mine in Huelva province, resulting in a seven-year battle with the English management that attracted considerable national sympathy and attention.

The return of economic slump in 1904 had a deleterious effect on the UGT. Fusi notes that "the unemployment rate between 1899 and 1903 for UGT members ranged from 6.05 percent to 7.21 percent, then rose sharply in 1904 to 16.28 percent and uniformly exceeded 20 percent over the next five years. The effects of economic recession, partly owing to deflationist policies followed by all Spanish governments since 1899 to restore the economy and to strengthen the peseta, were visible throughout Spain."[58] From a high of 57,000 in 1904–5, membership plummeted by 1908 to 36,612. Membership rolls declined from February to October 1905 by 10,000 and by a similar number the following year. The loss in local affiliates was particularly severe in the provinces. Strike failures in 1906 at the Asturian coal mining stronghold of Mieres and in the Vizcayan iron zone also dimmed prospects for expansion in these regions. Though party and union leaders attributed the organizational crisis confronting the UGT to the economic downturn, a lack of tactical astuteness in exploiting the extreme privation to which many wage earners were subjected was also evident. It would take six years before the UGT would recover the membership levels attained in 1904–5.

Growth after the 1905–11 slump led to important changes in the UGT's composition and structure. At the century's outset it had been a trade union movement in which skilled and semiskilled workers predominated. Roughly half the membership was concentrated in building construction, 10 percent in shoemaking and clothing manufacture, and another 8 percent were typographers. By 1911, however, transportation workers, especially railroad employees, constituted half the membership and those in the mining sector made up 10 percent. As Fusi remarks, "No longer was UGT a trade union organization of brick masons, shoemakers, and typographers; it had become transformed into a veritable industrial labor center."[59]

The entry of increasing numbers of industrial workers made it necessary to institute structural changes and to establish nationwide and regional trade and industrial federations. The Asturian Miners Union was constituted in 1910, followed by the creation of the National Mineworkers Federation. The Railroad Workers Federation was established several years later, and the Vizcayan Metalworkers Federation was formed in 1913–14. Its counterpart, the Vizcayan Mineworkers Federation, operated virtually as a regional industrial union. In 1916 the Typographers Federation expanded its jurisdiction to include all elements of the printing industry. Thus by 1914 fourteen national federations were in existence, which supports Morato's assertion that that year should be used as the takeoff point for labor organization.

The high membership of 1904–5 was regained by 1911 and then surpassed. Aided by the outlawing of the fledgling CNT, the socialist labor center experienced substantial growth and expansion. From 77,749 adherents in 1911, membership almost doubled to reach 147,729 over the next two years, a new high that would not be surpassed until 1919. Much of the new recruitment was from the ranks of railroad workers and miners and further reinforced the increasing industrial composition of the organization.

Organizational growth came in a climate of heightened labor conflict. A rise in labor disputes and strike activity that had been gathering force for several years reached a peak in 1913. "One can observe in 1913," notes Tuñon de Lara, "a peak year for strikes; in addition to those caused by wage issues there were an elevated percentage that had union recognition as their principal objective."[60] The wave of industrial unrest in Spain paralleled a general European trend.

The century's second decade saw generational changes in labor leadership. Outlawed in 1911, the National Confederation of Labor continued to function semilegally despite official harassment. Anarchist and syndicalist leaders of the Catalonian railroad workers union in 1912 forced the socialist-controlled Unión Ferroviaria reluctantly to call an industrywide strike in their support that ended in partial victory. The following year's textile strike in Catalonia gave further evidence of the gathering momentum of a reviving trade union movement. But until the CNT was permitted to resume activity in 1914, there was no guiding center or national leadership for anarcho-syndicalist organizations, although local CNT affiliates in Barcelona, Zaragossa, Gijón, Valencia, and La Coruña continued to operate. Manuel Buenacasa relates: "Until early 1918 the various national committees, one after the other, were incapable of maintaining continuous and necessary contacts with organizational affiliates because of constant persecutions by the authorities. Except for the Catalonian confederation that regularly maintained its committee, those of the other regions were not similarly constituted."[61]

This hiatus not only made for unstable trade union life, it was also responsible for the delay in the development of a new generation of leaders of national stature. At the time of its formation just two years after the Tragic Week that had greatly depleted the ranks of anarchist and unionist cadres, the CNT "possessed few leaders of distinction. Except for José Negre, Francisco Jordan, and Francisco Miranda, one can observe no first-rank figures until 1914. The future anarcho-syndicalist leaders were being formed in obscurity and would emerge to full view during 1918–19."[62]

During this time, however, a more stable leadership succession was evolving in socialist trade unionism. Boasting greater organizational cohesiveness and less subject to police repression, the UGT was nurturing a full-time corps of trade union professionals, and it was primarily from their ranks that a new generation of leaders arose.

Outstanding among them was Francisco Largo Caballero, the quintessential Madrid trade union professional and leading exponent of "Pablismo," who after Iglesias became the UGT's best-known and respected figure until the end of the civil war. Born into a poverty-stricken working-class family, Largo began his working life at the age of eight after only several years of formal schooling. He became a stucco plasterer, a craft he practiced for thirty-one years, joined the UGT in 1890, and organized his fellow journeymen. He learned to read and write at age twenty-two and in 1894, at the age of twenty-five, became a member of the PSOE. By 1905 he was one of three socialists elected to the municipal council and, after occupying a variety of union posts, gained his livelihood as the longtime director of Mutualidad Obrera, the preeminent Spanish society created by union members for medical, pharmaceutical, and burial services.

By the early years of this century Largo was second only to Pablo Iglesias in party and trade union affairs, and as the latter's failing health increasingly restricted his activities, Largo assumed a correspondingly larger role. He became the longtime UGT spokesman in the Institute of Social Reforms' directing committee and in 1918, following imprisonment for his leading role in the abortive revolutionary attempt of the previous year, was elected to the Chamber of Deputies. He was also named UGT general secretary that year, a post he occupied for many years.

As a product of the Madrid labor aristocracy and the socialist trade union bureaucracy, Largo generally followed the ideas and practices of Pablo Iglesias. Julián Gorkin, the veteran left activist and leader of the Workers Marxist Unification party (POUM), has left us a memorable portrait:

> Francisco Largo Caballero was indisputably the most representative and most popular among the leading figures. Of extremely modest origins, educated within the [socialist] organization to which he was exclusively devoted, he had always appeared to me both complex and linear; linear in defending UGT against the rivalry and attacks of the anarcho-syndicalist CNT and from the communist split in 1921 and its persistent infiltrations or destructive maneuvers. His many years of total devotion to worker demands as UGT general secretary made him the most reformist of socialist leaders. He seemed to us a bureaucratized leader of narrow views, lacking in imagination and ignorant of the history of the international labor movement; in a word, excessively secluded within the walls of the People's House, the fortress of Madrid laborism, where he had passed half his life. From whence came his enormous popularity, he, who was neither writer, journalist, nor even a brilliant orator? Undoubtedly it was due to the rectitude of his character, the firmness of his convictions, his austere modest life, and his total dedication to the workers' cause. Even his physical appearance, serious, somewhat stern, sparing in words and gestures, was characteristic of a man who inspires confidence and respect. I have in my life as an international militant listened to innumerable orators, but never have I known one with such a sparing and sober manner that so identified with his listeners and exerted such a total impact on them. He gave the image of an authentic mass man. Workers regarded his fifty years of militancy, his personal qualities, his identification with them and their cause, and were convinced he would never betray them.[63]

At this time the UGT also acquired support from middle-class intellectuals. With a few exceptions, most notably Jaime Vera, both the UGT and PSOE had been led by blue-collar autodidacts. But with the movement's coming of age, the political alliance with the Republicans, and Iglesias's entry into the Cortes, a growing number of intellectuals began to enter the party and to assume important responsibilities. They included men such as Fernando de los Rios of Granada, Luis Araquistáin, Manuel Nuñez de Arenas, and Julián Besteiro. Entering the party in 1912 at the age of forty, Besteiro, a professor of logic at the University of Madrid and a prestigious figure in academic and political circles, rose rapidly in the party and trade union hierarchy. He became a member of the UGT executive committee in 1916, and when in 1918 Largo Caballero became general secretary, Besteiro replaced him as vice-chairman. Upon the death of Pablo Iglesias in 1925, he assumed the chairmanships of both the UGT and PSOE.

5

THE TRIALS AND TRIBULATIONS OF LABOR IN CATALONIA

The ferocious repression of the mid- and late 1890s had had a profoundly disruptive effect not only on organized anarchism in Catalonia but on trade unions as well. The sense of disarray was further intensified by the war and its aftermath. The loss of Spain's colonies deprived the textile industry of a fifth of its cotton market. One estimate in 1900 placed the number of laid-off workers in the region at sixty thousand, including ten thousand in Barcelona.

"The labor crisis under way since 1898 reached a nadir in 1901 and 1902. During this five-year period work was in short supply and badly paid because of the joblessness and the labor surpluses. Wage rates were at a standstill and fell behind the price levels of basic necessities. The accompanying chart and indice [see figure 5.1] show in fact that the employees of La España Industrial, the large cotton mill of Sants, lost around 20 percent of their purchasing power during this period. This is without taking into account an extremely burdensome sales tax imposed by the Barcelona municipality on those residing in the general vicinity. As the workers' situation deteriorated," note Jordi Nadal and Carles Sudrià, "because of unemployment and declining profits, toward the end of the century the Catalan labor movement was radicalized."[1]

Spurred by rising discontent, labor organizations began to display a renewed vitality. From 1898 strikes took place on a hitherto unprecedented scale in response to mass layoffs and wage cuts. Hence it was no coincidence that the first pieces of protective social legislation, the laws regulating industrial employment for women and children and industrial accidents, received parliamentary approval in 1900, a year of cascading labor conflict.

Figure 5.1.   Wages and Prices in Barcelona, 1894–1905 (1896 = 100)

Source: Jordi Nadal and Carles Sudrià, *Historia de la caixa de pensions* (Barcelona: Edicions 62, 1981), p. 23.

A wildcat strike in Manlleu during 1899 quickly spread through the Ter and Fresser valleys, an area of cotton-spinning production, involving seven thousand workers. Its victorious conclusion led to the formation of the Spanish Textile Workers Federation, an umbrella organization of anarchist and socialist-led unions and those affiliated with the Tres Clases de Vapor Federación that claimed a membership of forty thousand. Rising labor militancy persuaded numerous anarchists to abandon their futile terrorist activities and to participate in the reconstruction of the labor movement. The Federation of Labor Societies of the Spanish Region, envisaged as the successor to the FTRE, was formed in Madrid in October 1900 with the anarchist leaders of the Ter valley textile union among its main sponsors.[2] But it never became an operative national center, for the failure of the 1902 Barcelona general strike and its disastrous consequences foredoomed it. By 1905 it practically ceased functioning and was formally dissolved two years later.

As the new century commenced trade union organization was still in its formative stage. Although workers were influenced by unions, only small numbers of them could be persuaded to become dues-paying members. "The dominant climate in our labor world," recounts Jordi Arquer, "was societarism under the ideological influence of a diffuse anarchism, more verbal than real, intermixed with a Federal Republicanism that animated the broadly liberal theories of Pi i Margall. This anarchist and liberal bourgeois convergence merged in the leftist politics of that period without precise indications where one commenced and the other ended."[3]

In compensation for the loss of colonial markets and to maintain profit levels while updating their plant machinery, the employers of the Ter and Fresser valley cotton-spinning mills instituted wage cuts and replaced male workers with women and children. Some mills reduced labor costs by as much as 50 percent by introducing electrical spinning machines and increasing the use of female labor. The Ter valley was one of the few remaining districts where men were still employed to run cotton yarn—spinning machines.

Backed by the region's powerful employers association, El Fomento de Trabajo Nacional, a lockout was declared in 1901 that became known as the "hunger pact" (*pacte de la fam*). The embattled textile employees received strong community support in Manlleu and Roda de Ter, but the factory owners were intent upon destroying the union. Sixty-three mills participated in the lockout, affecting fourteen thousand employees.

Their large inventories enabled employers to endure a prolonged shutdown, but the union felt constrained to call an industrywide strike. As Joan Ullman recounts, "When the factories reopened in 1902, employers could claim a partial victory; the union in the yarn factories had been almost destroyed but not all men had been replaced by women. Manufacturers now set about to augment productive capacity of the new machinery by maintaining an eleven to thirteen hour work day. Children were extensively employed, including those under twelve years of age despite legislation prohibiting them."[4]

The threat that these actions represented and the precedent they set aroused intense concern among organized workers throughout the region. Not only was the largest part of the industrial work force in cotton textile manufacturing, but wages and working conditions in that industry set the pattern for others. Ullman notes: "Following the example of the yarn producers in the Ter Valley, cotton fabric manufacturers in Barcelona and in cities throughout Catalonia attempted to impose a lower wage scale and harsher working conditions. So did employers in other industries, confronted with the same economic crisis."[5]

Despite this setback, worker militancy was by no means extinguished. Some unions, activated by the improving economic situation, recovered their previous losses in purchasing power. The atmosphere in 1901 in Barcelona has been described as one of "vertiginous worker mobilization," and Tuñon de Lara recounts that "the bricklayers' society grew to 13,000 members and the carpenters to 3,650. Meetings were held by the Barcelona local federation in 1901 assembling thousands upon thousands of workers."[6] In December of that year the metalworkers struck, demanding a reduction of the workday from ten hours to nine to create more jobs for those on layoff. Tensions rose as weeks went by without any resolution of the dispute. Employers refused a compromise settlement. A general strike called on February 17 in solidarity with the embattled metalworkers soon affected eighty thousand workers. The city was completely shut down, and the strike rapidly spread to the nearby industrial towns of Sants, Sabadell, Tarrassa, Tarragona, and Reus. The stoppage proceeded in an atmosphere of moderation and nonviolence. The spectacle of workers of the country's principal industrial center paralyzing all commercial and industrial activity was an unprecedented landmark in Spanish working-class mobilization.

It has been claimed that anarchists were responsible for the general strike because they had influence with the metal unions and considered it a weapon of almost mythic proportions. Albert Balcells is probably correct, however, in emphasizing that the great mass of participating workers were motivated by practical issues: "What was at issue," he points out, "was to assure the right of workers to bargain collectively with employers and to counter the employer offensive initiated by the cotton spinning sector."[7] The government reacted by instituting martial law, closing union offices, and imprisoning 371 labor leaders. In clashes between strikers, the Civil Guard, and the army, 17 were killed and 44 injured.

The strike momentum, however, had not yet run its course. Barcelona experienced a series of strikes at the century's outset that were the culminating point in the battle between workers and employers. Influenced by improving economic prospects, employers, despite having gained the upper hand, often reached compromise settlements with their workers.[8]

Having failed to reestablish a mass base in the labor movement, some libertarians, against the urgings of more moderate anarchist leaders, resumed terrorist acts in 1904. Their actions included failed assassination attempts in 1905 and 1906 on Alfonso XIII and a cause célèbre when bombs were placed in several thoroughfares of Barcelona by former anarchist Joan Rull, whom the police paid to tell them the locations of the bombs he himself had placed.

Though unprecedented numbers of workers were mobilized in the general strike, at its end organized labor had been destroyed. One reason for the movement's failure was the acute shortage of experienced, seasoned leaders. The repression of the preceding decade had decimated an entire generation of labor activists, anarchists and nonanarchists alike. Their replacements all too often were raw and untried, and new leaders were likely to be more inclined toward risky, impetuous actions.[9]

Only a handful of debilitated worker societies survived. White-collar workers in 1903, in an effort to overcome the effects of the previous year's disaster, established in Barcelona the Autonomous Center of Commercial and Industrial Employees (CADCI) under the guise of a mutual aid society. During the following year, after the estrangement between the unions and the anarchists that led to the collapse of the Federation of Labor Societies of the Spanish Region, a new Local Federation of Worker Societies was formed. This effort also proved abortive, for it was now clear that the wave of militancy had subsided as numerous union supporters lost their jobs or were blacklisted, eight hundred alone in the Ter-Fresser valley.

The leadership vacuum would not long remain unfilled. Sensing the opportunity, Alejandro Lerroux, a talented populist demagogue, transferred his base of operations from Madrid to Barcelona, where in 1901 he was elected a Republican member of parliament. Soon thereafter he was leading a revived Republicanism that dominated the political life of Barcelona from 1903 to 1914. Lerroux masked his essentially moderate sociopolitical views with a virulent anticlericalism, and his hyperbolic, pseudo-revolutionary rhetoric appealed to the city's proletarian masses, especially the recently arrived immigrants and the petty bourgeoisie. He was also able to capitalize on the revival of Republicanism in the 1900s that, in conjunction with the trade union revival, was an expression of popular social protest.

Lerroux sought to become the voice of the city's wage earners. One of the anarchists' objectives in the 1902 general strike had been to counter Lerroux's influence on workers. The strike's failure allowed him to appear as the sole spokesman for Barcelona's working class in both labor and political dealings with the government. [10] Two-thirds of the membership of his Progressive Republican party consisted of workers. The populist caudillo's hold on the popular imagination, despite the venality of many Lerrouxist leaders, received a potent assist when in 1906 a *casa del pueblo* was established in the center of the city and began to offer a formidable array of social services. By providing an alternative to bourgeois welfare, then in ecclesiastical hands, it ensured the workers' support. The program was underwritten by subsidies from the Republican-controlled municipality to welfare centers, consumer cooperatives, educational programs, and politico-cultural activities conducted by a chain of Republican centers. [11]

Many historians and researchers have claimed or suspected that Lerroux's timely appearance on the Barcelona political scene was either directly sponsored by the government or at least supported so as to wean the local populace away from regionalist sentiments and anarchist influences. Circumstantial evidence is persuasive, but actual proof of the existence of any such Machiavellian arrangements has not appeared. But it is of marginal interest whether Lerroux did in fact receive government assistance. He accomplished the political mobilization of virtually the entire working class of Barcelona, something no one in Spanish political life before him had been able to do.

The fin-de-siècle wave of social unrest that swept the country also reached Andalusia, where most previous labor disputes had originated with craftsmen and industrial workers in the towns and urban areas. Now, however, the rural zones were displaying signs of ferment, and they became the principal arenas of labor conflict. The resurgence of 1901–5, was characterized by the same abrupt surges followed by an equally rapid extinction of rural worker organization as had happened with similar movements during the latter part of the previous century and would persist until the 1930s.

Few if any agricultural strikes had taken place before 1902. By 1901, however, tensions in the countryside began to simmer as the region became increasingly caught up in an agricultural crisis resulting from the peninsula's economic difficulties following the Spanish-American War. The livelihoods of thousands of *braceros,* which were very sensitive to the fluctuations of inflation or to any loss in purchasing power, were equally vulnerable to the vagaries of the harvest. With wages abysmally low, the slightest downward trend in earnings because of adverse climatic conditions spelled disaster, and such a situation was the source of periodic outbursts of popular exasperation expressed through riots, assaults on bakeries and granaries, street demonstrations, and banditry.

Worker organization and rural labor disputes on this occasion served as an added form of social protest. Upsurges in labor militancy would usually begin, as Antonio Maria Calero writes, with "an intense propaganda campaign in the villages and the fields, a burgeoning increase in worker associations, the planning and carrying out of strikes and other forceful actions, initial worker victories, the ensuing reaction of the government and employers, then worker defeats and the complete prostration of the movement."[12]

Workers tended to be more assertive in years of good harvests. In 1901, however, though there were bad harvests and many workers lacked jobs, the soaring price of bread and other basic commodities led to numerous street demonstrations, riots, and violence, which attracted considerable national attention. With much improved harvests the following year fewer demonstrations were held and there were few rural labor disputes. By 1903, another year of bountiful harvests and full employment, large numbers of *braceros,* aware of their enhanced bargaining position, joined unions and engaged in work stoppages. Union-sponsored shutdowns were especially numerous in the valley of Guadalquivir near Seville, the Córdoba campiña, and Jerez. To save their abundant harvests, many landowners acceded to the workers' demands, as unionization mushroomed in the region.

By the following year, however, the incidence of rural labor disputes dropped sharply. An attempt to resume organizational activities and work stoppages ended as the effects of a drought became felt. Violence flared in some zones. The PSOE/UGT sought to launch a general work stoppage as part of a national protest against the high cost of living and to demand the creation of public works projects for jobless rural laborers, but it was supported only in areas where socialists possessed some influence. The gravity and duration of the agricultural crisis led to the collapse of most of the rural labor unions and, as always, to a resurgence in banditry and smuggling (*bandolerismo*).

In Andalusia 1904 was a tranquil year, underscoring the regional and often discontinuous nature of labor developments. But as Edward Malefakis notes, "For the first time bitter struggles over the right to organize were fought in such provinces of Old Castile as Avila, Zamora, Palencia, León, and Valladolid. For the first time Socialist labor organizations began to compete with the Anarchists for peasant support."[13]

The ephemeral nature of rural organization makes it difficult to ascertain the unionization rate in southern Spain. Tuñon de Lara tells us that "a majority of agricultural workers were conjuncturally organized. Membership in the Andalusian countryside oscillated between 10 and 15 percent of rural wage earners, but the declines, I believe, are much more important than those that occurred among industrial workers, although this phenomenon among the latter should not be minimized."[14]

Anarchist influence was considerable in certain zones, especially in western Andalusia. The lengthy successful general strike of 1902 at Moron de la Frontera that involved virtually the entire working population, even the municipal employees, was a wholly libertarian affair, but its importance has been exaggerated, for a variety of political and trade union currents were also in evidence at the time. In the province of Málaga, for example, the main rural labor movement, known as La Federación Málagueña, was Republican in orientation and led by a woman, Belen Sañaga. A smaller group, El Faro de Andalucia, was anarchist-led, and there were scattered socialist organizations in the province. Furthermore, many worker societies in the region's urban centers were nonpolitical, some under Republican tutelage and a lesser number socialist-oriented. Writing in 1910, Angel Marvaud observed that Andalusian anarchists "merely constituted small circles dispersed in the cities and villages of southern Spain where they aid in maintaining the revolutionary flame. But in the Andalusian ambience these small nuclei represented an organizational core around which strikes and other actions would take place, often involving large masses of participants."[15]

Solidaridad Obrera

The formation in 1907 of the Barcelona Workers Solidarity Local Federation (Solidaridad Obrera—SO) marked a watershed in the evolution of the Spanish labor movement. The destruction of many labor unions following the 1902 general strike had demoralized wage earners and labor activists. It underscored the bankruptcy of anarcho-communist tactics and strategy. The failure to endow the 1902 general strike with an insurrectionary character heralded the close of an epoch in the evolution of the anarchist movement that had originated with the creation of the FRE. As Joaquín Romero Maura remarked, "By 1907 the anarchists in Catalonia were more lonely and forsaken than they had ever been, more so than in the 1890's."[16]

Nor were the libertarians the only ones experiencing disarray. The failure of repeated attempts by the socialists to penetrate Catalonia had generated equally intense feelings of isolation among Pablo Iglesias's local followers.[17] The sense of shared adversity was all the more keenly felt when the rise of Lerrouxism threatened to displace both anarchists and socialists in Barcelona working-class affairs.

The reconstitution of a local labor body capable of rallying most of the surviving worker societies was also urgently needed for purely trade union reasons. The absence of a central coordinating federation made it impossible to pool available resources and undertake joint collective bargaining actions against employers, who often acted in unison. Socialists, anarchists, and "pure" trade unionists had all failed in their efforts to establish local federations. Thus SO represented a sort of mutual assistance pact.

The socialists initially promoted SO for political reasons as well as in hopes of improving their fortunes. Their first attempt in the 1890s to establish a foothold in the region ended disastrously, and the PSOE/UGT's stiff-necked refusal to support Barcelona's beleaguered metalworkers in 1902 boded ill for future prospects. The Catalonian socialist movement in 1907 was a small, inconsequential force. But several of its leading figures, including Antonio Fabra Ribas, an intimate of Jean Jaures, Antonio Badia Matamala, the head of the city's commercial workers union, veteran labor leader José Comaposada, and typographer Arturo Gas Belenguer did not share Iglesias's animosity to the anarchists and favored a modus vivendi in Catalonia with laborites and anarchists.

The local leadership of the PSOE/UGT, which was headed by Fabra Ribas following his return in 1908 from a seven-year sojourn in various western European countries, suggested creating a central labor body based on broad trade union principles and political neutrality so that socialists, Republicans, anarchists, and trade unionists could collaborate in an umbrella organization. Fabra Ribas, who had been active in the French socialist movement, had been influenced by men such as Hubert Lagardelle, who sought a reconciliation between syndicalism and socialism.[18]

The name Workers Solidarity (Federación Local Solidaridad Obrera) was chosen to indicate that the organization would serve as a proletarian counter to Catalonian Solidarity (Solidaridad Catalana), the broad region-alist political coalition that dominated the political scene following its landslide victory in the 1907 general elections.

Such an innovation naturally stirred mixed feelings. Among both an-archists and socialists some gave only grudging support, and others openly opposed the new venture.[19] An element in persuading anarchists was the recommendation by the Amsterdam international anarchist congress held that year favoring participation in trade union activities. The ultimate acceptance by both movements indicated the extent to which the working-class movement had deteriorated and the increasing irrelevancy of old ideas. Indeed it took such a desperate situation to surmount the legacy of mutual antipathy between the two movements.

Lerrouxists saw Workers Solidarity as a potential threat and sought to preempt it by launching a new labor body called Unión Obrera Re-publicana, but after it proved a resounding flop, Radical activists agreed to participate in the founding on August 3, 1907, of Solidaridad Obrera.

Displaying a prudently moderate, nondogmatic outlook, though unable readily to dispel the aura of apprehension and resignation that reigned in working-class quarters, the new organization was successful in garnering a certain prestige and popular sympathy. Economic conditions were un-favorable from 1907 to 1909, and unemployment was high in several industries. Consequently, strike activity in those years was at low ebb and few of them ended in victory for the workers. But even the civil governor, Angel Ossorio y Gallardo, who promoted moderation in the labor movement, regarded the fledgling federation with a certain protective benevolence.

SO consisted at its formation of fifty-seven affiliated unions with ten thousand members. When its first congress was held in September 1908, it had been converted into a regional body and had expanded modestly to fifteen to twenty thousand members, representing more than a third of all worker societies in Catalonia. The single largest contingent was made up of nonpolitical unionists, followed by the anarchists and their sympathizers, Lerrouxists, and socialists.[20] Workers often abstained from joining unions out of fear of retributions by their employers, though many supported the new labor center. Labor organization in Barcelona textile manufacturing was virtually nonexistent. Nor did the persistence of ter-rorist incidents and frequent bomb explosions on the city's thoroughfares make life any easier for Solidaridad Obrera. By the most optimistic estimates, it exercised influence over only half of all labor societies in Barcelona. Fifty to sixty societies preferred to remain outside SO.

Thus the movement involved only a tiny fraction (5 percent) of the work force.[21] The Republican journalist and historian Antoni Rovira i Virgili, a sympathetic observer, wrote on January 9, 1909, in the Barcelona periodical *La Campana de Gracia* that "Workers Solidarity has been converted into the Catalonian General Confederation of Workers Resistance Societies. It consists in all Catalonia of 67 societies, 53 of them in Barcelona. The total number of workers that compose it is 12,500, a paltry number since Catalonia possesses some million and a half workers. There are 200,000 in Barcelona."

Despite its unremarkable progress, the mere existence of the labor center was to have a seminal effect in the shaping of trade union and doctrinal attitudes. Anarchists, still mostly wedded to anarcho-communist ideas, had not joined SO because of any intrinsic change in doctrine or strategy but simply because all existing alternatives—terrorism, general propaganda activities, and the like—had proven unproductive. And Catalonian anarchism, with its proletarian composition, could not long survive without the mass support of organized labor. The new ideas of revolutionary syndicalism then in vogue in France, though significant, were of secondary importance. Thus what began as an act taken out of dire necessity became a theoretical rationale.[22] The anarchists were following Hubert Lagardelle's dictum, "Theory arises out of practice, action creates the idea." A process was thus begun that would reach full bloom in the anarcho-syndicalist views elaborated by SO's successor, the National Confederation of Labor (CNT). It is, indeed, ironic that Spanish socialists, so consistently unsuccessful in Catalonia, nonetheless served as the unwitting handmaiden in bridging the gap between anarcho-communism and trade union realities.

SO leaders in mid-1909 sought an issue that would enable the organization to reverse the trend of intimidation of workers, ineffectuality in labor disputes, mass layoffs, and economic recession. A campaign to revive organization in the textile industry had met with little success. Ultimately it was not a trade union issue but the escalation of the Moroccan war that catapulted the small SO into the forefront of a massive popular upheaval.

The Tragic Week

Intermittent guerrilla attacks and high casualties among the incompetently led military forces in the Riffian zone of the Spanish protectorate raised government concern over the zone's security. Normally sensible and prudent in such matters, Prime Minister Antonio Maura acceded to pressures and on July 10 agreed to dispatch a twenty thousand–man expeditionary force that was to be formed by mobilizing reservists. Anticipating the angry reaction that this would provoke, on June 4 he decreed the closure of the Cortes.

Maura had made a fatal misjudgment. Not yet recovered from the bloodletting of 1898, Spaniards were in a pacifist mood. The prospect of another colonial war in barely a decade aroused considerable opposition. Yet government officials paid little attention to the outcry.

Social and political temperatures in Barcelona were on the rise. Nationalist resentments against Madrid among upper and middle classes had intensified, and unemployment and economic slump, including an overproduction crisis in the textile industry, had worsened the plight of the lower classes. Only a pretext was required to set off a massive outburst.

The mobilization order that again placed the burden of an unpopular war almost exclusively on the poor furnished that reason. Economically well-off young men could avoid service by paying 1,500 pesetas. Conscription was onerous because many of the reservists were married with children, and virtually no provision had been made for the sustenance of their families while they were on active duty. Deprived of their breadwinners' earnings, many families faced destitution. The announcement of the mobilization had an electrifying effect on Barcelona and the region, for War Minister Arsenio Linares chose to call up the Third Mixed Brigade, made up of reservists from Catalonia, Valencia, and Aragon. Barcelona served as the port of embarkation.

The Socialist party fiercely opposed the war and spearheaded the national opposition movement.[23] In Barcelona, Fabra Ribas, the Catalonian Socialist Federation, and the UGT joined with leading Radicals and anarchists in Solidaridad Obrera to oppose the war. The PSOE/UGT had planned for a nationwide work stoppage to take place on August 2, but at the insistence of the anarchists the Catalonian socialists advanced the date and agreed to a general strike in Barcelona on July 26, hoping that it would be extended and eventually merge with the strike being readied in Madrid.

Tensions mounted around the country as mobilization proceeded amid a rising popular clamor. On July 18 the Riffian guerrillas inflicted heavy casualties on Spanish army units, making a mockery of the government's claim that the Moroccan affair was merely a police action. In Barcelona the climate grew increasingly taut as local newspapers, especially Republican ones, violently denounced the war. Street demonstrations had become a daily affair and steadily swelled in size and stridency. The police seemed powerless to deal with them.

Most workers struck on July 26, the general populace was sympathetic, and few factory owners discouraged the participation of their employees. The life of the city quickly ground to a halt as other towns joined the general stoppage.

The strike committee, with a small network of activists directing matters, lost control as the antiwar protest became submerged in a chaotic popular upheaval. The strike had turned into a plebeian rising similar to those that had taken place in preindustrial times. In a state of wonderment and disbelief, the veteran anarchist leader Anselmo Lorenzo wrote, "What is happening here is amazing. A social revolution has broken out in Barcelona and it has been started by the people. No one instigated it. No one has led it, neither the Liberals, Catalan nationalists, Republicans, Socialists, nor Anarchists."[24] Street barricades were thrown up in slums and working-class districts, the republic was proclaimed in nearby Sabadell, and revolutionary juntas were constituted in other localities. A participating labor activist described it as "the last romantic revolution . . . with its barricades, the hunting shotguns, nickel-plated revolvers, with the red flags affixed atop the barricades alongside posters reading 'death to looters.' "[25]

Joan Connelly Ullman tells us that as the general strike began to take on an insurrectionary character the leaders of Lerroux's Radical party (Lerroux had left the country to escape prosecution on a pending litigation) sought to defuse the situation by directing rebellious elements into anticlerical activities such as burning and pillaging church buildings, with the result that forty religious schools and churches, convents, and welfare centers were put to the torch together with twelve parish churches, less than half of the city's church buildings.[26] Only three priests perished, however.[27]

The pacific antiwar protest degenerated into a leaderless popular revolt largely because of the incompetence of the authorities. Civil Governor Ossorio y Gallardo had originally proposed letting the protest run its course under close police supervision, but he was overruled by his superior, Juan de la Cierva, minister of interior, a rigid law-and-order advocate, who declared martial law under the authority of the commanding general of the military region. According to Juan Benet, "Its declaration aggravated the situation for Luis de Santiago, captain general of Catalonia, who lacked sufficient military forces owing to the departure of part of his troops for Morocco and the fear of fraternization of the soldiers with the people who were hailing them, was apparently impotent in seeking to overcome the strike movement."[28] Many soldiers did begin to fraternize with the protesters and passively observed the depredations of the rebellious throngs. With nothing standing in their way, the workers acted out the demagogic revolutionary rhetoric of their political mentors, who were nowhere to be seen.

With the situation hopelessly out of control, some SO leaders, including Fabra Ribas, appealed to the Lerrouxists and the regionalist Federal Nationalist Republican Union (UFNR) to assume direction of the movement. By that time, however, the government had succeeded in preventing the antiwar protest from spreading beyond Catalonia (the PSOE's planned August 2 shutdown had been aborted by preemptive police detentions) and in giving the impression that the rebellion had been fomented by Catalonian separatists. With the end in sight, the Republicans prudently avoided public identification. With the arrival of troop reinforcements on July 28, the insurrection was quickly and severely put down. It had lasted one week, from July 26 to August 1, one day short of the planned national strike. Nine policemen and soldiers died and an additional 125 sustained injuries; 104 civilians were killed and 216 wounded. More than 2,500 persons were imprisoned, of whom 1,725 were indicted. Seventeen received death sentences, but only five, including the anarchist-oriented educator Francisco Ferrer, were ultimately executed. SO had not officially sponsored the call for a general strike, but its headquarters was sequestered by the authorities for having instigated a revolution in league with the French General Confederation of Labor (CGT) and international Freemasonry. Union offices and all nonsecular schools and Republican centers were closed down, numerous publications were suspended, and large numbers of labor and political activists, Fabra Ribas among them, crossed the Pyrenees to France to avoid imprisonment. Many others were exiled to remote rural hamlets. Thus once again the Catalonian labor movement lost important leaders. Martial law in Catalonia remained in force until November 7, though it was lifted on September 27 in the rest of the country.

Count Romanones in his memoirs observed that "Spanish governments carried on subject to Catalonian vibrations." Nowhere was this more in evidence than in the events surrounding the Tragic Week. The excessive harshness with which the rebellion was suppressed stirred considerable disapproval among many of the country's leading political figures.[29] The decision to make an example of Francisco Ferrer, founder of the Modern School educational movement, by naming him as the mastermind behind the uprising, followed by his execution, sent shock waves throughout Spain and the rest of the world.[30] This hitherto little-known anarchist-oriented educator became a martyr; his fate aroused worldwide indignation, similar to that generated by the Sacco-Vanzetti affair several decades later. The attempt to make Ferrer, who had no formal role either in the general strike or in the subsequent insurrection, into the guiding genius of a genuinely spontaneous popular explosion was grossly untenable. Ossorio y Gallardo termed it "laughable."

For many Spaniards the ensuing foreign outcry stirred memories of "La Espagne Inquisitorial," and this bruising of national pride provided an opportunity for opposition forces to oust the Maura government. Alarmed by the rising clamor, King Alfonso XIII "accepted" the prime minister's resignation, which had not been tendered, thus bringing to an inglorious end Antonio Maura's attempt to modernize the country's institutional infrastructure through "a revolution from above." Maura's arrogant style of governing, his perceived insensitivity to civil rights, his misbegotten Moroccan involvement, and the heavy-handed treatment of the Tragic Week participants also persuaded Pablo Iglesias and his followers to abandon their long-held policy of noncollaboration with the bourgeois Left and to enter into a broad political and electoral coalition that same year with the Republicans (La Conjunción Republicana-Socialista), a move that made possible Pablo Iglesias's entry into the Congress of Deputies the following year.

Normalcy returned with the lifting of martial law and other restrictions following the replacement of the Maura regime by a government headed by Liberal Segismundo Moret. Those convicted of misdeeds during the Tragic Week were amnestied and Solidaridad Obrera was permitted to resume its activities.

But SO's fifteen thousand members had now shrunk to some four thousand. Out of fear of further persecutions or concern over possible adverse effects of continued affiliation with SO on prospects for collective bargaining, several moderate-led unions withdrew. Many of the remaining affiliates experienced substantial losses in membership. Because many of SO's key figures and activists had fled Barcelona to avoid persecution, the anarchists' representation increased markedly, though not to the point of complete dominance. The Tragic Week, moreover, gave added impetus to the process of radicalization among labor militants and strengthened their reliance on direct action tactics rather than more pacific means of collective bargaining and labor relations.

For employers the Tragic Week confirmed their resolve not to seek peaceful coexistence with the unions but to brandish the clenched fist with even more severity than before.[31]

Founding of the National Confederation of Labor

There had been talk well before July 1909 of making Solidaridad Obrera into a national organization, especially among anarchist elements, who keenly felt the absence of an ideologically compatible labor center. Their numbers had increased substantially through the entry of additional anarchist activists following the Tragic Week, who had been persuaded that their former attitudes were untenable. Furthermore, in both SO and its successor, CNT, nonpolitical laborites tended to concern themselves primarily with the affairs of their local unions and trade federations and less with what transpired in regional and national labor bodies, thus permitting anarchists to exercise a disproportionate influence in the organizations' direction and policy making.

Despite its sponsors' protestations to the contrary, turning SO into a national labor confederation placed it on a collision course with the UGT. Catalonian socialists found themselves in an unenviable position. Fabra Ribas, in exile in France, together with Jean Jaures, pleaded with Iglesias and the party leadership not to return to the blood feuds of former days and to continue to seek ways of bridging differences with the Catalonian syndicalists and anarchists by participating in the new center's founding congress. Some socialist unionists attended but merely for tactical purposes, and they withdrew from the organization shortly thereafter, thus ending any hope of ultimately inducing SO to become the regional adjunct of the UGT. With the socialists and the Lerrouxists absent there were correspondingly fewer restraints on the anarchists to maintain the former moderate SO outlook.

The congress SO originally planned for September 1909 finally took place October 30 to November 1 of the following year. By an overwhelming margin the delegates voted to constitute a national body, and the newly formed center held its founding congress in Barcelona during September 1911. Symptomatic of the influence exerted by French syndicalism, the name CGT (General Confederation of Labor) was initially adopted but then later changed to the National Confederation of Labor (Confederación Nacional de Trabajo—CNT). The founding membership consisted of 140 affiliated locals representing some 26,571 adherents. Almost half hailed from Catalonia with the others representing unions in Valencia, Aragon, Andalusia, Rioja, and the northern anarchist enclaves of Gijón, La Felguera, and La Coruña. Of the 62 non-Catalonian unions at the congress 30 were from Zaragossa, attesting to the rising importance of the Aragonian capital as a CNT bastion second only to Barcelona. Anarchist influence was becoming strong in Valencia and Aragon and was evident in official policy pronouncements and in the tactics that were adopted.[32] French revolutionary syndicalist ideas were not merely transposed, they were intermixed with anarcho-communist concepts.

The ideological trade union pluralism that had been the distinguishing hallmark of SO was abandoned as prejudicial to the practice and implementation of direct action. Support for a minimum wage and sponsorship of cooperatives and mutual benefit societies (*sindicalismo a base multiple*) were abandoned. As César M. Lorenzo observes, "The foundations of a revolutionary syndicalism were laid, viewed as a means for attaining libertarian communism, in other words, of the old anarcho-syndicalism but now situated within a more severe, more intransigent ideological set. The National Confederation of Labor—CNT came into existence replete with all its armor: insurrectionary general strike, boycott, sabotage, the riot, antiparliamentarism, and a virulent antipoliticism."[33]

Though the official trade union vocabulary was permeated with anarchist jargon, as before, apolitical "pure" trade unionists were the largest component of the new organization. The return of numerous anarchist militants to trade union participation and their espousal of many of the postulates of revolutionary syndicalism (read anarcho-syndicalism) made possible a renewed convergence between the two currents. Anarchists acknowledged the legitimacy of the day-to-day struggle for trade union demands, and laborites generally acquiesced in the adoption of anarcho-syndicalist policies. In this waxing and waning of anarchist influence, as Francesc Bonamusa has emphasized, "The constant that emerges is that the Catalonian labor movement remained anchored in social and economic reality and was generally apolitical and federalist. To the degree that the various theoretical or pragmatic anarchist tendencies approached these realities did they succeed in gaining, if not hegemony, its leadership."[34] A process of pragmatic rapprochement had begun in 1910 that was to reach fruition in 1918–19.

It is almost impossible to gauge the extent to which anarcho-syndicalist ideas influenced trade union activists. Val Lorwin's comment on the impact of anarchist ideas on French CGT militants is probably equally applicable to many in the CNT of 1911: "The adoption of congress resolutions calling for the general strike and other articles of anarchist faith are not to be taken at face value. Certainly some of the men who voted for these resolutions were simply being as militant . . . as the next fellow."[35]

Its inability to check anarchist insurrectionist propensities was to make the CNT's initial existence extremely brief.[36] Further resistance during the summer of 1911 to Spain's attempt at consolidating control over its Moroccan protectorate again necessitated a sizable increase in the number of troops assigned to the expeditionary force. The Republican-Socialist Conjunction launched a national campaign opposing another colonial war in North Africa that was supported in Catalonia by the left Republicans of the UFNR. The PSOE again threatened to call a nationwide shutdown, but this time the Lerrouxist Radicals supported the government.

Not to be undone, the newly formed CNT decided at its first congress to call a general strike to protest the Moroccan intervention and to express its solidarity with strikes under way in the iron mines of Vizcaya, in Sabadell, and in Tarrassa. Preemptive mass detentions by the government, which was now headed by José Canalejas, caused the general strike to abort in Barcelona, while in the region of Valencia, in the town of Cullera, where a commune was proclaimed, and in Jativa, general shutdowns took on a violent character. It was in this context and government action to prevent a national railroad shutdown that Canalejas was gunned down by an anarchist in November of the following year. The CNT was outlawed and did not regain legal status until four years later.

During this period Lerroux's hold on the Barcelona proletariat began to decline. His party's ambiguous conduct during the Tragic Week, corruption, and its subsequent support for the government's actions in Morocco probably contributed to its loss of popularity. The growing influence of anarcho-syndicalist antipolitics that helped foster a renewed political alienation among workers was also the end result of popular disenchantment with Lerrouxism. At the height of Lerrouxist influence in

1907 close to 60 percent of all eligible voters in Barcelona cast their ballots; by 1910 the proportion of voters had declined slightly to 58 percent, but by 1914 it plummeted to 43 percent, and at the height of CNT power in 1920 it would sink to 29.5 percent.

6

CATHOLIC LABOR: ECCLESIASTICAL
MYOPIA AND DISASTER

Few European institutions in the nineteenth century found themselves in greater turmoil than the Catholic church. The secularizing effects of socioeconomic and political modernization that had deprived Catholicism of its privileged position under the old order, the "alliance of throne and altar," had forced the church to face the emerging reality. It was torn "between fidelity to a state of things whose impossibility of restoration ended in the imposition of a group of values, of a cosmovision that essentially replaced it."[1]

The Spanish Catholic experience was distinctive for the implacable tenacity with which it clung to its ancien régime outlook. Nowhere in the European church were conservative traditionalists so dominant and moderates so few in numbers and influence. Many within the church hierarchy and the lay faithful remained incorrigible ultramontanes and *integristas* intent on returning Spain to a confessional society ("the Catholic unity of Spain").[2] William J. Callahan speaks of "an ecclesiastical mentality deeply rooted in the quasi-medieval scholastic interpretation of social organization that had long dominated clerical thinking."[3] Resistance to change persisted long after most other national churches had reached some degree of accommodation with modernism, thus delaying the Spanish church's entrance into the new liberal order until well into the present century.

A pastoral strategy open to collaboration and dialogue was impossible. This extraordinary rigidity was reinforced by the church's prominence for many centuries in influencing not only morality, education, and social welfare but the country's politics as well. Callahan declares: "Few institutions have played so central a role in the history of a people as has the

Spanish church."[4] Even in the Restoration period (1876–1923) the church retained an extremely privileged social and political status. The lesser-evil argument advanced by some conservative Catholics to justify the church's integration into the Canovist political system was rejected by many in the hierarchy and in the lay faithful as an unacceptable retreat from integrism. Nor did Pope Leo XIII's proddings change matters greatly.

As a result, when public attention and political deliberations began to focus on social reform, the Catholic church was otherwise engaged. Its concern was with the "religious question," with the confessional character of the state that had been ever so slightly abridged in the 1876 constitution, by measures taken to counter the relentless advance of secularism, Catholic education, the religious orders, and other matters.

Such issues together with the difficulties in arriving at a policy consensus among the various fractious tendencies absorbed most of the church's energies. Catholic cohesion was consequently much diminished by serious doctrinal and policy differences. Integrists and Carlists, who represented the largest segment, rejected any accommodation with the new liberal order. The neo-Thomist proposal encouraged by Pope Leo XIII, whose most prominent advocates were the "Unionists" who collaborated with Restoration conservative governments, envisaged a church role more in keeping with contemporary realities. The ideological rather than the political presence of the church was stressed, with the new social Catholic doctrine to serve as an element in expanding its influence. The "secular" group, a small minority that included some of the Christian Democrats, had acknowledged the irreversibility of secularization and consequently argued in favor of a greater anonymous confessional presence.

Catholic Worker Circles

In western and central Europe the swelling ranks of factory proletarians and the growth of working-class movements generated a confessional response. The first Catholic worker organizations that emerged were varied in function and represented differing departures from traditional ecclesiastical practices. Before 1880, according to Michael Fogarty, "They tended either to be or become patronages under middle class or upper class control, directed to keeping the workers out of Socialist mischief or to mobilizing them for general political ends. The workmen's club movement of de Mun and la Tour du Pin never claimed to be anything other than a protective measure provided by the paternal solicitude of, to quote an early statement of the very upper class French Association of Catholic Youth, 'what is known as the ruling class.' The Catholic or mixed workers associations in Germany tended to become political centers for the general purposes of Kulturkampf."[5]

With a distracted clergy that had no tradition of social Catholic consciousness, the first Spanish Catholic initiatives in worker organization tended to be sporadic and locally inspired. Information is lacking concerning the full extent of these early efforts. They clearly were small in number and dispersed. The first known Catholic Worker Circle was established in the factory town of Alcoy, where in the 1870s a large number of workers had enrolled in labor organizations, resulting in the town's choice as the headquarters of the FRE. The circle had been formed by Jesuit priests in cooperation with local factory owners for the express purpose of countering the growing influence of secular trade unions and the anarchist-led FRE. Its life span was brief. In the general strike of 1873 that preceded the Cantonalist uprisings, an edict decreeing the "compulsory suppression" of all labor organizations forced it to cease operations for the next three years.

A Catholic Workers Society was constituted in 1871 in the Canary Islands city of Las Palmas, but it turned out to be a black sheep in the fold. Instead of serving an exclusively confessional purpose, it permitted membership regardless of religious belief or political orientation and had the temerity to enter into friendly relations with the FRE. A pastoral letter was disseminated by Bishop José Maria de Urquinaona (subsequently named bishop of the Barcelona Diocese and considered an early exponent of social Catholicism) placing the organization outside the pale by announcing the formation of a new rival association under formal church sponsorship.

The most notable among these early initiatives took place in 1877, one year before the ordination of Pope Leo XIII. Ceferino González, bishop of the Córdoba Diocese, a leading church thinker and a pioneer in Spanish social Catholicism, launched a campaign to create a chain of Catholic Worker Circles both in urban areas and in the countryside. Within six months forty-two circles had been established in a diocese that contained some one hundred populated centers. But it was one thing to engage church resources in the creation of such organizations and still another to acquire the know-how and infrastructure necessary for their functioning and survival. Many soon collapsed, and only a few managed to establish themselves on a relatively firm footing. When the movement was at its peak in 1879, there were, according to Juan Díaz del Moral, sixteen circles with 3,060 workers and 545 honorary members in addition to sixteen schools that were attended by 865 children. Their primary purpose was to counter anarchist and socialist influences. But "the collapse of the proletarian movement following the Black Hand repression caused a loss in interest in the Catholic Circles that were then gradually extinguished."[6] When in 1891 the circles were revived, they met with little enthusiasm among wage earners.

Of the small handful of clerics who pioneered in church social action during the late nineteenth century none was more influential and indefatigable in his proselytizing zeal than the Jesuit Antonio Vicent. "Virtually all our social-Catholic works," observed Severino Aznar, the leading social Catholic thinker of this century, "are his or have come from his disciples."[7]

Vicent was born in Castellon de la Plana in the region of Valencia on October 2, 1837. After a brief career as a lawyer, he became a Jesuit at the age of twenty-four. Upon completion of his novitiate he entered the University of Seville to study biology, a discipline that was to become one of his two abiding passions. He joined the faculty of Saint Ignatius College of Manresa in 1865. Already interested in social action, he organized a local worker circle, probably the first in Spain. Little is known of its existence except that it was short-lived.

At the time of the 1868 revolution he was studying theology at the Maximus College of Tortosa, and when religious orders were banished, he went into exile and completed his studies in France, where he was ordained. The Catholic Worker Circles movement was just developing in that country (Count Albert de Mun and René de la Tour du Pin founded the Oeuvre des Cercles Catholiques d'Ouvriers in 1871), largely as a reaction to the trauma evoked by the Paris Commune. Firsthand exposure to the concepts and operations of this movement profoundly influenced and shaped Vicent's outlook. To be sure, Spanish borrowings from French initiatives or concepts over the years have been the rule rather than the exception. Iberians of all social stations and outlook have frequently sought inspiration from French ideas and movements. Pablo Iglesias borrowed heavily from Jules Guesde, anarchists and left Republicans from Proudhon, and conservative Catholics from their Gallic counterparts, including the initial forays of social Catholics from the formulations of men such as de Mun, La Tour du Pin, and Leon Harmel.[8]

Upon his return to Spain in 1879, Vicent reestablished himself in the

Levantine city of Tortosa, a region that he would make the principal focal point for the launching and development of the peninsular Catholic Worker Circles.

The French Catholic Worker Circles were created through a coordinated national effort by social Catholics supported by church authorities. In Spain, however, the movement began in a sporadic, local fashion without any hierarchical guidance, "the fruit of preoccupations to which some sought a solution and as the result of echoes that were beginning to be felt from across the border, echoes which . . . at each latitude arrived with differing intensities and fidelity."[9] Thus the resulting groups were heterogeneous in form, content, and nomenclature. Some called themselves Catholic Worker Circles, others centers, patronages, institutes, or societies. Outlooks, emphases, and curricula varied considerably, a confusion that has contributed to the difficulty in ascertaining the size and scope of the movement during this period. When in 1893 a national coordinating body was formed, it had little success in systematizing the function and denomination of these groups.

At the end of 1892 the Tortosa Diocese was able to claim eleven operating circles with five subsidiary patronages and seventeen schools. In Valencia province there were forty circles with 16,893 members as well as twenty-seven patronages and seventy-seven schools. Most were located in rural areas. The average membership in Valencian circles was 422 (but only 244 if the "protectors" are excluded) and 245 in Tortosa Diocese (192 without the "protectors").[10]

José Andrés Gallego has written, "The Levant nucleus was, to be sure, not the initiator of the movement (contrary to what has been said) nor did it form the first important group (recall the previous one of Córdoba), neither did it constitute an isolated phenomenon. But what we do underscore is that the organizational spirit of the region and Vicent's zeal made it the base for the launching of a definitive impetus. The statutes for Vicent's Levantine Circles, of course, served as a model at the time for most of the other peninsular ones."[11] Vicent's book, *Anarquismo y socialismo,* a traditionalistic exegesis of the social doctrine contained in *Rerum Novarum,* enjoyed a wide circulation. It is dedicated to the Marquis of Comillas, who financed the printing of a second edition.

The early circles had as their principal mission countering the influence of secularist and anarchist workers and the loss of religiosity among the lower classes by means of devotional programs and beneficent-charitable activities. Some were little more than mutual aid societies, but most functioned simply as recreational centers. Carr observes, "They degenerated into friendly societies, clubs to keep the workers from the pernicious influence of the tavern and the socialists, organizations of working class piety more concerned with the suppression of blasphemy than with the improvement of working conditions."[12]

Consonant with official church doctrine, Vicent maintained that the "social question" was not simply a matter of social justice and meeting the economic grievances of wage earners; it was, rather, a moral and religious question that could best be solved through spiritual formation and religious observances rather than bettering working conditions. The proferring of services to dissuade workers from joining radical secular labor organizations was regarded as of secondary importance. But those who joined the circles often did receive special benefits such as welfare services, mutual benefit society memberships, job placement facilities, low interest loans, primary school education for their children, and recreational facilities.

An upper-class mentality that was little affected by the changing times directed the founding of the circles. Subordination, resignation, charity, antisocialism, and corporatist social harmony (strikes were considered anathema) were enjoined. Implicit in the organizational structuring of the circles was the notion that workers were either incapable or untrustworthy of assuming leadership responsibilities. In the name of Christian paternalism and the natural ordering of society, therefore, the circles were to be directed by wealthy patrons, employers, and clerics. Membership was divided into the "protected" (workers) and "protectors" (wealthy patrons and employers). In the statutes that Father Vicent prepared in 1887 for the Tortosa Diocese Worker Circles, of the fifteen voting members who constituted the executive committee (*junta directiva*), six represented the protectors, an additional six the regular members, and the remaining three the protector women and co-participants.[13] Even this modest worker presence was often further diluted and, in some instances, eliminated. The key figure in all circles, the one who invariably controlled and directed their activities, was a priest named by the local bishop, who served as "councillor."[14] This oligarchical, castelike distribution of functions and duties was, of course, consonant with church doctrine and hierarchical orderings and mirrored the configuration of Spanish Restoration society. Approximately 70 percent of urban wage earners in late nineteenth-century Spain were illiterate. Feliciano Montero García observes that two elements, "the persistence of a rural Spain and the privileged acknowledgment of Catholic Spain, help explain the permanence of the integrist thesis and concomitantly the persistence of a fundamentally welfarist-charitable approach to the social question that more properly belonged to the old regime."[15]

By the closing decades of the last century, the church's fortunes had begun to take a turn for the better. Its general influence and standing had partially recovered from the grievous decline it had suffered earlier in the century. Much of upper and secondary education came under clerical control, the church's coffers were rapidly replenishing, and a rechristianization of the upper classes had been accomplished. But among the thronging plebeian masses crowding into the burgeoning urban centers and among the landless of the rural south, areas that had become increasingly alienated from the organized church, the situation was more troubling than ever.

Pope Leo XIII's encyclical of 1891, *Rerum Novarum,* and *Immortale Dei e Libertas* that preceded it, signaled major efforts by the church to regain the allegiance of Europe's estranged working class and to respond more positively to the social challenges of the new industrial age and the human problems of mass society. The pontiff equally sought to disabuse the faithful of the notion that the tide of secularist socialism could be stemmed through the hurling of anathemas, as his predecessor had done, but rather through the formation of rival Catholic worker organizations dedicated to the fulfillment of an authentic Christian quest for social justice untainted by crude materialism. Mixed employer-worker associations were given preference, although purely worker unions were acceptable.

Though failing to grasp the full import of the new approach to Catholic social doctrine, the Spanish hierarchy nevertheless was dutifully effusive in endorsing it. The church hierarchy had no experience with or understanding of the social consequences of industrialism in a society where the factory proletariat outside Catalonia had barely begun to make its presence felt, or of the oligarchical setting of which it served as a leading apologist, but it gave lip service to the postulates of *Rerum Novarum.* "The initial reception . . . in official Catholic circles and publications," observes Feliciano Montero García, "was weak and paltry. Other than a few exceptions, without entering into its substance, in presenting the encyclical to their dioceses, the commentaries of most bishops displayed little comprehension for its contents and directives." *Rerum Novarum* heightened awareness of the social question but produced little real change in mentality and outlook.[16]

One thing did change for the better. Father Vicent and the Worker Circles movement received official blessing, and the indifference and hostility displayed by industrialists was somewhat allayed. In the five years following the issuance of *Rerum Novarum,* the circles were expanded. Because of their organizational and functional heterogeneity and often sporadic, fleeting existences, it is difficult to estimate their numbers and membership or those of related groups. José Andrés Gallego has calculated that the number of worker members in 1892 possibly exceeded 30,000 and may have reached 100,000 in 1903, compared with a claimed UGT membership in 1899 of 15,264 and the 30,000 attributed to the CNT in 1911.[17] That so formidable an institution as the Catholic church attracted so small a percentage of the labor force attests not only to the church's social myopia but to the massive apathy and passivity of most of the population.

Catholic Action, directed primarily to the lower classes, was another organization resulting from revived interest in the social question. A national coordinating body, the National Council of Catholic Worker Corporations (Consejo Nacional de las Corporaciónes Católico-Obreras), was founded in 1893. Its first major undertaking was the organization of a huge, costly workers' pilgrimage to Rome the following year in which more than eighteen thousand participated. It had no effect on Spanish social affairs, and one Catholic historian has aptly termed it "ecclesiastical triumphalism."[18] Pope Leo XIII used the occasion mainly to urge political unity of Catholics, underscoring the relatively little concern that the social question had for Spanish Catholics.

The National Council had been largely organized and financed by the second Marquis of Comillas (Claudio López Bru), heir to a great fortune and owner of many important industrial and commercial enterprises. A supporter of the Alfonsine monarchy and a fervent adherent to conservative Catholic social ideas, the marquis emerged as the moving force behind Catholic Action, and until his death in 1925 he dominated the policies and activities of the Worker Circles and allied forms of social action. Much of his great wealth was devoted to the financing of numerous church-sponsored social labor programs. His power was so pervasive that the church's intrinsically conservative social outlook during his lifetime probably evolved in a more reactionary direction than it otherwise would have.[19] At his behest and with his funding, the General Association for the Study and Defense of the Working Class was formed in Madrid during early 1895. Almost exclusively composed of aristocrats and upper-class individuals—its officers included a duke, two marquis, an admiral, and a general—it encouraged and supported the formation of Worker Circles. Though the projected goal was twenty-five circles, it organized only five in Madrid with an enrollment of five thousand during the first year of its existence. Most of them expired after brief periods of activity.

Nor were efforts to establish Worker Circles in Barcelona any more fruitful. Colin Winston concludes, "Unenticed by the rudimentary social services offered, humiliated by the 'continuous vigilance' exercised by ecclesiastical authorities and repelled by the compulsory religious observance required in most centers, Barcelona's workers avoided the Catholic Circles in droves. At most the city's centers provided a place of refuge for some 7,500 Catholic workers, some 4 percent of Barcelona's blue-collar force in 1914. The true percentage of the Catalan metropolis's manual workers affiliated with the centers was probably even smaller since even the circles' partisans recognized that a large segment of their members were shop assistants and sundry white-collar employees."[20]

The headquarters of the National Council of Catholic Worker Corporations had been located in Valencia but at Comillas's urging was transferred to Madrid. The National Council, writes Domingo Benavides Gómez, "and the General Association for the Study and Defense of the Working Class that had been founded a year earlier in the same city, though separate organizations, ended up being virtually jumbled, as revealed in the similarity of the names heading both entities. Moreover, the overwhelming presence of the aristocracy and bourgeoisie in the leadership of national organisms charged with promoting Catholic worker organization in Spain offers a most eloquent expression of the orientation of this movement."[21] Either out of skepticism or a lack of confidence in the efficacy of the Catholic circles in warding off socialist and anarchist labor influences among their employees, relatively few factory owners or industrial magnates took part in these organizations. Nor did the Marquis of Comillas have much success in organizing a group of Catholic employers.

The Worker Circles movement was at its height during the early years of this century, and it made its most meaningful contribution in the field of education, establishing numerous schools for workers and their children. The circles played a minimal role in establishing savings banks, cooperatives, and mutual benefit societies, though they later were active in that field in rural areas. Both the circles and the General Association for the Study and Defense of the Working Class helped create favorable public opinion and impetus for the adoption of protective social legislation. Eduardo Dato and others who led in the passage of the first laws were well-known social Catholics. It was, moreover, no coincidence that the first measures to receive legislative attention were those of high priority to social Catholics, namely the establishment of Sunday as an obligatory day of rest and restrictions on the industrial employment of women and minors.[22]

Fanciful hopes that the circles would serve as a mechanism to resolve labor-management differences were bound to be dashed. Father Vicent, who had been deeply influenced by his study of medieval guilds and the more contemporary notions of French confessional corporativism, had envisaged a Worker Circles movement whose primary function would not be welfare associationism but formation of a tripartite pyramidal structure. One section was to be composed of workers separated according to trade or occupational category, another similarly distributed for employers, and an overarching *jurado mixto* (a joint labor-management commission) would be composed of representatives from the two groups charged with mediating differences between them. The primary concern was assuring class harmony, and the economic improvement of working conditions was to result from education and moral uplift. Cooperativism and friendly societies were therefore regarded as of secondary importance.

By 1904 Father Vicent admitted to failure: "What have we accomplished with all those Catholic Circles that we have founded? In reality very little, all that has been gained is that the secretaries made out lists of members of those in the same trade, craft, or industry, but it has not been possible to form authentic corporative guilds [*gremios*]. Employers have always demanded absolute freedom to hire, and workers have rejected joining with the employers to constitute the Christian association. An abyss of hatred separates one from the other."[23] Two years later, not long before his death, he acknowledged the unsuitability of mixed unions, at least for urban workers.

The greatest failure of the Worker Circles movement was its inability to provide a credible alternative to secular labor organizations. The inauguration in 1907 of the UGT's *casa del pueblo* in Madrid, which was housed in an impressive former ducal mansion and financed by worker contributions, came as a disturbing revelation to Catholic activists, whose centers could be sustained only through contributions from the wealthy. Severino Aznar, the leading ideologue of modern social Catholicism, on that occasion wrote an article for a prominent social Catholic review consisting of a scathing interview (probably apocryphal) with a socialist worker:

> I spoke to him of the various Catholic patronages established in Madrid to care for the needs of the poor. I spoke of the Catholic Worker Circles. . . . My interlocutor smiled with infinite disdain. I cannot put into words the enormous sense of contempt in his gestures upon mention of the circles. "They don't exist," he said and challenged me, to be sure, to show any traces or influence they had had on the life of the Madrid worker. "What have they accomplished? What wage increases have they won? When did they intervene to reduce the workday or to improve working conditions? What strikes have they organized?"
>
> Most tellingly he added: "Believe me, at the beginning we were very fearful. We were few and we were not able then to establish strong trade societies. Fortunately they fiddled around with something or other and today they only inspire an immense disdain. They don't exist.
>
> "We never have had to overcome a single opposition mounted by these circles with all the enormous power that the formidable lists of dukes, counts, generals, bankers, ex-ministers, monks, etc., appear to represent, and that protect them or are said to protect them."[24]

Domingo Benavides Gómez concludes: "What remains is an effort of questionable religious formation and some cultural and vocational contributions to the worker and his children to which ought to be added some charitable works that more or less were worthwhile and efficacious. In many instances it amounted to less than that. The circles frequently became converted into meeting places, a sort of cheap clubhouse, useful at the most for separating the worker from less recommendable premises or establishments."[25]

The movement's failure vividly underscored the plight of a church caught between two worlds. "In the end," observes William J. Callahan, "the Church was puzzled by a society in ferment. As a result it fell between two stools. Its dream of a return to the charity of the past was impractical; its horror of radical social forces made it a defender of private property and the existing social order in an economic system the clergy fundamentally disliked."[26]

Beyond this failure to assist workers in erecting effective instruments of social and economic defense lay an even graver, self-inflicted stigma that foredoomed subsequent efforts to form an authentic, autonomous Catholic labor movement. The spectacle of so-called worker organizations directed and dominated by aristocrats and employers had made most Spanish workers see Catholic labor organizations as synonymous with "yellow" company unionism.[27] As late as the 1920s and 1930s, when employers had been formally excluded from most union memberships, they often continued to serve as "honorary" members (*socios protectores*). The identification of the church with such endeavors in an increasingly polarized society further alienated workers from organized Catholicism and fanned the flames of anticlericalism. One can understand why for many workers the struggle against clericalism and the struggle against employers went hand in hand and found its ultimate stark expression in the Tragic Week, when virtually all the Catholic Worker Centers and buildings housing the patronages and Worker Circles were vandalized or burned.

In addition, the movement was intrinsically incapable of developing an indigenous working-class leadership. The history of Catholic labor is replete with the names of clerics who led the various organizations, but the names of worker leaders are notably absent. By insisting on a high degree of confessionalism in all aspects of social action, the church assured an intrusive, almost exclusively ecclesiastical role in the organization and direction of worker groups.

Still another asynchronism resulted from the church's tardy involvement in social affairs. When the Catholic Circle movement in Spain was gathering force at the turn of the century, important changes were already well under way in the rest of western Europe. As Fogarty describes it, "There were still much middle and upper class initiatives in the workers movement and often the desire to protect the workers or to use them against Socialism. But more and more the movement came to be led by workers themselves in what they saw as the interests of their class, though within the general framework of the Christian social movement as a whole. These were the years when the working class as a whole, not merely its Christian section, was awakening all over Europe and becoming conscious of its strength. And this reflected itself among the Christian workers as elsewhere."[28] Because of these developments traditional paternalistic pastoral and apostolic approaches began to give way, permitting the various Catholic interest groups, especially workers, semiautonomy in directing and promoting their specific professional interests.

Their most glaring shortcoming was possibly that they regarded workers as a flock of errant sheep in need of trustworthy shepherds. Left to their own devices, workers were easy prey to the demagogic appeals of socialists and anarchists. As Severino Aznar has put it, the role of the Worker Circles was "to domesticate and pacify" workers.[29] Hence the church's prescription for social harmony and conciliation was tantamount to class subordination made even more blatant by its virtual silence, especially before 1902, regarding workers' efforts to obtain improved wages and working conditions.

Until well into this century the church rather than the state was the principal dispenser of charitable undertakings and welfare activities. The introduction of the Worker Circles consequently did not break new ground in the fields of cooperativism or mutual benefit associationism. And the tradition-bound Spanish church was unable to go from a charitable outlook to cooperative mutualism as other European confessional movements had done. As Montero García explains, "The mutualist principle in the Madrid Circles seems to have encountered difficulties of implantation, accustomed as both the association members and the circle founders and supporters were to defraying workers' material necessities through the giving of alms and other charitable means. Small deposits in the savings accounts were made for good behavior, regular attendance, and the like."[30]

The church did recognize the need to cater to the special needs of wage earners and small farmers. But because they viewed solutions to labor problems through the prism of traditional Catholic values, church conservatives and social Catholics were incapable of truly comprehending the realities of working-class life. For this reason more than any other, the effort to accomplish a rechristianization of urban wage earners through the formation of confessional labor organizations, despite the highly favorable setting that the Alfonsine Restoration offered for a renewal of the church's social influence, turned out to be a dismal failure.

Under the impact of rising socialist-oriented worker movements in France, Holland, Belgium, Germany, and Italy, the imperative to provide more effective competition through the encouragement of authentic confessional trade unions grew ever stronger. The belated development in Spain of a mass socialist labor movement and the failure of anarcho-syndicalism to emerge as a potent force in Barcelona until World War I tended to reduce the sense of urgency among the clergy and the wealthy to support a Catholic workers' movement similar to those then developing in other European countries.

Differences among Catholics on how to deal with the social question complicated their response. Differing attitudes toward the liberal state underlay the political rivalries between Carlists, integrists, and unionists.

Varying views on how to achieve rechristianization inevitably led to the formulation of distinctive strategies for promoting the Christian alternative in dealing with social problems and in pastoral methodologies. Carlists and integrists vehemently insisted upon the strict confessionality of Catholic social works; unionists, more prone to accommodation with the liberal world, progressively came to accept the idea of a confessional collaboration.

Social policy, nonetheless, remained firmly in the hands of ultraconservatives. For all practical purposes, the church hierarchy turned over direction of social action and labor programs to Comillas and the Jesuits, who shared his outlook and maintained close ties with Catholic industrialists and financiers. This assured that the Worker Circles movement would remain wedded to a philosophy that was being increasingly discarded by Catholics in other countries. Even such outstanding protagonists of corporativist paternalism in France as de Mun, Leon Harmel, and la Tour du Pin had conceded the inefficacy of mixed "vertical" labor organization and supported the formation of "pure." worker unions.

Occasional Worker Circles such as those in Burgos, Pamplona, and Valladolid began gradually to resemble workers' organizations. But the conversions that took place then from circles to *uniones profesionales* and *sindicatos* were mostly cosmetic in nature. In place of "mixed" organizations the concept of "parallel" unions was introduced. But under the influence of the Comillistas mixed unionism and employer domination continued to characterize most of these ostensibly restructured groups. This attempt at plastic surgery was prompted by the desire to secure representation on the various tripartite organs of the Institute of Social Reforms that had been formed in 1904. Organizations in which employers exercised direct or indirect dominance were disqualified from voting for the selection of IRS worker representatives.

In response to a query in 1913 on how to form a Catholic trade union, the editors of *La Paz Social,* by that time under the control of Comillas's supporters, used words that varied little in substance from the views of advocates of mixed unionism: "It would be advisable to form a mixed union with the consent of the majority of employers. But inasmuch as Spanish social legislation denies the right of occupational representation to societies in which employers directly or indirectly exercise compulsion or influence on workers, it is preferable to form an employers union [*gremio*] and a workers union."[31] But even this meager concession did not go very far, and the clerical "counselor" remained in place as did employer "protector" members.

Other Catholic Workers' Groups

Concern over mounting social conflict and increasing worker radicalization finally persuaded the church hierarchy to take a greater role in social affairs. A major effort was undertaken in 1908 with the establishment in Barcelona of Popular Social Action (Acción Social Popular—ASP). Largely the brainchild of Jesuit father Gabriel Palau, it represented an effort to replicate in Spain the German Volksverein (People's Union) that had been instrumental in mobilizing popular support for the German Catholic Center party. Winston characterizes it as "the most serious and sustained effort prior to the Civil War to propagate social Catholicism among the Catalan—and also Spanish—urban working classes," and José Andrés Gallego terms it "the great propagandistic entity of Spanish social Catholicism."[32]

Modeled to serve as an umbrella body to promote and direct a variety of social programs and projects, ASP was backed by the entire church establishment, including Comillas and the bishop of Barcelona. Through its outpouring of publications and ambitious propaganda activities, it amassed a national following. Starting out with 3,000 member-associates, it had grown to 27,352 seven years later at the time of its dissolution. A large part of this membership was non-Catalan. Only following the traumatic experience of the Tragic Week did it undertake in earnest the organization of confessional unions.

Some Catholic activists saw the need for a clear demarcation between ASP, with its conservative upper-class identification, and the promotion of authentic autonomous working-class *uniones profesionales* (UP), if efforts in this field were to prosper. But this was too much to expect. The unions were completely under the thumb of the ASP labor office, which was directed by Palau and his collaborators. According to Winston, "The UP's autonomy was further eroded by the unions' ultra-clericalism and obsessive concern with religious at the expense of syndical aims." A clear distinction had been intended between the Worker Circles, "formed by good people who want to protect the workers," and labor organizations, "founded by the workers to protect themselves." Nonetheless, despite the lip service given the idea of forming truly autonomous worker unions, "the emergence of pure Catholic syndicalism in Catalonia represented a continuation not a break with past social Catholic practices. . . . It was futile to hope that these decrepit institutions, utterly vitiated by paternalism and employer intervention, could provide the basis for authentic worker organizations . . . the UPs came no nearer to being genuine worker creations than were the Catholic Centers . . . social Catholics continued to rely on the owners' good will not on the workers' own efforts."[33]

A modest success was registered in the formation of the Unión Profesional de Dependientes y Empleados de Comercio, composed of white-collar workers and salesclerks. An insignificant number of blue-collar workers were enrolled in other UPs, many of which were merely paper organizations. The Marquis de Comillas not only funded the UPs, but he supplied many of their members. When in 1918 the Dependientes Union membership had shrunk to two hundred, more than an additional one thousand employees of three firms owned by Comillas were added. Reliable membership figures cannot be ascertained for most years of the UPs' existence. Fairly trustworthy estimates, however, place total UP membership in 1916, on the eve of the ASP's breakup, at approximately six to seven thousand, including some four to five thousand manual workers who at best represented 2 percent of Barcelona's blue-collar work force.

An important factor in the failure of the Catholic union effort was its inability to receive the support of employers. Because UP workers were regarded as "yellows" and strikebreakers, their employment was countered by both Cenetistas and independent unionists "by boycotts, strikes, and a general upsurge of industrial conflict."[34]

It is not clear why the church decided to abandon the ASP effort in 1916. A conflict between Comillas and Palau over which of them would exercise control over the Catholic labor effort in Barcelona (Comillas prevailed) was undoubtedly a factor.[35] Palau's difficult personality was another. His removal and the dismantling of the ASP coincided with the decision of the church hierarchy, urged on by Papal Nuncio Francesco Ragonesi, who shared the ultraconservative social views of Comillas and the Jesuits, to place severe restrictions on the clerics who were then leading figures in the effort to promote "pure" Catholic trade unionism. But beyond these and other internal difficulties, there was precious little to show for so great an outlay in church money and manpower. It was perhaps best summed up in the observation of the director of the Spanish pontifical college of Rome, who wrote that the ASP expired from "consumption."

The outcome in Madrid was even worse. The most rigidly conservative wing of social Catholicism had envisaged Madrid as a showplace for employer-clerical paternalism. A cornucopia of equipment and funds was lavished on the Worker Circles; libraries, gymnasiums, night schools, savings banks, and mutual benefit societies with medical and pharmaceutical services were established. Nowhere else in Spain did Worker Circles possess more well-endowed and efficiently operated welfare and recreational programs. Yet the impact of this bountiful outlay was indiscernible.

The first confessional union to be founded in Madrid in 1907 consisted of a small band of typographers. Further expansion proved difficult. After ten years, when the UGT had emerged as the incontestable hegemonic force among proletarian Madrileños, all the Catholic unions could show for their extravagant efforts was a possible two thousand adherents to unions grouped in the Catholic Workers Center. At least some of them probably also were members of UGT unions.[36]

Catholic *sindicatos* also were formed in the early twentieth century in Santander, Bilbao, Oviedo, Orense, Zaragossa, and numerous other localities. Those of Zaragossa were particularly noteworthy; in 1913 Catholic unions with a membership of a thousand represented about a third of all organized workers there. Most, however, appear to have been parallel rather than horizontal labor organizations. The National Secretariat of Labor Unions, one of Father Palau's ASP creations, noted that "worker unions are extremely few in number. There are those that do not appear to be mixed, but actually are so. And there are those that seem to be *sindicatos* but are semimixed, and others semiworkers or rather institutions of some other type."[37]

Reliable figures for membership in those years of confessional membership have not been established. In 1913 Severino Aznar estimated that the then existing 226 Catholic unions throughout the country, not including those in agriculture, had a membership of at least twenty thousand and possibly as high as one hundred thousand.[38]

Burgos, where one of the country's thriving Catholic Worker Circles was founded in 1883, was among the first to form nearly authentic labor organizations, of which it had eighteen by 1920. Probably the closest to authentic trade unions were established in Valencia. A federation of five local unions was formed that was quartered in the House of Workers of St. Vincent Ferrer, a sort of Catholic *casa del pueblo*. Uncharacteristically, it maintained friendly relations with the local UGT with which it cooperated in labor disputes and strike actions. Valencia's greater sophistication, in spite of the vociferous objections of local conservative Catholics, was attributable to the tolerance and support of the bishop of Valencia Diocese, José María Guisasola, who later was named cardinal primate.

The quintessentially Castilian city of Valladolid also became an important hub of Christian labor organization. The Jesuit father Sisinio Nevares took the lead in 1912 in converting the well-established Worker Circles into labor unions. An imposing structure, the Casa Social Católica, paid for by local wealthy aristocrats, was inaugurated in 1915 to direct the flourishing organized provincial rural movement (two years earlier Nevares had established the Valladolid Federation of Agrarian Unions) and the city's confessional worker organizations. Various labor organizations, ostensibly composed only of workers, had been constituted in 1913. By far the most important among them was the Railroad Workers Union of the Compañía del Norte and other lines that had banded together to form a national federation with headquarters in the Casa Social Católica. The federation claimed a membership of six thousand affiliated with eighteen branches. Comillas, who owned Compañía del Norte, had financed and supported it with the express purpose of opposing the increasingly potent UGT Railroad Workers Federation (Unión Ferroviaria).[39] The Compañía del Norte was one of the leading exponents in Spain of welfare paternalism. The Catholic union invariably went out of its way to oppose strikes called by its UGT counterpart. Its president, Agustin Ruiz, a cousin of Nevares, was awarded the Cross of Isabella the Catholic, at the company's urging, for the union's role in helping break the 1917 general strike.

Church-sponsored popular social action in the Basque provinces began with the formation in 1887 of the Patronatos Obreros de San Vicente de Paul (Worker Patronages of St. Vincent de Paul), soon followed by the formation of similar bodies elsewhere in Vizcaya province. Their principal functions, as with Worker Circles, were apostolic and welfaristic, and their activities were financed by contributions from employers.

The formation in 1905 of the *uniones profesionales* in Bilbao came as an outgrowth of the work conducted by the St. Vincent de Paul Patronage and consisted of small numbers of workers employed in various trades and crafts.[40] In 1909 the Bilbao Federation of Uniones Profesionales possessed 709 members. The following year, however, largely because of the expanding influence of the UGT, the UPs began to decline and were finally dissolved in 1916.

The UGT's general strike in 1910 and the development of Basque political nationalism led in 1911 to the formation of the Basque Workers Solidarity (SOV). Based initially in Vizcaya province, the SOV founded additional branches in the Basque provinces of Guipúzcoa and Alava over the next few years. Basque nationalists viewed the UGT as a union for "Maketas," a pejorative expression for non-Basque workers who predominated in local industry. The SOV, therefore, was intended to serve as the guardian of the interests of ethnically indigenous workers, who were the only ones eligible for membership. Its basic aims were threefold: laborism, nationalism, and Catholicism. But because it was more interested in combating socialist influence than in defending workers against employer injustices, these concepts during the initial decades of its existence remained diffuse and unarticulated.

The Basque Workers Solidarity was distinctive in that it was founded by workers, and because it was not organically linked to church institutions, clerical counselors were not able to exercise as suffocating an influence as they did elsewhere. Until 1929 its primary role consisted of welfare, mutual benefit, and cooperative activities rather than the usual heavy emphasis on exercises in piety. Primarily a friendly society with a nationalist orientation, it had little interest in collective bargaining. In conformity with Catholic doctrine, strikes were generally frowned upon, and "the mere fact of a strike having been called by the socialists was sufficient reason to oppose it." The SOV's evolution after 1929 from an essentially mutual assistance society with a nationalist outlook into a trade union has been compared with that of the Barcelona white-collar union, CADCI.[41]

Membership categories included not only the customary "protectors" but "cooperators" as well, worker members who had become self-employed, or shopowners, nationalist sympathizers, and the like. It is not known to what extent employers were also included. Regular members were divided into journeymen and apprentices. Self-employed artisans were also eligible for membership. Available data suggest a membership at inception of 178, rising to a thousand by 1914 and to more than two thousand in 1919. Membership was mostly recruited from small shops, self-employed workers, artisans, and white-collar employees, and because the SOV had a special relationship with employers, it did not foster development of a class or trade union consciousness. The only large industrial enterprise in which it gained majority support was at the Eskalduna shipyard, whose proprietors were fervent Basque nationalists.

Why was Catholic unionism (and Christian Democracy as well) successful in the Basque region at a time when it was encountering very little success elsewhere? The noted French Catholic labor intellectual Paul Vignaux has observed that "the preferred territories of Christian Democracy are regions with a strong autonomist tendency: Belgian Flanders, Alsace, the Basque provinces of Spain."[42] In addition, Basque clergymen enjoyed a popular mass prestige to an extent unknown elsewhere in Spain. Thus clerical support and the strong sense of communal solidarity served to vitiate the opprobrium attached to Catholic labor organizations in other parts of the country. And finally, by the 1930s the SOV took on the attributes of an authentic trade union.

The extraordinary sterility of the church's effort despite the expenditure of considerable funds and energies to stem the advance of secularist influences among wage earners and to win recruits to labor confessionalism led a handful of clergymen, influenced by the examples set by Belgian, German, and French social Christians, increasingly to question the validity of the hierarchy's approach and to advocate the formation of horizontal labor organizations. In lieu of charity and welfare, the emphasis, they argued, had to be shifted to the struggle for social justice.

Outstanding among such clerical dissidents were the Dominican priest Pedro Gerard and the Canon Maximiliano Arboleya. Of mixed Spanish-Belgian parentage, Gerard became a fervent supporter of Catholic unionism after a stay in Belgium in 1910, when he came under the influence of the Dominican Father Dominique Rutten, a seminal figure in the development of that country's Christian labor movement. Upon his return to Spain the following year, he settled in Jerez de la Frontera, the principal center for sherry vineyards and wine cellars and also one of Andalusia's anarchist strongholds. Widespread radicalization among workers most probably accounts for the financial assistance given Gerard by Patricio Garvey, one of the area's most prominent landowners and sherry producers, despite a distaste for horizontal Catholic unions that most local employers shared. Following the Belgian example, a House of Labor (Casa de Trabajo) was inaugurated in 1912 that served as the headquarters for the first Catholic Resistance Societies, which extended membership to workers regardless of their religion. The seven unions that formed the Jerez Catholic Trade Union Federation included wine cellar workers, locksmiths, carpenters, barrel makers, white-collar employees (*dependientes*), rural laborers, and others. Shortly after its formation, it had enrolled more than a thousand workers. A strike of vineyard field workers ended in half a peseta increase in the daily wage.

Gerard's call for the formation of an authentically working-class confessional labor movement received widespread sympathy and support. Catholic activists attending the social week conference of 1912 in Pamplona were electrified, wildly applauding his impassioned, eloquent defense of the workers' interests and his bristling denunciation of those who sought to stand in the way of the workers' struggle for social and economic justice. Father Gerard introduced a new element into Spanish social Catholicism, less a doctrinal revision than a major tactical shift. He was noted for his oratory in which he stressed the need of workers for independence to organize without interference from Christian morality.

But Gerard's tactics were bound to raise the hackles of the Catholic establishment because they involved a repudiation of virtually all that the church had done in social action for many decades and of its close identification with employer interests. His strong advocacy of the strike weapon and aggressive collective bargaining, regarded by his opponents as an espousal of the class struggle, incensed Catholic conservatives, who launched a bitter campaign to denigrate him.

To avoid exacerbating the hostility he had provoked in conservative quarters, Gerard left for Belgium to study the work and concepts of Father Rutten. Upon his return to Spain, he plunged with redoubled vigor into addressing worker audiences throughout the country. Organizations inspired by his ideas took the name of Sindicatos Libres, inspired by their Belgian counterparts and intended to connote their independence from employers and leftists.

The Libres Union recruited more than five thousand followers by 1913 and shifted its main base of operations from Jerez to Madrid. The Dominican Father José Domingo Gafo, an Asturian of modest origin who in 1914 had become the driving force behind the formation in Madrid of a Catholic Free Workers Union Center, worked closely with Gerard. The Madrid center's principal affiliate was the Catholic railroad workers union. Thus two rival groups in Madrid bitterly competed for the small available confessional clientele.

Once Gerard's group was committed to the development of still another national Catholic labor center, a clash with their conservative rivals became unavoidable, especially in areas such as Madrid, where Comillas and the Jesuits possessed some influence. Palau and his ASP collaborators joined in denouncing the Libres. Gerardistas were labeled "white anarchists"

(Dominicans wore white habits), and they countered with epithets about "yellow" company unionists. It was a rivalry that pitted one religious order against the other, Dominicans and Augustinians in support of the heterodox horizontalists and Jesuits on the side of the verticals.

The outcome was never in doubt. Not only did Comillas and his Jesuit allies receive the support of most of the Catholic establishment, but the scales were tipped in their favor by the vigorous assistance of Monsignor Ragonesi, the papal nuncio. The Vatican in those days had great influence over decision making in the Spanish hierarchy. In May 1916 a decision was made to put an end to the festering internecine squabbling within Catholic social action by a general crackdown on labor reformers. Father Gerard was ordered to cease his labor activities and was restricted to Jerez. Even the moderate Father Palau was dismissed and the Barcelona ASP virtually dismantled.[43]

But the absence of Gerard did little to stem the progress of *sindicalismo libre,* which was then beginning to attain modestly sizable proportions. Father Gafo replaced Gerard, and a national conference was called in Pamplona during late 1916, which was attended by representatives from twenty unions that claimed a combined following of ten thousand and formed the National Federation of Catholic Free Unions. Its main areas of influence included Madrid, Bilbao, Pamplona, Palencia, Zaragossa, and Jerez. When Father Gerard recovered his freedom in 1918 and was named general secretary of the federation, there were more than fifty affiliated unions. Unable to settle their differences with the Libres despite numerous attempts, the Comillistas in 1919 sponsored the formation of a rival national center, the National Confederation of Catholic Unions. Neither of the two confederations ever gained significant support among workers with the possible exception of the Barcelona Libres.

Maximiliano Arboleya agreed with Gerard and Gafo on the need to establish autonomous trade unions devoted primarily to the improvement of wages and working conditions.[44] But he had a better intellectual grasp of the problems involved and was less abrasive in dealing with his conservative opponents. He was of Asturian origin and became canon of the Cathedral of Oviedo in 1896, the year following his ordination. His interest in labor developed from years of study in Rome, where he first learned of the new Catholic social doctrines enunciated by Pope Leo XIII. Nonetheless, until 1914 he devoted himself primarily to writing on social problems, drafting numerous review articles, editing the leading Asturian newspaper, *El Carbayon,* and producing a steady stream of books.

A travel grant from the Junta de Ampliación de Estudios in 1913 to study social and labor programs in Italy and Belgium proved to be a turning point. Upon his return to Oviedo he took a more active part. Catholic social action in the region had till then generally followed the usual pattern, and Worker Circles were first established in various parts of the region following *Rerum Novarum*. Arboleya's initial effort in 1903 to infuse the Oviedo circle with an approach more favorable to labor was rebuffed, and his desire to institute social reforms was opposed by employers. After the 1906 strike that had been called by Llaneza's socialist miners union was crushed, the owners of the large Mieres factory decided to sponsor and finance the formation of the Catholic Syndicate (*agremiación*) under a Jesuit priest. Structured along the lines of a Catholic Worker Circle, it enrolled thirteen hundred worker members. By 1912, however, with the socialist UGT in the ascendancy, it declined to the status of an employer prop. Meanwhile, in industrial Gijón, then the center of Asturian worker militancy, a Catholic Social Center was established by Jesuits that grouped a handful of Catholic unions with pitifully little influence or membership.

The influence of Comillas, who owned one of the region's largest coal mines, Hullera Española, proved to be a major stumbling block. Despite Arboleya's urgings, the mine executives (the managing director was a nephew of Comillas) sought to stem the socialist tide through the formation of a company-controlled Catholic Mine Workers Association.

Under Arboleya's guidance, the Independent Union Federation was founded in Oviedo in 1914. Housed in a Catholic *casa del pueblo,* it incorporated his ideas of "pure" confessional unionism. The five affiliated unions included 661 commercial employees, railroad workers, arsenal employees, and white-collar workers, a respectable membership for a labor organization in a nonindustrial city. The new venture, however, soon ran into difficulties, emanating more from fellow Catholics than from socialist rivalry.

Employers had no more use for authentic Catholic trade unions than they did for the others. When the Agremiación of the Mieres factory sought to join the Oviedo federation, the plant executives made sure that it did not do so. And when Arboleya pleaded with employers of other enterprises to consider the moderate demands of the Catholic unions, they ignored his advice and ultimately were forced to accede to much tougher ones levied by the socialist unions.

Arboleya's followers thus found themselves in an impossible situation.

If they made more aggressive demands, Catholic conservatives would accuse them of rabble-rousing and bring pressure on the church to order them to cease their incitements. And if they failed to do so, they would lose to the socialists what credibility they possessed.

By 1916 the Catholic Mine Workers Association was at the point of extinction as workers increasingly shifted loyalties to the socialist SMA. Desperate, association leaders sought Arboleya's assistance in converting their organization into an authentic trade union and affiliated with the Oviedo Independent Union Federation. Arboleya consented and spoke at large, well-attended mass meetings. Membership recruitment rose as the organization gained popularity.

Comillas then complained bitterly to Cardinal Primate Guisasola about Arboleya's activities, and when the association submitted its demands to the company it was shabbily treated, suggesting that Comillas and his mine executives regarded Arboleya and his unsettling ideas to be as great if not a greater evil than the detested socialists. In 1917 during an industrywide strike a vote conducted among the miners by the Institute of Social Reforms ended in defeat for the confessionals and as a decisive triumph for the socialists. Dispirited, the Catholic Association a year later severed ties with Arboleya and his Oviedo federation and the Jesuits presided over the formation of the successor Spanish Catholic Mine Workers Union, which served as a main nucleus for the formation of a Comillista national federation headquartered in the Casa Social of Valladolid.

Disheartened, Arboleya withdrew from any further active participation. His departure and the unabating hostility of Catholic conservatives and employers led to a progressive decline of the Oviedo federation. The surviving remnants eventually affiliated with the Gerardista free unions.

The rebuke suffered by Arboleya and others was part of a larger failed effort to induce Spanish Catholicism to take a fresh approach to social problems. It was their misfortune, however, that the attempt to modernize social policies took place during the pontificate of Pius X, when Vatican policy once again reverted to a hard-line integrist confessionalism. It was also calamitous for the comparatively enlightened José María Guisasola, who as bishop of Valencia had promoted the development of authentic Catholic worker organizations. Upon his designation as primate, he sought out progressive moderates such as Severino Aznar, Arboleya, and Canon Francisco Moran to collaborate in reinvigorating social action programs. In private he spoke of the "obsolescence" of the concepts of the ultraconservatives. Endeavoring to regain control over social action policy making, he issued a pastoral letter, *Justicia y Caridad,* that approved the formation of authentic confessional unions. He also sought to constitute a labor secretariat with Arboleya as its executive director. but the combined opposition of church conservatives, the Jesuits, Comillas, employers, and their powerful ally, the papal nuncio, could not be overcome. Guisasola was forced to abandon his high hopes, and the direction of church social policy continued to remain largely in their hands.[45] When Comillas died in 1925, Arboleya wrote that "the Marquis of Comillas was the insuperable barrier upon which all our advances of Christian Democracy were pitifully dashed." During the 1930s, as the specter of civil war approached, Luigi Sturzo, the patriarch of Italian Christian Democracy, mournfully observed, "My homage at this moment goes to three Spaniards well known to European Christian Democrats: Professor Severino Aznar, the lawyer and former Minister Angel Ossorio y Gallardo, and the Canon Arboleya. They knew what hostility, suspicion, and struggle they had to sustain to accomplish their social program. But if they had been listened to, Spanish Catholics would not today be regarded by the workers as defenders of employers, even the unjust ones."[46]

Movements began to emerge within European Catholicism starting in the early twentieth century that combined an adherence to Catholic dogma with a radical critique of bourgeois society. Spain was not to experience such a breakthrough until the 1960s under the impulse of the Second Vatican Council and the efforts of Pope John XXIII.

Until the first years of this century the main emphasis had been given to the recruitment of urban wage earners, though in some areas, most notably Valencia, the principal base of Father Vicent's operations, the main result was rural circles, largely composed of tenant and small farmers. Elsewhere church social action in the countryside at the turn of the century mostly consisted of the formation and support of rural credit mutualities (*cajas rurales*), especially in Castile. Toward the end of the first decade, however, a change in emphasis became evident, largely as a result of the difficulties encountered in the organization of city proletarians, the successes registered by French Catholics and others in rural organization, and, above all, the opportunities created by the enactment of the 1906 Agrarian Syndical Law, which had been in gestation for several years.

Spanish Catholicism, like other national church movements, found its greatest popular following in rural areas that were strongholds of conservative traditionalism, most notably in Castile, Navarre, and the Basque country. Therefore, organization in the countryside began in a more propitious setting than that in the secularizing urban areas. Moreover, the failure of the underdeveloped, inefficient Spanish public administration to provide essential logistical, financial, and technical services to the many thousands of small and medium farmers enabled Catholic social action to play a meaningful role.

The passage of the 1906 law and subsequent modifications provided an impetus for the rapid expansion of confessional rural organization, which also benefited from the extensive support of the conservative government headed by Antonio Maura. From that time until his death in 1912, Father Vicent devoted most of his energies to organization in the countryside. Furthermore, because the agricultural unions (*sindicatos agrarios*) were constituted within a specific legal context and performed certain essential services, they were able to avoid the structural and functional ambiguities that characterized Catholic urban worker groups.

The greatest organizational success, with the exception of Valencia, occurred in the central and northern parts of the country, in Navarre, Palencia, Old Castile, León, Santander, Rioja, and Zaragossa. Under the impulse of a wealthy Castilian landowner, Antonio Monedero, who had been converted to social activism by Father Vicent, and the Jesuit Sisinio Nevares, an imposing number of farm unions were formed in Old Castile. They joined in 1912 to constitute the influential Catholic Agrarian Confederation of Old Castile and León. This federation was established in Valencia that year and renamed in 1917 the National Catholic Agrarian Confederation (CNCA) with Monedero as its founding chairman.

The CNCA claimed five hundred affiliated rural unions in 1914 with a total membership of 150,000. By 1920 the number of local affiliates had risen to five thousand, with some 600,000 adherents. In his study of the CNCA, Juan José Castillo alleges that these figures grossly exaggerate the confederation's real strength. He cites, for example, a report issued in 1917 by the government's General Directory of Agriculture, Mines, and Forests, indicating that all agricultural associations, Catholic and non-Catholic, possessed a combined membership of 142,506 whereas the CNCA alone was then claiming 250,000 followers. Castillo admits to the CNCA's growth and development during the years 1915 to 1920 but finds its membership figures fallacious.[47]

The success of Catholic rural organizations in the Meseta and adjoining areas was assured by the continued hold of traditional values and beliefs on the peasantry of these regions and the acute distress experienced by impoverished small landowners who predominated in much of the zone.[48]

The agrarian unions, whose activities were permeated with pious exercises and were directed by clerics, also often provided vital services such as relatively low-interest loans through rural savings and loan mutuals (*cajas rurales*), seed and fertilizer services, warehousing, and marketing and machinery cooperatives. The Bank of Leo XIII was created in Madrid with funds provided by the Marquis of Comillas to assist the *cajas rurales*. Referring to them as unions (*sindicatos*) was a misnomer. As one contemporary commentator observed, "What in Spain are called unions are referred to in Germany, Italy, and other countries as rural banks, agricultural cooperatives, guilds, and the like."[49]

Structurally they were mixed unions. According to the norms set by the Institute of Social Reforms, mixed unions in industry and services were unacceptable. The 1906 law, however, established no such criteria, allowing societies of farmers, tenants, big landowners, and farm laborers to be formed functionally, horizontally or vertically. Big landowners and clerics almost always directed the *sindicatos*. Benavides Gómez observes, "They were generally mixed unions since their by-laws excluded neither employers nor workers. In practice, however, they were employer unions for two reasons: in many regions almost all the cultivators to a greater or lesser degree were landowners or tenant farmers, but very few of them subsisted exclusively from day labor. Moreover, the services provided by the unions could hardly be used by those who were not farmers."[50] Though they were not devoted to the defense of wage earners, they did prevent the proletarianization of many farmers and tenants.[51] Josefina Cuesta Bustillo sums up the effects of agrarian Catholicism: it "was an effort in the development of small landholdings without destroying the foundation of established large landholdings through a reform of technique and not of the socioeconomic tenets of ownership."[52]

7

LABOR'S COMING OF AGE, 1915–1923

World War I

The downfall of the czarist regime in February 1917 persuaded Lenin that the great conflict was destined to act as "a mighty accelerator of events." Presumably it was a prediction mainly with his native Russia and the belligerent countries of western Europe in mind. Its repercussions, however, were to cut a much wider swath. Though "enclosed in a cellaphonous neutrality," Iberia was to figure prominently among those engulfed by the tidal wave of postwar social and political upheaval.

World War I brought to the fore a process of institutional deterioration that had been under way in Spain for some time. The shock waves emanating from the debacle of 1898 had generated much anguished soul-searching and talk of renovation. In the end, however, its principal effect was to strip away any lingering pretensions that Spain harbored concerning its status as a leading colonial power. To be sure, the post-1898 years gave rise to a period of sharp economic and political buffeting and to the first manifestations of generalized industrial strife. In retrospect, however, the institutional fabric of the Restoration government experienced a rude battering but not to the point of seriously imperiling its continued viability. The consequences of the world war were to prove much more devastating. After successfully surmounting the trauma of defeat in 1898, the Canovist constitutional monarchy entered a period of gradual enfeeblement so that the coming of the war precipitated a state of ineffectuality, somewhat akin to an incapacitated person whose bodily resistance had become so reduced as to make him vulnerable to infection.

Initially the war cut off traditional export markets and raw material imports for certain sectors of the economy. Financial and banking institutions were hurt, and panic spread among Catalonian textile manufacturers, who, fearing the worst, laid off large numbers of employees and placed the rest on short workweeks. Throughout the country factories and mines closed down or went on reduced production schedules, causing widespread layoffs and diminished take-home pay. Steep rises in the prices of basic necessities created increased hardships for wage earners.

By 1915 a profusion of orders from the belligerent nations, mostly France, England, and Italy, which had been forced to produce war matériel, fueled an unprecedented economic boom. Latin American countries that had also suffered from a loss of regular supply sources such as English textiles also turned to Spain. Exports of cotton, wool, and jute products, metal fabrication, leather and shoes, paper products, machinery, chemicals, and foods soared. The astronomical prices they commanded caused domestic shortages of basic commodities. The loss of normal supply channels also led to the establishment of a number of import-substitution industries. La Maquinista y Terrestre, the big metalworking firm in the Barcelona area, became the main domestic supplier of railway locomotives.[1]

A crazy quilt of economic winners and losers was created; some sectors benefited hugely while others, such as the export of oranges on which much of Valencian agriculture depended, as well as other agricultural products and some mineral ores, suffered because of inadequate transport facilities. Among the large numbers of Spaniards who emigrated to southern France to seek employment in those years were more than 125,000 Valencians.

In prewar Vizcaya, 80 percent of the iron ore had been exported, a quarter of it to Germany. As a result of the German submarine blockade and the gradual exhaustion of prime iron ore deposits, much of the work force had to seek employment elsewhere. But though the war led to a decline in iron mining, it generated a corresponding increase in the metalworking industries and shipbuilding. "The war," observed Salvador de Madariaga, "carried much gold and much poison along with the vivifying ferments of a new life."[2]

The great beneficiaries of the war were Asturian coal mine owners, whose profits trebled with the loss of British coal (40 percent of domestic coal needs previously came from imports), and the merchant marine and shipbuilding industries, which underwent a huge increase in tonnage production to replace Spanish ships sunk by German submarines and to fill foreign orders. Between 1915 and 1918 seven new shipyards were

Table 7.1.   The Spanish Economic Structure, 1910 and 1920 (in percent)

Year	Agriculture	Industry	Services
1910	66	15.82	18.80
1920	57	21.94	20.81

Source: Manuel Tuñon de Lara, *El movimiento obrero en la historia de España, 1900–1923*, 3 vols. (Barcelona: Laia, 1972), 2:294.

constructed in the Bilbao estuary and the port of Pasajes. Iron mining revived once the metal industries went into full production. The high cost of coal provided a strong impetus to expand hydroelectric power installations. Large landowners who raised olives, sugar beets, and grains also benefited, as did Catalonian textile manufacturing, especially woolens, because the German army had occupied northeast France, where many of that country's textile mills were located. Orders from France by March 1915 totaled 350 million pesetas.[3]

Spanish industrial production underwent substantial growth, outstripping agriculture as the leading element in the economy. But it was expansion geared to war. Neutrality created opportunities especially in speculative ventures so that the profit rate was proportionally far above the increase in industrial output. Industrial growth tended as before to be almost exclusively confined to Catalonia and Vizcaya, with Madrid emerging as an ever more important banking center and source for capital financing.

Rural folk flocked to the cities by the thousands, particularly to Barcelona and Bilbao, where many of the war orders were being produced.[4] The number of gainfully employed nationwide rose from 1,133,839 in 1914 to 1,384,947 in 1920, a fifth of them women. The public exchequer also handsomely benefited, converting a prewar deficit of 100–200 million pesetas into a 200–500 million surplus.

Substantial alterations in the country's economic structure also took place. During the decade from 1910 to 1920 the number engaged in agricultural work declined by 9 percent while those in industry increased by 6 percent and in services by 2 percent (see table 7.1). But despite the boom in industrialization, Spain remained economically backward. A modest structural change had taken place with clothing manufacture decreasing proportional to metalworking and chemicals. For the distribution of the industrial labor force see table 7.2.

In a society with great economic and social disparities the war made

Table 7.2.   Industrial Labor Force, 1910 and 1920

Industry	1910	1920
Building construction	283,422	307,899
Clothing manufacturing	276,743	
Textiles	133,959	243,651[a]
Food products	112,493	
Mines, quarries, salt pits	99,158	172,703

Source: Manuel Tuñon de Lara, *La España del siglo XX* (1966; rpt. Barcelona: Laia, 1981), p. 84.

[a] 134,00 women.

the rich richer and created greater privation for many of the less fortunate. The corrupting effect of easy enrichment and its ostentatious display added to the general dissatisfaction. Wage earners in Barcelona, Madrid, and Bilbao were comparatively better off than the rest of the working population, partaking to some extent of the income redistribution that favored the big urban centers and generally worsened the plight of those in small towns and rural areas.

Social discontent was also fueled by growing shortages of basic commodities and an inflationary cycle that went out of control. Shortages appeared everywhere in the wake of speculative hoarding, uncontrolled exports, and an inefficient, inadequate railway system that was totally unable to handle the movement of export goods and at the same time maintain normal supply channels.[5] Table 7.3 indicates that, with 1913 prices and wages at an index of 100, prices had risen by 1916 to 128.8 whereas wages were only at 107.8, and by 1918, with prices at 218.2 and wages at 125.6, the disparity had reached explosive proportions.

Despite innumerable attempts to contain the inflationary spiral and assure the availability of necessities, the government was powerless to stem the excessive exports of foodstuffs and the steady erosion of purchasing power. Various control systems were legislated, surveillance commissions formed, and rationing quotas established, but all ended in failure because of the inability of weak governments to control speculation, prevent illegal transactions, and resist the pressures of powerful interest groups.

Rural areas were hard hit, forcing many peasants to emigrate. Part of the rural exodus that had been intensified by the spread of phylloxera in wine-growing districts as well as by the grains crisis was absorbed by the industrial boom in Catalonia and the Basque country, increase in coal

Table 7.3.   Index of Wages, Prices, and Profits, 1913–1921

Years	Prices	Wages	Profits
1913	100.0	100.0	100.0
1914	99.7	98.2	86.8
1915	109.2	108.7	116.7
1916	128.8	107.8	153.5
1917	150.1	110.6	187.8
1918	218.2	125.6	223.4
1919	222.7	146.7	206.7
1920	227.6	179.3	214.0
1921	183.4	207.1	189.6

Source: José Luis García Delgado, José Sánchez Jiménez, and Manuel Tuñon de Lara, *Historia de España, la población, la economía, la sociedad (1898–1931)* (Madrid: Espasa-Calpe, 1984), p. 52. Sources for each category are as follows: wholesale price index, Barcelona Chamber of Commerce, *Report of the Gold Standard Commission*, p. 47; indices for male wage rates compiled by the Institute of Social Reforms, *Movimiento de los precios al por menor en España durante la guerra y la posguerra, 1914–1922* (Madrid, 1923), p. 36; profits calculated for eighty-five representative companies from seventeen industrial and service categories in Santiago Roldan and José Luis García Delgado, *La formación de la sociedad capitalista en España, 1914–1920* (Madrid: CECA, 1973), 1:102–24.

production in Asturias, and services and small industries in Madrid. During the ten-year period from 1910 to 1920 some 40,000 persons, mostly from nearby rural provinces, emigrated to the Basque country, 18,639 to Vizcaya province, and 7,954 to Guipúzcoa. Others sought employment in neighboring France; from January 1916 to March 1918 some 219,801 Spanish workers crossed the Pyrenees to work in the vineyards of the Midi. By war's end a semipermanent Spanish colony had been established that numbered more than a quarter of a million, and by the end of the 1920s had grown to 350,000.

Until 1919 most workers found themselves unable to catch up with the ever-rising cost of living. Even in Barcelona province, one of the higher wage areas, the General Labor Directorate (Dirección General de Trabajo) reported that real wages fell from an index of 100 in 1914 to 83 in 1920.[6] The Wool Textile Manufacturers Association found that the weekly requirements for a family with three children, which had been 59.79 pesetas in 1913, had soared to 95.54 pesetas by 1919, an increase of 60 percent. Wages in Sabadell, the principal center for wool textile production, rose by 36.2 percent between 1914 and 1918, representing a loss in purchasing power of 23.8 percent. A specialist on the Sabadell

wool manufacturing industry in this period has concluded that "the diminution of real wages was the principal element in the maintenance of
profit margins during the years of the first world war." "The inflation
produced by the first European war," observes economist H. Paris Eguilaz,
"whose greatest effect on prices was felt in 1920, led to a diminution in
wage earners' living standards of 21 percent compared to 1914."[7]

The two-party rotational structure managed for a time to engineer
election results, but the system of tightly controlled electoral constituencies began to show signs of wear and tear. In the early twentieth century
universal manhood suffrage was making its effects felt in an increasing
number of urban areas. Despite their inveterate divisiveness, the Republicans had reemerged as a popular force in the cities. Though still negligible, organized labor was becoming visible in episodic outbursts of
unrest and a gradually swelling union enrollment.

The Restoration's experiments at reform of the political system proved
short-lived. Antonio Maura's "revolution from above" had sought to accomplish renovation by weakening the grip of political bossism (*caciquismo*)
by fostering greater popular participation in local administration and
broadening the scope of social and labor legislation. His inadvertent
mishandling of the Tragic Week led to the demise of the reforms. José
Canalejas's valiant try at social and political renewal was of even briefer
duration, ending with his untimely death in 1912 at the hands of an
anarchist assassin.

As the world conflict neared, the absence of first-class political leadership
was all the more sorely felt because neither the Conservative nor Liberal
parties were true "parties" but merely congeries of political bosses and
notables whose cohesion owed more to loyalty to a forceful leader than
to shared political philosophies.[8] The Conservative political family was
reduced to a fractured, loosely knit assemblage consisting mainly of the
Datistas, led by Eduardo Dato, the Mauristas, and the Ciervistas, loyal
to ultraconservative Juan de la Cierva. In like fashion the Liberals divided
into Romanistas, linked with Count Romanones, an old-fashioned Andalusian wheeler-dealer, the Prietistas of García Prieto, and those grouped
around the progressive-minded Santiago Alba. To complicate matters
further, the Catalonian ruling elite abandoned the dynastic parties, which
catered primarily to landed and financial interests, and transferred its
loyalties to the Lliga Regionalista. The Chamber of Deputies became even
more unmanageable when, in addition to the Carlists, it included a sizable

minority of Republicans and the socialist parliamentary group that numbered six by 1918.

"By 1913," observes Javier Tussell, "from a political point of view any possible regeneration of the system from within had vanished. The rotational parties did not enunciate such an objective, limiting themselves to much more modest ones while their continuing fragmentation made Spanish politics much more complicated than it had been during the preceding decade. An added element was the increased complexity of political problems. By 1917 fragmentation had become so customary that King Alfonso XIII would consult with faction leaders of both parties before naming a new prime minister. Neither party was capable of forming stable, cohesive cabinets. Almost without exception, succeeding governments remained in office for brief periods, powerless to bring order to the country or to resolve its pressing problems. Governments unable to count on parliamentary majorities were increasingly forced to rule by decree."[9] Thirteen different governments with an average life span of five months held office between 1917 and 1923.

Spain adopted an official policy of neutrality, but most people had strong sympathies for one or the other belligerent, usually based on domestic concerns and ideological affinities. The more conservative sectors of society—large landowners, senior military officers, much of the business community, Carlists, and political conservatives—tended to identify with the Central Powers. Support for the Allies came from wage earners, the petty bourgeoisie, intellectuals, those in the liberal professions, some army officers, enlightened clergymen, bankers, and industrialists of Catalonia and Vizcaya. Most were followers of the Liberal party, Republicans, Catalanistas, and the left-wing parties. Some seven thousand young Catalans volunteered to serve in the French army. To many, the Allied cause was synonymous with liberty and democracy and the German side with authoritarianism. Many Catalonian businessmen who ostensibly sympathized with the Allies were, nonetheless, convinced that Germany would emerge victorious and therefore invested wartime profits in German bonds.

The issue of wartime loyalties so engrossed the Socialist party that for a time it neglected burning issues such as food shortages and the high cost of living. A minority sought acceptance of a policy of neutrality, but the party formally favored the Allies. At first, anarchists suffered confusion and disarray because of the strong pro-Allied position taken by such international luminaries as Peter Kropotkin, Charles Malato, Jean Grave, and numerous others. Distinguished Spanish anarchists including Federico Urales (father of Federica Montseny), Ricardo Mella, and Eleuterio Quintanilla followed suit. In the end, however, anarchists reaffirmed their traditional policy of "a plague on both your houses."

The governments of the belligerent countries conceded substantial advances to organized labor to assure trade union support for the war effort. Workers' real earnings, especially for those in the strategic economic sectors, kept up reasonably well with inflation. In Spain labor gained in strength, though on a much more modest scale than elsewhere, because of the chaotic economy and rising proletarian anger over a painfully diminished purchasing power.

By 1913 unionization in industry and transportation reached a prewar high of close to 20 percent. But the ensuing economic disorganization and the readjustments of the initial war years for a time led to a sharp downturn in union activities and enrollments. The UGT and CNT—the latter's legal status was restored in 1914—both lost around half their adherents, the UGT falling from a membership of 147,000 in 1913 to 76,000 in 1916 and the CNT shrinking to 15,000 by 1915. It would take three years for the UGT to rebuild its numbers.

The war's full impact was not felt before 1915, when commodities began to be scarce and the accelerating rise in the cost of living encroached on working-class well-being. Protest that year was generally limited to impromptu, spontaneous demonstrations of irate housewives and assaults on bakeries and granaries. By the following year, however, popular discontent increasingly took the form of labor disputes as workers sought cost-of-living wage adjustments. There were 91 officially reported strikes in 1915 affecting 30,591 workers with 383,885 workdays lost; by 1916 the number of shutdowns almost doubled, soaring to 178 involving 96,882 strikers and a loss of 2,415,305 workdays.

Trade union activity in Catalonia was modest during the years immediately preceding the war. The most notable event was the industrywide strike of 1913 in the textile industry, called by the Textile Workers Federation, La Constancia, which led to the issuance of a royal decree limiting the workweek for female textile operatives. Though the union suffered serious reverses, women workers showed a new interest in unionization.[10] Restoration of the CNT's legality coincided with the outbreak of the war and the accompanying economic difficulties suffered by many workers. The Regional Labor Confederation (CRT) was reorganized, but it functioned as simply a contact organization for the various worker societies, of importance mainly in Barcelona.[11] In October 1915 a CNT national committee was reconstituted in Barcelona, the first truly operative one since 1911. *Solidaridad Obrera,* the weekly paper of the Workers Solidarity Federation from 1907 to 1909, resumed publication in 1913 as the CRT's official organ and later served the same function for the national CNT.

At the outset, therefore, the new CRT and CNT merely consisted of committees with few formal links with the unions, serving occasionally to bring together anarchist-oriented as well as nonlibertarian-led local unions. There were no formal affiliations or regular dues payments. The CNT national committee functioned as a mail drop for anarchists in various parts of Spain. Regular membership books did not come into use until 1916. But such an amorphous atmosphere allowed men such as Angel Pestaña, Manuel Buenacasa, and many others to rise to positions of prominence within a short period.

Anarchism in Barcelona in the immediate prewar period tended to be ascetic and doctrinally dogmatic. All anarchists were vehemently anticlerical; many practiced vegetarianism and scorned the use of alcohol and tobacco. The movement encompassed a highly varied group including theoreticians and doctrinarians, those devoted to intellectual, literary pursuits or pretensions, the trade union leaders who furnished a link between anarchists and unions, those more strictly concerned with trade union work, the anarchist agitators and propagandists, and last but not least, the bohemian fringe. The theoretical innovations and discussions of the Parisian anarchists were avidly followed. Agitators and propagandists played a more important role in the CNT's 1915–16 reorganization than those who were more clearly linked with the unions.[12]

Most strikes in 1914–15 took place in towns outside Barcelona, especially in the textile mills, to gain wage increases and improvements previously granted to Barcelona workers. As inflation accelerated in 1916 a strike wave of unheard-of proportions erupted. In the demands for cost-of-living adjustments, large numbers of workers turned to the unions.

The formation of a cost-of-living committee in 1915 composed of the cooperatives and numerous unions, including the CNT, led to the sponsorship of a labor assembly held in Valencia on May 13, 1916, the first nationwide conference organized by the CNT since 1911. The assembly decided to launch a national campaign against the rising cost of living and to seek the UGT's cooperation. The UGT, which was then holding its twelfth congress in Madrid, decided to undertake a national work stoppage. Representatives from both organizations met in Zaragossa on July 16 and 17 and agreed to a formal alliance known as the Zaragossa Pact.

A large number of workers in urban areas and mining centers participated in the twenty-four-hour national work stoppage on December 18, 1916. Many shopkeepers shut down in sympathy. The strike was effective in Bilbao, Madrid, and various Catalonian factory towns but only partially successful in Barcelona, where, according to Pere Gabriel, "the more doctrinaire anarchists in the CNT did little to assure its success because of its pronounced 'laboristic' character and because CNT's influence, though decisive, was, nonetheless, of secondary importance."[13] This strike was the most successful national protest action yet undertaken by the labor movement.[14] The Romanones government responded by suspending constitutional guarantees and closing the Cortes.

The two labor organizations managed to surmount their traditional mutual hostility because a joint campaign was imperative if they were to have any effect on the cost of living. Furthermore, despite anarchist opposition, sentiment within Catalonian organized labor had always strongly favored trade union unity, and these sentiments were intensified by wartime economic developments. Salvador Seguí was the moving spirit behind the CNT's effort to engage in joint actions with the UGT, exemplifying his role in bridging the differences between the Catalan labor movement and the anarchists. (It should be kept in mind that UGT membership was then more than three times that of the CNT.)

A generational changing of the guard was also under way during this period. Beginning in 1917 the more doctrinaire anarchists such as José Negre and Tomás Herreros, who had been prominent in the formation of *Solidaridad Obrera* and in the CNT of 1910–11, began to be eclipsed by younger men, most of them recent arrivals to Barcelona: Pestaña, born in León province, came from Algeria, Evelio Boal from Valladolid, Buenacasa from Zaragossa, Francisco Jordan from Andalusia, Emili Mira from Alcoy, and Enric Valero from Madrid.

Foremost among them was Salvador Seguí, the embodiment of Catalonian trade unionism. Around him coalesced a group of authentic, practicing trade union leaders, men such as Camil Piñon, Simó Piera, Enric Valero, Joan Pey, and Josep Molins, as well as those who combined trade union backgrounds with theoretical, intellectual capabilities: Salvador Quemades, Josep Viadiu, Emili Mira, and Augusti Castella. Quemades, the group's leading intellectual, is reputed to have ghost written many of Seguí's speeches and articles. Mostly in their twenties and thirties, they were self-educated men "imbued with a great spirit of sacrifice, a devouring desire for culture, and an enormous idealism."[15] Frequent imprisonments gave them the opportunity to read and to teach fellow activists in jails.

Salvador Seguí stands out among the leaders of the Catalonian labor movement for his acute political insight, strong personality, and great moral force, which made him a formidable asset for anarcho-syndicalism. He was possibly the most important labor leader of this century. His father, a Catalan peasant, worked as a baker in Lérida. His family emigrated to Barcelona when he was a child, settling in the city's fifth district, a working-class tenement neighborhood where anarchists were influential. Like many working-class leaders of his generation, he left school at the age of twelve to supplement the family income, taking the trade of house painter. During his teens he first made contact with anarchists and soon became part of the libertarian bohemian milieu, joining a nietzchean group that flamboyantly called itself Hijos de Puta (Whore's Offsprings). He became increasingly drawn to labor activism and occupied a succession of posts in building construction unions. In 1911 he participated in the founding of the CNT, but it was not until World War I that he rose to prominence.

The origin of Seguí's nickname, "Noi del Sucre" (Sugar Boy), is unknown, but he had acquired it by the age of seventeen in 1904, and he used it as a byline for his articles in his union's publication, *El Pintor*. Victor Serge, who knew him as a fellow libertarian, has provided us with an engaging portrait:

A worker and usually dressed like a worker coming home from the job, cloth cap squashed down on his skull, shirt neck unbuttoned under his cheap tie; tall, strapping, round-headed, his features rough, his eyes big, shrewd and sly under heavy lids, of an ordinary degree of ugliness, but intensely charming to meet and with his whole self displaying an energy that was lithe and dogged, practical, shrewd, and without the slightest affectation. To the Spanish working-class movement he brought a new role: that of the superb organizer. He was no anarchist, but rather a libertarian quick to scoff at resolutions on "harmonious life under the sun of liberty," "the blossoming of the self," or "the future society"; he presented instead the immediate problems of wages, organization, rents, and revolutionary power.[16]

He must have been one of the great popular orators of his time. Manuel Buenacasa, CNT general secretary, who often found himself on the opposite side in policy debates, recounts, "Tall and corpulent, this man with his vigorous, powerful voice aroused and captivated the masses. . . . Seguí in his manner was a grandiloquent orator, especially in mass rallies."[17]

Seguí early became convinced that the nurturing and survival of a mass labor movement was paramount and that the independence of the CNT had to be safeguarded from those who sought to give it an exclusively anarchist character. Isidre Molas argues that "possibly the most notable trait of Salvador Seguí was the importance he accorded to the problems of strategic alliances and his refusal to accept the doctrinal leftist simplifications of the 'purists.' A constant throughout his life was an acknowledgment of the confederation's political role and its necessity, views that elicited eternal accusations from the 'radicals,' from the 'ultrarevolutionaries.' "[18] His "libertarian possibilism" was based on the convictions that the working class was unprepared to assume power and had to undergo a process of formation and that it was not antipolitical but antibourgeois political. To survive, the CNT had to contract alliances with intellectuals, farmers, and technicians, as well as with progressive bourgeois political sectors such as the left Republicans. The forging of such alliances had to accompany the building of a mass labor movement, a process that would prepare the working class for the direction of a future society.

Since his death a debate, much of it self-serving, has raged over what Seguí sought in rapprochement with progressive labor and political forces. He was constantly denounced by anarchists as an ideological backslider. Some have maintained that his actions were primarily defensive tactical moves in response to the severe repression to which the CNT was subjected. Others, in contrast, claim that he became politicized and allege that he was a party to plans being readied by Francisco Layret, Lluis Companys, and others to form a labor party and engage the CNT rank and file in political participation and that only the untimely deaths of Layret and Seguí prevented its realization.[19]

The truth probably lies somewhere between these two contentions. Salvador Seguí, like Francisco Largo Caballero, was first and foremost a trade unionist concerned with the survival and consolidation of the anarcho-syndicalist labor movement.[20] Joaquín Maurín considered him the Spanish counterpart of a French revolutionary syndicalist or an American Wobbly (International Workers of the World). Had he not died, Seguí might have abandoned apoliticism as did many of his collaborators.

Second only to Seguí in stature and ability though of a markedly different temperament was Angel Pestaña, whose rise in wartime Barcelona anarchist and trade union circles was meteoric. Like so many who gained positions of leadership in the Spanish labor movement, Pestaña's suffering, loneliness, and hardship commenced when he was very young. He was born in a coal mining town of León province that adjoins Asturias. His mother, the victim of frequent beatings, abandoned the household with his sister when he was a small child. With little formal schooling, he began his working career as a child laborer (*pinche*) in the mines at the age of eleven, and three years later, upon the death of his father, an itinerant, illiterate railway tunnel construction laborer, was left to his own devices. Years of wandering and privation followed, the effects of which could be observed in his wistful, mournful demeanor, prompting Seguí to dub him "the knight of the woeful countenance."

Pere Foix, a leader of the CNT commercial workers union, described him as follows: "Angel Pestaña was a man of romantic countenance and essence. Within him there persisted an anarchist mysticism that was then in decline, displaced by modern syndicalism. He couldn't comprehend the Parisian anarchist bohemianism transplanted to Barcelona by those who had spent a good part of their youth in Paris. He was a methodical man, a puritan, not very talkative, taciturn, sometimes irascible. Had he lived in the times of the conquistadores he would have made a fine missionary. . . . When one recalls his solitary existence in Algiers, surrounded by books, with little to eat, one can say that he had the makings of an ascetic."[21]

Pestaña's first contact with anarchists and anarchist ideas came during his adolescent wanderings. While in Algiers he submitted his first contribution to *Tierra y Libertad*, the leading organ of doctrinal anarchism. Almost immediately following his arrival in Barcelona in 1914, he joined the anarchist and trade union movements, combining activism with the occupation of watchmaker, a trade he acquired in Algiers. He contributed regularly to *Tierra y Libertad*, and following his release from jail in 1916 he became an editor of *Solidaridad Obrera*, which was then being revived as the official organ of the Catalonian Regional Confederation. He also joined Seguí that year as a member of the CNT delegation that met with UGT representatives in Zaragossa to plan the national strike. With his designation as director of *Solidaridad Obrera* in 1918, he acquired an

important role in CNT policy making, and he was a leading figure at the
Sants conference that launched the concept of industrial unionism (*sindicatos unicos*).

For a time following his arrival in Barcelona, Pestaña sided with the
more doctrinaire labor anarchists, who deprecatingly labeled Seguí "the
Spanish Jouhaux." But he subsequently moved toward a centrist position,
between the more rigidly sectarian purists and the pragmatically inclined
trade union—oriented supporters of Seguí. By the war's end, as Pestaña
acquired more day-to-day leadership responsibilities, he moved ever closer
to Seguí's point of view.

The Failed 1917 Revolution

Similarities have been cited between the revolutionary environments of
Russia and Spain during 1917. Both nations had in common deteriorating,
archaic sociopolitical structures. Military disasters provided the catalyst
for the Russian revolution while the war's economic consequences led to
Iberia's breakdown.[22]

The unfettered enrichment of entrepreneurs and speculators and the
privations imposed on the masses were more than a sick country could
bear. Trapped by a narrowing national consensus, increasingly impotent
governments proved incapable of relieving the burdens placed on the
people. The unraveling of the always tenuous social fabric began in earnest
as social and economic groups faced off to protect their interests.

Those who had been deprived of their share of power then joined in
challenging an ostensibly moribund regime. As the Restoration government seemed increasingly vulnerable, Francesc Cambó, at the head of the
Catalonian industrial and commercial elite, took the lead in forging a
coalition that included middle-class supporters of Republicans and Reformists as well as the business community of the industrial north. In a
parallel action, wage earners rallied under the aegis of the UGT/PSOE
and the CNT. Both groups sought the elimination of the landed oligarchy's power monopoly by openly calling for the downfall of the Canovist
Restoration regime and the installation of a more modern parliamentary system. With Cambó as its main spokesman, the two groups merged
into a broad reform movement that included among its luminaries
Melquiades Alvarez, Alejandro Lerroux, and Pablo Iglesias. Anarcho-
syndicalists gave their tacit cooperation.

With its proposed plan to tax wartime profits facing parliamentary defeat, the beleaguered Romanones government suspended the Cortes in February and had to rule by decree. By spring, goaded by the relentless rise in the cost of living, wage earners began a series of strikes. An intensification of the German submarine blockade and the torpedoing of Spanish ships brought fresh humiliations to national pride and severe economic repercussions that accelerated further an already dangerously high rate of inflation. By April the Romanones government withdrew from office, to be replaced by still another Liberal cabinet headed by the all-too-familiar figure of García Prieto. One writer termed it "a cabinet of mediocrities and incompetents."[23]

Revolutionary appetites were whetted by the appearance of military opposition. Taking a leaf from the unions, officers below the rank of colonel banded together in Barcelona, where social and political tensions were greatest, and formed the Juntas de Defensa Militar within the army. This movement spread rapidly, first to military units stationed in Catalonia and then throughout the country. Colonel Benito Marquéz, commander of the Vergara regiment stationed in Sabadell—Raymond Carr calls him a political simpleton—emerged as its leading spokesman. Subordination was sparked by growing resentments over changes in the military promotion system and the low military salaries, which had not kept pace with the cost of living. The virus was infectious; postal employees and other civil servants formed *juntas de defensa,* and noncommissioned officers followed suit.

Urged on by Alfonso XIII, the government imprisoned Colonel Marquéz and others in early June and sought to dissolve the military juntas. The officer corps responded with redoubled defiance, giving an ultimatum that amounted to open rebellion. Incapable of mounting effective countermeasures, a humiliated government liberated the arrested officers and capitulated to junta demands. By June 9 the García Prieto government had been driven from office. The emboldened Junteros began to intrude in government policy making, exercising a veto power over the selection of prime ministers. As Carolyn Boyd sums up the situation, "The government and the Crown were too shaken by the prospect of political and social revolution to offer effective resistance. Civil supremacy was thus sacrificed to secure army loyalty."[24]

One observer noted a shift in public sentiment from "we are badly governed" to "this cannot continue much longer." A revolutionary overthrow of the government began to appear attractive. Cambó and the Catalonian bourgeoisie had until then sought to accomplish change mainly through legal processes (convocation of a constituent Cortes), but now that the regime's principal support—the military—could no longer be relied upon, "he was resolved to take advantage of it." "Considering the circumstances in which the country finds itself," declared Cambó, "the most conservative thing is to be a revolutionary."[25]

Catalonian members of parliament petitioned the conservative Dato government to reopen the Cortes. To underscore its refusal, the government suspended constitutional guarantees throughout the country. Cambó and his fellow Catalonian parliamentarians then openly defied the government by announcing the convening of an assembly of members of parliament to be held in Barcelona on July 19.

As the day of reckoning approached, the military emerged yet again as the political arbiter. But it was unclear just where the Juntas stood. The ambivalence of their political declarations and their regenerationist rhetoric led many in the opposition to hope that even if they did not give direct support, they might remain neutral in the coming confrontation. Cambó avidly courted Colonel Marquéz and others. Ortega y Gasset, Pablo Iglesias, and Julián Besteiro may have hoped for a Spanish version of the Russian revolution. Melquiades Alvarez went so far as to call it "the beginning of a national renovation." But as Raymond Carr concludes, "Once more Spain suffered one of its periodic spasms of the military delusion, the conviction that the army could effect salutary change in the face of the impotence and indifference of the political establishment."[26]

The CNT and UGT prepared for a second national work stoppage, this one of unlimited duration and with revolutionary intent. The UGT/PSOE had adopted a strategy of mobilizing the working class through a revolutionary general strike in conjunction with the CNT and arranging a formal alliance with the bourgeois Left, the Reformists and Republicans, for the eventual installation of a provisional bourgeois democratic government and the convening of a constituent Cortes. The CNT planned an armed uprising but was willing to acquiesce in the UGT's political strategy.[27]

As early as March 27 the UGT-CNT issued a joint manifesto denouncing the government for its continued failure to arrest the corrosive effects of inflation, called for fundamental political changes, and announced their intention to launch a general strike. The Romanones government responded defensively by imprisoning the leaders of both organizations and padlocking union offices, then shortly thereafter releasing those imprisoned and permitting the *casas de pueblos* and other labor centers to reopen.

Strife then arose within the labor coalition. CNT leaders chafed at what they perceived as excessive caution on the part of the UGT and demanded that an early date be set for the launching of the general strike. Great confusion and disarray prevailed when the UGT railroad union of Valencia prematurely called a strike. While en route to Barcelona to attend the Parliamentary Assembly organized by Cambó, Marcelino Domingo, a firebrand Catalonian Republican member of parliament, told the local railroad workers (Republicans dominated the Valencia labor movement) that the convening of the assembly was the signal for the general strike. They struck on July 18, followed the next day by a walkout by the employees of the Northern Railways Company as well as those in Aragon. Both groups were employees of the company owned by the Marquis of Comillas.

The Parliamentary Assembly, attended mainly by members from Catalonia and a scattering of Republicans and others from the rest of the country, dispersed peacefully at the order of the civil governor shortly after its opening. In sympathy, many of the city's shops shut down spontaneously, and large numbers of workers walked out.[28]

This gross act of indiscipline prompted PSOE/UGT leaders to arrange a quick return to work but not before two workers were killed and fourteen wounded in clashes with the Civil Guard. Workers in Valencia and Valladolid returned to their jobs, but the company, which bitterly resented the presence of a socialist-led union among its employees, insisted on the discharge of thirty-six activists it held responsible for the work stoppages, stripped striking workers of their seniority, and awarded nonstrikers with promotions.

Cambó, the socialists, and others have maintained that the Dato government secretly induced the company executives to assume an attitude that would launch the general strike prematurely, thus making it easier to assure its failure. This allegation is supported by Dato's close relations with Comillas, a fellow social Catholic, and by his membership on the board of directors of the Madrid-Zaragossa-Alicante Railway Company. An examination of what is presently known about the incident and the accompanying climate leads one to believe, however, that instead a confrontation occurred with neither side the victor. The owners of Compañía del Norte had long bitterly opposed recognizing the Unión Ferroviaria, and they probably saw the walkout by the Valencia employees as an excellent opportunity to weaken the union. The leaders of the Railroad Federation had walked into a trap of their own making. Daniel Anguiano, the federation's national secretary and one of the most important executives of the PSOE/UGT, went along with the decision of the federation's national board by a one-vote margin to call an industrywide strike on August 10 if the company did not reinstate the discharged workers as well as the seniority rights of union supporters. Anguiano and some of his colleagues were convinced that the government eventually would be obliged to arrange a mutually face-saving solution. Initially the government sought to persuade the company to negotiate a compromise with the union and then thought better of it and withdrew. Largo Caballero and Besteiro quickly realized that their railroad comrades had unwittingly walked into a trap. In his memoirs Largo bitterly calls Ramón Cordoncillo, Unión Ferroviaria general secretary, a "cretin."[29]

The socialists were placed in an intolerable situation. Preparations for the general strike were not complete, and coordination with the Reformists and Republicans had not been sufficiently developed. November had been considered a reasonable target date for the general strike. But the unyielding attitude of the Compañía del Norte and the decision by the railroad workers' federation, the UGT's most powerful and prestigious affiliate, to call an industrywide sympathy strike on August 10 left little alternative but to support such an action. Furthermore, the alliance during June and July with the Cenetistas twice came close to a breakdown, and they would not wait much longer. From his sickbed Pablo Iglesias urged the party and the UGT to cut their losses by limiting action to economic objectives and solidarity with the railroad federation.

Anguished debates finally ended in a unanimous decision by the leadership to proceed with a revolutionary but peaceful strike. Largo Caballero, Besteiro, and Andrés Saborit feared that the strike would end in disaster and needed to find a way to allow the workers to act spontaneously without destroying the movement. It was no longer possible for a defensive holding action such as Iglesias preferred to work. The pull of the reigning revolutionary mood was sufficiently impelling to have caught up Largo Caballero and Julián Besteiro, men of essentially moderate temperaments.

With heavy hearts, the leaders scheduled the strike to begin on August 13, three days before the convening of the second Parliamentary Assembly. Despite the great difficulties in communicating the date of the strike to affiliates and political allies throughout the country in the midst of martial law and censorship, the shutdown was initially successful in most urban and mining centers, where union strength was concentrated. Its effectiveness was greatest in Bilbao, Oviedo, Barcelona, Madrid, the Asturian coal fields, Catalonian and Valencian factory towns, and mining centers such as Linares, Peñarroya, Rio Tinto, Cartagena, León, and Palencia. Numerous provincial capitals were paralyzed. Outside Catalonia the strike was peaceful. Residents of rural Spain, especially the farm laborers of Andalusia, who had not yet recovered from the disastrous events of 1904–5, did not participate.

Ironically, only part of the membership of Unión Ferroviaria heeded the strike call; it was effective only among the employees of the Compañía del Norte in Asturias and in Galicia and Andalusia. The most impressive responses came from the workers of Bilbao, where virtually the entire work force of one hundred thousand laid down their tools, and in Asturias, where in solidarity many farmers ceased making deliveries of milk and vegetables to the towns. In Madrid, whose thoroughfares teemed with armed police and soldiers, the shutdown was total in building construction, the bakeries, local transport, and the printing trades; many shopkeepers closed down in sympathy. Soldiers opened fire on workers and their families in the popular districts of Ventas and Cuatro Caminos, inflicting numerous casualties.

On the eve of the shutdown, the UGT/PSOE national strike committee, composed of Largo Caballero, Besteiro, Saborit, and Anguiano, went into hiding but was arrested not long thereafter, leaving the strike leaderless. The directing committee in Barcelona, headed by Pestaña, was unable to exercise much control over developments. The city's life came to a halt, but the strike was directed by isolated groups, and strikers often found themselves on their own. Some workers and anarchists set up street barricades and engaged in armed skirmishes with soldiers and civil guards. The strike in Barcelona was even more disorganized and leaderless than during the Tragic Week and became known as the Comic Week. In nearby Sabadell, the only locality where an insurrection was attempted, casualties mounted as cannon fire was directed at the local labor federation headquarters, where some strikers had barricaded themselves.

The leaders of both the UGT and CNT had hoped that the military might not carry out the government's instructions,[30] but they were disappointed. Colonel Marquéz led the Vergara regiment in the bloody quelling of the Sabadell strike. In all major strike zones that were under martial law—Catalonia, Vizcaya, Asturias, and Madrid—troops frequently fired on striking workers, and casualties were high. The otherwise peaceful shutdown in Asturias was marred by brutal gunfire against workers in an effort to break the strike.

The strike had its greatest impact during the first two days, but the harsh repressive measures that followed exacted an increasing toll. In Madrid the shutdown came to a sputtering conclusion on the eighteenth, and in Barcelona it steadily lost steam and was extinguished by the seventeenth. It was more or less ended in Vizcaya on the twentieth. In Asturias, however, the miners resisted severe army repression until the thirty-first. Casualties were substantially greater than official estimates. According to the official count, 71 died, including 37 in the Barcelona area, with 150 wounded. The number of wounded in fact was in the hundreds. Reportedly 2,000 strike participants were taken into custody, though one report cites that number for Catalonia alone, and many more than that number were detained in Asturias. Army court-martials ordered the execution of some leaders and consigned many others to internal exile.

Having failed to enlist the support of Antonio Maura or the dynastic parties, the assembly movement was practically reduced to a Catalan initiative, which made Cambó vulnerable to the exigencies of his left-wing allies. Horrified at the possibility of becoming the Spanish version of Kerensky, Cambó and the Lliga Regionalista quickly dissociated themselves publicly from their socialist allies. Sensing the strike's imminent collapse, Lerroux slipped over the French border, as did Catalan separatist Colonel Francesc Maciá. Marcelino Domingo in Barcelona and Melquiades Alvarez in Asturias remained faithful to their political commitments.

Only a timely intervention by government authorities prevented the military from summarily executing Largo Caballero, Besteiro, Saborit, and Anguiano, who were sentenced to life imprisonment in an army court-martial. In Barcelona Marcelino Domingo was saved from the firing squad by Colonel Marquéz's pleadings.

The strike's failure affected the two labor organizations in different ways. Cenetistas were now "convinced that their objectives could not be attained through political change. Without quarreling with them they distanced themselves from the Madrid socialists, their indifference toward the Catalanist Republicans increased, and their hostility toward the Lliga exacerbated. The 1917 failure alienated Catalonian workers from political action and strengthened their anarcho-syndicalist apolitical attitude, which was to express itself in a growing electoral abstention and in an increased reliance on direct action."[31] Voicing the sentiments of many of his fellow Cenetistas, Simó Piera wrote, "We learned that not even for political change were we able to count on anybody. We found ourselves alone."[32] Cenetistas felt confirmed in their direct action, but Ugetistas emerged deeply chastened by their disastrous experiment with revolutionary politics. The experience would serve as a constraint during the "Bolshevist Triennium" and in their subsequent acquiescence to the military coup of General Miguel Primo de Rivera.

Organizationally, however, both movements suffered only temporary setbacks. By mid-1918 UGT membership fell to 89,601 from 100,000 in large part because of the mass discharges of 6,000 union supporters from the Compañía del Norte. The Unión Ferroviaria for a time suffered from disorganization. Asturian coal mine owners took advantage of the strike to institute a 10 percent wage cut. But these were not permanent dislocations, and when constitutional guarantees were restored on October 19, 1917, the two labor centers were able to reorganize and resume regular activities. The Barcelona strike fiasco, nonetheless, underscored the CNT's continued organizational weakness.

Though the regime won a respite, the fundamental problems remained as intractable as ever. Their harsh treatment of striking workers brought the Junteros a notable loss in prestige. Incensed, the military sought to shift responsibility to the Dato government, which on December 3 was forced from office and replaced by an unstable national union cabinet headed by García Prieto that included leading Conservatives and Liberals and whose strongman was ultraconservative Juan de la Cierva, the darling of the Juntas. In a successful effort to divide the opposition, the Lliga was persuaded to permit two of its leaders to accept portfolios.

The excessively harsh sentences meted out to the socialist strike leaders and others met widespread public disapproval. Social unrest and labor strife meanwhile were growing. The outcome of the February 24, 1918, parliamentary election, one of the cleanest elections in recent years, was a bitter pill for those in power. Socialist representation increased from one (Pablo Iglesias) to six, among them the four imprisoned strike leaders. Besteiro and Iglesias were elected to represent Madrid, Largo Caballero in Barcelona despite the virtual nonexistence of the PSOE there, Anguiano in Valencia, Saborit in Asturias, and Prieto in Vizcaya.[33] A large number of Republicans were also elected to the Cortes. By March the government could no longer remain in office, and at the king's urging yet another multicolored cabinet was formed with the aging Antonio Maura as prime minister and Cambó in charge of finance. An amnesty was declared in

May, and the four imprisoned PSOE leaders were released and permitted to take their seats in the Cortes.

The reasons for the collapse of the revolutionary general strike have been best summed up by historian Juan Antonio Lacomba: "Why did the strike fail? Because basically it had not been adequately prepared, because the army opposed it, and because the bourgeoisie and the Republican parties would have nothing to do with it. The proletariat, moreover, was disunited and the peasantry did not participate."[34]

CNT Expansion

Gross inequities and the ravages of inflation fueled trade union growth after the general strike. The CNT's vast expansion beginning in spring 1918 derived to a large extent from its vigorous campaigns against the high cost of living and its militant demands for cost-of-living adjustments. In the process the labor movement was transformed from weak, disunited unions sustained by small groups of committed activists into powerful mass organizations.

The CNT's conversion into the personification of Catalonian worker protest was greatly aided by the absence of credible labor or political rivals. As the CNT grew in numbers and power, it became imperative to shed the social guerrilla philosophy and acquire the organizational norms of mass trade unionism. Heretofore organized labor mostly consisted of a generally uncooperative mass of small craft or trade societies— in 1917 there were 495 separate labor organizations in the city of Barcelona—many of them with overlapping and competing jurisdictions. Much of their energy was spent in protecting jurisdictional turfs from would-be interlopers. Seguí, for example, was a member of the broad brush (*brocha gorda*) painters union that possessed seventy-five adherents. To persuade them to engage in joint actions for purposes of collective bargaining or trade union solidarity was a daunting task. Some of the unions also organized on a neighborhood basis as, for example, in the *barriada* of Gracia, which were strongly motivated by a sense of community solidarity that sometimes took precedence over broader trade union concerns.

The dispersal of trade union organization had its roots in the plethora of small shops and factories that made up Barcelona industry and services. But unlike the unions, employers in many instances had formed trade and industry associations that afforded greater cohesiveness in responding to the demands of labor.

Increasingly conscious of this deficiency, the emerging new generation of labor leaders as early as 1915 inaugurated discussions on how to re-structure the labor movement. A local federation of building construction unions formed in 1913 at the urging of Salvador Seguí and Simó Piera was to facilitate its conversion in 1918 into an industrial union. But intervening developments, the general strikes of 1916 and 1917 and repeated periods of persecution, prevented a coming to grips with the problem until mid-1918. By that time, a new breed of labor leader had acquired a dominant influence and the CNT was growing by leaps and bounds.

The Rationalist Atheneum in the Barcelona district of Sants was the site for the first conference of the Regional Confederation of Labor, which was held from June 28 to July 1, 1918. This gathering marked a historic landmark in the development of Spanish anarcho-syndicalism. To attract the greatest possible participation, all unions of the region were invited. Some 164 delegates attended, representing 73,860 unionized workers, with the Barcelona contingent making up close to three-quarters of the delegates. By far the greatest number of delegates were nonideological *sindicalistas* whose main interest was organizational and economic prob-lems. The anarchist ideologues were scarcely to be seen, and politico-ideological issues were of secondary interest.

Seguí and his entourage concentrated their efforts on convincing the participants that dispersed union strength could be unified only through the creation of industrial unions called *sindicatos unicos* (one big union) that would possess broad industry or trade jurisdictions.[35] The various trade or crafts and neighborhood branches within the *sindicatos unicos* would maintain separate sections or departments and be equally represented on the union's executive board. Strike authorization for any of the constituent sections required the prior approval of the *unico* board, but once that approval was given the entire union was obligated to provide support either in the form of industrywide trade union action or through financial assistance.

Restructuring along industrial lines had been inspired to some extent at least by external trends. Industrial unionism had been gaining ground among trade unions outside Spain, especially among those of an anarcho-syndicalist orientation. The French General Confederation of Labor, whose actions and policies much influenced its Spanish counterpart, had since the turn of the century converted to industrial unionism, and the Sants congress emulated its precepts. The American Industrial Workers of the World, then in its heyday and whose hallmark was the "one big union," was undoubtedly well known to Barcelona trade unionists and may have been the source for the term *sindicato unico.*

The idea of *sindicatos unicos* generated long and impassioned debate, for such a restructuring seemed to negate the traditional spirit of autonomy and federalism cherished by the Catalonian labor movement. Reality prevailed, however, and the proposal was accepted by a large majority. Seguí was elected CRT secretary general, and at the end of the congress thirteen industrial unions were formed. Membership books were issued, and monthly dues payments of ten centimos established. Though the doctrine of direct action was reaffirmed, sufficient latitude was given to permit local affiliates to deal with third parties in labor disputes when appropriate. Apoliticism was strengthened by prohibiting unions from maintaining offices in party headquarters and, to lessen the meddling of anarchist ideologues, the proviso was added that unions could be represented only by their own members.[36] The desire for labor unity through an eventual merger of the CNT and UGT was reaffirmed. Angel Pestaña was named director of *Solidaridad Obrera,* which became a daily paper.

Many labor activists were moving from a diffuse laborism to an anarcho-syndicalist outlook, best exemplified by Joan Peiró. For them the building and survival of the labor movement were paramount. Seguí and others who made up the mainstream of CNT leadership represented a blend of anarchism as a broad ideological frame of reference and Catalonian unionism. In this sense, as Manuel Lladonoso describes it, the Sants congress epitomized a "convergence between a societary tradition and French syndicalist influences on the one hand and the dialectical tension between reality and libertarian idealism on the other. The fundamental concern of the men of the Sants congress was to find means and methods for transforming the unsatisfactory socioeconomic situation, and they were nourished by an anarchist mystique."[37]

Organized anarchism in Barcelona over the years remained a small movement with limited influence. But libertarian preachings and educational activities had gradually inculcated such concepts as collective property, the superiority of manual labor over any other, and the need to destroy constituted society and replace it with a superior, egalitarian one. Though doctrinaire anarchists strongly rejected the new trade union approach formulated by the Sants congress, labor activists became increasingly receptive to anarcho-syndicalism. In 1917 they conceived of the CNT primarily as an instrument to combat the high cost of living, but by mid-1918 many began to think in terms of a social revolution.

During the winter of 1918 a national anarchist conference took place to determine their attitude toward the CNT. Heretofore many libertarians had refused to participate in the labor movement. The assembly voted to recommend the active enrollment of their supporters, and many of them subsequently decided to enter the CNT. Among those who did enter were numerous Malatestians, proponents of "propaganda by the deed," who ultimately joined the action groups within the CNT.[38]

Though the CRT had succeeded in enlisting a substantial part of organized labor, it had by no means made the conquest of the movement in its entirety. Its principal strength resided in the key industrial sectors: building construction, woodworking, metal industries, and textiles. Its single largest component was the textile union known as La Constancia, which represented eleven thousand workers. Workers in these industries included large numbers of recent immigrants, whereas the unions that did not participate in the Sants congress generally were those representing the more stable skilled trades.[39] One estimate places CRT membership at roughly thirty-four thousand or 25 percent of the 40 percent union membership with the remaining 15 to 16 percent outside the CNT/CRT orbit.[40] The cohesion and bargaining power derived from the industrial union restructuring and the growth of the CNT the following year would almost totally overwhelm the remaining holdouts. At the time of the Sants conference the CRT existed primarily in Barcelona, but local federations in the leading industrial towns gradually affiliated so that by the end of 1918 the CRT was transformed into a veritable regional body.[41] Much of the spectacular expansion had come from the affiliation of numerous independent unions outside Barcelona. In other respects, however, Cenetismo provided a mirror image of general social mores. Its rebirth had given rise to a resurgence of unionization in the textile industry, whose work force was overwhelmingly made up of female operatives (more than 80 percent), yet the union's delegation to the Sants congress did not include a single woman.

The industrial union restructuring gradually took hold, not without some resistance, and by early 1919 many of the city's unions had been absorbed by the *sindicatos unicos*. The *unicos* in Barcelona and other larger industrial towns were structured along industry or trade lines. In smaller towns of the region and elsewhere, especially in rural Andalusia, the new unions became a sort of general union encompassing workers of all trades and crafts, making it a community labor organization. People began to refer to workers affiliated with the CNT as "those of the one big union" (*los de los unicos*) and to Ugetistas as "those of the people's house" (*los de los pueblos de casa*).

Presumably as a sop to the anarchists following the Sants congress, the Seguí-dominated CRT named a five-man committee to serve as a provisional CNT national committee, to which he appointed libertarians. "The five," recounts Manuel Buenacasa, who was one of those named, "formed an anarchist group that directed the confederation until the Madrid congress."[42]

The congress also formally constituted action and propaganda committees under the control of local union executive committees: "Such committees are the support on which the organization rests, their veritable guides and sustainers. They should, wherever possible, constitute standing committees composed of volunteers or, for obvious reasons, be named by the executive committee rather than by general membership meetings."[43]

Such strong-arm groups had previously existed in unions of various ideological persuasions to deal with strikebreakers and to conduct violent actions. But what was new was to accord them formal status and permit not only CNT activists but anarchist groups to participate in their activities. Later, of course, a variety of shady elements were also co-opted. In so doing, the leadership unwittingly deposited Pandora's boxes whose opening ultimately would lead to the movement's undoing.

The Bolshevist Triennium

The war brought prosperity and greatly increased profits to many landowners, though not at the extravagant levels attained by manufacturers in Barcelona and Bilbao. Nor did food shortages disrupt the daily lives of the working poor because many farm laborers possessed small garden plots. By late 1917, however, prices accelerated markedly and inflationary pressures spread to the rural zones as the lure of high export prices drained off large amounts of foodstuffs. In 1919 the price increases were even more precipitate. For example, in Jaen province the price of bread increased between the summer of 1914 and fall 1920 by 203.9 percent.[44] In neighboring Córdoba province it rose even higher. When the full brunt of inflation was felt in the countryside, the *braceros* were probably the most hard hit of the entire population.[45]

In Andalusia shortage of rail transport and the loss of export markets forced mine owners in Almeria and Granada to institute sharp production cutbacks and mass layoffs. Those in Linares, La Carolina, and the big Peñarroya mine, whose products were eagerly sought after by manufacturers engaged in the fabrication of import-substitution goods, benefited from the wartime bonanza. Labor disputes in the region's urban centers during 1918 were similar to those occurring in the rest of the country.[46] Demands for cost-of-living wage adjustments often tended to merge or overlap with housewives' protests against food shortages and the high cost of living.

Despair turned to resentment in rural Andalusia. New organizations sprang up as *braceros* displayed a new-found assertiveness. The agricultural economist Pascual Carrión observed that during 1903–4 local unions were formed in most towns, but by 1918 most landless Andalusian peasants had become members.[47] Almost every pueblo had its CNT *centro obrero* or socialist *casa del pueblo* or both. But compared with 1904–5 a notable change had taken place. No longer were there insurrectionary takeovers, the burning of land registers, the assaults on church buildings, or the plethora of work stoppages and sporadic labor agreements between individual landowners and their field hands.

The new unionism espoused by the Barcelona anarcho-syndicalists and to a lesser degree by the socialists led to greater emphasis on organization and concerted trade union action. As before, there was a lack of coordination and no attempt was made to concert urban labor actions with rural campaigns, but collective bargaining units now generally included an entire community or zone, though rarely did they go beyond the confines of a province. Most bargaining demands and strike disputes centered on economic issues and were often accompanied by talk of social revolution and land redistribution. Solidarity strikes and demands for the release of prisoners were also frequent. The Bolshevik October revolution, which took place as peasant militancy was approaching its height, was exuberantly cited by anarchist activists as the wave of the future. Still, there was much less violence than in the past.

In early 1918 the authorities reacted with restraint, and most strikes and disputes ended peacefully with landowners generally assenting to wage increases, for it had been a good harvest year. But the growing strength of the peasant unions created widespread apprehension and generated a rush by employers to form local and provincial associations. By 1919 as wartime demand lessened, employers' resistance stiffened. Union demands for a fixed day rate instead of the universally detested piecework system (*destajo*), the use of union hiring halls to replace the village square, and extension of the eight-hour day to cover farm labor following its promulgation in October ran into determined opposition. Government officials also began to exhibit a tougher policy toward labor unrest, imposing martial law and dispatching army units to the more seriously affected areas.

Labor unrest did not reach southern Spain until 1918. Andalusia had been conspicuously absent from the strike movements of 1916 and 1917. Over the next three years, however, a veritable avalanche of strikes known as the Bolshevist Triennium swept over the Andalusian countryside, as well as parts of Valencia and Aragon.

After the labor movement's almost total extinction in 1904–5, only small nuclei of ideological activists managed to keep their groups alive. The formation in 1913 of the National Agriculturists Federation (Federación Nacional de Agricultores—FNA) was inspired by the Catalonian anarcho-syndicalists, and most of its initial modest membership was centered in Valencia and Catalonia; Andalusian components came primarily from the traditional anarchist pockets of Jerez de la Frontera and the *campiña* of Seville province. The first signs of renewed activity in 1914–15 came from these areas where anarchist activists were leading strikes to obtain wage increases and other improvements. But it was an isolated phenomenon. In Córdoba province labor organization reached its nadir in 1917 with FNA membership in the province at only three hundred. Nor did the socialists fare much better. PSOE membership declined during 1915–16 and grew only moderately during 1917. Both labor organization and party membership were weakened further by the 1917 disaster, though not to the point of extinction. By November of that year the situation improved somewhat when, benefiting from the widespread sympathy elicited by the amnesty campaign, the number of elected socialist city councilmen increased from nine to eleven.

A conference held in Seville during 1918 before the Sants congress to constitute the CNT's Andalusian Regional Labor Federation (Federación Obrera Regional Andaluza) claimed 30,000 members. The FNA dissolved the following year to become part of the CNT. By 1919 the anarcho-syndicalists were claiming a membership of 92,995 that included 20,492 in agrarian unions. Despite the growth of rural unionism, however, the CNT in Andalusia was predominantly an urban workers' movement accounting for 47.5 percent of the membership compared with 22 percent in the agrarian sector. Cities such as Málaga and Seville became CNT strongholds. Furthermore, when repression led to a sharp decline in rural labor organization during 1919, unions in the urban areas were able to operate until 1921, when the effects of the Barcelona labor crisis were also felt in Andalusia.[48]

Peasant unionism suffered from the usual problems that afflict such labor organizations in underdeveloped traditional societies. Long periods of apathy and resignation broken by brief moments of intense agitation were followed by yet another plunge into lethargy. Regular dues payments were unknown. CNT unions charged the paltry monthly fee of two centimos, yet many if not most of their supporters paid dues regularly only when wage negotiations were under way or when some other vital matter arose.

Socialist influence in the region, the PSOE in particular, had always possessed an importance that went well beyond Andalusia's demographic standing. Andalusia, with a fifth of the peninsula's population, in good times contributed half the party's entire membership and in bad times declined to barely 10 percent. In 1918 the UGT could claim a membership of only 8,572, but it mushroomed to 36,759 by 1920. Because of the transience of farm labor organization, UGT membership tended to oscillate wildly as opposed to the PSOE's stability.[49]

The reason for this juxtaposition, according to Antonio Maria Calero, is that before 1918 the UGT practically ignored organizational work among the *braceros* and thus was unprepared to deal with rural problems. A separate national federation in this field, the National Federation of Land Workers (Federación Nacional de Trabajadores de la Tierra—FNTT), did not materialize until 1930. UGT membership tended to concentrate in towns, cities, and mining centers. But with the coming of the war increasing numbers of peasant societies joined the UGT so that by 1918–19 half its enrollment consisted of farm laborers and small landholders, and those groups in the PSOE constituted an even larger proportion (by 1932 the CNT would attain similar ratios).[50] In 1919 the party possessed a regional membership in excess of 25,000 or 60 percent of the national total, but by 1923 its proportion plummeted to 15 percent. Socialist influence was particularly notable in Granada, Jaen, parts of Córdoba, and neighboring Extremadura, whereas Cenetistas predominated in southern

Córdoba, Seville, Málaga, and Cadiz. Fernando de los Rios, a recent recruit from the Reformist party, was elected deputy representing Granada in 1919, the first socialist from Andalusia to enter the Cortes (another socialist won in Jaen but was officially disqualified).

The National Catholic Agrarian Confederation (Confederación Nacional Católico Agraria—CNCA) was unable to gain many adherents because it catered primarily to small farmers and therefore had little appeal for farm laborers. Andalusia consequently remained the region with the smallest CNCA presence. Once the red peril had passed and the union movement was plunged in crisis, the few existing Catholic unions quickly vanished.

The most stirring national labor conflict of the period took place at the huge Rio Tinto copper mine in Huelva province with its labor force of fourteen thousand.[51] The ebullient young Madrid socialist leader Eladio Fernández Egocheaga was sent in 1913 by the railroad workers federation to Rio Tinto to deal with problems in its local affiliate. The labor situation was tense and a number of disputes and work stoppages had taken place earlier that year. An ardent advocate of radical labor tactics, Eladio Fernández Egocheaga began to organize the entire work force. Over the years anarchists and others had made sporadic efforts, but unionizing the employees was no easy matter for the company paid relatively high wages and provided low-cost housing and a variety of fringe benefits. But discontent simmered for it was a tightly controlled company town that was run by its British overseers with a benevolent despotism that generated an ever-widening gulf of alienation and hostility between management and labor. Egocheaga's efforts came at a time of full employment, high production, and record profits. Preparing for the inevitable shutdown, he assembled a hefty strike defense fund to which all members contributed, and as the union gained support it was able to oust company-supported city councillors in the neighboring community of Nerva and replace them with socialists. Even local shopkeepers began to side with the union. Against the advice of UGT moderate leaders Largo Caballero, Iglesias, Barrios, and Llaneza, Fernández Egocheaga launched a general walkout in October to November 1913. Many in the party and UGT leadership were reluctant to endanger their organizations by assenting to Fernández Egocheaga's pleas for a nationwide solidarity strike by the miners federation. When a strike agreement was to take effect at the beginning of the following year, the company instead launched massive reprisals, and a prolonged battle ensued.

World War I forced Rio Tinto to institute sizable production cutbacks and layoffs, which weakened the union. Nonetheless, Rio Tinto was one of the few localities in the region where participation in the 1917 general strike had been substantial, resulting in 10 dead, 150 imprisoned, the *casa del pueblo* closed down, and the socialist city councilmen jailed. With the subsequent virtual collapse of the UGT union, labor peace of a sort prevailed until 1919. In 1920, however, Rio Tinto became the site of one of Spain's most bitterly fought labor battles. This time the anarcho-syndicalists took over the leadership of the mine workers, and UGT supporters were relegated to a minority status. The conflict originated with the company's refusal to grant a wage increase to miners in one section. The ensuing walkout spread like wildfire throughout the mine works with white-collar employees and even domestics employed by British families joining in. The mine shut down, while the leaders of the *sindicato unico* and socialist unionists fought over the conduct of the strike. The Cenetistas in control were a particularly radical lot, direct actionists who opposed letting the CNT national office help settle the strike. Strike demands initially included eighty-six items but were later pared down to three basic ones: a general increase of three pesetas while maintaining prices in the company stores at their current levels, a 10 percent adjustment bonus, and reimbursement for days lost during the strike. The company rejected the demands, pleading inability to pay such added costs at a time of business downturn. With its large stockpile, it could afford a lengthy shutdown. The strike dragged on for six months. Many of the workers preferred to leave Rio Tinto and look for work elsewhere rather than give in. Soon the strike became a national issue as strikers' children were farmed out to union supporters throughout the country. Numerous conciliatory efforts were undertaken by labor leaders including Salvador Seguí, the Institute of Social Reforms, and the newly appointed minister of labor. All were rejected by the strike leaders. By year's end, after six months of impasse, the strikers were forced to return to work under conditions dictated by the company.

The peasant revolt was centered in Seville (Guadalquivir valley) and Córdoba provinces. It began in 1918 as entire working populations in innumerable communities of the latter province, including artisans, enrolled en masse in the local labor centers, not always of their own free will. At the 1918 annual FNA conference, rural unions from Córdoba outnumbered all the rest combined. It is impossible to gauge the extent of the mobilization during this period because many unions of socialist or syndicalist sympathies did not affiliate with their respective national labor centers and the unions shifted from the CNT to the UGT and back again. We do know that unions existed in sixty-one of the province's seventy-five townships, claiming a membership of 55,382 and representing more than a third of Córdoba province's rural working population.

In 1918–19 Cenetista peasant leaders launched a series of general shutdowns in the area. The city of Córdoba was paralyzed in March 1919, and in April thirty-two pueblos were shut down by a month-long strike despite the declaration of martial law. In the aura of violence that accompanied the strikes many landowners gave in to union demands, which they later refused to honor. Others, frightened by the spectacle of a peasant reawakening, abandoned their farms and sought refuge in nearby cities. As the situation seemed to get out of hand the authorities abandoned their attitude of benevolent restraint and army units were sent into numerous pueblos, labor centers were closed, and activists jailed. According to Juan Díaz del Moral, an important element in the militancy and radicalism of the Córdoban rural organizations was "the great number of small farmers and sharecroppers both in the rank and file and in the leadership."[52]

By 1919 rural Andalusia seethed with labor unrest. Córdoba, for example, appeared to be in the midst of a volcanic social eruption with 184 work stoppages, some of them involving entire farm towns.[53] The total number of strikes in those years will probably never be known, least of all those in the countryside, where record keeping and reporting were at their worst. The number of days lost from strikes for the entire country rose, according to the Institute of Social Reforms, from 1,784,538 in 1917 to 7,261,764 in 1920, with the number of strikers going from 71,440 to 244,684. These figures suggest the great increase in conflict, but they grossly understate the true reality. Juan Díaz del Moral in his classic study of the Córdoba rural movement suggests that in that province alone substantially more than the IRS's figure of 27,514 workers had participated in strike actions.[54]

The combined effects of official countermeasures and increasing opposition from employers had a dampening influence so that by 1920 the number of strikes had fallen to only sixteen. Workers' societies began to disintegrate, a process intensified because 1921 and 1922 were bad years for olive growing. Though peasant organization was not entirely extinguished, it was nearing its end. And as the movement subsided, the number of crop burnings increased, leading to a royal decree against such action. By the early 1920s the eruption was over. Another ten years would elapse before southern farm labor would again dare to raise its head.

The moderation practiced by Seguí and his followers during the Bolshevist Triennium had exerted a wholesome restraining influence on the traditional insurrectionary penchants of Andalusian anarchism. Lamentably, it was short-lived. The physical destruction of the Catalonian labor movement placed anarcho-syndicalism in the hands of the most alienated, who reverted to apocalyptic insurrectionism. Its effects were to be felt on Cenetismo throughout the country and especially in Andalusia.

Socialist Identity Crisis

The economic difficulties and institutional crisis that had brought Spain to the brink of revolution radicalized the entire Spanish Left, including the socialists.[55] The UGT, which for years had taken pains to maintain at least formal political neutrality, now openly declared itself a socialist trade union.

Elements within the UGT led by Fabra Ribas, Fernández Egocheaga, and Facundo Perezagua had begun to press for more militant action before the war but acquired substantial support only during and after the war. The foremost need was to combat the erosive effects of uncontrolled inflation on wage earners' purchasing power. Following the war a radicalized opposition arose to oppose Llaneza's moderation in the Asturian coal fields, especially among younger miners, as jobs and wage standards were threatened. In Vizcaya, with the loss of wartime prosperity and easily won wage increases, Facundo Perezagua rallied the more militantly inclined from his shrinking iron mine union base. Within the Madrid party organization as well, especially among intellectuals and young activists, a clamor for greater militancy arose. Its most radical exponents were to be found in the seven thousand-member Socialist Youth Organization centered in Madrid and Bilbao.

Since few in the Left opposition had any clear notion of how they wished to change the party's outlook, differences separating so-called moderates from dissidents sometimes were difficult to discern. But the cleavage in party ranks was real enough. The termination in 1920 of the Republican-Socialist Alliance, a longtime grievance of the socialist Left, and a collaborative pact with the CNT can be regarded as an attempt by the party leadership to defuse growing left-wing sentiment and preserve party unity.

The UGT's postwar expansion from 89,601 in 1918 to 211,342 in 1920 coincided with a gradual diminution of Pablo Iglesias's autocratic control. Since 1916 failing health prevented him from participating in

UGT congresses, and he gradually relinquished direction of the day-to-day life of the organization. Much of the directing role was assumed by Largo Caballero, who was named UGT general secretary in 1918. He was joined by a second generation of socialist leaders, including Besteiro, Anguiano, Saborit, and Ramón Lamoneda, who gave the organization new flexibility and dynamism.

The debate over the future orientation of the party centered on whether the PSOE should remain affiliated with the reconstituted Second Socialist International or join the recently formed Third Communist International. Those favoring Comintern membership were known as the Terceristas. The sometimes inchoate, sometimes articulated desire for a more militant radical orientation crystallized around this issue. A similar debate was under way within the CNT. The Spanish Left radicalized as the revolutionary tide washed over the European Left in the early 1920s, motivated by postwar economic and social turbulence and the example of the Bolshevik triumph. Both the German Independent Socialist party and the French socialists voted in 1920 to become member organizations of the Third International. A large minority of the Italian party had constituted itself as the Communist party. Revolutionary Marxism-Leninism was making deep inroads throughout the European labor movement.

To convert the PSOE to a Bolshevik-style revolutionary vanguard party as required by the Comintern's twenty-one conditions to qualify for admission would have practically led to its complete undoing. As a movement, Spanish socialism possessed little doctrinal cohesion, housing a broad gamut of outlooks including Marxists, social democratic trade unionists, Krausist humanists (de los Rios), and pragmatic liberals (Prieto), as well as old-fashioned radical labor leaders (Perezagua) and Fabian parliamentarians such as Julián Besteiro. To impose a rigid doctrinal conformity on such a heterogeneous assemblage, as Moscow insisted, was unrealistic.

Yet many within the party were intent upon doing so though they were not aware of the possible consequences. Supporters and opponents were closely matched, causing great tensions within the organization. This controversy arose, ironically, when organizational and electoral prospects were brighter than ever. In 1919 the PSOE's membership swelled to 42,000 and the UGT's to 160,000, attaining the highest postwar level in 1921 with respective enrollments of 45,000 and 240,000. The number of elected city councilmen by 1920 had reached 578 (in 1917 it had been only 28), attesting to the growth of an impressive nationwide local infrastructure. It was a trend that lent even greater credence to the party's reformist electoral character. But intense social and labor turmoil enveloped the country. In 1919, for example, not only were Barcelona and Andalusia aflame with labor agitation, but the spreading rash of violent work stoppages had led the government to institute martial law in numerous localities, including Palma de Mallorca, Madrid, and Santander.

By a strange twist, the Bolshevik triumph had first been enthusiastically taken up by the Cenetistas while the PSOE leadership viewed Lenin's exploits with displeasure. But as the radical mood overtook various party sectors, the official attitude changed to warm support for the Soviet regime.

It seemed all but certain as the party congress opened in December 1919 that the Terceristas would carry the day. But differences arose, with some urging a pure and simple affiliation, others calling for a prior unification of the two internationals, and a group sponsored by the Asturians proposing that the party join the Moscow international only if the two did not unite. The last formula was adopted by a narrow margin. Another congress was held six months later, and once again it appeared that the Terceristas would emerge victorious, but again a final decision was put off, this time to await a report from an inquiry commission composed of Fernando de los Rios and Daniel Anguiano, who were dispatched to Moscow.

This proved to be an astute delaying tactic employed by moderate leaders Iglesias, Largo Caballero, and Besteiro. Tercerista fortunes then began to decline. Their cause also suffered from the arrival in the country of Comintern emissary Michael Borodin in January 1920, which led to the ill-conceived break engineered by the leadership of the Socialist Youth and their formation of the Spanish Communist party (PCE). The behavior of these impulsive sectarian extremists alienated many sympathizers in the party and created bitter divisions among the proponents of *tercerismo*. Meanwhile, growing numbers of militants became apprehensive of the possible adverse effects of the application of the twenty-one conditions.

Finally, after two years of intense controversy and bitter wrangling, yet another turbulent, disorderly congress was held in April 1921. As Gerald Meaker puts it, "If the majority approved Moscow's terms, schism by the right wing on the French pattern was a certainty, and if the Conditions were rejected, schism by the left wing, in the Italian manner was probable."[56] By now, the balance had shifted in favor of the moderates, and the congress voted 8,808 to 6,025 to join the Vienna second and a half international, which had been formed by a number of European socialist parties. Pablo Iglesias's warning against Comintern affiliation was an important factor in its defeat. Many of the Terceristas then left the party to form the Spanish Communist Workers party (PCOE). Both the PCE, formed by socialist juveniles, and the PCOE, whose main support came from small enclaves in the mining districts of Asturias and Vizcaya and from Madrid, came into existence when the radical moment had already passed, at a time of mounting economic dislocation, when a severe repressive wave had been launched following the assassination of Prime Minister Dato by anarcho-syndicalists and Primo de Rivera's dictatorial takeover was in the offing. Furthermore, the hopelessly unrealistic, extremist tactics and policies the parties embraced assured their consignment to political limbo. Spanish communism would remain a small, insignificant movement until the advent of the Second Republic.

Following the unification of the two Communist parties, a major effort was undertaken to strengthen and extend its trade union salient in the UGT. Largo Caballero and his fellow moderates till then had successfully prevented the spread of Tercerista influence. Moderate control was confirmed at the organization's 1921 congress by a lopsided vote—110,902 to 17,919—endorsing affiliation with the International Federation of Trade Unions (IFTU), which was closely linked with the Socialist International. Communist labor influence was concentrated in the mine unions of Asturias and Vizcaya and among some Madrid local unions. A tense showdown came at the UGT congress of November 19–21, 1922. Out of a total of 160 delegates, the communists could muster only 24. As tempers rose and UGT security guards sought to quell disturbances created by communist supporters, shots rang out and one of the Ugetista guards, a young socialist, fell dead. Largo Caballero and Besteiro immediately pointed to a PCE militant as the perpetrator. The true identity of the assassin has never been clearly established, but the UGT leadership held the communists responsible and voted the expulsion of their delegate supporters; fifteen unions that they controlled were also expelled. Disaster for the new communist movement had now come full circle.

Though PSOE moderates had successfully bested a challenge from the Left, which had nearly won control, the struggle drained the party of much of its membership and of its hegemonic role within the movement. By 1923 membership was down to only nine thousand. Though much of this loss came from Andalusia, where repression following the great agitation led to a precipitate drop in party adherents, many others throughout the country, disheartened by the fratricidal warfare, also dropped out. In contrast, the UGT leadership was able to maintain its influence and membership while successfully defending itself from internal assault.[57] The locus of power now clearly shifted to the UGT, and UGT General Secretary Francisco Largo Caballero would be the dominant figure of Spanish socialism throughout the 1920s.

The Rise of Anarcho-Syndicalism and the Barcelona Labor Wars

Powerful surges of working-class militancy have often served as a catalyst for trade union movements. The strike that began at the La Canadiense power company in Barcelona in 1919 is such an example in Spanish labor history.

Between 1914 and 1916 prices spiraled and profits skyrocketed while real wage earnings in the textile industry remained generally stationary. In 1916 proletarian disgruntlement burst forth as labor disputes and the number of strikes reached unprecedented heights. CNT membership that year rose to thirty thousand, double that of 1914, when it regained legal status; at the same time the UGT membership rose to one hundred thousand. The gap between prices and wages between 1916 and 1919 remained sizable enough in the Barcelona area for employers to reap considerable profits. The worker militancy of 1919–20 was brought to a halt by the advent of the 1921–23 economic crisis. Even the ranks of nonagrarian confessional labor swelled from twenty thousand in the early war years to roughly sixty thousand by 1919. Workers were most aggressive not in the heyday of wartime bonanzas but during the years immediately following, when profit taking lessened, causing wages to rise appreciably from 1919 to 1922. As labor unrest and strike fever reached their zenith in 1919 and 1920, Spain rose to fourth among European countries in strikes and numbers of workdays lost. Its impact on national life was without precedent. For the first time the country was forced to give major attention to labor problems and the role of organized labor. But the labor relations crisis could not have come at a worse time, for the regulatory powers of civil government had already undergone considerable erosion.

During the period starting with the La Canadiense strike in early 1919 to the toppling of the Restoration parliamentary system in 1923, except for the army's stunning disaster at Annual in Morocco, the country remained transfixed by the explosive breakdown in labor relations and the emergence of organized labor as a redoubtable factor in national affairs.

Trade unions in Barcelona and throughout the country were expanding prodigously. By December 1918 membership in the CRT/CNT had soared to 345,000, with far more in Barcelona alone than the UGT possessed nationwide. The CRT was spoiling for a major confrontation to force its acceptance as a bargaining entity. A seemingly banal dispute at Barcelona's principal electric power company, which previously had successfully resisted unionization, furnished just such an opportunity.[58]

Popularly dubbed "La Canadiense" because of its Anglo-Canadian ownership, the Ebro Irrigation and Power Company reduced the wages of some of its white-collar employees, and when objections were raised it discharged six (or eight) who had sought assistance from the CNT water, gas, and power workers union, which was conducting an organizing campaign at the company. A delegation of employees then appealed to the civil governor, the head of the Mancomunitat (semiautonomous regional government), and the mayor to intercede on their behalf. Incensed by the company's high-handedness, the 140 employees of the billing department went on a sit-down strike (*huelga de brazos caidos*) the following day. When police were called in, the bill collectors walked off the job.

What had taken place at La Canadiense to that point differed little from what had occurred at countless other companies intent upon preventing the unionization of their employees. But the fact that it took place amid widespread social unrest and when CNT strength was reaching its zenith, the challenge to the right to organize that it posed, as well as the CNT's desire to demonstrate its hegemonic sway transformed it into a historic three-way confrontation the likes of which had not been seen in twentieth-century Spain.

Most of the company's white-collar employees joined the walkout by February 8, and it soon spread to other companies owned by La Canadiense: power plants, electrified railway lines, and the Barcelona tramways. Two weeks later, the company's entire blue-collar force, which was responsible for the generation and distribution of electric current, joined the strikers, depriving the city of power. Workers at the other power companies also walked out on February 27. Electric power continued to be transmitted to Barcelona from hydroelectric installations in the Pyrenees, but no one was available to distribute it. Deprived of electric power, 70 percent of the industrial enterprises closed down.

The city's politicians and business community had paid little attention to mounting social tensions and the rise in CNT enrollment, preoccupied by the public clamor over the campaign for regional autonomy. A Catalonian autonomy statute drafted by the Mancomunitat had been presented to the Cortes and a date set for a popular referendum. Labor unrest throughout the country and the autonomy issue in Catalonia led the Romanones government to close down the Cortes on the very day of the referendum. Constitutional guarantees had been suspended on January 16 in Barcelona, accompanied by the jailing of seventy-nine CNT leaders, closing down *Solidaridad Obrera* and *Tierra y Libertad,* and the padlocking of union offices. Many labor leaders, however, including Pestaña and Piera, managed to elude the government net.

Repressive measures had little effect on the rising tide of worker militancy. Labor disputes and strikes continued as before, and *Solidaridad Obrera* appeared clandestinely. Seguí and the other imprisoned leaders managed to maintain close contact with the organization. A second line of leadership cadres took over, and workers continued to pay their dues to the shop delegates.

Cenetistas quickly grasped the potential the Canadiense dispute possessed to display their power and influence. A successful conclusion of the dispute would open up greater opportunities for the recruitment of white-collar workers, who hitherto had not responded to organizational appeals. And last but not least, it provided an ideal opportunity to respond to the government's vindictiveness.

Moving with deliberation and diligence, the CNT leadership conducted a modulated, gradual general shutdown. Unions in allied fields first conducted walkouts in water, gas, and other power companies. To prepare for the showdown, pending strikes were called off, including a shutdown in the textile industry. The strike committee complied with the eight-day advance notification that was legally required before taking strike action. Violence was kept to a minimum.

Specialized army units arrived on February 22 to take over operation of the electric power stations. The city presented an eerie aspect, shrouded in darkness, the shops shuttered. Municipal police directed traffic with lanterns and flashlights. Industrial activity was at a standstill. Fearing arrest, the strike committee refused to meet with the authorities.

Army specialists restored some power by early March, permitting some factories to resume operations, but the strike then spread to the provinces. Unable to resolve the dispute, the government took over operations of the electric power company on March 8 and placed its employees as well as those employed in railways, water, gas, and other power facilities under military mobilization. The Graphic Arts Union responded by instituting "Red Censure," prohibiting any newspaper from publishing the mobilization order or any comment prejudicial to the strikers under pain of fines or shutdowns. The attempt to force workers to return to work was an almost total failure. Some who returned refused to work. With no other coercive means left, martial law was declared on March 13.

The government then dispatched José Morote, subsecretary to the president, and a new civil governor, Carlos Montañes, a Catalan who formerly had been employed by La Canadiense as an engineer, with instructions to obtain a negotiated settlement. At long last, an accord was reached with the management of La Canadiense that met most of the strikers' demands, including the eight-hour day. Montañes pledged to free three thousand strikers who had been jailed and to expedite the processing of those few held by military authorities.

On March 19 the CNT held a mass meeting of twenty thousand union members in the local bullfighting arena. At issue was the liberation of prisoners still in military custody. Many in the audience, urged by the extremists, loudly demanded that the general strike be continued until the remaining prisoners were released. In what was his finest moment, confronting a hostile audience, Seguí, through sheer dint of oratory and character, succeeded in convincing the workers to return to work the following day, although he apparently felt constrained to promise that if the prisoners were not freed by the twenty-fourth, a general shutdown of the entire region would commence.

The CNT emerged from its forty-four-day struggle with unprecedented power and prestige. No labor organization in Spain had ever acquired such massive popular support, and Barcelona must have been one of the most highly unionized cities of the Western world. Its leadership, made up mostly of young men, had demonstrated remarkable tactical ability. The accord ending the strike called for the readmission of all strikers without reprisals, general wage increases, reimbursement for half a month's wages lost during the strikes, the release of most imprisoned strikers except for those awaiting disposition by military court-martials, union recognition, the reopening of union halls, and a pledge to extend the eight-hour day, which was already in force in the building construction industry, to all wage earners.

Many of these considerable achievements were soon to be tragically frittered away. Seguí's ill-advised pledge to resume the general shutdown if the handful of unionists who remained in military custody were not freed may have been regarded as necessary to prevent an overstimulated mass from assaulting the nearby Montjuich prison and forcibly liberating the jailed strikers. In the retrospective judgment of CNT General Secretary Manuel Buenacasa it was "the worst possible mistake and with disastrous consequences."

The CNT's stunning conquests left many employers in a state of panic and shock. Traditional structures of industrial control and authority were considered under mortal threat. A climate of polarization took over. Factory owners favoring coexistence were pushed aside in the desire by the more intransigent elements to be rid of the unions once and for all, an attitude that was taken up by the political Right, most notably the Lliga Regionalista. They found a natural ally in the military commanders of Barcelona, who bitterly resented the conciliatory approach of the Romanones government. During the strike Captain General Joaquín Milans del Bosch and Military Governor Severiano Martínez Anido had dissuaded F. Fraser Lawton, the head of Barcelona Traction and Light Company, from seeking a negotiated end to the dispute. Though the promulgation on April 3, 1919, of the eight-hour day by the Romanones government was consistent with the decision taken by the conferees at the Versailles Peace Conference, it infuriated the Catalonian bourgeoisie.[59] Thus as the date for the resumption of the general strike approached, the CNT found itself confronted by a formidable array of powerful opponents.

Commencing at midnight March 24, the general strike completely shut down the city. Other towns followed suit. Civil Governor Montañes, the architect of the government's new conciliatory line, was dumbfounded by the CNT's decision. Martial law was reinstituted, and army detachments took up positions at strategic points in the city. An eight thousand-member voluntary armed citizens militia, the Somaten, composed of upper-class persons, patrolled the streets to supplement the regular police. Class tensions were visible. Balcells writes, "Panic overcame those who had something to lose, a time of decision seemed to have arrived, and the classes in conflict erected an unbridgeable chasm."[60]

Shops and stores were forced to remain open, and a manhunt was launched to track down union leaders and activists. Even political moderates who favored conciliatory labor policies were taken into custody, including the chairman of the Barcelona Institute of Social Reforms Committee and attorneys representing the CNT. Some thirty-four thousand striking workers were jailed. By the second week the strike began to lose support. The two hundred officers of the various local unions that composed the strike committee were arrested and placed in Montjuich military prison. Unions were declared illegal and dues payments prohibited, and members of the CNT executive board were subject to arrest on sight. A CNT face-saving proposal to end the strike if reprisals were not taken was rejected. The shutdown ended on April 7, fifteen days after it began.

As workers streamed back to work, countless numbers of known union supporters were discharged and police continued to hunt down activists. Prestrike wage levels were maintained, but unions were no longer permitted to operate in the workplace and, to punish their employees, building construction employers instituted a two-week lockout. Martial law was retained for an additional four months, and as late as the following August some fifteen thousand workers were still being held in custody.

The CNT paid bitterly for its disastrous action. For having "committed the imprudence of giving in to the most impassioned ones," observes Balcells, "all that had been gained was compromised by engaging in a strike over a matter of honor and prestige. The labor organization without any perceptible benefit ended up bringing about the unification of businessmen in the Employers Federation under the leadership of the most aggressive and intransigent among the bourgeoisie, who responded to worker pressures and demands with lockouts and drove them to befriend and acquire the army's assistance."[61]

The government's peacemaking role also came to an end. On April 14 Civil Governor Carlos Montañes and Police Commissioner Gerardo Doval announced their resignations and abruptly departed for Madrid. In fact, they had been forced to resign by Generals Milans del Bosch and Martínez Anido and placed on the first train to Madrid. Acting in concert with the Lliga, the Employers Federation, and the Catalonian bourgeoisie, the local military with the support of the Military Defense Junta, bound by a shared fear of the proletarian challenge, joined in defying Madrid and imposing a mailed-fist policy. For upper-class Catalans this meant abandoning any further hopes of attaining full self-rule, which was anathema to the military centralists.

A movement that finds itself, after years of unrelenting persecution, transformed into a powerful mass force carries the earmarks of its upbringing. Numerous activists whose only prior experience had been in guerrilla labor activity now found themselves possessed of great power and responsibility in the conduct of labor relations. Such power proved to be heady wine. Nowhere was this more apparent than in the comportment of shop delegates.

As a decentralized, grass-roots movement, Cenetismo's hallmark was embodied in the key role accorded shop delegates, who were expected to assure rank-and-file participation in trade union affairs and in the collective bargaining process. In a period of almost constant persecution and frequent jailings of local union and regional officers, their abuses became flagrantly widespread. Shop delegates received less and less supervision and guidance, permitting them to assume greater autonomy of action and power of decision. Some became virtually de facto factory directors, and many often employed violence and intimidation against recalcitrant employers or uncooperative employees. Such excesses intensified employers' opposition to the CNT.

A veteran trade unionist recounts that, "against all logic," those named by the unions to fill these posts

> were not the most qualified for such a delicate responsibility but the most daring ones. This naturally led to a series of absurd conflicts because the delegates believed themselves endowed with absolute power and resolved any dispute that arose or pretended to do so according to their criterion or caprice. On innumerable occasions a delegate would call a strike of the entire personnel because of petty differences arising between a worker and employer. Union leaders consequently were confronted with unwarranted disputes and had to settle them as best they could, not always with a true sense of justice. Libertarian vapors rose to the heads of numerous unionists, who having become intoxicated felt that all such efforts were unnecessary. Believing themselves en route to · proletarian emancipation they accorded scant importance to "matters of little account." The worst of it was that the best prepared and perceptive ones, those who had the responsibility for keeping the organization on a common sense course, let themselves be carried away by the easy way out or prudently remained on the sidelines. They did not grasp that such an accumulation of errors would seed winds that would unavoidably end in tempests.[62]

Intent upon restoring labor peace through direct talks between the two sides, Civil Governor Julio Amado lifted martial law and released the imprisoned labor leaders. Many of the seventy thousand workers who had been rendered jobless were permitted to return to work. The liberation of Cenetistas and permission to resume trade union activities were made contingent upon the CNT's agreement to accept a truce and participate in talks leading to the creation of a new organism designed to assure peaceful outcomes of labor-management disputes. What Amado and his superior, Minister of Interior Manuel Burgos y Mazo, an old-fashioned Andalusian conservative politician and a social Catholic, had in mind was the issuance of a royal decree establishing the Catalonian Labor Commission, composed of five representatives each from management and labor and presided over by the local labor inspector. It was to be given broad powers to settle and mediate labor disputes, set industry wage rates, and so on.[63] By its explicit recognition of the CNT as the spokesman for labor, it represented the most advanced formulated system of government-sponsored labor relations.[64]

Had the commission been established much earlier, it might have had some chance for acceptance. But the lines were tightly drawn, especially on the employers' side, and the rising tide of terrorism and counter-terrorism foredoomed efforts at social pacification. Cenetistas were ready to sue for peace, but the employers, or at least their spokesmen, would settle for nothing less than the union's total destruction. A miniature civil war was in the offing.

Seguí quickly grasped the virtues of participation. Only through discussion and negotiation with employers and the authorities could the CNT's survival be assured. But for a sizable minority such conciliation represented a rank betrayal of the principles of direct action. Seguí finally prevailed over vociferous objections.

A good deal more is known about what transpired in labor circles than among the employers. The Spanish Employers Confederation was formed in 1914 at the instigation of building construction employers in Madrid and Barcelona. In both cities unions in this sector traditionally had been labor strongholds and often set area wage patterns. The uneasy labor-management relationship had become more strained than ever during the war years, when, despite limited profits because of wartime material shortages, building contractors still had to contend with the demands of militant, well-organized unions.

As the labor situation in Barcelona grew more ominous, the Spanish Employers Confederation became primarily the instrument of the Catalonian industrialists. Felix Graupera, Francesc Junoy, and other Barcelona building contractors who headed the city's employer federation also occupied leading posts in the national body.

Graupera, an obscure builder, seemed an odd choice as spokesman and putative head of the country's largest and most important group of industrial employers. But combative intransigents were to be found in greater numbers among the managerial nouveau riche, who had benefited from wartime speculation, than among "old money," and they were especially numerous in the building construction industry. Employers traditionally set policies through the Fomento de Trabajo Nacional, which was controlled by the region's leading families, who dominated the textile and metalworking industries. They had decided in August 1919 to form the Barcelona Employers Federation and to turn over the implementation of the tough antilabor policy to industrial newcomers such as Graupera. Communication was maintained, however, between Madrid and the Catalan bourgeoisie through Cambó, who acted as the employers' political spokesman, and not through Graupera's coterie, who were referred to as "law and order bolsheviks."

One reason for this curious arrangement may have been the desire of industrial magnates to remain outside the limelight. A compelling reason for their anonymity was to avoid being targeted by CNT and anarchist gunmen. Indeed, although Graupera and other factory owners and managers became victims of armed attacks (*atentados*), the members of the leading families, with few exceptions, remained unharmed.[65]

Simó Piera, who headed the CNT building construction *sindicato unico,* described his adversaries:

> As in any group there were all sorts of people in the employers' federation. The three factions within it shared a common objective but differed on how to achieve it. One group very diplomatically, through legal means, "sought to box us in" as comrade Seguí so aptly put it. The second wished with great urgency to follow a violent course, to put an end to us. There was also a third group composed of liberal petty bourgeoisie that was not very much in accord with them and sought to make use of their rights while respecting ours, insisting that negotiations be conducted honestly, to seek solutions. . . . The liberal group of the employers' federation was not taken into account, and it was the fat cats that ran things. Moreover, the first two groups complemented each other quite well; those who began the *allioli* [Catalan

salad dressing] were the diplomatic ones, and the others, advocates of violence, added the garlic. These were two ingredients that complemented each other perfectly.[66]

Obtaining unanimity in carrying out antiunion policies was no easy matter. The officers of the employers' federation often had to use financial and physical intimidation to secure compliance. Those who did not comply were cut off from supplies of raw materials or threatened with fines and physical injury. The degree of noncompliance is suggested by the annual report of the Catalonian Employers Federation issued in February 1921, which states that "the Infractions Committee is processing 400 cases" and that "a total of 234 violations were awaiting decisions."[67]

As the situation moved toward a climax, hard-liners in the Employers Federation all but silenced a minority that included some textile manufacturers who favored conciliation instead of bloody confrontation.[68] Because a national employers' congress was to open in Barcelona on October 20, Graupera and other officers pretended to cooperate with the civil governor and the commission. But it was a ruse; the employers had secretly decided to initiate a lockout in Barcelona and to extend it throughout the country to check rising trade union strength and force the government to return to a repressive policy.[69]

Finally, the federation agreed to an accord establishing a mixed commission. Though all employees were supposed to be rehired, many enterprises, including one owned by a federation leader who had signed the accord, excluded known activists and union supporters. Indignant over the deception, Seguí and the CNT delegation withdrew from the commission.[70] In the meantime plans were readied for the lockout, which was ostensibly for the purpose of eliminating CNT shop delegates and creating a joint labor-management committee to settle labor disputes. Its real purpose was to elicit labor violence that would provide a pretext for resorting to harsh countermeasures.[71] Seguí and the moderates lost control of the CNT and were forced to abandon the mixed commission. The seeds had been sown for the extremism that would burst forth at the upcoming national CNT congress in Madrid.[72]

On November 25 some 150,000 workers found themselves locked out and were informed by their employers that they could return to work only if they surrendered their union cards.[73] The CNT was sharply divided on how to respond. Manuel Buenacasa, a leader of the woodworkers union and CNT national secretary, urged a militant approach, including occupying factories; Seguí argued for calm and believed the organization could withstand the lockout's effects. Seguí's policy of passive resistance may have been the only realistic alternative, and though the attempt to crush the CNT failed and the momentum of the anarcho-syndicalist movement continued for a time, the exhausting seven-week lockout brought severe privations to the city's wage earners and drained organizational strength and morale.[74]

Despite the CNT's battle for survival in Barcelona, the groundswell of Spanish anarcho-syndicalism continued unabated. The CNT's second national congress was convened in December 1919 at Madrid's Comedia Theater while the Barcelona lockout was under way. Though affiliations had spread to many parts of the country, the Catalonian behemoth with 427,000 members out of a total membership of 700,000 clearly eclipsed all other regions.[75] Others of importance were the Levant, Andalusia, and Zaragossa, although in the north, beyond the enclaves of Gijón, La Felguera, and parts of Galicia, the CNT offered little competition to the socialists. By contrast, though UGT strength was centered in Andalusia, Asturias-León, Vizcaya, and Madrid, its overall membership was more nationally distributed than the CNT's. The UGT generally had more rural affiliates and greater strength in mining, transport, and heavy industry whereas the CNT's main support came from workers in light industries and consumer goods manufacturing, which were usually small and medium-sized enterprises.

Many of the 450 delegates were trade union novices attending a congress for the first time, and thus the gathering was rather disorganized and occasionally adopted contradictory policy resolutions. Moderates often found themselves outflanked. Young militants from Catalonia exploited the reaction to the repression, causing a shift toward extremism.[76] The Catalonian industrial union model was adopted as the national prototype, and, faithful to their federalist principles, regional and local federations continued to hold organizational authority. National executive committees were to be named by the unions of the locality in which they resided. The CNT was now three times the size of the UGT, and the former spirit of trade union unity was much less in evidence. A proposal sponsored by the Asturian and Castilian delegations in favor of a merger with the UGT was defeated by a two-to-one margin. With considerable hubris a countermotion was adopted calling upon the UGT to become part of the CNT.

The leadership of the Catalonian Regional Confederation supported a resolution reaffirming the principle of direct action and acknowledging its error in having agreed to participate in the ill-fated mixed commission. Like their socialist rivals, anarcho-syndicalists were divided over the question of affiliation with the Communist International. Seguí and Eleuterio Quintanilla of Asturias sided with those opposed. In contradictory fashion the delegates approved provisional adherence to the Comintern but declared libertarian communism to be the CNT's ultimate objective.

The new unionism tended to underscore existing organizational and philosophical differences between socialist trade unionism and anarcho-syndicalism. Cenetismo conferred the greatest possible autonomy and authority on its regional bodies. Each *sindicato unico* determined its own collective bargaining policy and when and where to call strikes.[77] CNT membership and influence were more concentrated in Barcelona and Catalonia than the UGT was in Madrid. Except in periods of severe repression, national CNT policy was set by the Catalonians.

In contrast, the UGT's policy-making authority, including the power to call strikes, resided with the national leadership, which was composed mostly of leaders in Madrid. Citywide local federations tended to play a larger role in UGT affairs than in those of the CNT. Craft unionism, especially in nonindustrial Madrid, continued to thrive alongside industry federations formed during the war in such industries as mining, railroads, and metalworking. Though some CNT leaders such as Seguí and Peiró favored the creation of national industry federations, they were rejected as prejudicial to the federalist structure of Cenetismo.

Consistent with its antireformist professions, the CNT employed only a few full-time paid officials and did not allow local unions to operate mutual benefit societies or cooperatives or to maintain strike defense funds, which were thought to have a bureaucratic corrupting influence on the proletarian spirit of combat. Leaders transacted union business on a lost-time remunerated basis.

Wartime expansion permitted the UGT to acquire the trappings of a European socialist trade union movement. A growing body of professional trade union functionaries presided over the movement's activities. Service organizations such as consumer cooperatives, mutualities, and medical clinics headed by full-time paid officials formed an integral part of the socialist labor movement, as did strike defense coffers. In times of crisis and stress, the UGT's structure proved to be more resilient and enduring.

CNT unions, which generally included a larger proportion of unskilled workers, charged lower dues and canvassed for voluntary contributions to support striking workers and sustain imprisoned workers and their families.[78] The UGT required higher dues payments, part of which was allocated to strike defense funds and to *casas del pueblos,* which served as union headquarters and also housed cooperatives, libraries, death benefit societies, and the like.

The collapse of conciliatory efforts by the Sánchez Toca–Burgos y Mazo government led in December 1919 to its replacement by yet another conservative administration, this one headed by Manuel Allende Salazar, which named Count Salvatierra (José Maestre Laborde) as civil governor and reverted to a policy of repression. This policy change followed the onset of a serious financial crisis the previous summer with the collapse of the important Bank of Barcelona, which created credit difficulties for many industrial and commercial enterprises, thus greatly increasing entrepreneurial apprehensions. The brusque change of course began ominously with an unsuccessful assassination attempt on Seguí in January followed by another against the Employers Federation head Felix Graupera (also unsuccessful). Again union halls were padlocked, leaders imprisoned, and the CRT declared illegal. This and the employers' lockout, which lasted until January 26, weakened the CNT. But the return to repressive measures was accompanied by increased social violence.

Upon discovering that the unsavory gang headed by German adventurer Baron Koenig employed as anti-CNT mercenaries was also engaged in a shakedown racket of employers, Salvatierra ordered its dissolution and Koenig (a.k.a. Colman) was deported. Meanwhile, as terrorism grew to menacing proportions, juries became subject to intimidation by both sides and consequently rarely convicted accused terrorists, a situation that eventually led to the abolition of jury trials.

When conservative Eduardo Dato became prime minister in June 1920, he first seemed committed to labor "normalization." A Labor Ministry was established for the first time, and various protective measures were adopted. The newly appointed civil governor for Barcelona, Federico Carlos Bas, the former director of the Customs Service, was instructed to pursue an even-handed policy in resolving the city's labor problems. The repressive measures instituted by his predecessor, Count Salvatierra, were gradually dismantled, press censorship lifted, and hundreds of CNT officials and activists freed from jail. Emergency rule was ended, and though CNT activities continued to be closely monitored, existing labor legislation and basic rights were honored. Emulating Julio Amado, Bas sought to extend a helping hand to Seguí and other moderates. But the situation was much less amenable to reconciliatory efforts than had been the case with Amado. A renewed groundswell of labor unrest and strike activity took place during mid- and late 1920, much of it accompanied by violence. Business activity and manufacturing were gradually slackening as the wartime boom was coming to an end. The rising toll of terror and counterterror was poisoning the climate and convincing ever larger sectors of the business community that little hope remained for a peaceful resolution. The bloody gun battles between the CNT and the Libre hit squads raged on.

CNT moderates had managed during the tenure of Julio Amado to exercise sufficient control to maintain labor terrorism (*pistolerismo*) at a reasonably low level. Now, however, despite a professed sympathy for Bas, they found themselves much less capable of maintaining control over their depleted ranks.[79] Bas's failure, therefore, owed less to the relationship between the restoration of basic rights and unabating social disorder than to bad timing. Strike activity and social turmoil were at their height in 1920. It was also a year of strikingly contradictory trends. Before slackening, inflation reached its highest level ever amid growing economic contraction and an increasing number of unemployed. The economic situation both exacerbated workers' discontent and stiffened employers' resolve to resist union demands.

Practically the entire moderate leadership had been jailed under the administration of hard-liner Salvatierra, making the union easy prey for extremists and action groups. Ironically, whenever a tough law-and-order policy was instituted, the CNT moderates, erroneously held responsible for terrorist activities, were almost invariably imprisoned, thus facilitating the takeover by those favoring violence. When Seguí and his collaborators were freed at Bas's direction, they discovered to their dismay that the presence and influence of the gunslingers had increased. Much of the organization's revenues now were being diverted to the financing of action squads and subsidizing jailed Cenetistas and their families. Years later Angel Pestaña was to write, "The organization lost control and was unable to direct its activities as it wished. It then lost its moral standing. . . . The CNT became so discredited that even today to call someone a *sindicalista* is synonymous with *pistolero*, criminal, outlaw, delinquent."[80]

The level of violence during both administrations therefore remained constant: fifty-six *atentados* took place in the first four months of Salvatierra's tenure compared with fifty-five for a like period under Bas.[81] The vacillations in government policy, with its crackdowns on the CNT followed by exercises in tolerance that attempted to imbue reconciliations with an impression of weakness and an accompanying loss in credibility, were responsible for this chaos.

To force a return to the iron fist the mayor of Barcelona convened a meeting on November 5 of community leaders, which adopted a statement denouncing the policy of even-handedness and calling for the replacement of Governor Bas. Belatedly alarmed, Seguí ordered an end to labor disputes—thirty-two thousand workers were on strike at the end of October—and by November 7 the lengthy and hard-fought strike in the Barcelona metalworking industry was finally settled. But it was too little too late.

Growth, élan, and forward momentum continued through 1920, the year of greatest labor unrest in postwar Spain. But as the year drew to an end the fortunes of Spanish anarcho-syndicalism were on the wane.

The origins of *pistolerismo* remain somewhat hazy, but its link with Barcelona's legacy of turbulent labor relations seems indisputable. Lacking relatively orderly channels of resolution, labor disputes had always been marked by an inordinately high quotient of violence. Scattered instances of assaults on factory owners and public officials predate the anarchists so the appearance during the late nineteenth century of the doctrine of propaganda by the deed provided some with a moralizing rationale. *Pistolerismo* thus emerged against a background of endemic violence engendered by indiscriminate hostility on the part of employers to collective redress of workers' grievances, leading to recurrent cycles of severe repression, the virtual destruction of labor organizations, and their subsequent rebirth. To avert total destruction through the hiring of strikebreakers, violence became a standard resort. With the introduction of anarcho-syndicalist ideas in 1907 anarchist terrorism ebbed, but its foundations had been laid and it would resurface on appropriate occasions.

Barcelona's populous underworld had been swelled by the wartime influx of riffraff from all over Europe—deserters, prostitutes, confidence men, criminals on the run, and the like. Labor terrorism first arose coincident with the general increase in social violence and criminality. Angel Pestaña dates its first appearance to 1916. The city had become one of the great wartime supply centers for France and other Allied powers. Germany mounted a considerable effort to harass and cripple this supply line. Barcelona was converted into a major battleground for rival espionage services, and the city teemed with foreign agents. Bombs were set off and manufacturers assassinated under German direction. Police Commissioner Manuel Bravo Portillo, who was in the pay of the Germans, provided the sailing schedules of Spanish ships laden with war matériel so that German submarines, laying in wait, could torpedo them. He also bribed several CNT local union officers, including the president of the metalworkers, to arrange the murder of a prominent factory owner engaged in the production of shell casings for France. Criminal elements were contracted to sabotage production and threaten factory owners. Some of the assaults in this period that had been attributed to Cenetistas later turned out to have been carried out by German mercenaries.[82] The local German consulate also provided funds to the financially hard-pressed *Solidaridad Obrera* in exchange for articles designed to discourage emigration to France, although Pestaña ended these subventions when he assumed direction of the paper.

As manufacturing prospered and the unions became stronger, some employers sought to avert costly interruptions of production by granting wage increases and recognizing the unions. Those who were less reasonable, especially in the textile industry, were subjected to bombings or accosted by armed groups acting under the direction of some union leaders. Those who made up these groups, recounts Pestaña, "were known members of the organization and of anarchist groups whom public opinion and the working class treated with the respect and consideration that any person might receive." They were "that special type of people who live in the twilight zone that exists between employment and common delinquency."[83] To some extent the initial two or three attacks that the anarchist militants undertook in Barcelona on behalf of the textile union represented a resumption of the old anarchist tradition of propaganda by the deed.

Some employers were killed and others injured. Many of the intimidated holdouts gave in to union demands, thus encouraging union enrollment but also providing greater incentive for the use of armed coercion. The great mass of workers observed these actions impassively if not with unconcealed approval.[84] More and more labor leaders consequently began to make use of action groups while employers hired bodyguards and counterterrorist gangs.

Pistolerismo remained at a low level during the war years and did not enter the mainstream of trade union life. Many of the anarchist action groups operated outside union control. Angel Pestaña tells of an encounter with several young men in 1916, members of an anarchist terrorist group, who offered to carry out assassinations of undesirable employers or public officials. As long as Seguí and other moderates remained physically in control of union affairs they were able to prevent terrorist extremists from making serious inroads in the organization. But it was impossible to immunize the entire organization. Within the space of a few years CNT membership had grown from thirty thousand to almost half a million, and there must have been an acute shortage of experienced, responsible leaders. Manuel Buenacasa comments, "Half a million dues payments in Catalonia alone filled the union treasuries; the ambitious ones, the hotheads . . . the rogues saw their opportunity arrive. All of us found ourselves caught up in a filthy whirlwind, unable to react against the huge influx of hoodlums and parasites who dominated in that climate."[85]

The murder of textile union leader Pau Sabater on July 19, 1919, marked the beginning of a series of wanton attacks and bombings that bloodied the streets of Barcelona. As in numerous similar instances his murderers were never identified nor did the police care. Their disinterest in uncovering the guilty parties, their incompetence, and their frequent complicity helped persuade unionists and action groups to take matters into their own hands.[86]

Employers and union officials alike hired bodyguards as social violence took on ominous proportions. In the beginning worker *pistoleros* mainly consisted of anarchist militants, but as terrorism increased, both sides recruited criminal elements. Hoodlums and toughs formerly employed by the Germans found new paymasters in the Barcelona Employers Federation as factory owners mounted a counterterrorist campaign. Before long terrorism and counterterrorism took on a life of its own. The murder of Pau Sabater led to the gunning down of Bravo Portillo by a Cenetista action squad. Portillo was then replaced by a particularly unsavory German adventurer known as Baron Koenig, who had worked for both the Germans and the French. Both the Bravo Portillo and Baron Koenig gangs worked closely with the local police and the Somaten. An estimated 843 *atentados* took place in Catalonia between 1918 and September 1923. For a graphic view of the violence between 1919 and 1925, see figure 7.1.

"Barcelona had to grow amid bombs, strikes, and assaults," recounts a journalist. "Economic, political, and cultural life, life in general, went on not without indifference to the agitation, rather in spite of it, being stronger than the daily disorder that occurred mainly in the industrial suburbs or in the famous fifth district. When it spilled over into the more gentrified parts of the city, it would last only a few hours when a com-

Figure 7.1.   Strikers and Social Terrorist Incidents in Spain, 1919–1925

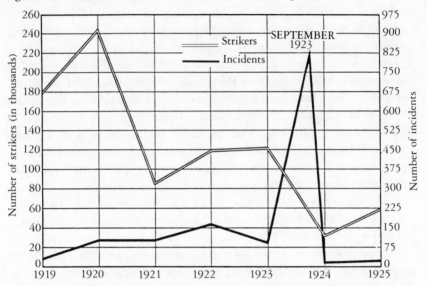

Source: Prepared by Latin Cartographic Institute in 1925, reprinted in Jaime Vicens Vives, *Historia de España y America, social y económica*, 5 vols. (Barcelona: Editorial Vicens, 1972), 5:361.

mando came through. Accustomed to this epidemic, the Barcelonite regarded it with trepidation, complaining of the government's inability to restore peace—always complaining against the government—and after having finished his day's work, better paid than before the war, devoted himself to his diversions and to soccer, which was then becoming a generalized passion."[87]

In a sort of retrospective mea culpa written in 1933 Pestaña mentions "collective complicity," placing much of the blame for the spread of the terrorist scourge on himself and his colleagues. Though vigorously repudiating the use or encouragement of armed terrorism, Seguí, Pestaña, and others tolerated it. When some union leaders hired armed gangs to enforce union discipline and to force reluctant employers to toe the line, these moderates tended to do nothing. None among them could bring himself to use force to stop the violence—after all, many of the *pistoleros* were idealistic anarchists and trade union activists. In 1920 Seguí called a meeting of union officers to denounce terrorist methods and secured a pledge from those in attendance to combat it, but nothing changed. And with violence widespread, to seek to end it was to risk life and limb. One day, for example, while en route to a meeting of the joint commission, Seguí was accosted by a well-known anarchist terrorist who angrily waved a pistol at him and threatened to kill him if he "betrayed" the CNT.

We have learned that once a sustained terrorist situation develops, its termination becomes extremely difficult. In common with the Basque ETA terrorists and other current prototypes, the Barcelona labor wars spawned and nurtured a genus of professional killers who became inured to their way of life and consequently had a vested interest in its perpetuation. Assassination squads changed loyalties and paymasters with alacrity.

The waxing and waning of terrorist activity throughout this period in large measure depended on whether at any given moment the authorities pursued a policy of repression or conciliation and whether the CNT leadership was imprisoned or permitted to exercise control. Once legal channels of activity were closed off, inducements to employ force of arms were greatly enhanced, stimulating "anarcho-syndicalist terrorism to the detriment of mass action and control by responsible leaders."[88] Numerous shop delegates who lost their jobs and were blacklisted, for example, lived off dues collections often made at gunpoint or joined action squads.

Persecution by the authorities and employers as well as the excesses committed by CNT supporters inspired the formation of a rival organization. A group of Carlist workers, most of them former members of the CNT, founded the Free Unions (Sindicatos Libres) in October 1919 for the purpose of wresting control from the anarcho-syndicalists. Denouncing the CNT for its adoption of libertarian communism and revolutionary objectives, rationalist schools, the increasing influence of action groups, and the general climate of coercion and strongarm tactics, the Libres emphasized a return to fundamentals. Though of a rightist orientation, it was characterized more by its opposition to the CNT than a coherent ideology of its own.[89]

Unlike most other Catholic-inspired ventures, the Free Unions were created and led by workers, and the group's confessional origins and its ties to Carlism were carefully played down. Though repudiated by much of the Catholic community, which regarded the Libres as another form of trade union thuggery, the group was befriended by Father Gafo's Católicos-Libres, who were in dire need of allies.

The Libres was a Catholic-oriented union sui generis. With its militant trade union action, tendency to violence, an adversarial attitude toward employers, celebration of May Day, and encouragement of strike actions and collective bargaining, it appealed to numerous wage earners.[90]

During its first year of existence its membership did not exceed ten thousand. By the end of 1920, however, the union expanded its recruitment beyond the core group of Carlists and Catholic workers. Workers in some factories joined en masse, as did a majority of the city's cooks and waiters. But further progress proved difficult largely because of a campaign of intimidation and murders by Cenetistas against Libre leaders and activists. CNT members also refused to work alongside Libre supporters.

The Libres then entered into a mutual assistance pact with the Employers Federation to combat their common foe. The authorities till then evinced little interest in encouraging a rival union but rather sought in some instances to work with Seguí and other CNT moderates. Even hardliner Count Salvatierra shunned the Libres.

Action groups of Carlist young men in their teens and twenties were formed, which, like the anarchist hit squads, were joined by members of the Barcelona underworld. While still in his early twenties, Ramón Sales, a rural Carlist and a former member of the CNT mercantile union, became the Libres' caudillo. Like their CNT counterparts most Libre leaders were in their twenties and thirties. General Emilio Mola describes Sales as "short, cross-eyed, with a round face from which jutted a carefully manicured mustache, curly black hair, an intelligent look, proper dress, correct manners, a facile tongue with a marked Catalan accent, and an energetic expression." His "extensive arsenal of explosive arguments" and his "rather violent character" were also noted.[91]

The interunion rivalry became all-consuming, with each side more intent on inflicting blows on the other than on the employers. Labor violence underwent a marked increase, especially during the first two years of the Libres' existence. Some 109 *atentados* were recorded in 1919, and in 1920 and 1921 the number rose to 304 and 254 respectively. Of the Libres' "martyrs" forty of some fifty-three were gunned down in the first two years of the union's life.

The terrorist plague soon spread to such industrial centers as Valencia, Zaragossa, and Bilbao (see table 7.4). But more than half of all *atentados* officially recorded between January 1920 and mid-1921 took place in Barcelona. "A madness took possession of Barcelona," labor activist Albert Pérez Baró tells us. "No longer were there isolated attacks. Gangs in broad daylight confronted each other with gunfire at the city's center.

Table 7.4. Social Assaults in Spain, January 1, 1917, to January 1, 1922

City	Deaths	Wounded
Barcelona	225	733
Valencia	57	120
Bilbao	24	145
Zaragossa	23	51
Seville	12	42
Madrid	8	62

Source: José Maria Farré Morego, *Los atentados sociales en España, las teorias, los hechos, estadisticas* (Madrid: Casa Faure, 1922).

Nobody went out at night. When the payment of dues to unions was made illegal, some of the workers who normally would have cooperated now refused to do so, consequently reducing material resources as well as the subsidies provided prisoners."[92]

Because of the deteriorating situation, "the period May to November 1920," avers Albert Balcells, "cannot be regarded as one of conciliation and authentic pacification as the previous one in 1919 but rather a time of truce during which the CNT proved incapable of recouping its former prestige and authority. It was, at the same time, a period in which the ruling classes ended up forming a united front intent upon its destruction."[93]

Dato, never known as a man of strong convictions, came under the strong combined pressures of the Catalan bourgeoisie, conservative party hard-liners led by Juan de la Cierva, and the military juntas. He reversed the government's labor policy, leading Interior Minister Francisco Bergamin to step down, to be replaced by Count Gabino Bugallal. But the shift was not fully implemented until November 8, when General Severiano Martínez Anido replaced Bas as civil governor.[94] Dato had apparently decided that though a crackdown might have little effect, it was much more risky for his weak government to incur the displeasure of such powerful groups. King Alfonso XIII was urging the renunciation of a mediatory role with the tacit approval of the Liberal party, the Lliga Regionalista, and the Employers Confederation. The CNT's expansion in southern Spain and other parts of the country, the great rise in labor unrest everywhere, and the bitter six-month strike at the huge Rio Tinto mine had prompted a broad consensus favoring harsh countermeasures.[95] Thus the lengthy debate in ruling circles over whether to employ peaceful means in dealing with the CNT or to rely on force, as Catalan big business demanded, was finally given a definitive response.

As the Dato government readied a shift in policy, a CNT delegation headed by Seguí hastened to Madrid to renew its alliance with the UGT and to obtain assurances of its participation in a national strike action being planned for December to protest repression of the Barcelona unions. The UGT leadership, embroiled in an internal crisis precipitated by the divisive debate over affiliation with the Third International, responded with caution. As a sop mainly to the PSOE left-wingers, a renewal of the alliance was agreed to as was UGT participation in the projected general strike. But as the date of the strike approached, the fear of any association with a defense of labor terrorism, the strike's possibly adverse effects on the PSOE's prospects in the parliamentary elections scheduled for December 19, and the chastening effects of the 1917 fiasco persuaded Besteiro, Largo Caballero, and other UGT moderates not to honor their commitment, thus assuring the strike's failure.[96] In parliament, however, Besteiro and Prieto strongly denounced the government's role in the Barcelona repression.

Dato's capitulation to the Catalonian industrialists by naming Severiano Martínez Anido as civil governor attests to the weakness of a Restoration regime that was no longer capable of following consistent, coherent labor policies.[97] The tragic mishandling of the Barcelona labor crisis and the Annual debacle in Morocco were to be the main culprits in the final collapse of parliamentary rule and the military takeover in 1923.

General Martínez Anido was a military ultraconservative everyman, convinced of the power of brute force in resolving complex social problems. The historian Jesús Pabón describes him as possessing

a simple, strong personality. Rather than the violent character attributed to him by his adversaries, he usually was calm and courteous but lacking in that personal human quality that so stood in good stead for Primo de Rivera. His intellectual and perceptual horizons were limited, but his will was strong and his effectiveness was based almost exclusively on tenacity. He was not very good at the written or spoken word. . . . His limitations account for his strengths and weaknesses, his way of viewing issues, his convictions, actions, and their ultimate outcomes. "He was the general," wrote someone who knew him, "a robust man though not stout, of medium height, strong gestures lacking in elegance

... deliberated ineffusive declarations ... with a vehement desire to impose his authority."[98]

A brutal crackdown based on a flimsy pretext was launched barely three weeks following his naming. CNT organizations were proscribed, union halls sequestered, and sixty-four labor leaders thrown into prison.[99] On November 20 a plant delegate was murdered by two members of the Somaten. An attempted general strike the next day proved only partially successful. The number of imprisoned Cenetistas soon rose to four hundred. The situation quickly took a macabre turn. Upon his return from Rio Tinto, Salvador Seguí was arrested and a flurry of killings by both Cenetistas and Libres followed. On the thirtieth Francisco Layret, a Republican deputy representing Sabadell, who also served as CNT counsel, paralyzed from the waist down, was murdered by Libre killers while en route to protest the imprisonment of Lluis Companys, a city councilman and fellow Republican. Thirty-six of the detained Cenetistas, including Seguí, were then transferred to Mola castle on the Balearic island of Mahón. A total of twenty-two killings by the two opposing bands took place during Martínez Anido's first month in office.[100]

Any semblance of official impartiality was stripped away as antiunion terrorism was applied with a vengeance. Libre *pistoleros* financed by the Employers Federation received official sanction and worked closely with the police and the Somaten in a concerted effort to annihilate the entire CNT leadership. Claudi Ametlla recalled, "One was consequently treated to the shocking, profoundly demoralizing spectacle of the government protecting a gang of mercenary killers."[101] Chief of Police Colonel Miguel Arlegui, whose more brutal impulses had been held in check by Governor Bas, now gave full vent to his more visceral propensities, personally torturing CNT prisoners. To relieve the congestion in the jails, weekly departures known as *conducción* took place, with manacled columns of prisoners forced to march to distant penitentiaries under the supervision of armed mounted civil guards.

The barbaric practice of *ley de fugas* (the escape law) was introduced in early 1921. Jailed Cenetistas were released in the middle of the night and were mercilessly gunned down before they had gone a few yards. Official reports listed them as killed while trying to escape. During the first twenty-two days of 1921 a total of twenty-one Cenetistas died in this manner.

Given carte blanche by the Dato government, Martínez Anido ruled

Barcelona with impunity. Most likely the government found it politically easier to distance itself from the dirty war and let Martínez Anido shoulder full responsibility. Nevertheless, it was Dato and not Martínez Anido who fell victim on March 8, 1921, to CNT gunmen who had been dispatched from Barcelona to avenge the *ley de fugas* atrocities.

The number of terrorist incidents during 1921 was only slightly lower than in the preceding year, but industrialists could take comfort that fewer factory owners and executives were now among the victims. Most were Cenetistas with a few Libre supporters.[102] The number of common crimes also rose, fostered by the climate of official lawlessness.

During the summer of 1921 the country was rudely shaken by news of a devastating defeat suffered at the hands of Moroccan guerrillas. As a debacle it was rivaled only by the Spanish-American War of 1898. Thousands had been killed or wounded. Spanish prisoners taken by the guerrillas numbered in the thousands, vast amounts of matériel were abandoned to the attackers, and General Manuel Fernández Silvestre, the expedition commander, perished in the ambush. To cope with this disaster, King Alfonso XIII called yet another coalition government headed by the aging Antonio Maura. Preoccupied with the military disaster, the new government kept Martínez Anido on as civil governor along with his implacable anti-CNT policy.

The unrelenting persecution of the CNT ate away at the organization's vitals. And the postwar recession caused strike activity to diminish. Through a combination of CNT demoralization and intimidation the Libre unions won over part of the former CNT following. To encourage recruitment, the Libres began to assume a more aggressive bargaining stance in the fall of 1921 and to sponsor work stoppages. Martínez Anido ignored the employers' complaints and continued to act as the Libres' patron-protector. By the following year they claimed a membership in excess of one hundred thousand.

When the Maura coalition cabinet was replaced by a conservative one led by José Sánchez Guerra, the beginning of the end loomed for Martínez Anido. Although he remained in office until October 1922, a new policy was adopted that led to the reestablishment of constitutional guarantees and the release of jailed CNT members, and the organization was gradually permitted to resume normal activities. For a time, therefore, official policy was contradictory, with the CNT resuming activities and Martínez Anido and Arlegui shielding the Libres and helping them retain the trade union following they had wrested from Cenetismo.

Martínez Anido's undoing came through a falling-out with Lliga Regionalista leaders and as a result of several crude terrorist conspiracies. Arlegui's agents and Libre gunmen attempted to assassinate Angel Pestaña during his visit to Manresa. The killers sent from Barcelona seriously wounded him and then stationed themselves around the hospital where he had been taken to finish the job upon his departure. A national outcry led Sánchez Guerra to order Martínez Anido to guarantee the safety of Pestaña. To make matters worse, a phony attempt on the life of Martínez Anido was concocted to serve as a pretext for the mass elimination of numerous CNT leaders through use of the *ley de fugas*.

A conciliatory policy was then instituted and yet another try made at persuading the CNT to forsake terrorist violence and operate within a legal framework. But as had been the case with Governor Bas, past repressions, CNT internal disarray, and the deep sense of alienation that had been instilled in many surviving activists could not be overcome.

Seguí's return to active leadership led to a moderation in CNT behavior. A national conference in Zaragossa in 1922 marked its high point. Following a report by Pestaña, who had returned from an inquiry mission to Moscow, affiliation with the Communist International was dropped, marking a defeat for the procommunist minority led by Andrés Nin, Joaquín Maurín, and Hilario Arlandis, which had gained control of the national committee following the murder of General Secretary Evelio Boal in 1921. Seguí was named national secretary, and the delegates voted to affiliate with the newly founded anarcho-syndicalist International Workingmen's Association (AIT) based in Berlin. At his urging, the conference also voted for the first time to create a full-time corps of paid trade union functionaries.

Seguí had long believed that it was strategically vital for the anarchosyndicalist movement to forge alliances with congenial labor and political groups. To move the organization in that direction, he drafted a balanced and somewhat contradictory resolution that declared the CNT to be "a distinctly revolutionary body that clearly rejects parliamentary and collaborationist action with political parties yet is undeniably political since its goal is to attain the prerogatives of review and oversight over the evolving values of national life; to such an end its duty is to exercise positive action by means of coercion derived from the resources and power of the CNT."[103] The resolution that was adopted disengaged the organization from communist and anarchist exclusiveness.

During the ensuing two-and-a-half-month truce with the Libres, the

CNT was able to recoup some of its losses. Some workers who had joined the Libres began to drift back. But this modest resurgence proved to be of short duration. In March 1923 Salvador Seguí was murdered by Libre *pistoleros* alarmed over the CNT's recuperation. A recrudescence of terrorism took place that featured exploits by a rising group of young anarchists. Headed by such men as Buenaventura Durruti, Juan García Oliver, Francisco Ascaso, Torres Escartin, and others, a number of secret affinity groups were formed bearing names such as Los Solidarios (the solidarists). These men were professional revolutionaries who hoped to convert the CNT into a totally anarchist organization and believed that coups executed by convinced minorities would be more successful than working with trade unions and sectors of the discontented middle class.

As the repression drained the CNT of its following and financial resources, Durruti and his fellow insurrectionists engaged in a series of daring armed holdups and bank robberies to raise funds for the unions and to purchase arms for the coming revolution. To avenge the murder of Seguí, Cardinal Juan Soldevilla Romero of Zaragossa and former Vizcaya civil governor Fernando González de Regueral were executed.

In an effort to regain lost ground, the CNT engaged in three major labor conflicts in Barcelona in 1923, all of them ending in disaster and further intensifying internal cleavages between laborites, anarchists, and procommunists. Thus when General Primo de Rivera launched his successful power bid later that year an extenuated CNT could offer little resistance.

The brutal suppression directed by General Martínez Anido unquestionably contributed greatly to the demise of the CNT. But perhaps of even greater importance were the economic crisis of 1921–22 and mass layoffs of workers that made use of the strike weapon for economic or political purposes much less practicable. The accompanying decline in worker militancy forced the CNT to assume an unaccustomed defensive posture.

8

THE SHAPING OF LABOR RELATIONS UNDER THE RESTORATION

Government and Labor

As elsewhere in western Europe, labor disputes and worker protest in Spain before the 1868 revolution were generally viewed as subversive challenges to the right of employers to preside in their establishments. Because few such disturbances attracted public notice, there was little reason to regard them otherwise. This attitude was reinforced by the endemic sociopolitical instability during much of the century and the tardy, only partial acceptance of modern industrial values. In France the Napoleonic Code of 1804 institutionalized a strong bias in the employer's favor, "le maitre est cru sur son affirmation." By 1868 this view had disappeared from French legal precepts. In Spain, however, a literal transcription, "el amo sera creido," was incorporated in Article 1584 of the Civil Code of 1889.[1]

The conservative response to worker protest was best expressed during the late nineteenth century by Antonio Cánovas del Castillo, the principal architect of the Restoration political system. "His social ideas," comments José Luis Comellas, "evolved less than his political ideas." During the 1870s he emphasized "Christian sentiments and private philanthropic charity, yet barely showed any awareness of an unjust social order or advanced any remedy other than what each person chose to apply with complete contractual liberty defined by the individualistic liberalism of the times."[2] His social conservatism reflected a pessimistic view of human nature. In one of his innumerable parliamentary addresses, he observed in 1871,

Your honor has declared, as I also hold, that the suppression of poverty is impossible. Nor do I hold that any practical person believes it possible, for to do so would require defending optimism that, to be sure, is the basis and constitutes the substance of certain political schools, the old ideas of Rousseau transformed, which is to imagine everything in the world to be good and all existing evil the work of men, as if someone other than men could have fashioned history. But evil exists, poverty exists today, inequalities exist, perversity exists within the human heart. There will always be poverty, always; there will always be an inferior estate, the final rung of the social ladder, and a proletariat that it will be necessary to contain by charity, enlightenment, and moral resources. And when these do not suffice, then with force.[3]

Cánovas, nonetheless, was a conservative, not a reactionary. The growth of industrial development and the attendant emergence of social conflict made it increasingly evident that traditional notions of individual Christian charity no longer sufficed. Cánovas became an ardent proponent of the Bismarckian carrot-and-stick approach: monopolization of social and political power by a select elite buttressed by a state-sponsored welfare paternalism sufficient to assure pacification of the masses, a belief that has much in common with the Franco regime. The neo-welfare state was a necessary adjunct to the *état gendarme*. "For a long time," Cánovas declared in 1890, a year of labor unrest, "perhaps for all time, armies will be the robust support of the present social order, and the invincible dike against illegal attempts by the proletariat who, through the use of violence, will only succeed in needlessly spilling its blood in unequal combat."[4] The military alone, however, could not ensure social tranquility. "One should not engage in wishful thinking," he warned in 1890, "the charitable sentiment and its like no longer are sufficient by themselves to care for today's exigencies. A complementary organization at the very least is necessary with individual initiatives emanating from the leading social forces."[5] Labor extremism could be held in check through the combined efforts of the state and Christian charity. In 1889 Cánovas declared, "Much that true workers ask, not those who lack a trade other than that of revolutionaries or who have it as their main one, civil society can grant, making use of the lesser or greater results of individual philanthropy that some call altruism. Accordingly, virtually all Europe hastens to the extent possible to favor workers."[6]

During his lifetime the grand design for a peninsular version of the Bismarckian welfare state remained largely theoretical. Priority had to be given to politics, to the elaboration of the Restoration party system, and to assuring order and control over his often fractious Conservative party. Insurrections in Cuba and the Philippines monopolized the attention of succeeding governments. Nonetheless, during the 1880s Cánovas supported the establishment of the Social Reforms Commission that eventually led to the creation of the Institute of Social Reforms, and in 1890 he sponsored legislation limiting the industrial employment of women and minors and establishing Sunday as a day of rest. Both measures failed to win the approval of the Senate. In 1896 he was struck down by an Italian anarchist. The social legislation he had sought was enacted in 1900 with the passage of laws regulating working conditions for women and children and for industrial accidents sponsored by his fellow conservative Eduardo Dato.

The right of association was formally acknowledged for the first time in the 1869 constitution, but Article 556 of the 1870 Penal Code made any collective action to alter the conditions of labor a felony. Throughout this period the government became increasingly tolerant of labor organization, but the repressive legal provisions were not repealed until 1909.[7] Legislation and ordinances tended to be drafted with calculated ambiguity to provide government authorities maximum discretionary powers in their interpretation and application.[8] It was not until the advent of the Second Republic in the 1930s that a legal statute specifically assuring labor's right to organize was promulgated.

The passage of the 1887 Associations Law marked a notable increase in tolerance for worker organization. Some idea of the situation unionists faced before passage of that law can be obtained from the following testimony of a Madrid stonemason given during hearings conducted in the 1880s by the Social Reforms Commission: "We were holding a meeting in the Recreo theater with the government representative present. We were discussing our by-laws. He disapproved and peremptorily adjourned the meeting and arrested those of us who were members of the executive committee. It then became necessary to have friends intervene and to thank the authorities profusely because we were released in three or four hours. The result is that nobody is willing to become a member of the executive committees of these societies. Of our eleven members, I am sure that if we were to hold a meeting today only five would show up because all of them are afraid of getting involved in a trial and ending up in jail."[9]

Changes in the government's role in labor disputes and the adoption of social legislation led to a kindred evolution in terminology. The first protective regulation (limiting employment of women and children), passed in 1873, was justified on grounds of Christian charity. Other laws cited gracious concessions granted by the monarch. By 1917, however, laws were adopted invoking social justice, government obligations, and "where formerly there had been humanitarian measures, we now observe juridical solutions." This awakening social awareness paralleled similar acknowledgments throughout continental Europe of workers' inalienable rights, which previously had been regarded as philanthropic concessions. Such a change of heart had been induced by the rising tide of labor organization and industrial strife during the final quarter of the nineteenth century. It came in Spain during the second and third decades of this century following a period of mounting labor unrest and an explosive growth in union membership.

As labor disputes became a regular feature of everyday life, the legal system proved incapable of responding to the new field of jurisprudence that was required.[10] Labor cases ordinarily require expeditious handling with minimal cost, an impossibility for a legal structure that was notorious for being dilatory, costly, and, above all, ineffectual. Judicial decisions, moreover, were often subject to pressures from government authorities and politicians. Labor organizations also had to overcome the antilabor, authoritarian cast of mind of most government functionaries. The passage in 1909 of a bill sponsored by the Maura government creating conciliation tribunals merely added to the growing number of inoperative regulations.[11] It was small wonder that the advocates of direct action were able to convince countless workers to reject legal recourse in resolving disputes and to rely solely on their own strength.

Government intrusion in industrial peacemaking followed an episodic, improvisational course engendered more by circumstance than design. Politics, of course, as well as differing philosophies, was often the influencing factor. Though the policies of the two ruling parties were generally indistinguishable and both included advocates of social reform and greater government intervention in the regulation of labor affairs, the approach varied depending on which of the two was in power. As the self-proclaimed heirs of 1868 and to compete with the Republicans for support among urban wage earners, Liberals tended to take a more tolerant attitude toward the development of autonomous, legal, moderate worker organizations and to strive for broadly acceptable solutions to social problems. In the resolution of labor disputes, Liberal governments, therefore, sometimes exhibited less of a rigid law-and-order approach and a slightly greater disposition to favor mediated outcomes. Conservatives, influenced by church social doctrine, displayed a greater skepticism toward the development of a nonrevolutionary labor movement. They often supported initiatives by employers and the church such as mixed worker-employer societies.

The first Catalonian industrywide textile strike occurred in 1890 while a Liberal government was in office. Partly at the urging of government authorities, the employers agreed to a compromise settlement with the Tres Clases de Vapor Federación. But the compromise proved to be a ruse. Six months later, following the replacement of the Liberal government by a Conservative one, the factory owners unilaterally abrogated the accord and proceeded to smash the union by instituting a lockout. Wage cuts and harsher working conditions followed the union defeat. By its refusal to intervene and its silence concerning the flagrant violation of an accord arrived at under the preceding government, the newly installed Conservative government openly assisted the employers in gaining the upper hand.

The Barcelona general strike of 1902, on the other hand, placed employers and government at loggerheads. Backed by a Liberal government that had returned to power, the local civil governor energetically sought to mediate a compromise settlement between the striking metalworkers and their employers. But the latter were not in a conciliatory mood and held out for the union's total demise, rejecting all compromise formulas. For his efforts, the civil governor was mercilessly pilloried, publicly accused of harboring an anti-Catalan bias, of being soft on labor extremism, and of failing to end the strike by calling in the armed forces.[12] When the employers' unyielding attitude transformed the metalworkers' dispute into a general strike, the authorities abandoned their peacemaking efforts and declared martial law, causing violent clashes, numerous casualties, and the collapse of the metalworkers' strike.

Another notable dispute of the period, the Gijón general strike of 1901, turned into a four-way battle, the employers on one side, the authorities as mediators, and the striking workers represented by contentious anarchists and socialists. It all began when the port workers' society presented formal demands during December 1900 for an increase in the daily wage, employment guarantees, and the institution of an eight-hour day. When the employers failed to respond, the port workers went on strike in January 1901, and strikebreakers were brought in from the nearby rural provinces of León and Palencia. An attempt at mediation by the civil governor was unsuccessful, and the ensuing employers' lockout elicited a general strike by the city's sixteen thousand wage earners. Differences meanwhile arose within the strike committee between anarchists and socialists, who were engaged in a fierce competition for dominance over the city's organized workers. An attempt at mediation by the noted writer and journalist Leopoldo Alas ("Clarín") proved unsuccessful because the anarchists had gained control of the strike committee and were intent on converting the shutdown into an insurrectionary general strike of indefinite duration. The civil governor then turned matters over to the military authorities, and on February 18 the strike committee was forced to accept the wage formula contained in the Alas formula but with a nine-hour day. The employers, moreover, were able to force the unions to bargain on an individual basis rather than through a citywide accord.[13]

Restoration governments were primarily concerned with the interests of landowners, financiers, and big industrialists. The differences over labor policy that sometimes emerged between the dynastic parties should not obscure their essentially upper-class orientation, as Montero García notes: "Declarations of social harmony as opposed to class struggle and the paternalistic protector-protected relation based on the acceptance of social inequalities as being something natural was upheld as much by Conservatives as the Liberals."[14] The inauguration of industrial strife, however, created increasing complications because government decision making had to take into account not only political considerations and client interests but also the maintenance of public order, the government's own survival, and its credibility as a mediatory agency.[15] Consequently, government and management sometimes adopted contrary attitudes. Illustrative of such a situation was the unfolding of the famous Vizcayan iron miners' strike of 1890 that paralyzed the province's mining operations and led to sympathy walkouts by large numbers of Bilbao factory workers. Previously, military intervention had invariably meant the smashing of a strike and vindication of the employers. The iron mine owners therefore enthusiastically welcomed the declaration of martial law and the takeover of the mining zone by military units.

This time, however, the military commandant, General Loma, unexpectedly forced the mine owners into accepting a compromise settlement by threatening to withdraw his troops. Why he did so is not known. The small size of available police forces in the mine zone compared with the thousands of striking workers and the fear that when the army contingents were withdrawn uncontrollable labor violence would recur must have been motivating factors. Fusi theorizes that "possibly acting on his generous impulses, Loma sought to carry out the instructions of a government (Sagasta), weakened by ministerial crises, that, therefore, needed to avert serious complications that might precipitate its downfall, and desirous of crediting itself with political merit by overcoming the much feared labor agitation of that May 1890."[16]

Thus while employers throughout Spain eagerly solicited military intervention to break strikes and crush labor organizations, for reasons peculiar to the Vizcayan iron zone, military intervention at a time when the government could ill afford serious incidents was astutely exploited by Facundo Perezagua and his fellow socialists. General Zappino in 1903 and 1906 and General Aguilar in 1910 likewise refused to crush strikes, both no doubt influenced by the mine owners' refusal to abide by accords they had agreed to. Such instances of intransigence and duplicity on the part of employers complicated matters for the authorities. When Prime Minister José Canalejas was laboriously engaged in seeking a negotiated solution of the lengthy 1910 Vizcayan strike, the mine owners sought to tip the scales in their favor by launching a back-to-work movement. Incensed by this untimely provocation, the authorities instructed the troops who were stationed in the zone to observe a strict neutrality and not to provide escorts for the strikebreakers. The strikers were then able to use force and intimidation to discourage any return to work.

A major reason for governments to seek rapid resolution of major labor conflicts was their general debility and the ever-present apprehension that latent political and social unrest might be set off by prolonged labor conflicts. Catalonia, the area of greatest political and social unrest, between 1814 and 1900 experienced no less than sixty years of a "state of exception" (*estado de excepción*) imposed by Madrid, during which constitutional guarantees were suspended and repressive actions taken. Furthermore, most urban centers possessed large numbers of "floaters," a lumpenproletariat that as in the Tragic Week helped transform labor protests into popular jacqueries. Most cities possessed small, untrained police forces that were incapable of coping with large mass actions.

But the primary impetus for industrial strife was the inherent weakness of civilian authority, which from early in the nineteenth century was forced to surrender the maintenance of public order to the military. The dispatch of army units and the suspension of constitutional rights became standard practice in dealing with sizable strikes and labor disturbances. Viewed by the military as something akin to sedition, strikes and collective bargaining disputes were frequently put down with brute force. When agricultural workers in Andalusia and Extremadura struck in 1919, Salvador de Madariaga recounts, "A general was sent to Andalusia to put down the farm workers' rebellion as if they were an army of invaders."[17]

From the initial phases of industrial development, enlightened politicians, clergymen, social reformers, employers, and labor leaders preferred to resolve labor disputes by creating joint worker-employer committees, *jurados mixtas* or *comisiones mixtas*. Such a committee was first requested by labor during the unrest in 1855 in Barcelona. In 1870 Pau Alsina, a Republican labor leader, delivered a petition to the Cortes signed by eight thousand Barcelona workers calling for establishment of a mediating committee. The Benot Law of 1873, which limited the employment of women and children in industry, is the first legislation to mention use of joint committees to monitor compliance. Another law was submitted that same year by the minister of development to create *jurados mixtas* for dealing with differences arising between owners and employees. Eduardo Dato proposed a law in 1891 that would formally establish such committees, but it did not pass.

Until 1873, the year the short-lived first Republican government was established, the term *joint committees* was loosely applied to various mediational or conciliatory bodies. Since at that time labor did not have the right to organize, joint committees were envisaged as mediating between employers and individual employees or groups of employees, not as conducting collective bargaining. Some were formally constituted industrial tribunals with defined jurisdictions. Others functioned informally, and still others were created on an ad hoc basis to resolve specific disputes. In the absence of effective alternatives, *jurados mixtas* were often used to settle labor disputes until the formation of parity committees (*comités paritarios*) under the Primo de Rivera dictatorship (1923–29).

The founders of the Institute of Social Reforms had expected it to operate at local, provincial, and national levels to mediate disputes. The 1908 law establishing arbitration and conciliation councils gave a key role to mayors, who also served as local IRS chairmen, thus creating confusion and overlapping in the functions of the two agencies. Neither proved capable of assuming this role because the requisite social climate was lacking; conciliation was impossible in a hostile, class-polarized environment.[18] The working class remained almost totally unintegrated in organized society. Nor would those who traditionally held power such as civil governors, political bosses (*caciques*), and Civil Guard commanders readily give up their authority to mediate labor disputes. In many communities the authorities ignored instructions to set up local IRS or arbitration and conciliation councils. In Catalonia, Valencia, Aragon, and the rural south many labor organizations under anarchist influence boycotted IRS activities; in Barcelona the chamber of commerce mediated between some of the employers and craft unions. When numerous labor organizations did have recourse to third-party mediation it was usually performed by the civil governors, local mayors, or ad hoc groups formed to seek a compromise solution for a specific labor dispute. Finally, most employers were strongly antiunion and had little use for the peacemaking efforts of the two agencies.[19] Between 1908 and 1914 the conciliation and arbitration councils resolved only 22 strikes out of a total of 986. The IRS did mediate labor conflicts such as the iron mine strike of 1911, strife at the Rio Tinto mine, and the bitter dispute between the Asturian miners union and the Hullera Española owned by the Marquis de Comillas.

Commentators have stressed the intransigence of Spanish employers. But were their attitudes all that different from those in other parts of Europe? France also experienced late industrialization, and the responses of French employers were in many respects remarkably similar. R. D. Anderson portrays the situation in France:

One reason for the weakness of trade unions was the almost unbroken hostility of employers, who refused to accept them as legitimate spokesmen. The atmosphere of French business was autocratic and employers were determined to preserve the "principle of authority", which they did by sacking militants, sponsoring company unions, hiring blacklegs, and organizing bodies for mutual aid in strikes. Collective bargaining had made little progress by 1914, being more or less confined to the printing trades (thanks to the powerful Federation du Livre) and to mining, though the northern coalowners had accepted it very reluctantly. On the other hand, government attitudes in labor disputes were less inflexible than the occasional bloody incidents suggested. Local officials often acted as arbitrators, and in major disputes the dependence of employers on the use of troops allowed the government to bring pressure on them to settle. Sometimes mediation came from the highest level, as when Waldeck-Rousseau intervened in Le Creusot in 1899. Despite this, strikes were seen in 1914 as a challenge to authority rather than a normal incident of disputes, and trade unions were not accepted as legitimate and respectable bodies or integrated into the machinery of bourgeois society.[20]

Progress was made toward the legitimation of labor disputes and increasing government's peacemaking role during the prime ministries of Antonio Maura (December 1903 to December 1904 and January 1907 to October 1909) and José Canalejas (March 1910 to November 1912), who, along with Cánovas del Castillo, are considered the outstanding political figures of the Restoration era. The Institute of Social Reforms was established during Maura's first term as prime minister, labor tribunals were created in 1908 during his second term, and laws were passed the following year legalizing strikes and lockouts and calling for the creation of arbitration and conciliation boards. Maura's ouster in 1909 following a mishandling of the Tragic Week ended his attempt at social and political modernization, his ill-fated "'revolution from above" (*revolución desde arriba*).

Maura was succeeded by a Liberal government under Segismundo Moret, a leading spokesman for progressive labor reforms, but it was short-lived. The following thirty-four months, during which José Canalejas was prime minister, can be considered a watershed in the evolution of government's role in labor affairs. A Republican turned Liberal, Canalejas was an anomaly within the Spanish political establishment, regarded in his own party as a political loner. The socialism he professed resembled English radicalism. Raymond Carr likens him to a failed Lloyd George. His political friends included Krausist intellectuals and others outside the liberal orbit. Some Republicans deserted their party to join him when he was named prime minister. Juan José Morato, a leading socialist, was an admirer, and Diego Abad de Santillan claims that the legendary Andalusian anarchist leader Fermin Salvochea maintained cordial relations with him until his death in 1907.[21] Of the leading post-1898 regenerationists he went furthest in his advocacy of sociopolitical modernization.

While serving as a cabinet minister in 1902, Canalejas unsuccessfully attempted to form a labor institute that became reality two years later as the Institute of Social Reforms.[22] He urged the Liberal party to seek support among the popular masses, not merely to secure a larger electoral following but to undercut the populist appeal of the Republicans. Government action was needed to promote a more equitable tax structure, protective legislation for labor, and social welfare. "When the social forces act with such enormously disproportionate influence and means as one observes in Spain," declared Canalejas, "the passivity of the state is synonymous with consenting to an absorption that, in the name of liberty, makes a clean sweep of all our liberties."[23]

As a political leader he brought to fruition many of the ideas he advocated. In a departure from Restoration dynastic practices, he sought political alliances with the Reformist Republicans led by Melquiades Alvarez and extended a cooperative hand to the rising socialist movement. He had offered the post of general secretary to Pablo Iglesias during his unsuccessful try at forming the labor institute in 1902. Upon entering office he had abolished two practices heartily detested by most Spaniards: taxes on primary necessities (*consumos*) and the discriminatory military conscription system that permitted the sons of the well-to-do to avoid military service by paying 1,500 to 2,000 pesetas (*las quintas*). He also tried to solve the Moroccan problem, to limit the power of the clergy, and to grant Catalans partial autonomy through the creation of the Mancomunitat.

During the Canalejas years government's role in labor disputes broadened, taking on a more distinctly mediational function. But for his untimely death, Spain would have acquired a ministry of labor much earlier. He permitted the Institute of Social Reforms to go beyond its investigatory and advisory functions and to take on a conciliatory role in resolving the 1910 iron mine strike in Vizcaya and the Andalusian rail stoppage of 1912. The government's imposition of mediation to end the 1910 iron mine strike came as a sobering blow to employers, who were accustomed to automatic government bias in their favor. "Its performance in the Bilbao strike of 1910," observes Carlos Seco Serrano, "was a forceful lesson for the companies, who considered themselves to be uniquely worthy of support from the authorities in opposing labor demands."[24]

Canalejas wanted to give organized labor a broadened institutional voice and presence, an endeavor that presupposed socialist willingness to participate. Yet despite the government's more favorable treatment of the unions and Canalejas's effort to build bridges to the socialists, it was doomed to failure from the outset.[25] With great animosity, Iglesias, who had been elected for the first time in 1910 to the Congress of Deputies, spurned all attempts at rapprochement. The PSOE and the Republicans were now politically linked through the formation of the Republican-Socialist Conjunction, and both viewed Canalejas's social reform agenda with mortal fear, for its success could well ruin them.

Iglesias demonstrated an incapacity to transcend doctrinaire rigidities and engage in pragmatic political transactions, a trait symptomatic of the deep class cleavages in Spanish society and a political puritanism reinforced by a Guesdist socialist vision. To make common cause with bourgeois parties (the Republican alliance was regarded as an unavoidable tactical exception) was virtually unthinkable. The PSOE's leadership persisted in believing that class differences were irreconcilable and that harmonious labor relations were impossible. The best that could be expected was to keep confrontations between the two natural adversaries as tractable as possible.[26]

UGT membership tripled during the years of the Canalejas administration, rising from 40,000 to well over 120,000. Improving economic conditions and the government's more lenient attitude contributed to rising labor assertiveness, much of it turbulent and violent. Canalejas's efforts to create a more modern structure of industrial relations ran into insuperable obstacles. Despite his prudent handling of the Moroccan problem, a crisis arose in 1911 forcing him to dispatch additional army units, an action that provoked the socialists and Republicans to organize a nationwide anticolonialist agitation. A socialist attempt to call a general strike made it necessary for Canalejas to suspend constitutional guarantees, jail a number of labor leaders, close the *casas del pueblo,* and ban the CNT, which had sought to organize a general strike. Canalejas became skeptical about the socialists' failure to cooperate and in an address on January 19, 1912, he declared that any joint action between the government and the Socialist party had become impossible.[27]

During 1912 strike activity rose to even higher levels. "Though most of the disputes were not politically motivated, they nevertheless catalyzed the Left's opposition to Canalejas, and they had at the very least political connotations," observes Juan Pablo Fusi. "It was not the strikes that preoccupied the Canalejas government but the possibility that, as in 1909, labor agitation might acquire the character of a general movement against intervention in Morocco."[28] Continuing tensions with the Catholic church added to the government's nervousness.

The intention announced by the UGT's Railroad Federation of calling an industrywide shutdown in September, which the UGT reluctantly felt obliged to call in solidarity with the independent Catalonian rail union that was under anarchist and Lerrouxist influence, came at a particularly inauspicious moment. The government responded by placing railroad employees in the active military reserve and dispatching military personnel to man key posts.[29] Canalejas nonetheless promised the strike committee that a law would be submitted to the Cortes substantially meeting union demands. Another law was also presented establishing mandatory arbitration for labor disputes in the railroad industry.

Shortly thereafter, at the government's prodding, the railroad companies reached compromise agreements with the union. But the combined opposition from Left and Right assured defeat of the mandatory arbitration bill. Before a vote could be taken, José Canalejas was gunned down by an anarchist assassin while browsing before the window of a Puerto del Sol bookshop.

Development of Collective Bargaining

Information on the true extent of labor disputes in this period is fragmentary,[30] but one may conclude that the incidence of strikes in Spain during the first third of the twentieth century was among the lowest in western nations, even taking into account the massive strike waves of 1919–23. The small size of the industrial work force throughout much of this period, the low unionization rate—5 percent early in the century and reaching an estimated 13 percent in 1920—and the persistent social and political demobilization of much of the population, of course, augured ill for labor agitation.

Yet industrial conflict in an underdeveloped society permeated with traditional outlooks inevitably led to extreme polarization in disputes between employers and workers. "As with many of the country's problems," observes Ignacio Olábarri, "the principal handicap for the organization of a stable system of labor relations came from the lack of accord among Spaniards on the fundamental basis to which a political system should conform." One result was the considerable violence that accompanied labor disputes and organizing efforts, which provided a fertile climate for the cult of violence preached by anarchists and anarchosyndicalists. When the police, Civil Guard, or military units intervened to put down popular risings or strikes among workers, their severity was such that the number of people killed, wounded, exiled, or imprisoned in such incidents was proportionately among the highest in western Europe.[31]

Collective bargaining in the late nineteenth century primarily took place between small or medium-sized employers and organized skilled craftsmen such as barrel makers, building trades journeymen, bottle cork operatives, typographers, skilled and semiskilled textile workers, and the like. Before 1914 there were few union recognition and bargaining agreements. The few exceptions included a bargaining breakthrough in 1912 by the Asturian miners union and regular collective bargaining with the employers achieved in 1913, after more than two decades of industrial warfare, by the Vizcayan iron miners union. In Madrid unions representing bakers, metalworkers, workers in the food products industry, typographers, building construction and woodworking craftsmen, and coachmen gradually won either formal or informal bargaining status. Bargaining arrangements in the Barcelona area prevailed mainly among the skilled and semiskilled trades—teamsters, carpenters, barrel makers, cabinetmakers, marble masons, bakers, and typographers—after the third quarter of the nineteenth century; spasmodic and tenuous relations also existed in parts of the textile and a few other industries. In Zaragossa the building construction and metalworking trades bargained with their employers. Unions in the semi-industrial sectors were the most likely to secure collective bargaining accords and recognition. And these were the sectors from which the organization and leadership of the Barcelona societary movement originated.[32]

The advance in union strength that took place between 1914 and 1923 led to the formation of UGT national industrial and craft federations and the restructuring of numerous CNT affiliates into industrial unions (*sindicatos unicos*).

World War I brought virtually all social and labor legislative activities to a halt. Santiago Alba, minister in a government headed by Count Romanones, had to abandon the idea of a separate labor ministry, which would not be formed until six years later. But the eruption of industrial strife and the formidable growth in union strength during and following the war gave renewed urgency to the extension of protective provisions and to the search for more effective ways to resolve labor conflicts.

Major advances were made in 1919 with the adoption of regulatory measures. Also that year, Spain, a signatory to the Versailles Treaty, became a founding member of the International Labor Organization (ILO) and party to various of the agency's international conventions. The eight-hour day was first decreed by the Romanones government for the building construction industry and then made generally applicable as part of the negotiated settlement of the Barcelona La Canadiense strike. Coal miners won an unprecedented seven-hour day. A mandatory pension system was introduced, and government subsidies were given to mutual benefit plans providing unemployment benefits. Other protective laws were either strengthened or added; maternity and sickness benefits were initiated in 1923.

But the most notable change took place in the area of labor relations and disputes resolution. The Catalonian Labor Commission sponsored in 1919 by the Sánchez Toca government and its interior minister, Manuel Burgos y Mazo, represented a valiant effort to bring peace to strife-torn Barcelona. Though this experiment failed, in the spring of the following year, the mixed commission for the Barcelona retail and wholesale trades not only succeeded but became the forerunner for similar ventures, including the system of parity committees that was subsequently established under the Primo de Rivera dictatorship.

Joint parity committees increasingly took over the formulation and monitoring of wage standards and labor relations. A royal decree in 1922 prescribed the establishment of parity committees to adjudicate labor-management problems, and in 1923 another decree ordered the formation of parity committees in all publicly owned industries and enterprises—railways, telephone, telegraph, local transport—empowered to resolve labor disputes. Though some of these initiatives proved to be of only symbolic importance, they clearly attested to the increasing acceptance of organized labor as a valid and necessary participant in a tripartite system of labor relations.

Collective bargaining and union recognition were also growing in importance. Labor-management relationships nevertheless rested on extremely fragile supports. Employers all too often had grudgingly entered into formal compacts. Yet as the Restoration neared its end, the system of industrial relations was gradually modernizing. But the sullen resistance of Spanish employers did much to reduce its effectiveness and consequently to hasten the destruction of parliamentary rule.

There is no reference in Spanish legal statutes before the Labor Code of 1926 to collective bargaining agreements, and even there little is said. Because collective bargaining lacked legal status, both parties to labor pacts were free to—and frequently did—abrogate the terms of the agreement. The absence of codified, enforceable contractual relationships contributed to the general climate of violence and adversarial confrontation that pervaded the country's industrial relations from its beginnings until the Second Republic.

Before organized labor's expansion in World War I, employers opposed any organized representation by their employees, except, of course, through company unions.[33] Unions generally were made up mostly of small nuclei of committed activists who conducted guerrilla actions to win the mass of workers to their side. Workers suspected of harboring union sympathies frequently were discharged. Strikes in such a setting often tended to degenerate into nasty confrontations. Owners recruited strikebreakers (*esquiroles*) to replace striking workers, who in turn employed violence to prevent scabs from working. As in France, some of the bloodiest clashes took place between strikers and police escorting strikebreakers. Employers sought to prolong strikes to starve the workers into submission, and strikers resorted to violence to force a quick end to the dispute. Factory owners sometimes provoked violent incidents to induce authorities to force an end to strikes through increased police intervention, arresting strike leaders, and closing union halls.

The obverse of employer union busting by provocation was what Eric Hobsbawm calls "collective bargaining by riot," a practice employed by Facundo Perezagua and the Vizcayan PSOE/UGT.[34] The mere threat of expanding a strike into an industrywide shutdown or a general strike was sometimes sufficient to bring the intervention of the civil governor or even Madrid.

To rid themselves of labor organizations or to force workers to accept reductions in wages, employers at times resorted to lockouts, especially in Catalonia. In the building construction, metalworking, and textile industries, Catalonian factory owners established joint defense funds that provided financial aid to companies engaged in lockouts of their employees. Appropriately dubbed the "hunger pact," this strategy could break unions that possessed few financial resources and whose members led a hand-to-mouth existence. Lockouts inevitably led to increased tensions and greater violence.

Pere Gabriel tells us that strikes in Catalonia were usually defensive actions and were used by employers to destroy the trade union movement:

> Strikes usually ended badly because of the intransigence of some employers, because of government repression for more general political reasons, or sooner or later because of terrorist provocations. The trade

union movement consequently became disorganized while the conditions previously agreed to were gradually accepted by the employers.
When reorganization appeared to be more or less established another
strike movement would develop and the cycle repeated. . . . This cycle
had many implications. Essentially it underscored the incapacity of
Catalonian, and more generally Spanish, society (ultimately the incapacity of Spanish capitalism) to permit the "orderly" development of
the trade union movement and of labor improvements which were the
great hope of the reformist intellectuals and, lest we forget, of many
trade unionists as well. A high degree of continuous trade union effort
took place in Catalonia but not the organizational stability of the labor
movement. The situation did not tend to strengthen the resolve of
labor leaders to avoid direct confrontations and avert disorganization
. . . but rather to reinforce the most intransigent outlooks.[35]

It is no coincidence that the most militant unions developed among
the workers of ailing industries—Asturian coal mining, building construction, and Catalonian cotton textiles. By contrast, the wool manufacturing industry of Sabadell, more prosperous and stable than cotton
textiles, was highly unionized and affiliated with the CNT and enjoyed
relatively peaceful collective bargaining relations.

In sum, aside from the years of the Primo de Rivera regime's experiment
in state-directed neoauthoritarian labor relations, modern forms of collective bargaining became only tentatively established in Spain. The leading labor law authority Alejandro Gallart Folch lamented in 1936 that
strike actions in Spain did not take place within an orderly collective
bargaining context and that joint trade union bargaining accords had not
taken root as they had in other countries.[36]

In common with many aspects of Spanish life, labor relations varied
in different regions. The incongruities of economic development that were
primarily responsible for this individuality also led to variances in the
evolution of workers' trade union consciousness. Managerial responses to
the problems of labor force recruitment, discipline, and stabilization also
varied. Such a situation was understandable in a country where textile
manufacturing was concentrated in Catalonia, iron mining and metal
fabrication in Vizcaya, coal mining in Asturias, copper extraction and
pyrites in the rural confines of Huelva province, and handicrafts, services,
and light manufacturing in Madrid. Each area and industry confronted
distinctive challenges and circumstances. Another reason for regional dif-

ferences in management's responses to labor was the government's prolonged disinterest in formulating a national industrial policy and the
absence until the Primo de Rivera dictatorship of a centrally administered
labor policy. A separate ministry of labor was founded only in 1920.

There were few national employer organizations because industrialists
usually preferred to have regional and local bodies pressure Madrid to
adopt congenial trade, industry, or tariff policies and to oppose labor
unions. The most powerful among them were the Catalonian Industrial
Institute (Fomento de Trabajo Nacional) (the name indicated its original
aspiration to become a national body) and the Spinning and Weaving
Manufacturers of Catalonia (Federación de Fabricantes de Hilados y Tejidos
de Cataluña). Others included the Mining Employers Association (Asociación de Patronos Mineros) and the Vizcayan Industry Center (Centro
Industrial de Vizcaya) as well as the employers associations of Barcelona,
Madrid, and Zaragossa.

None of the various attempts to form a national employers body proved
successful. The Spanish Employers Confederation (Confederación Patronal
Española—CPE), was formed in 1914 at the initiative of building construction employers,[37] who hoped it would coordinate labor policies and
pool resources for combating worker organizations and strikes. But its
formation coincided with the outbreak of World War I, and in the ensuing
economic boom employers' ardor to pursue confrontational labor policies
underwent considerable sedation. By 1919, however, labor unrest and
strike activity resumed, and at the behest of employer groups in Barcelona
and Madrid, the confederation was converted into a managerial combat
force for mounting a counterattack and sustaining lockouts. (Because of
its confrontational labor policies Basque employers avoided the CPE.) But
as the wave of strikes began to ebb by 1921, employers no longer needed
a confrontational organization except in Barcelona, where they used it in
violently opposing the now powerful anarcho-syndicalist CNT.

Innumerable elements contributed to the shaping, thrust, and configuration of the various managerial responses. Vizcayan iron mine owners,
for example, found it easy, especially during agricultural off-seasons, to
recruit Castilian small farmers and casual laborers to work their open pits.
Asturian colliery entrepreneurs, in contrast, had great difficulty not only
in converting seasonally employed farmers into stable, productive, full-
time operatives but in attracting workers from outside the region. Vizcayan iron mining was a lucrative business and made possible substantial
profit margins, whereas the Asturian coal industry was undercapitalized,

produced inferior coal that was difficult to extract, and yielded big profits only when the country's coal imports were cut off or sizably reduced. Thus, though both employer groups shared a common animus for labor unions, their respective responses were largely shaped by the economics of their respective industries.

Replicating the pattern of labor development common to most Western industrial countries, the initial clash between managerial authority and worker protest in the Vizcayan iron pits and the Bilbao steel mills and shipyards took on the character of unrestrained class warfare—Olábarri calls it "a war without quarter"—that began with the great worker outburst of 1890 and continued unabated until 1913, when collective bargaining was instituted. A change in the leadership of the Basque socialist movement several years earlier in which the rough-hewn militancy of Perezagua was replaced by the more moderate, conciliatory approach of Indalecio Prieto facilitated the gradual conversion to regularized labor relations patterns.

Asturian colliery owners, in a vulnerable economy and with meager capital resources, were limited in their ability to resist trade union encroachments. They resisted until 1912, encouraged by the disastrous strike of 1906 that nearly destroyed the Asturian UGT/PSOE. By 1910, however, as labor was visibly recuperating, the opportunity for reaping a windfall in profits as a result of the cutoff of British coal exports was too much to resist. To ensure labor peace the owners recognized the Asturian Miners Union (SMA) as the sole bargaining agent for the region's work force. The presence of Manuel Llaneza, a trade union moderate aware of the frailties of Asturian coal mining, at the head of SMA doubtless was pivotal in converting this industrial sector into one of the most advanced in national collective bargaining during the years 1912 to 1919.

Madrid's Ugetistas required more than three decades of laborious effort to achieve their much sought breakthrough. Union recognition was largely confined during the early years to a small number of skilled trades—printing, building construction, food products, local transport, and the railways. Others acquired bargaining status only after years of sustained effort. Employers generally were no less antiunion than their counterparts elsewhere in the country, and the process of securing recognition at times was more violent and confrontational than is commonly believed.[38] Madrid employers joined with their Barcelona colleagues in 1919 in converting the Confederación Patronal Española into a militant antilabor combat arm. The bakers union, forged in a lengthy violent struggle against hostile employers, developed a toughness and militancy that became legendary in Spanish labor annals. By the 1920s, however, collective bargaining was more accepted in the Madrid area than in the rest of the country.

Workers during much of the nineteenth century often found it expedient to align with political parties as vehicles for their demands even though the parties did not necessarily represent their views. Such linkages were particularly important in the extremely politicized Spanish environment, not only in securing ameliorative legislative and economic objectives but in assuring the survival of working-class organizations. Most Catalonian labor leaders in 1868 and even earlier were left Republicans in politics and pragmatists in trade union affairs. Only a very small minority chose anarchism. With the decline of Federal Republicanism and rising employer hostility, the leaders of the Tres Clases de Vapor, the region's largest labor organization, turned to the newly formed Socialist Workers party (PSOE) as a possible alternative. Socialist trade union practices were close to those of the Catalonian labor mainstream, but differences in outlook and temperament between the PSOE's Madrid leadership and the Catalonian textile trade unionists proved to be insurmountable. A crushing defeat not long thereafter of the Tres Clases de Vapor in a bitterly contested strike and its subsequent debilitation was a near mortal blow for Catalonian labor moderation. Workers then shifted their loyalties to the populist demagogue Alejandro Lerroux, but trade union organization and campaigns for improved wages and working conditions—it was a time of economic downturn—remained at low ebb. Nor did workers evince much interest in a regional nationalist creed then on the rise that was regarded as a strictly upper-class affair. Little then remained but the anarchist option.

When at long last the anarchists achieved control of the workers' movement in 1919, although it was adulterated by anarcho-syndicalism, they could look back on half a century of fragmented, diffuse, and chaotic gropings. The abnegations of anarchist worker militants, their unceasing promotion of adult education programs, libraries, popular atheneums, and literary and recreational circles together with the publication of a remarkable array of journals, newspapers, pamphlets, and books had succeeded in implanting a popular subculture among some inhabitants of working-class districts in Catalonian factory towns, yet only rarely had they managed to situate themselves in the labor mainstream. Persuading the Barcelona trade union core to join them in a common endeavor had proven extraordinarily difficult and required them to make extensive doctrinal concessions.

When the war came, the accommodative process was already well under way, and when the accompanying business bonanza obliged Catalonian industrialists to curb their antiunionism, the anarchists were well positioned. Most important, they had no serious political or trade union competition to contend with. Their task was made easier because a process of temperamental rapprochement had taken place. Years of continued employer hostility, the lack of enforcement of social legislation, and police persecution had converted increasing numbers of Barcelona unionists into militant practitioners of direct action. Anarchist efforts had been helped more than anything else by the undifferentiated, relentless determination of leading factory magnates to extirpate all worker organizations, moderate and extremist alike.[39]

The annual strike surveys prepared by the social Catholic Miguel Sastre provide some telling statistics. From 1903 to 1914 some 10,216 strikers lost their jobs in Barcelona while 4,749 strikebreakers were hired and more than 1,200 union supporters were jailed. These figures, of course, do not include the 1,500 workers discharged following the defeat of the metalworkers' strike in 1902, the innumerable union supporters who were fired, or those victimized following strike defeats. Over this period 425 strikes took place, of which only 87 were won by striking workers, 75 were concluded through compromise accords, and 263 were totally lost, most of them ending in the destruction or serious debilitation of the unions involved.

Most labor activists did not share anarchist dogma regarding insurrectionism, libertarian communism, and the like. They as well as the overwhelming majority of the CNT rank and file were of a moderate disposition. But in trade union temperament and in the use of combative labor tactics, they moved fairly closely over the years to anarcho-syndicalism. Cenetismo provided labor militants not so much with a *Weltanschauung* as a trade union idiom and a mode of action that seemed appropriate to their situation. Under differing circumstances they might have evolved into militant nonrevolutionary trade unionists as their counterparts had done in other European countries and as the rise to prominence of men such as Salvador Seguí, Joan Peiró, and Angel Pestaña suggested.

But moderation was not to be the answer. The workers had been nurtured in a climate of employer intransigence and violence, and Pestaña recounts how, even when the CNT became a powerful mass movement after the war, capable of winning essential trade union demands through the exercise of its formidable economic power, many of the leaders, still locked in a social guerrilla mentality, frequently sought to force employers to accede by brandishing the threat of terrorism.[40]

The employers' reaction in dealing with their labor problems is notable for the absence of the much vaunted Catalan virtues of *seny* and *pactisme,* common sense and a reputed inborn penchant for negotiating compromises rather than seeking confrontations. Good sense and enlightened self-interest in this instance seem to have abdicated to an overriding visceral hostility. At one point Francesc Cambó, the leading political representative of Catalonian business interests, sought to dissuade employers from continuing to oppose unionism, but upon observing the intransigence displayed by the leading textile families, he lapsed into a discreet silence. Was it indeed the panic and alarm that anarchist terrorism (*pistolerismo*) and militancy evoked that brought out the worst in employers?

Employers, to be sure, cannot be treated as a monolith. Some did bargain with unions. Numerous local and government leaders sought at times to build bridges between labor and management. Owners of small and medium-sized enterprises sometimes displayed less truculence. But much of the Catalonian industrial elite, those who controlled the production of cotton yarn, the large metalworking companies, and other major enterprises, ultimately determined basic attitudes toward labor and exercised a dominant voice in employer organizations. And they harbored an implacable aversion to organized labor.[41]

One of the most intriguing enigmas of Spanish labor history is why anarchism and anarcho-syndicalism succeeded in becoming so deeply rooted in the Catalonian working class. The reasons for the rise of anarchism in rural western Andalusia are more obvious and have been dealt with elsewhere. Was it that Catalonian employers' antilabor obtuseness gave rise to the kind of unions they merited? Or conversely, was anarchist influence responsible for employers' extreme response?

The Catalan historian Jaime Vicens Vives poses the question in the following manner: "The conservative classes of Spain, much more than those of other western European countries, were intransigent in their attitudes toward labor demands because of the presence of a violent and destructive anarchist movement. It still remains to be clarified whether anarchism developed as a consequence of the lack of vision and the harshness of Spanish employers or whether employers adopted a position of strong resistance when confronted with anarchist syndicalism's tendency toward lawlessness or avowedly revolutionary action."[42]

Spanish historians of all political and conceptual points of view are unanimous in indicting Spanish employers as a group for their myopic, undiscriminating opposition to social legislation and worker organization.[43]

The attitudes of management did not derive solely from innate authoritarian convictions; they were also grounded in economics. And the fusion of an inherent aversion for labor organization with an inordinate intransigence in large part arose from the peculiarities of the Catalonian textile economy. It was an industry hobbled by elements that inhibited its full growth and modernization. The inferior quality of its products, a lagging technology, low productivity, and high production costs meant it had extremely limited access to export markets. Domestic demand was circumscribed by a market composed mainly of a poverty-stricken rural population. The industry's prosperity was captive to the ups and downs of good and bad harvests from an inefficient, semifeudal agriculture. Inadequate capital investments—the industry was made up of family firms rather than joint stock companies—and a lack of credit facilities made mechanization, which would have rendered Catalonian textiles more competitive on the world market and improved quality, difficult. The industry's predicament was compounded because it had little or no control over the price of raw cotton, which had to be imported from the United States, and coal, from England. Technological improvements consequently had to be financed from profits, and labor was one of the very few cost components that could be manipulated. And in a labor-intensive industry like textiles, the cost of labor was of considerable importance, amounting in Sabadell wool manufacturing in 1934, for example, to 50 percent of production costs. That profits were not always plowed back to sustain financial and technical improvements but invested elsewhere in speculative ventures did not help either.

The industry faced even more obstacles. Jordi Maluquer argues that the introduction of labor-saving machinery in a large surplus labor economy elicited sharp reactions from workers: "The textile industry found itself restrained . . . in the introduction of both technological and organizational innovations by determined worker resistance to any reduction in industry employment. This—the struggle against innovation or, rather, the maintenance of the industry labor market size—is one of the strongest reasons for the solid implantation of trade unions in Catalonia and also for their radicalism."[44]

Albert Balcells emphasizes that

industrialization took place in an area lacking in basic materials, with a modest peninsular market, and a rail network of limited efficiency that increased the prices for its products. . . . Moreover, the central administration was ignorant of the social problems that were created by Catalonian industrialization and tended to disregard them. Catalonia's nascent proletarian movement was an uncomprehended phenomenon in Madrid. Trade union movements, from their initial emergence till well into this century—so extensively prevalent throughout Europe—were attributed to such diverse origins as Carlism, Republicanism, socialism, or separatism. . . . Barcelona and Catalonia were the nightmares of Madrid governments. Viewed as public order concerns, the problems of a complex industrial society were dealt with by resorting to forcible means.[45]

Industrialization had subjected the inhabitants of the principality to a profound accelerated sociocultural transformation and an uprooting of traditional values that went well beyond anything experienced elsewhere in the country. The massive incorporation of large numbers of illiterate rural emigrants, their preindustrial folkways intact, rootless, unintegrated, and unattended, helped transform Barcelona and nearby factory towns into social powder kegs. It is no coincidence that the anarchist appeal was strongest among the city's dispossessed and among young proletarians.

In his *Unfinished Revolution* Adam Ulam speaks of the inherent anarchism of the popular response to industrialism. The reasons he offers to explain the persistence of anarchist ideas in fin-de-siècle France are remarkably similar to those in Spain: "The incomplete victory of industrial values, when coupled with political instability, did not let the anarchist sentiment die out among the French proletariat and the progress of industrialization reproduced the feeling under the new form of syndicalism."[46] The extraordinarily slow pace of economic progress gave wage earners the worst of both worlds, especially in Catalonia. "The rebellion of the Spanish masses," observes Franz Borkenau, "was not a fight for better conditions inside a progressive capitalist system which they would admire; it was a fight against the first advances of capitalism itself, which they hated."[47]

The erection in 1906 of high tariff walls and the ensuing oligopolistic control of textile production that fostered high domestic prices assured reasonably ample profits for the industry. Income was increased by paying low wages and the use of a high proportion of female and child labor.

But the maintenance if not the enhancement of profit margins during cyclical economic downturns, bad harvests, or to help finance the costs of further mechanization was largely underwritten by reducing the size of work complements and labor costs.[48]

Catalonian cotton textile products were almost completely unable to develop an export capability, but early in this century some of them successfully penetrated South American markets, most notably in Argentina, despite American, German, English, and French competition, through lowering labor costs to such an extent that inferior quality became a secondary consideration. Meeting this competition meant, of course, imposing ever more regressive conditions on a group of workers who since the 1840s had developed a tradition of organization and resistance. Such practices made it extremely difficult for stable labor organizations to exist or for union leaders to evolve into temperate, responsible collective bargaining representatives. When the moderate-led Tres Clases de Vapor Federación collapsed in the 1890s, it was replaced in the Ter-Fresser valleys by a more combative movement led mainly by libertarians, which similarly became a casualty of employer intolerance. Labor organization by this century's first decade had been practically decimated in the textile industry, and its resurgence took place as part of the great wave of unionization that occurred during and immediately following the war years. Then the presence of a strong militant union in the textile mills became an important factor in the determined vendetta by employers against the CNT of the early 1920s.

Managerial determination to eradicate labor organization created a vicious circle. The destruction of moderate-led unions inevitably ended in their reconstitution under more militant auspices. Terrorism and radical labor tactics greatly increased employers' undifferentiated aversion for all labor organizations. This hostility, in turn, impelled normally pragmatic trade unionists, despairing of obtaining better treatment through peaceful, legal channels, to embrace a militant, extremely combative outlook. Thus when the great bonanza of World War I ended and a period of stringent industry retrenchment began, labor and management became locked in deadly combat.

It would appear that merely determining who had thrown the first stone would not tell us very much. It is clear that a dynamic set in that ultimately led to the tragic denouement of the early 1920s. The presence within organized labor of a large anarcho-syndicalist current that reinforced managerial antiunionism undoubtedly retarded the overall integration of trade unionism in Spanish society. But this is a matter of degree and not of fundamental import. Had a large extraparliamentary working-class movement not existed, were there not other inherent obstacles barring the path to labor and social progress? Was not the persistent appeal of anarchism an a priori expression of underdevelopment, of the violent encounter between Spain's past and present?

Why, then, did socialist rather than anarcho-syndicalist labor organizations become preeminent in the industrial districts of the Basque country and Asturias? Juan Pablo Fusi points to a number of contributing factors, including the structure of Basque industry and the distinctive character of a work force that included a large proportion of immigrants. The crucial element, he argues, was "the capacity and drive of the first generation of socialist leaders . . . their trade union activity as much if not more than political and historical circumstances such as, for example, the 1890 strike . . . combined to give the leadership of the Basque labor movement to the socialists and to establish a tradition that in the eyes of thousands of workers in the region identified labor action with the Socialist party."[49] An analogous development, of course, also took place in the industrial and mining zones of Asturias, where anarcho-syndicalism survived only in Gijón and La Felguera in an otherwise socialist area.

The collision in Catalonia of the two worlds was greatly exacerbated by the structural debilities of the textile and metal industries and employers' stratagems to enhance profitability not by market expansion and technological improvements but through a physical reduction in labor costs with all its portentous social and political consequences.[50] Not in Vizcaya, Asturias, or anywhere else did the rate of return depend so heavily on low wage rates and the exploitation of female and child labor. The chances under such circumstances for eventually arriving at a reciprocal accommodation of interests necessary for the successful functioning of a stable trade union movement and employer-employee relations were always a good deal less in Barcelona than in any other major urban industrial center.

9

THE PRIMO DE RIVERA DICTATORSHIP, 1923–1930: A JANUS-FACED LABOR POLICY

Primo de Rivera's Takeover
of the Government

By 1923 the parliamentary system seemed more responsive and representative. Left to its own devices it might have evolved into a viable form of government. But the preceding six years of almost constant social, political, and economic turmoil had exacted too great a toll. The ensuing debilitation of civilian rule encouraged a growing military presence as well as a swelling popular disillusion with parliamentary rule.

Sentiment in favor of strongman rule grew in both civilian and military circles. The savage repression under Martínez Anido and Arlegui weakened the trade union power of the CNT, placing the remnants of the organization in the hands of anarchist extremists. The resulting terrorist carnage prompted Catalonian industrialists in 1923 to appeal with renewed urgency for the military to topple the Liberal government of Prime Minister García Prieto, which had abandoned the hard-line approach in favor of a policy of conciliation toward the unions.

The results of a parliamentary inquiry to assign responsibility for the Annual disaster were to be made public on October 1 upon the resumption of the Cortes sessions. The report implicated various senior members of the military hierarchy and compromised the royal palace. King Alfonso XIII was known to have been actively involved in planning the ill-fated offensive that ended in the Annual debacle. Anger and resentment grew as rumors spread that the politicians were seeking their exoneration by blaming the military for the Moroccan failure.

Military conspirators had planned on the installation of a government headed by General Francisco Aguilera, president of the Supreme Council of Military Justice, but his last-minute involvement in a demeaning incident with the García Prieto government forced them to look elsewhere. An unlikely candidate, Miguel Primo de Rivera, captain general of the Catalonia military region, then made his bid.

Assured of the king's acquiescence if not his active support, Primo de Rivera issued a pronunciamiento in Barcelona on September 13, on the eve of the disclosure of the commission's findings. Deriding the politicians for their failure to maintain public order and pledging honest, effective government, he called on the officer corps and the public to support his military takeover.

When the king accepted the military coup d'état, the government submitted without offering serious resistance. Opposition came only from the weak CNT and the minuscule Communist party. Never before had a dictator taken power so effortlessly with so much popular approval and so little opposition. José Ortega y Gasset wrote approvingly in *El Sol,* "The alpha and omega of the military directory's task is to do away with the old politics. Their goal is so excellent as to preclude reservations." Manuel Azaña spoke of liberation from a state "of impotence and imbecility." The enthusiastic reception of the coup attested more to the debility of civil authority than to any perceived superior virtues of military rule. "In the final analysis," observed Joaquín Maurín, "the army merely put an end to an unstable situation that had persisted since 1917."[1]

Warm, bluff, well-meaning Miguel Primo de Rivera came from a military family of Cádiz landowning gentry. His uncle Fernando, the Marquis of Estella, had been an influential political general in the army and a life member of the Senate. Through his service record and family connections, he had risen by 1919, at the age of forty-nine, to the rank of lieutenant general.

Miguel Primo de Rivera fancied himself a Liberal (and a devout Catholic), but his political outlook reflected a melange of often conflicting views. His life span fittingly was equally divided between the last three decades of the nineteenth century and the first three of the twentieth. A self-proclaimed disciple of the leading regenerationist writer, Joaquín Costa, he envisioned reforms that reflected nineteenth-century caudillismo, imbued with an authoritarian, nationalistic cast and a deep-seated prejudice against parliamentary rule and politicians. His slogan was "Patria, Religión, Monarquía" (Country, Religion, Monarchy). He was much closer in spirit to the nineteenth-century progressive caudillo General Juan Prim than to his contemporary Benito Mussolini. Admittedly intuitive in approach and without an operative political outlook, he practiced a free-wheeling benevolent despotism that allowed occasional innovation, especially in dealing with labor and economic problems.

The new government consisted initially of an eight-man military directory headed by Primo de Rivera. Each general was charged with overseeing ministerial functions with administration delegated to technicians and bureaucrats. Partly to assure his supporters among the Catalonian bourgeoisie and partly to indicate his no-nonsense approach to law and order, he named General Martínez Anido undersecretary of interior and Arlegui director general of national security. The directory declared its intention to remain in office for a "brief parenthesis" of three months, long enough to cleanse the political system and to place government in the hands of "people uncontaminated by the vices which we attribute to political organizations." Primo saw himself as Joaquín Costa's "iron surgeon." Once the surgery had been completed, "following a period of convalescence," the patient would be permitted to resume a normal life.[2]

The new government's authoritarian intent was clear from the outset. Martial law was instituted, a rigid press censorship invoked, political parties banned, the Cortes dissolved, and dissenters muzzled or imprisoned. Elected officeholders at all levels were summarily dismissed and replaced with military personnel. The posts of civil governors and mayors were taken over by military officers, and some five hundred to six hundred military commissioners known as *delegados gubernativos* were assigned to assure the probity of local governments and to oversee the elimination of political bossism. The ensuing politicization of an entire generation of officers opened a Pandora's box that had fateful consequences not only for the dictatorship and the monarchy but for the Second Republic as well.

To strengthen support among the Catalonian industrial and political elite, Primo pledged before the coup to maintain and extend regional self-rule. But within five days of his assumption of power, presumably to curry favor with military hard-liners for whom any departure from a rigid Castilian centralism was anathema, to the consternation of Cambó and his fellow Catalan bourgeoisie, the use or teaching of Catalan was banned and any activity smacking of "separatism" (even the dancing of the Sardana) was prohibited. And by 1926, the Mancomunitat, that partial concession to self-rule, was dissolved.[3]

Upon taking power, authoritarian regimes often proclaim their intention of remaining in power only long enough to effect needed reforms. Once they are ensconced, however, "national interest" invariably demands their retention of power. Primo was no exception. Nonetheless, neither Primo nor his collaborators had any preconceived notion of how precisely to carry out their intended regeneration, and because their assumption of power had been primarily regarded as a corrective action, the 1876 constitution had not been abrogated, merely suspended.

Fortunately for Primo, except for the aftermath of the Annual disaster, the country faced no pressing crisis. The economy was gradually emerging from the postwar slump, and serious public order problems were limited to a few areas. Labor conflict had declined, and though political instability persisted, no immediate institutional crisis threatened. An institutional overhaul, therefore, had not been contemplated.

Postwar Europe experienced a parliamentary identity crisis that saw the rise of comparable authoritarian regimes in several countries, especially in central and eastern Europe. The Iberian variant, however, seems unique, and categorizing it has not been easy. One recent study of this period is entitled *Fascism from Above,* another *Revolution from Above;* others regard Primo as a second-rate Mussolini. The socialist historian Ramos Oliveira considers him to be an enlightened despot. Josep Fontana's and Jordi Nadal's depiction probably comes closer to reality: "It was a regime of landowners, of order-loving people and small gentry, which would follow a policy of pure conservatism, varied with flashes of paternalism."[4]

At once populist and traditionalist, modernizing and authoritarian, the regime tended to reflect Primo's hazy, freewheeling outlook. Has there ever been another authoritarian dictatorship that disdained brutal methods and determinedly sought collaboration with the socialists? And though it attracted the loyalties of diverse elements within the Spanish Right— Carlists, Maurists, social Catholics, conservatives, industrialists, large landowners, the military, and the church hierarchy—the dictatorship was incapable of fusing these groups into a coherent, articulated authoritarian ethos. A more cohesive ideological base would have enabled Primo to legitimize his rule with a more legal basis. In the end it remained an authoritarian *mestizo* (of mixed racial parentage), a sort of halfway house between Canovist constitutionalism and the more rigorous authoritarianism of the Franco regime. Francoists and Falangists were later to censure Primo's rule for its "liberal illusions."

The curious ambivalence of Primo's authoritarianism is best exemplified by his treatment of the labor problem. Widespread, unregulated labor strife had been one of the catalysts for the military takeover, and consequently major goals of the regime were to restore public order by taking stern measures against CNT labor extremism and to extinguish the last vestiges of terrorism. The white terror employed by Martínez Anido was abandoned, and the enfeebled CNT was subjected to systematic persecution, yet some of its unions were permitted to operate semiclandestinely. As a benevolent patriarch, Primo promised social legislation "that defends the worker, provides for his livelihood and old age, and favors his cultural development." Class struggle would be eliminated by government intervention to assure labor peace and equity. "But," according to James H. Rial, "concern for the less fortunate did not mean that as a soldier he tolerated insubordination from workers who did not act in accord with their place in society."[5]

Primo placed the CNT in limbo but extended the olive branch to the UGT. It is said that he admired the honesty and dedication of socialists in defense of wage earners. His conciliatory attitude also reflected the view commonly held by enlightened social reformers and political leaders of differing persuasions that since trade union representation had become an integral part of modern society, labor extremism could best be prevented by encouraging the development of moderate, reform-minded labor organization. This was the view of those who formed and collaborated with the Institute of Social Reforms. Though many of Primo's advisers would have preferred a Catholic labor movement, they realized that the Católicos were inconsequential except in a few localities. The Sindicatos Libres of Barcelona could be used as a counterforce to prevent a CNT resurgence, but they had an unsavory reputation. Therefore, the brand of unionism practiced by Pablo Iglesias was regarded as the safest alternative, and it would also provide the regime with much needed popular support.

Within weeks following the installation of the dictatorship, Primo summoned Manuel Llaneza, the moderate leader of the Asturian Coal Miners Union, and offered to collaborate with the UGT.[6] The socialist labor center and PSOE would be permitted to operate more or less as before and an active labor-management conciliation policy would be pursued through the parity committees.

The socialist reaction to the military takeover had been guarded.

Though the Bilbao UGT conducted a twenty-four-hour protest strike, the party denounced the military takeover but refrained from calling on the population actively to oppose the destruction of the parliamentary system. Appeals from the CNT and the communists to join in sponsoring a general strike fell on deaf ears. The socialists did not want to repeat the foolhardy revolutionary attempt of 1917. Why, moreover, should proletarian blood be shed in defense of a corrupted bourgeois parliamentary system? To men such as Largo Caballero, first and foremost was the survival of the unions and the welfare of their members. Furthermore, the movement had not yet recovered from the prolonged internal battle over affiliation with the Comintern and the departure of some leaders and activists to found the Communist party. The 210,000-strong UGT managed to emerge unscathed, but party membership rolls had plunged from a high of 45,000 in 1921 to 8,215.

The response to Primo's offer deeply divided the socialist leadership. Fernando de los Rios and Indalecio Prieto, whose local party organizations in Granada and Bilbao maintained close ties with the Republicans, urged total opposition to the dictatorship, but the majority led by Besteiro, Largo Caballero, Trifón Gómez, Saborit, and Llaneza, men involved in trade union work, won approval for a policy that ostensibly kept the dictatorship at arm's length but permitted the UGT to participate in public functions considered of advantage to the UGT, PSOE, and their followers.[7] The prospect of profiting from the CNT's disfavor was undoubtedly an influencing factor.

The political price exacted in exchange for the UGT's privileged position in trade union representation and the PSOE's relative liberty of action was the willingness to permit leading figures to accept high-visibility advisory posts in the government. UGT Secretary General Largo Caballero became a member of the prestigious Council of State (Consejo de Estado) and also served as principal worker representative on the Council of Labor (Consejo de Trabajo), an advisory body that replaced the Institute of Social Reforms. Others served on numerous government boards. City councilmen representing other political parties had been purged, but PSOE councilmen were continued in office. It amounted to an unstated policy of collaboration.[8]

Primo's policy of benevolent tolerance and cooperation was also dictated by his regime's need for international recognition. Spain had been a founding member of the League of Nations' International Labor Organization, whose director general was French socialist Albert Thomas.

Ignoring the persecution of the CNT, Thomas encouraged the dictatorship's collaboration with the UGT and praised its progressive labor policies and its observance of ILO international conventions. Spain won a seat on the ILO governing body.[9] A Madrid ILO regional office was established, and Antonio Fabra Ribas, a member of the UGT Executive Committee, was named office director.

Collaboration with the socialists may have been Primo's idea, but the architect of the regime's labor policies was Eduardo Aunós, who at age twenty-nine became undersecretary for labor and one of the dictator's principal aides. Of a Lérida conservative middle-class Catholic background, Aunós had been active in the Lliga Regionalista and had served as Francesc Cambó's political secretary. As an alumnus of the Augustinian University of El Escorial, his approach to labor problems was deeply influenced by social Catholic convictions. Labor priest José Gafo is said to have been his adviser. Also important in the framing of labor policies were men such as the venerable General José Marvá, an enlightened social reformer and leading figure in the Institute of Social Reforms and the Social Security Institute (INP), which he headed,[10] as well as specialists and staff members of the IRS and the Labor Ministry, many of whom were sympathetic to the UGT. Counsel and assistance from the ILO were helpful in drafting labor legislation. The increasingly warm relationship between the dictatorship and the ILO was evident when Aunós was named presiding chairman of the 1929 ILO annual meeting. Largo Caballero continued as Spain's worker delegate to the ILO.

The dictatorship's preferential treatment did have limits. Martínez Anido instructed civil governors not to obstruct UGT activities, but this guideline was not always carried out uniformly and was applied only when Martínez Anido and the government chose to do so. Many of the dictatorship's appointees at local and regional levels were from the extreme Right or Carlists who had little love for the socialists. Moreover, Martínez Anido, who was not happy with the UGT collaboration, sometimes sided with labor groups opposed to the UGT and permitted his underlings to obstruct and harass socialist activities. UGT Executive Committee minutes of meetings held during the years of the dictatorship reveal a good deal of time spent dealing with appeals from local unions and federations complaining of the heavy-handed obstructionism of military and government authorities in organizational and collective bargaining matters.[11] Though the UGT enjoyed a near monopoly of worker representation in many areas, it was forced to settle for little or no role in others. The

Catholic unions predominated in the province of Navarre, and an electoral bloc of Catholic unions in the socialist bastion of Bilbao managed to score a partial victory in the metal industry parity committee elections. The UGT was practically frozen out of Catalonia by Martínez Anido's protective patronage of the Sindicatos Libres, and the directory's favoritism toward the large landowners of Andalusia had a chilling effect on trade union organization in that region.

The consolidation of the regime was aided by the successful joint Franco-Spanish military campaign in the summer of 1925 that crushed Abd el Krim's Moroccan guerrillas, who had inflicted the Annual disaster. Primo's resolution of the eternal Moroccan problem took his popularity to new heights. The military presence in the government was replaced by a civil directory with a cabinet composed mainly of nonpolitical technocrats. Martínez Anido and Eduardo Aunós were elevated to full cabinet status, and Maurist José Calvo Sotelo, the architect of the local administration reform, was named to the key post of finance minister. These administrative changes had been preceded by the creation of the dictatorship's amorphous and largely ineffectual political arm, the Patriotic Union (Unión Patriótica).

Primo de Rivera's Approach to the Labor Problem

The year 1926, therefore, marked a high point in new policy initiatives, especially in the field of labor. Under Aunós's direction, Spain's first unified labor code was adopted. Though primarily a compilation of hitherto dispersed pieces of legislation and despite little added coverage (mainly in individual labor contract provisions), its formulation gave greater coherence to the administration of labor legislation and juridically represented an upgrading in the status of labor matters.[12] Activism in the labor field included increased social spending and the broadening or strengthening of protective provisions such as those covering night work for women, the creation of maternity benefits, and a paid hour daily for nursing mothers to feed their infants. Steps were also taken to initiate unemployment compensation benefits, greater protection for emigrant workers, and an expansion of vocational training facilities.

The dictatorship's most notable contribution was the establishment on November 26 of the National Corporative Organization (Organización Corporativa Nacional—ONC), which was hailed as inaugurating a "new labor order." But the new labor order was not really new. Essentially it represented a more cohesive, more effective use of the various initiatives that had preceded it. Aunós did acknowledge his debt to previous experiences, especially the successful Barcelona Mixed Commission for Commerce that, in his words, "can be regarded as the veritable laboratory for the incubation of the germ of Spanish corporative organization."[13] In the decree formally establishing the ill-fated Catalonian Labor Commission of 1920 Interior Minister Burgos y Mazo, a social Catholic, had clearly indicated his intention to employ the Barcelona initiative as a model for restructuring the country's labor relations along corporatist lines.[14] What was innovative in Aunós's initiative and made it more effective than its 1919–22 predecessors was its juridical authority (and that of a dictatorial government) and its obligating labor organizations to conduct virtually all their collective bargaining functions within the framework of the corporatist structure.[15] It had the ancillary effect of spurring employer organization that had languished.

The labor corporatist idea was supported by a diversity of interests. During the interwar years it became an ideological stalking-horse for fascist and other authoritarian creeds that advocated "organic democracy." Supporters were also to be found among at least some liberal social reformers, Krausists, and even some social democrats. Guild socialism also contains corporatist connotations.[16] Though its antecedents can be ultimately traced to the medieval guilds, it became a major ingredient of Catholic social doctrine and neo-Thomist ideas, expressed in the late nineteenth century in Pope Leo XIII's encyclical *Rerum Novarum*.

Not surprisingly, therefore, it possessed an enthusiastic constituency among the various Catholic groups that were a prime support for the dictatorship. Many Spanish social Catholics, including Eduardo Aunós, were influenced by the corporatist ideas of René la Tour du Pin. And since it was voluntary in nature, cloaked with trade union pluralism of a sort and tripartism, and maintained the right to strike, it also received the support of a broad spectrum of social reformers, among them former leading figures of the Institute of Social Reforms, senior Labor Ministry specialists, and the ILO, all of whom participated in its refinement.

The parity committees, representing twenty-seven principal industrial and trade categories, constituted the basic unit of the National Corporative Organization. Each committee contained equal numbers of employer and worker representatives and was chaired by a Labor Ministry appointee.[17] The committees, constituted by mutual accord of employer and worker organizations, were empowered to deal with a variety of economic and labor problems such as fixing wage rates, establishing the basic norms of individual labor contracts and imposing sanctions on violators, and preventing and resolving collective bargaining and individual disputes. Some also set up placement services.

Next in the hierarchical ordering were the intermediate mixed labor commissions and the corporative councils to coordinate trade or industry operations of the parity committees on a zonal and national basis. Only a few mixed labor commissions and few if any corporative councils were ever formed. A provisional Corporate Commission functioned as a high-level advisory body to the Labor Ministry.

Despite its social Catholic inspiration, political realpolitik and circumstantial necessities made the UGT the main beneficiary of the new system. The means for selecting worker representatives to the parity committees was the same as that employed previously by the Institute of Social Reforms. The majority labor organization was granted almost exclusive worker representation, thus assuring the UGT of close to a monopoly of labor spokesmen on the committees, a practice that was bitterly opposed by the Catholic unions, which unsuccessfully sought to obtain minority representation. "Catholic ideas govern," mourned Jesuit labor priest Sisinio Nevares, "but not Catholic workers."[18]

Only 26 parity committees were in operation before the formation of the ONC. By 1930, however, Aunós claimed that 460 existed and another 250 were in the process of formation. They represented more than a million workers, approximately one-fourth of all industrial and service employees.[19] Though the economic upturn clearly had some effect, labor corporatism must be credited with helping to lower the level of labor conflict. The number of strikes between 1924 and 1928 declined to roughly half that of the preceding two years with a comparable reduction in the number of workdays lost. The aggressive mediatory role of the Labor Ministry also contributed to reducing labor conflict. A high point in strike activity was reached in 1927, when employers in the ailing industries of coal mining in Asturias, textiles in Barcelona, and building construction throughout the country sought relief by increasing the workweek without corresponding wage adjustments. The following year, however, only eighty-nine work stoppages were registered, which Aunós claimed was the least number of strikes ever recorded in Spain.[20]

Though strike activity during the dictatorship was undeniably at low ebb, official figures should not be taken at face value. The Labor Ministry's 1930–31 annual report informs us that "it has apparently been ascertained that some authorities concealed the occurrence of strikes, possibly to create artificial triumphs by the as yet insufficiently matured organs," an obvious reference to the parity committees.[21]

Primarily conceived to suppress labor radicalism and to impose peaceful industrial relations, labor corporatism and the repression of anarcho-syndicalism did bring a greater measure of social peace but at the cost of vitiating the role of trade unions and of collective bargaining as the determination of wages and working conditions became increasingly bureaucratized. Direct negotiations between employers and workers or through the Labor Ministry steadily declined so that by 1929 26 percent of all conflict resolution took place through parity committees or arbitration tribunals. Nor were labor relations techniques extended to new areas. Bargaining through parity committees further institutionalized existing labor-management relationships while the suppression of the CNT and other dissident labor organizations had reduced the number of organized workers and those covered by collective bargaining.[22]

The decisions adopted by parity committees regarding wages and allied issues tended to favor workers and caused a widespread outcry among employers accusing the government of UGT favoritism. Some went so far as to dub Aunós "the white Lenin." Furthermore, a fair number of strikes in this period arose from refusals by employers to honor parity committee decisions. Nonetheless, as profits rose, a moderate loss in per capita income took place after 1925 that was at least partly offset by a drop in the cost of living. Employers, who shouldered the burden of financing the committees' activities, were dissatisfied because equal status was accorded to labor and management and the committees were concentrated in the highly unionized areas of Barcelona, Madrid, Vizcaya, and Asturias, where wage levels remained much higher than in the rest of the country. (Those of Valencia, Zaragossa, and Seville formed an intermediate group.) The partial realization of labor corporatism was all that was accomplished of an ambitious plan to corporatize much of Spanish social and economic life.

Was Primoriverist labor corporatism a stepchild of the Italian fascist chambers as some writers have claimed? The evidence strongly suggests only the slightest coincidental relationship. By its free selection of labor and employer representatives, its relative freedom of association (except for the revolutionary Left), and its retention of the right to strike, Iberian corporatism stood in marked contrast to its fascist prototype. Only in 1938 with the adoption of Franco's Labor Charter (Fuero de Trabajo) was Mussolini's fascist model truly evident. What made Spanish labor corporatism so unique was that, unlike its counterparts in Italy, Portugal, and Austria, it did not involve a homogenous labor organization of a clearly collaborationist tint. "Only in our country," observes labor specialist Alejandro Gallart Folch, "has such a far-reaching revolution taken place going from a socioeconomic individualistic ordering to a corporatist one without the ardor and dynamism of a strong ideological, emotional motif."[23]

Primo and Aunós sought to place Spain in the vanguard of European social policy making and therefore established close ties with the International Labor Organization. Shortly after taking power, Primo ostentatiously invited the ILO to hold its next governing body meeting in Madrid. Not only was there ample Spanish precedent, but Aunós sought external inspiration not from Italian corporatist theoretician Giuseppe Bottai but from the Belgian model. "The Directory," observes Anthony McIvor, "was actually anxious to dissociate Aunós's legislation from the Italian organization because of European disapproval of Mussolini's methods."[24] Barely a month following Primo's coup, the European worker group that included the UGT presented a resolution to the ILO's October 1923 labor conference calling for an investigation of violations of the freedom of association in member countries with Mussolini as the principal target. Moreover, the dictatorship's labor reforms were generally based on the social teachings of the church and on ILO norms.

A concerted effort to revitalize and modernize the economy was launched following military success in Morocco. Well before the advent of the dictatorship nationalism and interventionism had become the guiding norms for economic policy making. Primo, however, went a step further and elevated them to the status of official doctrine. "Like his regenerationist mentors," notes Shlomo Ben Ami, "Primo de Rivera was permeated with a deep frustration at Spain's economic *retraso*."[25] A forced march was needed to bring Spain into the twentieth century.

Faced with the implacable opposition of his latifundista political allies to any change in the agricultural status quo, the dictatorship gave its main attention to the industrial sector. In any event, Primo's regime was much more committed to industrial expansion than to the prosaic needs of agriculture. Industrialists, moreover, proved to be enthusiastic collaborators; since the turn of the century they had come to depend heavily on tariff protection and government handouts. Furthermore, an economy barely emerged from the postwar slump required a national industrial policy to direct its priorities and achieve stability.

Primo's recipe for economic modernization contained a curious mix of admirable projects drafted by competent technicians, pork-barrel ventures, and personal idiosyncrasies. Whereas Mussolini acquired a dubious notoriety for making Italian trains run on time, Primo's well-deserved fame came primarily from improvements in the railway system and from the construction of an excellent network of all-weather highways. Improving transportation facilities had the salutary effect of linking town and country as never before and expanding a national industrial market.[26] Automobiles also came to Spain; their number mushroomed from 135,000 in 1927 to 250,000 in 1930.

Unorthodox fiscal policies and worldwide prosperity permitted Primo to accelerate the process of social and economic change that had begun with World War I. Until the advent of the world depression in 1929, he was able to ride the high tide of prosperity. Spaniards would nostalgically look back to that period as the "blissful twenties." Vast public works programs, the underwriting of industrial expansion, the modernization of transport, and increased social spending were potent economic stimuli. Between 1923 and 1930 per capita industrial production, including a large building construction boom, grew by 31 percent. Many of the large structures that one observes in Spain today were erected during those years. Cement output reached 120 percent and steel 150 percent of their 1923 levels, and the use of electricity, the number of telephones in use, and the number of savings accounts doubled. Literacy and health standards also improved as illiteracy was reduced by an impressive 10 percent and mortality rates, especially those of infants, began to approach European levels. Increased spending on educational facilities resulted in a 22 percent rise in school attendance.

Such an industrial upsurge caused significant changes in the composition of the working population. In 1930, of the working population of 8,773,000, 4,150,000 were engaged in agricultural pursuits; roughly half of them were propertyless farm laborers. The number of industrial wage earners during the 1920s rose from 21.4 to 30.9 percent.[27] Two million were employed in transport and industry. Metal manufacturing displaced building construction and textiles as the leading industrial category.[28] The number of gainfully employed had grown by almost a million (see tables 9.1, 9.2, and 9.3).

Table 9.1.   Spanish Labor Force, 1920 and 1930

Sector	1920	1930
Services[a]	20.4%	21.7%
Industry[b]	21.4	30.9
Agriculture[c]	58.2	47.3
Total working population[d]	7,962,000	8,773,000

Source: Manuel Tuñon de Lara, *Historia de España: La población, la economía, la sociedad (1898–1931)* (Madrid: Espasa-Calpe, 1984), p. 601.

[a]The number engaged in domestic service in 1933 has been estimated at 360,000.

[b]"Industry" includes transport and communications.

[c]Approximately 20 percent of the working populations of western and central Europe in 1930 were engaged in agricultural pursuits.

[d]Total population in 1920 was 21,303,000 and in 1930, 23,677,095.

The 1920s witnessed a liberalized European attitude toward women and their status and Primoriverist Spain shared in this trend. Greater participation of women in public life was officially sanctioned, and protective social legislation was especially notable in its extended coverage for working women and children. The number of women attending universities almost doubled (4.79 to 8.3 percent) between 1923 and 1927 while their participation in the active labor force grew by 8.7 percent over the decade. Women's wages increased more rapidly than did those of their male counterparts as their percentage among skilled workers advanced from 22.6 in 1925 to 26.7 in 1930, and over the same period the proportion of women in apprentice programs rose from 32.6 to 36.4 percent.[29]

Companies and stock markets were doubly blessed; economic boom and government subsidies were accompanied by relatively stable wage costs and little labor trouble. Real wages between January 1925 and January 1930 declined by 2.5 percent.[30] That many workers were losing ground probably accounts for the failure of the UGT, despite its privileged position, to register substantial membership gains.

Industrial expansion with its accompanying increase in the number of marginal firms and in the enlarged employment of rural, mostly illiterate migrants helped to raise the industrial accident rate. Reported accidents (many, to be sure, were never reported) between 1923 and 1930 rose

Table 9.2.   Labor Force in Barcelona Province, 1930 (sectors employing more than 10,000 workers)

Sector	Number	Percent
Textiles	167,453	39.3
Commerce	73,084	17.2
Metal industries	52,561	12.3
Building construction	47,989	11.3
Local and national civil servants	23,776	5.6
Garment manufacturing	19,537	4.6
Dyeing and preparations	18,537	4.4
Printing	11,450	2.6
Food products	11,205	2.6
Total	425,592	99.9

Source: Albert Balcells, *Crisis económica y agitación social en Cataluña*, (Barcelona: Ariel, 1971), p. 32.

sharply. The largest number of accidents, as always, took place in building construction, followed by transport, mining, and metalworking.[31]

A predilection for grandiose undertakings resulted in the mounting of costly international expositions in Barcelona and Seville. Extensive public works programs were undertaken. Government development policies led to a substantial increase in the capacity of the electric power supply from 802,000 kilowatts in 1925 to 1,200,000 kilowatts in 1930 as a result of an increase in the construction of hydraulic power installations. Autarkic protectionist policies were undertaken partly to curry favor with Basque and Catalonian industrialists and with Asturian colliery operators. Already steep tariff barriers were raised to dizzying heights, prompting a denunciation of Spain in 1927 by the League of Nations as the most protectionist nation in the world.

The public works program lessened hardships for many *braceros,* alleviating unemployment in Vizcaya's iron mining district, among textile workers of Barcelona, and in other Catalonian mill towns. The International Exposition in Barcelona gave employment to more than fifteen thousand day laborers, and the Seville Ibero-American Exposition similarly gave work to large numbers of otherwise jobless rural work hands. Although industrial firms prospered, inaction on land reform and in raising rural incomes condemned consumer industries, especially cotton textiles, to stagnation and endemic crisis.

Table 9.3.   Labor Force in Madrid, 1930

Sector	Number	Percent
Agriculture	1,840	0.5
Industry	128,000	36.5
Commerce and transport	76,300	21.7
Domestic service	69,750	19.9
Police, civil servants, clergy, liberal professions	74,400	21.2
Total	350,290	99.8

Source: Censo de la población de España, 1930, cited in Santos Juliá, Madrid, 1931–1934: De la fiesta popular a la lucha de clases (Madrid: Siglo Veintiuno, 1984), p. 65n.

The ambitious industrial development program required huge outlays of public investment capital and subsidies. Because the government believed that large units made the economy more efficient, big business received the lion's share of subsidies and assistance that aided the growth of monopolies. Economic nationalism inspired denunciations of the evils of foreign capital and led to the expropriation of oil refineries owned by Dutch Shell and Standard Oil and the creation of the petroleum monopoly Campsa. It did not, however, prevent the granting of a concession to International Telephone and Telegraph—a bribe of $600,000 was reportedly involved—in the vital communications industry or to doing business with AEG-Iberica, Siemens Schubert Española, General Electric, Pirelli, and other foreign firms.

The financing of this program became a matter of fiscal sleight of hand. Calvo Sotelo sought to increase the government's income by eliminating the notorious tax evasions practiced by wealthy landowners and introducing a progressive income tax, but the ensuing outcry was so loud and intense that he had to settle for modest changes in the tax system. A "balanced" budget was created by dividing it into two parts, the "ordinary" and the "extraordinary," which ended up being a deficit budget. Frustrated in its attempt to secure greater tax revenues, the government sought alternative funding sources by establishing special accounts and floating bond issues that not only substantially added to the overall operating deficit but also fueled inflation. Then Calvo Sotelo declared that an expanding, prospering economy would take up the slack and make up the budgetary shortfall. But instead of genuine growth, the economy had experienced an uneven, short-lived spurt, and the dictatorship's practice of living beyond its means ultimately led to its downfall.[32] Primo's application of palliative remedies instead of major structural reforms fatally flawed his attempt at development. The mishandling of the peseta's valuation proved to be the crowning blow that confronted the dictatorship with an economic and political disaster. By December 1929 Primo de Rivera was forced publicly to acknowledge the government's bungling of the peseta intervention, and Finance Minister Calvo Sotelo was sacked. By month's end the dictator also had to tender his resignation.

Primo's reliance on economic development as an alternative to social change resulted in little substantive change in Spain's economic status. The public works program failed to stimulate private investment or to create the infrastructure required for self-sustained growth. Agricultural productivity stagnated, and the underlying structural deficiencies were exacerbated. Protectionism and price fixing allowed innumerable inefficient manufacturing and agricultural firms to survive. Short-term profits increased, but purchasing power was reduced. There were more social reforms than under previous regimes, but they fell far short of meeting the needs of an extremely inegalitarian society. "His economic legacy to the republic," observes James Rial, "consisted of artificial distortions, a large debt, and a host of unfinished projects."[33]

Socialism under the Dictatorship

The socialists' reaction to the dictatorship was shaped by the political conditions under which they had to function and the vagaries of economic developments.[34] Though mostly conducting a holding operation during these years, they were able to emerge in the postdictatorship period relatively well prepared to expand their influence and following. Neither the PSOE nor UGT experienced much progress in attracting new members during the dictatorship. At the regime's outset the PSOE had shrunk to a membership of 8,215, a fifth of its 1921 numbers. In 1928 its enrollment was virtually the same (8,251). The UGT in 1923 claimed 210,000 adherents, and by 1928 it numbered only 258,000.[35]

The PSOE's problems also derived from the political demobilization fostered by the dictatorship and the UGT's role as the principal liaison to the regime. The UGT leadership increasingly assumed decision-making roles that normally belonged to the party. Deprived of its electoral and representational roles, the party languished. There were few jurisdictional disputes between the two organizations, however, because much of the remaining party faithful were trade union activists and officials and eight of the eleven members of the executive committees of both groups were the same persons.

Influenced by these developments and by the electoral victory in December 1923 of the British Labor party, a party based on the trade unions, and the naming of Ramsay MacDonald as prime minister, Largo Caballero promoted greater politicization of the UGT through the formation of a joint coordinating body with the PSOE. Though his proposal was rejected by his peers, who feared that greater political identification might alienate UGT members who supported Republican and other parties, political realities ultimately led to a de facto realization of Largo's proposals.

Though in aggregate numbers the UGT experienced only modest growth during the dictatorship, significant changes in its composition and geographic distribution did take place. Its strength was no longer concentrated in the Madrid-Asturias-Vizcaya triangle. Madrid remained the union's paramount stronghold, but the prolonged crisis during the 1920s in the coal mining industry had sorely depleted the ranks of the Asturian Miners Union and spurred the growth of small, radicalized splinter groups led by communists and anarcho-syndicalists.[36] In 1922 the UGT possessed a regional membership of 18,147, but by 1928 it had declined to 12,808. In Vizcaya, where decline was hastened by the disruptions caused by small communist and anarcho-syndicalist enclaves, the loss was even more pronounced, going from 17,575 in 1922 to 9,938 in 1928.

The UGT had even greater difficulties in maintaining its rural following. At the behest of the big landowners in the south, the government excluded rural farm laborers from coverage by the parity committees despite UGT urgings. Though a decree was eventually issued in May 1928 extending corporatist coverage to the countryside, strong pressure from landowners, the National Catholic Agrarian Confederation, and the National Peasants League obliged the government to relent and to sabotage its implementation. These groups feared that the committees might serve as the means for socialism to infiltrate the countryside by allowing the minority representation afforded by the decree.[37] Richard Herr observes, "The dictator was sympathetic to the exploited rural laborers but to have attempted serious reform would have meant an attack on the rural oligarchy, and Primo was not one to awaken sleeping dogs, especially if they were big."[38] Between 1922 and 1928 the UGT lost sixty-five local affiliates with fifteen thousand members, most of them in farming areas.

It had boasted a farm membership in 1922 in excess of 65,000, but by 1928 its numbers had fallen to 50,000.

These losses, however, were compensated for in other areas largely as a result of the UGT's representational role in the parity committees and in reinforcing its influence in other districts. In the process it became a more nationally representative urban workers' movement.[39] The decline in the northern triangle was in large part made up by advances in the Levant. In order of importance the provinces with the largest memberships in 1928 were Madrid, Valencia, Castellon, Asturias, Alicante, and Vizcaya. The movement's increased urbanization and more equally distributed national membership also led to structural reforms that gave greater authority to national trade and industry federations and less to local federations.[40] Furthermore, to prepare for the 1928 decree extending the jurisdiction of labor corporatism to rural laborers, the UGT had engaged in an extensive organizing campaign in the countryside so that even though the decree was never implemented, the expansion of organizational cadres at that time facilitated the explosive expansion in rural recruitment that would occur in the early 1930s.

The labor violence and turmoil in Barcelona came to an end when widespread unemployment and economic slump in the early 1920s sapped the combative spirit of most workers. Close to one of every three employed in the textile industry was laid off, and by the spring of 1924 more than half the entire Barcelona work force was on shortened work schedules. At the time of Primo's coup, a last-minute attempt to organize a protest general strike fizzled, further intensifying the confusion within the CNT. After forceful action by the police against both CNT and Libre action squads, plus swift exemplary executions of three anarchist gunmen nabbed during a holdup in Sabadell, there were only 8 terrorist incidents in 1924 compared to 819 in all Spain the previous year, including more than 700 in Barcelona province before Primo's September pronunciamiento.[41]

The CNT was not banned outright, but steps were taken to make the continued functioning of its unions virtually impossible.[42] All labor organizations were required to reapply for legal permission to operate and to submit detailed financial reports, membership lists, and other material. Those engaged in the collection of dues were made liable to prosecution for fraud. A deeply divided CNT was incapable of agreeing on how to respond. Anarchists, who controlled a majority on the Executive Committee of the Barcelona local federation, pushed through a vote suspending the publication of *Solidaridad Obrera* and dissolving the organization in preparation for going underground. Others, however, including anarcho-syndicalists and communists, intent upon maintaining some form of legal existence, refused to acquiesce. The metalworkers and transport unions, in which the communists possessed some influence, as well as the public service and textile unions, sought to retain their legal standing through negotiations with the authorities.

Fierce competition ensued between the various factions and subfactions in a power struggle within an increasingly prostrate CNT with the pure anarchists holding the upper hand.[43] The controversy came to a forced halt by the murder on May 28, 1924, of the Barcelona court executioner, causing the authorities to adopt a harsher stance. All CNT organizations were banned, *Solidaridad Obrera* was suspended (a suspension that lasted until 1930), and many activists and leaders were imprisoned. Measures taken against the CNT no longer were confined to Barcelona and were felt throughout the country, although in Asturias, Galicia, Vizcaya, and the Catalonian province of Gerona, CNT unions managed to retain a semiclandestine existence. Some public meetings were permitted and directing committees met furtively.[44] The anarcho-syndicalist press ceased to exist, but theoretical philosophical journals such as *Revista Blanca* edited by the Urales family were permitted to publish. Some local CNT publications also managed to continue on a sporadic, precarious basis, especially after the lifting of martial law in 1925.

The increased persecution led to the mass exodus of Cenetistas and anarchists to France, which soon became the main operating center as it was for others opposed to the regime. Others migrated to Argentina to join forces with the anarchist labor organization there, the Argentine Regional Labor Federation (FORA), led by Spaniards such as Diego Abad de Santillan and Emilio López Arango. In November 1924 an armed group organized by the Solidarists and led by Buenaventura Durruti crossed the frontier at Vera de Bidasoa with the intention of starting an insurrection against the dictatorship. This scheme was intended to coincide with a rising within the Atarazanas military barracks of Barcelona. Not only did it turn out to be a tragic comedy of errors, but apparently it was a planned entrapment by the authorities.

The bloody events at Vera de Bidasoa brought to a halt painstaking efforts by Pestaña and Peiró (both were in prison) to promote the CNT's return to legality. With normal trade union activities no longer possible, the militants turned their energies to ideological debates. The perennial cleavage between those who accepted the "spiritual hegemony" of anarchism yet insisted on the fundamental economic function of trade unions and their independence (Peiró, Pestaña, Piñon, Quintanilla) and advocates of an exclusively anarchist trade union movement (Buenacasa, Abad de Santillan) reasserted itself. The theoretical indigence of anarchist militants led them to depend heavily on Spanish leaders of the Argentine FORA such as Abad de Santillan and López Arango for ideological sustenance.[45]

The creation in November 1926 of the corporative parity committees brought the controversy to a head. It came at a time when anarcho-syndicalists were again trying to reorganize the CNT and had formed a national committee in Mataró. Anarchist groups had also formed a national revolutionary committee that participated in various plots to overthrow the dictatorship. The two leading anarcho-syndicalists, Pestaña and Peiró, came to a parting of the ways when the latter balked at the former's proposal that the CNT seek legal recognition even at the price of accepting the parity committees. This split once more plunged the organization into disarray. More than ever frustrated in their quest for legalization, anarchist and anarcho-syndicalist factions increasingly directed their energies to collaboration in the various attempts to bring about the downfall of the dictatorship.

Differences separating purists from the more pragmatically inclined in the immediate postwar years deepened under the dictatorship. As always, there were men such as Buenacasa and Abad de Santillan who kept their anarchist faith pure. Midway stood Joan Peiró, who, though continuing to claim fealty to the anarchist idea, gave it an increasingly nondogmatic, reformist interpretation ("Unions are not affinity groups"). Pestaña gradually abandoned his anarchist convictions and by the early 1930s had, for all practical purposes, jettisoned them.[46] In a totally separate category were the violence-prone desperadoes—the "anarcho-bolsheviks" such as Durruti and García Oliver—who were proponents of a dour authoritarian revolutionary socialism.[47] On the tactical level, these groups were divided into those who sought an exclusively libertarian uprising to overthrow the dictatorship (Solidarios), those who favored some means for the unions to operate legally (anarcho-syndicalists), and those who desired to conduct the struggle against the regime clandestinely (anarchists).

The controversy over the nature and function of the CNT prompted anarchists such as Buenacasa, Eusebio Carbó, and Abad de Santillan to endeavor to preserve the confederation's anarchist identity through the formation of joint anarchist-CNT bodies, initially in the prisoner aid and confederal defense committees that wielded considerable policy-making influence, a formulation that was copied from the Argentine FORA and was known as the *trabazon* concept.[48] To this end the Iberian (it also included the Portuguese) Anarchist Federation (Federación Anarquista Iberica—FAI) was constituted in July 1927.

The formation of the FAI essentially represented a reorganization of the National Federation of Anarchist Groups that had been created in Madrid in 1923.[49] Contrary to some accounts, the FAI did not operate as an ideological phalanx nor did it conduct sustained organizational activity. Even moderates such as Joan Peiró were members. It merely brought together a large part of the highly dispersed and fragmented anarchist movement, ranging from activists bordering on common delinquency to high-minded idealists.[50] Until 1930 the FAI exercised little or no discernibly meaningful role. The insurrectionist Thirty/Solidarist group, later known as Nosotros(us), chary of organizational discipline, remained formally outside the FAI until 1934. Yet another abstainer was the *Revista Blanca* group of Federico Urales and his daughter Federica Montseny, zealous guardians of anarchist orthodoxy.

Although the main force of its crackdown was directed at Cenetistas and anarchists, the dictatorship initially took a stern attitude toward the Libres. Their leader, Ramón Sales, was arrested, and military censors showed little mercy in blue-penciling issues of their newspaper, *Unión Obrera*. By early 1924, however, the Libres became willing to collaborate. From then on, Libre corporativism began to take on a para-fascist coloration. A new municipal statute calling for partial corporatist representation led to the appointment of several Libre representatives as city councillors.

A conference held in Pamplona from December 30, 1923, to January 1, 1924, effected the merger of the Barcelona Libres and the Católicos Libres of the north led by Father Gafo to form the National Confederation of Sindicatos Libres of Spain (Confederación Nacional de Sindicatos Libres of España—CNSL).[51] For both it represented a marriage of convenience: the Católicos Libres, whose meager strength was centered in Navarre and in the Basque provinces, were suffering from anemia. In 1926 the Confederation of the North of the CNSL could claim only 3,825 followers. The Barcelona Libres needed the legitimacy of a national organization. At that time the CNSL listed a membership of 111,252, of which a lopsided 95 percent was concentrated in Catalonia.[52] By 1929 it claimed to have grown to 197,853.[53] In an effort to outdo the UGT, the new center lost little time in declaring its support for Primo de Rivera, who rewarded it with favors including the advisory posts that the UGT had turned down.

During the first stage of their existence, 1920–22, the Libres' main preoccupation was the intense rivalry with the banned CNT, whose members it tried to attract. Beginning in 1923, however, it turned to the articulation of a more authentic trade union function. Colin Winston discerns three distinct groups of workers attracted by the Libres: (1) the founding nucleus (ten to fifteen thousand) of Carlists, Catholics, and conservative elements repulsed by the CNT's anticlericalism and radical extremism; (2) those who, following the banning of the CNT, turned to the Libres for union representation (mostly workers from the large industrial factories and mills); and (3) those who had a long tradition of professional or trade association, particularly white-collar employees, blue-collar workers in smaller firms, and those in the artisanal and service trades. Many of them were attracted to the Libres for lack of alternative representation.[54] In 1927 Joan Peiró wrote, "Well or badly, falsely or sincerely, the Sindicatos Libres now preoccupy themselves with the problems of the working class, and during the last five years [the working class] has seen no force other than the Sindicatos Libres addressing the problems that affect it."[55]

The Libres proved least successful in such key Barcelona industries as textiles, chemicals, metalworking, transport, and building construction, which had been the source of much of the CNT's strength. It found greater success in a variety of lesser industrial and artisanal sectors and from white-collar employees such as cooks and waiters, barbers, graphics workers, bank employees, some among the building construction skilled journeymen, jewelers, and utility workers, including the employees of La Canadiense who had abandoned the CNT following the 1919 general strike fiasco. Aided by Interior Minister Martínez Anido, the large white-collar association CADCI, which had been closed down for its Catalanism, was turned over to the Libres, to the disgust of many of its members.

Efforts to expand in Catalonia beyond Barcelona province produced scanty results. Only in the Carlist strongholds of Igualada, Tortosa, and Lérida did it develop substantial influence. "Sindicalismo Libre emerged from the special ambiance of Barcelona Carlism," comments Colin Winston, "and it did not travel well."[56]

Despite the more favorable conditions offered by the dictatorship, confessional labor organization continued to lead a generally sterile existence. The Confederación Nacional de Sindicatos Obreros Católicos never surpassed the fifty thousand membership it claimed in 1922. Its counterproductive practice of giving precedence to religious rather than economic problems was reaffirmed by Cardinal-Primate Reig Casanova. Only under the Second Republic was confessionalism finally abandoned. Furthermore, despite the efforts of Father Gafo and Canon Maximiliano Arboleya, attempts at cooperation between the CNSL and the Católicos failed.

Downfall of the Dictatorship

Whatever the shortcomings of the regime's economic policy, they pale in comparison with the dictator's political obtuseness and naiveté, his "enormous capacity for self-delusion." Calvo Sotelo regarded him as a political babe in the woods. He tried to replace the old politicians with fresh new faces unsullied by the sordid activities of the past. The Patriotic Union (UP) had been formed to replace the rotten party system, but an incorruptible class of public servants simply did not exist, and the UP attracted few idealists but hordes of time servers, whom Calvo Sotelo called "the soup and spoon men." As before, corruption continued unabated.

Primo seriously misjudged his erstwhile socialist collaborators. He sincerely believed that he could incorporate them into a bipolar political structure consisting of the UP and UGT/PSOE. But the UP never furnished the needed popular support for the regime, and the socialists would not permit their marriage of convenience to be more than that. In 1927 a crucial turning point in the relationship took place when the socialists were forced to decide whether to go beyond a selective collaboration and engage in a more or less institutionalized linkage. The directory, in preparation for the convocation of a national consultative assembly, had issued a royal decree on September 13, 1927, naming among its four hundred members eight leading socialists. Neither the party nor the trade union leadership objected to representation in the assembly, but they insisted that these delegates be chosen by them and not the government. Primo refused to allow this. Special congresses of the PSOE and UGT then unanimously rejected participation, beginning a gradual estrangement from the regime.

It was not long before censorship and high-handedness in dealing with the intellectual and cultural life of the country such as the closing of the

Madrid Ateneo elicited the opposition of virtually the entire intellectual and academic community. Miguel de Unamuno went into exile to conduct a campaign against the regime, and men such as José Ortega y Gasset, who had initially hailed the advent of the "iron surgeon," became its adversaries. Students formed the University Students Federation (FUE), which was in the forefront of antiregime activities.

The heavy-handed muzzling of all forms of Catalanism led to a wholesale loss of ardor for the regime by the region's upper and middle classes. The dominant political party, the Lliga Regionalista, lost most of its popular support to various forces of the antidictatorship Republican Left. Increasingly critical of the regime, Cambó became persona non grata to the dictator. Primoverist support was soon confined to marginal rightist groups and the Libres.

Only part of the old political establishment supported the directory. Some chose to withdraw from the political scene to await better times. Others, most notably former conservative Prime Minister José Sánchez Guerra, sought to rally opposition forces against the government. The dictatorship's tenure was marked by numerous plots and conspiracies.

Again in 1929 Primo sought to install a new constitution and convoked the National Assembly.[57] This time, he gave in to the socialist demand that they name their own representatives. But the quest for political legitimacy had come too late. By July 1929 the directory's troubles were deepening. The economic prosperity that had mitigated Primo's political shortcomings was coming to an end, the peseta had undergone a disastrous devaluation, rumbles of discontent were heard increasingly from the army, ever larger sectors of the middle class were alienated, and students were in open rebellion, forcing a closure of the country's universities. The Valencia pronunciamiento of Sánchez Guerra, which had the support of monarchists, Republicans, assorted members of the military, and Cenetistas (a planned Barcelona general strike failed), was subdued, but his subsequent acquittal by a military court dealt a severe blow to the government's faltering prestige.

Visibly affected by the regime's declining popularity and growing unhappiness in their own ranks, especially among Asturian coal miners adversely affected by the economic downturn, the socialist leadership no longer was able to maintain a majority consensus favoring continued cooperation. Ever sensitive to grass-roots sentiments, Largo Caballero now joined forces with Prieto and De los Rios in opposing participation in the National Assembly. Only Besteiro and Enrique Sánchez continued to support cooperation. In deserting the sinking ship, the socialists sealed Primo's doom. Finding that his military support had evaporated, Primo left office in January 1930 and went into exile in Paris, where he died several months later.

With Primo's downfall the changes that had taken place in social and political life became apparent. Seven years of dictatorial rule had not only obscured these changes, it had destroyed the Restoration party system, leaving only the vaporous Patriotic Union. The former royalist parties were hopelessly sundered. Some leaders of the Conservative and Liberal parties nursed resentments against Alfonso XIII for having taken part in their political downfall while others continued to regard the survival of the Alfonsine monarchy as essential to their political salvation. The military tradition of unquestioning loyalty to the throne had been eroded by political fragmentation and institutional ambivalence. The apathy of the popular mass, especially of those residing in the urban areas, was subsiding.[58]

The Berenguer Government Adrift

Having failed to recruit a suitable civilian to head the new government, the king had to settle for yet another general, Dámaso Berenguer, the portly, ailing head of the royal military household.[59] A respected military figure, known for his intelligence, culture, and balance, he lacked the political acumen required to restore political stability. His declared commitment to a return to constitutional legality and some liberalizing measures set the right tone and were well received. But before long this initial store of goodwill was needlessly squandered. Temporizing to gain time, Berenguer soon found himself trapped in the political quicksands. The agonizingly slow pace of controlled decontrol, with rule by decree and censorship, merited his government the nickname of *dictablanda* (the gentle dictatorship). Unmindful of the changed political climate, Berenguer and the king deluded themselves into believing that it was possible to return to the status quo ante 1923 constitutional monarchy.

Neither the government nor Alfonso truly perceived the loss of prestige the monarchy had suffered. "In Catalonia," Raymond Carr tells us, "the dictatorship had damaged the monarchy beyond repair."[60] Many in the monarchist camp refused to be identified with a government headed by the tarnished king's former military aide. Efforts to induce promonarchist and opposition figures to accept ministerial posts or to head the government mostly proved unsuccessful. Political support was limited to fragmented elements of the Liberal and Conservative parties, Cambó's Lliga Regionalista, and supporters of the Patriotic Union, now renamed the National Monarchical Union. Even more disquieting was the mounting loss of support from the middle classes, which was underscored by the defection of leading conservatives such as former Prime Minister José Sánchez Guerra and Manuel Burgos y Mazo, who, though not embracing the Republican cause, emphasized the need for a return to constitutional government and conspicuously abstained from defending the king. Niceto Alcalá Zamora, a former Liberal minister and devout Catholic, and Miguel, son of Antonio Maura, openly repudiated the monarch and joined in the formation of a conservative Republican party.

Seven years of enforced lethargy along with the deteriorating economic situation dramatically gave way to widespread political effervescence. A veritable political sea change was in the making as Spain moved closer to twentieth-century mass politics. Berenguer compared the situation to the uncorking of a champagne bottle. Student rebellion that sparked the opposition to Primo assumed a similar role against the *dictablanda;* noted antiregime figures such as Miguel de Unamuno returned from exile amid a great pro-Republican resurgence. Street demonstrations and mass rallies were a frequent occurrence, and labor peace was shattered by a wave of work stoppages and general strikes.

After years of ineffectuality, Republicanism reveled in its new lease on life. Now that part of the Restoration political establishment had been attracted and it had gained respectability, the movement no longer consisted of social clubs (*tertulias*) of politicians, middle-class professionals, and assorted bohemians. It had become an imposing popular force with a new mobilizational capacity. The six Republican parties joined in the formation of a Republican Alliance. To map revolutionary strategy the alliance held a gathering on August 30, 1930, at San Sebastian of leaders of the opposition. Among those in attendance were Alejandro Lerroux, Manuel Azaña, Alcalá Zamora, and the leaders of the Catalan and Galician nationalist Left. CNT representatives came but took no part in the deliberations. Socialist leaders Indalecio Prieto and Fernando de los Rios attended in a personal capacity, not as official party representatives. Cautious and prudent, the alliance's leadership was deeply split over the extent of Republican collaboration (offers of collaboration with the Berenguer government had been spurned and support for a future Republican government endorsed).[61] Policy differences had not yet been resolved. By

October, however, the Republican-Socialist Conjunction was formally reconstituted.[62] The Pact of San Sebastian called for the holding of a constituent Cortes, the establishment of a republic by resorting to force if necessary, the restoration of full civil and religious liberties, and the granting of regional self-rule. A Central Revolutionary Committee was formed with headquarters in Madrid, which, in the months ahead, would increasingly take on the features of a provisional Republican government.

The sense of impending institutional crisis was especially felt in the economic and labor fields. The repercussions of the dictatorship's disastrous mishandling of the peseta's international standing and the growing impact of the worldwide depression set off by the October 1929 crash of the New York Stock Exchange could not be stemmed despite urgent efforts of the Berenguer government. A continuing drop in the value of the peseta and the ensuing flight of capital, as well as the huge budgetary deficits inherited from Primo de Rivera, provided little room for maneuver. Policy vacillated between an attempt to balance the budget by sharply cutting back on public works programs and the justified fear that such actions would further inflame social tensions. Growing unemployment and shortened workweeks sparked a wave of labor strikes during the latter part of 1930 comparable to that of 1920; four times as many work stoppages occurred in 1930 as in 1929 with corresponding increases in the number of workers involved and the loss of workdays.[63] Such proletarian discontent might have been manageable under ordinary circumstances, but growing political turmoil and the government's fragility magnified the effects of labor troubles.

To avoid worsening an already difficult situation, Labor Minister Pedro Sangro y Ros de Olano persuaded General Berenguer to ignore the urgings of employers that the parity committees be jettisoned. But there was no easy solution to the situation in Barcelona. The Sindicatos Libres had long served as the dictatorship's chosen instrument. Following its downfall, the CNT made an astonishing resurgence as Barcelona wage earners again demonstrated their affinity for the *sindicatos unicos*. A request by the CNT in February 1930 for legalization confronted the government with a dilemma.[64] General Emilio Mola, director general of security, urged a policy of ostensible neutrality and the granting of legal status. Berenguer, however, opted to continue favoring the Libres and giving the CNT limited permission to resume normal activities. Mola correctly regarded this decision as playing with fire.[65] When the CNT received legal sanction on April 30, 1930, its membership in Catalonia quickly soared to seventy-five thousand, eclipsing the Libres. Meanwhile, labor tensions and strike activity in Barcelona rose as the CNT exercised its strength. Work stoppages increased threefold compared to the previous year, partly because of a concerted effort to force employers to get rid of Libre supporters and activists. The more CNT strength grew the less were the despised parity committees able to function. By June the CNT's reorganization had advanced sufficiently despite official harassment that it was able to direct strikes in Catalonia, Aragon, and the Levant. Widespread unrest in Andalusia sparked by false rumors of the death of a woman olive picker in a labor dispute at the hands of police ignited a spate of general protest strikes that month throughout the region, most of them fomented by anarcho-syndicalists. Nonetheless, the resurgence in that region was hampered by the defection to the communists in 1927 of a number of activists and unions in the traditional stronghold of Seville.[66] Cenetista resentment at the government's partiality spurred an even more active role in inciting labor unrest and revolutionary conspiracies. It also served to strengthen the hand of anarchist intransigents against CNT moderates Pestaña and Peiró, who sought to convince their comrades to operate primarily as a mass trade union movement. The refusal of the authorities to authorize legalization of a CNT *sindicato único* for the entire transport industry in Barcelona led to a bitter dispute that culminated in a general strike in November. As a result, the CNT's legal status was again withdrawn and was not restored until the advent of the Second Republic.

The quickening political climate also witnessed the birth in November 1930 of the Workers and Peasants Bloc (Bloque Obrero y Campesino— BOC), a merger of the small Catalan Communist party led by Jordi Arquer, a leader of the Barcelona white-collar union, CADCI, with the much larger Catalonian-Balearic Communist Federation (FCCB), headed by Joaquín Maurín. The FCCB, which had been the largest regional unit of the Spanish Communist party, separated over the party's ultraleftism. It opposed forming a separate communist trade union instead of working within the CNT, refused to cooperate even minimally with progressive bourgeois political parties such as the Catalan Left, and was not interested in the Catalan national problem. "Despite its smallness," observes Albert Balcells, "it was the most dynamic party of the labor Left during the Second Republic."[67]

Most labor conflicts during 1929 and early 1930 were directed to economic issues, but by mid-1930, as political tensions increased, most of the strikes began to contain political overtones or indicated opposition to the regime. Stimulated by economic slump, the growing assertiveness of the rank and file, and the militant resurgence of the CNT, the UGT leadership, including Largo Caballero, belatedly took on a more aggressive trade union outlook that led to a more positive attitude toward collaboration with the Republican revolutionary movement.

Meanwhile, the Central Revolutionary Committee readied plans for an insurrectionary takeover to be initiated by military risings directed by General Gonzalo Queipo de Llano and Air Force Major Ramón Franco, brother of Francisco, and closely followed by a general strike to be sponsored by the two labor centers. Despite their growing popular support, the various Republican parties consisted merely of small groups of organized followers. Success of the revolutionary effort consequently depended heavily on the military response and the cooperation of the country's mass popular movements, the UGT and the CNT.

The leaders of the two labor confederations were initially divided over the nature of their intended collaboration. In March 1930 a number of CNT moderates, including Peiró, Foix, and Carbó, were signatories to a public manifesto, "Inteligencia Republicana," linking most of the Catalan Left with the national movement for a Republican government, but at anarchist urging they were overruled by a majority vote of the CNT committee, which rejected collaboration in such a political venture.[68] At a plenum the following November, however, the assembled delegates, including Faistas, approved cooperation with the insurrectionary effort. In October the Revolutionary Committee and the UGT/PSOE had formalized Republican-socialist joint action.

Seeking to stop these preparations for revolution and the opposition's growing strength, the Berenguer government promised to hold early parliamentary elections but persisted in rejecting the opposition's demand for the convocation of a constituent Cortes to draft a new constitution. When elections were set for March 1, 1931, threats from leading political groups to boycott them forced their suspension.

The revolutionary coup finally was set for December 15, but it was upstaged by a premature rebellion four days earlier directed by two captains at the Aragonese military garrison of Jaca who had not been informed that the coup had been postponed until the fifteenth. They were not the only ones to act prematurely. The CNT organized a massively heeded general strike in Barcelona that was called off after three days at the urgent pleadings of an emissary from the Central Revolutionary Committee. The abortive action at Jaca was quickly put down, and the two officers were executed. This draconian action dissuaded many would-be military participants but ultimately provided the Republican cause with popular martyrs. Aware of the planned action, the government imposed martial law and arrested some of the leading conspirators in Madrid and Barcelona.

Leaders of the CNT and UGT proceeded cautiously, chastened by bitter memories of 1917 and intent on confirming the promised military participation before committing their followers to a general strike. Military collaboration turned out to be far short of expectations with only scattered garrisons and some air force units under Ramón Franco and Hidalgo de Cisneros's command at the Madrid Cuatro Vientos air base taking part. Though few military units joined, numerous others took a neutral position, abstaining from directly participating in quelling the rising.

The shortfall in military support caused the socialists in Madrid to hesitate in ordering a general shutdown, and the morning of the fifteenth found them still debating the pros and cons of carrying out their commitment. An important element in their reticence was the declared opposition of the Besteirist faction, which controlled the Madrid party organization, to participation in the revolutionary undertaking.[69] The strike, however, was effective in Barcelona and other Catalonian towns, and shutdowns occurred in Vizcaya, Asturias, Andalusia, Levant, and Zaragossa, but the government had little difficulty in putting down scattered instances of rebellion.[70]

The quelling of the badly organized uprising did little but momentarily brake the momentum for political change. Popular agitation continued throughout the country, fueled by the deteriorating economic situation, declining agricultural output, and the accompanying social malaise made worse by a disastrous drop in the olive harvest during the winter of 1930–31 that caused widespread unemployment in the provinces of Córdoba, Granada, Huelva, and Cádiz.[71]

On the advice of Count Romanones and Francesc Cambó, Alfonso finally consented to the election of a constituent Cortes, but one that was to be preceded by municipal elections, whose outcome, it was confidently believed, would be determined by local issues and subject to the usual manipulations of the Interior Ministry. Sánchez Guerra was designated on February 14, 1931, to create a multiparty "national" government that would include some of the imprisoned members of the Revolutionary Committee. Strong objections from right-wing conservatives and the committee's refusal to cooperate caused the project to miscarry. Once more the king was forced to settle for a military candidate, this time the well-meaning but politically ingenuous Admiral Aznar. A political wag said of him, "Geographically he hails from Cartagena, politically from the moon."[72] His cabinet was made up of familiar faces from the past: La Cierva, Romanones, Bugallal, and others. Romanones served as the prime minister's eminence grise.

The principal purpose of the new government was to schedule and conduct the elections in a manner to protect and preserve monarchist political hegemony. Municipal elections on April 12 were to be followed two months later by parliamentary balloting. With less than two months remaining, monarchist forces were dispersed and divided. Though the chances for success were not promising, an aura of optimism pervaded government circles. Republican fervor in the country's main cities was greater than ever.

Though municipal elections traditionally focused on local issues and personalities, this one quickly became a national plebiscite on the monarchy. Unlike the monarchists, Republicans and socialists presented joint slates. The outcome took both sides by surprise. The Republican-Socialist Conjunction emerged victorious in forty-one of fifty provincial capitals, in Madrid, in the mining and factory towns of the north, in Andalusia, and in many areas of the Levant. Equally unexpected was the crushing defeat of the Lliga Regionalista in Barcelona at the hands of the recently formed Republican Left (Esquerra Republicana Catalana—ERC). Republicans there, as in other parts of the country, were much aided by Cenetista votes, benefiting, in the words of a CNT leader, from "the massive support of Confederation members for the Republic." More than two-thirds of the municipal councillors elected in Catalonia were Republicans or various kinds of socialists; only 20 percent of the vote went for the Lliga and allied groups. Sixty-nine percent of those voting in Madrid cast their ballots for the Socialist-Republican Conjunction. Nationwide 39,501 Republican-Socialists and 32,237 promonarchists were elected. But because the election of municipal councillors in the larger urban centers entailed many more votes than those in less populated areas, where most monarchist support was concentrated and countless numbers of "boss-ridden villages automatically turned in monarchist majorities," little doubt remained concerning the political implications of the election.[73]

No longer could the Republican juggernaut be checked. It had become abundantly clear that neither the military nor the country's upper classes was willing to shed blood in defense of a discredited monarchy. Romanones counseled the king to leave, and amid popular rejoicing in the streets of Spain's main cities, Alfonso hastily departed for Cartagena and exile.

10

THE SECOND REPUBLIC, 1931–1936

Labor Reform and the Trade Union Upsurge

The Second Republic, *La niña bonita* (the pretty child) as it was called, stirred great expectations. Few institutional transformations in Spanish history had been accepted with such tranquility. It was the first time in recent memory that a change in government had occurred without military intervention. General Mola observed, "The revolutionary spirit has invaded everywhere, from the humblest to the highest social class; workers, students, civil servants, industrialists, merchants, rentiers, men of liberal professions, the military, even priests."[1] To have suggested then that Spain's exhilarating experiment in popular rule was to end five years later in a bloody holocaust would have strained credulity. Its exuberant partisans saw the democratic parliamentary regime as the crowning of more than a century's strivings to bring political and social modernity to Spain. As its model, the framers of the new constitution looked to that of Weimar Germany, the most democratic of Europe.

There were few clues to the political and labor storm that was to overwhelm the Republic, yet saner minds would have realized that meeting the enormous expectations would be daunting. A successful transition from authoritarian rule to parliamentary democracy depends on proper timing, as the return to popular rule following the death of Franco demonstrated. In contrast, the Second Republic began with an extremely disadvantageous situation. Government finances were in a sorry state, and the world depression was straining trade and general economic activity. In retrospect, Manuel Azaña considered economic difficulties more important than anarchist uprisings or monarchist plotting in the tragic outcome of the Republican experience. Furthermore, the sudden collapse of the Restoration monarchy eliminated an entire ruling elite. The resulting vacuum momentarily immobilized the political opposition and permitted Republicans and socialists to govern unhindered. The abrupt political change, however, left few in power with governing or administrative experience. Of the forty-nine political groups that participated in the elections, most had been recently formed and a mere handful of deputies had ever served before in parliament.[2] To make matters worse, the undoing of the old political system had sharply tilted the political balance to the left.[3]

The new regime thus faced a situation with a high potential for division and conflict. Its opponents had not been vanquished, merely disarmed temporarily by the monarchy's totally unexpected downfall. In the old regime high finance and landed interests predominated, whereas the new ruling elite was made up of the urban bourgeoisie and enlightened sectors of the middle class, sustained in part by the organized working class. Yet because wealth and economic structures remained unchanged, social and economic reforms encountered sharp opposition even though from a European perspective they were modest.

Despite their new-found popularity, Republicans remained splintered into numerous competing parties and personality cliques. Only the PSOE could be regarded as a truly solid political movement with a nationwide organizational network, a dues-paying membership, an activist corps, and a powerful trade union arm. Therefore, it constituted a vital component of the governing coalition, all the more important because it was backed by a politically mobilized working class that furnished decisive support for the Republic. The Republic could not have been sustained or survived very long without its support.

A provisional government with Niceto Alcalá Zamora at its head took office on April 14, 1931. The cabinet included Manuel Azaña, civil servant and Madrid belle lettrist as war minister, Lerroux in charge of foreign affairs, Miguel Maura as interior minister, and three socialists, Francisco Largo Caballero as labor minister, Fernando de los Rios at justice, and Indalecio Prieto as finance minister.

Since the electoral system awarded an inordinate advantage to the victorious joint electoral slate, the governing coalition obtained a commanding majority in the June 28 constituent Cortes election.[4] In a 446-member chamber the PSOE with its 117 seats was the single largest parliamentary group; the left-of-center Radical Socialists had 59 seats, Lerroux's centrist Radicals 89, Azaña's leftist Republican Action 27, and Alcalá Zamora's conservative Republicans, the "progressives," also 27.

Radical Socialists, Radicals, and especially the Catalan Esquerra benefited from CNT votes. The government would count on the support of the Esquerra with its 33 deputies and the 16 Galician Nationalists. The non-Republican Right was able to muster only 57 seats, reflecting a fraction of its strength in the country. The election outcome, nonetheless, confirmed support for the infant Republic by a large majority of the electorate.

Over the objections of Alcalá Zamora and Maura, the socialists and left Republicans pushed through a series of restrictive measures against the church. The subsequent resignations of these two men led in December to the formation of a new government with Azaña as prime minister and Alcalá Zamora appointed to the newly created post of president, Largo Caballero remaining as labor minister, de los Rios moving to education, and Prieto to public works. Throughout its two years in office it followed a distinctly left-of-center course. The figure in that government who stands out is Azaña, who more than anyone else embodied the democratic aspirations of the Second Republic. An introverted man of superior intelligence, exquisite sensibility, and literary talent, he was incapable of tolerating fools. His opponents often felt the sting of his mordant, cruel sallies. He considered socialist participation in government essential to the preservation of political stability and "reconciling workers with Spanish society."[5]

Azaña's tenure, which became known as the "reform biennium" (*bienio reformista*) saw the adoption of an abundance of decrees, laws, and regulations. Many aspects of Spanish life were affected: church-state relations, education, popular culture, labor relations, and the drafting of a new constitution calling for democratic parliamentary government based on the equal rights of all individuals. Notable among his government's achievements were the adoption of Spain's first divorce law, a reduction in the size of the officer corps and civil service, the construction of thousands of new primary schools (illiteracy was still running at 30 to 50 percent), and an autonomy statute for Catalonia. With the possible exception of the Jacobin attack on church privileges, none generated greater divisiveness and controversy than the sweeping changes in the country's system of industrial and labor relations.

Responsibilities were tacitly divided. In exchange for granting the Republican ministers a relatively free hand in areas such as economic policy, foreign affairs, military administration, internal security, and commerce, socialists were given a wide berth in instituting changes in the field of labor.[6] Direction of the education and public works ministries was considered important, but it was through the Labor Ministry that the socialists' most cherished objectives were to be realized. The UGT believed that through social legislation, the authority of the ministry, the strengthening of the former parity committees, and oversight by a small army of prosocialist functionaries, a process of social change could be initiated that would integrate its unions into the socioeconomic fabric. Passage of a workers control law, a long-standing UGT aspiration, ultimately would enable the unions to participate in the system of production and distribution.

To appease the socialists, the preamble to the constitution was given a distinctly populist flavor: "Spain is a democratic republic of workers of all kinds [*de toda clase*], organized in a regime of liberty and justice." Article 46, which Salvador de Madariaga describes as the socialists' intent "to put all their wares in the window from the first day of the fair,"[7] represented a veritable catalog of socialist labor objectives under the Second Republic: "The Republic will guarantee to every worker the necessary conditions for a dignified existence. Its social legislation will regulate the labor of women and children and in particular, the protection of motherhood, the working day and minimum wages and family wages, yearly paid vacations, the conditions of Spanish workers abroad, cooperative institutions, the economic-juridical relations among the several elements that make up production, the participation of workers in the management, administration, and profits of business, and all that concerns the welfare of workers."[8]

The architects of the reform program were Largo Caballero and his chief aides, Luis Araquistáin, the ideological brain truster for Caballerism, who served as undersecretary, and Antonio Fabra Ribas, a former member of the UGT Executive Committee and more recently director of the Madrid ILO office, who headed the Directorate General of Labor, which supervised the ministry's field operations. That program consisted largely of borrowings from projects prepared by the Institute of Social Reforms and sought to bring Spanish norms and practices more in line with International Labor Organization standards and conventions.[9]

The reforms constituted a signal advance in the rights and well-being of wage earners, far exceeding any previous legislation. The stated intention of the socialists was not to tilt the scales excessively in favor of the workers but to instill a greater sense of class equity. But to an oligarchy accustomed to exercising almost exclusive political and social control, the spectacle of government power and legality employed in favor of organized labor was deeply troubling. The enfranchising of 2 million agricultural field hands by providing them coverage under protective legislation and their mass unionization amounted to a virtual social revolution in rural Spain.

A plethora of regulatory decrees and legislative projects was turned out. During eight months in 1931 some fifty-one decrees and laws were promulgated, and the pace quickened the following year.[10] The more salient changes included the following:

The Labor Contract Law, modeled along the lines of its Weimar prototype and recommendations of the Institute of Social Reforms, replaced the 1926 labor code. It modified and broadened individual terms of employment and for the first time regulated joint labor-management organisms as well as collective bargaining. Annual paid vacations were established and employers' obligations in cases of employees' illness were defined.[11]

The eight-hour day and forty-hour week that had been established by a 1919 decree became law and was extended to include agricultural workers. It resulted in a sizable increase in wages because landowners were now required to pay an overtime premium whenever extra hours were called for. The new law and increased enforcement also were intended to alleviate growing unemployment.

The Municipal Boundaries Law (Ley de Terminos Municipales) required farmers employing hired labor preferentially to recruit *braceros* resident in the municipality in which the work was performed. Obviously popular with local farm workers, the law's main purpose was to guard against wage reductions and to maximize the bargaining power of farm unions by restricting sources of labor and thus preventing the recruitment of outside strikebreakers. These restrictive hiring practices also caused wage levels to rise, and though they substantially benefited local inhabitants and UGT rural labor enrollment, they created great difficulties for Galicians and thousands of others who traditionally were employed as migrant harvest labor.

The Professional Associations Law conferred legal standing on both employers' associations and labor organizations and set basic norms for their accreditation. Oversight was carried out by provincial labor delegates responsible to the Labor Ministry. Furthermore, by depriving civil governors and mayors of their traditional mediatory roles in resolving labor disputes and transferring jurisdictional authority to the regional labor delegates, the Labor Ministry strengthened its control over all aspects of labor affairs.

Existing protective laws were strengthened and broadened as, for example, workmen's compensation provisions and inclusion of agricultural wage earners, the creation of a national unemployment compensation fund, improvements in maternity insurance coverage, minimum wages for rural field hands, and the establishment of May Day as a national paid holiday.

Discarding some of the more overtly corporatist features such as the pyramidal decision-making structure and instead empowering local and provincial bodies, the renamed *jurados mixtos* (mixed juries) still retained the dictatorship's parity system of labor relations and conciliation. They were vested with a threefold authority: to resolve labor disputes peacefully, to fix the conditions of employment in each trade (*bases de trabajo*), and to oversee compliance with social legislation. Their enforcement powers and oversight of compliance with social legislation were strengthened substantially. Findings could be appealed to the Supreme Court's Social Law Chamber. The *jurados* were made more responsive to direction from the Labor Ministry, and because most chairmen and vice-chairmen were named by the ministry (when worker and employer jury members were unable to agree, the ministry made the appointment), most decisions would favor the workers and the UGT in particular since it practically monopolized *jurado* labor representation.[12]

The mixed jury system tended to short-circuit the collective bargaining process and to make the ministry the ultimate arbiter in labor disputes. It was, consequently, often difficult to tell where the union ended and government began. In 1934, when the socialists had left the government, most of the important bargaining disputes in Madrid continued to be decided by the ministry. Moreover, since the conciliatory functions of the juries often proved to be inoperative, the ministry was forced to issue numerous arbitrational findings (*laudos*). Collective bargaining, as under the dictatorship, rarely went beyond the plant level.

For the craft unionist, power over the hiring and firing of workers is equivalent to control of the workplace. The mutually reinforcing effects of the *jurado* labor relations structure, such legislative initiatives as the Municipal Boundaries Law, and the stipulations of collective bargaining contracts greatly increased the authority of UGT unions.[13]

Surely the single most important innovation was the extension of *jurado* jurisdiction to include the countryside. Under the dictatorship the parity committees had been empowered to operate in rural areas, but they had been essentially inoperative. Now, however, *jurados* became a key factor in enfranchising farm laborers and promoting their entry into the UGT in 1931–32.

The cumulative effect of the labor legislation was to modernize considerably the country's labor relations system. But the construct of institutional machinery and its uses betrayed the unmistakable stamp of a labor minister whose overriding priority was not enlightened industrial relations but strengthening and extending the power and affiliation of the UGT. Largo continued to serve as UGT general secretary.[14] In this respect at least, he was eminently successful as UGT enrollment skyrocketed from 287,330 in December 1930 to more than a million by mid-1932. In the rural areas the UGT's National Federation of Landworkers far outstripped the CNT as its membership soared almost overnight beyond 400,000. UGT trade union practice had practically become official government policy.[15] With the UGT in the role of privileged interlocutor, the socialist dream of ridding social conflict of its usual hatreds and rancors seemed about to become reality.

Largo's grand design was flawed by his expectation that by government fiat he could eliminate the CNT as an effective rival.[16] Since the CNT was constitutionally unable to accept such a labor relations system, half of organized labor was consigned to an illegal status.[17] Socialist control of the mixed juries and other agencies of the Labor Ministry, it was held, would co-opt the anarcho-syndicalist masses. Contrary to plan, however, the CNT reemerged as a potent force and, though the UGT succeeded in attracting large numbers of farm laborers who formerly had been under CNT influence, its overall following not only remained generally intact but managed to expand in most of its traditional preserves.[18]

Great difficulty was encountered in making CNT unions adhere to legal requirements. Threats by the CNT to bomb *casas del pueblos* and other violent reprisals at times obliged the Labor Ministry not to force CNT unions to comply with formal legal requirements such as submission of financial data, membership lists, statutes, and *jurados'* bargaining procedures or to enforce the eight-day advance notice to authorities before going on strike. Responsibility for providing mediation had been taken from civil governors and mayors and vested in the provincial labor delegates, who were directly responsible to the ministry. Nonetheless, numerous civil governors continued to carry out this function, some to mediate in disputes involving interunion differences, others to curry favor with Cenetistas, who sometimes permitted their followers to vote for Republican candidates. In Catalonia, where the CNT was all-powerful and where for a time the Generalitat courted CNT favor, civil governors and local authorities, to the disgust of Largo, continued to act as mediators. When the labor conciliatory function was turned over to the Generalitat in 1934, Martí Barrera, a former CNT leader, was named labor counselor and functioned successfully as a third-party mediator between CNT unions and employers.

In responding to the demands of the lower classes, Republicans generally conceded a broad mandate to the socialists to undertake labor reforms. But the socialists' inability to meet all these demands had a corrosive effect on the cohesion of the coalition. The constituencies of Republican parties included the urban bourgoisie as well as large numbers of small and medium-sized entrepreneurs. Furthermore, although radical in religious and military matters, Azaña and others tended to be moderate if not conservative on fiscal and economic questions. These attitudes became even more pronounced as the flight of capital from the country took on serious proportions.

Apparently troubled by employers' dissatisfaction with Largo's sweeping labor reforms, Azaña sought during the formation of the December 1931 cabinet to name a less partisan labor minister. But when he learned that continued control of the ministry was a nonnegotiable socialist condition for its participation in the cabinet, he did not pursue the matter.

The refusal of the Cortes in October 1931 to pass a workers control bill backed by the cabinet seemed to mark the limit of socialist efforts to institutionalize UGT predominance through government authority. The initiative embodied a UGT aspiration dating back to 1919, when it was first presented to the Institute of Social Reforms. Calling it "workers control" may have given it a Marxist ring, but in reality, it was something much less. Inspired by the Weimar Republic's works council structure, it was a Spanish version of codetermination. Works councils were to be established in all enterprises employing more than fifty employees and were to assure compliance with existing social legislation, labor contracts, and plant regulations, to have a consultative voice in hiring and firing, to be provided access to company financial records that affected wages, and to be represented on the company board of directors in a consultative capacity. Consistent with prevailing notions of European social democratic labor economics, Spanish socialists expected such councils to foster a greater sense of responsibility among workers in the management of enterprises and a consciousness that their freedom was linked with the prosperity of the firm they worked for. But Largo and his advisers knowingly or unknowingly ignored the fact that the Weimar codetermination system had been the product of a social compact between industrialists and trade unions, exchanging growth and stability for higher wages and welfare benefits.

The entire notion was unpalatable to most employers (and to many Republican parliamentarians), who especially objected to the provision requiring works councils to submit quarterly reports to the UGT as official spokesman for the working class with carbon copies to the company, employer associations, and the appropriate labor delegate evaluating the general state of labor-management relations. From a general European perspective Largo's initiative was not terribly advanced or radical. In the Spanish context, however, it amounted to a quantum leap for a society and a working class barely emerged from preindustrialism and still oriented toward agriculture. Fierce opposition from employers caused the bill to be pigeonholed in committee, thus preventing the Cortes from voting on it.[19]

Conflicting demands resulted in skewed economics. The government's monetary and economic policies were deflationary, partly to overcome the enormous budget deficits inherited from the dictatorship, a misbegotten fixation with balanced budgets, and the slackening of economic activities caused by the worldwide depression. Logic would have required an accompanying effort to reduce real wage levels, but political and social imperatives dictated otherwise. Wages during the reform biennium rose steadily.[20] One estimate places the average increase in urban wages at 16 percent at the same time that prices fell from an index of 172 to 117; another claims an overall rise of approximately 20 percent. Agricultural wages virtually doubled.[21] Spain was the only country where real wage earnings actually rose during the world depression.

Clearly a sizable income transfer was taking place in a deteriorating economic climate. Spanish economists disagree over the extent of the decline. A Bank of Spain estimate put the loss in industrial production from 1929 to 1933 at 15 percent, though more recently Albert Carreras placed the decline at only 7.3 percent. In any event, consumer industries such as textiles for a time benefited from increased popular purchasing power while others, particularly building construction, metalworking, mining, railways, and export-oriented agricultural sectors, wine, citrus fruits, olive oil, dried fruits, and nuts, suffered acutely. Especially hard hit by inflated wage costs were thousands of small and medium-sized businesses and agriculturists, who in a time of declining profits sustained substantial increases in operating costs. Yet nothing was done to soften the impact of higher wages on vulnerable entrepreneurs. Bountiful cereal harvests in 1932 had an initially positive effect but then led to price collapses and the subsequent ruination of numerous small farmers in Old Castile, León, Navarre, and Aragon. Crisis in steel- and ironmaking industries was hastened by a policy shift away from heavy financial support by the dictatorship, which had underwritten the supply and equipment of the equally subsidized railways. The transfer of public capital allocations to labor-intensive programs such as road construction fell well short of fulfilling its objective of reducing unemployment.

Not since has Spain experienced such an extraordinary political and social mobilization. The Republic's encouragement of popular participation provided a powerful impetus to the growth of labor organizations. One estimate places the level of unionization by 1931 at 45.5 percent compared to a 1920 high of 13 percent. Sixty-five to 70 percent of Madrid's wage earners carried union cards, as did 60 percent in Seville and well over that proportion in Barcelona. In the Asturian coal fields unionization reached 69 percent, and in the heavily industrialized Vizcaya province, it was 40 percent.[22] Increased politicization also signified a heightening in workers' political commitment. The UGT and PSOE collaborated more closely in electoral campaigns and other political actions.[23] More than in the past, when a worker joined the UGT he had a sense of belonging to the socialist movement. Roused from their torpor by the glittering expectations that the new Republican government evoked, many workers were in no mood to take their places quietly in a well-ordered bureaucratic labor relations system. For some, especially the young and the unskilled, the flamboyant, agitational militancy of the anarcho-syndicalists and the direct action of the Cenetistas were very attractive.

For the socialists the rash of strikes, many of them fomented by CNT militants, was totally irrational. They saw the creation of the mixed juries as the crowning achievement of years of laborious incremental progress to improve wage earners' well-being. Now with the bargaining balance heavily tilted in the workers' favor and the mixed juries everywhere churning out prolabor findings, why should any right-minded worker wish to imperil this hard-won achievement by engaging in what Araquistáin termed a "tragic striking frivolity"?

The unabashed exploitation of ministry faculties and legislative powers

Table 10.1. Strikes, 1929–1933

Year	Number of strikes	Number of strikers	Days lost	Average days lost
1929	96	55,576	313,965	3,261
1933	1,127	843,103	14,440,629	13,806

	Strikes won	Compromised	Lost
1929	18%	47%	35%
1930	17%	49%	29%
1931	22%	45%	11%

Source: Labor Ministry.

to advance UGT interests was regarded by the CNT as an open declaration of hostilites assuring that the CNT would try to weaken and render inoperative the *jurados* structure.[24] In numerous instances CNT unions forced employers to circumvent the mixed juries and deal directly with them. The benefits the UGT reaped from Largo's favoritism thus were counterbalanced by intensified interunion friction and stiffened employer opposition that provided an impetus for a resurgence of the Right and seriously undercut CNT moderates who favored a modus vivendi with the government.

The advent of the Second Republic opened new vistas of political consciousness for great masses of people. Its outstanding contribution was the powerful sense of awakening and liberation it evoked among urban wage earners and the rural poor. It fostered exceptional trade union organization in an underdeveloped, politically unstable society. By mid-1932 the UGT alone possessed a larger membership than the French CGT. For thousands, especially those under anarcho-syndicalist influence, the antistrike policy of the Primo de Rivera dictatorship had built up a reservoir of resentments and unfulfilled wage claims. With the downfall of the authoritarian regime, the situation began to change dramatically. According to Labor Ministry statistics that are admittedly incomplete, the rise in strike activity between 1929 and 1933 was, indeed, without precedent.[25] The number of strikes in those years soared elevenfold, the number of strikers fifteen times, and the number of days lost a staggering forty-six times (see table 10.1).[26] The 1930–31 Labor Ministry annual report ascribes the huge jump in strike activity to the end of the dictatorship and the release of workers' grievances. It states that compromises were more easily obtained in strikes over wages than in those involving demands that discharged workers be rehired.

The industrial strife that swept the country in 1931, receded the following year, and then reached even greater heights in 1933 had been generated by several factors. Some have described this outburst as primarily "political" or "passional," mirroring the general political ebullience following the Republic's birth and the revolutionary putschist activities of anarchist extremists.[27] Such factors undeniably influenced the rise of social upheaval and worker unrest, but it is excessive to give them such weight. An important element in the strike incidence of 1933 was that many of the collective bargaining agreements that had been negotiated in 1931 were for two years and were due for renewal in 1933, a time of deepening economic difficulties and stiffened employer opposition to union demands.[28]

Many of the strikes, as the Labor Ministry report asserts, resulted from the period of enforced inhibition. Accounts of the period, especially from CNT sources, often refer to the chaos and loss of control (*desbordamiento*) experienced by union leaders as countless worker groups and activists engaged in spontaneous work stoppages. Roughly a million workers and rural laborers joined the two labor confederations during the reform biennium. Ugetistas were able to maintain a fair amount of discipline over their rank and file. Many of their strikes were in support of wage demands and union recognition as workers strove to obtain adjustments previously denied them. Wage levels rose appreciably and tended to brake wage reductions prompted by the growing economic crisis. Extremists sometimes tapped worker militancy for political, insurrectionary ends. Unemployment was another source of strife as workers tried to prevent layoffs.

Largo's conduct as labor minister and his strong labor bias outraged employers, who now had good reason to strengthen their representative organizations.[29] The single-minded pursuit of working-class improvement without taking into account the increasing economic difficulties this entailed for innumerable small and medium-sized firms, especially at a time of economic slump, inevitably contributed to solidarity among employers and polarization of the different classes. Under the dictatorship employers had showed their aversion for the parity committees, and the mixed juries' prolabor behavior now became the focus of their grievances. They formed coordinating bodies to press their claims. A meeting was held in Madrid on July 19, 1933, with representatives from more than a thousand employer associations throughout the country to demand reforms in the mixed jury system that would afford greater impartiality in their decision making.

A political shift had also taken place. Many of the employers had supported the first two Republican governments, but as the reform biennium neared its end, large numbers of them turned to the Radicals, whose battle cry had become ouster of the socialists from government and reform of the mixed jury system.[30]

Although the new government generally expanded the citizens' liberties, its policies regarding public order, its respect for civil rights, and the behavior of police and military personnel varied little from those of previous regimes. What had changed, however, was the object of harassment. Monarchists and other rightists were subjected to harsh treatment just as they, in former times, had dealt with those now in power.[31] This behavior was to some extent attributable to inexperience, the public order norms of an underdeveloped, politically turbulent country, and egregious shortages of police and their lack of training, all of which made it extremely difficult to effect reforms over the short term. Instead of doing away with or overhauling the Civil Guards, the rural constabulary noted for brutality and a reactionary outlook, they were retained without major changes because they were regarded as vital to the maintenance of civil peace in rural areas. But a Republican Assault Guard was formed as an elite force the government could count on to be politically reliable and which would act without the usual heavy-handed brutishness.[32] Formation of the Assault Guard was part of a large increase in police forces that took place during the first year of the Republic in response to rising social unrest and anarchist depredations.

Civil Guards and military units continued to be employed in quelling labor disturbances, and martial law was declared frequently. An unauthorized CNT demonstration in Pasajaes, the port town adjacent to San Sebastian, was fired on by Civil Guards after the crowd defied an order to disperse. Eight died and fifty were wounded. During the latter half of 1931, numerous incidents in the countryside also ended in casualties. A particularly grisly incident that became a national cause célèbre took place in the tiny hamlet of Castilblanco in the southern part of Badajoz province. Differing versions exist as to what actually happened, but the most plausible one is that Civil Guards, at the urging of the mayor, sought to break up a demonstration of peasants by firing first in the air and then into the assembled crowd, killing one and wounding another. Not content with killing the four guards, the enraged crowd gruesomely mutilated their corpses. The Civil Guard wreaked terrible vengeance: three days later strikers were coldly fired upon in numerous rural areas, and in Arnedo in Logroño province, the guard fired repeatedly on a crowd of peacefully demonstrating industrial workers, killing seven and wounding thirty.[33]

The government's undistinguished record on public order was partially attributable to a lack of consolidation in its control and influence and the need almost immediately to confront a rise in labor unrest, anticlerical outbursts, and other problems. The FAI-inspired violence in the September 1931 Barcelona general strike led to the enactment of the harsh Law for the Defense of the Republic that gave the government sweeping emergency powers in dealing with illegal strikes.[34] The law reflected Azaña's dictum "No liberty for the enemies of liberty." The unfortunate choice of Miguel Maura as the first interior minister did not help matters any. An old-fashioned conservative, he generally employed hard-line law and order practices that were little distinguishable from those of the Restoration era. His lack of political sensitivity, his unavoidable reliance on inexperienced civil governors, and the excessive use of armed force in dealing with labor disturbances were frequent concerns for Azaña.[35]

The climate of persistent social agitation and labor unrest and emerging signs of political regrouping on the Right prompted General José Sanjurjo, the country's most popular military officer but a political ingenue, to launch a pronunciamiento from Seville in August 1932. It was, of course, much too early to hazard such an attempt, and it collapsed when the local UGT called a general strike in defense of the Republic that was supported by Cenetista and communist unions.[36] Sanjurjo's failed coup did rally support for the Azaña government, which benefited from a much needed new lease on life.

Anarcho-Syndicalism: The Insurrectionary Self-Immolation

CNT leaders and militants almost without exception hailed the coming of the Republic. Both Cenetistas and anarchists had taken part in revolutionary conspiracies to overthrow the dictatorship and tacitly sanctioned voting for the Republican-socialist alliance in the April 12 municipal elections.[37] And when the new government took office on April 14, *Solidaridad Obrera* declared that "the triumph of the Republicans demonstrated the people's will."[38]

Moderates who headed the CNT assumed an attitude of condescension. Angel Pestaña was national secretary, Joan Peiró directed *Solidaridad Obrera,* and many other key posts were occupied by men of similar persuasion. Although they avoided direct collaboration—Pestaña turned down an invitation from Francesc Maciá, who headed the Generalitat, to serve as its labor counselor—tacit coexistence to aid in the consolidation of Republican rule was the order of the day, a posture that was also intended to help the anarcho-syndicalist movement conduct its reorganization and extend its mass following. Social revolution could come only after an extended period of preparation and organizational consolidation. The Republican takeover permitted a much more amenable environment for attaining these goals.

CNT membership during the early years of the Republic was around 250,000 of which 150,000 were concentrated in Barcelona,[39] representing a regional unionization rate of 30 percent and more than 50 percent in Barcelona. In neighboring towns such as Hospitalet, virtually the entire working population joined the CNT. The Sindicatos Libres almost disappeared as most of their members rejoined the CNT and many of their leaders fell victim to anarchist vengeance.[40] Despite Largo's manipulations and the UGT's success in reducing the CNT's rural following, the confederation remained the dominant element in many Andalusian cities and in the countrysides of Cádiz and Seville provinces. Seville, the region's largest city and a traditional anarcho-syndicalist fief, experienced a massive unionization involving almost 60 percent of the labor force with the largest segment (22,000) affiliated with CNT unions. Málaga also emerged as an important stronghold. Zaragossa and the Valencian region (Levant) were equally important areas of influence, and traditional enclaves flourished in the northern regions of Asturias, Galicia, Bilbao to a substantially lesser extent, and among the vineyard workers of La Rioja.

Soon the initial Republican euphoria dissipated and doctrinal cleavages reappeared. The principal bone of contention this time was the leadership's tacit coexistence with the authorities, a policy that numerous anarchists regarded as backsliding into "reformist possibilism" with an accompanying lack of revolutionary ardor. For them the new Republican government was merely another oppressive bourgeois regime and was not to be viewed as a lesser evil. Nothing less than its total destruction was required. Moreover, socialists were using that government to annihilate the CNT. The downfall of the monarchy, anarchists argued, had created a prerevolutionary situation, and CNT resources should be marshaled to assure its overthrow and the immediate establishment of libertarian communism.

An unbridgeable gulf separated anarcho-syndicalist "constructionists," who sought attainment of the ultimate objective through mass action and the building of a large popular movement capable of assuming the direction of a libertarian syndicalist economic order, from those intent upon armed struggle directed by a small conspiratorial elite. Once insurrectionary action was initiated, the masses would spontaneously join in. To acquiesce in the Republic's consolidation, they insisted, ran the risk of seeing workers become corrupted by social reformism. For many among them the confederation was a training ground for inculcation of a proletarian spirit of rebellion. A future libertarian communist society, in any event, would not be based on the unions but on the arcadian anarchist concept of rural "communes" or "free municipalities." The anarchists lacked any clear notion of how the new order would be structured; only after joining the enemy in street combat would some thought be given to the planning of the new society.[41]

With only a small number of followers in the Barcelona area, the Iberian Anarchist Federation had led a marginal existence.[42] Though deficient in theoretical or organizational talent, it had begun to emerge by the summer of 1931 as the rallying center for a variety of anarchist militants opposed to the "revisionism" of the CNT leadership. Its augmented role, however, did not result in an enlarged following or in greater policy cohesion. Its unifying force was "the ideological intransigence of its members, fierce opponents of authority, hierarchy, politics, the state, legal action, and 'temporizing.' "[43] Anarchist extremists of diverse views, purists such as Federica Montseny and the anarcho-bolshevik Nosotros group that included Durruti, Ricardo Sanz, Juan García Oliver, and Gregorio Jover, did not join the organization but now called themselves Faistas.[44] As they gained in influence, the level of violence, *pistolerismo,* and *atentados* rose.

A fierce rivalry marked by considerable violence commenced, centered in Barcelona. The traditional dispersal of authority, the total lack of discipline, and the decentralized organizational structure—confederal regional affiliates were bound only by voluntary agreements—made it extremely difficult to fend off a Faista onslaught and to prevent unions from engaging in insurrectionary actions once the opposition gained control.[45] During the spring of 1931 the FAI and the Nosotros group persuaded the CNT national committee to entrust them with the formation and manning of the paramilitary secret defense units that customarily conducted armed actions in support of the unions.[46] These groups were already well ensconced in the influential Comites Pro-Presos, the prisoners' aid organizations, and they served as an excellent vantage point from which to gain control of the various *sindicatos unicos.* The bravura and flaming demagogy of extremist firebrands all too often proved to be more appealing to the unsophisticated, ill-educated rank and filers than reasoned discourse. Not all Faistas supported the insurrectionist tactic, or what in anarchist argot was known as "revolutionary gymnastics," but it was a policy imposed by the Nosotros zealots, and all collaborated in organizing revolutionary strikes, *atentados,* and other armed actions.[47]

From June 10 to 16 a special national congress, the "Conservatory Congress," was held in Madrid.[48] It was the first since the 1922 Zaragossa conclave. Though less than two months had passed since the birth of the Republic and the recovery of the CNT's legal status, the congress assembled 418 delegates representing 511 affiliated unions speaking for an aggregate membership of 535,565.[49] More than half were from Catalonia (291,240). The congress took place as the confrontation between the embattled factions was intensifying. Several important Barcelona unions were already under Faista control and were represented by Durruti, García Oliver, and Sanz. Two issues dominated the deliberations: whether to accept the leadership's "possibilist" attitude toward the government and the formation of national trade and industry federations. The discussions were marked by considerable tumult and verbal violence.[50]

The conversion of the organizational structure from loosely federated regional entities to a more cohesive one based on national industrial federations had been sought by trade union–minded militants since the confederation's inception. Regional autonomy with its wide scope for independence had given the CNT a strong popular appeal and permitted the movement to include such diverse elements as Andalusian peasants and field laborers, Catalonian industrial workers, Asturian steelworkers, and Galician fishermen. But this diversity was a serious impediment to unified action.

Since greater cohesion had been rejected in 1919, it had been unceasingly advocated by its main exponent, Joan Peiró, one of the more capable and thoughtful anarcho-syndicalists. It was imperative, he argued, not only to permit a more effective challenge to the power of modern capitalism but to rid the organization of its archaic particularist mentality (*patria chica*), an excessive regional autonomy that all too often nullified any possibility for coordinated action. The fundamental issue was whether the confederation was to give greater priority to trade union collective bargaining goals or to revolutionary action. A vertical restructuring would mean strengthening the former; perpetuating the loose federal system would facilitate the conduct of spontaneous revolutionary struggle.

The congress endorsed the formation of industry federations and, though approving the leadership's conduct of policy, failed to adopt a positive attitude toward the constitutuent Cortes that Peiró and other moderates sought.[51] Pestaña and a moderate majority were returned to national office, but the congress revealed the depth and intensity of the differences between the rival factions. Furthermore, totally ignoring the congress's decisions, Durruti and his Nosotros comrades proceeded to impose their tactic of armed struggle, and it became impossible to form national trade federations until 1936, when the insurrectionist strategy was finally abandoned.[52]

During July thousands of workers flooded into the unions and bargained aggressively for wage boosts while extremists diligently pursued their revolutionary tactics, to the chagrin of CNT moderates. The relatively quiescent Andalusian *campo* became restive. The CNT telephone workers union called a nationwide strike on July 4 against the International Telephone and Telegraph–owned phone system (which was then taken over by Faistas) that led to a head-on clash with the authorities. The CNT union was only one of four unions claiming to represent the telephone employees, and the other three, including the UGT, refused to join the strike. The main purpose of the walkout was to embarrass the socialists and the government by portraying them as kowtowing to Yankee imperialism. The government was intent on maintaining phone service and insisted that a strike settlement could be obtained only through mediation by a mixed jury. The CNT had sufficient support to cut most of the services only in Barcelona and Seville. To keep the strike afloat, CNT activists resorted to violence, an armed assault on the Madrid telephone exchange, sabotage, and intimidation.[53]

The telephone conflict took place amid growing labor turbulence in Seville. Extremists had gained control of the local CNT federation in June as labor disputes and shutdowns, on the increase since May, were becoming more intractable and violent. Seville was the only major city in the country where the communists, who sought to outdo the Cenetistas in ultraradicalism and violent tactics, possessed a sizable trade union following. Consequently, the telephone strike only served to aggravate social tensions.

The death of a brewery worker in a fight with strikebreakers led to a pitched battle at his funeral, resulting in the deaths of three Civil Guards and four workers and hundreds of injured. An insurrectionary general strike was called on July 20 with the support of the communist Unión Local de Sindicatos. Forty thousand workers dropped their tools, completely paralyzing the city. Armed groups of anarchists, communists, and persons in the pay of employers, as well as police, roamed the city engaging in shootouts. Street violence and gun battles became daily events. More violence occurred than at any time since the Barcelona labor wars of the 1920s.[54] The pitifully small police force—they numbered forty-nine in a city of a quarter of a million—was totally overwhelmed, and on July 22 Interior Minister Maura declared martial law and dispatched military and Civil Guard units. If the depredations of strike activists had reached outrageous proportions, the measures taken to quell them, including the artillery bombardment of an alleged CNT hangout, were no less excessive. The general strike had begun as a twenty-four-hour action and was then extended indefinitely, finally dying out on the twenty-sixth, and the national telephone stoppage was abandoned on the twenty-ninth. The cost was appalling: thirty dead, two hundred wounded, and two thousand in jail.

Increasingly violent confrontations with the government, the continuing bloody rivalry with the UGT for control of the Barcelona waterfront, and exasperation over government insistence upon acceptance of the despised mixed juries joined to produce great hostility toward the Republic among CNT militants, which fostered support for the radicals. A regional plenum that was held in Barcelona in early August showed a sizable increase in Faista influence.[55]

Barely two months after their Pyrrhic victory at the national congress, thirty of the leading moderates, in a supreme effort to stem the alarming spread of Faismo, issued a public statement on September 1 that became known as the Manifesto of the Thirty. Among its signatories were such luminaries as Pestaña, Arin, Juan López, Camil Piñon, Sebastia Clará, and Ricard Fornells. Most were in their thirties and forties, men of the Seguí generation, whereas the Faistas were in their twenties and their views had been shaped during the Primo de Rivera dictatorship.[56]

The moment was particularly favorable for younger militants, whose formative years occurred in a time of street brawls and gunfights and who were much more accustomed to action and audacious exploits than to debates over ideology and strategy. None could rival the "three musketeers," Buenaventura Durruti, Francisco Ascaso, and Juan García Oliver as strong, action-oriented, charismatic leaders. Gerald Brenan describes Durruti as "a powerful man with brown eyes and an innocent expression and Ascaso a little dark man of insignificant appearance. They were two saints of the Anarchist cause, showing the way by their merits and their example."[57] Their exploits—bank robberies, years in prison and exile, reprisal assassinations, and daredevil insurrectionary undertakings—had made them heroes in the eyes of many Catalan workers. García Oliver, who had a superior political mind, has been likened to a 1919 Irish revolutionary.[58] He became the insurrectionists' leading tactician and the organizer of numerous strikes and revolutionary putsches.

"We propose revolutionary action," declared García Oliver, "without concerning ourselves whether or not we are prepared to make a revolution and to introduce libertarian communism. We do not conceive the revolutionary problem to be one of preparation but of will, endeavoring to carry it out when social decomposition such as presently affects Spain fertilizes any revolutionary effort."[59] The Republic's lack of consolidation, he argued, created an opportunity for its immediate overthrow.

In what was intended as a belated declaration of hostilities but ended up as a *cri de coeur,* the Treintista manifesto responded:

All is entrusted to chance, all awaits the unexpected miracle of holy revolution as though the revolution were some sort of panacea and not a tragic cruel event that forms man through the suffering of his body and the sorrow of his mind. Offspring of the purest demagogy, this concept of the revolution possesses advocates among us. . . . Should we, must we submit ourselves and the National Confederation of Labor to this catastrophic concept of revolution that is merely a revolutionary gesture?

Do not entrust the revolution exclusively to audacious minorities but to the great mass popular movement of the working class marching toward its definitive liberation with the unions and the Confederation deciding the appropriate moment for revolution.

We wish a revolution born of the deepest feelings of the people, as it is today taking shape; not a revolution that is offered us, conducted by a handful who, were they to succeed, would, however they label it, inevitably convert themselves into dictators the day following their triumph.[60]

What Cenetista moderates sought in essence to accomplish was to adapt anarchist ideas of the nineteenth century to the realities of twentieth-century industrial society.

The initiative had already passed to the maximalists, and, to quote García Oliver, the Treintista riposte had been "overtaken by events." On the very day of the manifesto's publication fifty Cenetistas in the Barcelona Modelo Prison went on a hunger strike. Rumors spread through the city alleging mistreatment and worse of the prisoners. Against the urgings of the national officers, the FAI-controlled city federation called a general strike on September 3. Barricades went up in working-class districts while police and armed militants exchanged gunfire. A police attempt to enter the headquarters of the building construction union to confiscate an arms store led to the death of three unionists. Faista actions may have been counterproductive, but over the short term they served to heighten resentments against the government and to increase radicalization.

The position of the national leadership became increasingly untenable, and Peiró and other moderates resigned on September 21, relinquishing control of *Solidaridad Obrera* to the FAI.[61] These events had taken place on the heels of a citywide meeting of union delegates that indicated that the extremists had become dominant in Barcelona, relegating the Treintistas to a distinctly minority status.

Growing Faista ascendancy coincided with the formation of the Azaña government in December, the reappointment of Largo Caballero as labor minister, and a reaffirmation of his labor policies. Labor unrest and insurrectionary attempts continued in many parts of the country. Azaña's response to the growing disorder was to adopt a tough public order policy. Recruitment for the newly formed Republican Assault Guards was speeded up, and the Defense of the Republic Law was passed, giving sweeping powers to the authorities in combating disorder and violence. Nonetheless, the violence continued as anarchists pressed their putschist tactics with undiminished vigor. By year's end differences between the two factions had reached the breaking point. Pestaña and Peiró passed their final months in office touring the country to rally support for the Treintistas. A last-minute intervention by emissaries from the International Workingmens Association to avert an open split proved unsuccessful.

How had it been possible for the extremists' seemingly irrational, destructive creed to take hold? Several factors worked in their favor. Besides providing a much more conducive climate for union recruitment, the prolabor policies of the Republic and the Generalitat also promoted sizable wage increases for farm laborers and urban wage earners. Improved purchasing power created a greater demand for textile products so that despite the worldwide depression Catalonia during the early Republican years enjoyed modest prosperity and unions found it fairly easy to force employers to grant wage boosts. Thus the Faistas came to power in the unions when union credibility and mobilizational capacity were at an all-time high. By late 1931 CNT membership in Catalonia may have exceeded four hundred thousand, making the confederation the single most powerful element in regional social, economic, and political life.

With its antipolitics, direct-action approach, Cenetismo had always possessed a special appeal for the untutored, recently arrived peasant immigrants. For that reason it has been referred to by some writers as a sort of left-wing Carlism. The overwhelming majority of anarchist activists, moreover, were of immigrant stock. At a time of upheaval they became the backbone of Faista support. In the Catalonian labor force of 514,000 in 1930, a third were immigrants with less than ten years' residence and one of every four Barcelona wage earners was of immigrant stock.

Large numbers of Murcian and Almerian peasants came during the dictatorship to seek work in government public works projects such as the Barcelona Universal Exposition, subway construction, and the nearby potassium salt mines. They came from Spain's most depressed, backward provinces, where illiteracy and living standards were at their worst and where political bossism was rampant. The deep hostility they harbored against politics and the attraction that a violent messianic creed held for them (and for their Valencian and Aragonese counterparts) is comprehensible.[62] In those rural districts the only way to oppose electoral corruption and intimidation was to refuse to vote. Protest in such repressive, semifeudal settings was usually expressed through primitive, violent outbursts. Extremist influence was particularly strong in the Barcelona building construction union and its counterparts in other cities. The construction industry employed a high percentage of unskilled immigrant workers (*peones*). Its influence was also strong in the suburb of Hospitalet, a predominantly immigrant workers community, and among the mining settlements of the Upper Llobregat valley, where the work force was almost exclusively made up of peasant migrants. The CNT construction union in Seville similarly became a Faista stronghold, and UGT dominance was broken in the Madrid building trades mainly by unskilled *peones* incited by Faistas. The industry was one of the hardest hit by abandonment of the large-scale public works programs of the dictatorship and the economic depression.

The final break was precipitated by an uprising in the Upper Llobregat mining town of Figols in January 1932. At the urging of Faistas, the potash miners of Figols and neighboring communities seized control of municipal buildings and proclaimed libertarian communism.[63] The action was taken without any prior notice to local, regional, or national union authorites.[64] The rising was supposed to spark off a revolutionary general strike throughout the region, but this never happened and the insurrection was snuffed out within three days.

The putsch was a minor nuisance and caused few casualties, but Azaña took strong countermeasures to demonstrate that revolutionary adventures would not be tolerated. Union offices were padlocked and a hundred CNT leaders deported to the Spanish Sahara and the Canary Islands. Among the deportees were Durruti and García Oliver. The government took care not to include Treintistas in its repressive actions, a policy that was also followed by Maciá and Companys in the Generalitat.[65] Protest strikes flared up in various localities, and on February 14, a few days following the deportations, anarchists organized an insurrectionary rising in the textile town of Tarassa that lasted a few days.

Disaster and setbacks did not generate soul-searching. Instead, Faistas heaped the blame entirely on the shoulders of their moderate opponents, calling them traitors for having refused to come to the aid of their embattled comrades. Following the flood of abuse and recriminations, Pestaña felt obliged to surrender his post of national secretary to a Faista. At an April 24 plenum in Sabadell the moderate regional secretary and several of his supporters tendered their resignations amid accusations that they had failed to support the Upper Llobregat risings. By this time insurrectionary strikes and putsches were beginning to exact a toll on the CNT's enrollment. Nonetheless, intent on a thorough ideological cleansing, anarchist zealots secured the expulsion of city federations in Lérida and Gerona (Tarragona was later added) that were under the control of supporters of the Marxist Workers and Peasants Bloc (Bloc Obrer i Camperol). The Sabadell federation, the most powerful and best organized CNT section with fourteen thousand dues-paying members, withdrew in protest over the dictatorial reign of the FAI and Barcelona centralism, declaring its support for the Treintistas, and was quickly emulated by the federations of Badalona, Valls, most of the Mataró locals, and many in Calella and Manresa.[66]

In September Treintistas formally constituted the Catalonian Anarcho-Syndicalist Opposition with a claimed adherence of twenty-six thousand CNT rank and filers. The Valencian regional federation, which was in the hands of the moderates, also began a process of gradual withdrawal from the confederation, as did most locals in Huelva. From the vantage point of the average member, the choice was not clear-cut. Both sides differed little on basic principles and ultimate objectives; the main difference was over tactics and strategy. Balcells writes, "Treintistas remained anarcho-syndicalists though less doctrinaire and violent than the Faistas. FAI accented the anarchism of the CNT, Treintistas trade unionism; both, nonetheless, were anarcho-syndicalists, anticommunists, and antisocialists."[67] Numerous local organizations and activists found it difficult to choose sides. Some of the pure anarchists such as Manuel Buenacasa were repulsed by the fanaticism, sectarianism, and violence of the Faistas. Disheartened by the fratricide, a number of unions left the CNT. Though in sympathy with the Treintistas, the regional organizations of Galicia and Asturias preferred to remain neutral, hoping ultimately to bring the two warring sides together.

A variety of elements combined in determining which faction to support. The influence of individual leaders and personal charisma often were key factors. There was, moreover, a correlation between the proportion within a given CNT union of immigrant unskilled workers and its ideological preferences. The bulk of those possessing predominantly immigrant members tended to side with the FAI while Treintista influence was generally greatest among unions in which those of Catalan ethnic origin were in the majority.[68] Barcelona with its large immigrant population became the FAI stronghold; industrial centers in the interior with much lower ratios of immigrant workers usually sided with the Treintistas. Tarrassa and Sabadell are neighboring wool textile manufacturing centers, but the former possessed a much larger immigrant worker component than Sabadell. The first became a hotbed of Faismo, the second a Treintista bastion. BOC found support in towns outside Barcelona and from white-collar workers in Barcelona. Meetings of the opposition unions tended to be conducted in Catalan and those under Faista control in Castilian. Many among the indigenous Catalans who supported the Treintistas did so to some extent to repudiate attacks by the FAI on the ruling Catalan Esquerra party, which they supported.

Upon gaining control of the regional confederation, Faistas expelled the Sabadell city federation on the pretext that it refused to pay dues to the national organization. In October the Levant confederation split into two rival bodies. A thorough purge of Barcelona unions then took place. Treintista supporters and sympathizers, including those holding union office, among them such renowned historic figures as Pestaña, Camil Piñon, Juan López, and many others, were expelled. A membership meeting of the food workers union in November voted to expel its president, Ricard Fornells. The inquisition also placed known supporters of BOC outside the pale. Ideological intransigence had now become absolute master of the Barcelona CNT.[69]

It is not possible to say with any precision what the membership of the CNT was in 1932 when it reached its zenith. Official claims place it at 1 million, but this figure was arrived at simply by counting the total number of membership books issued between April 1931 and June 1932, and it also included Opposition Union adherents as well as those under BOC influence who had been expelled. Angel Pestaña believed that the total may have approached 1 million. It does seem likely, however, that the number of workers in the CNT orbit at that time was fairly close to that in the socialist camp.[70]

With organizational control firmly in Faista hands, preparations were begun for a nationwide rising. This time greater pains were taken to provide coordination and planning. García Oliver, who headed the defense action groups, was its chief architect. The major battle was to be fought in Barcelona, preceded by a national railway strike to immobilize government countermeasures. Uprisings in the Andalusian and Aragonese pueblos were to serve as tactical diversions to avert any possible concentration of police and army forces. Arms, explosives, and personnel were gathered. After initially agreeing to a strike, the CNT railroad federation, which represented a small minority of the work force, finally decided against it. Amid confusion over whether the CNT national committee had given its authorization, García and his *cuadros de defensa* assumed direction. Thus "once again, as in 1930, the CNT was pulled into a revolutionary venture by the actions of the Iberian Anarchist Federation."[71]

On January 8, 1933, armed groups launched attacks on several Barcelona military barracks and assaulted police stations and military installations in Lérida and Valencia, scattered localities of the Levant, La Rioja, and Catalonia. The authorities were alerted in advance and rapidly subdued the uprisings. Nowhere did the hoped-for mass support materialize. Yet the cycle of uprisings and repression was repeated with mass detentions, punitive fines against *Solidaridad Obrera,* the closing of union offices, and other actions. Once more the human toll was high: thirty-seven dead and three hundred wounded.

Uprisings occurred in several Andalusian villages, especially in the province of Cádiz, where events at the hamlet of Casas Viejas (population one thousand five hundred) took a macabre turn. Assault Guards had been sent in after the local CNT peasants union seized control and proclaimed libertarian communism. Two Civil Guards were mortally wounded while attempting to retake the village. Resistance collapsed when reinforcements arrived. Several of the defending *campesinos* were killed. When an Assault Guard sought to enter the hut of a person named Seisdedos, where a group of resisters was holed up, he was felled by a shotgun blast. Calls for surrender were rejected. To break the stalemate a fresh unit of Assault Guards was brought in with orders to overcome resistance by any means. Unable to storm the hut (*choza*) without incurring further casualties, the guards set the hut afire when its occupants rejected a final demand to surrender. Altogether twenty-two peasants were killed, including those incinerated in Seisdedos's hut, several children who were gunned down while fleeing the burning shack, and the twelve *campesinos* who were killed in the reprisal massacre. Three Guards were also dead and four others wounded. The ferocity of the fighting, the torching of the besieged hut, and the slaughter of innocents shocked the country.

As the details of the tragedy became known, the Azaña government came under strong attack not only from the extreme Left but from disturbed Republican supporters as well; Lerrouxist Republicans and conservatives also joined in the assault. The atrocities were especially shocking because they were committed by the Assault Guards, a security unit formed precisely to avoid the excesses usually associated with Civil Guards. Socialists found themselves in the painfully compromising position of being forced to mute their revulsion for fear of toppling the government. Azaña's policy of vigorous suppression of anarchist revolutionary actions to save the Republic had come up painfully short.[72] The tragedy of Casas Viejas was a body blow to the government, which was branded "the government of Casas Viejas" and was to fall before the year was out.[73]

Despite the Casas Viejas incident, the CNT showed little interest in the rural confrontation at a time when the FNTT was embroiled in a power struggle with the rural oligarchy. The Barcelona Faistas, who were in control, were urban-oriented and conducted their revolutionary exploits from the cities, where their influence was greatest.[74] Consequently, during the Republican years Cenetista rural organizations conducted only sporadic militant actions.[75] Nor was any attempt made to form national or regional peasant bodies to challenge socialist strength. Cenetismo paid dearly for its rejection of the Republican labor reforms and land redistribution projects, causing it to lose the support of countless rural laborers who would have otherwise joined its ranks rather than those of the FNTT. In Andalusia, where most of its rural membership was concentrated, it numbered only fifty thousand at the time of the Conservatory congress.

The insurrectionary strikes and rebellions inflicted serious damage on the Republic's reputation in 1931. No regime had ever been subjected to such an unrelenting assault. It also had a ruinous effect on CNT organizational prospects and enrollment. The powerful appeal of anarcho-syndicalism as a popular movement so dramatically underscored in the massive influx during the first eight months of the Republic was now unraveling. Supporters by the thousands began to leave. By 1933 one-third of its 1931 membership was gone.

The FAI's control of the CNT and the violence of its actions depleted union ranks but generated further militancy. Estimates of FAI membership for this period conflict. At the outset of the Second Republic there were about four hundred FAI adherents in the Barcelona area and perhaps an equal number distributed throughout the rest of the country. The report issued by the October 1933 FAI plenum claimed 5,335 supporters, but the number was probably appreciably smaller.

Pestaña and his supporters sought to counter the growing ideological influence of the FAI by forming the Libertarian Syndicalist Federation (Federación Sindicalista Libertario—FSL). But instead of advancing their position, this initiative demonstrated that Treintistas, like their rivals, possessed little cohesion or philosophical homogeneity.[76] A first attempt to hold a public meeting in Barcelona was broken up by FAI supporters. The Catalonian Trade Union Opposition did, however, succeed in convening its first regional plenum on June 14, 1933, with more than twenty-six thousand CNT members represented. A conference the following August claimed to speak for thirty-five thousand at a time when CNT regional membership had shrunk to one hundred thousand.

Treintistas permitted their followers to participate in the national elections of November 1933, while the CNT-FAI plastered the country with posters urging "Instead of voting, social revolution," calling on their supporters to boycott the election. The abstention campaign appears to have had mixed results. Nonvoting rates in Barcelona hardly varied from those in the June 1931 elections, but in other traditional centers of influence, Seville, Cádiz, Málaga, and provincial towns of Catalonia, the abstention rate was high. The CNT undoubtedly contributed to the crushing defeat suffered by the Left and was widely excoriated for its actions. To atone for their negative role and to demonstrate their even-handedness, anarchists embarked on still another insurrectional attempt, this time against the newly installed center-right government. Zaragossa was the main center for the December rising led by a committee composed of Durruti, Cipriano Mera, and Isaac Puente. Since most of the regional federations were exhausted from previous insurrectionary attempts, Zaragossa, an anarchist stronghold, was selected to spearhead the rising. Other federations were to lend assistance in the form of strikes, seizures, and the like.

The notion of engaging in rebellious uprisings without the slightest chance of success is difficult to comprehend. Spanish anarchism imparted to workers a strong moral fervor that was its primary motivating force, a certain heroic quality that allowed its militants to engage in actions despite their seeming hopelessness. Nowhere is this ethos better exemplified than in the general strike at Zaragossa in March 1934, barely three months after the stern repression of the last insurrectionary effort. The strike was called to protest the mistreatment of Cenetistas jailed during the December actions and to demand their release. UGT unions joined in, and the city was totally shut down for four weeks. To alleviate the strike's hardships—there were no strike defense funds—many of the strikers' children were taken to other towns to be cared for. It was a remarkable display of resistance and courage.

Why, in the face of the dramatic failures of the insurrection tactic and its destructive effects on the movement, was it not possible for the moderates to advance an effective, reasonable alternative and to win over many more CNT members to their side? Faistas and Treintistas grossly overestimated the strength of their respective appeals. The coming of the Republic did not herald the opening of a prerevolutionary era, and the Spanish working class paid little heed to Faista entreaties. Nor was the timing of the Treintista challenge opportune. By 1933 the effects of depression and unemployment were being felt on a wide scale. Employers were fiercely resisting union demands, and a sense of beleaguerement pervaded union ranks. For the average rank and filer this was a time to close ranks against hostile employers and not to weaken their defenses by engaging in divisive activities.

Pestaña's miscalculated formation of the Syndicalist party in February 1934 seriously threatened the always fragile cohesion of Treintismo. Moving further from his anarcho-syndicalist roots, he now urged the trade unions to take political action and participate in elections.[77] Pestaña's new position represented such a wrenching doctrinal and psychological break with the anarcho-syndicalist tradition that few among his Treintista colleagues were willing to follow his lead. To join him in this heresy was to abandon any hope for a reconciliation in CNT ranks. The overwhelming majority of FSL members, including Peiró and López, refused to follow him, preferring to maintain hope of a reconciliation. But a process of fragmentation had begun that ended with Pestaña and his small band of Syndicalist party supporters becoming marginalized. It also led to the disillusionment and desertion of a number of distinguished leaders. Sebastia Clará, Martí Barrera, Simó Piera, Pere Foix, and others went over to the Catalan Left and still others ended up in the procommunist Unified Catalonian Socialist party (Partido Socialista Unificado Catalan—PSUC). After the July 1936 military rebellion the important federations of Sabadell and Manresa decided to join the UGT (and PSUC). The remaining Treintistas rejoined the CNT.

The Socialists: From Republican Reformism to Revolutionary Incoherence

The Republic's honeymoon period lasted eight months, from April 1931 to parliamentary ratification of the new constitution the following December. The enthusiasm generated during that period created optimal conditions for carrying out key social and political reforms. And as these changes took effect, Spain's system of government began to approach that of a modern European democratic state.

The deep cleavages in Spanish society soon resurfaced, however. In December the Azaña government lost the support of Lerroux's Radical Republican party, a major historic Republican entity and the second largest in the Cortes. Its support had come mainly from middle-class entrepreneurs, manufacturers, and farmers, but it now sought to become the rallying center for discontent over rising labor costs and socialist control of the Labor Ministry by demanding the PSOE's ouster from government.

The departure of the Radicals left the socialist—Left Republican coalition with only a slender majority, but it made the cabinet more cohesive. It was possible to govern with only a small majority because the opposition parties did not agree on major issues. But relations between the executive and the Cortes were unstable. As Edward Malefakis notes, "Azaña's legislative program was constantly in danger of being undermined by the defection of a handful of his own deputies or by the determined opposition of the parties outside the coalition."[78]

It is in this light that the government's failure to seize the moment to enact an authentic agrarian reform can be seen as its single most tragic shortcoming.[79] Land redistribution even under the best of circumstances was fraught with great difficulty and controversy.[80] Yet during those early euphoric months it could have been accomplished had not the Republicans exhibited a singular lack of urgency. Before the formation of the new regime Republicans had given little thought to the land problem. Only the socialists had bothered to formulate an agrarian reform program. Alcalá Zamora, pressed by his own supporters and the Radicals, shied away from endorsing a highly regarded reform proposal. Most Republican legislators were urban-minded and did not give agrarian reform a very high priority. In their view, the principal obstacle to Spain's modernization since the early nineteenth century was not its retarded agriculture but the exorbitant power of the church and the military. Consequently, these two institutions now became the main objects of attention.

Though fiercely opposed by the episcopate, the formal separation of church and state was not terribly controversial and was accepted even by many enlightened Catholics. What rankled, however, was the accompanying restrictions such as the withdrawal of financial subsidies to the secular clergy, registration and taxation of the orders' properties and financial holdings, and banning of the Jesuits and confiscation of their property. Article 26 of the constitution, furthermore, severely restricted the activities of the orders by denying them participation in commerce, industry, or nonconfessional teaching. Secondary education was largely in church hands and a source of considerable revenue. Solely from a practical political point of view, to alienate so many people before dealing with the agrarian issue, particularly since the church's main source of support came from the rural areas, was to make passage of land redistribution all the more difficult.[81]

Within the European context the measures taken against the church were not particularly radical. But in Spain, where church and state had functioned as virtual coequals since the fifteenth-century reconquest, an abrupt secularization with perceived punitive measures attached was charged with considerable emotional and institutional implications. Passage of Article 26 caused a notable loss of pro-Republican sentiment among many Catholics and led to the resignations of Catholic Republicans Alcalá Zamora and Maura in October, heralding the first major fissure in Republican ranks.

Though lacking much knowledge about military affairs, Azaña, who served concurrently as prime minister and war minister, undertook a major military reform. The bloated officer corps was reduced and those remaining on active duty were given enhanced status and pay. The voluntary retirement at full pay of large numbers of officers was a heavy drain on the public exchequer. Azaña sought to exempt the armed forces from any further intervention in matters concerning domestic public order and to concentrate on external defense. But the vindictive way in which church and military reforms were carried out did little to strengthen the Republic. Catholics grew increasingly alienated and many officers who had been undecided in their attitudes toward the new regime became hostile.

By the time Azaña and his agricultural minister, Marcelino Domingo, confronted the agrarian reform problem the optimal moment had passed. No longer were they able to marshal parliamentary support or finances. Forces opposed to agrarian reform had mounted a strong campaign on the eve of parliamentary debate. They held an imposing rally and meeting in Madrid in April 1932 sponsored by the Unión Económica, a consortium of employer associations, to advertise their opposition to the government's agrarian reform bill.

Throughout the spring and summer of 1932, the issue was bogged down in parliamentary obstructionism and maneuvering made possible by Republican lassitude. The opposition included the Radicals, and the small rightist Agrarian party representing landholding interests conducted a parliamentary filibuster that for many weeks prevented the Cortes from acting on pending bills. After the successful quelling of the Sanjurjo military pronunciamiento of August 1932, the government gained sufficient support to pass the Catalan autonomy statute and agrarian reform legislation, although not without an impassioned appeal from Azaña.

Republicans hoped the legislation would enable large numbers of small farmers to become independent, while the socialists argued for collectivized farming. Neither, however, possessed much real understanding of agricultural problems. The bill adopted by the Cortes in September contained many of the essential ingredients for conducting land reform, but because of the prolonged parliamentary haggling and compromise it emerged a flawed and exceedingly cumbersome legislative mechanism. The annual appropriation of 50 million pesetas allocated to the Agrarian Reform Institute to implement the law and indemnify owners for the purchase of their lands represented barely more than 1 percent of the national budget and less than half the sum allocated for the Civil Guard. Parliamentarians were more concerned with fiscal regularity than with effective land redistribution. Yet another year was lost in inventorying expropriable landholdings and in bureaucratic mismanagement.

The reform that finally emerged was a far cry from what had originally been envisaged. A well-drafted, nonideological, politically astute plan had been presented on July 15, 1931, by the Agrarian Technical Commission headed by the jurist Felipe Sánchez Roman and including agronomist Pascual Carrión and economist Ricardo Flores de Lemus. Land redistribution was to be concentrated in southern Spain, where land hunger and social distress were greatest. Instead of expropriation, "temporary occupation" of unlimited duration was recommended for substantial portions of large landed estates for which settlers would pay modest rental fees. The goal was to settle sixty to seventy-five thousand families annually over a twelve-to-fifteen-year period. An estimated 7 percent of the national budget (220 to 250 million pesetas yearly) would underwrite the program. To avoid the foot-dragging that did occur later, the commission recommended that the program be put into effect immediately by decree and submitted to the Cortes for approval only later, when it had become a fait accompli. The sweeping nature of its recommendations and tactical blunders by commission members prevented it from mustering much support.

The bill could not have been passed at a worse time. Its implementation came amid increased labor costs and a fall in agricultural prices. Discontent from all sides began to boil over. Landowners bitterly resisted implementation and the prolabor findings of the *jurados*. Peasants and *braceros*, frustrated and increasingly victimized by sharp increases in unemployment, gave vent, often violently, to their resentments.

Throughout this period agriculture was in the doldrums. The Republic came into existence on the heels of a disastrous harvest year and 1931 had not been much better. Thousands of destitute peasants greeted the advent of the Republic as an act of deliverance. Moreover, during the June 1931 election campaign the Republican-Socialist coalition parties had made extravagant promises to relieve the peasants' plight.

Then came sweeping changes in farm labor relations and the increase in rural labor organization. Countless strikes flared throughout Andalusia and Extremadura as new bargaining agreements (*bases de trabajo*) were negotiated and many landowners tried to avoid compliance with the Terminal Boundaries Law. Despite high expectations, union leaders were able to restrain their followers.

The 1932 harvest was good, but the labor climate began to deteriorate as landowners resisted the prolabor decisions of the mixed juries; some employer representatives withdrew from further participation. Fear of agrarian reform and land redistribution caused many to cut back on cultivation. The failure of the government to take action against infractions by landowners because many small and medium-sized farmers were Republican supporters added to growing socialist resentments. Strike actions and the level of violence rose steadily; the number of work stoppages in Andalusia escalated from twenty-one in 1931 to ninety-eight the following year.

By the time the agrarian law went into effect, the situation had reached alarming proportions. Harvests of olives and cereal grains in 1933 were only half those of the previous year and unemployment mushroomed. Profit-squeezed landowners confronted desperate, hungry field hands in countless acrimonious disputes, and there were 115 strikes in the region. Conflict became widespread and, as in past troubled times, unharvested fields were put to the torch.

Socialist peasant leaders rejected the more violent anarcho-syndicalist tactics, but the momentum of social change produced considerable tension and conflict. By October 1932 a wave of land invasions by *yunteros* (peasants owning mule teams) swept over Extremadura and countless incidents occurred elsewhere, many of them violent, as FNTT supporters sought to wrest control of local governments from entrenched conservative oligarchs. Socialists at times lost control of their more ebullient followers, and landowners occasionally took the law into their own hands to conduct reprisals. Then came the gruesome Castilblanco incident.

Caught in the middle of a rapidly escalating polarization, the government sought to defuse the situation by expropriating the lands of the nobility without compensation because of their support for the Sanjurjo rebellion and to use those lands for initial distributions. But the amount of land thus made available was not very large. To prevent the alarming spread of land invasions, especially in Extremadura, an emergency Cultivation Intensification Decree was issued in November 1932 permitting idle lands in Badajoz and eight additional provinces to be ceded to landless peasants for a two-year period.

Particularly damaging was the extraordinary slowness and timidity with which agrarian reform was implemented.[82] By the end of 1934 only 12,260 peasant families had been resettled. The focus by that time had shifted to coping with sharp increases in rural joblessness in the south. Close to two-thirds of total unemployment in the country between the latter half of 1933 and the outbreak of the civil war in 1936 was in rural areas. By the first half of 1936 it probably exceeded half a million. Reverse migration had swelled the number of unemployed as thousands, no longer able to find work in France and elsewhere, returned to their native villages. Efforts to alleviate unemployment by doubling the public works budget had little effect in forestalling the increase in the number of jobless. Calamity also visited the Castilian Meseta grain farmers. A combination of overabundant wheat harvests in 1932 and the misbegotten decision by Agriculture Minister Domingo to purchase foreign wheat (he anticipated a shortfall in grain yields) led to a price collapse and ruin for many small cultivators. For all their well-meaning rhetoric, Azaña and his fellow Republicans lacked a sufficiently strong resolve to carry out agrarian reform and, after precious months had been frittered away, time ran out.

By the end of 1932 the political capital the government acquired for putting down the Sanjurjo putsch had been largely expended. The disquieting events of the following January were to cast a permanent pall over the remaining months of the Azaña government's time in office. That month Faistas mounted their third insurrectionary uprising, seizing some Andalusian pueblos and proclaiming libertarian communism. The savage repression that followed in the village of Casas Viejas and the ensuing uproar seriously damaged the government's credibility. It also gave added impetus to a conservative shift under way in a populace increasingly impatient with economic malaise, social turmoil, and industrial strife. The outcome of the April 1933 municipal elections underscored this trend, registering renewed support for monarchists and rightist parties as well as major advances by the Radicals, mainly at the expense of the socialists. Government action to close Catholic schools was yet another self-inflicted wound. Industrial strife and interunion rivalries reached a high point that summer. The governing coalition began to fear for its future.

As the Azaña government entered a time of trouble, the conservatives saw their chance to launch a political comeback. Notable among them were the highly vocal and wealthy Alfonsine monarchists, the Agrarians, the Carlists, and the small profascist extreme right-wing fringe. The most important was Acción Nacional (later changed to Acción Popular), the political wing of the Catholic opposition that was formed in 1931 and whose principal figure was the politically adroit social Catholic lawyer and former Agrarian José Maria Gil Robles. During its formative period it stressed adherence to social Catholic ideas inspired by Pope Leo XIII's encyclical *Rerum Novarum*. But in the absence of a sizable Catholic labor movement and to maintain the support of diverse conservative groups, Gil Robles and his supporters moved to the right. Gil's original intention was to operate within the system and to work toward securing a dominant parliamentary position. At first there was little alternative but to operate within Republican legality. To accommodate his supporters on the anti-Republican Right—Alfonsine and Carlist monarchists, young followers infatuated with the ideas of Mussolini and Hitler—he embraced the concept of "accidentalism," which viewed the existing form of government as immaterial. He held that the most important feature of a regime was its socioeconomic philosophy. Their slogan, "Religion, Fatherland, and Property," placed these conservatives on the side of traditional Catholic values, the same position to which Restoration monarchists adhered.

The main goal was to effect cooperation among the elements of the political Right to achieve electoral victory over the combined forces of left Republicanism and socialism. This goal was accomplished at the end of February 1933 when a congress was held sponsored by Acción Popular and attended by 500 delegates claiming to represent 735,058 adherents of forty-two different conservative organizations. From this gathering came the Spanish Confederation of the Autonomous Right (Confederación Española de Derechas Autonomas—CEDA), a right-wing conglomerate.[83] Its announced goals were the "defense of the principles of Christian civilization"[84] and revision of the constitution, especially those sections dealing with religion, education, and property. Past efforts to form a Catholic party had failed. This time, however, anticlerical legislation provided the binding element.

Though the new party professed a commitment to social Catholic reforms, the composition of its support and its electoral clientele reduced its words to empty rhetoric. CEDA sought a return to the socioreligious values of traditional Spain and to exploit the discontent with government policies. Its support base ranged from moderate social Catholics to authoritarian reactionaries. A substantial part of its mass following came from the Catholic peasant organization CNCA, which was influential among the small traditionalist farmers of the Castilian provinces, and from the large landowners of south and central Spain, who opposed land redistribution and rural labor organization. Gil Robles earned his political spurs in 1932 leading the resistance of the Landowners Federation in his native Salamanca province to Largo's interference in the *jurado* findings on *bases de trabajo* and hiring practices, as well as FNTT bargaining power. CEDA, moreover, had the blessings of the church hierarchy and of King Alfonso. In essence, it was a marriage of religion and reaction.

Policy divisions within Spanish socialism had not changed since the final years of the dictatorship. An uneasy triumvirate presided, composed of PSOE and UGT chairman Julián Besteiro, the party's leading thinker "with his astonishing British allure"; the handsome, austere UGT General Secretary Largo Caballero, imperious man of action, more trade unionist than politician;[85] and corpulent Indalecio Prieto, undisputed chief of the Basque region, the party's finest orator and most astute political tactician. Besteiro spoke for a substantial sector that felt that proletarian underdevelopment, among other reasons, made it imperative that though the socialists might support the Republic, they should not serve in any government ministries. The factions headed by Largo and Prieto together constituted a majority, which for differing reasons favored full collaboration with the government. Largo and Prieto (and his supporter de los Rios) consequently accepted cabinet posts and Besteiro resigned as party chairman following his defeat but agreed to serve as head of the Cortes.

The socialists had acquired political power and governing responsibility unexpectedly before any consensus had been reached defining the nature of the collaboration. Differences remained unresolved concerning participation, and both short-term and longer-term expectations remained diffuse and unclarified. Socialists as a result were both unprepared and deeply divided on the issues confronting them as well as in the framing of an overall political strategy. Finally, Largo and his fellow trade unionists were more adept at day-to-day realpolitik than at devising more distant goals and strategies.

Neither the socialists nor any of the other leading political figures possessed much experience in democratic government or in consensus building, which might have enabled them to reject the destructive "winner take all" tradition that remained deeply entrenched in political mores and practices.[86] It was a failing that has been described as "recurrent themes in the Spaniards' history—their reluctance to sacrifice any part of their own interests to the common good and their intolerance of other people's views."[87]

Spanish socialism in the 1930s had moved beyond its initial trade union orientation. Its working-class character had become diluted by the entry of middle-class elements who were conspicuous among the leadership. One-third of its parliamentary delegation consisted of intellectuals and academics whom Javier Tussell calls "one of the most brilliant governing groups that Spain possessed at that time."[88] Of the four thousand people who entered the party organization in Madrid following the formation of the Republic, a substantial number were white-collar employees, professionals, and intellectuals.

The socialists' lack of experience in government administration or in making the harsh choices required by political responsibility resulted in much illusion and exaggeration concerning the feasible parameters of social and political change. Moreover, few among them possessed any training in or grasp of economic problems. Republican politicians, however, were not in a much better position. At the outset, socialists were able to introduce reforms that substantially improved the well-being of urban and rural wage earners. With the Labor Ministry acting as recruiting agent, the UGT gained many new members. Party membership also reached new heights, rising to sixty to eighty thousand. The Socialist Youth Federation (Federación de Jurentud Socialista—FJS) with its sixty to eighty thousand supporters had become a large popular organization.[89]

Such prodigious growth bespoke a fundamental alteration in the composition of the membership that was to have repercussions on organizational priorities and policy. In the past the union had catered mainly to semiskilled and skilled workers, railwaymen, and miners, with an ethos and trade union practice derived almost wholly from their needs and psychology. By June 1932 the UGT contained 445,414 rural members, 287,245 industrial workers, 236,829 white-collar employees (commerce, hotels, banking, liberal professions), and 72,051 civil servants and railway employees. No other western European trade union center possessed so large a percentage of agrarian members (see table 10.2).

As the UGT's composition became more diffuse, it also became more centralized. Increasing emphasis was placed on the formation of national trade and industrial federations at the expense of local bodies, a process

Table 10.2.   UGT National Membership by Occupational Categories, 1932

Occupational Category	Number
Agriculture	445,414
Building construction	83,861
Railroads	49,117
Mining	40,635
Urban transport	34,435
Metalworking	33,287
Food products	28,519
Bank employees	27,600
Commerce	25,603
Maritime transport	17,003
Woodworking	14,397
Public service	13,500
Teamsters	11,823
Fur and leather	11,560
Printing trades	9,347
Waiters	8,814
Theatrical trades	8,387
Textiles	7,705
Street lighting	7,545
Chemicals	6,855
Sandal making	6,640
Liberal professions	6,612
Tobacco	4,813
Clothing manufacture	3,959
Portworkers	3,007
Paperworkers	2,932
Fishermen	2,864
Barrelmakers	2,219
Barbers	2,057
Sanitation	1,856
Glassmaking	1,517
Ceramics	1,194
Fine metalwork	363
Lithographers	251
Vehicle builders	239
Miscellaneous	117,240
Total	1,041,539

Source: Manuel Tuñón de Lara, *El movimiento obrero en la historia de España, 1924–1936,* 3 vols. (Barcelona: Laia, 1972), 3:119–20.

Table 10.3.   Geographical Distribution of FNTT Membership, June 30, 1932

Area	Number	
Extremadura	65,389	
La Mancha	64,072	
Upper Gaudalquivir ·valley	69,063	} Andalusia total: 100,997
Eastern Andalusia	31,934	
Levant and southeast	56,649	
All other regions and provinces	105,846	

Source: Edward Malefakis, *Agrarian Reform and Peasant Revolution* (New Haven: Yale University Press, 1970), p. 292.

that had begun in 1914. Close to three-quarters of its million adherents were in national federations. It was an almost exclusively male movement with only forty-two thousand female members.

Farm locals had always existed, and their number grew appreciably during the early years of the dictatorship when the problems of agricultural labor had received only fleeting attention. When the National Landworkers Federation was constituted in April 1930, it possessed a membership of only 36,639.[90] By June 1932, however, far exceeding the leadership's fondest hopes, it passed the four hundred thousand mark, twice the UGT's entire membership under the dictatorship. By the following year it may have reached half a million. For the FNTT's geographical distribution see table 10.3.

After four decades of catering to skilled and semiskilled urban workers and miners, the UGT found itself representing the most primitive section of the Spanish proletariat. Constituting more than 40 percent of the rank and file, this group was the single largest component. Though recruitment gains were made in the Castilian province of Salamanca, in Toledo, and elsewhere, the bulk of the UGT's peasant members were in Andalusia and Extremadura. These were traditionally areas of endemic land hunger and simmering social tensions and were now experiencing great social upheaval as a result of the combined effects of government-sponsored reforms, peasant organizational mobilization, rising unemployment, the declining profitability of land exploitations, and the shifting power balance that these changes were provoking or threatening in countless pueblos and hamlets. Many of the peasant recruits were the same elements, unlettered and prone to elemental forms of protest, that had adhered to anarcho-syndicalism. The massive rural influx also enormously increased the disparity between nominal adherents and dues payers.

During the first two years of the Republic the FNTT had served as a moderating force in Andalusia and Extremadura.[91] Socialist moderates, followers of Julián Besteiro, then headed the organization. Despite the turmoil generated by the labor reforms, FNTT challenges to entrenched oligarchical interests, landowner resistance, and unemployment, socialist peasant leaders strove valiantly to keep the lid on. Even with this restraining influence, however, from April 1930 to June 1933 FNTT unions took part in no less than 925 strikes. The slow pace of agrarian reform and its paltry results did little to mitigate the sense of deception that by the end of 1932 began to displace the exhilaration and promise felt at the Republic's birth.

The increasingly acrimonious confrontation between landlords and peasant organizations soon became a major concern for the UGT. Until then the socialist trade union center had been regarded with some benevolence by numerous employers. Government authorities and even some conservative politicians at times supported the UGT in hopes of preventing the spread of anarchosyndicalist sympathies among workers. But a UGT in control of the Labor Ministry and acting as spokesman for mobilized land-hungry farm laborers was regarded with sullen hostility by the financial-economic elite.

The reforms and hefty wage increases sponsored by Largo Caballero generated vast changes in southern rural society, provoking hundreds of disturbances in Andalusian villages. Yet these reforms left much to be done. Without extensive land redistribution, the latifundia provinces would remain smoldering powder kegs capable of igniting into wholesale class warfare. Socialist peasant leaders rejected the use of violent anarcho-syndicalist tactics, but the momentum of social change inevitably fostered tension and conflict. A wave of land invasions by *yunteros* swept over Extremadura in 1932 and countless incidents occurred elsewhere as FNTT supporters sought to wrest control of local governments from entrenched conservative oligarchs. The gruesome Castilblanco incident took place in this rancorous social context.

Azaña felt powerless to reduce rural tensions as social turmoil steadily worsened. Labor Ministry statistics for the period are incomplete, but they generally reflect the rising tide of conflict. During the latter half of 1930, there were 27 agricultural strikes, but by the following year, with the advent of the Republic, there were 85, and in 1932, 198. Until

September 1933, when Azaña relinquished the post of prime minister, there were 245 strikes, and the total for the year was 448. As the number of work stoppages increased, so did the level of violence. Having consented to socialist labor reforms, the Azaña government had unwittingly unleashed a powerful social dynamic whose ramifications it was unwilling or incapable of dealing with.

Rural chaos probably could not have been averted through an adequate program of land transfers. "The importance of the failure to distribute land more quickly lay elsewhere," observes Edward Malefakis. "So long as the Socialists remained committed to the democratic regime, peasant unrest in most of the nation remained uncoordinated and ineffective. But because Azaña offered them no concrete achievement, some Socialist leaders and many of the rank-and-file members became disillusioned."[92]

Lack of timely action permitted the situation in the southern countryside to degenerate into explosive polarization. When the full impact of Largo's reforms and wage increases was being felt in the south by 1933, the profit squeeze brought on by higher labor costs and falling agricultural prices led to a further increase in already high unemployment levels. The situation was exacerbated when many landowners demonstrated their opposition by cutting back cultivation and hiring field labor. Violations of protective legislation and mixed jury decisions became widespread. The failure of the government to take action against landowners for their infractions added to socialist frustration and bitterness.

A full recounting of the radicalization of Spanish socialism in the 1930s is a task for future historians.[93] Gaps persist in our knowledge, especially concerning the personal political evolution of Francisco Largo Caballero, who played a central role in propelling the movement toward self-destruction. As a trade union leader he had acted throughout his long career with great caution and prudence. But he was overly preoccupied with short-term advantage and unable to take fully into account broader, long-term implications. Though his shift to extremist radicalism in his mid-sixties was to some extent prompted by a fear that workers would desert to more radical organizations, the stunning break with his past in the twilight of his career can be attributed, in the words of Franz Borkenau, to his having become "a revolutionary by disappointment."[94]

Various factors have been cited to explain Largo's political extremism, which began in July 1933.[95] Indeed, the problems socialists confronted by the summer of 1933 were daunting: imminent exclusion from power, the increasing ineffectiveness of the mixed juries, the UGT's loss of influence, the political offensive of the Radicals, mounting combativeness among employers, and the CNT's bitter hostility. These issues were coming to the fore at a time when political extremism on both Left and Right was on the rise throughout Europe and the postulates of revolutionary Marxism were attracting substantial numbers of converts within many socialist parties.

A large factor was Largo's disarray upon viewing the wreckage of a lifetime trade union credo. He believed that the condition of the working class could be improved only through a strong trade union within a state-supported corporative organization.[96] Hence the loss of the Labor Ministry was construed as the traitorous abandonment by the Republic of its commitment to social justice. A Republic stripped of its social reforms no longer was worthy of support. Once the political legitimacy of the Republic had been denied, what remained?

The socialists had little alternative but to engage in a defensive rearguard action to preserve the loyalty of the workers and to accommodate the growing radicalization of activists in the face of rising opposition from employers and to defuse workers' frustrations. For Largo and his fellow union leaders this meant sparking renewed militancy among workers and radical rhetoric. It was not the most reasoned way to checkmate employers' aggressiveness since it would have a polarizing effect on national political trends. Nonetheless, it would aid in preserving UGT strength, mollify the growing number of radicalized militants, and was popular within the movement, and therefore would strengthen Largo in his power struggle with the Besteiristas for control.[97] But it was a two-edged sword: revolutionary hyperbole might provide tactical benefits, but its prolonged employment affected the outlooks of numerous impressionable militants.

The Azaña government's failure to enact adequate and timely agrarian reform and land redistribution and its contribution to the turbulence and radicalization that gradually enveloped Spanish socialism have been admirably documented.[98] The growth of urban employers' opposition to the *jurados* and other prolabor measures of the reform biennium have also been the subject of recent scholarship.[99]

The corporative bargaining system experienced enormous strains as did Largo's ability as labor minister to direct and shape labor relations.[100] Less attention has been given, however, to the crisis of labor corporativism in the triangular heartland of socialist trade unionism, Madrid, Asturias, and the Basque country, which must have contributed greatly to the growing identity crisis in the UGT.[101]

The Madrid UGT had been primarily devoted to the interests of journeymen and crafts tradesmen. Since the 1920s it had depended on a relatively well-defined collective bargaining structure in which labor market arrangements, wage standards, and hiring practices were stipulated in a negotiated protocol between unions and employers. This system, shaped and bureaucratized by parity committee bargaining reinforced by Primoriverist corporatism, tended to pay little attention to the casual unskilled laborers and downplayed adversarial bargaining tactics and worker militancy.

As loyal members of the governing coalition, the socialists directed their efforts in 1931 and 1932 toward assuring labor peace and minimizing work stoppages. Madrid became a comparative oasis of labor tranquillity. No industrywide or general strikes took place there. The city's employers could obtain labor peace by raising wages. The solidity of the well-ordered labor-management relationship seemed secure. But an unforeseen combination of factors—a decline in building construction, discontent in Madrid's suburban shantytowns, CNT competition, and the UGT's inability to cope with mass joblessness and with a changing working-class mood—soon were to shatter that calm.

Before the coming of the Republic the CNT had never given serious thought to competing with the UGT in its own backyard. Madrid was the acknowledged bastion of Ugetismo, and CNT priorities and resources did not permit such a costly and dubious undertaking. Now, however, the ambitions of a rapidly reviving CNT to become a truly national movement made it imperative that its influence be extended to the capital. The CNT was doing its utmost to render the *jurados* inoperative, and its leaders decided to respond to Largo Caballero's hegemonic pretensions by challenging him on his own turf. The CNT and FAI moved experienced activists into Madrid. Symbolically, the first congress to be held following the inception of the Republic took place in Madrid, and the editorial office of a new daily, *CNT,* was also located there.

At the outset, the Madrid CNT was modest in size and influence with a membership by its own account of no more than 6,000, hardly a serious threat to the 190,000-member UGT. More than half were either construction laborers or bar and restaurant waiters. In both occupations employment was casual and personnel turnover high, making them difficult to organize. The UGT had made little effort to unionize them or to improve their sorry working conditions. The leadership of the Regional Confederation of the Center, whose core membership was in Madrid, was made up exclusively of anarchists and Faistas.

Various factors contributed to the traumatic shocks sustained by Madrid Ugetismo from 1932 to 1934. Roughly one of every two city wage earners was a member of the union. Such explosive growth within a short time span placed severe strains on organizational structures, welfare benefit facilities, and available cadres. The traditional preponderance of blue-collar workers was diluted by the entry of large numbers of white-collar employees (bank employees, office workers, members of the liberal profes-sions), which changed trade union discourse and organizational priorities. The number of unskilled workers in the UGT also increased substantially. In addition, the large influx into the Madrid labor market of migrants from rural areas since the early 1920s meant that *forasteros* (outsiders) outnumbered those of local origin and that the ratio of youthful wage earners was disproportionately high. The building and public works boom of the 1920s had attracted thousands of job seekers, mainly from the impoverished villages of the Castilian Meseta. Young women usually found employment in domestic service or as shop assistants; men tended to become building construction laborers or day workers. Most resided in the unhealthy, densely packed suburban communities or in the city's working-class *barrios*.

The difficulties of administering a much larger and more diverse trade union clientele were more than enough to bedevil a harried union offi-cialdom, but the added burden of coping with layoffs and mass unem-ployment made the situation untenable. The building boom had reinforced the role of construction as the city's principal economic mainstay, func-tioning much as cotton textiles did in the Barcelona economy. Other key industrial activities such as metalworking and woodworking became heav-ily dependent on building construction for their sustenance. More than eighty thousand of some three hundred thousand gainfully employed in the province of Madrid were in building construction, a larger number than the combined work force of all other industries. More than a third of UGT membership was similarly concentrated, and many of its leading figures, including Largo Caballero, came from the ranks of the building trades unions.[102]

With the birth of the Republic the dictatorship's ambitious, expensive public works program was abandoned. The sharp cutbacks in public works expenditures had a serious impact on the building construction industry, especially in Seville, Valencia, Zaragossa, Barcelona, and Madrid. For Madrid, whose economic well-being was linked to this activity, depression in the building industry was profoundly unsettling. Reliable figures on unemployment in the city's building construction industry are unavailable, but there are indications that by 1933 it had reached massive proportions, not only in Madrid but in most other large urban centers. One estimate sets the percentage of joblessness among Madrid bricklayers in late 1931 at 30 percent, and by mid-1932 industrywide layoffs had reached 28,786.[103] A survey conducted by the UGT of ninety thousand of its members in early 1934 concluded that 35 percent of them had lost their jobs and that more than half of these (18,441) were in construction. In a July 1933 report submitted to the International Building Construction Workers Federation, a trade secretariat of the International Federation of Trade Unions, the Madrid Building Trades Labor Federation (Federación Laboral de Edificación—FLE) reported, "We would not be greatly in error to assert that more than 50 percent of our comrades in all the building trades have been without work for many months and among the other half many work so intermittently that neither of them can be said to be in satisfactory conditions as in former times."[104]

The loss of a job was devastating to unskilled workers, who lived from hand to mouth and almost invariably resided in rented quarters. Job loss meant almost instant destitution. A British worker could count on a government dole to make ends meet, and a jobless American might find employment in the New Deal's public works projects, but in Spain no provision existed on a national level for unemployment assistance and the aid provided by local and national authorities fell far short of meeting actual needs. Because many employers were experiencing economic difficulties and they would have had to bear the brunt of the financing, socialists decided not to press for the introduction of unemployment compensation, a decision Republicans were happy to concur in. The public works programs aided only a few of the jobless, food chits were distributed, and food kitchens set up, but these were palliatives that did little to defuse the sense of desperation and bitterness of residents of the working-class suburbs adjoining the capital. Harassed by conflicting demands and intent on balancing the budget and reducing the huge deficit inherited from the previous regime, the Azaña government provided woefully inadequate allocations.[105]

The inglorious end to the reform biennium in 1933 came amid unprecedented industrial strife and social unrest. The labor-capital confrontation grew sharper as the economic depression made strikes more difficult to win, and they tended to last longer and to be accompanied by increased violence. The hard-hit building construction industry became a focal point of labor conflict with one-third of all strikes that year taking place in most of the leading cities. The worst and longest was in Barcelona, where the union, a Faista stronghold, had called an industrywide shutdown involving thirty-five thousand workers. Though it was an inappropriate time to engage in a work stoppage, the union leadership managed, partly through violence and intimidation, to maintain the strike for three and a half months, a truly remarkable achievement under such trying circumstances. The principal demand was for a thirty-six-hour week to create more job opportunities for the many laid-off workers. The strike was concluded when an agreement was reached to reduce the workweek by four hours to forty-four.

In Madrid, where the UGT exercised complete control, the situation was entirely different. The Federación Laboral de Edificación, which directed its attention mainly to the concerns of skilled and semiskilled workers, was unprepared to deal with the problems of mass unemployment, the most vulnerable victims of which were the unskilled *peones*. The collective bargaining machinery with its *jurado* structure and control of labor supply through union hiring halls depended on a full employment economy. Before joblessness reached massive proportions, the FLE muddled through with its mutual benefit funds and by distributing subsidies provided by the government. But in 1933, as unemployment reached crisis dimensions, the UGT's bureaucratized unionism became vulnerable, providing the CNT with its long-awaited chance.

At the time of the birth of the Republic, Cenetistas had attempted to challenge the UGT's hegemony, but its initial efforts among telephone workers failed dismally, as did a subsequent attempt to call a citywide general strike. But the construction industry was to prove infinitely more fruitful. Though its affiliate, the Sindicato Unico de Construción (SUC), possessed few members, its leaders were tough Faista street agitators of verve and talent, men such as the craggy-faced Cipriano Mera, David Antona, and Teodoro Mora, who were to emerge during the civil war as among the CNT's outstanding military commanders.

Before 1933 the SUC, in a series of violent skirmishes, sought to break the FLE monopoly by obtaining recognition from employers and forcing the hiring of its supporters. The UGT was virtually the only supplier of workers to contractors, especially to small and medium-sized companies. Gradually, however, the SUC succeeded, often with the help of pistol-brandishing militants, in carving out a modest degree of recognition and placing some of its people.

The decisive breakthrough came in September at several large building firms that employed large numbers of workers and were not as dependent as smaller firms on the UGT hiring halls for their labor supply. Using the pretext of opposing layoffs, the SUC engaged in an aggressive campaign to prevent them, thus becoming a champion of the issue of greatest concern to the workers. Almost five thousand workers laid down their tools, and the SUC succeeded in converting the walkout into a three-week industrywide strike despite frantic efforts by the FLE to prevent it. As UGT members joined the strike committee, the FLE lost control of its following to a small band of anarchist agitators.

The SUC gained an advantage by eliciting support from unskilled laborers and from laid-off workers, who had not received much attention from the FLE-UGT. Once the walkout became effective, the UGT was unable to resist the intimidating violence and mass mobilizational tactics of the Cenetistas. The CNT practiced an agitational form of unionism with daily pep rallies, some attended by as many as twenty-five thousand strikers, street parades, and union decisions taken by a show of hands at mass assemblies, a vicarious trade union theater that must have come as a refreshing change for untutored workers more accustomed to the dour impersonality of UGT bureaucratic bargaining and ratification by referendum. Ironically, construction workers had benefited handsomely from the *jurado* collective bargaining process, but these improvements, paradoxically, often increased unemployment as higher labor costs forced building contractors to lay off workers.[106] Thus the *peones,* who in Barcelona had served as the Faistas' battering ram, also became crucial in Madrid in the successful assault on the UGT. The strike settlement brought no major gains for the workers but forced employers to accord the CNT equal bargaining and representational rights, thus breaking the UGT's historic job control monopoly in the construction industry, a development that was to cast a shadow over the ensuing course of the city's labor relations and the UGT's trade union philosophy.

The mixed jury collective bargaining system received a serious setback in Madrid with the result that until the civil war began in 1936 it grew steadily weaker. Unable to stem the trend, many UGT labor leaders began to emulate the CNT style of strident strike calls, mass mobilizations, and aggressive behavior. As Santos Juliá observes, "Workers and employers ceased confiding in [the mixed juries] and in the policy as they became aware that their interests could not be adequately defended. The mixed juries were unable to resolve unemployment or layoffs, nor could they avert strikes or obtain the return to work of thousands of strikers. The juries could channel and resolve craft or trade disputes but were completely inadequate to deal with class confrontation."[107]

Crisis was not limited to Madrid. In Asturias the breakdown of corporative bargaining came as a by-product of industry crisis that led directly to the fierce insurrection of October 1934. The advent of the Republic and socialist collaboration with the government helped reverse the sagging fortunes of the Asturian Miners Union (SMA), which had persisted throughout the final years of the dictatorship. Coal miners returned en masse to the SMA when the government restored the seven-hour day, which had been abandoned in 1927. Socialist control and authority reigned briefly. But soon the economic situation worsened and the chronic debilities of the coal mining industry recurred despite government subsidies and coal purchases.[108]

Production cutbacks followed as well as shortened workweeks, wage cuts, and layoffs. One of the region's largest coal operators, Hullera Española, left its employees unpaid for two months. Discontent and rage spread throughout the work force as union leaders, following socialist policy, sought to preserve labor peace. Unable to express their distress through the *jurados* or official union channels, workers conducted wildcat strikes in 1932 and 1933. In an effort to defuse the situation, beleaguered labor leaders called several industrywide strikes with little effect. Asturias in those two years led the nation in the number of strikes. Union leaders increasingly lost control over their rank and file. The party daily, *El Socialista*, reported on January 3, 1933, that the coalfields were "charged with passion and folly; the only restraint is that provided by our comrades."[109]

Nor was the situation much more encouraging in the Basque region. From 1930 to 1934 Vizcayan heavy industry was a casualty of the economic crisis and shifting government priorities. Pig iron output in 1932 was at only 56.7 percent of its 1929 level, and from 1930 to 1931 shipbuilding plummeted by 81.7 percent. Iron mining was hit even harder.[110] By late 1933 unemployment ranged from twenty-four thousand to twenty-seven thousand with metals and building construction the most affected.

Hard times also brought a serious challenge to the UGT's historic dominance. At the beginning of the Republic the Catholic Basque Workers Solidarity (SOV) gained members and began to turn from a mutual benefit function to a moderate trade union outlook. By the early 1930s its numerical strength was second only to that of the UGT.[111] Close links with the Basque Nationalist party (PNV) were also important as employers tended to encourage their employees to join the SOV. In 1931 the UGT claimed a provincial membership of nineteen thousand drawn largely from the iron and steel plants and the shipyards of the Nervion estuary, and the SOV estimated its following at fourteen thousand; by July 1936 the two organizations were fairly closely matched.[112]

Viewing the SOV's growth as a grave threat, the UGT engaged in a bitter and often violent rivalry. The added presence of small but active groups of communists and anarcho-syndicalists, who on occasion joined forces with the SOV to challenge the UGT in the early 1930s, created considerable industrial strife and tension, especially in the factory districts of the estuary adjoining Bilbao. The mixed juries, which were regarded as an instrument of the UGT, were debilitated.

President Alcalá Zamora, observing the rightward drift of the national mood and the decline of the Azaña government, began to cast about for a replacement. His attempt in June 1933 to do so failed, but it made clear that the end was near for the socialist-Republican governing alliance. The following month Largo unveiled his new leftist approach in a speech to a gathering in Madrid of the Socialist Youth Federation, the movement's most radical section and a main source of support. Using the conservative triumph in elections for the Tribunal for Constitutional Guarantees (the Spanish equivalent of the U.S. Supreme Court) as a pretext, Alcalá Zamora asked Lerroux on September 11 to form a new government. When it was clear that the socialists would be excluded from future governments, Prieto declared in the Cortes that Republican "disloyalty" toward their socialist partners precluded any further cooperation between them.

The Radicals soon discovered that they were unable to govern until a new Cortes was elected. The president had little confidence in Lerroux's probity and chose Diego Martínez Barrio, Lerroux's lieutenant, to preside over a caretaker government and to supervise the holding of new elections in November. Both ephemeral governments were made up of representatives from all the Republican parties except the socialists.

The Azaña coalition parties went into the election dispirited and fragmented. The socialists, bitter over the Republicans' shabby treatment of them, decided to run on their own, rejecting invitations to reconstitute a broad electoral coalition. Despite internal differences, the Right presented a united slate. And because parties engaged in coalition slates had the advantage, the outcome, though it showed only a slight conservative shift, nonetheless marked a clear triumph for the Right and a disaster for the Azaña Republican Left and the socialists. CEDA, a formidable mass party, ran a well-orchestrated, well-financed campaign and won 110 seats with an additional 71 divided among three smaller rightist parties that ran separate tickets. The Radicals took 102 seats, and the Left Republicans retained only 5. Azaña held his seat only by running on a coalition slate with socialists in Bilbao. The socialists paid dearly for their self-imposed electoral sectarianism; their overall share of the vote remained more or less intact, but the number of their seats fell from 117 to 58. With only half the votes received by the socialists, the Radicals garnered 46 more seats. It was a disaster that Prieto years later called "a terrible mistake." Women, given the franchise for the first time, voted in large numbers for CEDA at the urging of the church, and the active CNT abstentionist campaign induced many workers not to take part in the balloting.

Socialist theory then held that the Second Republic represented a bourgeois democratic revolution, a necessary intermediate stage on the road to socialism. The socialist transformation consequently would evolve out of bourgeois democracy.[113] Since radical talk before the November election was primarily directed toward discouraging Republicans from ousting socialists from the government, little was done to tinker with this concept. Maximalist hyperbole helped drive Besteiro and his moderate followers from the dominant positions they occupied in the UGT, in the Socialist Youth Federation, and in parts of PSOE. Besteiristas vigorously denounced the new leftist tack as a suicidal course for the movement. Party members remained moderate in outlook, but the dynamism and activity of the radicals enabled them to gain control of an increasing number of key posts. The sweeping victory of the Caballerists discouraged Besteiro and his followers. Symptomatic of the general trend, the FNTT, previously a moderate stronghold, fell into radical hands. Ricardo Zabalza, a Pamplona schoolteacher and prominent Socialist Youth ally of Largo, became its general secretary. The first statement by the FNTT's newly installed Caballerist national committee in February 1934 carried the headline "We declare ourselves for the revolution."

As socialists became more politically isolated, Largo declared in April that it was no longer possible to achieve socialism through parliamentary means. "The only course is by revolution."[114] Republicans had become another bourgeois foe. The socialist conquest of power, with revolutionary violence if necessary, was now the order of the day. Luis Araquistáin, Largo's intellectual alter ego, spoke of "Azaña's noble error, his beautiful republican utopia of thinking that it was possible to construct and then rule over a state which was not a class state."[115] Largo had burned his bridges behind him and saw revolution as the only option, to be invoked if the Right chose to trespass constitutional norms and seek to establish a fascist dictatorship. By now the term *fascist* had become a loosely applied epithet for a wide variety of political opponents, be they monarchists, conservatives, Catholics, or authentic fascists. Should the Right move in this direction, socialists would respond with armed insurrection. But insurrection had different connotations. For old-line UGT trade unionists it meant calling a general strike, but to Marxist-Leninists of the Socialist Youth and radicalized intellectuals it was armed uprising and the establishment of a dictatorship of the proletariat.

The two years following the November 1933 election, a period of indecision, unstable governments, political reaction, and social retreat, have been dubbed *el bienio negro* (the black biennium). The period began inauspiciously with a minority government of Lerroux and his fellow Radicals taking office but dependent on CEDA parliamentary support for its survival. Emboldened employers ignored established legal labor standards and assumed a more pugnacious attitude toward the unions. The unpopular Terminal Boundaries Act was rendered almost inoperative, and rural labor unions found themselves under assault. Socialist appointees to the mixed juries were replaced with more amenable personnel, and the rotational hiring system (*turno riguroso*) in rural areas that had been imposed by the Labor Ministry was voided. Nonetheless, the government's actions provided little confirmation for socialist predictions of the coming apocalypse or justification for the growing radicalization in the socialist movement. Nor was the Lerroux government's behavior altogether negative. The agrarian reform law was fairly administered, and more peasants received land grants than under Azaña. Labor policy was not totally anti-union; several Labor Ministry decisions and mixed jury findings to resolve strikes in Madrid during 1934 were favorable to the workers, exasperating employers who were Radical supporters.

To determine whether socialist leaders were merely playing at revolution to defuse radical sentiment in their midst and to prevent the Right from going too far, the socialist reaction to the Faista-sponsored uprising of December 1933 is instructive. To demonstrate anarchist even-handedness

Table 10.4.   Agricultural Unemployment in Spain, 1932–1936

Year	Agricultural unemployment	Total unemployment
1932 (June)	258,570	446,263
1933 (July–December)	382,965	593,627
1934	409,617	667,263
1935	434,054	696,989
1936 (January–July)	522,079	796,341

Sources: Germaine Moch Picard and Jules Moch, *L'oeuvre d'une revolution: L'Espagne republicaine* (Paris, 1933), p. 289; Sindicato Vertical de Olivo, *El paro estacional campesino* (Madrid, 1946), p. 3, cited in Edward Malefakis, *Agrarian Reform and Peasant Revolution in Spain* (New Haven: Yale University Press, 1970), p. 286; Julio Alcaide, "Una revision urgente de la serie de Renta Nacional española en el siglo XX," in Instituto de Estudios Fiscales, *Datos basicos para la historia financiera de España, 1850–1975* (Madrid, 1976), 1:1136, all cited in Joseph Harrison, *The Spanish Economy in the Twentieth Century* (New York: St. Martin's Press, 1985), p. 93.

in opposing all bourgeois regimes and to atone for having contributed to the Left's debacle in the recent election, an insurrectionary uprising was directed against the Lerroux government. A joint UGT-PSOE statement was issued denouncing the rising and carefully dissociating themselves.

Nonetheless, socialist leaders in 1934 were in an excruciating situation. Unemployment was at its highest ever, causing widespread suffering, and the number of jobless in the rural districts was double that in urban areas (see table 10.4). The conservative social reformer Vizconde de Eza estimated that more than 150,000 rural families lacked the basic necessities of life. Resentment ran high in the countryside as landowners and authorities joined in wreaking reprisals on union activists and supporters. Wage levels declined, and Civil Guards reverted to their traditional role as protectors of the oligarchy (*poderosos*). Urban workers also suffered as unemployment and employers' increased power eroded their previous gains. UGT unions experienced some loss of support and were put on the defensive, but they remained generally intact, and wage standards, though under attack, did not decline appreciably.[116]

As militants became more radical, especially in the countryside, Largo tried to keep control through reassuring revolutionary homilies. But if his motives were primarily defensive, those of his more fervent followers were not. Leading party intellectuals and far leftist Socialist Youth ac-

Table 10.4. (*continued*)

Agricultural unemployment as percentage of total unemployment	Percentage of active labor force employed in agriculture
57.9	46.6
64.5	45.6
61.4	45.2
62.4	44.6
65.6	–

tivists, exponents of "bolshevization," took talk of armed seizure of power seriously. For them a return of the Republic to its original purposes was of little import; they wanted the immediate establishment of a socialist regime. Much of their revolutionary talk never went beyond rhetorical posturing, but such ideas were gradually acquiring legitimacy and a growing audience within the movement. Many of the radicalized young militants gained key party and trade union posts that were vacated by the ousted Besteiristas, who made up a large proportion of the old-line labor leadership. A significant number of them also became members of the Caballerist-controlled UGT Executive Committee.

The Lerroux government lived on borrowed time. Since the CEDA, a minority party, was in no position to insist on representation in the cabinet, its next best political stratagem was to keep Lerroux on a short string. In any event, the socialists had given notice that any inclusion of Cedistas in cabinet appointments would oblige them to take up arms against the government.

The violent tone of socialist political discourse had its counterpart in that employed by Gil Robles and other CEDA spokesmen. As a Catholic party embracing a broad spectrum of conservative political viewpoints, CEDA was suspected by many socialists and Republicans of harboring anti-Republican authoritarian intentions. Just as Socialist Youth militants flaunted their bolshevism, Gil Robles's juvenile phalanx, the Popular Action Youth Federation (Juventud de Acción Popular—JAP), voiced sympathy for Hitler and Mussolini. The victory of the authoritarian Catholic Engelbert Dollfuss in Austria and his bloody crushing of socialist resistance in February 1934 inflamed many socialist militants, who were convinced that Gil Robles was his Spanish clone and that a similar fate awaited the Spanish Left once CEDA gained access to power. There may have been reason to doubt Gil Robles's Republican loyalties, yet there was little to suggest that the formation of a CEDA government or the appointment of some CEDA ministers spelled Armageddon as the Socialist Left proclaimed.

Throughout the spring of 1934 socialists sought to straddle revolutionary and reformist options. The party continued to sit in the Cortes and to be represented in numerous government agencies such as the mixed juries and the Institute for Agrarian Reform. At the same time it permitted an increasing number of strikes and its leaders made inflammatory speeches. Their immediate objective was to dissuade the Lerroux government from undoing legislation passed under Azaña. They were also trying to prepare workers for a future insurrection. Arms were secretly stockpiled.

The FNTT, also caught up in a mixture of defensive and aggressive motives, embarked on an exceedingly risky strategy. The approaching harvest season was seen as an opportunity to check the landowners' growing ascendancy and to preserve labor conquests. A series of actions led to a nationwide rural strike. When the strike action began, the FNTT escalated its demands, insisting upon the surrender of expropriable land in the IRA inventory to collectives and the fulfillment of agrarian reform. After trying to dissuade the FNTT leadership, both PSOE and UGT executives gave their grudging approval to the strike.

Confronted by a serious challenge to its authority, the government responded cautiously. Rafael Salazar Alonso, the hard-line interior minister, was given carte blanche in dealing with a strike that he viewed as possessing revolutionary intent. Strikes at harvest time were banned, the FNTT's paper, *El Obrero de la Tierra,* was suspended, and strike meetings were prohibited. Others in the government, however, urged a compromise settlement to avert a general shutdown. These moderates included Cirilo del Rio, the agriculture minister, José Estadella of the Labor Ministry, and Ricardo Samper, who had replaced Lerroux as prime minister. Concessions were tendered before the June 5 strike deadline, including steps to prevent discrimination in hiring, urging local arbitration boards to expedite the conclusion of harvest agreements favorable to the workers, and authorizing field inspectors to require landowners in areas hard hit by unemployment to hire additional labor.

Such concessions and government desires to bargain with the FNTT provided a dignified way out for both sides. But the FNTT leaders overplayed their hand; to accept anything less than their original demands from the hated Salazar Alonso amounted to capitulation. They also had to deal with pressures from radicalized militants. Politico-ideological concerns took precedence over trade union good sense. Furthermore, their fiery exhortations led many *campesinos* to believe that the social revolution was at hand. On June 3 the FNTT renewed its demands for several patently impossible concessions, thus ending any possibility of averting a strike. "The question to be decided," observes a leading historian, "was whether Socialist labor organizations could compel the state to do their will. Isolated and alone (not a single Left Republican leader or journal supported the strike), the Socialists took their first stumbling step along the road Largo Caballero had pointed out to them."[117]

Zabalza's misbegotten strike strategy, the confusion arising from frequent changes in strike demands, the loss of ardor among many workers attracted by the government's offer of concessions, and the repressive measures combined to assure the strike's defeat almost from its start on June 5. Within five days the Caceres federation broke ranks and ordered its members back to work, an action that was soon followed by a succession of provincial federations. By the twentieth the strike came to an end. Socialist restraint kept casualties low: thirteen dead, several hundred injured, and seven thousand strikers temporarily jailed. For a movement that trumpeted its revolutionary credentials and a strike action pursuing quasi-revolutionary ends, it was conducted in a remarkably moderate fashion. Firearms or other materials of violence were not much in evidence, and no attempts were made to seize control of municipalities. Violence was kept to a minimum by the Samper government's moderation.

Not only was the strike defeat a catastrophe for the FNTT, but the rural labor force was left totally defenseless. Until 1936 the socialist rural following was to remain in a state of demoralization because the strike had "squandered all of the organizational gains made since 1931 and gave the rural oligarchy complete control of the Spanish countryside."[118] For the balance of 1934 and 1935 few rural strikes occurred.

When the Cortes reconvened in September, Gil Robles presented his political due bill—the inclusion of CEDA in a ministerial reorganization. That he chose to make this move following the FNTT fiasco was surely no idle coincidence. The prospect of CEDA ministers thoroughly alarmed the socialists and the entire Republican political community. As President Alcalá agonized over his response, Republicans of all hues (other than the Radicals), from Maura on the Right to Azaña on the Left, fearing that CEDA's entry into government heralded an eventual emasculation of the constitution, urged Alcalá not to permit their accession to power. Lluis Companys and his ruling Catalan Esquerra, embroiled in a conflict with

Madrid over the Generalitat's authority to legislate regional agrarian reform to aid tenant farmers (*rabassaires*), regarded the prospect of CEDA entry as a serious threat to regional autonomy.

The socialists found themselves thoroughly cornered as the hour of decision approached. The destruction of their formidable rural organization in June had greatly reduced the credibility of their threat to rise in rebellion should the Catholics gain power. Directives had been issued ordering a lessening of strike activity and labor disputes to husband energies, morale, and material resources. But the FNTT was not the only organization to pay little attention. Intense labor conflict occurred in 1934.[119] Some arms had been stockpiled, and efforts had been made to form a paramilitary militia among the Socialist Youth. A more fundamental question arose: could labor leaders dedicated to reform suddenly transform themselves into revolutionaries? Directing an insurrectionary assault was quite different from managing a general strike, and, as Paul Preston puts it, "even the most verbally radical of the Socialist leaders viewed with considerable trepidation the prospect of actually organizing a revolution."[120]

Efforts by Fernando de los Rios and others to mediate a peaceful face-saving solution met with little success. Although Largo defiantly announced the coming revolutionary confrontation, privately he could not bring himself until the last minute to believe that Alcalá Zamora would not be dissuaded by socialist revolutionary threats. The UGT-PSOE revolutionary committee spent the last three days before the rising nervously awaiting Alcalá's decision. By the time word was passed to commence the rebellion, the new cabinet had already decreed martial law.[121] The incongruency of the situation was reflected in Largo's return to his home following the commencement of revolutionary resistance to await the arrival of the police.

General strikes occurred in most of the leading cities. In Seville, where the UGT was weak, the CNT refused to take part and the communist unions were in disarray so the shutdown was only partially successful. In Madrid, where the main force of the Caballerist Left and the Socialist Youth was centered, the rising that began on October 3 was a complete failure. No operational plan was in force, nor were arms distributed. Instead of taking to the streets, most workers stayed home, and the plan to seize the Interior Ministry building miscarried. Few if any signs of resistance were observed in the rural districts, which were still suffering from the demoralizing effects of the failed June strike. In the Basque provinces of Vizcaya and Guipúzcoa, except for Mondragón and Eibar, where the movement became an armed insurrection, a peaceful general shutdown closed down the two provinces. On October 6, two days after the formation of the new Lerroux cabinet, all the Republican parties except the Radicals formally severed institutional ties. In Barcelona and most other localities the CNT refused to participate, viewing socialist revolutionary pretensions as suspect. Generalitat chief Companys's act of defiance in proclaiming Catalonia a separate entity within a federal Spanish state received working-class support only from the Workers Alliance (Alianza Obrera), formed at the instigation of Joaquín Maurín's Workers and Peasants Bloc, which included the Treintista opposition unions and various small socialist and other left-wing groups, none of which had much influence in Barcelona, where the CNT dominated.[122]

Aided by the sympathy of the Generalitat, the general strike was effective on October 5, the day following the formation of the new government, in much of the region. But it was impossible to challenge Madrid effectively without resorting to arms, and Companys's supporters wanted to prevent the CNT from taking a leading role in the rebellion. Thus the action lacked sufficient force to confront the central government, and it ended in failure and its leaders' imprisonment.[123]

The events of October 1934 are remembered for the extraordinary resistance shown by the workers of Asturias, especially the coal miners. Nothing like it had been seen in Europe since the Paris Commune of 1871. Their heroic stand resulted from events peculiar to that region. Unlike the Madrid leadership, which immediately became radicalized, the Asturians took a generally moderate position as advocated by the Prieto wing of the party. Though unhappy with the UGT's radicalism, they loyally carried out its policy and were driven to militancy by the union's rank and file. The national uprising became a vessel for the outpouring of pent-up frustrations by the region's coal miners. Workers' militancy had reached a peak when the call came for insurrection. Six industrywide strikes had taken place during the preceding eight months, including an impressive general strike to protest the holding of a mass CEDA rally at the town of Covadonga. Wildcat strikes had become common. Since late 1933 both the CNT and UGT had quietly amassed arms to augment the always ample supply of dynamite in coal mine warehouses.

The newly formed Alianza Obrera included socialists, anarcho-syndicalists, communists, and non-Stalinist leftists. The Asturian CNT had always favored joint action with the UGT and followed the Treintista trade union philosophy. The rising could, therefore, count on forty thousand UGT members, twenty thousand Cenetistas, and sixty-eight hundred under communist leadership. This unprecedented example of working-class unity in a movement hitherto characterized by bitter divisions gave rise to the slogan "Unios hermanos proletarios" (Let us unite, proletarian brothers) that was to resonate through leftist politics in the years ahead.

The basic cause of the workers' militancy was their disillusionment with the Republic for its failure to revitalize their ailing industry.[124] Miners expected the Republic to bring full employment, high wages, and job security. But Asturian mining suffered from bad management and produced poor-quality coal at prohibitively high production costs and could not be constantly propped up by government financial support. Severe economic crisis forced a cutback in government assistance, and once again the industry suffered from wage cuts, mine closures, short workweeks, and mass layoffs. By 1934 several large collieries had fallen as much as four months behind in the payment of wages. Consequently, the accumulated rage and bitterness of the miners exploded on October 5.

After seizing control of the mining districts, armed detachments of miners converged on Oviedo, the provincial capital. Following sharp exchanges with defending army units and Civil Guards, most areas of the city fell to the revolutionaries. At the uprising's height at least one-third of the province was in rebel hands.

An action that began as a general strike quickly became a full-scale insurrection, giving rise to a veritable popular commune. Law and order, transportation, hospitals, and the operation of manufacturing plants were taken over by local revolutionary committees. Some metalworking factories were converted to the assembly of armored cars and others to produce munitions. Overall direction of the rebellion was in the hands of a socialist-controlled provincial committee headed by mine union leader Ramón González Peña. But because the insurrection failed elsewhere, the government could concentrate on putting down the Asturian rising.

General Francisco Franco, who had been placed in charge of the military operation, brought in large contingents of the Foreign Legion (*Tercios*) and Moroccan troops notorious for their brutality.[125] When by October 9 it became clear that Asturias stood alone, socialist leaders began to seek ways to end the insurrection. By the eleventh troops forced their way into Oviedo, and the ensuing street fighting reduced much of the city to rubble. Despite their leaders' urgings and the hopelessness of their situation, several local committees refused to give up. Bitter resistance forced the army to take the mine towns one by one, house by house. Intent upon ending the useless carnage, socialist Belarmino Tomás met with General Eduardo López Ochoa on October 17 to propose a truce in exchange for a promise not to take reprisals or to permit the Moorish troops to enter the mine towns. The promise was given but not kept.

Workers generally behaved well, though "uncontrollables" murdered about forty employers and priests. The ferocity of the reprisals by the victorious military and police forces far overshadowed excesses committed by rebel supporters. The rebellion had resulted in about four thousand casualties, most of them workers. A vindictive repression began immediately after the surrender. To avenge their fallen comrades, Civil Guards executed many prisoners without benefit of trial. (As was their custom, Tercios and the Moors had executed those taken during the fighting.) To extract information about hidden arms caches, a special Civil Guard unit tortured numerous prisoners.[126] The ferocity of the fighting and the brutality of the reprisals prefigured the conduct of the civil war and its aftermath. As details of the repression filtered through the tight censorship, the public was horrified. Leading intellectuals, writers, and political figures petitioned the president to intercede. Inquiry commissions from various European countries were dispatched to the area, and their findings confirmed the grisly facts.

The Right found its opportunity in 1935. With its principal adversaries in disarray and with Azaña, Largo, and Companys imprisoned and facing jail sentences, it had no political opposition. A succession of suicidal guerrilla uprisings had shattered the anarcho-syndicalist movement. Socialists had paid an appallingly high price for having permitted revolutionary threats to become reality. The net result had been the resurgence and strengthening of the reactionary Right, with no special effort on its part.

Radicals and Cedistas could look forward to unobstructed rule. Urban wage earners and the rural poor, the political foundation of the Left, were defenseless. Municipalities were stripped of their socialist elected officials, the remaining mixed juries (as many as half ceased functioning) displayed a bias toward employers, labor activists were behind bars, and the *casas del pueblo* were padlocked. CEDA membership, in contrast, was growing by leaps and bounds. Even the economy was beginning to show signs of recuperation, despite continuing high levels of unemployment.

But the parties of the Right were no more capable of holding in check their vindictive impulses or maintaining internal cohesion than their adversaries on the Left. By the end of the year Gil Robles and his cohorts were ruefully to survey the wreckage of a lost opportunity. Determined to destroy their opponents politically, conservative reactionaries flooded the country with lurid accounts of Asturian atrocities such as the raping of nuns and gouging out the eyes of infants, but the desired effect of these horror stories was largely vitiated by the reprisals in Asturias. Public sympathy began to emerge for the victims of the repression and the thousands languishing in prison. More counterproductive still was the attempt to blacken the name of Manuel Azaña. He had been in Barcelona at the time of Companys's rebellion and had scrupulously distanced himself from the insurrectionaries, urging them not to undertake such an ill-advised action. Nevertheless, at the urging of rightists intent upon his political destruction, the government labeled him a ringleader of the rebellion. His vindication came first through hearings conducted on April 6 by the Tribunal for Constitutional Guarantees and then in a vote in the Cortes, in which even disgusted moderate conservatives, including the Radicals, voted on July 18 for his exoneration.

Socialists were saved from total ignominy by the inspiring example of the Asturian resistance and unchecked rightist vindictiveness. Workers were moved to renew their support for the socialists by the brutality of the government toward the coal miners, and Largo's imprisonment gave him a certain sympathetic appeal. The aura of martyrdom bestowed on Azaña by his right-wing inquisitors improved Republican prospects. A meeting he addressed outside Madrid was attended by more than three hundred thousand people, and he spearheaded a reinvigoration and re-groupment of progressive Republicanism before October 1934 that unified parties led by Marcelino Domingo, Azaña, and Santiago Casares Quiroga into a Republican Left, although a section of the Radicals, headed by Martínez Barrio, discontented over Lerroux's clerical concessions, left earlier that year to form the Republican Union.

Much more damaging was the government's sorry record on social and agrarian reform, A resurgent far Right blocked all efforts by more enlightened members of parliament to legislate moderate relief for the less fortunate. Wage standards and social reforms were rolled back while a severe drought in southern farm areas deepened the plight of *braceros*.[127] The balance of power in the Cortes was now firmly in the hands of its most reactionary elements—monarchists, agrarians, and the right wing of CEDA.

As employers vengefully ignored established legal and negotiated standards the Labor Ministry was flooded with appeals concerning violations of wage agreements. Social Catholic Federico Salmón, who became labor minister in May 1935, sought valiantly to restore some measure of equity but was overwhelmed by the sheer number of the petitions. With the labor arbitration system in a virtual state of collapse, he attempted to revive the *jurados* by appointing qualified civil servants to chair them. But the situation had gone too far. The UGT boycotted new jury elections, and Salmón had to all but acknowledge that those juries that still operated had become antilabor instrumentalities.

What little chance existed for a rebirth of Catholic labor organization was foredoomed. The great upsurge of anarcho-syndicalist and socialist trade unionism during the reform biennium and the government's dissolution of the National Confederation of Free Unions (Confederación Nacional de Sindicatos Libres—CNSL) obliged the confessionals to bide their time. With the rise in 1932–33 of organized political Catholicism, social Catholics attempted to stimulate the growth of a trade union adjunct. The stunning socialist reversal of October 1934 inspired a major effort to merge the small, scattered forces of confessional labor. In December 1935 a unification congress was held in Madrid to form the Spanish Confederation of Workers Unions (Confederación Española de Sindicatos Obreros—CESO). Claiming to speak for 276,389 followers, most of them members of the National Catholic Agrarian Confederation, it opposed political strikes and, though affiliating with the International Federation of Christian Trade Unions (IFCTU), rejected confessionalism. Ostensibly independent politically, it was meant to serve as CEDA's labor arm. Having come into existence under the worst possible conditions, CESO's prospects proved to be exceedingly meager.[128]

Manuel Jiménez Fernández, another well-meaning social Catholic, who served as agriculture minister in the first CEDA-Radical government, sought to salvage parts of the agrarian reform plan and to extend the leases of the thousands of *yunteros* in Extremadura who faced eviction and destitution.[129] Such modest initiatives were greeted with invective from conservatives, including many of Jiménez Fernández's fellow CEDA deputies. Along with Eduardo Aunós, Primo de Rivera's labor minister, he earned the sobriquet "white bolshevik." Father Gafó, the Catholic labor leader, urged Gil Robles to provide relief to the stricken areas and to restrain the landowners, who were vindictively controlling wage levels, tenant leases, and working conditions.[130] Decrying the owners for their "suicidal egoism" yet fearing the alienation of his more powerful supporters, he turned a deaf ear. Gil Robles used the cabinet reorganization of April 1935 to drop Jiménez Fernández as agriculture minister and replace him with a more reactionary Agrarian. Malefakis observes, "The transformation of the CEDA into a socially conscious Christian Democratic party, which was Jiménez's central purpose, was never accomplished. The polarization of Spanish society, which might have been checked by a show of generosity on the part of the triumphant Right, continued apace."[131]

The government had to decide what to do with the thirty to forty thousand prisoners taken during the abortive uprising.[132] A decision became unavoidable in March 1935, when González Peña, socialist deputy for Oviedo, and nineteen other revolutionary leaders were sentenced to death by a military court-martial. To appease his more extreme followers, Gil Robles demanded their execution, but Alcalá Zamora, acting on the advice of Lerroux, commuted their sentences to life imprisonment. CEDA and Agrarian ministers resigned in protest. Since the Radicals could not continue governing without CEDA support, Gil Robles used the situation to extract concessions. Now that the socialist threat no longer existed, CEDA pushed for the number of cabinet posts that it merited. The cabinet that took office in April saw Gil Robles in the key post of war minister plus four other CEDA occupants and two Agrarians. A commitment had also been extracted to initiate the desired changes in the constitution nullifying the separation of church and state. Cedistas dominated the new government in all but name.

Gil Robles used his increased influence in the cabinet and the War Ministry to conduct a purge of suspect political military elements and to install officers who shared his outlook in key positions. In carrying out these objectives he had a close ally in General Franco. To gain total control over the armed forces, Gil Robles then sought to have the Civil Guard transferred from the Interior Ministry to his own. Alarmed over this bold attempt to concentrate power over the military, Lerroux and Alcalá intervened.

In the fall of 1935 major scandals led to the downfall of the CEDA-Radical coalition. The *straperlo* affair surfaced in September, implicating several Radical dignitaries and Lerroux's nephew in taking bribes to secure authorization of illegal roulette (*straperlo*) gambling establishments. Radical ministers were forced to resign and a new government was constituted that same month with independent Joaquín Chapaprieta as prime minister. Yet another scandal broke out in December involving several cronies of Lerroux who had made illegal profits from army supply contracts. Despite Gil Robles's last-minute maneuvers to be named prime minister without resorting to new elections, Alcalá Zamora decided in favor of the latter course. Manuel Portela Valladares was named interim prime minister on December 14, the Cortes was dissolved, and the date of new elections was fixed for February 16, 1936.

The Popular Front: The Approaching Holocaust

The Left was overcome by chaos. In the wake of the bungled October rising, socialists were in disarray. The country's prisons bulged with those arrested in October and in the anarchist insurrections. Prieto had fled the country, and numerous party and trade union leaders, including Largo Caballero, spent most of 1935 behind bars. Unions and *casas del pueblo* were padlocked. UGT Executive Committee meetings were held in the Madrid Modelo Prison, where Largo and others were confined. Formulating a plan of action was out of the question; they could only wait passively for a change in fortune.[133]

The socialists' uneasy consensus on strategic and tactical goals was shaken. Largo's supporters could not consider a return to a policy of collaboration with the Republicans. Though chastened and more cautious, Largo reaffirmed his revolutionary faith. The Asturian Commune was merely a stage on the road to a victorious socialist revolution. Prieto "centrists" and Besteirists argued that the events of October had furnished dramatic proof of the bankruptcy of the movement's extremist binge and the need for the party to come to its senses.

The revival of Republican prospects and Azaña's call for the reconstitution of the old coalition stirred renewed interest in socialist circles. With most Caballerist leaders in jail, a new party executive had taken over. Most, including acting general secretary Juan Siméon Vidarte, were sympathetic to the idea of reforging the alliance.

With Largo immobilized, Prieto seized the initiative to induce the party to respond positively to the Azaña proposal. He had always favored a return to the alliance and later regretted temporarily setting it aside to collaborate with Largo in mounting a revolutionary threat to restrain a resurgent revanchist Right.

In the spring of 1935 the Prieto proposal received the unanimous endorsement of the party Executive Committee, including that of chairman Largo Caballero. But the accord was short-lived, broken by the resentment of left socialist leaders who felt that Prieto was exploiting the issue to consolidate his control over the party. The fact was that he was intent on elbowing aside the youth leaders, Caballerist intellectuals, and labor leaders, whom he regarded as politically irresponsible, so as to have a free hand in arriving at an understanding with the Republicans. Azaña formally tendered his proposed electoral conjunction on November 14. Responding to grass-roots clamors for united action, though fearful that such a move would undermine their position, left socialists grudgingly acceded. But it was a Pyrrhic victory for, as Santos Juliá concludes, "Prieto ultimately was able to conduct conversations with the Republicans but at an extremely high price since it meant losing the support of the Socialist Youth and of party branches that still regarded Largo Caballero as the unquestioned leader."[134]

The debate over policy was soon transformed into an acrimonious personality conflict. Largo's memoirs reveal a man who never forgave his rivals. Any position taken by Prieto almost invariably inspired the socialist Left to take a contrary view. Hostilities between the two factions soon went beyond the point of no return, and only the restraining hand of Caballerist labor leaders prevented an open split. Tensions during the summer reached a climax when Prieto, risking his authority and influence, sought to provoke Largo's resignation from the party executive. Largo, in turn, finding himself in a minority yet confident that his personal prestige would rally most of the rank and file to his side, tendered his resignation as party chairman at the end of the year. The gambit backfired, but it was a tactical move that did not involve policy differences since he had by that time already indicated his acceptance of a Popular Front slate in the next election.

Spanish socialism had become deeply fractured.[135] A conceptual and temperamental gulf separated Prieto and the moderates from those who demanded nothing short of a socialist government. And as Caballerist trade unionists relinquished party posts, the traditional party–trade union bond evaporated. The UGT took on the dual function of a labor organization and the politicized mouthpiece of the socialist Left. Thus an unexpected by-product of Prieto's success in securing the party's support for a reconstituted electoral alliance was a party and trade union working at cross-purposes.

Prieto and his followers controlled a sizable minority of the parliamentary group and found some support in the UGT, the party's leading organs, and its daily, *El Socialista*.[136] Their main strength came from Asturias and the Basque region. The Caballerists could count on the overwhelming support of UGT cadres and leaders, numerous intellectuals and publicists, the FJS, and the influential Madrid party organization. What ultimately tipped the power struggle in Largo's favor was his control of the UGT and the fealty that his charismatic figure evoked in socialist ranks, advantages Prieto could not compete with.

The socialist Left had hoped to avoid further collaboration with the Republicans and to await an appropriate moment for the formation of a socialist government. But the developing political momentum within the Left conspired against it as the general political trend both in Spain and in many parts of western Europe was moving in the opposite direction. The united action pact between the French Communist and Socialist parties to counter a rising threat from the extreme Right had been extended on July 1, 1934, to include the Radicals, the French counterpart of the Spanish Republicans. French Communist party General Secretary Maurice Thorez on October 10 launched the idea of a broad popular coalition against fascism. The seventh congress of the Communist International, meeting in July and August 1935, gave official blessing to the shift in international communist strategy and formally launched the Popular Front tactic.

The change in Comintern policy made possible the gradual emergence of the Communist party (PCE) as a significant element within the Spanish Left. Ever since its constitution in the early 1920s, its wildly extremist policies and lack of support assured its alienation from the political and trade union mainstream. Its only success in the 1920s had been capturing part of the CNT leadership and unions in Seville, where it sought to outdo the anarchists in violent insurrectionary exploits. In compliance with the Comintern's ultraleftist "third period" line, the socialists were branded "social fascists." The creation of the Second Republic inspired the slogan "Down with the Monarchy—yes, the same for the bourgeois Republic." At the advent of the Republic, General Mola, who was then serving as director of the National Police, referred to the PCE as a "phantom."

The Popular Front strategy provided a way for the party to improve its fortunes. Its timely advocacy of a broad political coalition, citing the French success, began to have increasing effect on supporters of the socialist Left and Prietistas alike. It began to court the PSOE-UGT in 1934, especially targeting the socialist Left by proferring a steady stream of proposals for united action. Though Largo and other UGT leaders studiously ignored them, they had a subtle influence on many in the rank and file. After a proposed formal merger of its labor front, the Confederación General de Trabajo Unitaria (CGTU), had been repeatedly rejected, the party dissolved its forty-six thousand–member labor adjunct and had its followers join the UGT.

Largo and the UGT leadership continued to be wary of communist ploys, but the Socialist Youth Federation exhibited some willingness to cooperate with its much smaller communist counterpart. Still, the PCE played only a marginal role in the reconstitution of the Republican-socialist electoral alliance. Azaña and Prieto kept communist participation at the lowest possible level so as not to scare off potential voters.[137] It was, however, able to play an increasingly manipulative role in the internal quarrels of the socialist movement.

The political climate following the October insurrection also produced significant political realignments in Catalonia. Elements of the Marxist non-Stalinist Workers and Peasants Bloc of Joaquín Maurín and the Communist Left led by Andrés Nin merged in September to form the Workers Marxist Unification party (POUM). Orthodox communists, in the meantime, initiated merger talks with the Catalonian Socialist Union (USC), the PSOE regional section, and others. By July 1936 the result was the creation of the Catalonian Unified Socialist party (PSUC), which became the regional Comintern affiliate.

Largo's endorsement of the Popular Front did little to alter his revolutionary rhetoric. Participation in the electoral alliance had been a tactical concession designed mainly to obtain the liberation of imprisoned militants. The vengeful behavior of landowners, employers, and conservative governments had greatly intensified class resentments and increased support among the socialist rank and file for radical policies. The socialist Left had little reason to moderate its attitude. Though sanctioning a common electoral front with bourgeois Republicans, socialists would enter an alliance only as part of a workers' alliance with other leftist groups. Socialists would vote for but not enter a future Popular Front government, thus providing a curious symmetry with the Besteirist thesis.

A "Popular Bloc" pact was reached on January 15 by the Republican Left, the Republican Union, the Catalan Esquerra, and the Socialist and Communist parties, as well as the smaller leftist parties, Pestaña's Syndicalist party and the POUM.[138] A moderate electoral platform called for the restoration of the religious, educational, and regional policies of the reform biennium, a thoroughgoing agrarian reform, and amnesty for all political prisoners. A pledge was made to restore the social legislation of the Azaña period, including the mixed jury system of labor relations, but the cherished UGT goal of "workers' control" was omitted. A joint slate of candidates for the Cortes was agreed upon that included representatives from the various participating parties. The future government was to be exclusively composed of Republicans but with the support of both Socialist and Communist parties.

Azaña and Largo, who shared a mutual antipathy, served as the leading spokesmen in the election campaign, and their appeals were jarringly discordant. Azaña exalted parliamentary democracy and peaceful reform while the veteran labor leader denounced bourgeois democracy and spoke in vague terms about emancipation through the coming socialist revolution. The Popular Front was maintained only because of the common fear that an open schism would lead to a right-wing victory.

A confident Right had amassed a huge campaign chest and mobilized a small army of volunteers. A massive publicity program was launched that included the posting of thousands of billboards bearing the image of Gil Robles, *el lider.* Preserving unity on the Right was as arduous a task as it was for the Left. Despite bitter differences within CEDA and with the monarchists and Carlists, who berated Gil Robles for his alleged softness toward Republican governments, the specter of a victory for the Left because of disunity on the Right ultimately forced disgruntled conservatives to accept a common slate.

Popular Front unity and the benevolent attitude toward it by anarchists and the CNT considerably reduced the level of violence surrounding the election. A publication edited by Peiró urged, "Worker, if you vote, do so against fascism." Landowners and their political allies throughout the country reverted to their traditional methods of intimidation to force peasants to vote for right-wing candidates while in leftist strongholds it took courage to vote conservative. Rightists possessed superior powers of intimidation and used them extensively.

The February 16 election elicited an unprecedented level of voter participation; more voters cast their ballots (72 percent of those eligible) than in either 1931 or 1933. The Popular Front won 4,555,401 votes or 34.3 percent; the Right and Center combined garnered 4,503,504 or 33.2 percent; and the Basque Nationalists and assorted centrists accounted for an additional 5.4 percent.[139] The Popular Front vote was particularly heavy in the larger cities, in the south, and in the peripheral regions, whereas the Right and Center did best in the northern half of the country, in Navarre, Palencia, Soria, Guadalajara, Cuenca, and the Balearic Islands. The 700,000 additional votes over the previous election in 1933 won by the Left came mostly from CNT supporters. In five urban centers where CNT strength was notable, Seville, Málaga, Murcia, Valencia, and Zaragossa, voter participation was particularly high. CEDA and other right-wing parties not only retained the votes received in 1933 but increased their overall support. But the Popular Front's greater electoral cohesion gave it the clear advantage, permitting it to benefit disproportionately from an electoral system that gave a big edge to the winning coalition. As a result, the Left, by comparison with 1933, increased its number of parliamentary seats from 97 to 264, the Center, the big loser, plummeting from 177 to 64 and the Right declining from 201 to 144. Both Lerroux, whose party was decimated, and Cambó lost their seats.

The peaceful conduct of the election and its outcome provided a clear mandate for dialogue and civility. The Popular Front won because many voters thought it was more moderate than its right-wing rival. Falange on the far Right won only forty to sixty thousand votes, and the PCE, benefiting from a disproportionate seat distribution decided upon by the coalition, won sixteen seats, four times as many as it would have normally received. Voters generally showed a preference for moderates; in Madrid, for example, Besteiro received the largest number of votes in the Socialist column with Largo lagging behind.

Despite the small difference between the two voting blocs, nobody challenged the legitimacy of the Popular Front's triumph. Many members of parliament elected as progressives, radicals, centrists, Basque Nationalists, and so on subsequently voted much more in accord with the Popular Front than with the Right. Furthermore, in spite of the close outcome, sweeping changes occurred in the composition of the Cortes, and, even more important, the political climate of the country had changed.

Rightist political supporters and many army officers reacted with shock and dismay. Army chief of staff Franco attempted to persuade government authorities to declare martial law, and rumors swept the country that a military takeover was imminent to prevent the Left from taking power.

Frightened by the growing climate of uncertainty, Prime Minister Manuel Portela, intent on vacating office as soon as possible, pressed Azaña to replace him on February 18 instead of waiting until the Cortes convened on March 16 as Azaña originally planned. Azaña finally relented.

The cabinet that took office on February 19 contained nine from the Republican Left, three of the Republican Union, a representative of the Catalan Left, and an army general. Within days, generals suspected of plotting a coup, among them Franco, Mola, and Manuel Goded, were transferred to more distant and less important commands, an action that only temporarily inconvenienced the conspirators.

Cenetistas and left socialists believed the Popular Front triumph gave them license to impose their demands. Before the government had time to take preventive steps, mobs in a number of towns forcibly liberated many political prisoners and replaced hundreds of conservative-run municipalities with leftist ones. Burning and sacking of churches and convents resumed. Workers and peasants with a rekindled militancy and a spirit of vengeance aggressively pressed their demands for higher pay.[140] Some work stoppages were organized by the unions, most of them to force recalcitrant employers to comply with the required reemployment of workers discharged for political reasons. Many were spontaneous expressions of pent-up proletarian resentments. Some were economically motivated; others had clear political ends. Unrestrained strike fervor and immoderate wage settlements prompted *Solidaridad Obrera* to editorialize on June 23 that excessive use of the strike weapon was detrimental to the workers' interest, which would be better served by seeking lower prices rather than wage increases. Militants of both confederations forced employers to discharge supporters of Catholic unions, leading to a general collapse of the movement.[141]

Labor unrest spread throughout the country, cresting in May and June, when half of Madrid's wage earners were on strike. Between May 1 and July 18 the Labor Ministry tallied 719 industrial work stoppages, and Malefakis estimates that as many agricultural strikes took place during this period as in the whole of 1932.[142] There were more strikes in those two months than in all of 1934 except for the October rebellion.

Despite its unprecedented scope, Spanish labor strife was not as intense as in neighboring France. Nor did it match the great strike wave and rural upheavals of the 1917–20 period. But what made it alarming was that it exacerbated the deteriorating sociopolitical situation.

An important factor motivating the intensified land redistribution and the officially ordered reemployment with back pay for workers discharged during the October 1934 uprising was the desire to assuage militant workers. It not only failed in this endeavor but generated a backlash among countless small and medium-sized urban and rural entrepreneurs.[143] The absence of a broad political consensus within the Popular Front made it impossible to contain wage increases within feasible limits. The CNT and UGT regarded their steep demands as a well-merited settling of accounts for past injustices, something many employers found intolerable, but these demands stimulated mobilization among a resurgent working class. "The problem," observes Santos Juliá, "was that no one had any clear notion of the ultimate consequences of this militancy."[144]

The most remarkable feature of the ebullience of that spring was the growth in trade union power and the corresponding decline in the leadership role of the political parties. The PSOE was incapable of taking political initiatives, and the PCE found itself powerless to induce trade union members to practice moderation. Juliá writes, "A strong feeling that the social revolution was both possible and imminent pervaded worker meetings and colored the speeches of labor leaders."[145]

Extremism also increasingly affected the Right. Before the February election, conservatism had been divided between those like Gil Robles who sought to attain power through parliamentary means and those who favored military intervention. Until then the former held the upper hand, but now the pendulum began to swing toward the *golpistas* as Gil Robles saw his control of CEDA slip away, with many youthful supporters defecting to José Antonio Primo de Rivera's violence-prone Falangists and still others joining the National Bloc of Calvo Sotelo, who declared, "The weapon of the Left is universal suffrage. The weapon of the Right bears another name; it is called 'authority.' "[146]

Only a month following the elections armed gangs of Falangists unleashed a reign of terror and political assassinations. The Socialist Youth and others responded in kind. Armed exchanges between gunmen of rival political groups became a frequent occurrence in the streets of Madrid. Violence began to spread through political life and labor relations. The government sought to prevent public knowledge of the full extent of the violence and disorder by imposing press censorship. Members of parliament and labor leaders armed themselves. During a particularly turbulent session of parliament in June, communist deputy Dolores Ibarruri uttered death threats to José Calvo Sotelo, the spokesman for the insurrectionary

Right. As Gil Robles steadily lost control, he passively accepted the inevitability of rebellion and did nothing to prevent it.

As government efforts to arrest the rising tide of lawlessness, labor indiscipline, and political polarization proved unavailing, events passed out of its hands. Government leaders tried to console themselves with the hope that the fervor of the revolutionary Left would soon die down, forcing it to enter into some sort of institutional coexistence or risk losing its followers. Students of this period are of two minds: those who believe civil war and social revolution originated in the outcome of the February 16 election and those who argue that had forceful steps been taken at crucial junctures following the election, Spain might have been spared the nightmare of civil holocaust. Those who defend the latter thesis may be right, but with virtually the entire organized working class unbound by any sense of restraint or loyalty to the government, with both labor organizations either driving toward social revolution or appearing to do so, and with an increasing disintegration of the economic and political fabric, the chances were extremely slim.

The Cortes retaliated against Alcalá Zamora for allowing CEDA to occupy cabinet posts in 1933 and 1934 by voting overwhelmingly on April 7 to unseat him and to replace him with Azaña. Then Prieto, with Azaña's aid and that of center-right moderates, made a bid for the vacant post of prime minister. The chances of restoring moderation with two such strong-minded men occupying the key posts of power would have been measurably enhanced. A governing coalition of the Republican Left and socialist moderates could have served as a counterforce to the destructive antiregime actions of anarchists, Caballerists, communists, and the *golpista* Right. In the end, however, the unseating of Alcalá Zamora turned out to be an ill-conceived move that damaged the Republic.

Azaña's attempt to install Prieto as prime minister was a supreme effort to deal with social chaos and conflict, especially in the southern countryside. Largo, a radicalized reformist rather than a true revolutionary, had not established a specific plan for revolutionary takeover but continued to espouse extremist policies, calling on the workers to ignore legal restraints and to take matters into their own hands. Though the government moved vigorously to redistribute land and resettle landless laborers, more land was distributed from March to July than at any previous time. Zabalza, who remained at the head of the FNTT, urged peasants not to await official action but to seize private landholdings. The countryside, especially in Andalusia and Extremadura, was increasingly subjected to waves of land invasions.[147] Powerless to check these land seizures, the government was forced to acquiesce in or formally condone them.

The land problem was exacerbated because much of rural Spain during the time of the election and the ensuing government changeover received record downpours, causing enormous crop losses. Countless tenant farmers and small landholders faced economic disaster, and *braceros* were plunged into destitution. During the first six months of 1936 rural unemployment rose by 20 percent. Farm unions, undeterred, continued to extract big wage increases. Malefakis estimates that labor costs, despite fierce landowner resistance, increased 300 percent during the early months of the Popular Front government. Thus the countryside that only a short time previously had suffered from abuse by employers now was the scene of equal immoderation on the part of labor. Malefakis concludes, "The enormous rise in labor costs and continuing social unrest began to make the traditional system of agriculture impossible."[148] In a climate of incipient civil war, landowners by the thousands deserted their farms to seek refuge in the cities.

The government found itself in desperate straits. It had won power with the support of workers. To take repressive action against them not only would erode its support base but would make the government susceptible to intimidation by the Right. Azaña, therefore, chose to move against the extreme Right by jailing José Antonio Primo de Rivera and many of his supporters, who were provoking terror against their political opponents. But the government's inability to check the revolutionary Left led to further social chaos.[149]

The quarrel over Prieto's designation as prime minister had been preceded by an airing of differences between the UGT and PSOE over basic policy attitudes. The socialist Left–dominated UGT sought a policy that promoted united action and merger of working-class organizations that were signatories to the Popular Front pact, an initiative ostensibly designed to monitor government accomplishments but actually intended to create an alternative to the "bourgeois" Azaña government. Regarding the proposal as a move to undermine the Popular Front government, the PSOE Executive Committee rejected the idea of constituting a coordinating body, arguing that the Cortes should oversee the government's fidelity to its commitments.

On May 1, on the eve of his bid for the post of prime minister, Prieto delivered a powerful address in Cuenca warning of the imminence of a military coup and naming General Franco as one of the ringleaders. Speaking against the destructive actions of the revolutionary extremists, he cautioned, "A country is capable of enduring the convulsion of revolution with a fixed end. What cannot be endured is the constant attrition of public order without any immediate revolutionary purpose, the erosion of its public authority and its economic vitality amid mounting anxiety, concern, and uneasiness." Union-sponsored wage increases, he added, that exceeded the capacity of the economy would lead to "a socialization of poverty."[150]

Largo's supporters regarded Prieto's admonitions as a betrayal as tensions between the two embattled factions reached the breaking point. When Prieto and his supporters González Peña and Belarmino Tomás, the heroes of the Asturian Commune, attempted to address a mass rally in the southern Caballerist stronghold of Ecija, they were greeted with gunshot volleys from Socialist Youth militants and barely escaped with their lives.

The socialist Left rejected Prieto because its strategy entailed awaiting the "inevitable" failure of the present government, which would make way for a socialist regime headed by Largo Caballero, and because of the vindictive personal relations between Largo and Prieto. Incapable of securing the support of the UGT or of a majority of the socialist parliamentary group, Prieto withdrew his candidacy to avoid provoking an open split of Spanish socialism. Azaña then named a close political associate, Santiago Casares Quiroga, as prime minister. A cultured, intelligent man but suffering from tuberculosis, Casares Quiroga lacked the drive and the political acuity the situation demanded. Prieto might have succeeded in forestalling and even preventing a military pronunciamiento, but the naming of Casares Quiroga increased its likelihood.

Only certain parts of the country were seriously affected by social disorder. The worst hit were Madrid and the southern regions, areas where Caballerist strength was concentrated and where CNT influence was on the increase. Catalonia and much of the north, including Asturias, remained comparatively quiet. One of the most damaging labor conflicts of this period began in Madrid on June 1 and involved more than seventy thousand building construction, electrical, and elevator repair workers. The strike was jointly sponsored by the UGT and CNT. Eventually a favorable government offer forced the UGT to call off the strike. The CNT refused to go along and tried to prevent UGT members from returning to work amid widespread violence and intimidation. Not even a military uprising on July 18 could end the strike, and it was finally brought to a halt in August.

In contrast, Catalonia was the Republic's oasis. Swift action by the Generalitat, once again headed by Lluis Companys, who had been released from prison following the amnesty, to implement the annulled Cultivation Contract Law restoring the tenant rights of thousands of tenant farmers (*rabassaires*) and the prompt ordered reemployment with back pay of forty-five hundred workers who had lost their jobs for political reasons did much to ease tensions. Even more important, the CNT's Faista leaders, chastened by their jarring reversals in 1932 and 1933, were engrossed in the reorganization of the confederation. Strikes were frequent in Barcelona and elsewhere, but violence was notably absent. The textile industry was in crisis, and employers tried to negotiate a social pact with the CNT to assure labor peace. In Zaragossa the coming to power of CNT moderates in this traditional center of violence-prone anarchism helped reduce the number of labor disputes and maintain them at collective bargaining levels.[151] In Seville, however, Faista extremism prevailed. CNT General Secretary Horacio Prieto, a relative moderate, urged striking construction workers to give up their outrageous demands lest employers be pushed into the hands of rightist extremists. His pleadings fell on deaf ears. Much of the strike fever that swept other parts of the country was motivated by the CNT.

The May 1 Zaragossa congress of the CNT registered 988 local affiliates and 550,595 members.[152] One-third of the affiliates were from Andalusia-Extremadura and made up the single largest bloc, followed by Catalonia and the Levant. Anarcho-syndicalism was expanding rapidly and may have had a million followers. Since February Treintista opposition unions had been in a process of reintegration that was finally completed by the Zaragossa congress. Exceptions were the local federations of Manresa and Sabadell, which chose after July 1936 to join the UGT and were subsequently an important element in the region's communist labor strength. The reunification gave the CNT sixty thousand new members.

Despite repeated past failures, the FAI retained firm control of the CNT.[153] One writer observed of the congress, "No one could resist this impressive display of revolutionary mystique, of optimism, and collective excitation."[154] The increasingly somber social and political situation received less attention than long-winded discussions regarding the future organization of a libertarian communist society and the exaltation of the virtues of the "creative spontaneity of the masses." Anarchist hard-liner

Madrid Faista Cipriano Mera, supported by Durruti, defeated an attempt by García Oliver and Ascaso to alert the organization to the imminent threat of a military coup and the need to form an effective paramilitary defense organization.

The days of Faista-inspired uprisings, however, were past.[155] No longer did Cenetistas claim a monopoly over labor. Several years earlier, Valeriano Orobón Fernández, a young anarchist, had argued that the CNT was incapable of carrying off a successful revolution. To overthrow bourgeois society and counter the rising threat of fascism required an alliance between the CNT and the UGT.[156] But until García Oliver's insurrectionary concept had been proved unworkable, little attention was given to Orobón's initiative. Only the Asturian CNT was influenced by his ideas. Now sentiment had shifted. In accepting the UGT's invitation to form a revolutionary alliance, the CNT ended its isolation and acknowledged the existence of two trade union movements of equal size and influence. Yet skepticism persisted concerning the UGT's conversion to a revolutionary philosophy.

As a precondition to its acceptance, the CNT required that the UGT abandon parliamentary activities and commit itself to the destruction of the existing regime. Though the warming of relations had produced increased cooperation at local levels, the proposed alliance remained unrealized until the advent of the civil war.

Revolutionary posturing by trade union reformists made the socialist movement with its rudimentary, diffuse ideology easy prey for Marxist groups with a more coherent political message. Socialist Youth leaders initially evinced sympathy for the ideas of Joaquín Maurín and his Marxist Workers and Peasants Bloc, but their influence was soon superseded by that of the rising Communist party. "A paradox occurred," notes Victor Alba. "At the very moment the Comintern readied its turn to the right and alliances with the very elements [bourgeois democrats] from which Spanish socialists were separating themselves, interest and sympathy arose within socialist ranks for the USSR.[157] Even more serious was the consistent underestimation of the communists by Largo and his supporters, who deluded themselves into believing that the communists could be exploited as a support in their bitter rivalry with the leaders of the PSOE.

The failure of the extremist adventure and Prieto created a vacuum in the national political spectrum normally occupied by the moderate labor Left that was exacerbated by the negative effect of the Caballerists in preventing socialist moderates from taking initiatives and yet failing to formulate an alternative. The socialists seemed to be waiting for the Azaña government to collapse so that a socialist government could be installed. It was an unrealistic hope because Azaña and most other Republican leaders would never permit the Caballerists, whom they regarded as politically irresponsible, to assume leading roles in any future government. For the socialist Left this also implied a refusal to take seriously the ominous preparations under way to overthrow the government.

Almost without exception, Communist parties in those years were under the rigid control of their Russian patrons. For weak ones such as the Spanish party, this control was absolute. Fernando Claudin, a leader of the Communist Youth at that time, recalls, "No one among the party cadres possessed even a middling theoretical formation. To overcome this deficiency the Moscow doctors and their emissaries in Spain took control. A cornerstone in the PCE's formation had been fidelity to the Communist International."[158]

Comintern emissaries Vittorio Codovilla of Argentina, the Bulgarian Vanini Stepanov, and the Hungarian Erno Gerö ("Pedro"), who decided and directed PCE political strategy, sensed the political opportunity and exploited it to the fullest. While maintaining a revolutionary rhetoric, the PCE moved to occupy the terrain of a left populist, more reasonable party, at a time when the socialist movement was experiencing acute internal disarray. The monolithic character of the PCE was reinforced. And as Largo and his cohorts reduced political options to a broad revolutionary worker alliance with the Faista-dominated CNT and sundry Marxist groups, the PCE issued a call for a coalition embracing both the proletarian Left and progressive Republicans.

As public order deteriorated in Madrid and other parts of the country and the government's authority came under daily assault, communist reasonableness and common sense attracted growing support. Aided by infusions of Comintern funding and political expertise, party membership and prestige made great strides as memories of the PCE's recent insurrectionist past receded.[159]

Left socialism was particularly vulnerable to communist encroachments. Caballerist "bolshevizers" proclaimed their leader the "Spanish Lenin" and took the Soviet model as their guide, seeking to replicate the 1917 Bolshevik seizure of power. According to Alba, "Instead of endeavoring to 'work' with CNT, the 'Treintistas,' or BOC, all of them stronger than the PCE, having embraced Marxism-Leninism, the Socialist Left sought Communist blessings and for a time exhibited the ardor of novices by seeking to be more Leninist than the PCE." Araquistáin, its principal ideological spokesman, boasted that Caballerists were more communist than the communists.[160] Ignoring Stalin's brutal repressions, the FJS "professed a total admiration for the soviet political system."[161]

A unified party of the Marxist Left was called for with the socialists serving as its core. The PCE also favored a united party but one that would be subservient to the Communist International. The UGT's approval of the entry of the PCE's trade union following and the merger that took place in April between the Socialist Youth and its much smaller communist counterpart were intended to initiate a process that would lead to ascendancy over the Prieto-controlled PSOE. But not long thereafter, to the consternation of socialist left leaders, many of the FJS leaders joined the PCE, especially following a visit to Moscow by Socialist Youth leader Santiago Carrillo. Thus the envisioned political merger turned out to be political cannibalism.[162] Some of Largo's close associates, especially Julio Alvarez del Vayo, became communist supporters.[163] A growing hostility toward the communists began to emerge.

After courting and manipulating the socialist Left, the PCE joined with the Prieto faction in calling for support of the Popular Front government and upheld the candidacy of Prieto for prime minister. It also abstained from participation in political violence. A strong shift to the right had been executed. "In 1936," observes Joaquín Maurín, "the CP was in fact a radical socialist party: populist, demagogic, and communist in name only. The politically immature mass that was Radical Socialist in 1931 became communist in 1936.[164]

Caballerists were equally discomfited by Faista extremism and a radicalizing rank and file. Pitched battles occurred frequently between supporters of the two labor centers in their efforts to enlist worker support. The month of June witnessed the eruption of a bloody vendetta in Málaga between elements of both organizations, and the Madrid construction strike that also began that month involved a nasty dispute with the CNT over the UGT's decision to accept a favorable settlement. Communists urged acceptance, but Cenetistas refused. Settlement terms were overwhelmingly approved by the membership in July. But fearing loss of support to the more militant appeal of the CNT, the UGT at first decided to ignore the vote and continue the strike. Protest from the rank and file led to an order to return to work. An irate CNT leadership responded by unleashing a campaign of extreme violence to prevent a return to work. Five workers lost their lives in one day as pistol-wielding toughs from both unions squared off. With weapons in hand, CNT leaders had their supporters eat in restaurants and collect their groceries without paying for them.

As the "Tragic Spring" neared denouement, "the Republican ship of state put into port in July 1936, its sails in tatters, its crew mutinous."[165] The country was suffused with a sense of expectation and polarization. Numerous conservatives and disgruntled Republicans joined supporters of the military conspiracy as lines grew tightly drawn and both sides girded for the coming showdown. In a recently published memoir, Cardinal Vicente Enrique y Tarancón, who headed the Council of Bishops during the post-Franco transition to democratic rule, recalls, "We were all convinced that the only solution lay in confrontation. For months Spain awaited the inevitable. Incapable of dialogue, one half of Spain confronted the other. Arms had the last word. What is clear, and this must be honestly admitted, is that all of us at that time believed in violence, blaming the other side for it, but, nonetheless, regarding it as indispensable."[166]

11

LABOR AND THE CIVIL WAR, 1936–1939

Plans for a military coup d'état drew increasing support throughout the spring. General Sanjurjo, who had lived in Portugal since his abortive 1932 pronunciamiento, was to head the rising. Conducting a successful insurgency, however, was one thing and forging a consensus on the nature of a successor regime was another. For a civilian support base that included such diverse political groups as protofascists, rival monarchist factions, Christian democrats, Primoriverists, and others to reach accord was impossible. Nor was it any easier among the military. Sanjurjo favored a monarchist restoration; Mola had in mind a Republican dictatorship that would preserve social reforms. Others wanted a wholly military dictatorship. But this discordance had the virtue of making it easier to rally the support of such a motley political constituency. More of a problem was the fence-straddling of numerous officers, Franco among them, who were intent on hedging their bets until success seemed assured.

The revolt began on July 17, 1936, with the seizure of the Moroccan garrisons of Tetuán, Ceuta, and Melilla, whose forty-five thousand troops, made up mostly of Moroccan regulars and Foreign Legionnaires, were the combat elite of the Spanish army. The murder of José Calvo Sotelo on July 13 by officers of the Assault Guard in retaliation for the Falangist assassination of their comrade Lieutenant Castillo had little to do with fixing the date of the uprising but did sway some vacillating elements to throw in their lot with the rebellion. On the following day, Franco and Queipo de Llano, then serving respectively as commander of the Canary Islands and inspector general of the *carabineros* (customs and border police), joined the rebellion, while garrisons in Burgos and Valladolid also declared for the rebels. Aided by Carlist Requetes, Mola, principal architect of the insurgency, then took control of Navarre province. Nonetheless, cautions

Stanley Payne, "The rebellion was not a generals' revolt but rather a midlevel officers' uprising that swayed many generals."[1]

Much conjecture exists regarding the reaction of the government, then headed by Casares Quiroga. The authorities surely knew of plans for a military rebellion but tended to discount the idea. Though military conspiracies were a frequent occurrence throughout the Second Republic, the only serious one, the Sanjurjada of 1932, had been a dismal failure. Casares, with his lack of knowledge of the military establishment, could not gauge the seriousness of the conspirators. As late as July 18 he dismissed the rumors as an "absurd conspiracy." Instead of forcefully dealing with the revolt, he turned its resolution over to police and military subordinates.

With small forces at their disposal, commanders such as Gonzalo Queipo de Llano in Seville, Miguel Cabanellas in Zaragossa, and Colonel Antonio Aranda in Oviedo, seemingly against great odds, gained control through sheer guile and audacity. But these were the exceptions, and indecision was the more common reaction. "The general tendency on both sides was an avoidance of commitments," military historian Gabriel Cardona informs us, "affecting figures such as General Sanjurjo and Franco. The former refused to leave his Portuguese refuge until Mola sent him a plane on the twentieth, and Franco's trip from the Canary Islands to Tetuán is a model of stalling and verification." Exasperated military colleagues dubbed him "Miss Canary Islands of 1936." Once bloodshed occurred, however, "all broke out in a sinister headlong race to suppress responsibility for the violence by assuring its definitive outcome."[2]

According to the coup d'état scenario, troops and matériel were to be transported by ship from Morocco to the mainland to assist in the seizure of strategic points along the Mediterranean littoral and the formation of a southern expeditionary column to take part in the conquest of Madrid. The failure of most naval units to join the rebels caused this part of the plan to miscarry. Responding to urgent appeals, Mussolini and Hitler furnished fleets of air transport and fighter support to ferry the troops. Moroccan regulars were then taken to provide the troop support for General Queipo de Llano to consolidate control over Seville and for use in the subsequent seizure of Córdoba and Granada, where insurgent forces were under siege by loyal army units and worker militias.

Republican military manpower greatly exceeded that of its Nationalist adversary, but quantity could not overcome quality. Spearhead forces led by Mola in the north, Juan de Yagüe in the south, and Cabanellas in

Aragon consisted mainly of experienced professional troops under the command of seasoned career field officers.

With an expeditionary force numbering three thousand, Yagüe moved swiftly through the leftist strongholds of Andalusia and Extremadura encountering only scattered resistance from the militias and loyal residuals of Republican security units. Within a few days following the suffocation of the Barcelona uprising, ragtag CNT militias under the command of Durruti and García Oliver, supported by POUM units and others, set out for Aragon to liberate the anarcho-syndicalist citadel of Zaragossa and to check any rebel advances that might threaten Catalonia. The rebels' superior military tactics and the inexperience of the militia commanders permitted the rebels to prevent the liberation of the lightly defended provincial capitals of Huesca and Teruel and to bring about a stalemate on the outskirts of Zaragossa despite the Republicans' four-to-one manpower superiority. Rural areas in eastern Aragon were retaken by the militias but otherwise failed to achieve their main objectives.

Accounts of the period reveal a glaring lack of reconnaissance, an egregious absence of coordination between Republican units, and panic under fire. Rebel artillery, air bombardments, and flanking movements often caused untrained militiamen to flee in disorder. Disputes between militias of rival political groups greatly hampered the conduct of military operations. Not until rebel forces reached the outskirts of Madrid were Republican defenders able to make a stand. As Franz Borkenau observes, "The same men who had been heroes in the streets of Madrid became cowards on the battlefields of Talavera and Santa Eulalia."[3] Militias could be effective in street fighting and in the defense of urban centers, but they were grossly deficient in open field combat. The rebels, by contrast, excelled in tactical skill and maneuver.[4]

The initial phase of the campaign ended with about one-third of the country's garrisons siding with the rebels, most of them concentrated in the conservative northern and northeastern areas. With their main operational bases in Navarre and Morocco, the rebels held a substantial portion of the country's grain-raising areas, containing 10 million of its 24 million inhabitants. Most of the industrial plants and the principal urban centers remained in Republican hands. Following the initial seizure of towns such as Huelva, Burgos, Badajoz, and San Sebastian, no other city except Málaga changed hands until spring of the following year. In the intervening eight months action centered on the rebel assault on Madrid, its capture their prime object.

Though the bulk of the population and resources remained in Republican hands, as did most garrisons, a large number of the armed forces had defected to the Nationalists. Of thirty-nine infantry regiments, twenty-five rallied to the rebel side, along with sixteen of twenty-seven artillery regiments, more than half of all army and navy commissioned personnel, and fifteen thousand of the twenty-two thousand Civil Guards.[5]

Casares and his cabinet resigned on July 19, giving way to a ministry headed by the moderate Martínez Barrio that made a last-minute effort to forestall civil war by attempting to form a broad national unity government with rebel participation. Had such a solution been proferred much earlier it might have been welcomed, but now it was too late.

Governing authority in the two zones stood in stark contrast. The rebels were in a much more advantageous position. The lack of bureaucratic infrastructures, the less complicated administration required for governing rural areas, and the formation of a unified military command greatly aided the military in gaining control. Once it became clear that a prolonged conflict lay ahead, political groups were shunted aside, a task made easier by the murder of Calvo Sotelo on the eve of the civil war, eliminating the most forceful, able civilian leader on the rebel side. Furthermore, the choice of supreme military commander had been facilitated by the untimely death of General Sanjurjo in an air accident on the day the rebellion began, followed by the capture and execution of General Goded in the failed attempt to seize Barcelona. Francisco Franco was named "generalissimo" of the Military Defense Junta on July 24 and subsequently elevated to caudillo of the Nationalist zone.

Chaos and confusion overtook much of the Republican zone as constabulary and military organizations disintegrated and the administrative fabric evaporated. Part of the military establishment remained loyal, particularly senior officers stationed in Madrid, some of the garrisons, most of the small air force, and the bulk of the navy, many of whose officers had been shot by loyal sailors and petty officers. Local police and Civil Guard units displayed divided loyalties. Most Assault Guards remained with the Republic.

Because the rebellion's initial successes and failures occurred in a totally haphazard fashion, large numbers on both sides found themselves in opposite war zones. To survive, many feigned loyalty to the locally victorious side. This was particularly true of numerous officers in the Republican zone, rendering some military units practically useless. The disintegration of what remained of the army was further hastened by

Prime Minister Casares's order on July 18 dissolving army units in rebel territory. The order was followed only in the loyal zone, however. To make matters worse, leftists intent on relying exclusively on "an armed people" promoted the dissolution of police and army units in favor of popular militias, incorporating some of the former but relegating them to advisory or generally subordinate roles.[6]

As the insurgency assumed alarming proportions, Largo Caballero in Madrid and CNT leaders in Barcelona urged the authorities to arm the workers. The refusal of some civil governors to arm labor organizations and loyal political groups had in several instances contributed to the success of the insurgency. Republicans were thus confronted by a long-dreaded dilemma. The Popular Front had gained power through an electoral pact with the labor Left, but bourgeois Republicans had not lost their great fear of its revolutionary pretensions. The insurgency brought to the fore the great differences separating the Popular Front governing parties from the revolutionary Left. Martínez Barrio's desperate effort to arrive at an understanding with the insurgents was partly motivated by fear of being overrun by the aroused masses. His failure led to the quick substitution of a new Republican party cabinet presided over by José Giral, an Azaña intimate, who, to save the tottering Republic, issued instructions to civil governors to provide arms to supporting organizations of the Popular Front. It was too late to put down the insurgency, but the belated arms distribution prevented rebel takeovers in some areas.

Security and military forces loyal to the government in Madrid managed to quash an attempted rising; popular mobilization, in Raymond Carr's words, merely "added enthusiasm."[7] In Barcelona, however, worker resistance was more important. The Generalitat had advance notice of the insurgency and conferred with the CNT leadership in planning countermeasures but did not furnish arms. On July 19 rebel military forces, whose ranks included small contingents of local Falangists and several hundred supporters of the Sindicatos Libres, marched on the city's center. They were met by gunfire from Assault Guards and CNT snipers. The fate of the rebels, however, was sealed with the decision of the Civil Guards and their commander to remain loyal. During the ensuing action CNT militants seized control of the Saint Andreu arms depot and acquired a large haul of weapons. Additional arms were obtained in the bloody assault on the Atarazanas barracks. Francisco Ascaso, an intimate of Durruti and one of the legendary anarchist "three musketeers," was killed in the action.

Asturian miners brought out their hidden arms and took control so that the region remained in Republican hands, but the garrison commander in Oviedo, through a ruse, managed to retain control of the city for the rebels. The indecisiveness of General Francisco Paxtot enabled the combined forces of the UGT, CNT, and Assault Guards to frustrate a rebel takeover of Málaga. Procrastination also led to insurgent defeat in the Basque provinces and in Santander. Playing for time in Valencia, rebel army units declared themselves neutral, thus affording local UGT, CNT, and political groups time to form a People's Executive Committee. The resulting standoff was broken in August with a successful assault on army barracks by worker militias, sailors, and Assault Guards. Despite considerable self-serving exaggeration, popular mobilization, especially that of trade unions, proved decisive in repulsing the rebels in Albacete, Pozoblanco, Guadalajara, San Sebastian, Toledo, and elsewhere. The mere presence of popular mass support was frequently sufficient to sway wavering police and military personnel in favor of the Republic.

Apologists of the Franco regime were later to justify the military rebellion as a contingency action to prevent an imminent insurrectionary takeover by the Left. The crowning irony was that, for all its inflammatory rhetoric, the revolutionary Left never gave serious thought to such a possibility. The police constabularies and the military had forcefully demonstrated their ability to foil such attempts by anarchists and socialists. The military rebellion and the resulting breakdown of law and order removed this barrier. Federica Montseny exulted that the military revolt "hastened the revolution we all desired but no one had expected so soon."[8]

The Trade Union Revolution

The melting away of the army and the virtual disappearance of the police from the streets of many communities created a void that within the space of a few days was filled by popular initiative. Worker organizations and political parties took over out of sheer necessity. Lacking directives from the labor confederations, trade union militants improvised, forming a bewildering variety of local governing bodies. Some were composed exclusively of representatives from the locally dominant labor organization, others consisted of coalitions of local labor and political groups, still others formed an amalgam with municipal authorities. Farm laborers and tenant farmers took over landed estates and those abandoned by their owners as workers in some cities became the collective proprietors of various enterprises. The new bodies assumed the functions of food distribution and popular justice and as popular militias, mostly formed by CNT and UGT unions, took over responsibility for local defense and security.

It was an astonishingly headless revolution conducted mainly by grass-roots activists of the two labor centers. Leon Trotsky called it "a confused hybrid revolution, partly blind, partly deaf."[9] Labor leaders merely followed the lead of their constituents.[10] The lack of national guidance and the revolution's pluralistic political character made it to a large extent a local affair. Each town and village formed a self-contained entity with its own military safe-conducts and militias. Some even issued their own currency and scrip. Economic, security, and administrative norms varied considerably from one locality to another. Spain's deeply ingrained local particularism was expressed in a crazy quilt of local separate governments.[11] Common to all was the core governing role of the local unions. Factories, commercial enterprises, utilities, and farm lands were converted into cooperatives or collectives managed and directed by the unions. Unions also formed the militias. Trade union power became so pervasive that the average citizen was unable to function without a union card.

The great transformations in land and factory ownership in this period have been given more or less perfunctory treatment in most accounts of the civil war. Anarchists and their apologists have greatly inflated their importance. If in one sense these changes gave the impression of a transcending flare preceding the eclipse of the revolutionary Left, they also expressed a more profound social transformation that for reasons of time and place could not be fully realized.

According to government estimates, the militias enrolled approximately ninety thousand during the first three months of the war. These popular militias were constituted in a matter of days and immediately forced to assume combat and policing responsibilities. They were pitifully deficient in the rudiments of military combat and leadership. Many militiamen had never before handled a gun. The few military professionals among them were usually relegated to the role of advisers while command functions were assumed by trade union and political militants. Discipline, coordination between units, and steadfastness under fire, qualities essential for military success, were in woefully short supply.

During July and August there seemed to be nothing to prevent the UGT and CNT from taking power. Republicans were in disarray, communists had not yet begun their swift political conquest, and the Prieto-controlled PSOE had lost the initiative. Proletarian militias ruled, and workers had taken over a large part of industry and agriculture. Union enrollments had expanded enormously by the end of the year, with each organization claiming a membership of 2 million. The unions did not take over completely, however, not merely because to do so would have endangered the Republic's survival but because they were constitutionally incapable of doing so. Neither labor confederation possessed the centralized control and policy-making structure necessary to carry out such an action. The CNT consisted of loose, unruly regional organizations, and though the UGT was more cohesive, its central authority was weak.[12] Local unions possessed considerable freedom of action, and crucial policy decisions were often taken not by the UGT Executive Committee but by the leading bodies of the various national industry and trade federations, many of them recently formed. They, in turn, lacked the organizational and financial resources necessary to assure adequate control and guidance of local affiliates. At a time when central control and direction were all-important, Spanish unions proved unable to exercise effective control over their followers.

In Barcelona and other Catalonian towns the CNT became the de facto ruling power. The POUM controlled Lérida and the PSUC Sabadell. With an arsenal of thirty thousand weapons, anarcho-syndicalists disposed of an armed militia six times larger than the security forces of the Generalitat. A watershed decision confronted the CNT leadership: whether to assume total control or to accept a compromise power-sharing arrangement.[13] Opting for the latter course signified a repudiation of its most sacrosanct beliefs—direct action, antistatism, and antipolitics. Brutal realities, however, left little choice. It was possible to install libertarian communism only in Barcelona and some other parts of Catalonia and, even there, it would have required considerable bloodshed, destruction, and the imposition of a political dictatorship, actions that not only went against the anarchist grain but would have deeply divided Republican forces, facilitated foreign intervention, and assured rebel victory.[14]

The formation of the Catalonian Anti-Fascist Militias Committee was a face-saving solution. It contained representation from the various labor and political organizations but was controlled by the CNT-FAI.[15] The Generalitat was permitted to function as the formal governing entity, but most of its vital functions were preempted. The militias, which had absorbed segments of the Civil Guards and the Assault Guards, took over the running of the economy and responsibility for public order and overall military operations. One reason the CNT consented to this arrangement was its desire to oblige comparable bodies in other parts of the country where its influence was not so great to be accorded a requisite participatory role.[16]

Once a decision had been made to share power, the anarcho-syndicalist movement found itself drawn into a web of institutional responsibilities, creating an ever-widening abyss between basic ideological tenets and the harsh necessities imposed by total war.[17] Arcadian communalist ideas were of little help in running the economy or in waging war. In such critical times, leaders and movements that prove capable of exercising an imaginative pragmatism without departing blatantly from doctrine are usually the more successful ones. Political elites in crisis situations have little time to ponder and refine basic political philosophies. The best they can do is to expend accumulated intellectual capital. Anarchists had precious little, appreciably less than left socialists, to draw on in guiding their political instincts.

Anarchist revolutionary utopianism in any case would have had to come to terms sooner or later with modern sociopolitical realities. As long as the CNT-FAI was able to pursue a policy of total opposition to the state and employers, anarchists could repeatedly turn back attempts to bring policies and conduct more in line with modern industrial society. First came disarray and retreat as the insurrectionary strategy confined the movement to a blind alley. The assault on anarchist faith and doctrine that wartime collaboration signified was to have a crushing effect that would continue to convulse the libertarian movement long after the final defeat of the Republic.

Great social upheavals almost always have unleashed waves of violence and terror, and the Spanish civil war was no exception. Following the collapse of public safety, the Republican zone succumbed to an orgy of bloodletting during the early months of the war. Political groups and labor organizations possessed their own prisons, their *chekas,* and lists of suspects. The CNT of Madrid, for example, functioned as a virtual state within a state, with its own militia, intelligence and security services, prisons, and publications. Assassination squads made daily sorties to do away with real or imagined enemies of the Republic. The climate of disorder and unlicensed killings also permitted others to settle personal accounts or commit criminal acts.

We will probably never determine precisely how many persons perished in the terror that raged throughout the summer of 1936. Gabriel Jackson sets the number at about twenty-five thousand, but other estimates are much higher.[18] No single group suffered more than the clergy, whose death toll was between six and seven thousand. Also singled out for retribution were known supporters of the rebellion and right-wing parties, landowners, industrialists, and members of the upper classes. In Barcelona the terror took on a distinctly class character with anyone considered a member of the well-to-do fair game for elimination.

As a backdrop to these developments, one should recall that violence in resolving sociopolitical differences had been a constant throughout Spanish contemporary times and that the civil war had been preceded by a rising number of political murders and vigilantism. More important in heightening the bloodlust was the strategy embarked upon by Mola and his fellow insurgents. During the initial phases of the conflict, rebel forces usually consisted of small armed groups charged with seizing control of key urban centers with large hostile populations. Quick strikes and mass killings were employed as a tactic to overwhelm and terrify local populaces. Terror in the Republican zone was only partially administered by official and semi-official bodies; to a much greater extent it was the work of "uncontrollables." In rebel areas it was official military policy.

Mass executions of Republicans and leftists were often conducted. The capture and consolidation of anarcho-syndicalist citadels such as Seville, Zaragossa, Cádiz, and Algeciras and of socialist strongholds in Extremadura involved the slaughter of thousands. Queipo de Llano is reputed to have carried out the executions of nine thousand in the working-class districts of Seville. The massacre of fifteen hundred to two thousand Republican defenders in the bullring of Badajoz caused infuriated vigilantes to raid the Madrid Modelo Prison and conduct reprisal killings of distinguished political and military detainees. The systematic slaughter of three thousand, mostly CNT members, in the city of Zaragossa must have stimulated the brutality of Durruti's militiamen in purging their Aragonese rear guard of suspected opponents.

Despite their well-earned reputation for violence and lack of discipline, anarchists and Cenetistas have received a disproportionate amount of blame for the "red terror." One has but to read Gerald Brenan's memoirs recounting the nightly *paseos* in the villages surrounding the city of Málaga by execution squads composed of libertarian youth to gain some idea of what actually took place.[19] Nonetheless, other groups also participated in the killings. Most of the terror occurred in Madrid, Catalonia, Valencia, Málaga, and parts of south-central rural Spain. The advance of Durruti's column through eastern Aragon left in its wake the massive elimination of hundreds of suspect villagers.

Following the defeat of the uprising, Barcelona was convulsed by a wave of random killings as execution gangs, some with organizational connections, others unlicensed, self-styled vigilantes and delinquents bent on self-enrichment, roamed the city streets in search of likely victims. Some clergymen and businessmen were given sanctuary by Generalitat officials. In Madrid as many as twenty thousand, often with the help of government and political leaders, sought refuge in foreign embassies.

The CNT-FAI for a time did not interfere with the murderous rampage. Then they issued a declaration in Barcelona threatening to shoot on sight any malefactor who took the law into his own hands or engaged in looting. To rid the city of its many "uncontrollables," some were rounded up by CNT security militiamen and shipped off to the Aragon front. The wave of unofficial killings then subsided greatly.

Anarchists had differing opinions on the uses of physical terror. Some urged its continued employment in dealing with suspect political elements. Faistas forced Federico Escofet, the Generalitat public order commissioner, who had publicly decried the terror, to flee to France for his own safety. In a series of articles in the Mataró daily *Llibertat,* republished in a book entitled *Perill a la retaguardia* (Peril to the rear guard), Joan Peiró refuted communist allegations and placed the main blame for the murderous rampage on the CNT. He denounced the terror for its corrupting effect on humane ethical values: "Human beings have been consumed as weaker animals in the jungle are devoured. . . . Men have been killed for the sheer sake of killing. . . . Many who have perished were shot out of personal vengeance or for old scores. . . . A people in rebellion has been infiltrated by amoral elements who rob and murder by profession and by instinct. . . . If all those who, to the common shame, call themselves revolutionaries, had their homes searched for stolen goods, there would not be enough room in the prisons to hold them." Such plain talk from the conscience of anarcho-syndicalism brought death threats and forced Peiró to acquire an armed bodyguard. In general, however, it is necessary to keep in mind that the legacy of animosities and the resort to the practice of individual violence inherited from the Barcelona labor wars of 1918–23, quiescent for a time, resurfaced following the failed military coup of July 19.[20]

Distant from the war front, Barcelona went on a revolutionary binge. Spaniards and foreigners alike marveled at the proletarianization of this great city, where no one any longer dared to wear a tie and people greeted each other with *"salud"* and the clenched, upraised fist. Memorable accounts of revolutionary Barcelona have been written by George Orwell, Franz Borkenau, and E. H. Kaminski.[21] Their accounts are in accordance with those contained in letters to family members and intimates from a resident British company executive, F. Fraser Lawton of the Barcelona Traction Light and Power Company, otherwise known as La Canadiense. Returning from a walk along the Ramblas one day, he wrote, "The town looks as though en fete, but en fete with the revolutionaries and workmen to the fore." The city's upper classes were "in a perfectly terrible plight. Like hunted rats, daren't go near their houses—hide and sleep anywhere but in their houses—dress in awful clothes and go unshaven, etc. . . . They have no protection, no one to appeal to. Perfectly tragic and awful."[22]

The Collectivizations

Predictably, Barcelona became the center of worker collectivization. The city's factory owners ran for cover when CNT activists took control following the heady days of street fighting. Many fell victim to the orgy of killing that followed, especially those who had engaged in antilabor reprisals after October 1934. The more fortunate ones succeeded in finding refuges, and others either went into hiding or donned plebeian dress. On their return to their workplaces, wage earners discovered that many owners and managers had disappeared. Having become de facto masters of their enterprises, workers attempted to resume operations,[23] taking over not only key economic sectors such as textiles, metalworking, chemicals, and transport but such unlikely enterprises as theaters, beauty shops, and greyhound racing.[24] One recent estimate counts forty-five hundred commercial and industrial establishments placed under workers' control in Catalonia and close to two thousand others collectivized as well as a further five to six thousand grouped together in six hundred collectives.[25]

The Generalitat, more concerned over the restoration of its own standing than the resumption of full production and labor discipline, took the lead from the equally debilitated Madrid central government in decreeing a reduction in the workweek to forty hours, a 15 percent general wage increase, and a big reduction in rentals of living quarters and quickly moved to resolve all pending mixed jury disputes in the workers' favor, much to the disgust of CNT leaders, who now had the main responsibility for reestablishing some order in economic life. Denouncing the Generalitat for undercutting their efforts to instill a greater sense of responsibility in the workers for sustaining the war effort, unions instructed workers to disregard the reduction in the workweek.[26] Meanwhile, workers elected plant committees and a director to manage operations in the seized enterprises, and starting in January 1937, an *interventor* designated by the Generalitat was added. Much confusion prevailed at the outset.

Having lost the initiative from the very beginning and having failed to furnish its *sindicatos unicos* with clear directions concerning coordination, the economy, and workers' control, the CNT allowed the Generalitat to pick up the slack, which further exacerbated differences among its supporters at the operating levels. Its inaction helped give the impression throughout the war that it was a libertarian movement woefully lacking in consistency and cohesion.[27]

The lack of policy guidance led to great variety in the structures adopted by the different worker-controlled enterprises. The Generalitat assumed a coordinating role toward companies that produced items of value to the war effort, permitting trade union participation in overall operations but retaining control. In some firms workers took complete control, and in others that still had managerial personnel present they tended to work out matters of control without clear union instructions. Where blue-collar militants proved unable to assume managerial responsibilities, white-collar and technical personnel often took over. CNT unions tended to do better in running plants where they had no political or labor competition. When they were unable to impose the idea of self-management, and because of the murkiness of the CNT position, Cenetistas were obliged to arrive at mutually acceptable accommodations with other forces, which often caused difficulties.[28]

Such a lack of consistency, at first glance, seems incomprehensible. All efforts during the first months, it should be kept in mind, were directed toward ensuring military and political control so that though the factory takeovers represented the realization of some of the movement's most cherished revolutionary goals, actually running them was left to the shop-floor militants. Few among them possessed any real understanding of fiscal and economic problems, and the movement was deeply divided over how to deal with such issues.

The civil war not only brought to the fore a host of problems involving military organization and defense as well as the economy, but it effected a great internal transformation. Republicans and socialists limited the number of new entrants, but the CNT and the communists welcomed anyone who wanted to join. At a time when a union card had become indispensable to employment and survival, the ranks of both organizations were enormously increased by the influx of countless opportunists and delinquents, in addition to the more idealistically inclined. The shortage of competent technicians became acute. Thus, for example, Joan Fabregas, who served as the Generalitat economic counselor, had joined the confederation after July 19. Before then, he had been a prominent figure in Barcelona business circles and in the conservative Lliga Catalana.

No longer could the CNT function as an egalitarian movement largely run by workers recompensed on a lost time basis. Overnight it became a big bureaucratic operation with hundreds of militants filling important posts in military and public administration and in the collectivized factories. With a membership in excess of 2 million, it controlled a string of daily papers in all the major cities.

The movement was suddenly thrown into ideological disarray and was unprepared to deal with its new power and responsibilities.[29] It was required to abandon any pretense of a unilateral seizure of power and to collaborate with other political and labor forces in repelling the military insurgency. The prevailing impression was that the quelling of the rebellion would take only a few weeks so CNT leaders tended to put everything else aside to concentrate on the organization of worker militias and the conduct of the Aragon campaign. And with so many cadre elements at the Aragon front or otherwise engaged in military tasks, few remained to assume other important responsibilities. The neglect of social revolutionary developments resulted in a disregard for economic issues in the zealous attempt to accomplish CNT goals at the political level.[30]

Cenetistas had always been divided over economic questions. During the May 1936 Zaragossa congress, on the eve of the civil war, cleavages concerning the nature of the future economic order had to be papered over. Now little agreement existed on how to deal with the factory collectivizations. Anarcho-syndicalists understood socialization to entail empowering each industrial union with managerial authority over collectives within its jurisdiction whereas anarchists insisted on the collectivization of industrial entities under worker self-management, namely the free initiative of individual producer groups.[31]

The POUM's Marxist prescriptions called for the socialization of the means of production with central economic direction. The newly formed PSUC and the UGT officially "defended the principle of nationalization in common with socialist organizations in other countries, but the residual of libertarian upbringing that many of their militants brought from their CNT past jumbled nationalization concepts with the most absurd social organization proposals so that its unions often acted in the same manner as those of CNT."[32]

Sensing an opportunity, the centrist Catalan Left–dominated Generalitat seized the initiative to promote a more orderly regulation of economic affairs and of the new socialist-oriented system. Overburdened as it was with military concerns, the Anti-Fascist Militias Committee was only too glad to shed some of its economic responsibilities. After consultations with the CNT, the Economic Council was constituted on August 14. Among its architects was Diego Abad de Santillan, leader of the FAI and a prominent exponent in anarchist circles of a theoretical renovation of economic concepts that borrowed from traditional anarcho-syndicalist notions.[33] The council contained a balanced representation of libertarians, Marxists, and the petty bourgeois parties and served both as a central economic coordinating agency and a channel through which trade unions were able to assume a more formal role in the management of individual enterprises and in the economy as a whole. It also enhanced the authority of the Generalitat and of its politically canny president, Lluis Companys. On the basis of his long experience with and knowledge of Cenetismo, Companys shrewdly opted for a policy of gradually channeling and containing CNT aspirations.

On September 29 the Anti-Fascist Militias Committee was dissolved and a new Generalitat government formed with three CNT members and three from POUM and PSUC, thus formally acknowledging the hegemonic role of the labor Left.

The Collectivization and Workers Control Decree of October 24, 1936, conferred legal status on the industry collectives, but it was carried out only in Catalonia. The new law required all enterprises employing a minimum of one hundred workers to be collectivized. Those posessing smaller work forces could collectivize by majority vote of the employees and the assent of the employer. Though the law's intent was to coordinate and supervise the operation of self-managed firms, it did little more than provide legal sanction for the existing situation. It did, however, give substance to a tacit understanding between Companys and the CNT. Collectivization was given legal protection in return for the CNT's tacit acquiescing in the Generalitat's quasi-separatist transgression of its statutory powers despite Madrid's howls of protest.[34]

It is impossible to judge the general efficacy of the Barcelona worker collectives. They were an experiment in worker control conducted under extremely difficult wartime conditions, and the paucity of research reduces any such evaluation to speculation. By the end of 1936 a growing number of enterprises were encountering serious problems as raw materials short-ages became ever more acute. The morale of workers deteriorated as food shortages appeared and inflation rose fourfold during the war and wages increased only half as much. The abandonment of the plants by their owners and managerial personnel left no alternative but for the workers to take over. In spite of the problems, the known successes of collectiv-ization in sectors such as urban transport, public utilities, chemicals, and the railway system are notable.[35]

The outstanding success story of trade union–Generalitat collaboration was the creation of a war industry. A War Industries Commission was formed, headed by Josep Tarradellas, to take control of and reconvert various enterprises to the mass production of war matériel. By October 1937 the commission had under its control five hundred factories and a work force of fifty thousand together with an additional thirty thousand employed in auxiliary firms.

In the nation's capital the situation evolved differently. Much of the governmental administrative machinery remained intact, and firms whose employers held rebel sympathies or whose production facilities were deemed important to the war effort were placed under joint government-union control. The UGT took over transport as well as telegraphic and telephone communications. Public security forces were able to prevent the purge of factory owners that had occurred in Barcelona. The UGT called for the collaborative management of owner-abandoned firms, work-ers' control in large enterprises, and the protection of small and medium-sized enterprises but did not conduct a campaign to nationalize all industry and transport, a restraint that was conditioned by the impending des-ignation of its leader, Largo Caballero, as prime minister. Though many establishments remained in private hands, all were subjected to worker (trade union) control. The growing threat of a rebel attack on Madrid also argued against any disruptive economic transformations. As a result, only 30 percent of Madrid's industry and services were placed in the hands of worker committees compared to 70 percent in Barcelona.

The reigning mood in the two cities also contrasted greatly, to some extent conditioned by the closeness of the war front. Other than the ubiquitous display of red flags and coverall-clothed militiamen, the city had experienced little outward change. Bourgeois high living and the ostentatious display of luxury and lavish dress were unaffected.

In the north, where the war front was perilously close, complete collectivization could not be effected. Factories and mines in Asturias were either taken over (*incautadas*) by revolutionary committees similar to those formed during October 1934 or placed under union control. A few collectives or cooperatives were created. No attempt was made to alter the basic industrial structure or property ownership because many companies and capital investments were of foreign origin and a takeover might have created diplomatic problems.

The Basque regional government was controlled by the conservative Basque Nationalist party, and Prietistas dominated both the UGT and PSOE. There, except for firms engaged in the production of war matériel, the economy remained largely untouched. The possibility of an attack on Bilbao by Mola's forces was a restraining factor. In Valencia, where the CNT was strong and the UGT in Caballerist hands, trade union takeovers were substantially greater, involving approximately 70 percent of local industry and commerce. The Levant Economic Council, in which both the CNT and UGT participated, decreed the collectivization of all enterprises employing more than fifty workers and all farm lands that could not be directly tended by their proprietors and family members.

As the body of research has expanded modestly in recent years, a more comprehensive picture of the urban workers' collectivization movement has emerged. But our grasp of what actually transpired in the countryside remains elusive and ill-defined. Local and regional studies are on the increase, yet our knowledge of the extent and efficacy of rural collectivization remains at best fragmentary.[36] Roughly 54 percent of expropriated lands were collectivized with the remainder either distributed to individuals or turned over to cooperatives.[37] Most of the land that was seized had been abandoned by its owners or they had been killed. Collectivization affected 70 percent of cultivated land in eastern Aragon, 80 percent of the expropriated lands in Jaen province, and virtually all of the 50 percent of cultivated land seized in Ciudad Real.[38] A larger proportion of land was collectivized in Spain than had been in Russia during its civil war.

Why collectivization was chosen over other forms of land resettlement varied from one area to another. Where there were large concentrations of landless peasants in latifundist areas such as Andalusia, Extremadura, parts of Castile, and La Mancha, where unrest had been running high on the eve of the insurgency, and where labor organization was strong, collectivization was favored. After his September 1936 visit to the La Mancha region of Ciudad Real, a well-known socialist stronghold, Borkenau told of observing the collectivization of 256 landed estates within slightly more than a month.[39] On the other hand, in Catalonia, a region of small and medium-sized farming plots and tenant farmers well organized in unions linked with the dominant Catalan Left party, anarchist attempts to conduct massive collectivizations failed dismally and were limited to a handful of scattered settlements.

Collectivization was sometimes more a political act than a grass-roots phenomenon. The presence of CNT unions, its armed militias, or both, as in Cuenca, eastern Aragon, and parts of Valencia, led to the formation of rural collectives even though the bulk of the farm populations in those areas consisted of small and medium-sized farmers. The formation of agrarian communes was the libertarian ideal, but circumstances and peasants' desires forced anarchists to accept not only collectivization but the coexistence of small landholdings as well. It was decided upon in other instances not so much as an ideological solution to the problem of land redistribution but as the most practical way to resume production as quickly as possible and avert costly harvest losses. The fate of seized lands was often determined by existing landholding patterns and the area's proximity to the war front. The coming of the war and its accompanying administrative breakdown led rural unions, like their urban counterparts, to take control of large numbers of farms or landed estates. Local militants usually decided whether or not to collectivize.

The CNT lacked both a national farm organization and a clearly enunciated agrarian policy, and it was not until well into 1937 that efforts were undertaken to overcome these crucial deficiencies. Benefiting from more favorable local conditions and possessing a more solid organization, socialists, who dominated the farm collectives of Jaen province and those of Castile–La Mancha, displayed better organizational skills than did the CNT in Valencia and Aragon.

Rural collectivizations, unlike urban ones, did not occur all at once. Though the bulk of spontaneous expropriations took place during August to September 1936, they continued throughout the remainder of that year. Thereafter, the number of collectives grew at an uneven pace, continuing until as late as 1939.[40]

The policies to be followed by collectives were usually determined in general membership meetings that also decided upon the distribution of profits and agricultural surpluses. A directing committee elected by member participants might also include representatives from one or the other labor organizations, sometimes both. In areas close to the war front the collective governing body, municipal administration, and militia committee were often one and the same. Where communalization had taken place, the collective coordinating committee was also synonymous with the political system of the territory.

Though collectives often suffered from improvisation and ignorance of the intricacies of commercial production and distribution, the orange export collectives of Valencia improved distribution methods and developed workable administrative procedures. In Catalonia, Valencia, and New Castile, where the UGT or other elements were influential, legal currency was used, although in CNT-dominated collectives it was often not used in the conduct of internal operations and was limited to external transactions. The greatest disparity was in the form of wage payments. CNT collectives instituted a "family wage" in which goods and services were distributed based on the number and needs of family members rather than work performed. In the other collectives wages were usually related to work performed and depended on the economic situation of the collective.

Nothing then or since has generated more controversy than the collectivizations of eastern Aragon. Anarchist apologists extol that experiment as the paragon of peasant revolutionary spontaneity.[41] Its detractors, especially Azaña and the communists, saw it as an egregious sabotage of the war effort. The advance of the predominantly anarcho-syndicalist Catalan militia columns into eastern Aragon created a power vacuum in the liberated villages, providing a unique opportunity to put anarchist collectivist ideas into practice. Large tracts of land had been abandoned by absentee owners and rebel supporters and by others who had been executed. A wholesale collectivization under the aegis of the militias was conducted in an area in which small and medium-sized farms predominated. The result was the single largest concentration of collectivized land in the Republican zone. According to Gaston Leval, an anarchist writer on libertarian collectivizations, three-quarters of all available land was divided into 450 collectives with more than three hundred thousand peasants. A recent study suggests that these figures should be halved.[42]

To ensure political control over the region and to facilitate production and distribution, CNT militia leaders and surviving Zaragossa militants set up the Council of Aragon in October 1936. It was the only truly anarchist governing body in the Republican zone. The council was formed with Durruti's encouragement against the advice of the CNT national committee and the POUM, which favored placing the area under the control of the Catalan Generalitat.[43]

Before July 1936 the CNT in Aragon had existed almost exclusively in urban areas with the great bulk of its strength concentrated in the city of Zaragossa. The eastern part of the region had been mainly under the influence of Republican parties and many peasants had been members of the National Catholic Agrarian Confederation. The collectivization program and local government administration largely became the responsibility of militants whose only prior experience had been as union officers in Zaragossa.

Furthermore, because the collectives were mainly run by anarchists rather than anarcho-syndicalists, the libertarian notion that trade unions should oversee them was often ignored. More often than not, collectives and unions were one and the same. Their different structures—some operated as cooperatives, others as virtual communes—and the problems encountered in improvising economic solutions made overall coordination and central administration extremely difficult.

Much has been made of the coercion employed by militiamen in forcing peasants to join the collectives, an allegation that was employed as the pretext in the summer of 1937 for their forcible dissolution. Intimidation was undoubtedly employed, yet numerous peasants did voluntarily join the collectives and a substantial number of them, especially the poorer ones, remained loyal to the anarchist collectives even after the dissolution of the Council of Aragon. An important inducement was the favoritism displayed by the Council of Aragon toward collective members in the distribution of supplies and other items. The degree to which collectivization was imposed by armed terror or was an indigenous revolutionary phenomenon remains unclear and undocumented.[44] Though it is impossible to generalize about the rural land takeovers, there is little doubt that the quality of life for most peasants who participated in cooperatives and collectives notably improved.

Largo Caballero as Prime Minister

The Madrid central government was able to preserve its administrative infrastructure but at a price. As soon as it became obvious that the rebels were in no mood to compromise, the ephemeral Martínez Barrio government was dissolved to make way for an all-Republican government headed by José Giral on July 19. Prieto was a key adviser to the Giral government. With the armed forces and police constabularies falling apart or being absorbed by the popular militias, power lay in the streets. The danger of a rebel attack on the nation's capital left the Giral government little alternative but to distribute arms to the unions and political parties. In Madrid the two unions were given arms and UGT militias took over the main responsibility for the policing and defense of the city.

Overrun by what Azaña called "a trade union revolution," the government had no choice but to accommodate to reality. It made little sense, in any event, to continue a government made up exclusively of Republican parties when most of the armed militias were under the control of the labor Left. A single choice presented itself: Francisco Largo Caballero. He was the only potential leader who held the affection and regard of the proletarian masses. Overcoming their personal dislike of the aging labor leader (he was sixty-eight) and serious doubts concerning his ability to lead the country at such a difficult moment, Prieto and Azaña accepted his designation as a necessity. For Largo, acceptance meant repudiating the political platform of the socialist Left, but it was difficult to turn down an offer to head a government of national unity in the interest of the common defense effort. Consciences were soothed with the rationalization that the interests of socialism would best be served by having a labor leader occupy the country's highest office for the first time.

A national union cabinet took office on September 4 that included figures from the various Republican parties and two communists for the first time. Key posts were reserved for left socialists with an additional three from the Prieto faction, among them Negrín and Prieto himself. Largo also assumed charge of the War Ministry. The CNT was invited to participate, but internal divisions prevented it from accepting the offer. Instead, the formation of a CNT-UGT national defense junta was proposed, a wholly unrealistic initiative, particularly since an assault on Madrid by Franco's army was becoming a distinct possibility.

Largo Caballero's parochialism was a matter of common gossip: his gruffness, his exasperating meticulousness that earned him the nickname *fraile sindical* (trade union monk), his great vanity, his imperiousness, and his secretiveness. Most of his political peers disliked him. Dolores Ibarruri's criticism, despite its self-serving intent, that Largo's governing style was more appropriate to a trade union secretary than a prime minister, contains some truth. Yet no one would deny his incorruptibility, courage, and rectitude. Largo's war leadership was on the whole highly creditable.

The delicate balancing act required of Largo in serving as the nation's war leader while preserving his credibility as leader of the socialist Left was no easy matter because it meant embracing moderate socialist positions without seeming to do so. If the nation and its resources were to be properly mobilized, some of the revolution's most notable conquests had to be minimized or abolished. His followers were comforted by the promise that once the war was won the postponed revolution would take place. His government intended for the time being to preside over a commingling of Republican legality and revolutionary achievements.

The first order of business was to reconstruct the shattered military organization. As a supporter of popular militias, Largo incorporated them in the new Popular Army rather than seeking their dissolution. It was the only practical alternative.

He held total responsibility for directing the war effort, beginning with the seemingly impossible task of transforming the unruly militias into a cohesive fighting force.[45] Putting Prieto in charge of the navy and the small air force, the first disabled by the wholesale elimination of its officer corps and the other of relatively minor importance, was a way of assuring that he would not interfere with major war policy decision making. A general staff was reconstituted under Largo's direct supervision. Key responsibilities were given to two energetic officers, General José Asensio as subsecretary of the War Ministry and as Largo's principal military adviser and General Sebastián Pozas as commander of the Madrid defense front. Military rank was restored and militiamen made subject to the military justice code. Largo avoided a head-on clash with the various political groups who sought to retain exclusive control of their armed units, and the militias were gradually drawn into the new army. Operational command authority (*mando unico*) was vested in the war minister, but reforms could be effectively installed mainly only in the Madrid sector; units under the control of the Asturian, Catalan, and Basque regional governments balked at integration. To afford greater combat flexibility, the traditional divisional system was abandoned in favor of the smaller mixed brigade units.[46]

But these were crucial reforms whose effects would be felt by the summer of 1937. In the meantime, the desperate military situation of the Republic remained unchanged. Largo's accession to the premiership had been preceded by the September 3 disaster of Talavera de la Reina, where Moorish troops took over by default as militiamen broke ranks and fled in disorder upon the approach of the regulars. Toledo also fell at the end of the month. In the north, with the capture of Irun, Mola tightened the noose around the increasingly beleaguered Basque Republican forces. The loss of Málaga in February through a combination of anarchist bungling, communist-anarchist infighting, divided army command authority, the spread of panic among defending militiamen, and an unwillingness by the government to divert men and matériel from the defense of Madrid was a particularly damaging setback. Nonetheless, in military historian Gabriel Cardona's judgment, "Considering the conditions under which the war was being fought it was well nigh a miracle that the Republic was able to resist at all. Having begun from scratch, the war leadership's improvisations generally proved efficacious. The fruits of its efforts were to be seen in the recuperation of government authority, a working accord between extremely disputatious forces, and the laying of foundations for a new military organization. All this was done without ceding control to the military or to the indispensable Soviet allies."[47]

Having encountered only scattered resistance, the rebel expeditionary force arrived at the outskirts of Madrid. Little preparation had been made for the city's defense, not even the emergency construction of breastworks and fortifications. Mola's strike to seize control of the capital through a quick advance had been blunted by the successful defense mounted by militias and regular government army units in the mountain passes northeast of the city. The Republic had managed to survive the summer of 1936 primarily as a result of the courage and ardor of the men of the popular militias. Nonetheless, Largo and most of his fellow cabinet members had become resigned to the eventual loss of the capital. General Pozas, who had replaced General Asensio as head of the Army of the Center on October 24, also counseled leaving the city.

Fearful of incurring anarcho-syndicalist wrath for having abandoned Madrid, Largo once more invited the CNT-FAI to join the government. As an added inducement, the number of available cabinet posts was increased from one to four. A debate then began within the CNT over the pros and cons of joining the Largo cabinet. Not long before, a decision had been reached to collaborate in a new Generalitat government, and participation at the national level seemed a logical extension of this policy.

Ignorant of Largo's intention to desert Madrid, CNT General Secretary Horacio Prieto, a prominent advocate of increased political involvement, successfully pressed the leadership to accept the government's offer.

The four chosen to serve as cabinet members were selected with an eye to assuring a balanced representation from the various currents within the CNT-FAI. Juan López, who was named minister of commerce, and Joan Peiró, who became minister of industry, were leading representatives of the moderate former Treintista group while Juan García Oliver, who became minister of justice, and Federica Montseny, in charge of public health, spoke for Faismo and orthodox anarchism. The selection also revealed the true locus of power in the libertarian movement: Juan López was the leader of the Valencian CNT, second in importance to that of Barcelona, while García Oliver and Montseny spoke for the dominant group in the Barcelona CNT. Though Peiró had not taken an active part in CNT affairs since the defeat of the Treintistas in 1934, he continued to write for the anarcho-syndicalist press and his highly acclaimed management of the Mataró glass-making cooperative was probably a factor in his selection. To their dismay, the four CNT ministers were sworn in on the very day the government commenced the evacuation to Valencia. Though the departure had been a collective decision of the cabinet and the military staff, primary responsibility lay with Largo. Criticism arose not so much of the city's evacuation as the clumsy, politically insensitive manner in which it was conducted.

Largo's subsequent ouster as prime minister and his descent into political oblivion resulted from his consistent underestimation of the communists and his mishandling of the defense of Madrid. The nonintervention policy adopted by the Western powers seriously undermined the Republic by robbing it of its international legitimacy and its foreign financial credit standing. It was powerless to prevent Hitler and Mussolini from supplying Franco in flagrant violation of the arms ban. Stalin decided to abandon his policy of nonintervention and to use the embattled Republic as a pawn in his attempt to mount a grand Western security alliance to counter the rising German threat. The decision to embark on a massive assistance program came after Largo had been in office for two months. It was to prove crucial in the spectacular acquisition of political hegemony by the Spanish Communist party, which till then had been a negligible factor in Republican political life.

Like other leftist groups, the Spanish Communist party grew rapidly after July 18, 1936. Nonetheless, it still lagged far behind the socialists and CNT in overall strength and influence. Since it proved extremely difficult to make any substantial inroads among blue-collar workers, most of the party's trade union strength was concentrated among white-collar and middle-class groups. Three factors were crucial in the PCE's expansion that commenced with the arrival of Russian military assistance: Soviet pressure and blackmail to assure that the PCE received favored treatment politically and in the distribution of military equipment; its increasingly prominent role (with the aid of Russian advisers) in military affairs; and a politically moderate program conducted with cohesion and discipline.

The wartime party was a largely artificial contrivance of Comintern agents to serve as a prop to Soviet foreign policy. Stalin's courtship of the Western powers required that the embattled Spanish Republic appear not as a hotbed of left-wing revolution but as a moderate Western-style democracy. Consequently, Spanish communists insisted that what was taking place was merely a "bourgeois democratic revolution." "To acknowledge otherwise," writes former communist Fernando Claudin, "was tantamount to admitting that Stalinist policy in Spain amounted to rolling back the revolution."[48] The party joined socialist moderates and Republicans in the slogan "First win the war."

Thus two fundamentally opposed camps faced off, one insisting that the war could be won only with a strong central government and the relinquishing of revolutionary conquests so as not to alienate the middle class and farmers. The other retorted that a successful war effort was possible only if the masses were given fundamental social and economic advances. Partisans of a return to social and political "normality" included the Republican parties, the Prieto wing of the socialist movement, and the communists. Opposing them were the CNT, the socialist Left, and the POUM, which maintained the primacy if not the unity of social revolution with the war effort.[49] But while left socialists and anarchists floundered in confusion, division, and uncertainty, communists proceeded to carry out their clearly enunciated objectives with cohesion and ruthlessness.

In carrying out Stalin's injunctions, the PCE became the champion of social conservatism. Communist political strategy was tailored to make the best of the existing situation. The bulk of the organized working class had a historic allegiance either to anarcho-syndicalism or to the socialists. The best that could be gained, consequently, was for the communists to obtain the support of fractional segments of organized labor, which could best be done by developing support and predominance in

Table 11.1.   Social Composition of the PCE, 1937

Category	Totals
Industrial workers	87,660
Agricultural workers	62,250
Peasants[a]	76,700
Middle class	15,485
Liberal professions	7,045

Source: José Diaz, *Por la unidad hacia la victoria*, pp. 13–15, cited in David C. Cattell, *Communism and the Spanish Civil War* (1956; rpt. New York: Russell and Russell, 1965), p. 94.

[a]Includes those who own land.

the military effort and joining with bourgeois Republicans in restoring the authority of the central government. Communists became the principal spokesmen for private property and orderly government. And, indeed, what better safe harbor existed for the middle class than a disciplined party with impeccable proletarian credentials, hence ideally situated to halt the spontaneous social upheaval?

Farmers, small factory owners, shopkeepers, and artisans flocked to the party.[50] Valencian cultivators, formerly supporters of the Catholic peasant confederation, now sought refuge in communist-controlled agrarian organizations. The Catalonian UGT, which came under the control of the procommunist PSUC, became a sanctuary for white-collar workers, merchants, and small factory owners terrified by anarcho-syndicalist aggression. Barcelona's leading white-collar and technicians union, CADCI, which had been directed by supporters of the Catalan Left, was won over by the local UGT. Government civil servants also joined the UGT.

Official figures on the social composition of the PCE in 1937 are revealing (see table 11.1). Probably never before had a European Communist party possessed such a large ratio of petty bourgeoisie in its membership and with an agricultural majority to boot.[51]

The great popularity of the Soviet Union for its assistance to the Republic increased the prestige of the PCE. And as Largo's role as war leader faltered, communists concentrated on enhancing their reputation as the most competent military defenders of the Republic. No other political group could match the PCE in material, technical, and political assets. The party's monolithic structure, its semimilitary discipline, the political capital gained from Russian military assistance, the counsel of Russian military advisers, and the political expertise provided by a host of Comintern mentors gave it an exceptional force. The famous "fifth regiment," which in fact was not a combat unit but a party military training school, turned out thirty thousand combat troops and commanders, far surpassing the CNT's modest resources.[52] Army of the Center units under party control received a disproportionately large share of Soviet military equipment with lesser amounts going to the CNT, UGT, and POUM. Impressed by the party's growing military role, numerous career military officers gravitated to it.

Largo belatedly awoke to the threat the communists posed to his liberty of action. He gave them free rein at the outset to please the Russians and to help rebuild a regular army. Only later did he realize that they were exploiting his permissiveness to form their own units and to undercut his authority in military decision making. The International Brigades had been formed and dispatched to Spain not as a result of a government decision but by the Comintern, and they operated autonomously, more responsive to PCE directives than to those of the government.

When the government evacuated Madrid in October, the PCE gained a key role in the city's Defense Junta, in which all Popular Front organizations were represented (the POUM had been excluded at Soviet insistence) and which was headed by General José Miaja and seconded by his able chief of staff Colonel Vicente Rojo. As Cardona concludes, "The battle of Madrid and the resistance offered took the government by surprise. Miaja, aided by the Defense Junta, retained supreme command, resulting in an autonomy totally unwanted by Largo Caballero."[53]

The PCE indeed contributed appreciably to the defense of Madrid, as did the International Brigades. But the formidable propaganda machine of the party and the Comintern magnified their exploits out of all proportion to the detriment of the substantial roles played by CNT and UGT military forces, the outstanding staff work of Colonel Rojo, and the valiant command role of professional officers loyal to the Republic.[54]

Largo increasingly came under attack for the bungled evacuation to Valencia and the debacle at Málaga as the communist star was in the ascendancy. Belatedly the aging labor leader became aware of the peril his government faced from Soviet attempts to dictate its conduct and from the expansion of communist power. Never one to be subtle, Largo went from extreme permissiveness to total opposition to the communists.[55] He fought back by ordering the dismissal of the many communist political army commissars who had been named by his collaborator, the procommunist Alvarez del Vayo, and who had assured PCE control of many army units. Infuriated by Soviet Ambassador Marcel Rosenberg, who had intruded in government policy making to the point of demanding the removal of General Asensio, Largo had him declared persona non grata. He gave further vent to his fury by floating a foreign policy initiative designed to secure western European support in an effort to reduce the government's heavy reliance on Soviet aid.

At Moscow's insistence the PCE worked to dislodge Largo from power. Blame for the fall of Málaga was pinned on General Asensio and his ouster obtained. Largo was asked to relinquish the post of war minister. The "Spanish Lenin" now became "*el viejo chocho*" (doddering old fool). He was subjected to criticism and vilification and found few defenders. His new anticommunism had led to a rapprochement between the PCE and the Prieto-controlled PSOE. Prietistas and Republicans were only too happy to assist in bringing about his downfall.

Largo and his military advisers had pinned great hopes on preparations for an offensive during the spring of 1937 in Extremadura aimed at gaining control of the cities of Mérida and Badajoz. If successful, this operation would have cut the Nationalist zone in two, relieving pressure on the north and Madrid and possibly permitting the recapture of Seville. It was an attractive scenario. But fearing that its success would make it impossible to dislodge Largo, the Russians torpedoed the project by refusing to furnish the necessary aerial support.

The ouster campaign soon found a particularly virulent outlet in the fierce power struggle under way in Catalonia. Formed on the eve of the military rebellion with a modest number of adherents, PSUC experienced a rapid expansion as did its labor adjunct, the Catalan UGT section.[56] The heterogeneity of its founding components permitted the new party to project a broad populist appeal that attracted elements of the Catalan middle class as well as those on the labor Left. Merchants, shopkeepers, and small factory owners, traditional supporters of the Esquerra Republicana, dismayed by its conciliatory attitude toward the CNT, increasingly defected to the PSUC, which more vigorously defended their interests and opposed the CNT and the POUM. The PSUC did not become thoroughly Stalinized before 1939, though it became a member of the Comintern, faithfully followed its international line, and took on a ferociously self-serving anti-Trotskyist attitude.

Before July 18 the Catalan UGT could lay claim to only a small fraction of unionized workers, twenty thousand compared to the CNT's six hundred thousand, and exercised little influence in regional affairs. It grew along with its parent body. The UGT was the principal beneficiary of the mandatory unionization decree. The important city federations of Sabadell and Manresa did not follow the Treintista unions' return to the CNT fold but joined the UGT instead, as did white-collar, public service, and various unaffiliated unions.

An important source for expansion ironically came from the entry of unions under the influence of the POUM grouped together in the Labor Federation for Trade Union Unity (Federación Obrera de Unidad Sindical—FOUS), which had been formed during May 1936 to serve as a rallying point for allied unions that had been ousted from the CNT by Faistas during the anti-Treintista purges. It probably possessed a larger membership in the region at the time of the military rebellion than did the UGT, most of it outside Barcelona in cities such as Lérida, Tarragona, Valls, and Gerona. The August 10 decree making union membership obligatory, which legally recognized only the two main labor centers, placed the POUM in a painful quandary. The party's entire strategy was based on attracting the anarcho-syndicalist mass, yet POUM militants were unwelcome in the CNT. They had no choice but to enter the UGT. But the POUM leadership had not bargained for the rapid domination of the organization by communist elements and the subsequent loss of many of its unions and their following. FOUS unions in Barcelona, especially those in the graphic arts and public utilities, were lost; some of the POUM's labor following in various provincial towns was salvaged, but a large part was irretrievably lost to its worst enemies.

The growing power of the PSUC-UGT produced important changes in the political balance. Companys, seeking to use the PSUC as a counterpoise to the CNT, favored the former. Meanwhile, through pressure and threats of withholding arms shipments, Soviet consul Vladimir Antonov-Ovséenko, forced Companys and the CNT to eject the POUM and its leader, Andrés Nin, who was serving as justice minister, from the Generalitat. It was a Kafkian irony that during his Moscow sojourn in the late 1920s, Nin and Antonov-Ovséenko had been friends and supporters of the Trotskyist Left Opposition.

The communist offensive was directed primarily against the POUM. The PCE's ascendancy coincided with Stalin's brutal purges of the old Bolsheviks and show trials designed to depict the exiled Leon Trotsky as a Nazi agent. The POUM had serious differences with Trotsky, who pilloried its leadership for its "centrism." The communists, nonetheless, branded the party "Trotskyist" for, among other things, it had been the only party in Spain that openly denounced the Moscow trials and had even sought asylum in Catalonia for the exiled Russian revolutionary.

The PSUC and Antonov-Ovsëenko then embarked on a vicious smear campaign against the POUM. The November 28 issue of *Treball,* official organ of the PSUC, carried an article by the Soviet consul accusing *La Batalla,* the POUM daily, of conspiring with international fascism as the campaign to expel the POUM from the Generalitat went into high gear. The crisis was finally resolved on December 17 with the formation of a new cabinet that excluded the POUM and increased UGT representation. The net result was to give the PSUC equal representation in the distribution of councillor positions with the ERC and to reduce the CNT to only one representative. The CNT was enticed with the promise of increased arms supplies for its military units.

The crisis came to a head with a bloody confrontation in Barcelona, known as the "May events," during the first week of May. Ever since July 1936 various forces, chafing under anarcho-syndicalist control, had been preparing for a showdown. Inflation had soared, and food was in short supply in the city, resulting in the establishment of food rationing. Frequent bread shortages had made long lines before the bakeries a permanent feature of the daily routine, sometimes resulting in violent demonstrations by irate housewives.

Industrial production plummeted as raw materials imports were sharply reduced and available reserves were consumed. An increasing number of worker-managed enterprises had to cease operations—much of the textile industry, for example—or operate on greatly reduced work schedules. Others that produced luxury articles either closed down or were converted to war production. Most enterprises not directly engaged in the production of military equipment were forced to lay off workers, leading to a sharp rise in unemployment. Popular discontent and war weariness were reaching disquieting proportions as leaders of the various labor and political groups jockeyed to pin the blame for the deteriorating conditions on their opponents.

Political tensions grew as the PSUC's growing muscle threatened to undo CNT political hegemony and conquests. With each passing month violence and assassinations increased as CNT leaders, apprehensive over the decline of their strength and rising popular discontent, sought to arrest the challenge of the PSUC and its Soviet patrons.

Internal differences arose between those occupying positions in government and in the management of enterprises, who tended to favor the emerging centralization of power, and those who clung to anarchist orthodoxy. The thirty-four thousand-strong Federation of Catalonian Libertarian Youth was prominent in the latter category, and the FAI was deeply divided. CNT popularity was adversely affected "for not having put an end to violence in the rear guard and for the appearance of a new bureaucratic and managerial group distanced from a rank and file that suffered meager rations, a black market, and the growth of joblessness despite conscription."[57]

In this climate of mounting confrontation the government sent Carabineros to retake control of Catalonian border stations that had been in CNT hands since July 1936. Eager to avert an armed clash, CNT leaders agreed to a compromise, but a succession of political murders by supporters of the two adversaries set the stage for a settling of accounts. The April murder of an important UGT/PSUC leader led to the staging of a funeral in Barcelona that served as an impressive PSUC show of strength. The imminence of a "civil war within a civil war" resulted in a breakdown of plans to hold a joint UGT-CNT May Day parade and to its subsequent prohibition by the authorities.

The spark that set off the conflagration came with the dispatch of police contingents under the command of PSUC Public Security Commissioner Rodríguez Salas to take control of the city's central telephone exchange, known as La Telefonica. The building had been in CNT hands and guarded by its militiamen since the commencement of the war. Both the Generalitat and the central government now in Valencia had considerable interest in its recovery for much telephone communication in the Republican zone had to be conducted through Barcelona, where all telephone calls were subjected to CNT eavesdropping.

Until then the CNT-FAI had sought to preserve its strength and protect its interests through temporizing and providing lip service to disagreeable government decrees. The tenuousness of this balancing act was dramatically exposed by the reaction generated by the attempted seizure of the Telefonica. For many CNT militants it had all the earmarks of a communist provocation. Armed Cenetistas spontaneously took over most of the city and erected barricades.[58] After vain efforts on May 3 to persuade the CNT leaders to abandon their policy of expediency and to take control of the city, the POUM, despite its sense of impending disaster, found no alternative but to call on its supporters to join the rising.[59]

The only other group to join the POUM in urging workers to take power was a small, relatively obscure group of extremists, bolshevized anarchists, known as the Friends of Durruti, who were seconded by a tiny number of authentic Trotskyists, the Bolshevik Leninists. Though of little importance organizationally, the Friends of Durruti, through its appeals for resistance, was able for a time to prevent the CNT leadership from regaining control of the insurgent workers.

Anguished appeals from local and regional CNT leaders to lay down arms went unheeded. Faista ministers Montseny and García Oliver as well as CNT General Secretary Mariano Vasquez rushed to Barcelona. The battle raged for four days, leaving 233 dead and a thousand wounded. Both sides considered it a defensive action, but the large casualty toll attests to the extreme bitterness that led to the execution of many prisoners. UGT General Secretary Antoni Sese was killed while en route to the Generalitat headquarters to assume his post as councillor in the newly formed emergency government. Montseny and Vasquez narrowly escaped death. Numerous outspoken anti-Stalinists were singled out for assassination by agents of the Russian NKVD, among them the Italian anarchist Camillo Berneri and Alfredo Martínez, head of the Libertarian Youth. Marc Rhein, a politically neutral foreign correspondent, was spirited away and presumably killed by NKVD agents because he was the son of exiled Menshevik leader Rafael Abramovitch.

By May 6 the POUM directed its militants to lay down their arms, and the uprising came to an end the following day. With its conclusion a political watershed had been reached. The May events marked the eclipse of the revolutionary Left and of trade union power. The ensuing erosion of anarcho-syndicalist strength also made it possible for the Valencia government to curtail the powers of the Generalitat. The main beneficiary was the Communist party, which now was able to assume a preeminent role in Republican affairs.

The humiliating spectacle of a CNT leadership incapable of controlling its followers and the gulf its weakness revealed between an increasingly bureaucratized upper echelon and the restive grass roots could only damage the movement's political standing. Many in the leadership who had pushed for a quick cease-fire were later to regret having done so without first extracting adequate political guarantees. As the CNT's star fell, that of the PSUC rose. The new Generalitat government gave equal representation to the ERC and PSUC and provided the CNT with only a nominal presence. In reality, however, the PSUC had displaced the ruling ERC as the predominant regional political force.

The Barcelona incidents also provided the pretext for Largo's ouster.

Communist ministers stigmatized the POUM as responsible for the armed uprising, labeling the party an agent of Hitler and Franco. Largo defended the POUM, refusing to declare the party illegal and imprison its leaders. The CNT ministers were the only ones to side with Largo. When the two communist ministers withdrew in protest, Prieto and other socialist moderates together with the Republicans also resigned, causing the government to fall. Subsequent efforts by Largo to form a new government ended in failure.

The Revolution Throttled

The new government took office on May 17 with socialist moderate Dr. Juan Negrín as premier. He also retained the post of finance minister, which he had occupied in the former government. Prieto assumed the newly created key slot of defense minister[60] with Julián Zugazoitia, another Prieto loyalist, taking over the Interior Ministry. Jésus Hernández and Vicente Uribe, the two communists, remained as ministers of education and agriculture. Republicans headed the Labor, Justice, and Foreign Affairs ministries. Both the UGT and CNT refused to take part. At the behest of the communists, the POUM was declared illegal, and on June 6 the party's leaders were imprisoned. POUM General Secretary Andrés Nin was seized by PCE and NKVD secret police and taken to a clandestine prison near Madrid, where he was tortured to extract a Moscow trials–style confession. When he refused to give in to his torturers, Nin was killed.

The savage persecution of the POUM at the hands of the PCE and Stalin's agents provided the more poignant aspect of its ultimate demise. Its political shortcomings also contributed to its downfall. At the beginning of the civil war the party seemed poised to emerge as one of the region's most potent political forces. Its leadership contained some of the brightest and most able men on the Spanish Left. Within a matter of weeks party membership rose from ten thousand to twenty to thirty thousand. But the initial promise soon began to fade.

The sudden loss of Joaquín Maurín was to have incalculable consequences. Maurín was in Galicia at the time of the July 18 insurgency and ended up spending most of the war in Francoist jails under an assumed name. Party leadership was then taken over by Andrés Nin, a man of considerable intellectual attainments and with an impressive background that included a prominent role in the CNT during the early 1920s, a number of years in Moscow as a secretary of the communist trade union international (Profintern), and as a leader of the Spanish Trotskyists, the Communist Left. But Nin and many on the POUM Executive Committee lacked the political acumen of a Maurín and generally tended to adopt relatively dogmatic political positions. A common failing that also prevailed in the socialist Left was not to consider Spanish political realities in their true light but to view them through the prism of the Russian October revolution. The POUM thus abdicated to the PSUC its great potential for becoming a broad leftist force—with predictable results.

Following his ouster Largo resumed an active role as UGT general secretary, but efforts to revitalize the socialist Left were unsuccessful. It had lost many of its original components. Much of the Socialist Youth had gone over to the PCE along with the Catalan sections of the PSOE and UGT. A number of Largo's trusted collaborators had defected to the communists. What remained were the party organizations of Madrid and Valencia and control of the UGT national and executive committees, but even these had become extremely vulnerable. Largo moved to form an alliance with the CNT. Fearing that a reconstituted trade union coalition could serve as a potential rallying center for malcontents, Prieto socialists and communists decided, once and for all, to assure Largo's downfall.

During Largo's final days in office the UGT Executive Committee had voted to withhold support from any government not headed by the aging labor leader. Negrín's designation consequently plunged the organization into acute controversy. A number of national federations under Prietista control challenged this policy. A rude rebuff was dealt *el viejo* (the old man) by a vote taken on May 28 during a special meeting of the national committee. It was decided by a vote of twenty-four to fourteen to censure the Executive Committee.[61] Shortly thereafter, a delegation visited Negrín to offer its support.

Largo then invalidated the vote, charging that a number of participating federations were in arrears in their dues payments and therefore ineligible to vote. Thirteen federations with some two hundred thousand members were suspended for failure to pay dues. An effort to call a special meeting of the national committee failed, and a delegation representing thirty dissident federations gathered in front of the UGT Valencia headquarters on October 1 but was refused entrance. The police then informed Largo that the delegation had government authorization to enter and meet. The delegates proceeded to meet and designated new national and executive committees, naming Prietista Ramón González Peña as chairman, José

Rodríguez Vega, secretary, and procommunist Felipe Pretel, treasurer. Most of the other members of the Executive Committee were Prietistas, and some were procommunists. The new committee was promptly recognized by the government and by the PSOE-PCE liaison committee. Not long thereafter the Interior Ministry suspended publication of *La Correspondencia de Valencia,* controlled by Largo's UGT supporters, and the Madrid daily *Claridad* was taken over by Prieto supporters.

Walter Citrine of the British Trades Union Congress and Léon Jouhaux of the French CGT, sent by the International Federation of Trade Unions to patch up the quarrel, found themselves in a difficult position. By temperament and ideology they felt closest to Prieto but shared Largo Caballero's animosity toward the communists. The compromise formula devised by Jouhaux that was adopted called for a new Executive Committee with representatives from both sides. González Peña and Rodríguez Vega would remain in the two principal posts and Largo would no longer be general secretary. To compensate for this loss, four Caballerists were added to the committee. Largo roundly rejected this cosmetic papering over of a surrender of control to Prieto and his communist allies.[62] A parallel effort undertaken by French socialist Vincent Auriol to effect a reconciliation between Negrín and Largo also foundered.

After the conflict had become public, Largo sought to rally support by holding congresses in the larger cities. Believing that his popularity was on the wane, the government at first acquiesced. But upon observing the huge turnout for his address in Madrid on October 17 and his biting criticisms of the Negrín government's policies, the government prohibited him from traveling and placed him under virtual house arrest, thus putting an end to the lengthy and eventful career of one of Spain's foremost working-class leaders.

Juan Negrín was a most improbable choice for prime minister. A member of a wealthy, pious Canary Island family, he had had a bourgeois upbringing, had traveled extensively in Europe, and had had a German education. He had never shown much interest in politics. Until the civil war, Broué and Témime tell us, he "had merely been a brilliant dilettante in politics."[63] He had succeeded his mentor, Nobel Prize winner Santiago Ramón y Cajal, to the prestigious chair of physiology at the University of Madrid. Like so many other distinguished intellectuals of his generation, little concerned with Marxist theorems and repelled by Republican pusillanimity and fragmentation, he joined the socialist movement during the late 1920s out of a sense of moral outrage over social injustices.

In spite of his political anonymity, a university reputation for enterprise—he had directed the construction of Madrid's university city—
merited his designation as finance minister in the Largo Caballero government as one of three Prietista representatives. While serving in that
post, he incurred the enmity of the CNT for his resolute opposition to
collectivization and his defense of private property.

His firm advocacy of Republican stability and his indefatigability made
him attractive to both moderates and communists. Communists preferred
him over Prieto, who, despite his flirtation with the PCE, had in the past
displayed anticommunist feelings. Prieto, in turn, was content to assume
the key post of defense minister, which gave him a vantage point from
which he hoped to serve as the power behind the throne. Negrín's irregular
working habits and his astonishing sensual appetites were counterbalanced
by great self-confidence, an acute intelligence, and an impressive vitality.
Because he was generally politically nonpartisan, he rapidly emerged as
a strong leader with near dictatorial powers. For a time at least, he seemed
to be the irreplaceable war leader.

Negrín was convinced that Republican survival depended on the creation of a strong centralized state and a return to political moderation.
With his communist allies he held that the revolution had seriously
damaged the alliance of workers and the middle classes upon which the
very life of the Republic depended. Thus freedom of worship and the
right to private property were reaffirmed. Lands seized in 1936 could be
reclaimed by their former owners, and the Catalonian collectivization
decree was suspended. By 1938 the centralization process had become so
pronounced that indignant Basque and Catalonian nationalists quit the
government. With a leader so firmly committed to moderation, hopes
rose, despite the extraordinary increase in communist strength, that France
and Great Britain would become more friendly toward the Republic.

To bring the anarchists to heel, a military expeditionary force under
the command of communist Major Enrique Lister was sent in August to
Aragon to dismantle the semiautonomous anarchist-controlled Council of
Aragon and to disband the agrarian collectives. Anarchists lost more
ground when police security in Barcelona was turned over to the communists and municipal councils replaced the CNT-FAI committees.

With Russia as the principal source of arms, his own party in shambles,
the Republicans in a comatose state, and his utter contempt for the
revolutionary Left, Negrín could see no alternative but to collaborate with
the PCE, the only disciplined, coherent, political force available. Despite

efforts to avoid too close an association with the communists, he had to give them considerable freedom and to suffer intolerable pressures from the PCE and Soviet military advisers. Communist power had reached extraordinary dimensions. Many ministries, much of the armed forces, and the police were in party hands, and even Negrín's personal staff included communist supporters. Hugh Thomas compares the relationship to that of Faust with Mephistopheles.[64]

Largo would not countenance repression of the POUM. Negrín, however, felt it necessary to submit to pressure, and in doing so cast an indelible stain on his moral stature. On June 21 formal charges were lodged against the POUM, including having slandered "a friendly country whose moral and material support had enabled the Spanish people to defend its independence" and, referring to the POUM's denunciation of the Moscow trials then under way, "for having attacked Soviet justice." Numerous political figures, including some in the PCE, were privately aghast at the clumsy forgery concocted by NKVD agents purporting to prove that POUM leaders were in connivance with Franco. Prieto and Justice Minister Manuel de Irujo unsuccessfully sought to restrict the charges to a political indictment of Poumists for their revolutionary opposition to the government. A pogrom was unleashed against Poumists, Trotskyists, anarcho-syndicalists, and other critics of the PCE.[65] The entire POUM leadership was imprisoned, its militias disbanded, and many of its militants persecuted or assassinated.[66] News of Nin's whereabouts was even kept from Negrín. Prisons in Madrid, Valencia, and Barcelona bulged with newly incarcerated anti-Francoists.

Parallel to the refashioning of the People's Army along more traditional military lines, the system of justice was tightened and the police given greatly expanded discretionary powers, making criticism of the government and the holding of oppositional rallies extremely difficult. As in former times, union meetings required prior authorization from the local delegate as public order and censorship became more binding. Increased censorship was especially instrumental in the UGT power struggle. Statements issued by Caballerist supporters could not be published, not even articles in the CNT press devoted to the subject.

Serious opposition to Negrín's sweeping centralizing measures failed to develop because by mid-1937 the Republic was enveloped by a sense of beleaguerment caused by a series of major military disasters, particularly the loss of the entire northern sector. Exhortations for a return to the revolutionary spirit of 1936 tended to fall on deaf ears. Many among even the most fervently revolutionary Cenetistas were now convinced that winning the war had to be given first priority.

The May events caused a marked decline in CNT influence, thus further exacerbating the libertarian movement's schizophrenia. The abandonment of some of its most cherished beliefs had not halted a steady political and organizational erosion. The goal of September 1936 to secure the formation of an all trade union government headed by Largo Caballero was now reduced to a humiliating entreaty to permit the two labor centers to take their places in the Negrín government, even as junior partners. The more enmeshed the movement became in the tawdry details of political power and responsibility the further it drifted from its ideological moorings.

To effect a healing process, in July 1937 the Catalonian Regional Confederation established political affairs committees at all organizational levels to deal with matters of political concern that stood outside the trade union ken. In such a highly politicized environment, these committees inevitably became the most powerful within the CNT, operating as veritable politburos.

Wartime centralization and government collaboration forced the CNT to take on the philosophy and characteristics of a traditional trade union movement. In August 1938 the CNT joined the newly constituted Labor Council, a government-sponsored joint labor-management body charged with the adjudication of labor relations disputes. In conformity with the decision of the 1931 Zaragossa congress, the national committee moved to abandon the organization's traditional federalist structure and form national trade and industry federations. The implementation of this plan was interrupted by the fall of Barcelona in January 1939.

Neither could the FAI escape the effects of the war. A plenum of "the specific organization" in July 1937 endorsed a sweeping organizational overhaul, converting it from a structure of loosely coordinated federations of affinity groups to something resembling a political party. The bastion of anarchist antipolitics found itself drawn into a political role. Nonetheless, the FAI remained essentially a small elite anarchist movement.[67]

Determined at all costs to gain entry into the Negrín government, the leaders of both the CNT and FAI, regarding it as the most efficacious means of fending off the aggressions of their enemies, displayed an uncharacteristic passivity during the violent dismantling of the Council of Aragon in August 1937. Nor did the divided Aragonese libertarians know how to respond. Encouraged by the anarcho-syndicalists' dilatoriness, communists redoubled their attacks, assassinating or jailing militants and forcing others to join the PCE. To bludgeon the CNT into submission, its military units were given few arms and little ammunition.

Government policy for a time was set through consultations between Azaña, Prieto, and Negrín. In March 1938, however, Negrín and Prieto became estranged over the latter's pessimism and his advocacy of a negotiated end to the war.[68] Communists demanded his removal as defense minister for his efforts to limit communist influence in the army and his balking at a proposed PSOE-PCE merger. The Bilbao socialist leader, who had served as the communist catspaw in expediting Largo's ouster, now found himself the subject of a similar political vendetta.

Although Prieto had personally directed the disbanding of the Council of Aragon, the CNT hastened to offer its support against its hated communist rivals.[69] Prieto's departure would signify an even more difficult time for confederal army units and a further intensification of communist harassment.[70] Anarcho-syndicalists, with his cooperation and that of other moderates, were prepared to take whatever steps were necessary to oust Negrín and his communist cronies. Prieto demurred, declaring that since the war was already lost such an action would be pointless.

The failure to topple Negrín and his communist allies meant that the only remaining alternative was to gain admission to the Negrín cabinet. Following the Nationalist breakthrough on the Aragon front, the prime minister urgently needed to bolster his political base. In preparation for their accession, a pact was made several weeks earlier with the UGT establishing a permanent liaison committee. The UGT pledged to support CNT entry into the government and formal recognition of what remained of the collectivizations. The CNT, FAI, and UGT were also admitted to the Popular Front, which functioned as a quasi-governmental body. The new cabinet that was formed on April 6 dropped Prieto as defense minister (Negrín took over) and included UGT chairman Ramón González Peña as justice minister and Cenetista Segundo Blanco in the inconsequential post of health minister. For the sake of appearances the PCE was given only one ministry.

A rapprochement between a bitterly anticommunist CNT, much closer in spirit to Largo and the socialist Left, with a UGT in the hands of Negrín socialists and procommunists seems paradoxical. The reason was the gravity of the military situation. Ever since mid-1937 the situation of Republican forces had grown increasingly bleak. In September of that year the entire northern front fell to the enemy, and from December 1937 to February 1938 failed offensives in Belchite and Teruel had resulted in great losses of matériel and manpower. In March 1938, while the CNT was negotiating its return to government, the Aragon front collapsed. Then came the fall of Lérida and Nationalist takeover of the Mediterranean fishing town of Vinaroz. The Republican counterattack on the Ebro to prevent the Nationalist seizure of Valencia, a massive engagement that lasted from July to October 1938, though initially successful, so drained men and matériel as to leave the Republican army too weakened to fend off subsequent Nationalist offensives. The CNT's reintegration in the government, therefore, was not only a defensive move to ward off communist persecution but a demonstration of national unity in the face of the military threat. It did little to improve military prospects, but it brought relief from the harassment of Cenetistas and allowed the CNT greater latitude in conducting organizational activities.

Differences within the movement sharpened, particularly in the wake of the May events, and the confederation was plagued by its habitual lack of cohesion and discipline. To resolve these problems the CNT, FAI, and Libertarian Youth held a joint regional conference on April 2, 1938, at which they agreed to form a unified directing committee of the Catalan Libertarian Movement vested with supreme authority over virtually all aspects of military and domestic activities. The CNT national committee objected, claiming that such an "authoritarian" initiative violated essential libertarian principles.

A further attempt to overcome internal differences and improve coordination took place at a national plenum held in Barcelona during late October. Three propositions were debated: (1) participation by all component parts of the movement in political activities; (2) formal conversion of the FAI into a political party that would represent the libertarian movement in government; or (3) renunciation of participation in government.[71]

Most agreed with the first premise, but the second, supported primarily by former CNT General Secretary Horacio Prieto, was rejected by many militants even though for all practical purposes the FAI was already functioning as a political party in all but name. The third proposition was supported by only a small minority of extremist youth leaders.

As was customary in such gatherings, a pro forma unanimity prevailed in the adoption of resolutions, which did little to dissipate antagonisms within the movement or to foster cohesion. Differences between CNT and FAI leaders remained as unresolved as ever. Overshadowing differences over politicization of the FAI and other doctrinal issues were the sharp divergences between the two organizations over military prospects and Negrín's strategy of resistance to the bitter end. CNT General Secretary Mariano Vasquez and minister Segundo Blanco were ardent supporters of the embattled prime minister, but many in the FAI, led by Abad de Santillan, opposed him. Anchluss in Austria, the invasion of Czechoslovakia, and the general European climate of appeasement foredoomed any hope for rescue by the Western nations. The war had become a lost cause. Faistas favored a negotiated peace arranged by Great Britain.

Negrín's strategy to gain support from the Western powers contained a self-defeating flaw. For both domestic and international reasons he had to rely heavily on communist support. But the resulting spectacular expansion of PCE power and the party's use of brutal Stalinist methods deeply alienated the noncommunist Left. Furthermore, the impression of an increasingly Stalinized Republican zone did little to enhance the Negrín government in diplomatic circles.

During May 1938 Negrín issued his famous "thirteen points" designed to curry favor with the Western democracies and to establish the terms for a negotiated peace. These points announced the government's intention to establish a modern Western "bourgeois" democracy, the right to private property, encouragement of business enterprise, and a broad war amnesty. The CNT gave its support, but Negrín's partiality toward the communists, permitting them further to strengthen their military dominance, rankled anarcho-syndicalists. The decline of Esquerra in Catalonia and the increasingly dominant role of the PSUC prevented the CNT's return to the Generalitat government.

By the end of the year the government's situation had gone from bad to worse. In a desperate attempt to win the favor of Western governments, a withdrawal of the International Brigades began in September. In December Franco's forces launched their Catalonian offensive against a smaller, ill-equipped Republican defending army. The fall of Barcelona on January 26 led to the mass exodus of more than half a million combatants and civilians who sought refuge in France. Azaña crossed the Pyrennees and resigned as president. After fleeing Barcelona, which had served as the Republican capital since October 1937, Negrín returned on February 10 to what remained of the Republican zone, seeking to rally the populace to continue resistance while still hoping for a last-minute change in the Allied attitude and the commencement of World War II. This policy was supported in the cabinet only by the communists. A reassignment of military commands on March 2 further strengthening the communist grip on the army proved to be the last straw.

Two days later, a coup led by Colonel Segismundo Casado, Julián Besteiro, General Miaja, and others, with the support of the UGT, CNT, all within the PSOE except Negrín supporters, the Syndicalist party, and Republicans, assumed control of Madrid. Negrín's collaboration with the communists had generated a deep bitterness in socialist ranks, especially in Madrid and Valencia. A bloody clash between communist-controlled units and those under the command of Faista Cipriano Mera ended in the rout of the former.

Casado and Besteiro's attempt to negotiate an honorable conclusion to the war was contemptuously rejected by a triumphant Franco, who insisted upon total capitulation. As the resistance collapsed, most of its leaders left Spain. Julián Besteiro stoically refused to join them and spent his last days in a Francoist prison. The Nationalists entered Madrid on March 28, thus bringing to an end the most searing national ordeal experienced by the Spanish people.

EPILOGUE

The consequences of defeat were felt mostly by workers and their organizations that had ardently supported the Republic. Trade union militants and members were singled out for vindictive persecution. Efforts by the CNT and UGT to maintain a clandestine presence met with savage repression. Many activists and leaders were subjected to torture, execution, and long prison terms. Between 1939 and 1954 seventeen national committees of the CNT and seven of the UGT were apprehended, and by the early 1950s both organizations had been reduced to scattered, ineffective groups. Those in exile, meanwhile, engaged in bitter recriminations over responsibility for the defeat and acrimonious disputes over anti-Franco opposition policies, leading to splits in both organizations. Demoralization was further abetted by a shattered economy, extreme hardships, and mass deprivation. The 1940s were the "years of hunger." During the five years following the conclusion of the civil war, the number of deaths from malnutrition and disease exceeded the pre–civil war mortality rate by two hundred thousand.

The authoritarian corporative labor structure that was instituted had as its primary purposes the imposition of social discipline and monitoring of a suspect working class. The authority of employers was reinforced and strikes categorized as seditious offenses. The regulation of industrial relations and setting of wages became an exclusive government prerogative, inspired by Falangist notions concerning the establishment of a national syndicalist state, social Catholicism, the Italian Carta dal Lavoro of 1927, and the 1933 Portuguese Estatuto do Trabalho Nacional. The Labor Charter of March 1938 established joint labor-management "vertical syndicates," not for the purpose of defending workers' interests but as "instruments of the state" under the direct supervision of the Ministry of Trade Union Organization and Action.

In the distribution of political spoils among the various elements supporting the Franco regime, the Falange was given exclusive jurisdiction over the corporative National Syndical Centers (CNS), which both employers and wage earners were required to join. Offices in the vertical syndicates were reserved for militants and fellow travelers of the Falange, and numerous prewar social Catholics, who converted to Falangism, were given important posts in the ministry. A 1940 reorganization creating the dictatorship's unique party, the Movimiento Nacional, converted the CNS (now renamed the Spanish Syndical Organization—OSE) into its labor arm.

Franco wished for a docile, submissive syndical organization with the result that the OSE had far less power than its counterparts in Peronist Argentina or fascist Italy. Efforts by some Falangists to afford the OSE a semiautonomous, populist appearance were repressed. Thenceforward labor representation consisted largely of a bureaucratic machine in the hands of a Labor Ministry–OSE army of thirty-five thousand self-serving, often corrupt political hacks, described by one observer as a "bureaucratic mastodon." To make up for the lack of collective bargaining representation, workers were given family allowances, and the 1944 Law of Labor Contracts made it almost impossible for employers to discharge them.

The OSE was viewed by many workers as a government agency favoring employers. It was able to dominate them but incapable of exerting any real influence, especially in the traditional strong trade union areas of Barcelona, Vizcaya, and Asturias. To overcome its lack of credibility, some Falangists and renegade Cenetistas sought to persuade the CNT to become part of the official labor structure. Joan Peiró, who was turned over to the Franco government by Vichy French authorities in 1942, was given the choice of supporting the OSE or being executed. The CNT rejected the overtures, and Peiró chose integrity and death.

Shop-level representation for a long period was practically nonexistent. *Jurados de empresa* (works councils) were established in 1947 but given only consultative powers. Company executives chaired the *jurados,* which did not become operational until 1953. *Enlaces sindicales* (shop stewards), whose selection had been limited to members of the Falange, were chosen after 1950 through enterprise elections. As the economy began to show signs of improvement in the 1950s, the combined effects of spiraling inflation, workers' eroding purchasing power, and government actions permitting employers to negotiate informal accords with their employees fueled outbursts of discontent among workers, most notably in Barcelona and Vizcaya. At the same time the dissent among students that was to haunt the regime throughout its remaining years began. Though there were some impressive displays of worker mobilization, strong repressive countermeasures and a few concessions prevented their extension. Nonetheless they served as harbingers of a wave of industrial strife that in the coming years was to sweep the country.

A dramatic turnabout came during the late 1950s stimulated by the introduction of a new system of labor relations. The Collective Bargaining Law of 1958 allowed *jurados* and *enlaces sindicales* to engage in plant-level contract bargaining with employers to determine wages and working conditions. It was part of a sweeping liberalization, an opening of the economy that featured abandonment of a defaulting autarkic economic policy to escape stagnation and to partake of the great prosperity and boom under way in Western Europe. It also represented an effort to defascizize Franco Spain to make it more acceptable to the outside world.

A massive influx of foreign capital investment and technology, the financial remittances of a million Spanish foreign workers, and the proceeds of a vastly expanded tourist industry fueled a spectacular industrialization that within a decade catapulted Spain into the company of Western European consumer societies. Industrial production and per capita income levels did not return to pre–civil war levels before the 1950s, but annual growth in gross national product from 1960 to 1965 reached 9.2 percent, the highest in Europe and second only to that of Japan. An accompanying demographic revolution transformed the country into a predominantly industrial, urban-oriented society. There were more people living in cities with populations exceeding twenty thousand by 1975 than in France. The fact that strikes by farm laborers, so prominent a part of the labor unrest of the 1930s, were nowhere to be seen in the bargaining conflicts of the 1960s and 1970s provided an eloquent testimonial to the sweeping changes under way.

Accelerated economic growth generated a host of social changes, especially a new generation of industrial wage earners who were younger, better educated, accustomed to a higher standard of living, and unaffected by the memories of the civil war. Most were immigrants from depressed rural regions. The workers' new aggressiveness was fostered by the fact that per capita growth and economic development in the early 1960s no longer depended on protectionism and wage squeezing but on achieving improved productivity, efficiency, and output. The new generation of workers, with their rising expectations, would no longer meekly accept authoritarian restraints, nor was the regime capable of accommodating to the exigencies of a modern industrial society. Wage earners were insistent upon gaining their share of the bounty promised by economic expansion.

Nor was the UGT or the CNT able to adapt to the new situation. The anarchists in particular proved unable to create an effective underground organizational structure and gradually disappeared, forced into an exile existence. And as the number of internal cadres grew smaller as a result of the brutal suppression directed against them, both movements became ever more isolated from the realities of a rapidly changing Spain. Increasingly the Socialist party became an exile organization. In 1968 a rival Socialist Party of the Interior led by Professor Enrique Tierno Galvan was formed. The initial impetus for the renewal came from two sources, the Catholic church and the Communist party.

The new collective bargaining system and the continued inability of the official unions to represent the workers adequately led to the grass-roots formation of independent workplace committees that dissolved after each bargaining round. From 1962 on these "workers commissions" began to assume a more stable, organized form. With the support of a wide spectrum of opposition groups, including the UGT and the left Catholic Unión Sindical Obrera (USO) as well as frustrated Falangists, the workplace committees were soon able to gain a collective bargaining role in a number of key industries. Industrial modernization and a more liberal labor relations system required effective worker representation, and employers had an interest in promoting wage agreements that increased productivity. Increased strike action was a logical concomitant of collective bargaining.

Some thought the grass-roots (*asembleario*) workers commissions movement had the potential to challenge the government unions. The communists saw them, however belatedly, as heralding a new unitary labor movement that might replace traditional organizations such as the UGT and CNT, thus enabling them, for the first time, to gain a predominant role in organized labor. And indeed, as the movement became more organized during the late 1960s, the communists gained a controlling position, prompting the UGT and then the USO to withdraw. The principal bone of contention between the UGT and the communists was the former's boycott strategy and the latter's infiltration tactic. The PCE's strategy proved successful as Comisiones Obreras (CCOO)–sponsored opposition slates emerged victorious in the metalworking plants of Madrid and Barcelona, though the UGT remained influential in Asturias and the Basque region, where the boycott policy received substantial support.

At first the government tolerated the workers commissions, and until 1968, when they were declared illegal, it permitted them to meet in OSE union halls. Policy makers were divided between those who thought they might invigorate an otherwise discredited official organization and the hard-liners wedded to a no-nonsense, get-tough attitude toward them. The growing strength of worker dissidence was evident in the September 1966 *jurados* elections, which registered a stunning breakthrough for the CCOOs. The government responded by launching an extensive crackdown in the late 1960s and early 1970s. Despite the crisis the CCOO experienced in those years, worker militancy continued undiminished. Mass jailings did not stem the work stoppages that officially numbered 777 in 1963, declining to 484 in 1964 and then mushrooming to 1,595 in 1970. Despite their continued illegality, close to 5,000 strikes took place from 1964 to 1974. Large wage gains were won, often exceeding official guidelines. Conflict was especially intense in the traditional labor zones of Barcelona, Madrid, Asturias, and the Basque provinces. Local and regional strikes, many of them with political overtones, were particularly widespread in 1973. The Franco regime expired amid an extraordinary display of proletarian assertiveness.

The response to mounting worker opposition and labor unrest was a combination of carrot and stick. "Troublemakers" were removed from the *jurados* (eighteen hundred from 1964 to 1966 alone), many leaders were given long prison sentences, and the mass firings of striking workers took place while, at the same time, employers assented to sizable wage settlements. Moderate reforms provided some autonomy to worker representatives on the shop floor and greater latitude for workers and employers within the OSE. Even the term *vertical syndicates* was dropped. Francoist conservatives balked at the reformist enthusiasm of Falangist labor boss José Solis. But reform was too little and came too late for it did little to stem the official unions' increasing irrelevancy. Only 16.6 percent of labor disputes were resolved by the OSE during 1963–64.

Suffering from an acute shortage of experienced militants, especially of the post–civil war generation, hobbled by perennial ideological cleavages, and experiencing great difficulties in coming to terms with life in a modern industrializing society, the CNT, after a brief period of clandestine reactivation in the late 1940s, lapsed into inconsequence. Its modest revival in Barcelona during the mid-1970s also fizzled out. In contrast, the UGT in company with the PSOE began to attract a new young generation of leadership during the 1960s that by 1974 wrested control of the movement from the aging civil war veterans in exile. From its surviving bases in the Basque region, Asturias, and parts of Andalusia, the UGT underwent a revival. Its subsequent expansion in the 1970s came in the wake of the emergence of the PSOE as the dominant party of the Left and the abrupt decline of communist influence. Socialist political hegemony and a more realistic trade union approach induced many workers, hitherto CCOO supporters, to transfer their loyalties to the UGT.

The strike wave that crested during 1974–76 took place at a time of huge increases in the price of imported Middle Eastern oil on which Spain was heavily dependent for its energy needs. It also spanned the death of Franco in November 1975 and the ensuing transition to democracy. The country's political elite was then engrossed with managing the passage to parliamentary rule and paid little attention to the deterioration of the economy. The provisional government felt too insecure politically to take unpopular austerity measures, especially since the sharp rise in inflation and reduced purchasing power came at a time of intense worker militancy. The workers reacted by aggressively pressing for big wage adjustments.

A further difficulty was that institutional change had not yet been sufficiently advanced to provide channels for orderly collective bargaining and to establish a consultative mechanism to forge consensual wage and general economic policy guidelines. Organized labor used its enhanced bargaining power to secure wage boosts that averaged 7 percent from 1974 to 1976, rising much more rapidly than the cost of living. The wage component in national income distribution rose between 1974 and 1977 by four percentage points.

The church, which had helped to legitimize the Franco regime, began in the 1960s to distance itself from the government. Modernization in Spanish Catholicism was encouraged by the Second Vatican Council and Popes John XXIII and Paul VI. As the belated *aggiornamiento* got under way, a growing number of priests and bishops openly called for the restoration of basic liberties. Cardinal-Primate Enrique Pla y Deniel, who had taken a leading role during the 1920s in organizing Catholic workers in Catalonia, publicly defended the right to strike and free labor organization. Various church-sponsored organizations, most notably the Young Christian Workers (JOC) and the Catholic Action Workers Brotherhood (HOAC), took the lead in the 1950s and early 1960s in the fight for workers' rights and trade union freedoms. Churches often served as sanctuaries for illegal meetings of dissident worker groups. Availing them-selves of the legal cover such organizations provided, numerous left-wing activists joined HOAC and other Catholic labor groups. A majority of bishops voted in 1971 to apologize publicly for the church's stance in the civil war.

The Communist party had abandoned armed guerrilla resistance during the early 1950s and shifted to a policy that stressed "boring from within." Unlike the socialists and anarcho-syndicalists, who refused to take part in plant elections as conferring legitimacy on the Francoist *jurados*, the PCE adopted a strategy of infiltrating the OSE at the lower levels. Its centralized structure and discipline, together with its superior financial means, placed the party in a good position to conduct such a tactic. Its main competitor in the early 1960s was the Catholic Action militants, who soon lost their leading role as the church hierarchy, under government pressure, reversed course and placed restraints on their activities. Fur-thermore, by the late 1950s the PCE was emerging as the leading force within the anti-Franco opposition.

After a decade of unparalleled expansion, a combination of ineffective government action to reverse the economic backslide, an excess of workers and production capacity in industry, falling profits, and the somber in-ternational economic climate joined in pushing the country into economic slump, inflation, and high unemployment.

To stem further decline, an economic package known as the Moncloa Pact was devised in October 1977 by the government and the opposition parties to hold wage increases below the rate of inflation. The persistence of economic recession and the critical situation confronting many firms led to a succession of implicit and explicit social contracts between gov-ernment, employers, and unions until 1986. Unions tended to trade off acceptance of wage restraint and enhanced productivity for improved job security and a promise to create more jobs.

Throughout most of the democratic transition, the two leading labor confederations have undergone a rude buffeting. The resounding failure of the Communist party's Eurocommunist strategy to assure its supremacy in the post-Franco Left led to a decimation and splintering of communist forces and a consequent debilitation of the Workers Commissions Con-federation. Furthermore, since gaining power in late 1982 the socialist government headed by Felipe González has been embroiled in an acri-monious dispute with the UGT that has also divided the ruling Socialist

Workers party. Nowhere in Europe has a socialist movement experienced such a bitter falling-out between the party leadership and its fraternally linked trade union organization. In its effort to accelerate economic modernization to prepare the country for greater competitiveness within the European Economic Community (EEC) by 1992 (Spain joined the EEC in 1986), when the EEC plans to eliminate remaining barriers to trade, employment, and the flow of capital across the twelve member states, government economic policy has encountered frequent reservations if not open opposition from the unions.

The economic boom of the late 1980s that gave Spain a 4.5 percent real growth in gross domestic product in 1987 and nearly the same in 1988, the highest in the EEC, has not been especially beneficial for the unions. After abandoning the economic austerity policy of the early 1980s in favor of expansion, the government gave priority to strengthening the productive infrastructure rather than social welfare. The financial burdens of private business were lightened to foster increased profitability, to encourage domestic capital investment, and to make Spain more competitive with its European counterparts. Popular purchasing power was to be maintained by lowering the inflation rate. Wages throughout the 1980s have lagged behind prices though business's share of net income rose from 10 to 14 percent. Bank profits in 1987 rose by 40 percent, and annual increases in private sector productivity from 1974 to 1986 were more than twice the Organization for Economic Cooperation and Development average. Impressive economic expansion has taken place but not without significant social costs.

An urgently needed industry reconversion program has been carried out in such key industries as steel, shipbuilding, textiles, and coal mining, which are also centers of union strength. The restructuring has led to the loss of 60,000 jobs at a time when Spain's unemployment rate is the highest in the EEC. The UGT has bitterly complained that the government has not done enough to create more jobs (370,000 new jobs were created in 1987, but 350,000 new job seekers entered the labor force) and that only 26 percent of the unemployed in mid-1988 were receiving unemployment benefits.

Unions also find themselves victimized by the need to eliminate rigidities in the labor market to enhance labor mobility. This is particularly galling because it involves the undoing at a time of extremely high joblessness of a Francoist paternalistic legacy that endowed workers with virtual lifetime job security. The inability of the unions to prevent this trend—it is required by EEC accords—is seen by many workers as a serious liability. Another effect of this liberalization has been a big increase in the number of temporary and part-time workers, from 15 percent of the labor force in April 1987 to 21 percent the following year, double the European average, a development that poses a worrisome threat to employment security and union wage standards.

This emphasis on reducing inflation, encouraging private investment, preventing increased labor costs from discouraging foreign capital investment (labor costs currently are half the EEC average), limiting social spending, restructuring industry, and readying the economy for open competition within the EEC left little room for a meaningful trade union role.

The net result is that although Spanish labor relations have been modernized and integration of unions within the economic and social fabric has been formally accomplished, an essential prerequisite remains unfulfilled. Unions lack sufficient weight and influence to represent the country's wage earners adequately. The singularity of post-Franco economic developments and the democratic transition have prevented unions from becoming full-fledged participants in social and economic affairs. Restraints on collective bargaining and gradually declining real wages since the late 1970s have produced a situation in which workers retain their trade union sympathies but rarely pay dues. A large part of the work force, 6 out of some 14 million, are covered by union wage agreements, but few carry union cards. A study commissioned by the EEC found the rate of unionization in 1989 to be only 11 percent.

This is not merely yet another instance of the general decline in union strength that has taken place everywhere among Western industrial nations since the economic recession of the 1970s. In Spain its roots go deeper for it is a manifestation of a developmental lag in the maturation of political and trade union consciousness. The low participatory rate is not unique to the unions. Membership in political parties is also the lowest in Western Europe. Nonetheless, on December 14, 1988, more than 7 million workers responded to a call for a twenty-four-hour work stoppage sponsored by the two labor confederations to protest government economic policies, making it the most imposing nationwide strike in more than half a century.

Democracy remains a novel experience for many Spaniards. The numbing effects of sociopolitical passivity inculcated during the four decades of dictatorial rule have not yet been totally dissipated. Nor has the relationship between trade unions and political parties attained the degree of maturity and sophistication that exists elsewhere in Europe. Political leaders all too often heretofore have tended to look upon kindred labor organizations as presumptuously submissive party appendages. Only when a broader popular participation occurs in the decision-making process can it be said that the consolidation of the democratic renewal has truly been accomplished.

BIBLIOGRAPHIC ESSAY

As with so much else in Spain, labor history has been a late bloomer. The civil war and the ensuing four decades of authoritarian rule inhibited research on labor history. To engage in such studies was regarded by the police as politically suspect, access to original sources was extremely limited, and all published work was subject to official censorship. Only a small fraction of the files of labor organizations and leading participants was spirited out of the country. Most such records were either destroyed to avoid confiscation by advancing Francoist military forces or subsequently seized by the authorities.

Records of local, regional, and national UGT and CNT organizations that fell into Francoist hands were mostly turned over to a military archive established in the city of Salamanca. Some were also placed in the National Military Archive of Madrid. For many years this material could not be consulted by outside researchers and was primarily used by the police to identify Republican and trade union supporters. Numerous documents considered of little use in this endeavor but of great historical value were destroyed. The Salamanca archive was opened during the 1960s to pro-Franco apologists, who selectively used its holdings in the preparation of proregime accounts of the civil war and other periods.

Documentation on earlier periods of Spanish labor history is equally sparse and contains important lacunae. Anyone who inspects the holdings of the National Historical Archive becomes immediately aware of this deficiency. Until very recently Spaniards did not overly concern themselves with the collection and preservation of historical material. To cite a few examples: in the past (and in the present as well) socialist leaders tended to regard party and UGT files as their personal property and to remove them to their private residences. The Ministry of Labor did not establish an archive section until 1930, and during the disastrous general strike of

October 1934 the government authorities seized UGT records, which subsequently disappeared, making the study of socialism in this and preceding periods all the more difficult. The decentralized organizational structure of the CNT and cavalier disregard for record keeping, fostered in part by the frequent seizure of union files by the authorities, has rendered research on anarcho-syndicalism a daunting venture. What is more, the internal correspondence and working papers of the Ministry of Labor during the 1920s, especially those of the Primo de Rivera dictatorship, were lost during the civil war.

Horror stories on the sorry fate of historical documents are legion. On a number of occasions I visited the library of the Ministry of Labor to which the records and files of the Institute of Social Reforms (1904–24) had been entrusted and which also contained rare holdings. When I tried to locate various items listed in the library's catalog, attendants informed me that many documents and books had been removed by ministry functionaries and never returned.

As the authoritarian regime became less repressive in its final decade and with political, cultural, and labor dissidence on the rise, historical research on the labor movement commenced in earnest. Encouraged by Spain's most eminent historian, Jaime Vicens Vives, young Barcelona scholars such as Father Casamiro Martí, Albert Balcells, and Josep Termes, making use of local and foreign archives and interviews with surviving union militants, produced trail-blazing monographs on such key themes as the origins of anarchism, the Barcelona trade union movement of the early 1920s, and the Spanish Regional Organization of the First International (FRE). Equally talented specialists from the faculties of the Madrid universities such as Manuel Pérez Ledesma, Juan José Castillo, José Alvarez Junco, and Antonio Elorza did further studies. Regional studies also began to appear; the most notable among them were those of Antonio Maria Calero Amor on Granada and Andalusia, David Ruiz on Asturias, and Juan Pablo Fusi and Ignacio Olábarri on the Basque region.

The 1970s were a halcyon time for the modestly growing band of labor specialists. Several first-rate monographs were produced, but many tended to be political statements rather than balanced evaluations. Writing labor history in the early 1970s was often construed as a political act in defiance of the regime. The quality of these works was marred by the difficulty in gaining access to original sources, a tendency to concentrate on the politics of trade union development and a consequent neglect of operational realities, the unavailability of adequate library resources and university financing to conduct field research, and a weak tradition of nonpartisan objective research; these and other factors made the preparation of high-quality studies an exceedingly arduous undertaking. It is truly remarkable that many excellent works were produced despite these obstacles.

A major stimulus came from the outside. The Center of Hispanic Studies at the University of Pau in France, where young historians and labor researchers from Franco's Spain could meet with fellow specialists commencing in 1969 and engage in exchanges under the aegis of the doyen of Spanish labor studies, Manuel Tuñon de Lara, played an important role. A succession of books were published in Spain starting in the 1970s containing the papers presented in seminar colloquiums at the University of Pau, many of them summaries of doctoral dissertations.

A key contribution was made by American Hispanists Joan Connelly Ullman, John Brademas, Gerald Meaker, and Edward Malefakis. Under the impetus of Raymond Carr, who was awarded a peership for his distinguished writing on Spanish contemporary history, Saint Anthony's College of Oxford University produced outstanding Spanish scholars such as Juan Pablo Fusi, Joaquín Romero Maura, Santos Juliá, and José Maria Maravall.

By the 1980s archival and foundation holdings became more accessible. The Pablo Iglesias Foundation, established by the Socialist Workers party, has become the principal repository for documents on Spanish socialism and the UGT. Arrangements are under way for the return to Spain of the important collection of papers of the CNT that has long been entrusted to the Amsterdam Institute of Social History. The Salamanca Civil War National Historical Archive is conducting a systematic inventory and cataloging its chaotically filed deposits.

Although facilities for conducting research are improving, the number of specialists engaged in the study of Spanish labor history has declined. The field no longer attracts as many young, earnest academics, and some labor historians have turned their attention to more academically rewarding fields or accepted positions with the socialist government as public office holders or civil servants. Those, however, who continue to work in this field and the small new generation of scholars no longer view the writing of labor history as an exercise in political vindication and tend to provide more balanced accounts of Spain's rich and complex labor past.

The General Socioeconomic Setting

For a general historical overview, especially on the nineteenth century, though written close to a quarter-century ago and thus unable to benefit from writing and research conducted in the intervening years, Raymond Carr's *Spain, 1808–1939* (Oxford: Oxford University Press, 1966; partially revised in 1982) remains unsurpassed. More recent studies include Miguel Martínez Cuadrado, *La burguesia conservadora (1874–1931)* (Madrid: Alianza, 1973); *Historia de España*, vol. 8, *Revolución, oligarchia, y constitucionalismo (1834–1923)*, edited by Manuel Tuñon de Lara (Barcelona: Editorial Labor, 1981); and *Historia de España*, vol. 37, *Los comienzos del siglo XX, la población, la economía, la sociedad (1895–1931)* (Madrid: Espasa-Calpe, 1984), also edited by Tuñon de Lara.

Jordi Nadal's *Spain, 1830–1914,* in the Fontana Economic History of Europe series, *The Emergence of Industrial Societies*, vol. 2, pt. 2 (London: Fontana/Collins, 1977), is an edited version of his now classic "El fracaso de la revolución industrial en España, 1814–1913." *Historia agraria de la España contemporanea*, vol. 2, *Expansion y crisis (1850–1900)*, edited by Ramon Garrabou and Jesús Sanz (Barcelona: Crítica, 1985), a more recent examination, should be read in conjunction with Pascual Carrión's older, definitive *Los latifundios en España: Su importancia, origen, consequencias y solución* (Madrid: Graficas Reunidas, 1932).

Possibly the best among recent general economic works is *La modernización económica de España, 1830–1930,* edited by Nicolás Sánchez Albornoz (Madrid: Alianza, 1985). Surveys in English are Sima Lieberman, *The Contemporary Spanish Economy: A Historical Perspective,* (London: Allen & Unwin, 1982), and Joseph Harrison, *The Spanish Economy in the Twentieth Century* (New York: St. Martin's Press, 1985).

General Labor History

The single most important gap in the literature on Spanish labor is the absence of an up-to-date, comprehensive historical survey. The only such work is Manuel Tuñon de Lara's three-volume *El movimiento obrero en la historia de España* (Barcelona: Laia, 1972), which covers the period 1832 to 1936. Though unique and a pioneering contribution to labor historiography, it suffers from a number of defects. It was published before the current substantive progress in monographic research had taken place.

It also displays a procommunist bias, and Tuñon de Lara's treatment of the anarcho-syndicalist movement leaves much to be desired.

Another major lack is a bibliographical compilation that incorporates the considerable body of published and unpublished work that has appeared during the past two decades. All that is available is *Bibliografía dels moviments socials a Catalunya, país Valencia, i les illes* under the joint editorship of Emili Giralt i Raventós, Albert Balcells, Alfons Cucó, and Josep Termes, published by Editorial Lavinia of Barcelona, but it dates back to 1972. The path-breaking study by Renée Lamberet, *Mouvements ouvriers et socialistes, chronologies et bibliographie, L'Espagne, 1750–1936* (Paris: Editiones Ouvrieres, 1953) is valuable for its bibliographic references on anarchism and anarcho-syndicalism, but the author's death prevented its updating and reissuance.

Among works devoted to the history of an individual movement Josep Termes's *Anarquismo y sindicalismo en España, la primera internacional (1864–1881)* (Barcelona: Crítica, 1972) remains the definitive study of the Federacion Regional Español as does Miguel Izard's *Industrialización y obrerismo, las Tres Clases de Vapor, 1869–1913* (Barcelona: Ariel, 1973). The doctoral dissertation of Manuel Pérez Ledesma that covers the UGT from inception in 1888 to the advent of the Second Republic in 1931, "La Union General de Trabajadores: Ideologia y organización (1888–1931)" (Madrid Autonomous University, 1976) is the major source. His collected essays, *El obrero consciente* (Madrid: Alianza, 1987), mainly deal with the early period of socialist trade unionism. A useful complement is *Historia de la Union General de Trabajadores (U.G.T.), 1888–1931* by Javier Aisa and V. M. Arbeloa (Bilbao: Zero, 1974). The two-volume *Historia de la UGT de España (1901–1939)* (Barcelona: Grijalbo, 1977), by Amaro del Rosal, a former left socialist turned communist leader of the UGT in the 1930s, can be profitably consulted but is often a subjective, self-serving interpretation. Juan José Morato's *El Partido Socialista Obrero, génesis, doctrina, hombres, organización, desarrollo, acción, estado actual* (1918, rpt. Madrid: Editorial Ayuso, 1976) is a prime source on the early years of the socialist trade union movement. Of equal if not greater importance is his *La cuna de un gigante: Historia de la Asociación General del Arte de Imprimir*, first published in 1925 and reissued in 1984 by the Ministry of Labor. Also of interest is his *Lideres del movimiento obrero español, 1868–1921*, edited by Victor Manuel Arbeloa (Madrid: Cuadernos Para el Dialogo, 1972). Antonio Elorza's essay "Socialismo y agitación popular en Madrid (1908–

1920)," *Estudios de Historia Social,* nos. 18–19, vols. 3–4 (1981) examines a little studied period in UGT history. On Pablo Iglesias, who shaped the philosophy and activity of the socialist movement during the first four decades of its existence, there is *Pablo Iglesias, escritos y discursos, antologia crítica,* with an introductory essay by Enrique Moral Sandoval (Madrid: Salvora, 1984).

The closest approximation to a full-length history of anarcho-syndicalism is César M. Lorenzo's *Les anarchistes espagnols et le pouvoir, 1868–1939* (Paris: Editions du Seuil, 1969), much of which is devoted to the 1930s and the civil war period. Though it is a work of major importance, some of the writer's judgments tend to justify and support the positions taken by his father, Horacio Prieto, who was a leading CNT figure during the years of the Second Republic. An important work on the evolution of anarchist ideas is José Alvarez Junco's *La ideologia política del anarquismo español (1868–1910)* (Madrid: Siglo XXI, 1976). Manuel Buenacasa, founder and leading figure of the CNT, is the author of the classic *El movimiento obrero español, 1886–1926* (1966; rpt. Madrid: Jucar, 1977). Barcelona labor activist Adolfo Bueso's two-volume *Recuerdos de un Cenetista, de la Semana Tragica (1909) a la Secunda Republica (1931)* (Barcelona: Ariel, 1976) contains interesting details and insights. José Peirats's three-volume *La CNT en la revolución español* (Paris: Ruedo Iberico, 1971) provides a valuable history of the CNT and its times from an anarchist perspective. Finally, Pere Gabriel Sirvent's doctoral dissertation, "Clase obrera i sindicats a Cataluyna, 1903–1920" (University of Barcelona, 1981), deals insightfully and informatively with the antecedents of the CNT and its history until 1920.

The Ministry of Labor's *Revista de Trabajo* occasionally published historical documents and studies during the 1960s and early 1970s. Since 1977 the *Estudios de Historia Social* has been the leading journal devoted to labor and social historical subjects.

The Nineteenth Century

A vital source on labor conditions in the late nineteenth century is the five volumes that contain the oral and written testimony presented to the Social Reforms Commision, 1889–93, and reissued in facsimile by the Ministry of Labor in 1987 under the title *Reformas sociales.* For working-class life in Madrid there is Carmen de Moral's *La sociedad Madrileña fin de siglo y Baroja* (Madrid: Turner, 1974). Juan Pablo Fusi's *Política obrera en el pais Vasco (1880–1923)* (Madrid: Turner, 1975) contains a section on life and labor in Bilbao and Vizcaya. Adrian Shubert's *Hacia la revolución, origenes sociales del movimiento obrero en Asturias (1860–1934)* (Barcelona: Crítica, 1984) includes a useful discussion of the social origins and working conditions of Asturian coal miners until October 1934 (there is also an English-language edition). The sections of Joaquín Romero Maura's *La rosa del fuego, republicanos y anarquistas: La política de los obreros Barceloneses entre el disastre colonial y la Semana Tragica, 1899–1909* (Barcelona: Grijalbo, 1974) that detail Barcelona working-class life at the turn of the century are also applicable for earlier decades.

For social reform and labor legislation recommended studies are those of Manuel R. Alarcon Caracuel, *El derecho de asociación obrera en España (1839–1900)* (Madrid: Revista de Trabajo, 1975); Luis Enrique de la Villa and M. Carlos Palomeque, *Introdución a la economía de trabajo,* vol. 1 (Madrid: Editorial Debate, 1978); and M. Carlos Palomeque, *Derecho del trabajo i ideologia: Medio siglo de derecho de trabajo español, 1873–1923* (Madrid: Akal, 1980). On social reform, Santiago Castillo's introductory essay to the five-volume compendium of submissions to the Social Reforms Commission (1883–94) is particularly useful not only for the information he provides but for his depiction of the climate and mentality of the times. Also useful are Ramon Casteras, *Actitudes de los sectores Catalanes en la coyunctura de los años 1880* (Barcelona: Anthropos, 1985), and Alfredo Montoya Melgar's *Ideologia y lenguaje en las primera leyes laborales de España* (Madrid: Civitas, 1975).

Accounts dealing with rural social and labor organization in the late nineteenth and early twentieth centuries are to be found mostly interspersed in works dealing with broader themes such as anarchism, labor movement studies of the period, and regional and economic studies. A pioneer in studying rural labor conditions was Bernaldo de Quiros, whose writings on the subject include reports he drafted for the Institute of Social Reforms early in this century on the plight of Andalusian farm laborers. His two most well-known works are *El bandolerismo Andaluz* (1933; rpt. Madrid: Turner, 1973), and *El espartaquismo agrario Andaluz* (1919; rpt. Madrid: La Revista de Trabajo, 1978). This edition also includes material on the social problems of Andalusia.

Gerald Brenan's *The Spanish Labyrinth* (Cambridge: Cambridge University Press, 1943) is an often brilliant evocation, despite occasional misinterpretations and factual inaccuracies, of late nineteenth- and early twentieth-century Spanish sociopolitical life. Though primarily focused on the province of Córdoba, Juan Díaz del Moral's *Historia de las agitaciónes campesinas* (1929; rpt. Madrid: Alianza, 1979) is one of the authentic classics of Spanish social history and contains much information and commentary on labor organization and peasant protest in the entire Andalusian area. The leading historian on labor in Andalusia currently is Antonio Maria Calero Amor, who has written a short but informative survey entitled *Movimientos sociales en Andalusia (1820–1936)* (Madrid: Siglo XXI, 1976). Also of interest is Temma Kaplan's controversial *Anarchists of Andalusia, 1868–1903* (Princeton: Princeton University Press, 1977), which discusses the anarchist-led peasant labor movement in Cádiz province. Though Edward Malefakis's outstanding *Agrarian Reform and Peasant Revolution in Spain* (New Haven: Yale University Press, 1970) is primarily concerned with the period of the 1930s, it also contains a good deal of material and data on the earlier decades. Antonio Miguel Bernal, a specialist in Andalusian agrarian history and social struggles, is the author of *La propiedad de la tierra y las luchas agrarias andaluzas* (Barcelona: Ariel, 1974). José Varela Ortega's *Los amigos políticos: Partidos, elecciónes y caciquismo en la Restauración (1875–1900)* (Madrid: Alianza, 1977) is particularly good in its portrayal of Castilian rural life, social structures, and labor organization.

Many regional studies have been published over the past two decades, inspired in part by the decentralization of ruling authority since the end of the Franco regime. By far the greatest number have come from Catalonia. Especially worthy of mention is Albert Balcells's *Historia contemporanea de Cataluña* (Barcelona: Edhasa, 1983), which not only provides a general historical survey of the region but includes substantial material on social and labor developments from the early nineteenth century to the end of the civil war. J. M. Huerta Claverias has produced a labor history handbook, *Obrers en Catalunya* (Barcelona: L'Avenc, 1982). Xavier Cuadrat's *Socialismo y anarquismo en Cataluña (1899–1911); Los origenes de la CNT* (Madrid: Ediciónes de la Revista de Trabajo, 1976) is a solid contribution. The works of Joan Connelly Ullman and Joaquín Romero Maura (see the next section) contain abundant references to the turn-of-the-century years. Pere Gabriel Sirvent's dissertation, "Clase obrera i sindicats a Catalunya, 1903–1920," is the outstanding study on this subject.

The Basque region boasts two first-rate books, those of Juan Pablo Fusi, *Política obrera en el pais vasco, 1880–1923* (Madrid: Turner, 1975), surely one of the two or three best labor studies in recent years, and

Ignacio Olábarri's *Relaciónes laborales en Vizcaya (1890–1936)* (Durango: Leopoldo Zugaza, 1978). The more recent monograph by Antonio Rivera Blanco, *Situación y comportamiento de la clase obrera en Vitoria (1900–1915)* (Vitoria: Universidad de Pais Vasco, 1985), is an original investigation by a young scholar.

The excellent *Hacia la revolución* by Adrian Shubert deals primarily with the evolution of trade unionism among Asturian coal miners. Also worthy of mention is Enrique Moradiello's *El sindicato de los obreros mineros de Asturias, 1910–1930* (Universidad de Oviedo, 1986). Antonio Maria Calero Amor's major work is his *Historia del movimiento obrero en Granada (1909–1936)* (Madrid: Tecnos, 1973), which is rightly regarded as one of the finest monographic studies of its kind. An overview of Valencian labor history is provided by *Trabajadores, sin revolución; La clase obrera valenciana, 1868–1936*, by Xavier Paniagua and José A. Piqueras (Valencia: Edicions Alfons el Magnánim, 1986). Labor in Aragon is dealt with in "Historia del socialismo en Aragon PSOE-UGT (1879–1936)" by Luis G. German, Santiago Castillo, Ignacio Baron, and Carlos Forcadell (Departamento de historia económica, Universidad de Zaragossa, 1979).

The Tragic Week and Prewar Labor Developments in Catalonia

In addition to Pere Gabriel's dissertation, the two best researched works on this period are Joaquín Romero Maura's *La rosa del`fuego* and Joan Connelly Ullman's *The Tragic Week: A Study in Anticlericalism in Spain, 1875–1912* (Cambridge, Mass.: Harvard University Press, 1968) (an expanded Spanish edition appeared in 1972). An interesting firsthand account comes from veteran labor activist Adolfo Bueso, *Como fundamos la CNT* (Barcelona: Avance, 1976).

Labor and the Catholic Church

José Manuel Cuenca Toribio has written extensively on the contemporary church. His *Aproximación a la historia de la iglesia contemporanea en España* (Madrid: Rialp, 1978) is especially useful. The best work in English is that of William J. Callahan, *Church, Politics, and Society in Spain, 1750–1894* (Cambridge, Mass.: Harvard University Press, 1984). Among the noteworthy studies on church social and labor policies are José Andres

Gallego's *Pensamiento y acción social de la iglesia en España* (Madrid: Espasa-Calpe, 1984): Feliciano Montero Garcia, *El primer católicismo social y la Rerum Novarum en España (1889–1902)* (Madrid: CISC, 1983); Domingo Benavides Gómez, *Democracia y cristianismo en las España de la Restauración, 1875–1931* (Madrid: Editora Nacional, 1978) and *El fracaso social de católicismo español, Arboleya Martinez, 1870–1951* (Barcelona: Nova Terra, 1973). The leading authority on confessional unionism is Juan José Castillo, and his principal works are *El sindicalismo amarillo en España* (Madrid: Edicusa, 1977) and *Proprietarios muy pobres, sobre la subordinación política del pequeño campesino en España (La Confederación Nacional Católico-Agraria, 1917–1943)* (Madrid: Servicio de Publicaciónes Agrarias, Ministerio de Agricultura, 1979).

Labor's Coming of Age, 1915–1923

The best single general work on this period is Gerald H. Meaker's *The Revolutionary Left in Spain, 1914–1923* (Palo Alto: Stanford University Press, 1974). Juan Antonio Lacomba's *La crisis española de 1917* (Madrid: Ciencia Nueva, 1970) provides useful background. On economic developments we have the solidly researched work of Santiago Roldan and José Luis García Delgado, *La formación de sociedad capitalista, 1914–1920*, 2 vols. (Madrid: CEIC, 1973).

Labor developments in Barcelona and Catalonia are dealt with in three first-rate works: Albert Balcells, *El sindicalisme a Barcelona (1916–1923)* (Barcelona: Nova Terra, 1965) (a Spanish-language version also exists) (see also relevant sections in his more recent *Historia contemporanea de Cataluña*); Pere Gabriel's dissertation; and Manuel Lladonoso, *El congres de Sants* (Barcelona: Nova Terra, 1975). Until a full-length study of Salvador Seguí is undertaken, we have to be content with dispersed writings. Most notable among them is the portrait-essay in Pere Foix's *Apostols i mercaders, quaranta anys de lluita social a Catalunya* (Mexico City: Edicións de la Fundación Sara Llorens de Serra, 1957). It also contains a particularly arresting portrayal of Angel Pestaña. Foix worked closely with both men in the leadership of the CNT. Of collateral utility is Salvador Seguí, *Escrits*, edited by Isidre Molas, who also provides an introductory essay (Barcelona: Edicións 62, 1972). For the general mood of the times see the recollections of a CNT leader in Joaquim Ferrer, *Simó Piera: Perfil d'un sindicalista;* and *Simó Piera: Records i experiencies d'un dirigent de la CNT* (Barcelona: Portic, 1975). Of inestimable importance are Angel Pestaña's reminiscences, "Lo que aprendi en la vida," written in 1933, in his *Trayectoria sindicalista* (Madrid: Tebas, 1974).

Pascual Carrión's celebrated *Los latifundios en España* (Madrid: Graficas Reunidas, 1932) provides the agro-socioeconomic setting of the 1918–20 Bolshevist Triennium, especially in the rural south. Manuel Tuñon de Lara in his *Luchas obreras y campesinas en la Andalucia del siglo XX; Jaen (1917–1920), Sevilla (1930–1932)* (Madrid: Siglo XXI, 1978) examines the events of this period in the province of Jaen; José Manuel Macarrro analyzes similar developments in the city of Seville in his *Conflictos sociales en la ciudad de Sevilla en los anos 1918–1920, seis estudios sobre el proletariado Andaluz (1868–1932), II premio de investigación "Diaz del Moral," sobre historia social de Andalucia (S. XIX–XX)* (Córdoba: Ayuntamiento de Córdoba, 1984). Malefakis, Calero Amor, Diaz del Moral, and Brenan also devote sections of their works to this period.

Meaker's book is particularly good on the UGT and the socialist movement, and Manuel Pérez Ledesma's dissertation includes an extended discussion of the early years of the UGT and its evolution in this period. Juan José Morato's *El Partido Socialista Obrero* furnishes a firsthand testimonial. Of interest also are relevant sections of Tuñon de Lara's *El movimiento obrero en la historia de España,* vol. 2, and the works of Calero Amor, Juan Pablo Fusi, and Juan Díaz del Moral.

The convulsive labor conflicts in Barcelona during 1919–23 are best treated in Balcells's *El sindicalisme en Barcelona.* A detailed account of the famous La Canadiense strike and its aftermath can be found in the two books of E. G. Solano, *El sindicalismo en la teoria y en la practica* and *El ocaso de sindicalismo, secunda parte* (Barcelona: Bauza, 1922). The social Catholic Burgos y Mazo, who served as interior minister, recounts his efforts at pacification in *Para otras paginas: El verano de 1919 en gobernación* (Cuenca: Emilio Pinos, 1921). Jésus Pabon's excellent *Cambó,* vol. 2 (Barcelona: Alpha, 1969), devotes considerable space to a discussion of the Barcelona labor wars and Cambó's role. Labor terrorism of the early 1920s has inspired a considerable literature, possibly the most fascinating and informative of which is the account of Angel Pestaña that is recounted in his "Lo que aprendi en la vida." An earlier work of his on this subject written in 1923, somewhat more guarded and less candid but of interest, is *Terrorismo en Barcelona* (Barcelona: Planeta, 1979), with a lengthy introduction by Javier Tussell. Colin Winston's *Workers and the Right in Spain, 1900–1930* (Princeton: Princeton University Press, 1985) deals largely with the rise and fall of the Sindicatos Libres. Joaquín Maurín, who was a leader of the CNT during the early 1920s, provides details on this period in his *L'anarcho-syndicalisme en Espagne* (Paris: Petite Bibliothèque de Internationale Sindical Rouge, 1924). Among the various memoirs of labor and political figures, those particularly worthy of mention are Claudi Ametlla, *Memories politiques,* vol. 2, *1918–1926* (Catalonia: Distribucións, 1979); Albert Pérez Baró, *El "Felicos Anys Vint": Memories d'un militant obrer* (Palma de Mallorca: Edicións Molls, 1974); and Adolfo Bueso's two-volume *Recuerdos de un Cenetista* (Barcelona: Ariel, 1978).

Labor Relations during the Restoration

Though its statistics must be treated with caution, the descriptive and general information produced by the Institute of Social Reforms, including its annual strike surveys, labor inspection reports, and special inquiries on major labor disputes, working conditions, and the like, between 1904 and 1924 are the single most important body of information on this period. For public order policies and government attitudes toward labor unrest, chapter 10 of Manuel Balbé's *Orden público y militarismo en la España constitucional (1812–1983)* (Madrid: Alianza, 1985) is particularly useful. On general official attitudes and formal policies see Alfredo Montoya Melgar's *Ideologia y lenguaje en los primeros leyes laborales* (Madrid: Civitas, 1975). Alejandro Gallart Folch, *Derecho español de trabajo* (Barcelona: Editorial Labor, 1936), is illuminating on this period, and Juan Montero Aroca, *Los tribunales de trabajo (1908–1938)* (Valencia: Universidad de Valencia, 1976), provides a good discussion and evaluation of the government's mediational and joint parity bargaining bodies in this period. An informative and interesting overview can be found in Ignacio Olábarri's "El mundo de trabajo: Organizaciónes profesionales y relaciónes laborales," in *Historia de España y America, revolución y restauración (1868–1931)*, vol. 1 of 16 (Madrid: Rialp, 1982). Also worthy of mention is "Estructuras sociales (1898–1931)" by Manuel Tuñon de Lara in vol. 37 of *Historia de España* (Madrid: Espasa-Calpe, 1984).

The Primo de Rivera Dictatorship, 1923–1930

The dictatorship period is one of the least studied of Spanish labor history. Two significant general historical studies have appeared in recent years, *Fascism from Above,* by Shlomo Ben Ami (Oxford: Oxford University Press, 1983), and *Revolution from Above,* by James H. Rial (Fairfax, Va.: George

Mason University Press, 1985). Though less ambitious in scope, the latter is particularly good on the dictatorship's social policies. A useful companion to these two books is the special issue of *Cuadernos Economicos de ICE,* no. 10 (1979), dedicated to the dictatorship. Making use of the correspondence and files of the International Labor Organization in Geneva, Anthony D. McIvor's doctoral dissertation, "Spanish Labor Policy during the Dictablanda of Primo de Rivera" (University of California, San Diego, 1982), is a major contribution to an understanding of labor developments in this period. Primo's labor minister and confidant Eduardo Aunós was a prolific writer and apologist of labor corporativism; his *Política social de la dictadura* (Madrid: Real Academia de Ciencias Morales y Políticas, 1944) is an authoritative defense of the regime's labor policies. Alfredo Montoya Melgar, in his *Ideologia y lenguaje en las leyes laborales de Espana: La dictadura de Primo de Rivera* (Murcia: University of Murcia, 1981), provides a useful overview, and the already cited study by Juan Montero Aroca offers an interesting examination of the parity committee structure and related conciliatory mechanisms.

Colin Winston's *Workers and the Right in Spain, 1900–1936,* examines in detail the collaboration between the Barcelona Sindicatos Libres and the dictatorship. Pérez Ledesma's dissertation discusses the role and evolution of the UGT, and Adrian Shubert, Juan Pablo Fusi, and Ignacio Olábarri (*Relaciónes laborales en Vizcaya*) chronicle developments in Asturias and the Basque region. In *The Coming of the Spanish Civil War: Reform, Reaction and Revolution in the Second Republic, 1931–1936* (chapter 1) (London: Macmillan, 1978), Paul Preston examines Spanish socialism in this period, as does Shlomo Ben Ami in chapter 3 of *The Origins of the Second Republic* (Oxford: Oxford University Press, 1978). Of less utility yet worthy of consultation is José Andres Gallego's *El socialismo durante la dictadura, 1923–1930* (Madrid: Tebas, 1977).

The books of César M. Lorenzo and José Peirats contain helpful accounts of this period. Antonio Elorza'a "La CNT bajo la dictadura (1923–1930)" in numbers 39–40, 44–45, and 46 (1972–74) of the *Revista de Trabajo* is a useful source for documentation and information. *El arraigo de anarquismo en Cataluña, textos de 1926–1934,* edited by Albert Balcells (Madrid: Jucar, 1973), reproduces a series of articles by leading critics and supporters of anarcho-syndicalism that originally appeared in the Barcelona periodical *L'opinio* on why this movement had taken root in Catalonia.

For the brief transitional government that was in power from the collapse of the dictatorship to the advent of the Second Republic, the

Berenguer *dictablanda,* we can count on Berenguer's memoirs, *De la dictadura a la Republica* (Madrid: Plus Ultra, 1935), which contains a chapter on labor. Of greater interest is Emilio Mola's *Lo que yo supe (memorias de mi paso por la Dirección General de Seguridad),* in *Obras Completas* (Valladolid: Libreria Santarem, 1940). Mola headed the national police agency and was deeply involved in the administration and framing of labor policies. Anarchist journalist Eduardo de Guzman's 1930 *Historia política de un año decisivo* (Madrid: Tebas, 1973) provides an account of the abortive revolutionary general strike of that year and related political developments. Albert Balcells's admirable *Crisis económica y agitación social en Cataluña (1930–1936)* (Barcelona: Ariel, 1971) provides both information and cogent analysis of the deteriorating economic situation in 1930, trade union development, and the rising incidence of social conflict.

The Republic and the Civil War, 1931–1939

The Spanish civil war has inspired a huge literature, but relatively little has appeared on social aspects and labor developments under the Second Republic. With few exceptions most leading studies provide little more than passing references. Among the few exceptions is Gabriel Jackson's *The Spanish Republic and the Civil War, 1931–1939* (Princeton: Princeton University Press, 1967). Malefakis's study remains the most distinguished work not only on agrarian-labor developments but on general political events. Balcells's *Crisis económica y agitación social en Cataluña (1930–1936)* is still the mainstay on themes such as unemployment, strike incidence, trade unionism, and related economic problems. The appearance in 1983 of Mercedes Cabrera's *La patronal ante la II Republica: Organisaciónes y estrategia (1931–1936)* (Madrid: Siglo XXI) was a major addition, the first such study on employers to appear in Spain. Santos Juliá's prolific and illuminating writing in recent years on socialism and Ugetismo in the 1930s has appreciably expanded our knowledge of the political dynamics on the Left in this turbulent period. His *Madrid, 1931–1934: De la fiesta popular a la lucha de clases* (Madrid: Siglo XXI, 1984) made available for the first time a well-researched and astute examination of socialist trade unionism in Madrid and of the CNT's efforts to break its monopoly. His essay "Estudio preliminar: Socialismo y revolución en el pensamiento y la acción política de Francisco Largo Caballero" in Francisco Largo Caballero, *Escritos de la Republica: Notas historicas de la guerra en España (1917–1940)* (Madrid: Editorial Pablo Iglesias, 1985) is indispensable for comprehension of the thinking and behavior of Largo Caballero. Paul Preston's *The Coming of the Spanish Civil War: Reform, Reaction and Revolution in the Second Republic, 1931–1936,* despite the writer's reservations on his depiction of the CEDA, is another major contribution to our understanding of the Spanish socialist movement, whose development and actions have long been shrouded in obscurity and hearsay. Juan Montero Aroca's chapters on the role and evolution of the *jurados mixtos* provides the perspective of a labor law specialist.

When the doctoral dissertation by John Brademas, "Revolution and Social Revolution: A Contribution to the History of the Anarcho-Syndicalist Movement in Spain, 1930–1937" (Oxford University, 1956) first appeared, there was neither the interest nor the possibility of publishing it in Franco Spain. In 1974, it finally was published under the title *Anarcosindicalismo y revolución en España (1930–1937)* (Barcelona: Ariel). Brademas's extensive interviewing of leading participants and keen analytical skills make his work, despite its age, an indispensable basic study of this subject. Reflecting differing libertarian outlooks, the previously cited books by César M. Lorenzo, *Les anarchistes espagnols et le pouvoir,* and José Peirats, *La CNT en le revolución española,* are required reading. Also useful are the proccedings of the 1931 CNT congress, *Memoria del congreso extraordinario celebrado en Madrid los dias 11 al 16 de Junion de 1931* (Barcelona: Tipografia Cosmos, 1932).

Among the various works dealing with the FAI-Treintista cleavage the two books of Eulalia Vega, *El trentisme a Catalunya, divergencies ideologiques en la CNT (1930–1933)* (Barcelona: Curial, 1980) and *Anarquistas y sindicalistas, 1931–1936* (Valencia: Edicións Alfons el Maganánim, 1984), focusing on the division within the Valencian CNT, are the most useful. The single finest study of this period is Albert Balcells's "La crisis de anarcosindicalismo y el movimiento obrero en Sabadell entre 1930 y 1936," a long essay in his *Trabajo industrial y organización obrera en la Cataluña contemporanea (1900–1936)* (Barcelona: Laia, 1974). Also valuable is Joan Peiró, *Escrits, 1917–1939* (Barcelona: Edicións 62, 1975) and the introductory essay by Pere Gabriel. The Faista point of view can be obtained from Juan García Oliver's memoirs, *El eco de los pasos* (Barcelona: Ruedo Iberico, 1978).

A fairly sizable literature has accumulated on the Casas Viejas affair, the best being Jerome Mintz's *The Anarchists of Casas Viejas* (Chicago: University of Chicago Press, 1982). On the disastrous consequences of communist ultraleftism and Faista extremism in "Red" Seville, see José

Manuel Macarro Vega's overblown but informative *La utopia revolucionaria, Sevilla en la Secunda Republica* (Seville: Monte de Piedad Caja de Ahorros, 1985).

On the radicalization of the socialist movement in the 1930s the previously cited works of Santos Juliá, Paul Preston, and Edward Malefakis, as well as Marta Bizcarrondo, *Araquistáin y la crisis socialista en la II Republica, Leviatán (1934–1936)* (Madrid: Siglo Veintuino, 1975), are the principal ones to consult. A collection of essays edited by German Ojeda, *Octubre 1934* (Madrid: Siglo XXI, 1984), is the most recent analysis by specialists on the revolutionary general strike disaster of that date and its repercussions. Also useful are the papers presented at a symposium conducted at the University of Oviedo, October 29–31, 1984, commemorating the fiftieth anniversary of the October 1934 insurrection. They have been reproduced in *Estudios de Historia Social*, no. 31, vol. 4 (October–December 1984). Adrian Shubert's *Hacia la revolución* traces and identifies the socioeconomic factors that led to the explosive outpouring that resulted in the Asturian Commune.

Among the countless general works on the civil war, four have particular relevance to this study: Gabriel Jackson's *The Spanish Republic and the Civil War in Spain, 1931–1939;* Pierre Broué and Emile Témime's *The Revolution and the Civil War in Spain* (Cambridge, Mass.: MIT Press, 1940); Stanley Payne's *La revolución y la guerra civil española* (Madrid: Jucar, 1976); and Ronald Fraser's *Blood of Spain: An Oral History of the Spanish Civil War* (New York: Pantheon, 1979). The collected papers entitled *Socialismo y guerra civil* (Madrid: Editorial Pablo Iglesias, 1987) are useful in discerning Spanish socialism's often confusing and complex behavior. Enric Ucelay da Cal's *La Catalunya populista: Imatge, cultura i política en l'etapa republicana (1931–1939)* (Barcelona: La Magrana, 1982) is a helpful guide through the seemingly impenetrable thickets of Catalonian political and social developments. Victor Alba's *El Partido Comunista en España* (Barcelona: Planeta, 1979) is insightful and informative on the PCE in this and preceding periods; his volume on the POUM in his four-volume *Historia de Marxisme en Cataluña* (Barcelona: Portic, 1979) is valuable as a firsthand account. *La guerra civil española, cinquenta años despues,* a collection of essays by leading specialists edited by Manuel Tuñon de Lara (Barcelona: Labor, 1985) is of generally high quality. On the anarchist role see Diego Abad de Santillan, *Por que perdimos la guerra, un contribución a la historia de la tragedia española* (Madrid: Plaza y Janes, 1977). For the non-Stalinist

Marxist point of view Joaquín Maurín's *Revolución y contrarrevolución en España* (Paris: Ruedo Iberico, 1966) is useful. Maurín arguably was Spain's outstanding Marxist writer and political figure of his time.

Among the accounts of the revolutionary upsurge that took place immediately following the military rebellion in the summer of 1936, Franz Borkenau's *The Spanish Cockpit* (1937; rpt. Ann Arbor: University of Michigan Press, 1963) remains the single most interesting eyewitness report together with George Orwell's *Homage to Catalonia*. (1938; rpt. New York: Harcourt, Brace and World, 1952). Also worthwhile is H. E. Kaminski's *Ceux de Barcelone* (Paris: Denoel, 1937), which contains interesting sidelights on collectivizations in Barcelona. *The Anarchist Collectives: Workers' Self-Management in the Spanish Revolution, 1936–1939*, edited by Sam Dolgoff (New York: Free Life Editions, 1974), a pro-anarchist interpretation, contains excerpts from the works of such anarchist writers as Gaston Leval and Frank Mintz. Albert Pérez Baró, who served as administrator of the Catalonian government's collectivization agency, has written *30 meses de colectivisme en Catalunya* (Barcelona: Ariel, 1974). *Els traballadors i la guerra civil* by Anna Monjo and Carme Vega (Barcelona: Empuries, 1986) relates the results of an inquiry into how collectivization fared in one of Barcelona's leading metalworking companies. A more ambitious undertaking is Walther Bernecker's *Colectividades y revolución social: El anarquismo en la guerra civil española, 1936–1939* (Barcelona: Crítica, 1982). A most useful guide in delineating the various strands of anarchist and anarcho-syndicalist economic ideas and social restructuring is *La sociedad libertaria: Agrarismo y industrialisación en el anarquismo español (1930–1939)* by Xavier Paniagua (Barcelona: Crítica, 1982).

Two recently published works have greatly increased our understanding of anarcho-syndicalism and the workings of the collectivizations: Aurora Bosch, *Ugetistas y libertarios, guerra civil y revolución en el pais Valenciano, 1936–1939* (Valencia: Institución Alfons el Magnánimo, 1983), and Julián Casanova, *Anarquismo y revolución en la sociedad rural Aragonesa, 1936–1939* (Madrid: Siglo XXI, 1985). Other regional studies include Luis Garrido González, *Colectividades agrarias en Andalusia: Jaen (1931–1939)* (Madrid: Siglo XXI, 1976).

The oft-cited books of César M. Lorenzo and José Peirats are mostly devoted to examinations of the CNT and the anarchist movement during the civil war period. Peirats's work includes extensive citations and the full reproduction of numerous FAI and CNT documents and declarations.

In addition to *Socialismo y guerra civil,* developments in the socialist sector are best followed in the sections devoted to this period in works by Broué and Témime, Edward Malefakis, Gabriel Jackson, Paul Preston, and Santos Juliá.

NOTES

CHAPTER 1: THE SOCIOECONOMIC SETTING

1. Paul Kennedy, *The Rise and Fall of the Great Powers* (New York: Random House, 1987), p. 54.
2. David Landes, *The Unbound Prometheus* (Cambridge, Eng.: Cambridge University Press, 1969), p. 7.
3. Javier Tussell Gómez, *La España del siglo XX* (Barcelona: Dopesa, 1975), p. 21.
4. Stanley Payne, "Spanish Conservatism, 1834–1923," *Journal of Contemporary History* 13 (1978): 787.
5. Nicolas Sánchez Albornoz, *España hace un siglo: Una economía dual* (Barcelona: Peninsula, 1968), p. 7.
6. Franz Borkenau, *The Spanish Cockpit* (1937; rpt. Ann Arbor: University of Michigan Press, 1974), p. 27.
7. Jordi Nadal, "Spain, 1830–1914," in the Fontana Economic History of Europe series, ed. C. M. Cipolla, *The Emergence of Industrial Societies,* vol. 2, pt. 2 (Glasgow: Fontana/Collins, 1973), p. 617. This is an abridged version of Nadal's *El fracaso de la revolución industrial en España, 1814–1913* (Barcelona: Ariel, 1974).
8. A leading historian comments: "The three horsemen of the Apocalypse made their appearance in Spain from 1866 to 1885 and considerably ravaged the population. . . . According to relatively modest calculations the Carlist wars and civil conflicts resulted in at least 250,000 deaths and a no less similar number of casualties who suffered the grievous consequences of mutilations, illnesses, and other scourges. The colonial war of 1868–1879 [in Cuba] among overseas military personnel produced. . . . between 75,000 (the lowest estimate) and 140,000 (the highest estimate) deaths" (Miguel Martínez Cuadrado, *La burgesía conservadora (1874–1931)* [Madrid: Alianza Universidad, 1973], pp. 82–83).
9. Quoted in Raymond Carr, *Spain, 1808–1939* (1966; rev. ed. Oxford: Oxford University Press, 1981), p. 430.

10. Salvador de Madariaga, *Spain, a Modern History* (New York: Praeger, 1958), p. 69.

11. "The fact that industrialization throughout this period was merely sporadic is explained by the existence of factors little conducive to the establishment and growth of a diversified manufacturing industry that was self-supported and regionally balanced. The country suffered politically from considerable instability; the lack of managerial spirit and motivation for industrial progress was not neutralized as would have been possible within a proper framework of economic inducements. The implantation of industrial activity was also held back by the lack of an adequate physical and technological infrastructure and, finally, the low population and demographic density together with a low per capita income critically limited the expansion of the internal market for manufactured products" (Jurgen Donges, *La industrialización en España* [Barcelona: Oikos-Tau, 1976], p. 26).

12. Miguel Izard, "Entre la impotencia y la Esperanza: La Union Manufacturera (5/7/1872–8/4/1873)," *Estudios de Historia Social*, no. 4 (1978), p. 52.

13. Tussell, *La España*, pp. 18–19. Miguel Martínez Cuadrado estimates that the top ruling elite numbered approximately 1,000 (0.28 percent of the total ruling class), "the nucleus engaged in making fundamental decisions in the social process—ministers, parliamentarians, big industrialists, financiers, latifundists, and big proprietors. Leading professionals and high functionaries in whose leadership make up an added 10–14,000 (3.84 percent) cooperated and a further 230–275,000 (95.89 percent) who in various forms also participated" (*La burguesía conservadora*, p. 349).

14. Manuel Tuñon de Lara, *Los comienzos del siglo XX: La población, la economía, la sociedad (1898–1931)*, vol. 37 of *Historia de España*, ed. Tuñon de Lara (Madrid: Espasa-Calpe, 1984), p. 441.

15. Raymond Carr, *Modern Spain, 1875–1980* (Oxford: Oxford University Press, 1980), p. 33.

16. Jordi Nadal, "Spain, 1830–1914," in Fontana Economic History of Europe series, ed. C. M. Cipolla, *The Emergence of Industrial Societies*, vol. 4, pt. 2 (Glasgow: Fontana/Collins, 1977), p. 537.

17. Gabriel Tortella, "La historia económica de los siglos XIX y XX: Ensayo bibliografico," in *Historiografia española contemporanea*, ed. Manuel Tuñon de Lara (Madrid: Siglo Veintiuno, 1980), p. 178. "Taking the population in 1877 of Catalonia as 100, it rose to 114.9 in 1900, to 144.5 in 1920, and 157.7 in 1930. In comparison with the last quarter of the nineteenth century, the demographic increase had accelerated considerably during the first third of the twentieth century. The number of inhabitants in 1877 of the principality was 1,975,555, 2,269,406 in 1900, and 3,116,037 in 1930" (Albert Balcells, *Cataluña contemporanea*, vol. 2, *1900–1939* [Madrid: Siglo Veintiuno, 1976], p. 59).

18. In 1930 in the eleven countries of western and central Europe 24.2 percent of the population was engaged in agricultural work. In Spain that figure was 56.6 percent. "By far agricultural output [was] the biggest component until the 1950s of the Spanish national income" (Gabriel Tortella Casares, *Banking, Railroads, and Industry in Spain, 1829–1847* [New York: Arno Press, 1977], p. 347).

19. Sánchez Albornoz, *España hace un siglo,* p. 8.

20. Edward Malefakis, *Agrarian Reform and Peasant Revolution in Spain* (New Haven: Yale University Press, 1970), p. 12.

21. Ibid., p. 17.

22. Carr, *Modern Spain,* p. 17.

23. Malefakis, *Agrarian Reform,* p. 25.

24. Pierre Vilar, *Spain, a Brief History,* 2d ed. (London: Pergamon, 1977), p. 69.

25. "Andalusia . . . consists roughly of the plains of the Guadalquivir and the mountains that enclose it like a shell. Taking it in all, it is overwhelmingly a country of concentrated settlements (pueblos), an empty countryside into which the peasants went for long periods to live in shelters or barracks, leaving their wives in the towns, of vast absentee-owned and inefficient estates and a population of almost servile landless braceros or day laborers" (Eric Hobsbawm, *Primitive Rebels* [Manchester, Eng.: Manchester University Press, 1959], p. 54).

26. Ramon Rodríguez, "El proletariado agricola Andaluz (1913–1920)," *Estudios de Historia Agraria/2* (1979): 171–93.

27. An estimated 84 percent of small proprietors throughout the country in the early 1930s needed wages to subsist. See Gerald Brenan, *The Spanish Labyrinth* (London: Cambridge University Press, 1943), p. 245.

28. Rodríguez, "El proletariado agricola Andaluz," pp. 171–93.

29. José Varela Ortega, *Los amigos políticos* (Madrid: Alianza, 1977), p. 225. For an informative depiction of Castilian rural life and social relations, see ibid., pp. 216–35.

30. A. Milward and S. B. Saul, *The Development of the Economies of Continental Europe, 1850–1914* (London: Allen & Unwin, 1977), p. 222. According to Malefakis, "It may be safely assumed that the annual earnings of agricultural day laborers were seldom more than half and never more than two thirds of those of even industrial workers (*Agrarian Reform,* p. 102).

31. Antonio M. Bernal, "La llamada crisis finisecular (1872–1919)," in *La España de la restauración,* ed. J. L. Garcia Delgado (Madrid: Siglo Veintiuno, 1985), pp. 250–51.

32. Antonio M. Bernal, "La agricultura Andaluza en el siglo XIX," in *Historia agraria de la España contemporanea,* vol. 2, *Expansion y crisis (1850–1900),* ed. Ramon Garrabou y Jésus Sanz (Barcelona: Crítica, 1985), pp. 438–39.

The farm crisis, which began with price instability in cereal grains, then enveloped vineyards with the spread of phylloxera and the loss of export markets for olive oil following the end of World War I.

33. Bernal, *La llamada crisis finisecular,* pp. 251–52.
34. Milward and Saul, *Development of the Economies of Europe,* p. 222. Tussell claims that the yield per hectare in the early twentieth century was estimated to have been five or six times less than that of Germany or England (*La España,* p. 15).
35. Varela Ortega, *Los amigos políticos,* p. 225.
36. Vilar, *Spain,* p. 70.
37. "They are totally illiterate; even the foremen, the 'operadores' who are in charge of farms of from 3 to 400 hectares, are hardly able to read and totally incapable of writing. . . . There are either none at all or insufficient primary schools. . . . In the villages neighboring Gibraltar, because of a lack of teachers, the children attend classes with the English, so that they learn English better than their normal language. The extremely high illiteracy rate in the south, the lack of schools, notwithstanding, occurred primarily because starting at age seven children of rural laborers accompanied their parents in the fields and worked with them, an absolute necessity given the very low wages paid to braceros" (Henri Lorin, "Les conditions du travail en Andalusie," *Memoires et documents,* Le Musée Social, 1905, p. 241). Illiteracy in France at the end of the century was about 24 percent.
38. Quoted by Tussell, *La España,* p. 19.
39. Eduardo Sevilla Guzman, "La cuestíon agraria Andaluz," *El Pais* (Madrid), August 11 and 13, 1981. Nowhere else in Europe was there such a high proportion of agricultural laborers. "The rural proletariat was also very large; 40% of the French agricultural population at the end of the 18th century, and a higher proportion still, of course, in the lowlands of northern, central, and eastern Europe" (J. F. Bergier, "Industrial Bourgeoisie and the Rise of the Working Class, 1700–1914," in Fontana Economic History of Europe series, ed. C. M. Cipolla, vol. 3, *The Industrial Revolution* [Glasgow: Fontana/Collins, 1977], p. 420). Miguel Artola calculates the ratio of rural day workers in Spain at 56 percent.
40. Casamiro Martí, "Afianzamiento y despliegue de sistema liberal," in *Revolución burguesa, oligarquia y constitucionalismo (1834–1923),* vol. 8 of *Historia de España,* ed. Manuel Tuñon de Lara (Madrid: Labor, 1981), p. 190.
41. Manuel Tuñon de Lara, "La economía española entre 1900 y 1923 por José Luis Garcia Delgado," ibid., p. 414.
42. Jaime Vicens Vives, *Coyuntura económico y reformismo burgues y otros estudios de la historia de España* (Barcelona: Ariel, 1968), p. 176.
43. Constancio Bernaldo de Quiros and Luis Arcilla, *El bandolerismo Andaluz* (1933; rpt. Madrid: Turner, 1973), pp. 85, 86, 258.

44. Antonio Maria Calero, *Movimientos sociales en Andalucia (1820–1936)* (Madrid: Siglo Veintiuno, 1976), p. 11.
45. Ibid., pp. 9–10.
46. Antonio Miguel Bernal quoted by Martí, "Afianzamiento," p. 191. "Anarchism, in fact, postulated a 'new' model of life values and social organization that 'corresponded' to and 'expressed' the peasant experience of rupture and continuity; the idea of land redistribution [*reparto*] stimulated by the experience of disamortization, hostility to the combination of centralism and *caciquismo,* to the new economic legislation and the rural police who represented the liberal order. Anticlericalism and the need not for an ethos of resignation but of rebellion including notions of solidarity and liberty, originating with or strengthened by these experiences, fused with the basic ideas of economic collectivism, political anarchism, and religious atheism" (Victor Pérez Diaz, "Teoria y conflictos sociales," *Revista de Occidente* 15 (1974).
47. Catalonian entrepreneurs and artisans were aided in acquiring technical knowledge during the initial stages in the development of textile making by French and Italian textile specialists who settled in Barcelona and eventually became assimilated Catalonians.
48. Vicens Vives, *Coyuntura económica y reformismo,* p. 149.
49. As early as 1857 Barcelona employed 20,700 people in cotton textiles, accounting for 12 percent of the city's population and 40 percent of its work force.
50. Half of all the wool-spinning looms in Spain were concentrated in Sabadell and Tarrasa.
51. Tortella, "Historia económica de los siglos XIX y XX," p. 180.
52. Barcelona province consists of the *llano,* the coastal plain, where the city and a number of nearby communities are situated, and in the interior, the *montaña,* a semimountainous area with riverine valleys.
53. Joaquín Romero Maura, *La rosa del fuego, el obrerismo Barcelones de 1899 a 1909* (Barcelona: Grijalbo, 1975), p. 52.
54. Lucás Beltrán Flórez, *La industria algodonera española* (Barcelona: Ministerio de Trabajo, 1943), p. 48.
55. Each worker in the mid-nineteenth-century Catalan cotton industry transformed 660 kilograms of cotton annually compared to 1,500 kilograms by a worker in the United States (Pau Romeva Ferrer, *Historia de la industria Catalana,* 2 vols. [Barcelona: N.p., 1952], 2:370).
56. Miguel Izard, *Industrialisación y obrerismo* (Barcelona: Ariel, 1973).
57. Francesc Bernis, *Fomento de las exportaciónes* (Barcelona: Minerva, 1920), p. 120.
58. Albert Balcells, *Historia contemporanea de Cataluña* (Barcelona: Edhasa, 1983), p. 150.
59. Beltrán Flórez, *La industria algodonera,* p. 106; Eduard Escarra, the author

of "Le developpment industriel de Catalogne," in 1908 noted that while western European textile-making establishments averaged forty to fifty thousand spindles, those in Catalonia possessed only five to fifteen thousand.

60. Jordi Maluquer de Motes Bernet, "La estructura del sector algodonero en Cataluña durante la primera etapa de la industrialisación (1832–1861)," *Hacienda Publica Española*, no. 38 (1976), pp. 133–48. See also Balcells, *Historia contemporanea de Cataluña*, p. 35.

61. Jordi Maluquer de Motes, "La revolución industrial en Cataluña," in *La modernisación económica de España, 1830–1930,* ed. Nicolas Sánchez Albornoz (Madrid: Alianza, 1985), p. 213.

62. Ralph M. Odell, *Cotton Goods in Spain and Portugal* (Washington, D.C.: U.S. Department of Commerce and Labor, 1911), pp. 23–25. Odell's description of textile working conditions is in general accord with that provided by Eduard Escarra.

63. Carr, *Spain, 1808–1939,* p. 434.

64. Beltrán Flórez, *La industria algodonera,* p. 107.

65. "Two of the most striking aspects of the relative backwardness of Catalan industry were the almost complete absence of joint stock companies and the limited recourse to borrowing of industrial enterprises. At the turn of the century the Barcelona stock exchange had only fifteen registered joint stock companies compared with a total of 1,000 for Spain as a whole (mainly assurance, public utility, and the mining companies). Moreover, although there were a number of banks represented in Catalonia including the Banks of Barcelona, Sabadell, Tarrasa, the Hispano Americano and the Hispano Colonial, not to mention branches of foreign banks, the role they played in industrial development was very restricted. It is difficult to know whether to blame the banks for antiquated procedures, or Catalan businessmen for their lack of financial acumen. Most of the family firms of the Principality financed their own development out of profits" (Joseph Harrison, *An Economic History of Modern Spain* [Manchester, Eng.: Manchester University Press, 1978], p. 71). For an examination of the family structure and value system of the Barcelona industrial oligarchy, see Gary W. McDonough, *Good Families of Barcelona: A Social History of Power in the Industrial Era* (Princeton: Princeton University Press, 1986).

66. Albert Balcells, *Cataluña contemporanea,* vol. 1 (*1815–1900*) (Madrid: Siglo Veintiuno, 1977), p. 84.

67. Jaime Vicens Vives and Montserrat Llorens, *Industrials i politics del segle XIX* (1958; rpt. Barcelona: Planeta, 1979), pp. 110–14.

68. Muriel Casals, "La primera guerra mundial i les seves conequencies, un moment clau del proces d'industrialisacíon a Catalunya: El cas de la industria llanera de Sabadell" (Ph.D. dissertation, Barcelona Autonomous University, 1983).

69. Nadal, *El fracaso de la revolución industrial,* pp. 213, 218.
70. Joseph Harrison, *The Spanish Economy in the Twentieth Century* (New York: St. Martin's Press, 1985), p. 20.
71. Balcells, *Historia contemporanea de Cataluña,* p. 34.
72. Joan Connelly Ullman, *The Tragic Week: A Study in Anticlericalism in Spain, 1875–1912* (Cambridge, Mass.: Harvard University Press, 1968), p. 70.
73. *Noticias de la Inspección de Trabajo relativa a la industria textil de España y la huelga del Arte Fabril de Cataluña en Agosto de 1913* (Madrid: Institute of Social Reforms, 1913), p. 93.
74. David Avery, *Not on Queen Victoria's Birthday* (London: Collins, 1974), p. 243.
75. Sánchez Albornoz, *España hace un siglo,* p. 24.
76. By 1914, on the eve of World War I, the situation was more or less the same. Exports were primarily agricultural products such as oranges, almonds, onions, wine, olive oil, and minerals, including iron, lead, and copper ores, exports typical of a nonindustrial country. See Sima Lieberman, *The Contemporary Spanish Economy* (London: Allen & Unwin, 1982), p. 132.
77. E. Témime, A. Broder, and G. Chastagnaret, *Histoire de l'Espagne contemporaine* (Paris: Aubier Montaigne, 1979), p. 69.
78. Quoted in Juan Pablo Fusi, *Política obrera en el pais Vasco, 1880–1923* (Madrid: Turner, 1975), pp. 31–32.
79. José Luis Comellas, *Historia de España—el siglo XIX* (Barcelona: Carrogio, 1981), p. 261.
80. Fusi, *Política obrera,* p. 29.
81. Henri Lorin, *L'Industrie rural en Guipúzcoa* (Paris: Musée Social, 1907), p. 216.
82. Fusi, *Política obrera,* p. 180.
83. Lorin, *L'Industrie rural,* p. 216.
84. Fusi, *Política obrera,* p. 181.
85. Francisco Erice, *La burguesia industrial Asturiana, 1885–1930* (Oviedo: Silverio Canada, 1980), pp. 214–15.
86. David Ruiz, *El movimiento obrero de Asturias* (Oviedo: Amigos de Asturias, 1968), p. 39. "Contemporary accounts are unanimous in attributing to these workers habits of indolence and absenteeism that are contrary to the exigencies of modern industrial labor" (Gregorio Santullano, *Historia de la mineria Asturiana* [Gijón: Ayalga, 1978], p. 125).
87. Adrian Shubert, "Mundos que Chocan: Los origines sociales de la militancia obrera (1860–1914)," *Estudios de Historia Social,* no. 15 (October–December 1980), p. 237.
88. Lenard R. Berlanstein, *The Working People of Paris, 1870–1914* (Baltimore: John Hopkins University Press, 1984), p. 11.

89. José Luis García Delgado, "La economía española entre 1900 y 1923," in *Revolución burguesa,* vol. 8 of *Historia de España,* ed. Tuñon de Lara, p. 420.

CHAPTER 2: A MODERN LABOR FORCE AND SOCIAL LEGISLATION

1. Interview, November 28, 1985.
2. "In a more modern sense the working population, those employed in sectors such as textiles, mining or metallurgy, did not go beyond half a million, some 200,000 working in textiles and mining around 1860, and some 500,000 workers engaged in textiles, mining, building construction, and furniture making around 1900. The evolution of the total population was as follows: 10.5 million in 1797, 15.5 million in 1857 and 18.5 million persons in 1900. Between 1860 and 1900 the active population made up around 40 percent of the total population" (Pere Gabriel, "El anarquismo en España," in the Spanish edition of George Woodcock's *Anarchism* (Barcelona: Ariel, 1979), p. 332.
3. Manuel Tuñon de Lara, *Los comienzos del siglo XX: La población, la economía, la sociedad (1898–1931),* vol. 8 of *Historia de España,* ed. Tuñon de Lara (Madrid: Espasa-Calpe, 1984), p. 441.
4. José Sánchez Jiménez, "La población, el campo y las ciudades," ibid., p. 406.
5. Jaime Vicens Vives, "El moviment obrerista Català (1901–1939)," *Recerques* 7 (1977–78): 12. The figures are taken from a master's thesis prepared by M. J. Sirera i Oliag.
6. Esparto grass traditionally has been used for the making of rope, mats, and the like. See Miguel Martínez Cuadrado, *La burguesía conservadora (1874–1931)* (Madrid: Alianza, 1973), p. 179.
7. Richard Herr, *Spain* (Englewood Cliffs, N.J.: Prentice-Hall, 1971), pp. 134–35.
8. M. Sans Orenga, *Els treballadors mercantils dins el moviment Català* (Barcelona: Portic, 1975), p. 42.
9. Enric Ucelay da Cal, *La Catalunya populista, imatge, cultural i política en l'etapa republicana (1931–1939)* (Barcelona: Ediciónes de la Magrana, 1982), pp. 58–59.
10. Jacques Valdour, *L'Ouvrier español, observatións vecue,* 2 vols. (Paris: R. Giard et A. Rousseau, 1919), 2:301–2.
11. Miguel Capella Martínez, *La industria en Madrid,* 2 vols. (Madrid: Camara oficial de la industria, 1963), 2:2.
12. S. G. Checkland, *The Mines of Tharsis* (London: Allen & Unwin, 1967), p. 171.
13. B. Seebohm Rowntree, *Poverty: A Study of Town Life* (1901; rpt. New York: Howard Fertig, 1971), p. 360.

14. Jaime Vicens Vives, *Historia social y económico de España y America,* 5 vols. (Barcelona: Editorial Vicens Vives, 1971), 5:158.

15. Juan Pablo Fusi, *Política obrera en el pais Vasco, 1880–1923* (Madrid: Turner, 1975), p. 40.

16. Cited in Jordi Nadal, *La población española (siglos XVI–XX)* (Barcelona: Ariel, 1984), p. 156n.

17. Angel Marvaud, *La question sociale en Espagne* (Paris: Felix Alcan, 1910), p. 122.

18. Joaquín Romero Maura, *La rosa del fuego, el obrerismo Barcelones de 1899 a 1909* (Barcelona: Grijalbo, 1974), p. 140.

19. Albert Balcells, *Trabajo industrial y organisación obrera en la Cataluña contemporanea (1900–1936)* (Barcelona: Laia, 1974), p. 41.

20. R. Joseph Harrison, "The Beginnings of Social Legislation in Spain, 1900–1919," *Iberian Studies* 3 (Spring 1974).

21. José Varela Ortega, *Los amigos políticos* (Madrid: Alianza, 1977), p. 221.

22. Sánchez Jiménez, "La población," p. 189.

23. Nadal, *La población española,* pp. 160–61.

24. Vicens Vives, "Moviment obrerista Catalá," p. 13.

25. Eduard Escarra in his "Le development industrial de la Catalogne" recounts that "general working conditions overall are extremely deficient, especially from the point of view of hygiene and worker safety. Outside of a few modern factories—the bottle cork industry as well—most establishments are badly maintained, filthy, and disorganized, the premises are too small and insufficiently lighted and ventilated, hazardous machines do not have protective devices" (*Bibliothèque de Musée Social,* [Paris: Rousseau, 1908], p. 122). Many workers, according to the regional inspector, because of illiteracy and "lack of culture," opposed the use of safety devices and did not "appreciate the virtues of hygiene." Consequently they did not insist that their employers comply with existing legal requirements (*Noticias de al Inspección de Trabajo relativa a la industria textil de España y la huelga del Arte Fabril de Cataluña en Agosto de 1913* [Madrid: Institute of Social Reforms, 1913], p. 83).

26. José Marvá, *Información sobre el trabajo en las minas* (Madrid: Institute of Social Reforms, 1909), p. 186.

27. Maximiano García Venero, *Eduardo Dato* (Vitoria: Diputación Foral de Alava, 1969), p. 105.

28. "The terrible gamut of illnesses and industrial accidents was interminable: fractures through falls for bricklayers and roofers, tuberculosis for the employees of large warehouses, pulmonary or intestinal carbuncles that Erichsein called the illness of woolens workers, the anthracosis of the stone-cutters, the frequent mutilations of fingers among female textile workers. . . . It is difficult to obtain reliable medical statistics for this city [Barcelona]; the lack of precise data, however, does not alter the somber panorama of thou-

sands of persons afflicted by illnesses and work accidents" (Romero Maura, *La rosa del fuego,* p. 140).

29. Emili Salut, *Vivers de revolucionaris; Apuntes historics de districte cinque* (Barcelona: Libreria Catalonia, 1938), pp. 46–47.

Late industrialization did not invariably signify gross exploitation. The French expatriate anarchist Pierre Piller (his pseudonym was Gaston Leval), who had worked in forging shops in both Paris and Barcelona, recounts: "A worker in France hammers ten-millimeter cold rivets. In Spain they are heated and an apprentice is employed. The worker does not tire so readily and the employer earns less. Before the war in Paris we worked ten hours daily, five in the morning and five in the afternoon. From morning to night we hammered away. . . . Here everyone works without competition, humanely. We rest every twenty rivets . . . [the journeymen] light up a cigarette while the apprentices clean the forges" (quoted in Xavier Paniagua, *La sociedad libertaria* [Barcelona: Crítica, 1984], pp. 201–2).

30. Raymond Carr, *Spain, 1808–1939* (1966; rev. ed. Oxford: Oxford University Press, 1975), p. 400.

31. Manuel González Portilla, *La formación de sociedad capitalista en el pais Vasco (1876–1913),* 2 vols. (San Sebastian, Spain: L. Haranburu, 1981), 2:136.

32. Jaime Vicens Vives and Montserrat Llorens, *Industrials i politics del segle XIX* (1958; rpt. Barcelona: Planeta, 1979), p. 165, notes that epidemics usually followed periods of economic crisis.

33. Quoted in González Portilla, *La formación de sociedad capitalista,* 2:206.

34. Peter Stearns, *European Society in Upheaval* (New York: Macmillan, 1967), p. 128.

35. For the condition of female labor in France see Michel Collinet, *Essai sur la condition ouvriere, 1900–1950* (Paris: Editions Ouvrieres, 1951), p. 52.

36. Balcells, *Trabajo industrial,* p. 15. I have relied heavily on Balcells's study of female labor in Catalonia during the early years of this century, pp. 7–121.

37. Juan Romero González, "Condiciónes de vida de la clase obrera en el pais Valenciano (1880–1923)," *Saitabi* 27 (1977): 11.

38. Práxedes Zancada, *El trabajo de la mujer y del niño* (Madrid: A. Pérez y Cia, 1904), pp. 165–67. In Catalonia in 1915 41.3 percent of the men were illiterate compared to 55.15 percent of the women. See Albert Balcells, *Cataluña contemporanea,* vol. 2 (*1900–1939*) (Madrid: Siglo Veintiuno, 1976), p. 7.

The legacy of the past has still not been completely eradicated. A study based on the 1981 census and completed in September 1984 by the Ministry of Education and Science revealed that 6.6 percent of the population ten years of age or older were totally illiterate. An additional 36 percent, more than 11 million, were functional illiterates, able to read and write but incapable of using these skills in written, verbal, or numerical communication. The situation is substantially worse among women than men; for every totally illiterate male, there are 2.6 women, and the number of functionally illiterate females is greater than their male counterparts. As before, though in appreciably lesser degree, the highest percentages of illiteracy are found in southern Spain.

39. *Noticias de la Inspección de Trabajo,* p. 83.
40. Juan José Morato, *Subsistencia en Madrid, la nueva era* (1901), pp. 433–38, quoted in *Pensamiento socialista español a comienzos del siglo,* ed. Manuel Pérez Ledesma (Madrid: Ediciones del Centro, 1974), p. 133.
41. Antonio Calero Amor, *Historia del movimiento obrero en Granada, 1909–1923* (Madrid: Editorial Tecnos, 1973), p. 60.
42. Romero González, "Condiciónes de vida de la clase obrera," p. 12.
43. A married woman required the authorization of her husband before she could accept employment, and she could legally receive her wages directly only if her husband did not object. To become a litigant before the Industrial Tribunal, a married woman required her husband's authorization, a procedural requirement that was also carried over into the labor code that was adopted in the 1920s during the dictatorship of Primo de Rivera. The Labor Contract Law that was adopted in 1906 made it possible for a woman worker to contest the refusal of her husband to provide such an authorization. See Mary Nash, *Mujer, familia y trabajo en España, 1875–1936* (Barcelona: Anthropos, 1983).
44. Emili Salut, *Vivers de revoluciónaris,* p. 44.
45. Stanley Payne, *The Spanish Revolution* (New York: Norton, 1970), p. 12. The labor historian Miguel Izard is somewhat less categorical: "The working conditions of Catalonian cotton workers were very harsh. . . . But they were no worse than those endured by most of the European proletariat during the development of the industrial revolution, though in general terms the laws that mitigated their severity—especially those concerning the employment of women and children—were promulgated in Spain with considerable delay in comparison with other European countries" (*Industrialisación y obrerismo* [Barcelona: Ariel, 1973], p. 82).
46. Henri Lorin, *Les ouvriers mineurs à Bilbao* (Paris: La Musée Social, 1903), pp. 348–51.
47. Fernanda Romeu Alfaro, *La clase trabajadores en España (1898–1930)* (Madrid: Taurus, 1970), p. 35. Fusi supports this contention: "Circumstantial evidence and statistical sources, which are extremely inadequate and almost always imprecise and contradictory, make one believe that for workers of rural Spain working in the factories and mines of Vizcaya signified the possibility of an unquestioned improvement in their standard of living, even within the following limitations: social segregation, insalubrious neighbor-

hoods and housing quarters, deficient food, poor garments, with leisure time confined to the tavern, fronton, and from 1910 to the cinema. The relatively high wages of Vizcaya were the result neither of employer profits nor of an income redistribution but of an elevated productivity accomplished through long workdays and a recourse to bonuses and piecework. One worked in the mines during the 1880s from five in the morning till nightfall" (*Política obrera en el pais Vasco,* p. 57).

Fusi's observation on the imprecision of various sources on workers' earnings is supported by Malefakis, who has pointed out that the average income for all employed individuals in 1902, listed at four pesetas in the National Statistical Institute's (INE) *Primera mitad del siglo XX,* includes upper- and middle-class earnings and therefore overstates the incomes of individual workers by roughly one-third. See Malefakis, *Agrarian Reform and Peasant Revolution in Spain* (New Haven: Yale University Press, 1970), p. 100.

48. Romero Maura, *Rosa del fuego,* pp. 144–45.

49. Escarra, "Development industriale de la Catalogne," p. 122.

50. M. Capella Martínez, *La industría en Madrid* (Madrid: Camara oficial de la industria, 1963), 2:752.

51. Institute of Social Reform, *Información sobre el trabajo en las minas* (Madrid: Imprenta de la sucesores de Minuesa de los Rios, 1909).

52. Jaime Vicens Vives, *Historia de España y America,* 5 vols. (Barcelona: Editorial Vicens Vives, 1971), 5:160.

53. Stearns, *European Society in Upheaval,* pp. 119–20.

54. Anselmo Lorenzo, *El proletariado militante* (1901, 1923; rpt. Madrid: Alianza, 1974), p. 53. This is a labor classic.

55. Stanley Payne surmises that these floaters made up 3 to 4 percent of the population and in the nineteenth century were prone to agitation (*Politics and the Military in Modern Spain* [Palo Alto: Stanford University Press, 1967], p. 3). Vicens Vives estimates that subproletarians during the early years of this century made up 20 percent of Barcelona's working population. See his *Moviment obrerista Catalá,* p. 12.

56. Angel Ossorio y Gallardo, *Barcelona, Julio de 1909: Declaración de un Testigo* (Madrid: Ricardo Rojas, 1910), pp. 13–14.

57. James Joll, *Europe since 1870* (Middlesex, England: Penguin Books, 1976), p. 27.

58. Robert O. Paxton, *Europe in the Twentieth Century* (New York: Harcourt Brace Jovanovich, 1975), p. 32.

59. Alfredo Montoya Melgar, *Ideologia y lenguaje en las a primeras leyes laborales de España* (Madrid: Civitas, 1975), pp. 41–42.

60. Krausism, inspired by the ideas of an obscure German philosopher of the early nineteenth century, was introduced into Spain by the noted educator Julián Sanz del Rio. It exerted a considerable influence on Spanish culture,

social reform, and education from the second half of the nineteenth century until the outbreak of World War I. It "provided intellectual capital for a generation . . . who wanted to 'open' Spain to 'modern' ideas. . . . German Krausism, by what must be considered an intellectual accident, became for an isolated intellectual world, a means of reunion with the stream of European thought." Though a hazy system of thought, "what was left was intellectual tolerance, a high moral concern for the cultural and educational regeneration of Spain, as a premise for her political and economic regeneration" (Carr, *Spain, 1808–1939*, pp. 303–4.

61. Quoted in Luis Enrique de la Villa Gil and Carlos Palomeque López, *Introducción a la económia del trabajo*, 2 vols. (Madrid: Debate, 1978), 1:208.

62. Melchor Fernández Almagro, *Historia política de la España contemporanea*, 2 vols. (Madrid: Alianza, 1974), 2:140.

63. Carr, *Spain, 1808–1939*, pp. 460–61.

64. León Martín Granizo, *Apuntes para la historia de trabajo en España* (Madrid: Sexto Cuaderno, 1952), p. 13. Indispensable to an understanding of social reformism is *El Instituto del Trabajo: Datos para la historia de la reformismo social en España*, ed. Adolfo Buylla, Adolfo Posada, and Luis Morote, originally published in 1902 and reissued in fascimile form by the Ministry of Labor in 1986. The new edition contains an introduction by Santiago Castillo. See also *Reformas sociales*, a 1987 fascimile reissued by the Ministry of Labor of the five-volume edition of the oral and written submissions to the Social Reforms Commission with an introductory essay by Santiago Castillo.

65. Salvador de Madariaga, *Spain, a Modern History* (New York: Praeger, 1958), p. 365.

66. "Until 1919 the amount of funds assigned to the IRS for its entire activity was less than a nation such as Belgium allocated solely for labor inspection; and in the most recent budget the Ministry of Labor that was already in existence had been assigned 16 million pesetas of which 3,847,000 was for the IRS to cover all its inspection and statistical services; analogous foreign organisms such as the Labor Ministry of England received 156 million pounds, the French 205 million francs, the Italians 294 million lira, and that of Belgium 150 million francs" (Conde de Romanones, *Las responsabilidades del antiguo regimen* [Madrid: Renacimiento, 1924], p. 189).

67. Posada quoted in Luis Enrique de la Villa and Carlos Palomeque, *Lecciónes de derecho de trabajo* (Madrid: Instituto de Estudios Sociales y Seguridad Social, 1977), p. 233; Montoya Melgar, *Ideologia y lenguaje*, p. 9.

68. Carlos Seco Serrano, *Viñetas históricas* (Madrid: Espasa-Calpe, 1983), p. 338. According to Balcells, in an effort to palliate Catalonian resentment over tax increases that had led to a taxpayers' strike in Barcelona (*el tancament de Caixes*), the conservative Silvela government in 1900 sought to mollify workers' discontent through the promulgation of two labor laws, the in-

dustrial accidents act and another that set maximum working hours for women as well as prohibiting employment of minors less than ten years of age. See his *Cataluña contemporanea,* 2:5.

69. M. Carlos Palomeque, *Derecho de trabajo e ideologia* (Madrid: Akal, 1980), pp. 55–56.

70. During the first decade of the twentieth century, a total of 531 dispositions of a social nature were promulgated in Spain: 30 laws, 101 royal decrees, 386 royal orders, 37 circulars, and 7 dispositions. See De la Villa and Palomeque, *Lecciónes de derecho de trabajo,* p. 234.

71. Carr, *Spain, 1808–1939,* p. 461.

72. Marvaud, *La question sociale en Espagne,* p. 288.

73. André Voyard, "Las institutions fondamontales de la nouvelle organisation du travail en Espagne," *La Musée Social,* no. 1 (January 1, 1920), pp. 13–14. Voyard's and Marvaud's assertion that the law on industrial accidents was the "best observed" is not shared by Miguel Sastre, the noted specialist on Barcelona labor affairs: "Nor do many employers comply with the labor accidents law, which requires them to inform the authorities within three days following the occurrence of an accident in their shops or factories; and, nevertheless, . . . many of them delay for months in doing so, and many also do not even accomplish this, even though they are threatened with fines that the law imposes in such instances. But it should be noted that these fines are almost never levied" (*Las huelgas en Barcelona y sus resultados durante el año 1905* [Barcelona: La Hormiga de Oro, 1906], p. 6).

74. *Memoria general de la Inspección del Trabajo—1907* (Madrid: Imprenta de la sucesores de M. Minuesa de los Rios, 1908).

75. L. San Miguel Arribas, *La Inspección de Trabajo* (Madrid: IEP, 1952), p. 66.

76. Maximiano García Venero, *Historia de los movimientos sindicalistas españoles (1840–1933)* (Madrid: Ediciones de Movimiento, 1961), p. 271.

77. Ibid., p. 314.

78. Joll, *Europe since 1870,* p. 213.

79. Antonio Ramos Oliveira, *Politics, Economics, and Men of Modern Spain, 1808– 1946* (1946; rpt. New York: Arno Press, 1972), p. 225.

CHAPTER 3: THE EMERGENCE OF MODERN LABOR ORGANIZATION

1. Albert Balcells, *Historia contemporanea de Cataluña* (Barcelona: Edhasa, 1983), p. 34.

2. In Alcoy, the textile manufacturing center in the Valencian region, there were also frequent attempts from 1821 to 1826 to destroy newly installed machinery. See Manuel Cerda, *Els moviments socials al pais Valenciá* (Valencia: Institució Alfons el Magnanim, 1981), pp. 43–44.

3. See Manuel R. Alarcon Caracuel, *El derecho de asociación obrera en España (1839–1900)* (Madrid: Ediciónes de Revista de Trabajo, 1975), pp. 79–86.

4. Indispensable for this period is Josep Benet and Casamiro Martí, *Barcelona a mitjan segle XIX, el moviment obrer durant el bieni progressista (1854–1856)*, 2 vols. (Barcelona: Curial, 1976). Still worth consulting is the pioneering study by Manuel Reventos, *Els moviments socials a Barcelona en el segle XIX* (1925; rpt. Barcelona: Crítica, 1987), with an introduction by Pere Gabriel.

5. Jordi Maluquer de Motes Bernet, *La era Isabelina y el sexennio democratico (1834–1923)*, vol. 34 of *Historia de España*, ed. José Maria Jover Zamora (Madrid: Espasa Calpe, 1981), p. 786.

6. Casamiro Martí, *Revolución burguesa, oligarquia, y constitucionalismo (1834–1923)*, vol. 8 of *Historia de España*, ed. Manuel Tuñon de Lara (Barcelona: Editorial Labor, 1981), p. 246.

7. Alejandro Gallart Folch, *Derecho español de trabajo* (Barcelona: Editorial Labor, 1936), pp. 35–36.

8. The anarchist Anselmo Lorenzo notes that not a single authentic labor organization existed in Madrid at the time of the 1868 revolution, only some cooperatives and mutual benefit societies. See his *El proletariado militante*, cited in Juan Díaz del Moral, *Historia de las agitaciónes campesinas Andaluzas* (Madrid: Alianza, 1977), p. 75.

According to Juan Pablo Fusi, in the 1880s, "Vizcaya lacked any tradition of labor organization and industrial conflicts. . . . Labor disputes that only by stretching the meaning of the term could be regarded as strikes were not totally unknown. . . . Worker societies with trade union objectives practically did not exist. There were throughout the Basque country twelve legally constituted worker societies, of which only one, the Typographical Society of Bilbao, had as its aim 'the betterment of its membership' " (*Política obrera en el pais Vasco, 1880–1923* [Madrid: Turner, 1975], pp. 67–68).

9. "Mutualism [mutual assistance societies], cooperativism [consumer and production cooperatives], and trade unionism [resistance societies]. The first responds to the notion of alleviating the sorry lot of the worker without attacking its roots, the second went slightly further; nourished by the myth of establishing a more just system of production paralleling the existing one, which would ultimately become predominant through its greater economic yield and superior ethical quality. The third presents its objectives as the struggle against the capitalist system and, as such, to secure for the worker the selling of his skin for as much as possible" (Manuel R. Alarcon Caracuel, *El derecho de asociación obrera en España (1839–1900)* [Madrid: Ediciones de la Revista de Trabajo, 1975], pp. 79–80). The advocates of cooperativism were moderates whose ideas were inspired by Robert Owen and the Rochdale experiment. They regarded cooperatives as the basis for the structuring

of economic society, opposed class struggle tactics, and favored conciliatory employer-employee relationships. In politics they supported the
Republicans.

10. The major work on Tres Clases de Vapor is Miguel Izard, *Industrialización
y obrerismo: Las Tres Clases de Vapor* (Barcelona: Ariel, 1973).
11. Martí, *Revolución burguesa*, p. 193.
12. Josep Termes Ardevol, *Federalismo, anarcosindicalismo y catalanismo* (Barcelona: Anagrama, 1976), p. 14.
13. Fanelli's visit to Spain had been preceded by exploratory surveys conducted
by the French geographer Elisée Reclus, who was well acquainted with the
country. Fanelli was joined in Barcelona by Reclus's brother Elie and by
Aristides Rey, a French doctor, both members of the Alliance for Social
Democracy, who had come to Spain to aid in the launching of a Spanish
anarchist organization. See Juan José Morato, *Lideres del movimiento obrero
español, 1868–1921,* Selection and notes by V. Manuel Arbeloa (Madrid:
Cuadernos para el Dialogo, 1972), p. 30n.
14. Ateneu Catalan del Clase Obrer was founded in Barcelona in 1861 to provide
a cultural life for workers. Toward the end of 1868 it was dominated by
progressive liberals, but after the September revolution, Bakuninists such
as Rafael Farga i Pellicer Paraire, Jaume Balasch, and Josep Llunas i Pujals
predominated. It was closed down in 1874 as was the Spanish section of
the First International following the coup d'état of General Pavía. See *Gran
Enciclopedia Catalana* (Barcelona: Edicións 62, 1969–83), p. 666.

    The two major works on this period are Casamiro Martí's excellent *Origines
del anarquismo en Barcelona* (Barcelona: Teide, 1959), and Josep Termes,
Anarquismo y sindicalismo en España: La primera internacional (1864–1881)
(Barcelona: Critica, 1972).
15. Fernand Pelloutier, *Histoire de bourses de travail* (1901; rpt. Paris: Costes,
1946), p. 77.
16. Quoted in E. H. Carr, *Michael Bakunin* (London: Macmillan, 1937), p. 38.
17. For an examination of anarchist ideas on economic organization see José
Alvarez Junco, *La ideologia política del anarquismo español (1868–1910)* (Madrid: Siglo Veintiuno, 1976), pp. 341–74.
18. Quoted in Juan José Morato, *El Partido Socialista Obrero* (Madrid: Ayuso,
1976), p. 22.
19. Balcells, *Historia contemporanea de Cataluña,* p. 84.
20. Supporters of Bakuninism from 1868 to approximately 1878 were known
as "Aliancistas"; thereafter, they began to refer to themselves as "anarchists."
The Marxist dissidents, originally dubbed the "authoritarians," later preferred the title "socialists." For the problems caused by the congress's apolitical orientation for the Barcelona Federation, which preferred democratic
Federal Republicanism, see Manuel Nuñez de Arenas and Manuel Tuñon

de Lara, *Historia del movimiento obrera español* (Barcelona: Nova Terra, 1970), p. 79.

21. Martí, "Afianzamiento y despliegue del sistema liberal," p. 106. That the Catalan labor movement was predominantly concerned with immediate problems, not with social revolution, is attested by Jaime Vicens Vives and Montserrat Llorens, *Industrials i politics del segle XIX* (1958; rpt. Barcelona: Planeta, 1979), p. 146.

22. Balcells, *Historia contemporanea de Cataluña,* p. 85. Claims vary concerning the membership of FRE, some ranging as high as 300,000. The 30 to 40,000 figure is the one most Spanish labor historians accept. It brings to mind a tendency by labor leaders to inflate their membership claims, which is underscored by this beguiling commentary offered by Gerald Brenan: "But the Anarchists, true Iberians that they are, have never attached much importance to numerical accuracy. 'Let us have no more' wrote the editor of *Solidaridad Obrera* in 1937, 'of those miserable statistics which only freeze the brain and paralyze the blood' " (*The Spanish Labyrinth* [London: Cambridge University Press, 1943], p. 155n).

23. Josep Fontana, quoted in Josep M. Huertas Claveria, *Obrers a Catalunya* (Barcelona: Colleccio Clio I, 1982), p. 49.

24. C. A. M. Hennessy, *The Federal Republic in Spain* (Oxford: Oxford University Press, 1962), pp. 155–66.

25. In the FRE's Málaga Federation, whose adherents from 1871 to 1882 encompassed more than half of the total Andalusian membership, slightly more than half were owners of small land parcels (*minifundistas*). In 1871 the leadership of the federation was almost exclusively made up of artisanal craftsmen: three pastry cooks, a shoemaker, a button maker, a molder, a mechanic, and a barrel maker. See Antonio Nadal, "La formación del movimiento obrero en Málaga," *Estudios de Historia Social,* no. 15 (October–December 1980), pp. 241–70.

26. C. A. M. Hennessy observes that "the main theoretical justification for federal republicanism came from Proudhon and it was in Spain that his political views found their first practical expression outside France. . . . Much of the profundity of his thought . . . eluded the Spaniards who merely used his concept of political federalism to justify their own tentatively formed views" (*Federal Republic,* pp. xiii and xiv).

27. Enric Ucelay da Cal, *La Catalunya populista* (Barcelona: Ediciónes de la Magrana, 1982), pp. 54–55.

28. Antonio Maria Calero, *Movimientos sociales en Andalucia (1820–1936)* (Madrid: Siglo Veintiuno, 1976), p. 19.

29. James Joll, *The Anarchists* (New York: Grosset and Dunlap, 1966), p. 238. "When they resorted to violence that is certainly part of their program, or subversion in the form of insurrections or rebellions, it did not differ at all

from those provoked by Republicans, Filibusteros [parties seeking independence in overseas colonies], Garibaldians, Carlists, Moderates, Alfonsin
monarchists, nationalists, and all parties and sects that generally despaired
of triumphing through legal means" (Diaz del Moral, *Agitaciónes, campesinas
Andaluzas,* p. 123).

30. Termes, *Federalismo,* p. 29.

31. Diego Abad de Santillan, *Historia del movimiento obrero español* (Vizcaya: Zero,
Algorta, 1967), p. 225.

32. Huertas Claveria, *Obrers a Cataluyna,* p. 54.

33. Termes, *Federalismo,* p. 44.

34. As conceived by Errico Malatesta and other leaders of Italian anarchism,
"propaganda by the deed" was understood as insurrection and not political
assassination. "In an ironic twist, the basis for the adoption of 'dynamite
terrorism' (by the London international anarchist conference of 1877) was
not to be found in any tradition of anarchism but in the powerful impression
the successful assassination of Tsar Alexander II by Russian nihilists had left
on Europe. Individual acts of terrorism became the new revolutionary hope
for anarchists" (Ulrich Linse, " 'Propaganda by Deed' and 'Direct Action,' "
in *Social Protest, Violence, and Terror in Nineteenth- and Twentieth-Century
Europe,* ed. Wolfgang Mommsen and Gerhard Hirschfeld [New York: St.
Martin's Press, 1982], p. 203).

35. Quoted in César M. Lorenzo, *Les anarchistes espagnoles et le pouvoir* (Paris:
Seuil, 1969), pp. 30–31. According to Manuel Buenacasa, the idea of setting
up a new national labor center as well as preparations for holding its founding
congress originated with fifty Barcelona "militants." See *El movimiento obrero
español, 1886–1926* (1962; rpt. Madrid: Jucar, 1977), p. 30.

36. Pere Gabriel Sirvent, "Clase obrera i sindicats a Catalunya, 1903–1920"
(Ph.D. dissertation, University of Barcelona, 1981). This study is the best
source on labor organization during the early part of this century. A contributing element to the smaller size of the Catalonian contingent was that
a large part of the Tres Clases de Vapor's membership, the largest and most
important union of cotton textile workers that had been affiliated with the
FRE, chose to remain outside the FTRE, as did the barrel makers' and
weavers' federations.

37. More than half the Andalusian membership consisted of farm laborers and
small farmers. Three-fourths were concentrated in the provinces of Málaga,
Cádiz, and Seville. Even at this early stage anarchist followings attained
mass popular proportions in certain rural towns; FTRE members in ten
localities constituted more than 10 percent of the entire population, which
meant that at least half of all heads of families were adherents. Affiliation
was sparse beyond Andalusia and Catalonia: 5 percent in the Levant, 4

percent in the Castilian provinces, and 1 percent each in Galicia, Aragon, and the Basque country.

38. José Alvarez Junco, a specialist in the ideological evolution of Spanish anarchism, views it from a somewhat different perspective: "Marxist historiography traditionally has stressed the agrarian roots of anarchism. Díaz del Moral or Brenan have linked the Spanish prototype with Bandolerism and Andalusian millenarianism. While, doubtless, this is so, it should not be forgotten that the anarchist agrarian ideal in no manner signified renouncing 'the advantages of modern industrial processes' as observed by Brenan and evidenced in Lorenzo's writings on progress. What distinguished it more as a modern utopia than millenarianism is the 'belief in progress'—a mix of technics and mystique—together with a faith in the reign of justice which, upon achieving a socialist consciousness, would not signify *reparto* (division of the land) but rather collectivization" ("El anarquismo en España," in *Los anarquistas,* ed. I. L. Horowitz, 2 vols. (Madrid: Alianza, 1975), 2: 266–67.

39. Josep Fontana, *Cambio económico y actitudes políticas en la España del siglo XIX* (Barcelona: Ariel, 1973), pp. 189–90.

40. Angel Marvaud, *La question sociale en Espagne* (Paris: Felix Alcan, 1910), p. 45.

41. See Temma Kaplan, *Anarchists of Andalusia, 1868–1903* (Princeton: Princeton University Press, 1977), for a discussion of the anarchist movement in Cádiz province. There is also a Spanish edition.

42. Clara Lida, *Anarquismo y revolución en la España del siglo XIX* (Madrid: Siglo Veintiuno, 1972), p. 251.

43. Díaz del Moral, *Las agitaciónes campesinas Andaluzas,* p. 122.

44. Joaquín Romero Maura stresses the unbridgeable gulf between theory and practice in the disintegration of the anarchist-led labor movement. The anarcho-collectivists insisted that trade unions under their control be purely anarchist, but they found it unavoidable to admit nonanarchist workers despite their disapproval of traditional trade union practices as detrimental to the main goal of preparing for the insurrectionary seizure of power. To retain the support of many textile workers in Catalonia who had joined the federation, it was necessary to allow regular trade union activities, partial strikes to secure improved wages and working conditions, and collective bargaining of a sort. In the south, however, where the *braceros* insisted on satisfying their land hunger, violence was a prerequisite. Thus, though the reformist transgressions in Catalonia could be tolerated, the subversive extremism of the Andalusians imperiled the existence of the entire movement. The end result of this contradiction on a theoretical level took the form of anarcho-communism. As the doctrine of propaganda by the deed became

increasingly dominant in the late 1880s and 1890s, though most anarchists viewed the turn to terrorist violence with repugnance, activists deserted the unions in increasing numbers and embarked upon the isolated, secretive existence of the *grupos de afinidad* (affinity groups) (*La rosa del fuego, el oberismo Barcelonés de 1899 a 1909* [Barcelona: Grijalbo, 1975], pp. 199–202).

45. Clara Lida, a historian of this period, considers the development of radical extremism, especially in Jerez province, not merely a response to the harshness of the repression in the 1870s but an extension of the peasant tradition of secret societies and of Bakuninism. According to J. A. Lacomba, the extremist mood that developed in Málaga province, where anarchist influence was substantial, coincided with the impoverishment of numerous small and medium-sized vineyard owners, who were ruined by the spread of phylloxera. See A. M. Calero, "El movimiento obrero en Andalucia," in J. A. Lacomba, ed., *Approximación a la historia de Andalucia* (Barcelona: Laia, 1978).

   In common with others of the anarcho-communist persuasion, the "Disinherited" believed that "any organization with its inevitable distinctions of leaders and led or administrators and administrated implies an inequality and engenders hierarchy; association is a form of authoritarian organization. . . . There should be an end to societies and labor congresses, in this manner only can the individual enjoy his uncoercive and unsubordinated sovereignty" (Díaz del Moral, *Las agitaciónes campesinas Andaluzas,* p. 122).

46. Romero Maura, *Rosa del fuego,* p. 202.

47. Díaz del Moral, *Agitaciónes campesinas Andaluzas,* p. 122.

48. Alvarez Junco, "El anarquismo en España," p. 271.

49. The novel *La Bodega* by Blasco Ibañez deals with the 1892 anarchist uprising at Jerez de la Frontera.

50. In France during 1892–94 there were an estimated thirteen anarchist attacks, eleven of them in Paris. In Russia, however, a much larger number of notables perished between 1881 and 1911 at the hands of the "nihilists of the deed." David Hannay, the British vice-consul at Barcelona and the author of *Twentieth Century Spain,* claims that much of the violence attributed to the anarchist movement was in response to the savagery of the police repression. See Brenan, *Spanish Labyrinth,* pp. 168–69.

51. The terrorist outrages of the 1890s and the resulting repression gave the term *anarchist* a sinister, forbidding connotation. To avoid this stigma and the suppression of their publications, anarchist groups began to refer to themselves as libertarians.

52. See R. Nuñez Florencio, *El terrorismo anarquista, 1888–1909* (Madrid: Siglo Veintiuno, 1983), p. 48.

53. Balcells, *Historia contemporanea de Cataluña,* p. 128. Anarchists also attempted in 1888 to create a successor organization to the FTRE. Doctrinal cleavages led to the formation of two separate entities; the anarcho-collectivists con-

stituted the Resistance Societies Solidarity Pact and anarcho-communists created the Anarchist Organization of the Spanish Region, conceived as the reincarnation of the old Alianza and as a predecessor for the future FAI. Both proved to be short-lived.

54. Ibid.

CHAPTER 4: EARLY DEVELOPMENT OF THE GENERAL WORKERS UNION (UGT)

1. Because of the small number of supporters, anarchists sarcastically dubbed it the "Federation of the Nine."
2. The Sociedad General del Arte de Imprimir began as a mutual benefit society. Moderate in outlook and nonpolitical, it received support from the mayor of Madrid and other government authorities. The subsequent radicalization of some typographers, including Anselmo Lorenzo and Pablo Iglesias, who soon rose to positions of leadership, led to its conversion into a resistance society.
3. Antoni Jutglar, *Ideologias y clases en la España contemporanea (1808–1874),* 2 vols. (Madrid: Cuadernos para el Dialogo, 1973), 1:274. There were, to be sure, underlying socioeconomic factors that made libertarianism a more readily accessible creed. In 1868, "85 percent of the men and 88 percent of the women were illiterate. Unskilled labor [peonage] predominated, and among the 19 percent [of the population] who were working, only 11 percent were industrial workers. According to Josep Fontana, this retarded structure explains the failure of Republicanism, and Marxism's lack of support in the rivalry for control of the International, the popularity of anarchism, as well as the rise of Carlism that resumed its armed struggle in 1873, the year of the founding of the Republic" (Josep M. Huertas Claveria, *Obrers a Catalunya* (Barcelona: Colleccio Clio 1, 1982), p. 4.

   Jutglar's judgment may be somewhat overstated. Though the anarchist activists did achieve an ascendancy, Albert Balcells has pointed out that "the extent of the labor movement's break with federal republicanism and toward the First International after 1870 has tended to be exaggerated. The truth is that the break in Catalonia was more theoretical than real. In 1873, during the final decade of the nineteenth century and in the early twentieth, worker electoral support for the federals, though not formalized and fluctuating was, nonetheless, effective." See his *Cataluña contemporanea,* vol. 1 *(1815–1900)* (Madrid: Siglo Veintiuno, 1977), p. 96.
4. The party's name was likely inspired by that of the German party, which until 1891 was called the Socialist Workers party of Germany. See Miguel Martínez Cuadrado, *La burgesia conservadora* (Madrid: Alianza Universidad, 1973), p. 359.

5. See Albert Balcells, *Historia contemporanea de Cataluña* (Barcelona: Edihasa, 1986), pp. 123–24.

6. The FRE's Madrid section never established a truly proletarian base and went out of existence in 1876. Anselmo Lorenzo recounts that at the time of the 1868 revolution not a single authentic labor organization (*sociedad obrera de resistencia*) was in existence in Madrid, only some cooperatives and mutual benefit societies. See his *El proletariado militante*, cited in Juan Díaz del Moral, *Historia de las agitaciónes campesinas Andaluzas* (Madrid: Alianza, 1977), p. 75.

7. "The elements Iglesias as leader had at his disposal with respect to resistance organizations were the nine hundred members of the printing arts and the groups of Madrid, Barcelona, and Guadalajara that in the political sphere together did not amount to a hundred adherents." Two additional party branches were soon constituted in Valencia and San Martin de Provensals. See Juan José Morato, *Pablo Iglesias, educador de muchedumbres* (1931; rpt. Barcelona: Ariel, 1977), p. 52.

8. The vanguard role of skilled craftsmen is, of course, a common denominator in the formative process of most labor movements. In Spain their leadership role was made even more imperative by the extremely high illiteracy among such workers. Typographers played a leading role not only in the socialist movement but among anarchists as well: men such as Anselmo Lorenzo, Rafael Farga i Pellicer Paraire, José Llunas i Pujals, and José Poysol; Tomás González Morago had been an engraver. Proudhon, incidentally, also had been a typesetter. During World War I the CNT leadership included numerous typographers, among them Salvador Quemades, Evelio Boal, Rafael Vidiella, and Adolfo Bueso.

9. Juan José Morato, *La cuna de un gigante: Historia de la Asociación General del Arte de Imprimir* (Madrid, 1925), p. 43.

10. Quoted in Manuel Pérez Ledesma, "La Union General de Trabajadores: Ideologia y organización (1888–1931)" (Ph.D. dissertation, Madrid Autonomous University, 1976), p. 173. Pérez's study is the most notable work available on the early years of the UGT. See also his book *El obrero consciente* (Madrid: Alianza Universidad, 1987).

11. Gerald Brenan, *The Spanish Labyrinth* (Cambridge: Cambridge University Press, 1943), p. 218. Even the Republicans had little faith in the electoral process. See Joaquín Romero Maura, "Terrorism in Barcelona and Its Impact on Spanish Politics, 1904–1919," *Past and Present*, no. 41 (1968), p. 138.

12. David Thomson, *Europe since Napoleon* (1957; rpt. London: Penguin, 1984), p. 406.

13. Gerald H. Meaker, *The Revolutionary Left in Spain, 1914–1923* (Palo Alto: Stanford University Press, 1974), p. 2.

14. Pérez Ledesma, "Union General," p. 166. The difficulties of reconciling theory and practice also produced an inordinate disparity between a professed doctrinal radicalism and a relatively reformist comportment. Such was Jules Guesde's unbending dogmatism that, in contrast to Jean Jaures, he disdained taking sides in the celebrated Dreyfus affair, considering it merely another quarrel between rival factions of the bourgeoisie.

    Few European socialist movements were as intensely proletarian in composition as was PSOE. Its simplistic theoretical underpinnings and its suspicion of middle-class intellectuals made the party unattractive to them. Jaime Vera, a doctor by profession, one of the very few in the early leadership to be equipped with a well-developed political intellect, became frustrated and dropped out of active participation during the first years of the party's existence. The collaboration of such outstanding figures as Miguel de Unamuno and José Ortega y Gasset during their youth early in this century was only of limited duration. By the second decade of this century the situation began to change as men such as Julián Besteiro and Fernando de los Rios emerged as leading figures.

15. European socialist parties and trade unions were known for ambiguity regarding their respective roles, but the ideological ingenuousness of the Spanish party was notable. At the Stuttgart congress of the Socialist International in 1907, where party–trade union relations were discussed and delineated, the Spanish delegates artlessly explained that "relations between the party and UGT are of an excellent friendship. Iglesias presides over both. Our union does not force its members to join the party" (quoted in Manuel Nuñez de Arenas and Manuel Tuñon de Lara, *Historia del movimiento obrero español* [Barcelona: Nova Terra, 1970], p. 170n). See also Juan Pablo Fusi, *Política obrera in el pais Vasco* (Madrid: Turner, 1975), p. 69.

16. Pablo Iglesias, *Escritos y discursos; Antologia Crítica,* ed. Enrique Moral Sandoval (Santiago de Campostela: Salvora, 1984), p. 25.

17. Morato, who collaborated closely with Iglesias for many years, described him in the following manner: "He possesses an acute understanding and discourses with logic and clarity. He is capable of overcoming his natural timidity and has enriched his intelligence with an uncommon general knowledge that subsequently became as specialized as possible at an appropriate point in order to better comprehend, defend, and propagate his ideals. But he is not a brilliant man or a forger of doctrines, principles, or theories" (*Partido Socialista Obrero* [Madrid: Ayuso, 1976], p. 221). A special issue of the review *Anthropos,* nos. 45–47 (1985), is devoted to a study of the personality and ideas of Pablo Iglesias.

18. The historian José Maria Jover has pointed out that the centralized control and authority in the PSOE mirrored the "centralism" that imbued so many

aspects of national life. See *Revolución burgesia, oligarquia y constitucionalismo*, vol. 8 of *Historia de España*, ed. Manuel Tuñon de Lara (Barcelona: Editorial Labor, 1981), p. 357.

19. Raymond Carr, *Spain, 1808–1939* (1966; rev. ed. Oxford: Oxford University Press, 1975), p. 447.

20. Brenan, *Spanish Labyrinth*, p. 218.

21. Iglesias's rejection of the general strike also reflected dominant sentiments in European socialist circles. Guesde's categorical opposition to the emerging revolutionary concept of the general strike of the French syndicalists must have been influential. Friedrich Engels expressed similar attitudes, and such authoritative figures as Wilhelm Liebknecht and August Bebel similarly opposed it. Bebel scornfully labeled the general strike as general anarchist nonsense. A middle position was taken by Eduard Bernstein, who contended that under appropriate economic or political circumstances the general strike could be a powerful instrument in influencing governments and securing reforms. Kautsky formulated the idea of the "mass strike," so named to differentiate it from the anarchists' and syndicalists' insurrectionary version, positing its utility as a tactical political weapon.

22. The UGT's refusal to support the 1902 general strike dealt a grievous blow to socialist aspirations in the region because the Barcelona trade unionists attached great importance to its outcome. "In its realization the influence of the new concepts of French revolutionary syndicalism which saw the general strike as a prologue to the social revolution . . . was less important than worker reaction to the employers' wage-cutting offensive in the midst of an overproduction crisis and technological immobility. The immediate effect was the solidarity movement with the metalworkers who had been on strike for two months demanding a reduction in the workday from ten hours to nine. During February 1902 the general strike took place, lasting eight days, and was surprisingly total and peaceful in Barcelona. What was basically at issue was to assure the right of workers to bargain collectively with the factory owners and to halt the employer offensive that had been initiated in the cotton thread spinning sector. The UGT leadership in Madrid opposed the strike so ostentatiously that the future of socialism in Catalonia was impaired" (Balcells, *Historia contemporanea de Cataluña*, pp. 178–79).

23. Pérez Ledesma, "Union General," p. 222. Pere Gabriel points out that though "it was a success to some extent for the anarchists, it would, nonetheless, be a mistake to attribute what occurred on May 2 exclusively to their actions. What essentially did take place was that because of the May first success, seeking to profit from the occasion in order to secure improvements from the eight-hour campaign and the parade that had brought it to the foreground, worker societies launched a struggle. In fact the strike underscored the socialist inability to control the societary movement as well

as the weakness of the anarchists, who had to observe the strike rapidly slip away onto the corporative terrain. The strike, however, did help impose on employers the negotiation of new standards" ("Clase obrera i sindicats a Catalunya, 1903–1920" (Ph.D. dissertation, University of Barcelona, 1981), pp. 370–71.

24. "In such a setting during the monarchy and under the dictatorship, Second International style socialism appeared as excessively legalistic and moderate. . . . From time to time the top leadership of PSOE and UGT put aside its gradualism and engaged in risky general strikes, despite having theoretically repudiated them. These exceptions to the traditional tactics of Spanish socialism—1911, 1912, 1917, 1934—indicate to what extent UGT's disciplined masses found themselves driven at times by Hispanic structures to embrace methods resembling those of anarcho-syndicalism" (Albert Balcells, *El arraigo del anarquismo en Cataluña, textos de 1926–1934* [Madrid, Ediciones Jucar, 1973], p. 23). The 1910 iron miners' strike in Vizcaya, which was transformed into a general strike to assure its success, was of spontaneous origin and was opposed by UGT national officers Largo Caballero and Lucio Martínez; the national railroad strike two years later, called in solidarity with a walkout in Catalonia, was also disapproved of by the national leadership. Balcells has noted that the impetus for socialist-directed general strikes in 1911, 1912, 1917, and 1934 invariably came from Vizcaya and Asturias, not from Madrid.

25. Val Lorwin, *The French Labor Movement* (Cambridge, Mass.: Harvard University Press, 1954), p. 42.

26. Morato, *La cuna de un gigante,* p. 323.

27. José Varela Ortega, *Los amigos políticos, partidos, elecciónes, y caciques en la Restauración (1875–1900)* (Madrid: Alianza, 1977), p. 384.

28. "What has to be essentially questioned is whether Catalonian economic, political, and social conditions were conducive for a trade union movement to attain the kind of moderate, stable existence that developed in England, Belgium, and Germany. Even the Barcelona anarcho-collectivists of 1881 had failed. This occurred despite the fact that their objective was, to a large extent, merely to obtain a legal, stable, moderate existence for the labor movement" (Gabriel, "Clase obrera i sindicats," p. 377).

29. In the 1880s, according to Juan Pablo Fusi, "Vizcaya lacked any tradition of labor organization and industrial conflicts. . . . Worker societies whose objectives were strictly trade unionist practically did not exist (*Política obrera en el pais Vasco,* pp. 67–68).

Until 1909 the majority of organized workers in the north were affiliated with Republican centers. See Manuel Buenacasa, *El movimiento obrero español, 1886–1926* (1962; rpt. Madrid: Jucar; 1977), p. 103.

30. Fusi, *Política obrera en el pais Vasco,* p. 66. Joaquín Maurín called him

"the most capable agitator that socialism possessed in the country" (*Los hombres de la dictadura* [1930; rpt. Barcelona: Anagrama, 1977], p. 178).

Strongman rule of local party and trade union organizations was the general rule. Caudillos such as Cabello in Valladolid, Lorite in Jaen, Sanchis in Valencia, Torrijos in San Sebastian, Vigil in Gijón-Oviedo, and Llaneza in Mieres ran their movements with an iron hand. Close ties of friendship aided in the coordination of and adhesion to national policy directives. See Juan Pablo Fusi, "El movimiento socialista en España, 1879–1939," *Actualidad Económica,* no. 145 (May 25, 1974), p. 63.

31. "It is in the canteens with their provisions stacked in piles and owned by independent, enriched foremen, that purchases must be made without complaint, provisions for which men left part of themselves at the bottom of the pits.

"Foremen and canteen keepers thrived at the cost of the Castilian, Extremaduran, Galician, or Andalusian peasants who are without alternative, for not to make their purchases in the canteen, one would lose his job in the pit. By paying the workers on a monthly instead of a weekly basis forces the workers to live on credit and the mine owners thus enrich the foremen and the canteen keepers.

"Close by are the housing barracks, company property where human beings are packed in like cattle.

" 'At night when the workers have retired, the barracks filled with the smoke of coarse tobacco and flickering light of an oil or kerosene lamp hanging in the center of the room, offered a Dantean spectacle. The faces of the partly naked men could be dimly perceived moving between the bunks or seated on sleeping mats in a pestilential atmosphere in which the odor of sweat, fermenting food, and urine joined with the nauseating detritus that overflowed the large chamber pots in small open areas adjoining the common room of each barrack.'

"Foremen and canteen keepers! Housing barracks owned by the companies. Company towns. Truck system. Dawn to dusk work days.

"Desks where the sales to England were formalized and where the local *caciques* purchased votes for their political patrons.

"Foremen and canteen keepers! Employers without consciences! On their side the law. And with the law the guns of the Civil Guard" (Dolores Ibarruri, *El unico camino* [Barcelona: Brugera, 1979], p. 25, reproduced in Alfonso Carlos Saiz Valdivieso, *Indalecio Prieto, crónica de un corazon* [Barcelona: Planeta, 1984], pp. 19–20).

The "truck system," which was a major source of the miners' discontent, was formally abolished by royal decree on July 19, 1907, some seventeen years after the explosive outburst of 1890.

32. Fusi, *Política obrera en el pais Vasco,* p. 93.
33. The lack of UGT cadres forced socialist local groups to assume this function. See ibid., p. 102.
34. Ibid., p. 130.
35. "The increase in production was particularly marked after 1885, coinciding with the appearance of three large companies, Unión Hullera and Metalurgica Asturiana in 1885, Hulleras del Turon in 1890, and Hullera Española in 1892. 'A new division of production appeared after 1888–1889,' as Chastagnaret has noted, 'and only the strong enterprises seemed to perform roles in the production process' " (Adrian Shubert, *Hacia la revolución: Origenes sociales del movimiento obrero en Asturias, 1860–1934* [Barcelona: Crítica, 1984], p. 18).
36. Ibid., p. 131.
37. Ibid., pp. 131–32.
38. In his *Hombres de Asturias* (1964) socialist leader Andrés Saborit notes that the 1903 official UGT figures indicating twenty-one affiliates and 2,956 members in the region were inaccurate and understated socialist trade union strength, for most of the Asturian party branches did not pay dues to the UGT even though they were often involved directly in labor disputes and collective bargaining.

    The blurring of party and trade union functions that took place in various parts of the country, according to Manuel Tuñon de Lara, "had always been accentuated by the fact that PSOE's statutes permitted the affiliation of craft societies [*sociedades de oficio*] in the same manner as socialist branches, thus creating confusion between the respective nature and objectives of the worker's political party and the union; this phenomenon—that of the so-called 'entities'—that were not branches, was to last a long time, especially in the Andalusian countryside where it was very difficult to distinguish between socialist militants and 'Ugetistas' and where undoubtedly the confusion between party and union became exceptional" ("Sobre la historia del pensamiento socialista entre 1900 y 1931," in *Teoria y practica del movimiento obrero en España (1900–1936),* ed. Albert Balcells [Valencia: Fernando Torres, 1977], p. 24).
39. "Llaneza upon his return to Asturias in 1910 was determined to avoid the decentralization that had characterized the early unions and had so greatly facilitated their destruction, and to organize a new union based on the model provided by those of northern France: 'The sections possessed no autonomy and could make demands or go on strike only with the authorization of the executive committee. Dues went to the union treasurer with the section retaining a portion, with the prior accord of the Mieres committee, that was indispensable for local expenses' " (Shubert, *Hacia la revolución,* p. 141).

40. The SMA's hegemonic status in the work force was incomplete for some years because of the bitter resistance by the management of Hullera Española, one of the region's major colleries, which was owned by the Marquis de Comillas, a leading conservative figure in Catholic social action affairs. A confessional union was set up and supported by the company in a costly and lengthy effort to prevent the entry of the socialists and SMA. The company also refused to become a member of the region's mine owners association and to become a signatory to regional labor accords with SMA. When the management in 1917 refused to accept an industrywide agreement, its employees walked out and the company ceased operations. After nineteen days of shutdown the Institute of Social Reforms dispatched General Marvá to mediate the dispute. A vote was then conducted among the workers that was easily won by SMA. When after two weeks the company refused to resume operations and accept the SMA, it was ordered to do so by the government. Though the bitter and often violent rivalry between the SMA and the Catholic union continued for some time thereafter, it was the beginning of the end for the Catholic organization.

41. Victor Manuel Arbeloa, *Las casas del pueblo* (Madrid: Editorial Mañana, 1977), provides a comprehensive treatment of their development and location.

42. Carr, *Spain, 1808–1939,* p. 455. The anarchist-sponsored Ateneo Obrero of Gijón also conducted educational and cultural programs. Manuel Buenacasa described it as "one of the most important cultural entities of Spain" (*Movimiento obrero español,* p. 142).

43. Promotors of the University of Oviedo's extension program included Adolfo Buylla, who later was to become a leading figure in the work of the Institute for Social Reforms; Adolfo Posada; the historian Rafael Altamira; Aniceto Sela; and Leopoldo Alas, "Clarin," Asturias's most illustrious writer and journalist.

Henri Lorin of the French social research institution Le Musée Social described the Oviedo Labor Societies Center in 1911: "The Oviedo center today possesses more than 1,100 members among the various affiliated societies. The building that it occupies has been constructed by the voluntary cooperation of affiliated masons, carpenters, and supported by the financial contributions of its members. It is a modest edifice but ingeniously constructed to permit an economic development; a large meeting hall on the ground floor, on the first floor a classroom, a library, a large room for the secretariats of the eleven societies of the central group, a consumer cooperative, which appeared to be stocked with good merchandise and well frequented, is situated in an adjoining building. . . .

"The center's primary school offers its courses in the evening after work;

it accepts as students both adults and children who are the offspring of society members. We have observed a young man of nineteen years who, several months ago, arrived totally illiterate and who today reads and calculates with ease. . . . He pays his society a monthly fee of 10 centimes and this payment gives him the right to enroll in the school. The center is currently attempting to organize a musical group with chorus and orchestra; it already possesses an actors' troupe.

"More original are the extension's public classes and lectures. In 1908–9 the first series included Spanish, arithmetic, physiology, French, grammar, and literary readings. . . . The participants, on the average aged thirty to fifty, are for the most part workers who arrive in their work clothes between the end of work and the evening meal.

"Regular lectures, originally bimonthly and now weekly, are given at the Worker Societies Center by the extension. Sometimes the lecturers speak on a single theme (the labor contract, notions on the center of gravity, etc.), sometimes with two to four lessons: the history of the earth, contemporary Europe. . . . The other day, a young teacher from Bilbao discoursed spiritedly before an audience of more than five hundred, including a number of female workers, on feminism" (*Dans les Asturies: L'Universite d'Oviedo et l'enseignement populaire* [Paris: Le Musée Social, 1911], pp. 212–15).

44. A power struggle took place in 1911 over whether to continue the militant radical policies of Perezagua or the more conciliatory ones advocated by Indalecio Prieto. Prieto finally won out, and Perezagua, embittered and frustrated, was expelled from the PSOE and later headed the newly created Communist party in Bilbao.

In the postwar years, as the precariously based Asturian mine economy underwent a steady decline, Llaneza endeavored to prevent radicalized elements in the SMA from engaging the union in extreme, destructive actions.

It should also be kept in mind that illiteracy in Asturias was much less widespread than in other parts of the country, and the general standard of living was somewhat higher than in central and southern Spain.

45. "Statutes of the [French] northern miners federation, for example, insisted that workers try conciliation procedures before any strike and undertake no effort without approval of at least two thirds of the membership. They worked for realistic demands that could be won without total conflict with management" (Peter Stearns, *Revolutionary Syndicalism and French Labor* [New Brunswick, N.J.: Rutgers University Press, 1971], p. 25).

46. Melquiades Alvarez had been a member of the University of Oviedo faculty and participated in the promotion of its extension service. Later he became a leading figure in Republicanism and founder of the Reformist party and

a prominent figure in national affairs until his untimely and tragic murder by pro-Republic zealots at the civil war's outset. He was regularly elected to the Chamber of Deputies, first representing Gijón and then Oviedo. During the abortive 1917 general strike, he directed the insurrection in Asturias and concealed Llaneza, who was sought by the authorities, in his home.

47. Raymond Carr and Juan Pablo Fusi, *Spain: Dictatorship to Democracy* (London: Allen & Unwin, 1979), p. 141.

48. José Luis García Delgado, "Cuarte parte, la economía española entre 1900 y 1923," in *Revolución burgesa,* pp. 420–21.

49. According to official census reports, from 1857 to 1900 the population of Barcelona grew from 215,000 to 533,000 and that of Madrid from 200,000 to 540,000.

50. Fernanda Romeu, *La clases trabajadores en España (1898–1930)* (Madrid: Taurus, 1970), p. 46.

51. Only by World War I would industrial workers outnumber those engaged in artisanal occupations.

52. Shubert, *Hacia la revolución,* p. 134.

53. Jaime Vicens Vives et al., *Historia de España y America, social y económica,* 5 vols. (1957; rpt. Barcelona: Ed. Vicens Vives, 1979), 5:327.

54. Manuel Tuñon de Lara, *El movimiento obrero en la historia de España (1900–1923),* 3 vols. (Barcelona: Laia, 1972), 2:51.

55. Figures on PSOE membership in its early years differ. Xavier Cuadrat in his *Socialismo y anarquismo en Cataluña (1899–1911)* (Madrid: Revista de Trabajo, 1976), pp. 17–32, 131–52, has made a critical survey of official and unofficial claims.

56. Morato, *La cuna de un gigante,* p. 424.

57. The historian Miguel Martínez Cuadrado has concluded that if the elections of 1901 had been honestly conducted, the PSOE would probably have elected two members to the Congress of Deputies, one from Bilbao and another from Madrid. See his *Elecciónes y partidos políticos, 1868–1931* (Madrid: Taurus, 1969), p. 643.

58. Fusi, *Política obrera en el pais Vasco,* p. 265.

59. Ibid., p. 315.

60. Tuñon de Lara, *Movimiento obrero,* 2:152.

61. Buenacasa, *Movimiento obrero español,* p. 42.

62. César M. Lorenzo, *Les anarchistes espagnoles et le pouvoir, 1868–1969* (Paris: Seuil, 1969), p. 48. The author points out that until 1920 many of the best minds within the Catalonian anarchist movement remained pure anarchists and opposed participation in trade union affairs.

63. Julián Gorkin, *El proceso de Moscou en Barcelona* (Barcelona: Ayma, 1974), pp. 64–65.

CHAPTER 5: THE TRIALS AND TRIBULATIONS OF LABOR IN CATALONIA

1. Jordi Nadal and Carles Sudrià, *Historia de la caixa de pensions* (Barcelona: Ediciónes 62, 1981), p. 21. Outbursts of protest by workers, occasioned generally by unemployment and declining real wages after 1900, also took place in France and in much of industrial Europe.

2. See Jaime Vicens Vives, "El moviment obrerista Català (1901–1939)," *Recerques* 7 (1977–78):16. Some of the anarchist labor activists must have been of a moderate persuasion for, much to the disgust of their Barcelona comrades, the organization publicly petitioned government authorities in Madrid to enact protective labor legislation.

3. Jordi Arquer, *Salvador Seguí (Noi del Sucre) treinta y seis años de una vida (1887–1923)* (Barcelona: C.I.B., n.d.).

4. Joan Connelly Ullman, *The Tragic Week: A Study in Anticlericalism in Spain, 1875–1912* (Cambridge, Mass.: Harvard University Press, 1968), p. 68. The agreement limited the replacement of men by women workers, included stipulations for the establishment of a joint labor-management committee (*jurado mixto*) to arbitrate future disputes, and created a *montepio*, a fund to which employers and employees would contribute to finance old age pensions. The two most notable studies of this period are that of Ullman (a slightly expanded Spanish edition is also available) and Joaquín Romero Maura, *La rosa del fuego, el obrerismo Barcelonés de 1899 a 1909* (Barcelona: Grijalbo, 1975).

5. Ullman, *Tragic Week*, p. 68.

6. Manuel Tuñon de Lara, *El movimiento obrero en la historia de España, 1900–1923*, 3 vols. (Barcelona: Laia, 1972), 2:47. According to social Catholics, union membership on the eve of the general strike in Barcelona stood at forty-five thousand, less than one-third of the entire work force. Ullman considers this figure slightly overstated (*Tragic Week*, p. 123). An unprecedented rash of labor disputes took place that year throughout much of the country, including anarchist-led general strikes in Gijón, La Coruña, and Seville.

7. Albert Balcells, *Historia contemporanea de Cataluña* (Barcelona: Edhasa, 1983), p. 178.

8. Vicens Vives, "El moviment obrerista Català," p. 17.

9. Manuel Buenacasa, the anarchist leader and chronicler, describes the inexperience and setbacks in *El movimiento obrero español, 1886–1926* (1962; rpt. Madrid: Jucar, 1977), pp. 29–45.

10. Balcells, *Historia contemporanea de Cataluña*, pp. 181–82.

11. Ibid., p. 182. In 1901 there were only two Republican centers in operation; by 1909 there were fifty. Joaquín Romero Maura describes the situation at the time of Lerroux's arrival: "When Lerroux arrived on the scene in 1901,

he found the working masses in desperate circumstances. Prices were rising much more rapidly than wages, and at the same time there was much redundancy and unemployment. Approximately 50 percent of the Barcelona working-class population was illiterate. Official statistics and sources reveal how awful their living conditions were. A very high incidence of tuberculosis, typhoid, and smallpox existed. These underprivileged masses had little contact with the established culture of the middle classes. The church did not take much interest. Lerroux offered these masses municipal patronage and established self-help organizations and schools, financed in part by funds provided by wealthy Republicans (until 1906 at least, when most of them, it seems, joined Solidaridad Catalana)" ("Terrorism in Barcelona, 1904–1909," *Past and Present,* no. 41 (1968), p. 164.

12. Antonio Maria Calero, "Movimiento obrero y sindicalismo," in *Historia de Andalucia,* 9 vols. (Barcelona: Cupsa-Planeta, 1982), 8:122.

13. Edward Malefakis, *Agrarian Reform and Peasant Revolution in Spain* (New Haven: Yale University Press, 1970), pp. 140–41.

14. Tuñon de Lara, *Movimiento obrero,* 2:51–52.

15. Angel Marvaud, *La cuestión sociale en España* (Madrid: Revista de Trabajo, 1975), p. 96 (Spanish edition).

16. Joaquín Romero Maura, "Spanish Anarchism," in *Anarchism Today,* ed. David E. Apter and James Joll (London: Macmillan, 1971), p. 70.

17. The Catalonian section of the UGT had declined by 1908 to a paltry membership of 469, all of it concentrated in Barcelona. The PSOE, whose greatest influence lay in the industrial town of Mataró, consisted of small branches in ten localities.

18. "Antonio Fabra Ribas was among those of a liberal profession who were attracted to Spanish socialism and who in France, Germany, and England had always been on the side of the socialists. . . . Like many socialists Fabra Ribas did not partake of the notion that syndicalism was a new incarnation of anarchism, and when he returned to Barcelona, encountering a strong syndicalist current and accepting the reality of the aversion of Catalonian organizations to join the General Union (UGT), believed that this nucleus created for mutual assistance against persecution should be converted into a (county) federation" (Manuel Nuñez de Arenas and Manuel Tuñon de Lara, *Historia del movimiento obrero español* [Barcelona: Nova Terra, 1970], p. 144).

19. See José Negre, *Recuerdos de un viejo militant* (Barcelona: Cuaderno 1, 1936?), p. 7.

20. Although SO attracted only fifteen thousand followers in all of Catalonia, Lerroux succeeded in winning thirty to thirty-five thousand proletarian votes in Barcelona, a majority of them from women workers. See Joaquín Maurín, *L'anarcho-syndicalisme en Espagne* (Paris: Petite Bibliothèque de Internationale Sindicale Rouge, 1924), p. 21. Anarchists in SO joined together to form

the Trade Union Atheneum (Ateneo Sindicalista) "to operate alongside worker societies, but lodged in their quarters, to provide a platform for propagators of revolutionary trade unionism, to advance the growth of sizable minorities of anarchist unionists to orient that splendorous organization along revolutionary lines" (Negre, *Recuerdos de un viejo militant*, p. 28).

21. The Barcelona metalworkers union, which on the eve of its 1901–2 industrywide strike had enrolled approximately four thousand of the twelve thousand in its jurisdiction, as late as 1909 had not been able to recuperate its strength and had only three hundred members. Despite their small numbers the union was able to spearhead the general strike of July 26.

   "Not more than 50 to 60,000 unionized workers existed in the entire country in 1909 compared with 900,000 in France, two million in Germany, and two and a half million in Great Britain" (César M. Lorenzo, *Les anarchistes espagnoles et le pouvoir, 1868–1969* [Paris: Seuil, 1969], p. 43).

22. French syndicalist ideas may have been of secondary importance in the shaping of Spanish anarcho-syndicalism, but they did exercise a certain influence. For example, starting in 1907, the term *sindicato* began to replace *sociedad obrera de resistencia al capital* (workers resistance society against capital). See Joan Connelly Ullman, *La Semana Tragica* (Barcelona: Ariel, 1972), p. 193.

   Only eleven strikes took place in Barcelona during 1909, ten before the Tragic Week, of which only three were won or resolved through compromises. The remaining eight ended in total defeat for the workers. Only one was settled through direct negotiations between an employer and a resistance society. See *Las huelgas en Barcelona y sus resultados durante los años 1910 al 1915* (Barcelona: Editorial Barcelonesa, 1915). Social Catholic Sastre prepared annual strike surveys of Barcelona between 1904 and 1914 that are key sources of information in those years.

23. During an antiwar rally on July 11 Pablo Iglesias declared, "The Moroccans are not enemies of the Spanish people; its government is. The government should be opposed with all available means. Instead of firing downward, soldiers should fire upward. If necessary workers will go on a general strike with all its consequences, without taking into account the reprisals that the government may levy against them" (quoted in Nuñez de Arenas and Tuñon de Lara, *Movimiento obrero español*, p. 171).

24. Quoted in Juan Benet, *Maragall i la Semana Tragica* (Barcelona: Edicións 62, 1965), p. 50.

25. Adolfo Bueso, *Recuerdos de un Cenetista*, 2 vols. (Barcelona: Ariel, 1976), 1:32.

26. Ullman's contention that the church burnings were a direct result of Lerrouxist manipulations is controversial. In *La rosa del fuego* Joaquín Romero Maura expresses doubt as to whether the church destructions were

so concertedly inspired by the Lerrouxists (see pp. 519–20). David Ruiz claims that the churches became the principal target of popular fury because industrial enterprises and public buildings were heavily guarded but the churches were left defenseless. See his "España 1902–1923: Vida política, social y cultural," in *Revolución burguesa, oligarquia y constitucionalismo (1834–1923),* vol. 8 of *Historia de España,* ed. Manuel Tuñon de Lara (Barcelona: Labor, 1981), p. 485. The journalist Claudi Ametlla, who was present in the city during the Tragic Week, avers that the churches were desecrated mainly by teenagers, many of them from the city's slum districts, who were joined by young Lerrouxist activists, members of the "Young Barbarians" (Jovenes Barbaros). See his *Memories politiques, 1890–1917* (Barcelona: Portic, 1963). Juan Benet has pointed out that on July 25, the day before the declaration of the general strike, the two dailies most read by the lower classes, the Lerrouxist *El Progreso* and the anticlerical *El Diluvio,* both carried leading articles exalting the burning of convents in 1835 as an event to be emulated. See Benet, *Maragall i la Semana Tragica,* pp. 23–24.

27. For the failure in general to harm nuns and priests, despite the incendiary anticlerical propaganda of the Lerrouxists, see Bueso, *Recuerdos de un Cenetista* p. 32.

28. Juan Benet, "Demogogia, catastrofes y desconocimiento," *El Pais Semanal* (Madrid), July 29, 1984, no. 381, pp. 23–24.

29. Count Romanones, *Notas de una vida, 1912–1931,* 3 vols. (Madrid: Renácimiento, 1947). Francesc Cambó told intimates that the repressive measures ordered by the Maura government were "worse than a crime; they were a great immense stupidity." "The manner in which the Maura government conducted the repression was another error. . . . he sent a new civil governor to Barcelona to substitute for Ossorio y Gallardo . . . a person who was a 'silent' deputy in the Cortes and who, according to Cambó, 'possessed an absolute ignorance of Catalonia. His conduct was a total disaster' " (Benet, "Demogogia," pp. 23–24).

30. A number of the country's leading intellectual figures, including Nobel Prize winner Ramon y Cajal, served as members of an advisory board of the Escuela Moderna, which collaborated with the anarchists' "rationalist" schools as well as those operated by the Lerrouxists.

31. See Jaime Vicens Vives, *Historia social y economic de España y America,* 5 vols. (Barcelona: Vicens, 1972), 5:340.

32. Anarchist influence had spread to Valencia and Aragon, probably because these two regions furnished the bulk of non-Catalonian immigrants to the Barcelona area.

33. Lorenzo, *Les anarchistes,* p. 45.

34. Francesc Bonamusa, *Congreso de Constitución de la Confederación Nacional del Trabajo (CNT)* (Barcelona: Editorial Anagrama, 1976), p. 10.

35. Val Lorwin, *The French Labor Movement* (Cambridge, Mass.: Harvard University Press, 1954), p. 44. Some idea of radical anarchist influence can be gained from attempts made during July and August 1910 to launch a general strike in solidarity with strikers in Bilbao and Zaragossa. At a meeting held on August 3 attended by representatives of forty out of the forty-five societies affiliated with the CNT, fourteen voted in favor, eight were opposed, and twenty abstained. After two further votes, eighteen voted yes, twelve no, and ten abstained. Then it was agreed to permit delegates to consult with their respective organizations and to take still another vote. The final vote reportedly stood at twenty-five in favor, fourteen opposed, and three abstentions. On August 5, when the general strike was to take place, only a relatively small number of workers responded to the strike call. See *Las huelgas en Barcelona.*

36. "The revolutionary strike was conceived in Barcelona as an insurrectionary act, in Paris as a virtually painless attitude assumed by the working class that would suffice for the corrupted foundation of present-day decrepit, unbalanced society to collapse. The Barcelonites were interested in the new techniques but not in the underlying philosophy of revolutionary syndicalism; that would come later. The new fervor for the insurrectional general strike was another version of the old anarcho-communist faith, as a revolutionary shortcut since terrorism had not brought the masses into the streets, perhaps the flame would spread if a general shutdown took place" (Maura, *La rosa del fuego,* p. 206).

CHAPTER 6: CATHOLIC LABOR: ECCLESIASTICAL MYOPIA AND DISASTER

1. José Manuel Cuenca Toribio, "Iglesia y poder político," in *Le era Isabelina en el Sexenio Democratico (1834–1874),* vol. 34 of *Historia de España,* ed. Manuel Tuñon de Lara (Madrid: Espasa Calpe, 1981), p. 571.

2. Father Casamiro Martí, the leading historian, who is currently engaged in research on the Spanish church in the late nineteenth century, has discovered that the conservative hierarchy was severely circumscribed by an even more conservative Catholic grass roots (interview, November 23, 1985). In 1910 Marvaud wrote that "the reactionary spirit is still that of the large majority of Spanish Catholics and especially of members of the clergy." See *La cuestión sociale en España* (Madrid: Revista de Trabajo, 1975), p. 222.

3. William J. Callahan, *Church, Politics, and Society in Spain, 1750–1894* (Cambridge, Mass.: Harvard University Press, 1984), p. 183.

4. Ibid., p. 1.

5. Michael P. Fogarty, *Christian Democracy in Western Europe, 1820–1953* (London: Routledge & Kegan Paul, 1957), p. 186.

6. Juan Díaz del Moral, *Historia de las agitaciónes campesinas Andaluzas* (Madrid: Alianza, 1977), p. 146. José Andrés Gallego claims that the 1883 repression was less responsible for the decline of the circles than the transfer that year of Bishop González to Seville. His successor as bishop of Córdoba evinced less interest in the promotion of social action initiatives. See Gallego, *Pensamiento y acción social del la iglesia en España* (Madrid: Espasa-Calpe, 1984), p. 189.

7. Quoted in Montserrat Llorens, "El P. Antonio Vicent S.I. (1837–1912); Notas sobre el desarrollo de la Acción Social Catolica en España," *Estudios de Historia Moderna* 4 (1954). Severino Aznar, originally a Carlist, was converted in 1904 to social Catholicism by Vicent.

8. For the French influence on the development of Spanish Catholic Workers Circles, see Gallego, *Pensamiento y acción social,* p. 178.

9. Ibid., p. 193.

10. Patronages or Patronages of Young Workers were usually devoted to education and occupational training of young workers and sometimes also conducted mutual benefit programs. Upon coming of age adherents would become circle members. The patronage of St. Vincent de Paul catered to the needs of the poor.

11. Gallego, *Pensamiento y acción social,* pp. 192–93. "*Economic objectives,* compared with religio-moral and educational activities, were often neglected and were, moreover, carried out more with paternalistic, welfarist initiatives than with authentically mutualist ones" (Feliciano Montero García, *El primer Catolicísmo social y la* Rerum Novarum *en España (1889–1902)* [Madrid: CSIC, 1983], p. 314).

12. Raymond Carr, *Spain, 1808–1939* (1966; rev. ed. Oxford: Oxford University Press, 1982), p. 457. See also Domingo Benavides Gómez, *Democracia y cristianismo en la España de la Restauración, 1875–1931* (Madrid: Editora Nacional, 1978), p. 215.

13. Though numerous members of the nobility, high-ranking military officers, academics, and leading conservative politicians participated in the circles movement, an appreciably smaller number of employers did so.

14. One reason for this extraordinary, persistent clericalization of confessional unionism, insists José Andrés Gallego, is that the disappearance of the old absolutist regime in which clerics played a prominent role as politicians and rulers was only a few decades removed and no clear doctrine had been subsequently established concerning the role of priests in temporal affairs. "The basic motivations for those who took part in social Catholicism was clearly resumed by the Jesuit Vicent during the early 1890s in his 'Socialism and Anarchism': the world is dechristianizing (and the proletariat with it),

its rechristianization is necessary. The clerics are the mediators par excellence between Christ and men. Consequently theirs is the principal function" (*Pensamiento y acción social*, p. 420).

15. Montero, *El primer Catolicísmo social*, p. 20.

16. Feliciano Montero García, "Reformismo conservador y Catolicísmo social en la España de la Restauración, 1890–1900," in *Resumenes de tesis doctorales* (Salamanca: University of Salamanca, 1980), p. 45. Domingo Benavides Gómez agrees that Spanish Catholicism was incapable of dealing with the problems of the modern proletariat but that *Rerum Novarum* "served to shift the attention somewhat of some Catholics to the social terrain" (Benavides, *Democracia y cristianismo*, p. 211).

17. Gallego, *Pensamiemto y acción social*, pp. 203–15.

18. Benavides, *Democracia y cristianismo*, p. 220.

19. See Gallego, *Pensamiento y acción social*, p. 417.

20. Colin Winston, *Workers and the Right in Spain, 1900–1936* (Princeton: Princeton University Press, 1985), p. 34.

21. Benavides Gómez, *Democracia y cristianismo*, p. 222.

22. Montero García, *El primer Catolicísmo social*, p. 329.

23. *Boletin del Consejo Nacional de las Corporaciónes Católico-Obreras* (1904), p. 14, quoted in Benavides, *Democracia y cristianismo*, p. 225. Still another reason for their failure was that "a large portion of the circles' membership consisted of country folk, artisans or workers from quasi-artisanal small industry. When he therefore sought to establish his trade associations—which were to be composed of employers and workers—he was inevitably drawn into forming artisans guilds and peasant associations. The term he employed in the statutes—*gremio,* guild—to designate this type of society is highly significant. It is a clear reference to medieval antecedents that he had studied intensely and which inspired him at the time. The result of this campaign, begun in 1893, that he called *agremiacion,* was highly irregular. The peasant associations were generally consolidated, and soon there developed a very important core of agricultural unions and rural banks. On the other hand, the artisans guilds, and those of workers even more so, languished and disappeared without a trace. From 1897 Father Vicent devoted his entire activity to the formation and organization of rural associations, independent of the Worker Circles, which he considered destroyed from the moment they demonstrated their incapacity corporatively to organize their adherents, employers and workers" (Casamiro Martí, J. N. Garcia-Nieto S.J., and Montserrat Llorens, "L'Espagne," in *150 ans de movement ouvrier Chretien en Europe de l'ouest,* ed. S. H. Scholl [Louvain: Editions Nauwelaerts, 1966], pp. 186–87).

24. "El palacio de los obreros," *La Paz Social* 1 (1907): 266–67, quoted in Gallego, *Pensamiento y acción*, p. 281.

25. Benavides Gómez, *Democracia y cristianismo*, p. 223.

26. Callahan, *Church, Politics, and Society in Spain*, p. 229.
27. Employers sometimes used Catholic labor organizations to recruit strike-breakers. "By 1900 the Church was a symbol of an unjust social order to many of the lower classes as it had been at the beginning of the century to liberals" (Richard Herr, *An Historical Essay on Modern Spain* (1971; paperback ed. Berkeley and Los Angeles: University of California Press, 1974), p. 122.
28. Fogarty, *Christian Democracy*, pp. 186–87.
29. Winston, *Workers and the Right in Spain*, p. 49.
30. Montero García, *El primer Catolicísmo social*, p. 317.
31. *La Paz Social* 4 (1913): 680, quoted by Gallego, *Pensamiento y acción*, p. 310.
32. Winston, *Workers and the Right in Spain*, p. 38. This book includes the most comprehensive overview currently available of the ASP; see chapter 2. See also Gallego, *Pensimiento y acción*, pp. 352–54.
33. Winston, *Workers and the Right in Spain*, pp. 45–47.
34. Ibid., pp. 55–56.
35. ASP's pretensions to serve as the principal fount of social action were viewed by the Comillas-led National Council of Catholic Worker Corporations as threatening its preeminence. Nor was it positively regarded by Cardinal Primate Guisasola, who in 1915 gave faint praise for the work accomplished by ASP, then added, "But Father Palau seeks to direct from Barcelona the Catholic Action of all Spain and this cannot be" (quoted in Domingo Benavides, *El fracaso social de Catolicísmo español: Arboleya Martínez, 1870–1951* [Barcelona: Nova Terra, 1973], p. 73).
36. As the UGT gained ascendancy among the workers of Madrid, young workers, after finishing their vocational studies at Catholic schools (*patronatos*), often found it necessary to join the UGT union of their trade to secure employment. Some workers belonged to both: to the Worker Circles to benefit from the various welfare and benefit services and to the socialist UGT to find employment and to protect their basic labor rights. A similar situation developed in Oviedo.
37. *Revista Social* 10, no. 136 (1911): 764, quoted in Gallego, *Pensamiento y acción*, p. 309.
38. Benavides Gómez, *Democracia y cristianismo*, p. 303.
39. In 1918 the railroad federation was merged with a miners federation to form the Railroad and Mining Secretariat, also based in Valladolid. With Agustin Ruiz and Nevares as its principal leaders, it sought to pool resources in its fierce rivalry with the UGT. Most of its efforts were concentrated in the north, in Asturias, León, Vizcaya, and Castile. Major organizational campaigns were also undertaken at Rio Tinto and at the big La Union mine in Murcia. Official membership claims for the two industrial federations were grossly inflated to conceal the small actual membership and to make them

appear as more credible rivals to their much larger socialist counterparts. In 1920, when the Sindicato Ferroviario Católico was at its height, a membership of 14,000 was claimed. Juan José Castillo has concluded that the true figure was less than 2,500. The Sindicato Católico de Obreros Mineros Españoles, according to a census conducted by the Institute of Social Reforms, possessed 8,900 adherents at the end of 1919. The combined membership of these two organizations represented somewhere between a quarter and a third of the entire membership of Catholic nonagricultural labor groups. For background see Juan José Castillo, *El sindicalismo amarillo en España* (Madrid: Edicusa, 1977), pp. 103–221.

40. In the 1907 election for members of the Bilbao local committee of IRS, the St. Vincent de Paul Patronage claimed 2,200 members, a figure that Juan Pablo Fusi believes to be somewhat inflated, "but it attested to the extent of Catholic progress." Some workers were attracted, particularly during this period of hard times, by the material benefits derived from joining the various Catholic groups such as the provision of two pesetas daily in case of illness, layoff, or accident, free medical and pharmaceutical services, and hiring preference by employers to Patronage members. See Fusi, *Política obrera en el país Vasco (1880–1923)* (Madrid: Turner, 1975), p. 266.

41. Margarita Otaegui, "Organisación obrera y nacionalismo: Solidaridad de Obreros Vascos (1911–1923)," *Estudios de Historia Social,* nos. 18–19 (July–Dec. 1981).

42. Paul Vignaux, "Introduction à l'étude historique de mouvement syndical chretien," *International Review for Social History* 2 (1937): 35.

43. A successor organization, Acción Popular, was formed to take the place of ASP, but it conducted a much scaled-down program of activities and exerted little perceptible effect on general social developments.

44. On Arboleya see Benavides, *El fracaso de Catolicísmo social español.*

45. The failure of labor priests Arboleya, Gerard, Gafo, Ibeas, and Yoldi and of Cardinal Primate Guisasola redounded unfavorably on the small band of Christian Democrats, men such as Angel Herrera, the editor of the Madrid Catholic daily *El Debate,* Severino Aznar, Ossorio y Gallardo, the left Maurists, and Pedro Sangro, whose efforts to form a modern Catholic party in Spain were brought to an abrupt end by the coup d'état of General Primo de Rivera in 1923.

46. From an article by Arboleya in *Asturias Agraria,* May 15, 1925, cited in Benavides, *El fracaso de Catolicísmo social español,* p. 573.

47. Juan José Castillo, *Propietarios muy pobres, sobre la subordinacion política del pequeno campesino en España (La Confederación Nacional Católico-Agraria, 1917–1942)* (Madrid: Servicio de Publicaciónes Agrarias, 1979), p. 116.

48. CNCA leaders Monedero and Nevares carefully maintained an attitude of neutrality between the two fractious social Catholic currents and included

leading representatives of both groups in various advisory and supportive bodies. They also benefited from the support of Father Vicent and many Catholic progressives for mixed unions in the farming areas.

49. "La obra nacional Católico-agraria," in *Ecclesia* 1 (January 6, 1941): 11, quoted in Castillo, *Proprietarios muy pobres,* p. 80.

50. Benavides, *El fracaso de Catolicísmo social español,* p. 298.

51. Maximiano García Venero, *Historia de los movimientos sindicalistas españoles (1840–1933)* (Madrid: Ediciónes del Movimiento, 1961), p. 334.

52. Josefina Cuesta Bustillo, *Sindicalismo Católico agrario en España (1917–1919)* (Madrid: D. L. Narcea, 1978), p. 310.

CHAPTER 7: LABOR'S COMING OF AGE, 1915–1923

1. The clearest example of import substitution was in the heavy chemical industry, which lacked superphosphates previously imported from France and the Netherlands and German aniline dyes. See Joseph Harrison, *The Spanish Economy in the Twentieth Century* (New York: St. Martin's Press, 1985) pp. 40–41.

2. Salvador de Madariaga, *Spain, a Modern History* (New York: Praeger, 1958), p. 314.

3. Joaquín Aguilera, "La guerra europa y sus efectos en la industria de Cataluña," *Revista Nacional de Económica* 1 (1916):39.

4. Annual immigration to Catalonia from 1910 to 1920 averaged 20,000; from 1900 to 1910 it had averaged 3,400.

5. For a firsthand account of the chaos, see Albert Pérez Baró, *Els "Felicos Anys Vint"; Memories d'un militant obrer, 1918–1926* (Palma de Mallorca: Moll, 1974), p. 11. In 1916 the export of foodstuffs was 50 percent greater than it had been in 1914, while imports had declined by 22 percent; livestock exports increased 82 percent while imports were down by close to 40 percent. Manufacturing exports rose by 126 percent with imports reduced by 10 percent. See Santiago Roldan and José Luis García Delgado, *La formación de sociedad capitalista, 1914–1920,* 2 vols. (Madrid: CEIC, 1973), 1:144–69.

6. The coal miners and the metal and steelworkers of Vizcaya, Asturias, and Alava reached or surpassed 1914 real wage levels. Building construction laborers continued to experience diminished real wage earnings, 18 percent less in Madrid and 28 percent in Barcelona. The loss in Catalonian textiles exceeded 30 percent (*Estadistica de los salarios y de jornadas de trabajo referida al periodo 1914–1925, Ministerio de Trabajo, Comercio y Industria, Dirección General de Trabajo y Acción Social; Sección de Estadisticas Especiales del Trabajo* (Madrid: Sobrinos de M. Minuesa de los Rios, 1927), p. cliii).

7. Muriel Casal, "Le Primera Guerra Mundial i les seves consequencies, un moment clau del proces d'industrialisacion a Catalunya: El cas de la industria

llanera de Sabadell" (Ph.D. dissertation, Autonomous University of Barcelona, 1983), quoted in Manuel Tuñon de Lara, *La España del siglo XX,* 3 vols. (Barcelona: Laia, 1972), 1:94.

8. "The sad state of government institutions in our Spain is that their operation and continuity are completely subordinated to individuals and when they fail, the entire system also failed" (Adolfo Posada, *Fragmentos de mi memorias* [Ovieda: University of Oviedo, 1984], p. 312).

9. Javier Tussell, *La España del siglo XX* (Barcelona: Dopesa, 1975), p. 95.

"Despite Spain's substantial trade surpluses between 1915 and 1919, finance ministers, both Liberal and Conservative, not only proved incapable of balancing the budget—always their prime objective—but in seven consecutive financial years from 1914 to 1920 no occupant of that portfolio managed to persuade the Cortes to approve his annual budgetary estimates" (Harrison, *Spanish Economy in the Twentieth Century,* p. 36).

10. Pestaña claimed that the 1913 textile strike went down to defeat because members of the strike committee had been bribed by the police to assure its failure. See his *Terorismo en Barcelona* (Barcelona: Planeta, 1979), p. 81.

11. Pere Gabriel Sirvent, "Clase obrera i sindicats a Catalunya, 1903–1920" (Ph.D. dissertation, University of Barcelona, 1981), p. 594.

12. Ibid., p. 605.

13. Ibid., p. 635.

14. Juan Pablo Fusi, *Política obrera en el pais Vasco, 1880–1923* (Madrid: Turner, 1975), p. 369.

15. Victor Alba, *Catalonia, a Profile* (New York: Praeger, 1975), p. 97.

16. Victor Serge, *Memoires d'un revolutionaire de 1914 à 1940* (Paris: Seuil, 1951), p. 64. The character Dario in Serge's novel *Birth of Our Force* is drawn from the real-life Seguí.

17. Manuel Buenacasa, *El movimiento obrero español, 1886–1926* (1962; rpt. Madrid: Jucar, 1977), p. 62.

18. Salvador Seguí, *Escrits,* ed. Isidre Molas (Barcelona: Edicions 62, 1972), p. 11.

19. Journalist Francisco Madrid, an intimate of Layret and Seguí, says that Layret and Companys, increasingly concerned over the possibility of a military coup d'état, sought to form a joint slate sponsored by the UGT and CNT in the coming parliamentary elections. Seguí told Madrid that the CNT would "momentarily" abandon its antipolitical policy so that he, Pestaña, and others could be included among the candidates. At the time of Layret's assassination, Antonio García Quejido and Ramón Lamoneda, leading members of the PSOE Executive Committee, were in Barcelona "with complete authority to sign such a pact." See Madrid, *Ultimas veinticuatro horas de Layret* (Buenos Aires: Patronato Hispano-Argentino de Cultura, 1942), pp. 54–

55. The idea of supporting such a joint electoral slate apparently was supported only by PSOE left-wingers, for whom García Quejido and Lamoneda were leading spokesmen. Once PSOE moderates regained control of the party executive, nothing further was presumably heard concerning this proposal.

20. Manuel Lladonoso believes that Seguí "was obsessed by the need for trade union unity and to build powerful organizations that could assure the workers' triumph. Toward the end, when the assassination of leaders and the social struggles disorganized the CNT, he became convinced of the need for a protective cover," which gave rise to his interest in the Catalan Left but "did not mean that Salvador Seguí sought to become a parliamentary politician, though his attitude aroused numerous accusations from the pure anarchists incapable of going beyond their revolutionary infantilism" (*El congres de Sants* [Barcelona: Nova Terra, 1975], p. 58). Jaime Vicens Vives calls him "a trade unionist fundamentally" and believes that "when he became aware of the impossibility of carrying out a social revolution with such a conglomeration of socially intolerant and very little educated activists. . . . he conceived a practical evolutionism" ("El moviment obrerista Català (1901–1939)," *Recerques* 7 (1978): 25.

21. Pere Foix, *Apòstols i mercaders; quaranta anys de lluita social a Catalunya* (Mexico City: Ediciónes de la fundación Sara Llorens de Serra, 1957), p. 137.

22. For a detailed account of the 1917 crisis see Juan Antonio Lacomba, *La crisis española de 1917* (Madrid: Ciencia Nueva, 1970).

23. Wenceslao Fernández Flórez, quoted in ibid., p. 98.

24. See Gerald Meaker, *The Revolutionary Left in Spain, 1914–1923* (Palo Alto: Stanford University Press, 1974), p. 70; Carolyn P. Boyd, *Praetorian Politics in Liberal Spain* (Chapel Hill: University of North Carolina Press, 1979), pp. 51–52.

25. Quoted in Meaker, *Revolutionary Left in Spain,* p. 71.

26. Raymond Carr, *Spain, 1808–1939* (Oxford: Oxford University Press, 1975), p. 501.

27. "The CNT clearly intended to radicalize the movement to a maximum. To be sure, the accords were circumstantial. The Cenetistas were intent upon pushing for the revolution to its fullest consequences and to overrun the political parties" (Lladonoso, *Congres de Sants,* p. 37).

28. Adolfo Bueso, *Recuerdos de un Cenetista,* 2 vols. (Barcelona: Ariel, 1976), 1:74.

29. Francisco Largo Caballero, *Escritos de la republica* (Madrid: Editorial Fundación Pablo Iglesias, 1985), p. 8. See also Andrés Saborit, *Asturias y sus hombres* (Toulouse: Dulaurier, 1964), pp. 162, 167.

30. An editorial in *Solidaridad Obrera* observed, "It remains to be seen whether the people will find themselves confronted by their own sons or whether,

as in Russia, [the army] takes up arms against the enemies of the Spanish people" (June 12, 1917, quoted in Lladonoso, *Congres de Sants* p. 38).

31. Albert Balcells, *El sindicalisme a Barcelona (1916–1923)* (Barcelona: Nova Terra, 1965), p. 46. This excellent study remains essential for an understanding of the period.

32. I. Joaquim Ferrer, *Simó Piera: Perfil d'un sindicalista,* sec. 2, *Simó Piera, Records i experiencies d'un dirigent de la C.N.T.* (Barcelona: Editorial Portic, 1975), p. 154.

33. In Barcelona, Largo Caballero appeared on a joint amnesty ticket with the Republicans. The unexpected defeat of Lerroux resulted from his increasing notoriety and the abstention of many anarchist sympathizers, who did not want to vote for a socialist. Nonetheless, the Republican Marcelino Domingo and Largo Caballero won enough votes to gain parliamentary seats.

34. Lacomba, *Crisis española,* p. 281.

35. The only *sindicato unico* in existence before the Sants congress was that of the woodworking trades (S.U. del Ram d'elaborar fusta), which had been organized by Manuel Buenacasa and Joan Pey.

36. "The congress displayed a preference for so-called 'direct action' that originally meant that workers in a given industry through elected committees were to run their own affairs without ever resorting to intermediaries. To some extent this concept originated from an 'apolitical' prejudice of a preoccupation to cast aside those whom the congress referred to as 'professional politicians.' The reality of the trade union struggle that is much more complex than such schemas led, however, to the emergence within the CNT of men who directed the actions of union sectors to which they did not belong and empirically imposed a necessity for permanent directing organisms" (Manuel Nuñez de Arenas and Manuel Tuñon de Lara, *Historia del movimiento obrero español* [Barcelona: Nova Terra, 1970], p. 201).

37. Lladonoso, *Congres de Sants,* p. 57.

38. "The admiration in Spanish anarchist circles for regicides and assassinations of leading figures has always been greater than in any other [national movement]" (Angel Pestaña, "Lo que aprendi en la vida," in Pestaña, *Trayectoria sindicalista* (Madrid: Tebas, 1974), p. 183.

39. Balcells argues that the great influx of rural immigrants is a key element in the rise of anarcho-syndicalism in Barcelona (*Sindicadisme a Barcelona,* p. 11). Victor Serge emphasizes the rapid expansion of the industrial proletariat that did not permit the formation of a labor aristocracy (*Memoires d'un revolutionaire,* p. 62).

40. See Gabriel, "Clase obrera i sindicats a Catalunya," p. 685.

41. A second regional assembly, held on December 8, 1918, registered 254 affiliates in the region—at Sants there had been 158—and the number of localities represented had grown from 23 to 30. By 1919, for example, the

textile union, La Constancia, saw its membership mushroom to eighty thousand. During this period regional confederations were constituted in Aragon, the Levant (Valencia), Murcia, Andalusia, and the north.

42. Buenacasa, *Movimiento obrero español,* p. 51.

43. Quoted in Gabriel, "Clase obrera i sindicats a Catalunya," p. 705.

44. Manuel Tuñon de Lara, *Luchas obreras y campesinas en la Andalucia del siglo XX: Jaen (1917–1920), Sevilla (1930–1932)* (Madrid: Siglo Veintiuno, 1978), pp. 41–42.

45. The agricultural economist Pascual Carrión tells us that during the winter of 1918–19 day wages in Seville province for farm laborers averaged 2.50 to 3.00 pesetas for males and 1.25 to 1.50 for females. According to another source, male wages in the province during 1917 ranged between 1.20 and 2.00 pesetas, while in Córdoba they were 1.50 to 4.00 pesetas. Tuñon de Lara estimates that before 1918 wage increases averaged 15 to 20 percent. See Tuñon de Lara, *El movimiento obrero,* 2:165. See also Roldan and Delgado, *Formación de la sociedad capitalista,* 1:246.

46. The cities of Jerez and Seville, whose labor movements were under anarchist leadership, tended to depart from the norm and to engage in quasi-insurrectionary general strikes. See Antonio Calero Amor, *Historia de Andalucia,* vol. 8, *La Andalucia contemporanea (1868–1981)* (Madrid: Cupsa-Planeta, 1981), p. 113.

47. Pascual Carrión, *Los latifundios en España* (Madrid: Graficas Reunidas, 1932), p. 414, cited in Edward Malefakis, *Agrarian Reform and Peasant Revolution in Spain* (New Haven: Yale University Press, 1970), p. 148.

48. For labor developments during this period in urban centers see José Manuel Macarro, "Los conflictos sociales en la ciudad de Sevilla en los años 1918–1920," in *Seis estudios sobre el proletariado Andaluz (1868–1939)* (Córdoba: Ayuntamiento de Córdoba, 1984).

49. The ratio between party and trade union membership in 1919 was much smaller in Andalusia than anywhere else—1:1.5 compared with Asturias-León's 1:20, the Basque country's 1:19, Extremadura's 1:2.4, and Madrid's 1:15, suggesting that functional differences between the political party and the labor organization were considerably blurred in rural areas. See Tuñon de Lara, *Movimiento obrero,* 2:278.

50. The eleventh PSOE congress in 1918 for the first time seriously took up the agrarian problem and called for special efforts in that field. Two years later, in 1920, the UGT sponsored an agricultural conference in Jaen for its affiliates in Andalusia and Extremadura that was chaired by General Secretary Largo Caballero, who later called it the first step in the ultimate formation of the National Federation of Land Workers (FNTT).

At the time of its 1920 congress the UGT possessed agricultural affiliates with a claimed total membership of 74,677, constituting the single largest category, followed by mining with 44,414, building construction, 27,638, and metalworking, 19,128. Overall adherence was 240,113 distributed in 1,078 local unions. First in importance was Madrid with 45,502 members, then Asturias with 39,470, and Vizcaya with 21,581. Membership in Andalusia had risen to 36,759 of which 3,879 were located in Jaen province, 15,400 in Córdoba. See Javier Aisa and V. M. Arbeloa, *Historia de la Union General de Trabajadores (UGT)* (Bilbao: Zero, 1975), pp. 93–94. Antonio Calero Amor, "El movimiento obrero en Andalucía," in *Aproximación a la historia de Andalucía,* ed. J. A. Lacomba (1979; rpt. Barcelona: Laia, 1981), pp. 291–92.

51. See Calero Amor, "Movimiento obrero," pp. 133–34; Fusi, *Política obrera en el pais Vasco,* pp. 346–50.

52. Juan Díaz del Moral, *Historia de las agitaciónes campesinas Andaluzas-Córdoba* (Madrid: Alianza, 1977), p. 286.

53. Malefakis, *Agrarian Reform and Peasant Revolution,* p. 147.

54. Díaz del Moral, *Historia de las agitaciones,* pp. 262–63.

55. Gerald H. Meaker, in his *Revolutionary Left in Spain,* chap. 12, provides a detailed account. Meaker's excellent work is particularly good on the socialists.

56. Ibid., p. 346.

57. The UGT at that time numbered 208,170, and the expelled unions possessed approximately 15,000. Party membership in Andalusia between 1921 and 1923 plummeted from roughly 22,000 to only 1,300. Furthermore, much of the party membership did not pay dues regularly. The 1920 party congress reported that only 19,526 paid dues out of a total of 52,887 members.

58. A detailed account of the La Canadiense strike is included in E. G. Solano, *El sindicalismo en la teoría y en la práctica* (Barcelona: Bauza, 1922). See also *Estadistica de las huelgas, memoria de 1919* (Madrid: I.R.S., 1922), pp. 37–84.

59. Spain had become a member of the International Labor Organization, and its action instituting the eight-hour day was in compliance with a general accord agreed to by member nations.

60. Balcells, *Sindicalisme a Barcelona,* p. 79.

61. Ibid., p. 91.

62. Bueso, *Recuerdos de un Cenetista,* 1:109.

63. Amado later explained that the formulation of a closely regulated labor relations structure was prompted by his discovery upon arriving in Barcelona that past accords between employers and unions had not been arrived at in a spirit of concord and had not been followed by either side. See E. G. Solano, *El ocaso del sindicalismo?—Segunda Parte* (Barcelona: Editorial B. Bauza, 1922), p. 24.

64. Manuel Burgos y Mazo subsequently wrote a book on his experiences as

interior minister and his efforts at social pacification, *Para otras paginas; El verano de 1919 en gobernación* (Cuenca: Emilio Pinos, 1921), that is essential reading for an understanding of the Barcelona labor wars.

65. Fernando Rey confirms that among the various social crimes that took place in Barcelona there were hardly any victims among the traditional employers: "Virtually all the attacks were directed against the newer employers" ("Actitu des políticas y económicas de la patronal Catalana (1917–1923)," in *Homenaje a Manuel Tuñon de Lara*, 2 vols. [Madrid: Ministry of Education, 1982], 2:34).

66. Ferrer, *Simó Piera*, pp. 173–74.

67. Quoted in Baró, *Els "Felicos Anys Vint,"* p. 38; see also Balcells, *Sindicalisme a Barcelona*, p. 117.

68. Pedro Gual Villalbí, a textile factory owner and general secretary of the Fomento de Trabajo Nacional, provides interesting insights on the evolution of employers' attitudes in his *Memorias de un industrial de nuestro tiempo* (Barcelona: Sociedad de Publicacíones, 1922?), esp. chaps. 15, 16, and 17.

69. A resolution sponsored by the Barcelona delegation to the meeting of the Spanish Employers Confederation national committee, held on September 3, 1919, was unanimously adopted. It declared that "the situation created by the development of unionism (*sindicalismo*) for national production is morally and materially unbearable. The governments of Spain apparently do not comprehend this. Granting one concession after the other has placed employers in an impossible regimen of humiliation and material burdens." Taking the lead from their Barcelona colleagues, the building construction employers of Madrid instituted a lockout in 1919 (*II Congreso patronal de la Confederación Patronal Española memoria general, Barcelona 20–26 Octubre, 1919* [Barcelona: Emprenta Elzeviriana, n.d.], pp. 9–10).

70. CNT representatives on November 2, 1919, agreed to the inclusion of a clause in the royal decree constituting the joint commission, stipulating that shop delegates would no longer have the right unilaterally to call plant shutdowns. The collapse of the joint commission talks nullified this concession made by Seguí.

71. "It must be clearly, forthrightly stated with a regard for the truth: the employers and other Barcelona leading groups are mainly responsible for the present horrible social situation. . . . Today's proletarian generation that is its victim and that has been unwittingly formed by them constitutes the expiation of a collective social transgression as others that history has recorded" (Burgos y Mazo, *Para otras pagins*, pp. 171, 196–97).

Civil Governor Julio Amado faulted the employers not for opposing Cenetista abuses and their desire to rid themselves of troublemakers but for their adversarial attitude just when the CNT appeared willing to resolve existing differences peacefully. See Solano, *Ocaso del sindicalismo*, p. 24.

72. Though the attempt to form a mixed labor commission ended in failure, the later creation of the Comision Mixta de Trabajo en el Comercio de Barcelona (Joint Labor Committee for Commerce) proved to be one of the few successful government-sponsored labor-management efforts. White-collar workers were mainly represented in the committee by CADCI, an unaffiliated union of moderate left Catalanist orientation.

73. A sizable drop in exports during the final quarter of 1919 made it possible for many employers to endure a lockout without incurring major financial losses.

74. The British consul in Barcelona reported that "the working class has been reduced to begging and it is impossible to walk the streets without being molested by beggars, mostly women—carrying infants in their arms—who appear to be half-starved" (quoted in Robert W. Kern, *Red Years, Black Years: A Political History of Spanish Anarchism, 1911–1937* [Philadelphia, Ishi: 1978], p. 46).

75. CNT membership claims should be regarded with skepticism. The seven hundred thousand figure, which was used at the time of the La Comedia congress, was based not on dues payers but on the claims of each local affiliate. Some of the participating delegates, moreover, were present as observers and did not represent CNT-affiliated organizations. For example, only fifteen thousand of the twenty-five thousand claimed members in Zaragossa were actually members of CNT affiliates. See Bueso, *Recuerdos de un Cenetista*, p. 128. UGT figures for this period are more accurate and are based to a greater extent on dues payments.

76. Tuñon de Lara, *Movimiento obrero*, 2:259.

77. Despite the CNT's ostensibly greater concern for rank-and-file participation and militancy, the late Luis Portela, a former activist in the Madrid UGT, founder of the Communist party, and leader of the POUM in the Valencia area during the civil war, contended that the UGT was operated in a more democratic manner than the CNT. Many CNT leaders were elitist and manipulative, with all the hubris of convinced ideologues (interview, March 14, 1982).

78. The monthly dues of ten centimos were to be allocated as follows: two centimos to the local federation, two to the regional committee, two to the national committee, two to *Solidaridad Obrera*, and two to an assistance fund to aid those in prison and their families. Unskilled, low-paid workers in particular chose membership in the CNT rather than UGT because of the former's lower dues requirements.

79. "During the early months of 1920, especially during the governance of F. C. Bas, a just and prudent man, the pistoleros took over the unions and conducted a shameful hunt for employers and workers in the streets of Barcelona; they in turn also became victims in reprisal actions undertaken in which

elements of the Free Unions were beginning to participate" (Vicens Vives, "Moviment obrerista Català," p. 25).

80. Pestaña wrote a number of articles and essays dealing with labor terrorism. The most candid and revealing is contained in his autobiographical account "Lo que aprendi en la vida" (p. 185), from which this quotation is taken.

The anarchist historian José Peirats explains the situation as follows: "The perceptive minority in the trade union camp found itself in the confrontation incapable of restraining the exalted, suicidal majority, which fell into the crass error of taking up the challenge under the worst possible conditions. Conscious instances of provocation aside, it succumbed to a sort of collective vanity represented by ostentation and the excessive use of force. And the response, which was possibly readied beforehand, was not long in coming" (*La CNT en la revolución española,* 3 vols. [Paris: Ruedo Iberico, 1971], 1:31).

81. Though the number of incidents remained at the same level, an important change had occurred in the composition of the victims. In comparison with the Salvatierra period, fewer factory owners, plant executives, and policemen were killed or wounded under Bas, while the number of affected workers had correspondingly increased, possibly reflecting the interunion warfare between CNT supporters and the Libres.

82. The employment of agents provocateurs, it should be kept in mind, was a time-honored police practice in dealing with labor organizations and political groups.

83. Pestaña, "Lo que aprendi en la vida," p. 174.

84. "Many people felt that these intimidatory actions made factory supervisors more lenient in dealing with worker infractions" (Claudi Ametlla, *Memories politiques, 1918–1936,* 2 vols. [Barcelona: Distribucións Catalonia, 1979], p. 31). Joaquín Maurín, a CNT leader in that period, estimates that more than four hundred employers were assassinated in Barcelona from 1917 to 1921. See his *L'anarcho-syndicalisme en Espagne* (Paris: Petite Bibliothèque de l'Internationale Sindicale Rouge, 1924), p. 31.

85. Buenacasa, *Movimiento obrero español,* p. 53.

86. Interior Minister Manuel Burgos y Mazo recounts that only one arrest took place in a six-month period during which twelve terrorist incidents had occurred (*Para otras pagins,* p. 449).

87. Ametlla, *Memories politiques,* 2:37.

88. Albert Balcells, *Historia contemporanea de Cataluña* (Barcelona: Edhasa, 1983), p. 212.

89. Colin M. Winston, *Workers and the Right in Spain, 1900–1930* (Princeton: Princeton University Press, 1985), examines the rise and fall of the Barcelona Sindicatos Libres.

90. Though adhering to Catholicism, the Libres joined radical Carlists in excoriating the Catholic establishment, accusing the Marquis de Comillas of supporting scab unions and labeling Acción Social Popular the "shoeshine boys of the Employers Federation" (ibid., pp. 120–21).

91. Quoted in ibid., p. 114.

92. Pérez Baró, *Els "Felicos Anys Vint,"* pp. 86–87.

93. Balcells, *Sindicalisme a Barcelona,* p. 132.

94. The choice of Severiano Martínez Anido as Barcelona's civil governor was made by King Alfonso XIII. See Madrid, *La ultimas veinticuatro horas de Layret,* p. 31.

95. Employers' growing sense of beleaguerment and intransigence must also be seen against the background of the rising wave of revolutionary developments and labor unrest throughout western Europe that reached its apogee in France and Italy during the summer of 1920, precisely when CNT power was running at full tide and when many of its activists were similarly caught up in the reigning revolutionary euphoria.

96. A moderating element in the UGT decision doubtless was the general ebbing in European labor élan. In May of that year a national solidarity strike, sponsored by the French CGT, ended in failure, as did the factory occupations in Italy.

97. Between 1917 and 1922 Barelona had eleven different civil governors.

98. Jesús Pabón, *Cambó,* part 2 (Barcelona: Alpha, 1969), p. 203. Cambó reportedly disliked Martínez Anido because of his brutal nature. See Joan Manent i Pesas, *Records d'un sindicalista llibertari Català, 1916–1943* (Paris: Ediciones Catalanes de Paris, 1976), p. 382.

99. The CNT was riddled with police spies and informers. During the 1921–22 repression, the confederation's legal counsel informed the police regularly concerning various confidential activities. See Maurín, *L'anarcho-syndicalisme,* p. 38.

100. During this period, outside Catalonia, the CNT continued to function more or less normally except for periodic crackdowns.

101. Ametlla, *Memories politiques,* p. 31.

102. An estimated more than five hundred workers fell victim in Martínez Anido's bloody campaign. See Maurín, *L'anarcho-syndicalisme,* p. 33.

103. The full text of the resolution appears in Meaker, *Revolutionary Left in Spain,* p. 532.

CHAPTER 8: THE SHAPING OF LABOR RELATIONS UNDER THE RESTORATION

1. See Alfredo Montoya Melgar, *Ideologia y lenguaje en los primeros leyes laborales de España* (Madrid: Civitas, 1975).

2. José Luis Comellas, *Cánovas* (Madrid: Ediciónes Cid, 1965), p. 316.
3. Juan B. Solervicens, ed., *Cánovas del Castillo, Antologia* (Madrid: Espasa Calpe, 1941), pp. 120–21.
4. Luis García Arias, ed., *Cánovas del Castillo, Antologia* (Madrid: Ediciónes Fe, 1944), p. 174.
5. Solervicens, ed., *Cánovas del Castillo,* p. 130.
6. Quoted in Melchor Fernández Almagro, *Cánovas* (Madrid: Tebas, 1972), p. 416.
7. The 1870 Penal Code and Article 556 had been inspired by similar provisions in the French Penal Code. Article 556, especially its antistrike clauses, essentially represented a continuation of a juridical formula dating back to 1848 and 1850, to a time when labor relations problems in their contemporary form did not exist. See Alejandro Gallart Folch, *Derecho español de trabajo* (Barcelona: Editorial Labor, 1936), p. 37.
8. Article 698 of the Penal Code that defined as illicit any association whose objectives or circumstances contravened "public morality" was invoked in 1884 to declare the Workers Federation of the Spanish Region (FTRE) illegal.

   In drafting the 1887 Associations Law parliamentarians purposely gave government authorities broad discretionary powers to permit the barring, dissolution, or otherwise to harass worker societies of an anarchist orientation as well as to prevent them from obtaining legal recognition. "The CNT consequently was constantly in danger of having its affiliates shut down by the government, and this occurred especially during periods of intense social conflict. If in other periods anarcho-syndicalists were able to operate without legal obstacles, it was because the authorities did not systematically apply a strict interpretation of the law to the full extent. A good example is the decree of March 1923, recalling the disposition permitting government authorities to inspect the financial records of labor societies, a decree that remained without effect because of passive resistance, starting with the 'legalist' UGT" (Ignacio Olábarri, "El mundo de trabajo: Organisaciónes profesionales y relaciónes laborales," in *Historia de España y America, Revolución y Restauración (1868–1931),* 21 vols. [Madrid: Rialp, 198], 16:621).
9. Quoted in Maximiano García Venero, *Historia de los movimientos sindicalistas españoles (1844–1933)* (Madrid: Ediciónes del Movimiento, 1961), p. 257.
10. For the changes in Spanish civil jurisprudence to deal with the growing number of labor conflicts, see Juan Montero Aroca, *Los tribunales del trabajo (1908–1938)* (Valencia: Universidad de Valencia, 1976), pp. 18–19.
11. The Maura government in 1908 also sponsored the passage of a law constituting industrial labor tribunals that were intended to handle disputes arising from breaches of individual work and apprentice contracts and those relating to the Work Accident Law of 1900. Local tribunals composed of

equal numbers of employer and worker representatives and presided over by an impartial chairman were to be formed at all appropriate levels. This legislation established the precedent of creating special legal procedures and organisms to deal with labor matters and providing a legal recourse that was materially accessible to worker litigants. It was, however, riddled with defects that rendered it largely inoperative. Even taking into account subsequent modifications intended to improve its functioning, S. Alarcon Horcas, a labor jurist, declared in 1929 that "in Spain the industrial commission is a failed institution and consequently prejudicial to the ends of justice. . . . Impartiality in decision making is not known or possible; employer members are not able to understand why workers participate and, on the other hand, worker members never admit to allegations made by an employer. With such prejudices, verdicts always end up in draws, whose decision depends on the chairman of the tribunal, obligating him to decide momentarily in a monosyllable without justifying his opinion" (*Codigo de trabajo*, 2 vols. [Madrid: Reus, 1929], 2:651–52).

12. The role of Civil Governor Miguel Socias has been variously judged. Joaquín Romero Maura points to the intransigence of employers and the governor's "total incompetence" as the major elements leading to the general strike. See *La rosa del fuego el oberismo Barcelones de 1899 a 1909* (Barcelona: Grijalbo, 1975), p. 210. Borja de Riquer, however, believes that the civil governor's handling of the metalworkers' strike and the tolerance displayed toward Lerroux in the Barcelona municipal elections of 1901 reflected a concerted attempt by the central government to counter the rising regional nationalist challenge of the Lliga Regionalista with which Catalan industrialists were closely identified. See his *La burgesia Catalana i el nacionalisme (1898–1904)* (Barcelona: Ediciónes 62, 1977), chap. 6.

13. An account of the Gijón strike can be found in the section contained in Manuel Tuñon de Lara, "Estructuras Sociales, 1898–1931," vol. 37 of *Historia de España* (Madrid: Espasa-Calpe, 1984), pp. 484–85. See also Angeles Barrio Alonso, *El anarquismo en Gijón* (Madrid: Bibliotica Julio Somoza, 1982).

14. Feliciano Montero García, *El primer Catolicísmo social y la* Rerum Novarum *en España (1889–1902)* (Madrid: CSIC, 1983), p. 405.

15. Alejandro Gallart Folch cited in Olábarri, "El mundo de trabajo," p. 629.

16. Juan Pablo Fusi, *Política obrera en el pais Vasco, 1880–1923* (Madrid: Turner, 1975), p. 100n.

17. Salvador de Madariaga, *España, ensayo de historia contemporanea* (1930; rpt. Madrid: Espasa-Calpe, 1979) p. 262; an English translation also exists. See also Manuel Balbé, *Orden público y militarismo en la España constitucional (1812–1983)* (1983; rpt. Madrid: Alianza Universidad, 1985), esp. chap. 10.

18. "It was not possible for a mechanism intended to seek compromises through

negotiations between the parties to function properly when both regarded compromise merely as another means of combat acceptable only to the extent that it yielded advantages in a strategy of global conflict" (Olábarri, "El mundo de trabajo," p. 624). The 1909 annual labor inspection service report, referring to the local and provincial IRS committees, observed that "the Committee sometimes does not dare make use of its inspection powers for fear of reprisals from influential persons who are the proprietors of the industries" (Institute of Social Reforms, *Memoria general de la inspección de trabajo* [Madrid: Imprenta de la sucesora de M. Minuesa de los Rios, 1910], p. 7).

19. The Catalonian Social Statistical Annual for 1914 states that twelve strikes were settled through the mediation of mayors, thirteen by civil governors, forty-two directly by employers and workers, eight through the intervention of the "governing authority," one by others, and only four by local IRS committees.

20. R. D. Anderson, *France, 1870–1914: Politics and Society* (London: Routledge & Kegan Paul, 1977), p. 138. Unlike Spain, although French employers were unalterably opposed to organized labor, workers had an increasingly effective voice in local and national affairs through elected representatives of left-wing parties, and public authorities were therefore more likely to act as mediators and to pressure employers to reach compromise settlements with the unions.

21. Raymond Carr, *Spain, 1808–1939* (1966; rev. ed. Oxford: Oxford University Press, 1975), p. 492; Diego Abad de Santillan, *Alfonso XIII, la II Republica, Francisco Franco* (Madrid: Jucar, 1979), p. 55.

22. Canalejas's interest in labor problems was underscored by his naming of Práxedes Zancada as his political secretary and sometime labor troubleshooter. A leading labor jurist, Praxedes was the author of several well-known books on labor problems and served as one of the senior officers of the Institute for Social Reforms.

23. Quoted in the introduction by Jesus Pabón in Diego Andrés Sevilla, *Canalejas* (Barcelona: Aedos, 1956), p. xviii.

24. Carlos Seco Serrano, *Viñetas historicas* (Madrid: Espasa-Calpe, 1983), p. 277.

25. Maria Teresa Martínez de Sas, *El socialismo y la España oficial: Pablo Iglesias, diputado a Cortes* (Madrid: Tucar, 1975), provides a detailed examination of the relationship between Canalejas and Iglesias and the attitudes of the UGT and the government in major labor disputes during the Canalejas administration.

26. Ibid., p. 180.

27. Ibid., p. 242. Canalejas expected the Socialist party to collaborate in labor relations, as it had in other European countries. "His error was not in a misunderstanding of socialist doctrine but in its interpretation and practice by Pablo Iglesias" (ibid., pp. 257–59).

28. Fusi, *Política obrera en il pais Vasco,* p. 327.
29. The Briand government in France and the Italians had set a precedent for militarizing railroad employees threatening an industry shutdown.
30. Official strike statistics provide only a partial picture. Data on labor disputes from 1906 to 1924 were compiled by the Institute for Social Reforms. Both during this period and when the Labor Ministry assumed responsibility for gathering statistics, the figures contained in the annual reports were based on frequently faulty reporting by local authorities. Strikes considered to have political motivations were excluded. The figures concerning strikes lost and won by workers are also suspect because labor organizations customarily submitted exaggerated initial demands and then settled for less. Such instances were often reported as "lost" strikes. Furthermore, local authorities had the self-serving tendency to minimize the number of workers taking part in a strike and to inflate the number of nonstrikers. See Manuel Tuñon de Lara, *Metodologia de la historia social de España* (Madrid: Siglo XXI, 1973), pp. 152–54.
31. Olábarri, "El mundo de trabajo," p. 560. A particularly cruel punishment accorded labor and political dissidents, especially anarchists, was to force them to walk manacled over long distances to their assigned places of internal exile guarded by Civil Guardsmen on horseback.
32. Pere Gabriel Sirvent, "Clase obrera i sindicats a Catalunya, 1903–1920" (Ph.D. dissertation, University of Barcelona, 1981), p. 869.
33. "Persistent employer opposition to explicit recognition of trade union representation doubtless explains why for decades resistance societies and unions considered strikes as the sole efficacious means . . . to change working conditions. Employers only took part in negotiations when no other means existed for avoiding a strike" (Ignacio Olábarri, *Relaciónes laborales en Vizcaya (1890–1936)* [Durango: Leopoldo Zugaza, 1978], p. 314).
34. For the use of violence as a negotiating tool for workers see Eric Hobsbawm, *Labouring Men: Studies in the History of Labour* (1964; rpt. Garden City, N.Y.: Doubleday Anchor, 1967), p. 9; and Fusi, *Politica obrera en el pais Vasco,* p. 98.
35. Gabriel, "Clase obrera i sindicats a Cataluyna," pp. 825–26.
36. Gallart Folch, *Derecha español de trabajo,* p. 151.
37. For a brief, comprehensive overview of Spanish employer organizations during this period consult Olábarri, *Relaciónes laborales en Vizcaya,* pp. 191–97.

"The general tendency in North America and Europe for employers to band together against the audacities of trade unionism has also come to Spain, where in the nation's capitol the first one has been constituted on November 18, 1911.

"In the report which the president of the Madrid Federation has kindly furnished it speaks of similar existing federations in Barcelona, Gijón, Seville,

Bilbao, San Sebastian, Palma de Mallorca, Cádiz, Orense, Logroño, and other important cities that are not cited.

"According to the report the result of the Madrid Federation's campaign has been to break pacts, contracts, and working conditions previously agreed to with the worker societies, asserting for the employer his liberty of action to hire and fire personnel without hindrances nor the recognition of outside authority as befits his dignity.

" 'We can affirm that the Federation's first year has been one of great adversity for strike agitators and professionals. Large desertions among their followers and the dissolution of some societies have been the consequence of sustained lockouts. To constantly weaken labor organization and to disallow its caudillos: this is our norm and our best defense.'

"An ardent employers federation movement has gotten under way. That of Madrid, according to the report, possesses 939 members, in Zaragossa 1,200. . . . Barcelona now follows this example, and, as is known, the Federation of Yarn and Cloth Manufacturers has been constituted. Madrid is actively urging that the greatest possible number of employers organize in order to form a general confederation" (*El Trabajo Nacional*, January 1, 1914; it was the official publication of the Fomento de Trabajo Nacional).

38. Interview with Luis Portela, March 8, 1982. Portela had been an activist in the Madrid UGT and a leading figure in the formation of the Communist party.

39. Albert Pérez Baró, who was a leader of the CNT Commercial Workers Union during the 1920s, claims that an important element in the popularity of the CNT was the aura of martyrdom acquired from frequent persecutions and repression (interview, March 14, 1982).

40. "What terrorism did was to aid in overcoming the tenacious resistance to a betterment of the workers' economic condition that the bourgeoisie opposed. But they could have come to this result without terrorism with the existence of a powerful trade union organization" (Angel Pestaña, "Lo que aprendi en la vida," in Pestaña, *Trayectoria sindicalista* [Madrid: Tebas, 1974], p. 184).

41. "From 1890 to 1895 five manufacturers owned more than 50 percent of all the spindles in the spinning industry, between eight and ten controlled 30 percent, and the remaining 20 percent was distributed among fifty industrialists. Some years later five manufacturers (two had disappeared and were replaced by others) were dominant, possessing 73 to 75 percent of the spindles. . . . This serves to some extent to explain the solidity acquired by the big industrial bourgeoisie of Catalonia" (Jaime Vicens Vives, *Industrials i politics del segle XIX* [Barcelona: Planeta, 1979], p. 114). See also Gabriel, "Clase obrera i sindicats a Catalunya," p. 867.

42. Jaime Vicens Vives, *Approaches to the History of Spain* (Berkeley and Los Angeles: University of California Press, 1972), p. 206.

43. Reinhard Bendix observed that employers acted as they did because their own self-esteem depended on the exercise of authority patterned after that of the landowners and the long absolutist legacy. See his *Work and Authority in Industry* (New York: Wiley, 1956), p. 206.

44. Jordi Maluquer, "Le revolución industrial en Cataluña," in *La modernización económica de España (1830–1930),* ed. Nicolas Sánchez Albornoz (Madrid: Alianza, 1985), p. 219.

45. Albert Balcells, *Cataluña contemporanea,* vol. 1 (Madrid: Siglo Veintiuno 1977), pp. 84–85.

46. Adam B. Ulam, *The Unfinished Revolution: An Essay on the Sources of Influence of Marxism and Communism* (New York: Random House, 1959), p. 129.

47. Franz Borkenau, *The Spanish Cockpit* (1937; rpt. Ann Arbor: University of Michigan Press, 1974), p. 20.

48. See Miquel Izard, "Entre la impotencia y la esperanza: La Union Manufacturera (5/7/1872–8/4/1873)," *Estudios de Historia Social,* no. 4 (1978), p. 52.

49. Juan Pablo Fusi, *El pais Vasco, pluralism y nacionalidad* (Madrid: Alianza, 1984), pp. 62–63.

50. "Regionalism and anarchism were but the expressions of an inability to resolve the problems of Catalonia's complex society and economy through the national structure." A major factor was the inability of Catalonian industry "to expand and diversify, together with its emphasis upon production of a low-price cotton textile that required minimal labor costs. A worker in these conditions, denied political redress of grievances as well as the right to bargain collectively with employers, had no recourse but the violent direct action extolled by anarchists. Violence, in turn, justified the contention of national politicians, and of industrialists throughout Spain that the 'labor problem' was merely one of public order" (Joan Connelly Ullman, *The Tragic Week: A Study of Anticlericalism in Spain, 1875–1912* [Cambridge, Mass.: Harvard University Press, 1968], pp. 61–62).

CHAPTER 9: THE PRIMO DE RIVERA DICTATORSHIP, 1923–1930:
A JANUS-FACED LABOR POLICY

1. Joaquín Maurín, *La revolución española* (1931; rpt. Barcelona: Anagrama 1977), p. 47.

2. Quoted in Shlomo Ben Ami, *Fascism from Above* (Oxford: Oxford University Press, 1983), p. 58.

3. A leading Catalonian historian says that "the Catalan bourgeoisie felt betrayed by [Primo's] actions" (Albert Balcells, *Historia contemporanea de Cataluña* [Barcelona: Edhasa, 1983], p. 226).

4. Ben Ami, *Fascism from Above;* James H. Rial, *Revolution from Above* (Fairfax,

Va.: George Mason University Press, 1985). Antonio Ramos Oliveira, *Politics, Economics and Men of Modern Spain, 1808–1946* (London: V. Gollancz, 1946), pp. 187–210; "Spain, 1914–1970," in Fontana Economic History of Europe, ed. Carlo M. Cipolla, Contemporary Economies, pt. 2 (London: Collins/Fontana Books, 1976), 6:473.

5. Rial, *Revolution from Above*, p. 68.

6. The singling out of Llaneza to proffer the offer of collaboration was fortuitous. The coal industry was suffering economic crisis and the union's bargaining power was virtually nonexistent. Llaneza was thus eager to circumvent growing employer aggressiveness by seeking the intervention of the civil governor or the Madrid authorities to secure acceptable compromises. See Adrian Shubert, *Hacia la revolución: Origenes sociales del movimiento obrero en Asturias* (Barcelona: Critica, 1984), p. 168.

7. Prieto's opposition was swayed by the decline of UGT influence in the Basque region under the dictatorship. The UGT's collaboration with the directory won the combined denunciations of the communists, anarcho-syndicalists, and the Basque Workers Solidarity (SOV). UGT moderation permitted communists and Cenetistas to assume an increasingly important role in labor affairs starting in 1927. See Ignacio Olábarri, *Relaciónes laborales en Vizcaya (1890–1936)* (Durango: Leopoldo Zugaza, 1978), p. 425. The minutes of the UGT national committee reveal an initial hostility to cooperative relations with the Military Directory and to Llaneza's more positive attitude, but under the pressure of numerous local affiliates that had become accustomed to dealing with government authorities, it relented and embarked on a limited working relationship. See Manuel Pérez Ledesma, "El movimiento obrero antes de Octubre," in *Octubre 1934,* ed. German Ojeda (Madrid: Siglo Veintiuno, 1985), p. 224.

8. The socialists were criticized by Republicans and many on the Left for their collaborationism. The brochure by Enrique Sánchez, *La Union General de Trabajadores ante la revolución* (Madrid: Saez Hermanos, 1932), offers a spirited defense of their collaboration. Sánchez was a leading figure in party and trade union affairs.

9. Upon losing its seat in the League of Nations general council to Germany in 1927, the Spanish government withdrew in protest, thus making its link with the ILO all the more valued.

10. On Marvá see Anthony D. McIvor, "Spanish Labor Policy during the Dictablanda of Primo de Rivera" (Ph.D. dissertation, University of California, San Diego, 1982), p. 64.

11. The minutes of UGT Executive Committee meetings for those years are unpublished and can be consulted at the Pablo Iglesias Foundation of Madrid. In an effort to hide the true extent of its collaboration, in 1932 the UGT issued a report that exaggerated the persecutions and harassments it expe-

rienced under the dictatorship. The report is reproduced in Javier Aisa and V. M. Arbeloa, *Historia de la Union General de Trabajores (UGT)* (Bilbao: Zero, 1975), p. 119.

12. Following a series of unsuccessful tries, most notably in 1906, the labor code included labor contract legislation replacing the leasing of services (*arrendamiento de servicios*). In addition to further modernizing Spain's labor legislation, it responded to long-expressed demands of moderate labor organizations, especially the UGT. The UGT, for example, in January 1919, called on then Prime Minister Romanones to draft a consolidated labor code. UGT Secretary General Largo Caballero served as a member of the drafting commission designated by Aunós's Labor Ministry.

13. Eduardo Aunós, *Estudios de derecho corporativa* (Madrid: Reus, 1930), p. 81. Aunós was a prolific writer on and defender of labor corporatism. Among his more notable publications are *La Organización Corporativa del trabajo* (Madrid: Consejo Superior de Trabajo, Comercio, y Industria, 1928); *Las corporaciónes del trabajo en el estado moderno* (Madrid: Biblioteca Marvá, 1928); and *La política social de la dictadura* (Madrid: Real Academia de Ciencias Morales y Políticas, 1944).

14. In a parliamentary address delivered in August 1919, José Calvo Sotelo, Primo de Rivera's future finance minister, declared that the parity committees, "as in all countries, were destined to serve as one of the essential supports of Spanish social policy."

15. But it was labor corporatism in an authoritarian context. If a worker was free to join the union of his choosing (providing it was not the CNT), his union, in turn, could effectively protect his interests only by operating within the corporatist machinery. Aunós described it as "free syndication within a system of obligatory corporatism" (see his *La reforma corporativa del estado* (Madrid: Reus, 1935), p. 130.

16. For the ideological basis of corporativism see Alfredo Montoya Melgar, *Ideologia y lenguaje en las leyes laborales de España: La dictadura de Primo de Rivera* (Murcia: Universidad de Murcia, 1980), p. 14.

17. For an official description of the purposes and operation of the ONC see Count Altea, "National Corporative Organization in Spanish Industry," *International Labor Review* 15 (June 1927): 828–41. For an examination of the parity committees from the point of view of a labor law specialist, consult Juan Montero Aroca, *Los tribunales de trabajo (1908–1938)* (Valencia: Universidad de Valencia, 1972), esp. chap. 2.

18. Raymond Carr, *Spain, 1809–1939* (1966; rev. ed. Oxford: Oxford University Press, 1975), p. 573.

19. Aunós, *Estudios de derecho corporativa,* p. 231. A year earlier Aunós claimed: "There are currently constituted 450 parity committees and the number of workers covered by corporate groups ... exceeds 320,000; the number

of employers eligible to take part in the elections [of parity committees] is 100,000. The sum total of those covered by the National Corporative Organization is estimated at 500,000" (*La organización corporativa y su posible desenvolvimiento* [Madrid: Ministerio de Trabajo, 1929], p. 54). Sánchez, *Union General,* pp. 31–38, provides additional statistical data.

20. Eduardo Aunós, *La organización corporativa y su posible desenvolvimiento* (Madrid: Ministerio de Trabajo y Previsión, 1929), p. 53.

21. Quoted in Albert Balcells, *Crisis económica y agitación social en Cataluña* (Barcelona: Ariel, 1971), p. 171.

22. "Aunós's project was enormously complex, and in attempting to implement it without a trained staff of administrators or adequate preparation among workers and owners, numerous mistakes were committed. By shying away from state coercion the system required a harmony of interest to be effective that was not present in the Spain of the late 1920s. Nevertheless, both Libres and Socialists did their best to make the system function, and the howls of protest from business and from certain political quarters indicated that they were not wholly unsuccessful" (Colin M. Winston, *Workers and the Right in Spain, 1900–1930* [Princeton: Princeton University Press, 1985], p. 267).

23. Alejandro Gallart Folch, *Derecho español de trabajo* (Barcelona: Editorial Labor, 1936), pp. 194–95.

24. See McIvor "Spanish Labor Policy," p. 46. This may also have been an important element in Primo's decision not to employ Martínez Anido's brutal methods in suppressing the CNT.

Some writers in support of their allegations of fascist influence in Aunós's labor corporatism have cited his visit to Italy in 1926 and subsequent exchange visits by Aunós and Giuseppe Bottai, the architect of Italian fascist corporatism. Aunós did make two trips to Italy, the first in 1926 and the second the following year. "The 1926 trip centered on the Milan Trade Fair and was very low key; Aunós was not feted by Fascist officialdom. Bottai did not even become Minister of Corporations until several months later, and Aunós did not have an interview with Mussolini until 1927." Fabra Ribas, then serving as the Spanish ILO representative, wrote to Director General Albert Thomas that Mussolini was actively courting Spain by dispatching numerous lecturers and cultural personalities. Bottai came in late 1926. "The Italians were politely received by elements of Primo's Union Patriotica," according to Fabra, "but could not come to an understanding even with them. As for the other sections of Spanish opinion," he wrote, "they never had strong sympathies for Italy and Mussolinism" (ibid., pp. 57–58). Aunós and other Catholics embraced fascism in the 1930s under the Second Republic. Also, even though the leaders of the Barcelona Libres were subsequently to take on fascist traits, at this juncture they supported the Italian Catholic unions and the Popolare in their opposition to Mussolini. See Winston, *Workers and the Right in Spain,* p. 158.

25. Ben Ami, *Fascism from Above,* p. 240.

26. From 1923 to 1929 9,455 kilometers of new highways were constructed compared to 2,796 over the preceding five years. Railway lines were extended a modest 800 kilometers, but extensive modernization of equipment took place.

27. See Manuel Tuñon de Lara, *Los comienzos del siglo XX: La población, la economía, la sociedad (1898–1931),* in *Historia de España,* vol. 37, ed. José Maria Jover (Madrid: Espasa-Calpe, 1984), p. 600.

28. "The Spanish cotton industry on a per capita basis was sixth in Europe at the outset of the Restoration. By the end of the Primo de Rivera dictatorship it had declined to tenth place. This textile specialty by the number employed and, more important, by gross value, continued at that time to be Spain's principal industry. But it was an industry with obsolete equipment, lacking vigor or prospects and on the defensive. After having imposed exclusivity of the domestic market (tariffs calculated in constant pesetas for foreign yarn and cloths—untreated, bleached, and dyed—were three times greater in 1925 than in 1913) in 1926 the creation of the . . . Regulatory Committee was demanded in July of that year, the numerous clauses were obtained by decree, namely, a ban on installing new manufacturing plants and the expansion of existing ones" (Jordi Nadal, "Un siglo de industrialización en España, 1833–1930," in Nicolas Sánchez Albornoz, ed. *Modernización económica de España, 1830–1930* [Madrid: Alianza, 1985], pp. 96–97).

29. Rial, *Revolution from Above,* pp. 193–95. Much of the increase in women's and apprentices' wages came from substituting them for better-paid male workers.

30. Juan Velarde Fuertes, *Política económica de la dictadura* (Madrid: Guadiana de Publicaciónes, 1968), p. 157; see also McIvor, "Spanish Labor Policy," p. 14; Manuel Tuñon de Lara, *El movimiento obrero en la historia de España, 1924–1936,* 3 vols. (Barcelona: Laia, 1972), 3:19–33, for a detailed discussion of wages and prices.

31. According to the Labor Ministry, the number of reported accidents rose steeply from 131,116 in 1923 to 225,988 in 1930, while fatalities increased during the same period from 337 to 650. See McIvor, "Spanish Labor Policy," p. 15.

32. In 1923 Calvo Sotelo claimed a surplus of 186 million pesetas, but the sum total of the two budgets revealed a shortfall of 859.8 million pesetas. See Ben Ami, *Fascism from Above,* p. 275.

33. Rial, *Revolution from Above,* pp. 180–83.

34. For socialist attitudes in this period see Paul Preston, *The Coming of the Spanish Civil War* (London: Macmillan, 1978), chap. 1. Also useful are José

Andrés Gallego, *El socialismo durante la dictadura, 1923–1930* (Madrid: Te-bas, 1977), and Shlomo Ben Ami, *The Origins of the Second Republic* (Oxford: Oxford University Press, 1978), esp. chap. 3. Largo Caballero's version can be found in his *Escritos de la republica* (Madrid: Editorial Pablo Iglesias, 1985).

35. UGT membership figures are taken from official sources. Enrique del Moral, who is currently preparing a study of socialism under the dictatorship, asserts that UGT/PSOE figures of this period are inflated by about 20 percent.

36. For a discussion of the decline of the Asturian Miners Union during the 1920s see Shubert, *Hacia la revolución,* esp. chap. 6.

37. Ben Ami, *Fascism from Above,* p. 301.

38. Richard Herr, *An Historical Essay on Modern Spain* (Berkeley and Los Angeles: University of California Press, 1976), p. 176. Siding with the UGT, Aunós sought Primo's authorization to activate the parity committees in the *campo,* but under pressure from the landowners, the dictator overruled him.

39. At the end of 1923 the UGT claimed a membership of 210,977 distributed in 1,275 local affiliates; by 1929 it had grown to 250,203 members with 1,617 locals.

40. According to Manuel Pérez Ledesma, the UGT's "theoretical outlook and organizational structuring underwent sweeping changes of great importance between 1888 and 1931. From a labor federation primarily devoted to the support of locals on strike, declaring itself apolitical, that was promoted and defended by Pablo Iglesias, the General Union was now distanced from the administration of strike solidarity and primarily concerned with the broadening of social legislation. Possessing a markedly socialist character that was reflected in its declaration of principles, it sought how best to intervene directly in political life. . . . The road traversed had been long and complex. More gradual in the hands of the first generation (Iglesias, García Quejido, Vicente Barrio) with its small number of affiliates and membership, with accelerated growth the new leaders (Largo Caballero, Besteiro, Saborit) could count on a relatively substantial following and with a certain weight in the country's public life" (Manuel Pérez Ledesma, "La Union General de Trabajadores: Ideología y organización [1881–1931]" [Ph.D. dissertation, Madrid Autonomous University, 1976]). The UGT conversion to national federations encountered some resistance, particularly from Madrid craft unions and from those in the printing trades.

41. In addition to forceful police countermeasures and the fear of military court-martials, the drop in labor terrorism was precipitated by "the disrepute among workers for violent methods and the exhaustion of trade union financial means that irregularly had underwritten anarcho-syndicalist terrorists. Armed struggle ceased with the exile of a large part of the anarcho-syndicalist terrorists and with the abeyance of the Sindicato Libre *pistoleros*

appeased by the dissolution of CNT and possibly orders from on high" (Balcells, *Historia contemporánea de Cataluña*, p. 233).

Primo established a division of labor in his cabinet. Martínez Anido was authorized to direct the persecution of the CNT and other labor dissidents while Aunós handled relations with the UGT and the Catholic unions. Martínez Anido continued to serve as patron-protector of the Barcelona Libres.

42. A return to Martínez Anido's brutal methods in dealing with the CNT would have made it impossible for the UGT to cooperate with Primo and also would have prejudiced his effort to secure the legitimizing sanction for his labor policies from the ILO.

43. A useful reference on the CNT in this period is "La C.N.T. bajo la dictadura (1923–1930) of Antonio Elorza," which appeared in nos. 39–40, 44–45, and 46 (1972–74) of the *Revista de Trabajo*. See also Eulália Vega, *El Trentisme a Catalunya: Divergencies ideologiques en la CNT (1930–1933)* (Barcelona: Curial, 1980), and John Brademas, "Revolution and Social Revolution: A Contribution to the History of the Anarcho-Syndicalist Movement in Spain, 1930–1937" (Ph.D. dissertation, Oxford University, 1953), chaps. 1 and 2.

44. Rationalist schools continued to operate in Barcelona and other Catalan industrial centers (interview with Juan Manuel Molina ["Juanel"], March 16, 1982). See John Brademas, *Anarco-sindicalismo y revolución en España (1930–1937)* (Barcelona: Ariel, 1974), p. 24; José Peirats, *La C.N.T. en la revolución española,* 3 vols. (Paris: Reudo Iberico, 1971), 1:39.

45. De Santillan, who returned to Spain in 1933, became a leading intellectual spokesman for the anarchists, and the FORA organ *La Protesta,* which carried articles dealing with the Spanish controversy, was disseminated in Spanish anarchist circles. The brochure *El anarquismo en el movimiento obrero,* written by De Santillan and López Arango (Barcelona: Cosmos, 1925), served as the principal exposition of the anarchist-*trabazon* point of view.

46. "While for Peiró and other anarcho-syndicalists, syndicalism constituted a modern expression of anarchism and the road to a realization of libertarian communism, Pestaña experienced no difficulty in viewing syndicalism as apart from anarchism, as a new force for revolutionary ends. Considered as a new ideological conglomerate and as the aspiration of human evolution, libertarian communism for him was the final end of a transitional stage that would come about validated through syndicalist ideas" (Xavier Paniagua, *La sociedad libertaria* [Barcelona: Crítica, 1982], pp. 166–67). This book provides a useful survey of doctrinal disputes and concepts during the 1920s and 1930s.

47. The writer César Lorenzo, son of the anarcho-syndicalist leader Horacio Prieto, provides a portrait of the Solidarists: "Young militants aged twenty

to twenty-five years on the eve of the Primo de Rivera dictatorship, they were more hardened than their elders. Having barely completed adolescence, they had already experienced imprisonment and police brutalities; they were no mere youngsters shouting revolutionary slogans for sport or to affirm their personalities and then hasten to become peaceable, resigned citizens. They were men of action, avid for justice and change. They were forged in strikes and riots and impatient to avenge their comrades assassinated by the defenders of 'order'. . . . Prepared for any sacrifice, rejecting all compromises, they possessed an unbreakable faith in libertarian communism. Often they were esperantists, naturists, and vegetarians who enjoyed reading Kropotkin's *Conquest of Bread,* admired the impassioned life of Bakunin (whose ideas, however, they disregarded), they read Nietzsche and, curiously, Schopenhauer." The twenty who made up the Solidarist group "were notable for their extraordinary daring, their energy, resistance and sense of adventure. . . . The influence of the Solidarists was to be immense in the domain of action but extremely wanting on the doctrinal level" (*Les anarchistes espagñols et le pouvoir, 1868–1969* [Paris: Seuil, 1969], pp. 52, 59, 62).

48. The polemic over the *trabazon* concept became a three-way affair. Ranged against its proponents were Italian anarchists Errico Malatesta and Luigi Fabbri, who favored anarchist participation in unions without formal collaboration in their direction, and syndicalists Pestaña and Peiró, who made a clear demarcation between ideological anarchism and trade union action.

49. Its most immediate precursor was the Federation of Spanish Language Anarchist Groups, which was constituted in France during 1926. Juan Manuel Molina ("Juanel"), its secretary general, later served in the same capacity in the FAI.

50. Until the Second Republic, organized anarchism in Barcelona remained a small movement. There were, according to Juan Manuel Molina, twenty-five *grupos de afinidad* in 1918–19 with each group numbering six to eight adherents. At the time of the formation of FAI in 1927, anarchists numbered two hundred with several thousand sympathizers. By 1930 there were four hundred to five hundred. The two leading anarchist organs, *Tiempos Nuevos* and *Tierra y Libertad,* then had printings of twenty thousand (interview, March 16, 1982).

51. See Winston, *Workers and the Right in Spain,* esp. chaps. 5 and 6, for a detailed account of the Libres under the dictatorship.

52. Both organizations had core memberships made up of Carlists. CNSL General Secretary Mariano Puyuelo, who succeeded Father Gafo, was also a Carlist.

53. Social Catholic Severino Aznar's estimate placing CNSL membership in 1928 at 68,344 suggests exaggeration in official claims. Winston concludes, "At its 1922 peak the union had spoken of between 170,000 and 200,000 members in Catalonia alone; the 1925 figures reveal the extent to which the

Libres had been decimated by the CNT resurgence. These losses were slowly recouped during the dictatorship. By 1929 the CNSL registered 197,853 workers in the entire peninsula" (*Workers and the Right in Spain*, p. 177).

54. Ibid., p. 178.

55. Joan Peiró quoted in ibid., p. 188.

56. Ibid., p. 205.

57. Raymond Carr writes that "the National Assembly was a non-elective consultative body. The constitution which it drafted expressed the current right wing hostility to the practices of liberal responsible parliamentary government. . . . The constitution was to be ratified by a plebiscite. This turned it into a *charte octroyée* which created a 'sterile and boring' caricature of parliamentary life" (*Spain, 1808–1939*, p. 586).

58. A detailed chronicle of that year's tumultuous events can be found in Eduardo de Guzman, *1930, Historia política de un año decisivo* (Madrid: Tebas, 1973).

59. Damaso Berenguer's memoirs, *De la dictadura a la republica* (Madrid: Plus Ultra, 1935), tells of his tenure as prime minister. Chapter 8, "El elemento obrero," discusses labor developments.

60. Carr, *Spain, 1808–1939*, p. 592.

61. The socialist leadership, preoccupied with trade union affairs, was on the fringe of these sociopolitical developments. Tuñon de Lara believes that "the majority of them were caught unawares by the amplitude of the 1930–1931 Spanish crisis" (Tuñon de Lara, *Movimiento obrero en la historia de España*, 3:63).

62. Though the party faithful and the entire UGT/PSOE leadership favored a Republican government, differences arose in the party's Executive Committee between Julián Besteiro and Andrés Saborit, who controlled the Madrid party organization, and the combined forces of Largo Caballero and Prieto over the nature of socialist cooperation with a future Republican government. Besteiro argued that the bourgeoisie should make their own revolution and, though giving support to the Republican cause, should refuse direct participation in a bourgeois government (they had been offered three ministerial posts). Largo and Prieto insisted that ministerial collaboration was essential to the success of such a government. Though the latter position ultimately won out in September 1930 by an eight to six vote, differences between the two groups persisted until the proclamation of the Second Republic.

63. According to the Ministry of Interior, in 1929 there were 96 strikes involving 55,576 workers and 313,065 days lost; in 1930 182 strikes involved 247,460 workers and 3,745,360 days were lost. These figures do not include the large number of general strikes, most of which took place in the latter part of 1930.

64. Following the February request, a CNT national plenum was held in Blanes

(Gerona) on April 17 and 18 during which the moderate leadership, despite strong Faista opposition, succeeded in securing formal endorsement of its efforts to obtain legalization.

65. Emilio Mola, *Lo que yo supe* (*Memorias de mi paso por la dirreción general de seguridad*), vol. 1 in *Obras Completas* (Valladolid: Librería Santarén, 1940).

66. At the time of the dictatorship's downfall the PCE abandoned its policy of working inside the CNT through the "reconstruction committees" to form its own trade union adjunct, the Unified General Labor Confederation (CGTU).

67. Balcells, *Historia contemporanea de Cataluña,* p. 233. The definitive study of BOC is that of Francesc Bonamusa, *El Bloc Obrer i Camperol (1930–1932)* (Barcelona: Curial, 1974). Also important is the volume on the BOC in Victor Alba's four-volume *Historia del marxisme a Catalunya, 1919–1939* (Barcelona: Portic, 1974–75).

68. Anarchist opposition forced Joan Peiró to resign from the CNT national committee and to withdraw his signature. A month later, however, Peiró was named director of Solidaridad Obrera. See Pere Gabriel, "El anarquismo en España," in *El anarquismo,* ed. George Woodcock (Barcelona: Ariel, 1979), pp. 378–79.

69. Santos Juliá argues that the failure of the 1930 Madrid general strike (repeated in 1934) was not caused by alleged shortcomings of leaders such as Largo Caballero or Besteiro but, as in 1917, by the "organic incapacity" of a movement shaped by its reformist craft trade union character to conduct a successful revolutionary general strike. See his *Madrid, 1931–1934, de la fiesta popular a la lucha de clases* (Madrid: Siglo Veintiuno, 1984), pp. 26–29.

70. Neither side "possessed accurate information regarding its resources or that of its adversaries. If the movement ultimately failed it would be proper to attribute it to the colossal errors of the revolutionaries than to the merits and good judgment of the monarchist authorities" (Guzman, *1930,* p. 469).

71. In a report by Constancio Bernaldo de Quiros prepared for the Labor Ministry in December 1930, the number of unemployed in Andalusia was estimated at 100,000 or 12 percent of the labor force in the region. Among the full-time agricultural field hands, one of every three and half of all casual laborers were without work (*La crisis Anduluza de 1930: Estudios y documentos* [Madrid, 1931], rpt. in his *Espartaquismo agrario Anduluz y otros ensayos sobre la estructura económica y social de Andalusia* [Madrid: Turner, 1973], pp. 99–126). The agricultural economist Pascual Carrión claimed that during nonharvest months in 1930 and 1931, the number of unemployed in Andalusia was as high as 200,000 (*Los latifundios en España, su importancia, origen, consequencias y solución* [Madrid: Graficas Reunidas, 1932], p. 366).

72. Quoted in Javier Tussell, *La España del siglo XX* (Barcelona: Dopesa, 1975), p. 227.
73. Gabriel Jackson, *Historian's Quest* (New York: Knopf, 1969), p. 47.

CHAPTER 10: THE SECOND REPUBLIC, 1931–1936

1. Emilio Mola, *Obras completas* (Valladolid: Librería Santarén, 1940), p. 480.
2. For a discussion of the weaknesses of the Republic's party system see Manuel Ramirez, "Los partidos políticos durante la II Republica," in *La crisis del estado español, 1896–1936,* ed. Manuel Tuñon de Lara (Madrid: Cuadernos para el dialogo, 1978).
3. Juan Linz emphasizes that among the Republic's founders, "one factor was central: the sudden installation of a new regime by a small conspiratorial group and the Socialist party after the disintegration of the dictatorship. This non-mobilised society created an upsurge of support for the regime that was amplified by the electoral system and created over-confidence in its strength and unity of purpose, as well as dangerous ignorance and scorn for its conservative and clerical opponents" ("Great Hopes to Civil War: The Breakdown of Democracy in Spain," in *The Breakdown of Democratic Regimes: Europe,* ed. Juan Linz and Alfred Stepan [Baltimore: Johns Hopkins University Press, 1978], p. 180).
4. "The continued refusal of the Anarcho-syndicalists to present candidates resulted in a parliament that was unrepresentative of the nation both on the Right and on the extreme Left" (Edward Malefakis, *Agrarian Reform and Peasant Revolution in Spain* [New Haven: Yale University Press, 1970], p. 172).
5. Manuel Azaña, *Obras completas,* 4 vols. (Mexico City: Oasis, 1966), 2:635.
6. Niceto Alcalá Zamora observes that "with the double privilege of a political party and as the only recognized, pampered trade union organization, the Socialist party received rather exceptional treatment" (*Memoria* [Barcelona: Planeta, 1977], p. 249).
7. Salvador de Madariaga, *Spain, a Modern History* (New York: Praeger, 1958), p. 411.
8. Ibid., pp. 410–11.
9. When Luis Araquistáin left his ministry post, Fabra Ribas replaced him as under-secretary and Carlos Baraibar, another intimate and political adviser of Largo, was named director general. Most of the drafting and formulation of the labor reforms was done by Fabra Ribas.
10. See Ministerio de Trabajo y Previsión Social, *Labor realizado desde la proclamación de la República hasta el 8 de Septiembre de 1932* (Madrid: Sucesores de Rivadeneyra, 1933?), for a comprehensive listing of the official actions accomplished during this period.

11. For an examination of the historical background and contents of this law consult Santiago González Gómez and Manuel Redero San Roman, "La ley de contrato de trabajo de 1931," in *La II Republica española,* J. L. García Delgado, ed., (Madrid: Siglo XXI, 1987), pp. 75–93.

12. The practice of using public office for partisan advantage was by no means a uniquely socialist shortcoming. The noted labor law professor Alejandro Gallart observed that the naming of *jurado* chairmen "was booty, the scant booty that changes in government provided parties and political groups to whose disposition the filling of the position of chairmen and vice-chairmen were given to the leaders who handed them out with alacrity" (Extracto oficial del Congreso de los Diputados, sesion de 5 de Julio de 1935, Numero 218, p. 22, quoted in Juan Montero Aroca, *Los tribunales de trabajo (1908–1938)* (Valencia: Universidad de Valencia, 1976), pp. 142–43. Gallart was then serving as a deputy from the conservative Catalonian Lliga.

13. "Labor representation on the mixed juries could in reality be channeled through the UGT craft unions. The greater role accorded their hiring halls strengthened their perceived role as workplace champions. In the labor agreements that were concluded during the early years of the Republic, a clause frequently appears stipulating union recognition and giving specific jurisdiction over the hiring and firing of workers" (Santos Juliá, "Organizaciónes y practicas obreras," *Arbor* 109 (June–July 1981). For union agreements in this period consult Mariano González Rothvoss, *Anuario español de política social, 1934–1935* (Madrid: Sucesores de Rivadeneyra, 1934).

14. For Largo Caballero's use of politics for trade union purposes see Santos Juliá, "Socialismo y revolución en el pensamiento y la acción política de Francisco Largo Caballero," in Francisco Largo Caballero, *Escritos de la República: Notas historicas de la guerra en España (1917–1940)* (Madrid: Editorial Pablo Iglesias, 1985), pp. ix–lxvi.

15. Ibid., p. 214.

16. "Through these conciliatory bodies the Socialist party, which controlled the Labor Ministry in the person of Largo Caballero, sought to increase party influence in Catalonia by occasionally issuing findings to resolve disputes that were even more favorable than the strikers' demands. The frenetic proselytism of the socialist leader, acting as an arm of the government, often prejudiced the legitimate interests of employers. Needless to say, such efforts scarcely proved successful" (Claudi Ametlla, *Memories politiques, 1918–1936* [Barcelona: Distributions Catalonia, 1979], 2:205). The author, a noted Barcelona journalist, served as civil governor during the early Republican years.

17. Compliance with the Professional Associations Law was violently rejected by the CNT with ample reason. The law prohibited minors less than eighteen years of age from becoming union members, and only those aged twenty-one or more could hold union office. Anyone convicted of a common crime

was barred from union membership. The anarcho-syndicalists held special appeal for the young and, in accordance with Spanish anarchist tradition, welcomed persons with criminal records. Additional provisions included the submission of financial records and membership lists to the labor delegate and, with the CNT in mind, stipulated that certain union actions had to be approved by general membership meetings. French socialist Jules Moch described the law as containing "rather rigorous obligations" (Germaine Moch Picard and Jules Moch, *L'Espagne Republicaine* [Paris: Reider 1933]).

18. The unexpected growth of CNT influence reinforced socialists' conviction in the rightness of their course and caused them to take even more stringent actions against their anarcho-syndicalist rivals. In cabinet discussions on how to deal with labor unrest fomented by the CNT, Labor Minister Largo Caballero pressed for more restrictive strike legislation than that proposed by Interior Minister Maura. See Azaña, *Obras completas,* 4:36–37.

19. Mercedes Cabrera, *La patronal ante la II Republica, organizaciónes y estrategia, 1931–1936* (Madrid: Siglo XXI, 1983), pp. 198–202.

20. A 1932 questionnaire circulated among the UGT's 5,107 local affiliates revealed that all had obtained wage increases since April 1931, ranging from half a peseta daily to five pesetas (Picard and Moch, *L'Espagne Republicaine,* p. 275).

21. Albert Balcells, *Crisis económica y agitación social en Cataluña (1930–1936)* (Barcelona: Ariel, 1971), p. 167; Cabrera, *La patronal ante la II Republica,* p. 132; Malefakis, *Agrarian Reform and Peasant Revolution,* pp. 263–64. Jordi Palafox estimates that real wage earnings between 1930 and 1933 rose more than 20 percent in most instances and in some sectors with especially strong unions the increase amounted to about 30 percent. See his "La gran depresión de los años treinta y la crisis industrial española," *Investigaciónes Económicas,* no. 11 (1980), pp. 5–46.

22. The 1934 unionization estimate is from M. Martínez Cuadrado, *La burguesia conservadora (1874–1931)* (Madrid: Alianza, 1973), p. 362; on Madrid, Santos Juliá, *Madrid, 1931–1934, de la fiesta popular a la lucha de clases* (Madrid: Siglo Veintiuno, 1984), estimate derived from author's data; on Seville, José Manuel Macarro Vera, *La utopia revolucionaria, Sevilla en la Secunda Republica* (Seville: Monte de piedad y caja de ahorros de Sevilla, 1985), chap. 3; for Barcelona, Balcells, *Crisis económica,* p. 192; on Asturias, Adrian Shubert, *Hacia la revolución: Origines sociales del movimiento obrero en Asturias* (Barcelona: Crítica, 1984), p. 181; for Vizcaya, Ignacio Olábarri, *Relaciónes laborales en Vizcaya (1890–1936)* (Durango: Leopoldo Zugaza, 1978), p. 431.

23. In areas such as Madrid and Aragon party membership remained relatively low compared to the great increase in UGT recruitment. In late 1931, for example, the PSOE in the region of Aragon numbered 1,471 while Zaragossa

province alone had 26,000 UGT members, including a substantial number of rural adherents. Arsenio Jiménez, then a leading figure in Aragonese socialism, in a 1979 interview, explained the lack of greater party recruitment as caused by peasant unionists regarding themselves as socialists and feeling that by joining the UGT they had also adhered to the party. He claimed that 95 percent of the peasant members were highly politicized. See Luis G. German, Santiago Castillo, Ignacio Baron, and Carlos Forcadell, *Historia del socialismo en Aragon, PSOE-UGT (1879–1936)* (Zaragossa: Departamento de historia económica, Universidad de Zaragossa, 1979), p. 102.

24. The proanarchist novelist Ramon Sender commented that "to continue empowering Largo Caballero with the new regulation of labor is like confiding religious freedom to the bishop of Madrid-Alcalá" (*El Sol,* August 5, 1931, quoted in Juliá, *Madrid, 1931–1934,* p. 214).

25. See Balcells, *Crisis económica,* pp. 166–85. See also Jordi Nadal, Jaime Vicens Vives, and Casimiro Martí, *Le mouvement ouvriere en Espagne en temps de depression economique (1929–1939), leurs consequences d'orde politique et sociale* (Assen, Netherlands: International Institute of Social History, 1961).

26. Labor Ministry statistics recorded only a fraction of the number of strikes that took place in rural zones not to speak of other forms of social protest. Only 27 were registered during the last six months of 1930, 35 in 1931 following the establishment of the Republic, and 198 in 1932. In 1933 the total amounted to 448, more than half before the September downfall of the Azaña government. See Malefakis, *Agrarian Reform and Peasant Revolution,* p. 313.

27. Nadal, Vicens Vives, and Martí, *Le mouvement ouvriere en Espagne;* and Gabriel Jackson, *The Spanish Republic and the Civil War, 1931–1939* (Princeton: Princeton University Press, 1965), p. 96.

28. See Balcells, *Crisis económica,* p. 174. Labor conflicts, especially in 1932–33, were increasingly marked by violence as the deteriorating economic situation resulted in stiffer employer resistance to union demands and it became increasingly difficult for unions to maintain strike discipline without resorting to violence and intimidation.

   Juan Hernández Andreu writes: "I wish to register my disagreement with those who attribute the strike movement of the Second Republic to political more than to economic reasons. Strikes increased with the economic depression of the 1930s. The precipitate increase in the number of strikes that took place in 1933 occurred when economic decline deepened and preceded the statistically recorded wage slowdown of 1934 during which large numbers of striking workers persisted" (*España y le crisis de 1929* [Madrid: Espasa-Calpe, 1986], p. 165).

29. In a June 1933 parliamentary interpellation the moderate Republican Sán-

chez Roman told Labor Minister Largo Caballero that "there is an extremely widespread belief among Spanish businessmen, so extensive that we cannot think of an exception, that within the parity committees that serve as government organs of social policy, a most grave class struggle is being incubated and these serious apprehensions are depressing our spirit of enterprise" (quoted in Mercedes Cabrera, "Las organizaciónes patronales ante la conflictividad social y los jurados mixtas," in *La II Republica, una esperanza frustrada, actas del congreso, Valencia, capital de la Republica (Abril 1986)* [Valencia: Edicións Alfons el Magnánim, 1987], p. 1987).

30. Cabrera (ibid., pp. 65–82) provides a comprehensive treatment of employers' evolving attitudes. See also Juliá, *Madrid, 1931–1934,* for a discussion of employers' attitudes in Madrid during the 1930s.

31. "For a hundred and twenty years the first act of every new regime has been to harass the outgoing party and to undo its legislation. . . . Judged by these standards the behavior of the Republicans was moderate. The Dictatorship had been much more vindictive but both made the same mistake of exasperating their enemies without disarming them" (Gerald Brenan, *The Spanish Labyrinth* [London: Cambridge University Press, 1943], p. 264).

32. "It was a frequent practice for the Guard to fire point-blank at strikers, and the Ministry of Interior invariably protected the anonymity of the marksmen if it could not entirely suppress the news. If for the landlords the Guard was indeed La Benemerita, for the landless peasants it was an army of occupation composed of 25,000 well-armed servants of the rich" (Jackson, *The Spanish Republic and the Civil War,* p. 68).

33. The Castilblanco incident was but a particularly grisly manifestation of "the unrelieved tension that gripped the Spanish countryside [and] exploded into an outburst of primitive savagery." Malefakis also cites landowner-sponsored acts of barbarism that took place in December 1932 at Castellar de Santiago (Ciudad Real) in which a band of landowners lynched a number of FNTT supporters (*Agrarian Reform and Peasant Revolution,* pp. 312–13).

34. For a discussion of the Republic's public order and civil rights record, consult Manuel Balbé, *Orden público y militarismo en la España constitucional (1812–1923),* 2d ed. (Madrid: Alianzo Universidad, 1985), chap. 11. Azaña sought to demilitarize the administration of domestic security, but he encountered nearly insuperable obstacles. "The Civil Guard was military and the police profession in the western European sense did not exist. The 1906 Jurisdictions Law had disappeared but in the absence of an efficient civilian police, the Civil Guard and the army were employed in dealing with serious public order situations. The civilian outlook that inspired the Republic evaporated whenever clashes took place between public order forces and civilians with the matter ending up before military tribunals. This had the effect of main-

taining the army in the front line of social conflict" (Gabriel Cardona, "Estado y poder militar en la Secunda Republica," in *La II Republica, una esperanza frustrada,* pp. 51–52).

35. Azaña noted in his diary, "What Unamuno once said of Primo can be applied somewhat; first fire and then aim" (*Obras completas,* 4:43). The ailing Santiago Casares Quiroga, a political intimate of Azaña, replaced Maura as interior minister in October 1931. In spite of his greater sophistication, "Time after time, he stated that the government was not going to make martyrs of the anarchists and time after time he had to call the Civil Guard and the Assault Guard, temporarily close CNT headquarters, and suspend anarchist newspapers" (Jackson, *The Spanish Republic and the Civil War,* p. 113).

36. For having participated in the anti-coup general strike, José Bullejos and other Communist party leaders were purged on orders of the Communist International. The ultraleftist "third period" had been prescribed by Stalin, and Spanish communists violently opposed the Republic, preposterously declaring that the formation of workers' and peasants' soviets was the order of the day.

37. John Brademas, "Revolution and Social Revolution: A Contribution to the History of the Anarcho-Syndicalist Movement in Spain, 1930–1937" (Ph.D. dissertation, Oxford University, 1956), remains the single most valuable general study of this period. A Spanish version has been published: *Anarcosindicalismo y revolución en España (1930–1937)* (Barcelona: Ariel, 1974).

38. An editorial in the April 25 issue of *El Luchador,* organ of intransigent anarchism published by the Montseny family, declared, "Spanish republicans should not count on anarchists in the consolidation of their form of government, but neither should they fear them so long as they have not consolidated."

39. These estimates are those of historian Albert Balcells. According to Helmut Rudiger, AIT secretary for Spain, affiliation in Catalonia during 1931 well exceeded 300,000 and then generally ranged between 150,000 and 175,000. See AIT internal document no. 13, circular 12, a discussion paper prepared by Rudiger on the situation in Spain for the June 1, 1937, plenum of AIT, available in the Archivo Historico Militar and the Pablo Iglesias Foundation.

40. See Stanley Payne, *The Spanish Revolution* (New York: Norton, 1970), p. 116.

41. Alexander Schapiro, a Russian anarchist who was sent to Spain in 1933 by the International Workingmen's Association (AIT—Spanish initials), observed in his report: "The instinct of revolutionary spontaneity continues among the militants to override other considerations. The notion that destructive revolutionary action in itself contains the germs of reconstructive revolutionary activity remains deeply rooted among our comrades and is an

ever present obstacle in the CNT's activities to the inoculation of the organizing virus" (quoted in Brenan, *Spanish Labyrinth*, p. 264).

42. Though somewhat unsatisfactory and tendentious, Juan Gómez Casas, *Historia de la FAI* (Bilbao: Zero, 1977), is the only work on this subject and provides useful background material.

43. César M. Lorenzo, *Les anarchistes espagnoles et le pouvoir, 1868–1969* (Paris: Seuil, 1969), p. 67.

44. "To avoid confusion with another anarchist group in Barcelona that had taken the same name, the older 'Solidarios' group took the name of 'Nostoros' " (Ricardo Sanz, *El sindicalismo español antes de la guerra, los hijos de trabajo* [Barcelona: Petronio, 1976], pp. 191–92).

45. Union general membership meetings at which election of officers took place were poorly attended. It was not uncommon for Faistas to assure that the sergeant-at-arms, who controlled access to the meeting, was a Faista supporter. He, in turn, admitted Faistas whether or not they were actually members of the union. Their presence in sufficient numbers assured the election of their candidates (interview, Luis Portela, March 14, 1982). Rafael Vidiella, a former CNT leader, observed, "In Catalonia the industrial unions no longer served as the federal bond between trade branches that the 1918 regional congress so clearly accorded. In detriment to the various trades, they were dominated by a total centralism. Membership meetings are always held jointly even at times permitting those not from the industry to take part and in which the *peones*, being more numerous than skilled workers, predominate" (*Leviatán*, October 1935, pp. 27–32, reproduced in *El arraigo de anarquismo en Cataluña, textos de 1926–1934*, ed. Albert Balcells [Madrid: Jucar, 1973], pp. 167–75).

46. "Each defense squad consisted of ten men with one of them acting as its head. . . . They were organized as self-contained units, and there were no contacts between them. A neighborhood defense committee maintained contact in each working-class district with the cadres and with the local defense committee. Without constituting a specific group, the local defense committee that performed the function of a Catalonian regional defense committee as well was composed of those of us who had been members of the Solidarios group: Aurelio Fernández, Gregorio Jover, Ricardo Sanz, Buenaventura Durruti, Francisco Ascaso, and myself" (Juan García Oliver, *El eco de los pasos* [Barcelona: Ruedo Iberico, 1978], pp. 129–30). The only viable groups were formed in Barcelona.

47. "Anarchist action groups that were not formally affiliated often adopted the name FAI (for example, Juan García Oliver and Buenaventura Durruti), and its area of influence became blurred with such publications as *La Revista Blanca* of Federico Urales and Federica Montseny" (Isidre Molas, *El sistema de partidos políticos en Cataluña, 1931–1936* [Barcelona: Peninsula, 1974], p. 116).

48. For the proceedings of the 1931 congress see *Memoria de congreso extraordinario de la C.N.T. celebrado en Madrid los dias 11 al 16 de Junio de 1931* (Barcelona: Cosmos, 1931).

49. Official membership claims are to be taken with caution. Taking into account local unions that failed to send delegates to the June 1931 congress, total CNT membership was claimed to go well above six hundred thousand. In this instance as before, figures are not based on actual dues payers but on membership figures submitted by each affiliate. Local unions usually determined the number of their adherents on the basis of how many membership books had been issued without making allowances for personnel turnover, dropouts, nonpayment of dues, and so on. Furthermore, voting at regional and national conferences sometimes was determined by a count of individual delegates or weighted according to the affiliate membership each delegate spoke for.

50. Angel Pestaña claimed that during the Madrid 1931 congress of the CNT, anarchist extremists made three attempts on his life. See Enrique Santiago, *La Union General de Trabajadores ante la revolución* (Madrid: Saez Hermanos, 1932), p. 105.

51. Peiró felt that the failure to specify a benevolent attitude toward the Republic foredoomed his proposed conversion to industrial federations. Instead of having a period of relative peace in which to carry out the organizational restructuring, the multiplication of local strikes lacking clear goals and the climate of confrontation provoked more repression and the CNT's disarticulation. See Joan Peiró, *Escrits, 1917–1939,* ed. Pere Gabriel (Barcelona: Edicións 62, 1975), p. 23.

52. Ignoring policy decisions whenever it was considered appropriate to do so was a well-established anarchist practice. Legitimation of actions and policies came not from organizational representative responsibilities but from strongly held ideological convictions. Writing in 1924, Joaquín Maurín, the independent Marxist and former CNT leader, observed, "The most crucial decisions are taken without consulting the mass, and regional conferences adopt decisions that contradict those voted in national congresses" (*L'anarcho-syndicalisme en Espagne* [Paris: Petite Bibliothèque del Internationale Syndicale Rouge, XIII, 1924], p. 30).

53. It was reported to the 1936 CNT congress that militants, not telephone workers, sustained the struggle.

54. Anarchist *pistoleros* from Barcelona came to Seville to assist their embattled comrades (José Manuel Macarro, *La utopia revoluciónaria: Seville en la Secunda República* (Seville: Monte de piedad y caja de ahorros de Sevilla, 1985), pp. 147–56). CNT militants were generally armed. To maintain public order and labor peace, the first civil governor of the Republic pursued a policy of accommodation with the anarcho-syndicalists and permitted them to possess

arms. "Those pistoleros who were arrested in late 1932 carried the most up-to-date machine pistols and often had as much as 2,000 pesetas on their person [about $200 at the exchange rate of the time or about six months' wages in a unionized factory]. The money came from union dues and shake-downs of small shopkeepers, and subsidies of the agent provocateur type. Many of these gunmen wandered from city to city, exploiting labor tension, now in Barcelona, now in Seville" (Jackson, *The Spanish Republic and the Civil War,* p. 100).

55. See Brademas, *Anarcosindicalismo y revolución en España,* p. 82.

56. Sanz, *El sindicalismo español,* pp. 91–96.

57. Brenan, *Spanish Labyrinth,* pp. 250–51. The power base of Durruti and the Nosotros affinity group was the big textile worker union of Barcelona, the single largest CNT affiliate.

58. Jaume Miravtlles, the Catalan writer who served with Durruti on the Anti-Fascist Militias Committee that was formed in Barcelona after the July 1936 military rebellion, recounts that after three days, unable to endure the committee's tedious deliberations, Durruti took off for the Aragon front, where he assumed the military command. García Oliver sought to emulate him by also going to the front at the head of a Faista column, but within days he was back in Barcelona. "He was not born for such a life. Essentially he was an intellectual. I do not know the breadth or depth of his baggage but he spoke well, articulating his ideas, making proper historical compar-isons with the terminology of a man possibly having drunk too exclusively from individualist anarchist philosophical springs. His thinking, nonethe-less, had a consistency, expression, and the virtue of conviction that appealed to the masses" (*Gent que he conegut* [Barcelona: Destino, 1980], p. 88).

59. The quotation is taken from a lecture given by Juan García Oliver to a trade union meeting in the Barcelona barrio of Clot, which was reproduced in an article in *La Tierra,* October 3, 1931. See the special number of *Cuadernos de Ruedo Iberico* entitled "El movimiento libertario español, pasado, presente, y futuro" (1974), pp. 312–15. Durruti and García Oliver's insurrectionary strategy represented an application of Bakuninist prescriptions. "Bakunin was a firm believer in immediate revolution. He rejected the view that revolutionary forces will emerge gradually, in the fullness of time. What he demanded, in effect, was 'freedom now'. He would countenance no temporising with the existing system. The old order was rotten, he argued, and salvation could be achieved only by destroying it root and branch. Gradualism and reformism were futile palliatives, and compromises of no use. Bakunin's was a dream of immediate and universal destruction, the leveling of all existing values and institutions, and the creation of a libertarian society on their ashes" (Paul Avrich, *Anarchist Portraits* [Princeton: Princeton University Press, 1988], p. 10).

60. The complete Treintista manifesto can be found in Brademas, *Anarcosindicalismo y revolución en España*, pp. 250–54.

61. How best to combat Faismo was a matter of considerable controversy among Treintistas. Peiró felt the best tactic was to turn over organizational responsibility to the FAI so that its culpability for the disastrous putschist policy would be more clearly exposed. With this in mind, he relinquished control of *Solidaridad Obrera* without offering much resistance.

62. "Apoliticism traditionally signified the right of individual members to support whatever political group they wished but with the union maintaining a strict political neutrality. Now, however, apoliticism came to mean an active hostility toward all parties, especially the socialists and communists" (Albert Balcells, *Historia contemporanea de Cataluña* [Barcelona: Edhasa, 1981], p. 265).

63. The notion of seizing control of a town or hamlet and proclaiming libertarian communism originated with the Italian anarchist Errico Malatesta, who prescribed, "Seize a town or a village, render the representatives of the state harmless, and invite the population to organize itself freely." It also neatly conformed to the Spanish pronunciamiento that was often employed in the nineteenth and twentieth centuries by would-be military dictators or republican revolutionaries. The Malatesta quote appears in *The Revolution and the Civil War in Spain* by Pierre Broué and Emile Témime (Cambridge, Mass.: MIT Press, 1970), p. 56.

64. For more detail on the Figols uprising see Adolfo Bueso, *Recuerdos de un Cenetista*, 2 vols. (Barcelona: Ariel, 1976), 2:61–62.

65. Growing FAI dominance and a corresponding increase in labor violence caused Maciá, Companys, and the Esquerra Catalana to abandon their policy of cordiality and accommodation once it became clear that the CNT no longer would act as a "loyal opposition."

66. The most reliable and detailed account of the Treintista-FAI split and the secession of the Sabadell federation is Albert Balcells, "La crisis del anarcosindicalismo y el movimiento obrero en Sabadell entre 1930 y 1936," in his *Trabajo industrial y organización obrera en la Cataluña contemporanea (1900–1936)* (Barcelona: Laia, 1974), pp. 181–320. See also Eulalia Vega, *El trentisme a Catalunya, divergencies ideologiques en la CNT (1930–1933)* (Barcelona: Curial, 1980).

67. Balcells, *Crisis económica,* p. 194.

68. From 1923 to 1936 immigrants represented 37 percent of Barcelona's population, while in Treintista strongholds their numbers ranged from 10 to 20 percent. Mataró, for example, possessed only 10 percent.

69. Referring to the Faista direction of the Barcelona CNT, the veteran anarchist trade unionist Manuel Buenacasa wrote: "During certain epochs serious people and ideas led our movement and things went well. But the frequent

inundations of newcomers have dashed our brightest hopes. They have many times in good faith engaged the Spanish labor organization in the most absurd undertakings" (*La CNT, los "Treinta" y la FAI, la crisis del sindicalismo en Cataluña, sus causas, sus efectos, su remedio* [Barcelona: Talleres Graficos Alfa, 1933], p. 75).

70. Germaine Moch Picard and Jules Moch estimated CNT membership in January 1932 to be 862,000. See *L'Espagne republicaine,* p. 312.

71. Brademas, *Anarcosindicalismo y revolución en España,* p. 101.

72. A negative result of the Casas Viejas incident was the outcome in Cádiz province of the November parliamentary elections. Urged on by the CNT, 62.7 percent of the voters abstained, permitting this anarchist bastion to be represented in parliament by a Center-Right coalition that was able to garner eight of the ten seats with only 20 to 30 percent of the vote. It also permitted José Antonio Primo de Rivera, founder of the fascist Falange, to win a seat with only a small number of votes. Earlier the UGT's farm union, FNTT, had succeeded in winning over a substantial part of the CNT rural following in the province. Now, however, the socialists lost three seats.

73. The available literature on the Casas Viejas affair contains much that is tendentious and inaccurate. I have relied primarily, though not exclusively, on the excellent *The Anarchists of Casas Viejas* by Jerome Mintz (Chicago: University of Chicago Press, 1982). Mintz takes Eric J. Hobsbawm to task for his allegedly misbegotten attempt to stereotype the Casas Viejas rising as a classic anarchist insurrection, "utopian," "millenarian," and "apocalyptic"; there are factual errors in his chapter on the Andalusian anarchists in *Primitive Rebels* (Manchester: Manchester University Press, 1959). Mintz asserts that Hugh Thomas's *Spanish Civil War,* rev. ed. (New York: Harper & Row, 1977) is "painted in heroic colors" in discussing Casa Viejas and also contains factual inaccuracies.

74. Strike activities in Seville province during 1932–33 by CNT rural unions often were in support of insurrectionary strikes called by Faistas in the city.

The UGT's increase in rural enrollment reduced the CNT's following in the *campo* to its traditional reservoirs of influence, principally to the lower Gaudalquivir valley, to Cádiz, and to parts of Córdoba province. In the Levant and in La Rioja, rural anarchism predominated in significant zones.

75. Other than the usual disputes over wages, CNT action in the countryside mainly consisted of local uprisings. But as a 1937 report of the International Workingmen's Association (AIT) noted, it was reduced to "only a loose union of local and regional organizations, each of which formulated its own policies and acted at decisive moments without a common plan," thus assuring a lack of power (Malefakis, *Agrarian Reform and Peasant Revolution,* p. 305).

76. Three currents can be discerned within the Treintista group: (1) those who

were distinctly more syndicalist than anarchist in outlook (Pestaña, Josep Moix, leaders of the Sabadell city federation), (2) partisans of a politically neutral syndicalism compatible with the conduct of political activities that did not directly interfere with trade union action, and (3) anarcho-syndicalists opposed to the FAI's intrusion in confederal activities and policy making (Joan Peiró, Camil Piñon). See Vega, *Trentisme a Catalunya*, p. 202.

77. For an exposition of Pestaña's rationale see his *Por que se constituyó el Partido Sindicalista* (1934; rpt. Madrid: Zero, 1969).

78. Malefakis, *Agrarian Reform and Peasant Revolution*, pp. 193–94.

79. The following account of the vagaries of agrarian reform is largely based on Malefakis's classic study, *Agrarian Reform and Peasant Revolution*.

80. The working agrarian population, according to the 1930 census, totaled 3.7 million of which approximately 1.9 million were farm laborers (including those with small plots who supplemented their earnings by working as field hands); sharecroppers and tenant farmers numbered 750,000, and there were more than a million small and medium-sized cultivators. Large landholders numbered 12,000 and relatively prosperous ones 72,000.

81. See Antonio Ramos Oliveira, *Politics, Economics, and Men of Modern Spain, 1808–1946* (London: Victor Gollancz, 1946), p. 339.

82. The "vacillations and disorder" that characterized the administration of agrarian reform were due partly to the incompetence of Agriculture Minister Marcelino Domingo, a well-meaning neophyte in agrarian affairs of whom Azaña noted in his diary, "His lack of knowledge of rural affairs is total" (Azaña, *Obras completas*, entry of July 6, 1933, p. 90).

83. A massive study of CEDA is available: José R. Montero, *La CEDA, el Católicismo social y político en la II Republica* (Madrid: Ediciónes de la Revista de Trabajo, 1977).

84. Quoted in Tuñon de Lara, "La secunda república" in *Historia de España*, vol. 9, ed. Tuñon de Lara, *La crisis del estado: Dictadura, república, guerra (1923– 1939)* (Barcelona: Labor, 1981), p. 158.

85. The French historian Jean Richard Bloch offers this portrait of Largo Caballero: "A robust sixty-seven . . . square bald head . . . massive face, stubborn forehead, bitter mouth, the lines of his body slim and handsome in its strength, bright eyes . . . terribly weary" (*Espagne* [Paris: Editions Sociales Internationales, 1936], pp. 79–80, quoted in Broué and Témime, *The Revolution and the Civil War in Spain*, p. 64).

86. "On the basis of civic culture, literacy rates, and economic development, it might be hypothesized that by 1930 Spain was at the level of England in the 1840's and 50's or France in the 1860's and 70's. Neither midnineteenth-century England nor even France at the beginning of the Third Republic had to face such severe political tests as Spain underwent in the thirties" (Payne, *Spanish Revolution*, p. 84).

87. John Hooper, *The Spaniards* (London: Penguin, 1986), p. 272.
88. Javier Tussell, *Hijos de la sangre* (Madrid: Espasa-Calpe, 1986), p. 40.
89. The spectacular growth of the socialist and anarcho-syndicalist movements during the Republic mirrored an extraordinary increase of popular participation in social and political affairs. The center and left Republican parties possessed an aggregate membership of possibly a quarter million, and CEDA claimed more than seven hundred thousand members.
90. The UGT originally planned to form a national farm workers federation in the early 1920s. Largo announced its forthcoming establishment at a conference of rural unions in 1922. By that time, however, the Bolshevist Triennium had petered out and many Andalusian farm unions had gone out of existence, indefinitely postponing its projected launching.
91. The Andalusian and Extremaduran rural oligarchies were strongholds of political bossism and among the most reactionary in the country. In the fateful April 14 municipal elections Alfonsine monarchists were elected to fill 42.4 percent and 39.4 percent respectively of the posts of municipal councillors. See Juan Linz, *El sistema de partidos en España* (Madrid: Narcea, 1976), p. 103. An English-language version is *Party Systems and Voter Alignments: Cross-National Perspectives,* ed. Seymour Lipset and Stein Rokkan (New York: Free Press, 1976).
92. Malefakis, *Agrarian Reform and Peasant Revolution,* p. 316.
93. The more significant studies of socialist radicalization are Paul Preston, *The Coming of the Spanish Civil War: Reform, Reaction and Revolution in the Second Republic, 1931–1936* (London: Macmillan, 1978); Santos Juliá, *La izquierda socialista (1935–1936)* (Madrid: Siglo XXI, 1977); and Marta Bizcarrondo, *Araquistáin y la crisis socialista en la II Republica, Leviátan (1934–1936)* (Madrid: Siglo XXI, 1975).
94. See Preston, *Coming of the Spanish Civil War,* p. 133; Franz Borkenau, *The Spanish Cockpit* (1937; rpt. Ann Arbor: University of Michigan Press, 1974), p. 285.
95. Largo embarked upon his radical course with a speech delivered at the 195 Socialist Youth's summer school in July 1933. Fernando Claudin, who was at that time a leading figure in the communist youth organization, recalls: "Besteiro and Prieto, who were regarded as the leading representatives of reformism, were coldly received, if not with open hostility. Largo was hailed with cheers for 'the Spanish Lenin.' The nickname had emerged a bit earlier, spontaneously apparently, at a UGT meeting and then spread like wildfire. Amaro del Rosal recalls that Araquistáin, the theoretical brain truster of Largo Caballero, among intimates argued forcefully the need to 'create a myth' to bring the masses to revolution" (quoted in Santiago Carrillo, *Crónica de un secretario general* [Barcelona: Planeta, 1983], p. 15).

96. See Santos Juliá, "Socialismo y revolución," Estudio preliminar to Largo Caballero, *Escritos de la Republica*, p. xliv.
97. Largo's victory over the Besteiro faction was aided by Prieto's passivity. Prieto understood the folly of Largo's revolutionary talk, but in the interests of party unity and at first not believing that its use in dissuading Lerrouxists and Cedistas from going too far would not cause great harm, he acceded. Later it was to be a matter of deep regret.
98. Edward Malefakis's *Agrarian Reform and Peasant Revolution in Spain* is a major study of this period.
99. Cabrera, *La patronal ante la II Republica*.
100. "Since in Catalonia they were repudiated by both classes the mixed juries failed as a collective bargaining instrument and as an element of social pacification. Influenced by anarcho-syndicalism, a majority of workers rejected them as a symbol of gradualism and state authoritarianism and employers rejected them as organs partial to wage earners. Both rejected them for being under the sectarian control of the socialists" (Balcells, *Crisis económica y agitación social en Cataluña*, p. 190). The 1931–33 minutes of the UGT Executive Committee meetings contain numerous complaints from affiliates of employers' violations of *bases de trabajo, jurado* accords, and collective bargaining agreements. The minutes are located in the Pablo Iglesias Foundation.
101. Santos Juliá's excellent *Madrid, 1931–1934* has narrowed this gap.
102. This account of the rise and fall of Madrid labor "possiblism" has relied heavily on Juliá's study (ibid.).
103. These figures are approximations provided in ibid., p. 64.
104. Ibid., pp. 99–100.
105. On unemployment in building construction see ibid., esp. chap. 3.

When unemployment benefits were first introduced on April 1, 1932, there were only 42 recognized mutual benefit societies and the like with 31,057 members. Twenty-four sought benefits for 6,105 laid-off workers. By the end of that year the number of unemployed exceeded half a million. Benefit data come from Anales de Instituto de Previsión, January–February 1933, cited in Santos Juliá, "Los socialistas en la crisis de los años treinta," *Zona Abierta* 27 (February–March 1983): 63–77. Malefakis writes: "The direct expenditures of the national government for the relief of unemployment remained infinitesimal. From 1931 to 1933 they must be expressed in tenths of one percent of the national budget. In 1935 they rose to approximately three-quarters of one percent. Only in the first quarter of 1936 did direct allocations increase significantly; even then they accounted for only two percent of all state expenditures" (*Agrarian Reform and Peasant Revolution*, p. 287).

106. "Possibly never in Madrid's industrial past had there been real wage increases so widespread within so brief a time as those of the Republic's first years. Employers first regarded them with astonishment and then entirely opposed them" (Juliá, *Madrid, 1931–1934,* p. 315).

107. Ibid.

108. Shubert, *Hacia la revolución,* pp. 179–205.

109. Quoted in ibid., p. 193.

110. See Maria Luz Sanfeliciano, "El sindicato obrero metalurgico durante la Secunda Republica: Contribución a la historia del movimiento obrero en Vizcaya," *Estudios de Historia Social,* no. 4 (1978), p. 162.

111. Delegates to the SOV congress of April 29 to May 1, 1933, voted to change the name to Solidaridad de Trabajadores Vascos (STV) as part of a general restructuring intended to give the organization a more trade union character. See Policarpo de Larrañaga, *Contribución a la historia obrera de Euskalerria,* 2 vols. (San Sebastian: Editorial Auñamendi Argitaldaria, 1977), 2:199.

112. See Ignacio Olábarri, *Relaciónes laborales en Vizcaya (1890–1936)* (Durango: Leopoldo Zugaza, 1978), pp. 423–30. UGT membership in the region (including the province of Navarre) by February 1936 totaled fifty thousand of which thirty-five thousand were in Vizcaya and twelve thousand in Guipúzcoa, the equivalent of 30 to 35 percent of the regional industrial labor force. The STV possessed an estimated following of thirty-seven thousand, eighteen thousand in Vizcaya and fifteen thousand in Guipúzcoa (Juan Pablo Fusi, "Movimiento obrero y nacionalismo vasco (1890–1936)" in his *El pais vasco: Pluralismo y nacionalidad* [Madrid: Alianza, 1984], p. 46).

113. Manuel Cordero, *Los socialistas y la revolución* (Madrid: Imprenta Torrent, 1932), p. 25.

114. In a declaration published in *El Socialista,* April 17, 1934.

115. Luis Araquistáin, "La utopia de Azaña," *Leviatán,* no. 5 (September 1935), p. 28.

116. Wage levels declined substantially in 1935 but not perceptibly in 1934. See José Manuel Macarro Vera, "Octubre, un error de calculo y perspectiva," in *Octubre 1934,* ed. German Ojeda (Madrid: Siglo XXI, 1985), pp. 269–82. The UGT and PSOE both experienced membership declines. Between June and December 1933, for example, the FNTT lost seven thousand members and the PSOE lost more than a quarter of its following, much of it probably in the southern rural areas. See Paloma Biglino, *El socialismo español y la cuestión agraria, 1890–1936* (Madrid: Ministerio de Trabajo y Seguridad Social, 1985), pp. 497, 427.

117. Malefakis, *Agrarian Reform and Peasant Revolution,* p. 340. For Tuñon de

Lara's version of the strike see his "La Secunda Republica," in *Historia de España,* vol. 9, *La crisis del estado: Dictadura, república, guerra (1923–1939)* (Barcelona: Labor, 1981), pp. 184–89.

118. UGT and FNTT leaderships shared equally in the ignominious strike failure. Largo Caballero had opposed the strike from the beginning and, consequently, rejected Zabalza's appeals for sympathy strike actions to forestall the imminent collapse of the FNTT shutdown. Since members of the UGT Executive Committee were Caballerists, they could not bring themselves to humiliate a fellow committee member (Zabalza) and fervent Caballerist by openly forcing him to call off the strike, even though they regarded it as foolhardy. During a strike postmortem that took place at the June 11 meeting of the UGT Executive Committee, Zabalza complained that it had not been enough for the committee to "counsel" against going on strike; it should have ordered him to call it off. Irritably, Largo responded, "What were we to do? Declare you traitors to the *campesinos?*" Zabalza replied, "We simply had no way out, they would have called us traitors." See Acta de la comision ejecutiva, UGT, June 11, 1934, Pablo Iglesias Foundation, Madrid.

119. Madrid experienced twenty-nine strikes in 1933. In the first half of 1934 alone there were thirty-seven.

120. Preston, *Coming of the Spanish Civil War,* p. 101.

121. The contemplated action was not meant to be a socialist revolution; its objective was land nationalization, dissolution of the religious orders and the Civil Guard, and reorganization of the armed forces and the tax structure. Largo's speeches, however, gave a different impression. See Tuñon de Lara, "La Secunda Republica," p. 189.

122. The PSOE and UGT sympathized with the notion of a national workers alliance that had been launched by BOC but preferred to conduct the October rising under their exclusive political hegemony. The CNT was opposed. After October, however, the socialist Left began to show more interest.

123. Companys had strong misgivings but, under the pressure of extremists in his party, was forced to go along.

124. See Shubert, *Hacia la revolución,* chap. 6.

125. Franco's role in putting down the Asturian rebellion was pivotal in advancing his military career. As a reward, he was named head of the armed forces in Africa, and when Gil Robles became war minister in 1935, he was appointed armed forces chief of staff.

126. The tortures were directed by Major Doval, who had learned his trade while serving under General Martínez Anido during the Barcelona labor wars of the 1920s.

127. "Seen from the countryside, in terms of actual lived facts, of bread on the

table for the landworker's family, the change was disastrous. Many, too many landlords, had forgotten nothing and learned nothing, and their callous and shortsighted policy of old had been sharpened by a tooth of vindictiveness for insults and injuries received while the Left had ruled— not very wisely, perhaps. The landworker saw his wages drop again to famine levels, the security of his employment disappear, his hope of land vanish. These facts, thousands and millions of them hidden away in villages, dales and hills of the center, south, and southeast of Spain, were some of the most potent seeds of the Civil War which two years later was to tear asunder the vitals of the country" (Madariaga, *Spain,* pp. 426–27).

128. CESO's principal officer, for the first time, was a worker and not a priest. Father José Gafo, the veteran exponent of nonconfessional Catholic trade unionism, served as its leading adviser. See Antonio Elorza, "El sindicalismo Católico en las Secunda Republica; la C.E.S.O. (1935–1938)," in his *La utopia anarquista bajo la Secunda Republica* (Madrid: Ayuso, 1973), pp. 295–350 (first published in *Revista de Trabajo,* no. 33 [1971]). Also Richard A. H. Robinson, *The Origins of Franco's Spain: The Right, the Republic and Revolution, 1931–1936* (Pittsburgh: University of Pittsburgh Press, 1970), pp. 214–15, and Salvador Carrasco Calvo, "Teoria y práctica de sindicalismo Católico, libre y profesional (1911–1936)" in *La crisis de la Restauración: España entre la primera guerra mundial y la II Republica,* ed. J. L. García Delgado (Madrid: Siglo Veintiuno, 1986.

129. During the summer of 1936 unemployment was at 732,000; by the following November it had reached 806,221, amounting to more than 20 percent of the work force (Tuñon de Lara, "La Secunda Republica," p. 205.

130. A moderate Spanish historian has written that "the behavior of the Right in the countryside . . . in the second six months of 1935 was one of the principal causes of the hatred in the Civil War and probably of the Civil War itself" (Carlos Seco Serrano, *Historia de España,* vol. 4, *Epoca contemporanea,* 3d ed. [Barcelona: Instituto Gallach, 1971], p. 138).

131. Malefakis, *Agrarian Reform and Peasant Revolution,* p. 355. A recently discovered diary of Fernández Jiménez makes it clear that his designation as agriculture minister was initially intended as a gesture to reassure the Left. After October 1934 and with the ascendancy of the intransigent Right, his usefulness in that post was at an end. See Tussell, *Hijos de la sangre,* p. 54.

132. Estimates of the number of imprisoned vary. Elena de la Souchere, a former official of the Republican government in exile, in her *Explanation of Spain* (New York: Random House, 1965), p. 248, claims that there were not more than 12,500.

133. See minutes of UGT Executive Committee meetings for 1935, Pablo Iglesias Foundation.

134. Juliá, "Estudio preliminar," in Largo Caballero, *Escritos de la Republica,* p. lvii.

135. For a comprehensive examination of the philosophy and development of Caballerism, see Santos Juliá, *La izquierda del PSOE (1935–1936)* (Madrid: Siglo XXI, 1979); also Bizcarrondo, *Araquistáin y la crisis socialista,* and Manuel Contreras, *El PSOE en la II Republica: Organización i ideologia* (Madrid: Centro de Investigaciones Sociologicas, 1981). Also worthy of mention is Gabriel Mario de Coca's *Anti-Caballero* (1936; rpt. Madrid: Ediciónes del Centro, 1975). Coca provides a strong defense of Besteiro and a blistering indictment of Largo Caballero's policies.

136. Control of *El Socialista* by the Prieto faction prompted the socialist Left to sponsor its own organ, *Claridad,* which first appeared as a weekly and then as a daily; the Besteiro group, in turn, edited the weekly *Democracia.*

137. Santos Juliá, *Origines del frente popular en España (1934–1936)* (Madrid: Siglo XXI, 1979), and Victor Alba, *El frente popular* (Barcelona: Planeta, 1976).

138. The electoral alliance was originally known as Bloque Popular and in Catalonia took the name Front d'Esquerres (Leftist Front). The Popular Front denomination came later.

139. There is little agreement among the experts regarding the outcome of the election. The figures I have used are those compiled by Javier Tussell, *Las elections del frente popular,* 2 vols. (Madrid: Cuadernos para el Dialogo, 1971), that are the ones most commonly accepted.

140. "14 April 1931 had been a political victory which the urban masses had celebrated with jubilation; 16 February 1936 was a social victory from which both they and the now fully aroused peasantry sought vengeance" (Edward Malefakis, "Parties of the Left and the Second Republic," in *The Republic and the Civil War in Spain,* ed. Raymond Carr [London: Macmillan, 1971], p. 38).

141. Robinson, *Origins of Franco's Spain,* p. 270.

142. Malefakis, *Agrarian Reform and Peasant Revolution,* p. 371.

143. "Employers were ordered to take back all men discharged after the strike of October 1934 and to pay them back wages and also to keep on or to indemnify the men taken on in their place. This was impossible. For instance, the newspaper *ABC* had discharged 300 men and taken on other employees in their place. It now found itself double-staffed and owing 75,000 pounds to the men who had returned. There was no strong attempt to cut through these problems which every day became worse. Every employer who could do so cut down staffs and unemployment was at 700,000 officially and probably 1,000,000 in reality" (Henry Buckley, *Life and Death of the Spanish Republic* [London: Hamish Hamilton, 1940], p. 198).

144. Santos Juliá, "Luchas obreras y políticas de frente popular en Madrid (1931–1936)," in *Estudios de Historia Social* 1–2, nos. 16–17 (1981): 140.
145. Santos Juliá, "De la division organica al gobierno de unidad nacional," in *Socialismo y guerra civil,* ed. Santos Juliá (Madrid: Editorial Pablo Iglesias, 1987), p. 233.
146. In an article by Calvo Sotelo that appeared in *Diario Vasco,* March 11, 1936, quoted by Souchere, *Explanation of Spain,* p. 163.
147. The land invasions occurred mainly in Andalusia, Extremadura, and La Mancha. Other parts of the country did not experience such high levels of social conflict. In rural Aragon, for example, UGT and CNT unions during the first seven months of 1936 continued to press their collective bargaining demands with a minimum of violence. See Julián Casanova, *Anarquismo y revolución en la sociedad rural Aragonesa, 1936–1938* (Madrid: Siglo XXI, 1985), pp. 51–59. In Córdoba province, a highly unionized zone, "conflict seemed greater than it was in reality because of the constant threat of hostility between social classes. The number and type of disputes were no higher than they had been in previous years but the stability of the existing social order was to some extent threatened" (Manuel Pérez Yruela, *La conflictividad campesina en la provincia de Córdoba (1931–1936)* [Madrid: Servicio de Publicaciónes Agrarias, 1979], p. 214).
148. Malefakis, *Agrarian Reform and Peasant Revolution,* p. 382.
149. The following survey of lawlessness and political violence that Gil Robles presented to the Cortes has generally been considered reasonably accurate: "From February 16 to June 160 churches were destroyed, 251 attacks or attempted assaults on churches, 269 dead, 1,287 wounded, 215 averted personal assaults, 138 robberies and 23 more attempted, 69 political offices destroyed, 312 assaulted, 113 general strikes, 228 others, 10 newspapers destroyed plus an additional 33 assaulted or attempted, 146 explosions, and 78 unexploded bombs retrieved" (quoted in Jackson, *The Spanish Republic and the Civil War,* p. 218).
150. The complete text of the address can be found in *Discursos fundamentales, Indalecio Prieto* (Madrid: Ediciónes Turner, 1975).
151. Casanova, *Anarquismo y revolución en Aragonesa,* p. 62.
152. For the proceedings of the congress, see *El congreso confederal de Zaragoza* (Bilbao: Zero, 1978).
153. In February 1936 the FAI had less than five thousand members. See Juan Gómez Casas, *Historia de la FAI* (Bilbao: Editorial Zero, 1977), p. 209.
154. Lorenzo, *Les anarchistes espagnols et la pouvoir,* p. 93.
155. The failure of the insurrectionary strategy permitted Abad de Santillan and his Nervio affinity group, in conjunction with its adjunct Z group, to assume a leadership role in the peninsular FAI, to dominate the Juventudes Libertarias de Cataluña, and to take the initiative in the reappearance during

February 1934 of the anarchist weekly *Tierra y Libertad*. The FAI at that time reportedly consisted of only a third of the country's anarchists. Abad de Santillan and his supporters placed less reliance on spontaneity of the masses and "improvization" in conducting the revolutionary transformation, stressing instead the necessity for organization and economic planning. Despite their growing influence, the Zaragossa May 1936 congress reaffirmed adherence to the traditional articles of faith in spontaneity and libertarian communalism whose principal exponents were Isaac Puente, Federica Montseny, and the Revista Blanca group. See the introduction by Antonio Elorza in Diego Abad de Santillan, *El anarquismo y la revolución en España, Escritos 1930–1938* (Madrid: Ayuso, 1976).

156. For a discussion of Orobón Fernández's ideas see Xavier Paniagua, *La sociedad libertaria* (Barcelona: Crítica, 1982), chap. 5.

157. Victor Alba, *El Partido Comunista en España* (Barcelona: Planeta, 1979), p. 156.

158. Fernando Claudin, *Santiago Carrillo, crónica de un secretario general* (Barcelona: Planeta, 1983), pp. 46–47.

159. Figures concerning PCE membership in this period are wildly contradictory. General Krivitsky, who directed western European operations of the NKVD, in his book *In Stalin's Secret Service* (New York: Harper, 1939) attributes a membership of three thousand to the PCE in early 1936 and of 200,000 by January 1937; Franz Borkenau agrees with these figures.

160. Alba, *Partido Comunista en España*, p. 156. For Araquistáin's political views see Bizcarrondo, *Araquistáin y la crisis socialista*.

161. Ricard Viñas, *La formación de las Juventudes Socialistas Unificadas (1934–1936)* (Madrid: Siglo Veintiuno, 1978), p. 26.

162. Realistic estimates place FJS membership at about eighty thousand and that of the Communists (UJC) at approximately five thousand. About half of FJS followers refused to accept the merger and remained in socialist ranks. See Alba, *Partido Comunista en España*, p. 172. For a detailed account see Viñas, *La formación de las Juventudes Socialistas Unificadas.*

163. A repentant Luis Araquistáin subsequently revealed that his brother-in-law Alvarez del Vayo, a member of Largo's inner circle, whom he calls the "Macbeth of the Spanish proletariat," was an undercover communist who secretly promoted the unification of the two youth organizations. See his *Sobre la guerra civil y en la emigración* (Madrid: Espasa Calpe, 1983).

164. Joaquín Maurín, *Revolución y contrarevolución en España* (Paris: Ruedo Iberico, 1966), p. 287. The term *Radical Socialist* does not mean socialist radicals but a variety of Spanish Republicanism personified by men such as Marcelino Domingo and Alvarez de Albornoz, who employed a radical populist rhetoric but were moderate in practice.

165. José Manuel Cuenca Toribio, *La guerra civil de 1936* (Madrid: Espasa Calpe, 1986), p. 26.
166. Vicente Enrique y Tarancón, *Recuerdos de juventud* (Barcelona: Grijalbo, 1984), pp. 184–85.

CHAPTER 11: LABOR AND THE CIVIL WAR, 1936–1939

1. Stanley Payne, *La revolución y la guerra civil española* (Madrid: Jucar, 1976), p. 116.
2. Gabriel Cardona, "La sublevación de Julio," in *Socialismo y guerra civil,* ed. Santos Juliá (Madrid: Editorial Pablo Iglesias, (1987), pp. 26–27.
3. Franz Borkenau, *The Spanish Cockpit* (1937; rpt. Ann Arbor: University of Michigan Press, 1974), p. 283.
4. "The real answer seems to be that militias could fight well only on the defensive and in cities; they could not mount an offensive, even against thinly held lines. Thus towns like Huesca, from the military point of view a seemingly easy target, survived serious attacks" (Raymond Carr, *Spain, 1808–1939* [1966; rev. ed. Oxford: Oxford University Press, 1982], p. 159).
5. These figures are taken from Bartolomé Benassar, *Histoire des Espagnoles,* 2 vols. (Paris: A. Colin, 1985), 2:317.
6. On the resulting chaos see Adolfo Bueso, *Recuerdos de un Cenetista,* 2 vols. (Barcelona: Ariel, 1976), 2:179–80.
7. Raymond Carr, *The Spanish Tragedy: The Civil War in Perspective* (London: Weidenfeld and Nicolson, 1977), p. 73.
8. Montseny, speech summarized in *Solidaridad Obrera,* December 22, 1936.
9. Quoted in Stanley Payne, *La revolución y la guerra civil española* (Madrid: Jucar, 1976), p. 74.
10. See Elena de la Souchere, *Explanation of Spain* (New York: Random House, 1965), p. 185.
11. Nowhere was the spirit of local particularism more in evidence than in the Republican zones of Andalusia. Catalans, Basques, and Aragonese possessed a regional identity; in Andalusia, however, a strong local spirit prevailed. "Each village became independent; neither centralization nor coordinated action was possible. In contrast with other large Spanish regions, no organism was formed to control the countless tiny local governments or attempted to do so. For example, it was not until November 1936 that an antifascist Popular Front was constituted in the province of Granada" (César M. Lorenzo, *Les anarchistes espagnols et le pouvoir, 1868–1969* [Paris: Sevul, 1969], p. 192).
12. The CNT possessed a revolutionary spirit but otherwise lacked the wherewithal of a truly revolutionary movement. "Everyone in the CNT had his

own opinion, each acted as he wished. Leaders were constantly criticized and questioned. The autonomy of the regional federations was sacrosanct, just as was that of local federations and unions. To obtain acceptance of a decision, to convince others that it was necessary to proceed in a given manner, a militant had to engage in exhausting speeches, personal contacts, and travels. Libertarians loathed taking votes, and unanimity required interminable debates. Anarchists lacked an efficacious combat organ as the insurrections of 1932 and 1933 had demonstrated" (ibid., p. 237).

13. Abad de Santillan was the leading spokesman in the deliberations for the "collaborative" position, and García Oliver argued in favor of an immediate establishment of *comunismo libertario*. It was generally agreed to postpone the launching of a libertarian communist regime until the end of the war. Peiró argued that the CNT-FAI was unable to impose libertarian communism immediately because the outcome of the struggle against fascism might be determined by assistance from foreign bourgeois democratic nations. It was, consequently, important to enter government to avert actions, in the economic sphere especially, that might damage the future interests of the proletariat. In any event, the CNT dominated only in Catalonia and parts of Aragon, and it shared power with the UGT in Valencia. Only by participating in government was it possible to assure protection of the Catalonian achievements and a voice in decisions affecting other parts of the country. See Pere Gabriel, Introduction to Joan Peiró, *Escrits, 1917–1939* (Barcelona: Edicións 62, 1975), p. 28.

14. The official rationale for the abandonment of antipolitics was as follows: "The CNT in principle and conviction has always been antistate and opposed to all governments.

"Circumstances, however, superior to human will, though determined by it, have changed the nature of government and the Spanish state.

"As a regulating instrument of state bodies, the present government has ceased serving as an oppressive force against the working class and as a divisive social class organ. With the intervention of the CNT it no longer oppresses people" (*Solidaridad Obrera,* November 4, 1936).

15. "Power in Catalonia, according to the libertarian schema, theoretically operated bidirectionally, from the periphery to the center, and from the center to the periphery. . . . In fact, however, the authority of the Militias Central Committee was not very great. Local committees paid little heed; relations among themselves and with the C.C. were very slack. A central power in fact did not exist, rather a swarm of autonomous microgovernments" (Lorenzo, *Les anarchistes espagnols et le pouvoir,* pp. 111–12).

16. Diego Abad de Santillan, *Por que perdimos la guerra. Una contribución a la historia de la tragedia española* (Barcelona: Plaza y Janes, 1977), pp. 95–96.

17. "Anarcho-syndicalist participation in the Catalonian government, the in-

evitable consequence of CNT-FAI strength and for having respected the constituted organs of power, was a veritable Trojan Horse in revolutionary precincts. The CNT presence in the Generalitat strengthened the latter's authority and ultimately fostered rather than undercut the recuperation of its powers at the expense of the Confederation and the FAI" (John Brademas, *Anarcosindicalismo y revolución en España (1930–1937)* [Barcelona: Ariel, 1974], p. 182).

18. See Gabriel Jackson, *The Spanish Republic and the Civil War, 1931–1939* (Princeton: Princeton University Press, 1965), pp. 526–40.

19. Gerald Brenan, *Personal Record (1920–1972)* (New York: Knopf, 1975), pp. 285–319.

20. The Peiró quote is from *Perill a la retaguardia* (1936; facsimile ed. Barcelona: Editorial Alta Fulla, 1987), pp. xx, xviii, xviv. On the repressive violence see Albert Balcells, "Violencia y terrorismo en la lucha de clases en Barcelona de 1913 a 1923," *Estudios de Historia Social* 42–43 (1987): 39.

21. George Orwell, *Homage to Catalonia* (1938; rpt. New York: Harcourt Brace and World, 1952); Franz Borkenau, *The Spanish Cockpit* (1937; rpt. Ann Arbor: University of Michigan Press, 1974); and H. E. Kaminski, *Ceux de Barcelone* (Paris: Denoel, 1937).

22. I am indebted to Adrian Shubert for bringing to my attention the correspondence of F. Fraser Lawton. See Shubert's paper "Civil War, Revolution, and Foreign Corporations: The Case of La Canadiense," which was presented to the 1988 annual meeting of the Spanish and Portuguese Historians Society, for an interesting insight into how an important foreign-owned company fared in the Barcelona worker takeovers.

23. "People took to the streets on July 19 to prevent a military coup. On the twenty-second, however, when they returned to work—especially in Catalonia and Levant—they learned that many owners or executives had disappeared. To avoid being left payless, workers the following Saturday agreed to 'collectivize' these companies, to designate committees to run them. They could have asked the government to provide credits to cover wage payments, which some unions did, especially where the CNT was weak. Where the unions were strong, workers preferred to assume the responsibility for running the companies" (Victor Alba, *El Partido Comunista en España* [Barcelona: Planeta, 1979], p. 181).

24. At the outset of the civil war forty thousand textile workers, almost the entire industry work force in Barcelona, were organized in the CNT. According to the textile workers union, out of an estimated five thousand employers, 40 percent had been "eliminated," another 50 percent had gone into hiding, and the remaining 10 percent continued working in their former establishments as employees. The entire industry was collectivized.

25. Pelai Pagés, *La guerra civil española a Catalunya (1936–1939)* (Barcelona: Amelia Romero, 1987), pp. 73–74.
26. Albert Balcells, *Historia contemporanea de Cataluña* (Barcelona: Edhasa, 1981), p. 297–98; see also Gabriel, Introduction to Peiró, *Escrits*, p. 28.
27. Anarchist contempt for money and usury, for example, led to a decision not to take over banks and other financial institutions, leaving the UGT to assume control in these areas. A meeting of the CNT regional federations approved a future government takeover of the banking system. By January 1938, however, having come to appreciate the importance of protected sources of credit and financing in a modern economy, the CNT proposed the creation of an Iberian labor bank to be jointly sponsored with the UGT.
28. See Anna Monjo and Carme Vega, *Els treballadors i la guerra civil* (Barcelona: Empúries, 1986), for a study of how worker collectivization fared in a prominent metalworking company in the Barcelona area.
29. "Before July 19 the CNT was a movement lacking internal cohesion or tactics, operating solely on spontaneity and improvisation. Today it is becoming a real organization, though, naturally, sentimentalism, pure revolutionary lyricism, the desire to do whatever one feels like, and 'putschist' tendencies play an important role" (Helmut Rudiger, May 8, 1937, Document No. 13, AIT Plenum, June 11, 1937, Archivo Historico Militar and Pablo Iglesias Foundation). Rudiger was the International Workingmen's Association (AIT) secretary for Spain resident in Barcelona.
30. See Walther L. Bernecker, *Colectividades y revolución social* (Barcelona: Crítica, 1982), p. 286.
31. "Realization of the impossibility of restructuring into self-sufficient communes made the trade union the key element in resolving the agricultural problem. Industrial workers, protagonists of the revolution, required other mechanisms, both in their struggle for daily demands and for a future construction. . . . For some this amounted to a radical deviation and the birth of a new authoritarianism, despite its utility in the destruction of capitalism. For others it represented a postponement of the revolution, contradicting the destruction of bourgeois society as Bakunin and other leaders had taught. . . . What really mattered was to overcome the contradiction between consumer desires and social necessities, between leadership and participation, between worker democracy and worker dictatorship. This was being debated in the midst of a civil war when the difficulty of accommodation was acknowledged" (Xavier Paniagua, *La sociedad libertaria* [Barcelona: Crítica, 1982], pp. 271–72).

The CNT leadership was never able to agree on the character and scope of collectivization. The CNT of Madrid favored the traditional anarcho-syndicalist concept of socialization of large industry, services, and transport under union control. Barcelona, however, supported the notion of total collectivization irrespective of size and with profits turned over to a common fund to be administered by the Catalan Economic Council. In a discussion held during the National Plenum of regional organizations on September 3, 1936, representatives for Levant spoke in favor of "socializing" factories and industries while Catalonians pushed for "collectivization." The UGT advocated the cooperative management of owner-abandoned firms, workers' control in large enterprises, and assistance to small and medium-sized privately owned establishments. The minutes of CNT regional plenums can be consulted at the Archivo Historico Militar and at the Pablo Iglesias Foundation.

32. Albert Pérez Baró, *30 mesos de colectivisme en Catalunya* (Barcelona: Ariel, 1974), p. 51.

" 'Incautacion' (seizure) signifies the expropriation of an enterprise by a group or a collective workers organism of a productive unit, unions, municipalities, Generalitat, or Republic. Expropriation does not affect the future juridical status of the enterprise.

"The term 'collectivization' designates the attribution of an enterprise, factory, or establishment's economic power to a collectivity of workers therein employed. Collectivization, therefore, is the equivalent of what currently is meant by worker self-management. Logically, collectivization implies, after the deduction of taxes, interest, and rentals, of providing surplus value to the workers in the form of wages and benefits.

"When a group or body other than those that possessed the economic power of an enterprise or factory intervened or was able to control some of their decisions, it is said that they 'controlled' the enterprise or factory. These firms remained under the control of their former owners or executives but some decisions were made by their employees.

"The term 'socialization' had differing meanings, depending on the party or political movement. From the anarcho-syndicalist point of view socialization was the effective expropriation by the *sindicato unico* for the industry of all companies in its jurisdiction; the socialists, however, regarded socialization as entailing the conferring of the political power of enterprises to a popular government" (Josep Bricall, "La economía española (1936–1939)," in *La guerra civil española, cinquenta años despues,* ed. Manuel Tuñon de Lara [Barcelona: Labor, 1985], p. 394).

33. For a discussion of Santillan's economic views see Paniagua, *La sociedad libertaria,* pp. 250–64.

34. When Joan Peiró became minister of industry in the Largo Caballero cabinet he sought the adoption of measures that would apply the Catalonian action to the entire Republican zone. Largo, however, feared antagonizing petit

bourgeois elements and adversely affecting relations with Western democracies and preferred that there be no regulation outside Catalonia.

35. "Notable efficacy was attained in some sectors, especially in the metalworking and chemical industries. But it was necessary to halt the creation of fictitious cooperatives by proprietors to avert taxes and controls. Furthermore, because of the individualism of some plant committees and the indiscipline of certain trade unions, it was always difficult to obtain compliance with the required regulation of wages and prices" (Balcells, *Historia contemporanea de Cataluña,* p. 314).

36. Among the more notable studies published in recent years are Julián Casanova, *Anarquismo y revolución en la sociedad rural Aragonesa 1936–1938* (Madrid: Siglo XXI, 1985); Walther L. Bernecker, *Colectividades y revolución social; El anarquismo en la guerra civil española* (Barcelona: Crítica, 1982); Aurora Bosch, *Ugetistas y libertarios, guerra civil y revolución en el pais Valenciano, 1936–1939* (Valencia: Institución Alfonso el Magnánimo, 1983); José Luis Gutiérrez Molina, *Colectividades libertarias en Castilla* (Madrid: Campo Abierto, 1977); Luis Garrido González, *Colectividades agrarias en Andalusia: Jaen (1931–1939)* (Madrid: Siglo XXI, 1976).

37. Malefakis estimates that roughly 55 percent of the arable land in the central region was expropriated and that "less than half of this 55 percent did not experience radical changes because all that took place was that it passed into the hands of its former tenants and sharecroppers who worked it, individually continuing its cultivation." Approximately 30 percent of all lands taken were collectivized, amounting to 8 to 10 percent in the Levant, 30 percent in Castile and La Mancha, possibly 45 percent in Andalusia and Extremadura, and reaching its highest proportion in Aragon. See Edward Malefakis, "La económia española y guerra civil," in *La económia española en el siglo XX, una perspectiva historica,* ed. Jordi Nadal, Albert Carrera, and Carles Sudrià (Barcelona: Ariel, 1987), p. 158.

38. These figures are taken from Bricall, "La económia española," p. 389.

39. Borkenau, *Spanish Cockpit,* p. 148.

40. The Agrarian Reform Institute in August 1938 tallied 2,213 collectives (Catalonia was not included) involving approximately 3 million persons.

41. For the anarchist point of view consult Gaston Leval, *Colectividades libertarias en España* (Buenos Aires: Proyección, 1972; another edition was published in 1977 by Aguilera, Madrid); Frank Mintz, *La autogestión en la España revolucionaria* (Madrid: La Piqueta, 1977); see also *The Anarchist Collectives,* ed. Sam Dolgoff (New York: Free Life Editions, 1974).

42. This estimate and other details concerning collectivization in Aragon have been taken from Casanova, *Anarquismo y revolución en Aragonesa.*

43. According to the Aragonese CNT leader Macario Royo, most of the militia commanders who were Catalans opposed the formation of the council. "Then

Durruti arrived. 'I have waited all these years for the revolution. Now it has happened. The 14,000 men in my column are with me, I believe, because they agree with me. My men and I are at the disposal of the villages and their unions. . . . while collectivization served both the war effort and our vision of the future, we were attempting to put into practice a libertarian communism about which, it's sad to say, none of us really knew anything" (quoted in Ronald Fraser, *Blood of Spain: An Oral History of the Spanish Civil War* [New York: Pantheon, 1979], pp. 350–51).

44. Fraser's account is probably closest to actual fact: "It did not happen on instructions from the CNT leadership—no more than had the collectives in Barcelona. Here, as there, the initiative came from CNT militants, here as there, the 'climate' for social revolution in the rearguard was created by CNT armed strength; the anarcho-syndicalists' domination of the streets of Barcelona was reenacted in Aragon as the CNT militia columns, manned mainly by Catalan anarcho-syndicalist workers, poured in. Where a nucleus of anarcho-syndicalists existed in a village, it seized the moment to carry out the long-awaited revolution and collectivized spontaneously. Where there was none, villages could find themselves under considerable pressure from the militias to collectivize—even if for different reasons. There was no need to dragoon them at pistol point; the coercive climate in which 'fascists' were being shot was sufficient. 'Spontaneous' and 'forced' collectives coexisted, as did willing and unwilling collectivists within them" (ibid., p. 349).

45. "That Largo regarded war leadership and policy his personal responsibility is well known. His own testimony is quite explicit. In addition to the war ministry he later formed a Superior War Council within the cabinet under his direction, made up of ministers Prieto, Alvarez del Vayo, García Oliver, Uribe, and Irujo. The council was of little use, rarely meeting and with decisions made by Largo Caballero. At first he confided in no one within the War Ministry's army staff headquarters and brought in trusted civilians. Later Colonel Asensio and General Martínez Cabrera became his advisers. A series of actions such as the Procurement and Arms Juntas were formed, presumably 'to unify the war leadership' in the absence of a supreme military head of the Republican army. The final decision remained, nonetheless, in the hands of the head of government, often without any prior consultation.

"What we have stated concerning the military question is applicable to other aspects of government. Through various testimonials, del Vayo, Prieto, Zugazagoitia, Koltsov, and others, the meticulousness with which 'the old man'—as he was called by his followers—examined all matters is well known" (Julio Aróstegui, "Los componentes sociales y políticos," in *La guerra civil española,* ed. Manuel Tuñon de Lara, pp. 71–72).

46. Hugh Thomas's contention—"When Largo Caballero took office, the orders

of the central government could often do no more than endorse faits accomplis by regional forces. When he left, orders from Valencia were customarily fulfilled"—is somewhat overdrawn but contains some truth. See his *The Spanish Civil War* (1961; rpt. London: Penguin, 1977), p. 673.

47. The greatest failure of the Caballerist military policy was the northern front, isolated, lacking organization, militarily and politically divided. The main preoccupation had been the Madrid front, whose defenders had been transformed by early 1937 into an army capable of foiling Franco's attempts to seize or surround the city. The impossibility of controlling the north and Catalonia persisted. In neither of those two zones was an authentic army formed. While the north was being lost, the government's military policy, despite grave deficiencies, proved to be successful in other regions" (Gabriel Cardona, "Largo Caballero y la dirección política de la guerra civil," in *Socialismo y la guerra civil*, ed. Santos Juliá [Madrid: Editorial Pablo Iglesias, 1987], p. 253).

48. Fernando Claudin, *The Communist Movement, from Comintern to Cominform* (London, Penguin, 1975), p. 224.

49. POUM leader Andrés Nin expressed it in the following terms: "What is happening in our country is not the defense of the independence of the homeland. . . . What is developing is the fight of the Spanish proletariat against the Spanish bourgeoisie" (quoted in Willy Brandt, *In Exile* (Philadelphia: University of Pennsylvania Press, 1972), p. 151.

50. "The Madrid Communist party in 1938 officially reported 63,426 members of whom only 10,160 possessed union cards. Its composition could be broken down in the following manner: first senior military and administrative personnel, then employers and well-to-do farmers, followed by white-collar employees, and finally, a worker minority. The case of Valencia can be cited, where almost all of Gil Robles's Cedistas joined the Communist party. Furthermore, career military officers, who at the most were lukewarm Republicans, such as Miaja, Pozas, Hidalgo de Cisneros, Galán, Cuitat, Gordón, Barceló . . . became party members" (Bueso, *Recuerdos de un Cenetista*, 2:225–26). Unregenerate members of the bourgeois elite including José Alcalá Castillo, a son of former President Alcalá Zamora, and Constancia de la Mora, granddaughter of Antonio Maura, became enthusiastic members of the PCE.

51. José Diaz, *Por la unidad hacia la victoria*, pp. 13–15, cited in David C. Cattell, *Communism and the Spanish Civil War* (1956; rpt. New York: Russell and Russell, 1965), p. 94.

52. See Pierre Broué and Emile Témime, *The Revolution and the Civil War in Spain* (Cambridge, Mass.: MIT Press, 1970), p. 233.

53. Cardona, *Largo Cabellero*, p. 252.

54. "It was the remaining units of the old army and security forces, and the

hastily improvised Spanish units, the new 'Mixed Brigades' commanded by professional officers who were loyal to the Republic, which 'saved' Madrid. . . . The role of the International Brigades was exaggerated by the Communists, who built up their commander, General Kleber, as the saviour of Madrid, an exercise not to the liking of Rojo and Miaja" (Carr, *Spanish Tragedy*, p. 156).

55. "Two factors led to Caballero's downfall, his congenital obstinacy that prevented him from properly accommodating the impossibility at that time of dispensing with aid from the USSR and a need to dominate and the Communist party's preoccupation with power that led it to give disproportionate importance to simple police problems as in the case of the POUM and its seeking to impose its will on a man whose nature was inflexible and who was personally and politically incorruptible" (Juan Siméon Vidarte, *Todos fuimos culpables* [Mexico City: Fondo de Cultural Económico, 1973], p. 668). Vidarte was a supporter of Prieto and served as PSOE deputy general secretary.

56. The founding organizations of the PSUC were the PSOE Catalonian Federation with six hundred to seven hundred members; Catalonian Proletarian party, eighty; Catalonian section of the Communist party, four hundred; and Catalonian Socialist Union (USC), twelve hundred to fifteen hundred. USC leader Joan Comorera was named general secretary and M. Valdes of the PCE secretary for organization. Its largest component, USC, was an independent moderate socialist party with a Catalanist orientation.

57. Balcells, *Historia contemporanea de Cataluña*, p. 312.

58. According to Victor Serge, the POUM leaders had long feared that the indecision, feebleness, and political inability of the anarchist leaders would result in a spontaneous uprising lacking leadership that would provide the counterrevolutionaries with the opportunity to inflict a bloody wound on the proletariat (Broué and Témime, *The Revolution and the Civil War in Spain*, pp. 287–88).

59. POUM leader Julián Gorkin, who took part in talks with the CNT, recounts having posed the issue in the following terms: "Either we place ourselves at the head of the movement in order to destroy the internal enemy or else the movement will collapse and the enemy will destroy us" (Julián Gorkin, *Canibales políticos* [Mexico City: Ediciónes Quetzal, 1941], pp. 69–70).

60. The War, Navy, and Air ministries were consolidated as the Defense Ministry.

61. Following the February 1936 Popular Front election victory, Largo invited the POUM to merge with the PSOE. Despite Maurín's pleadings, the unity proposal was defeated in a party Executive Committee vote. When after the war Maurín was liberated from prison, he privately voiced his disagreement with the POUM's decision. He disapproved of the party's having given

priority to social revolution instead of first assuring that the war was won. With the benefit of hindsight, he reiterated his regret that the POUM had not merged with the PSOE so it could be semiautonomous in Catalonia, which would have made it much more difficult for the Stalinists to single out the POUM for persecution and would have enhanced the POUM's ability to compete politically with the PSUC. See Victor Alba, *Dos revolucionarios, Joaquin Maurín, Andreu Nin* (Madrid: Semin Arios y Ediciòns, 1975), pp. 285–92. For a discussion of the rivalry for the role of left populist spokesman, see Enric Ucelay da Cal, *La Catalunya populista: Imatge, cultura i política en l'etápa republicana (1931–1939)* (Barcelona: La Magrana, 1982), p. 303.

62. "The vote was not truly representative of the sentiments of the UGT grass roots. The fourteen federations that supported Largo possessed large memberships while the 24 opposed were mostly organizations of professional and skilled workers with much smaller followings. . . . The National Committee vote did two things. In the first place, it was a propaganda victory for the Communists and their allies. Secondly, it showed that Caballero was still very strong among the mass of workers and that his opposition was a threat to the stability of the Negrin government" (Cattell, *Communism and the Spanish Civil War*, p. 175).

63. Broué and Témime, *The Revolution and the Civil War in Spain*, p. 298.

64. Hugh Thomas, *The Spanish Civil War*, rev. ed. (New York: Harper & Row, 1977), p. 668.

65. In Valencia, the seat of the government and CNT-left socialist stronghold, the POUM was shielded from the brutal persecution it was undergoing in Barcelona and Madrid.

66. "When the leaders of the POUM were tried in October 1937, the cases against them were dismissed for lack of evidence. Five, however, were convicted and imprisoned for taking part in the Barcelona uprising in May 1937. In spite of the final vindication of the POUM, the Communists had achieved their desired end, the complete elimination of the POUM from the political scene of Spain" (Cattell, *Communism and the Spanish Civil War*, p. 173).

67. At the close of 1937 the FAI claimed a membership of 150,000. Victor Alba, then a leading activist in the Barcelona POUM organization, insists that enrollment never went beyond three to five thousand (letter to author, July 3, 1988). Alba's estimate is probably closer to reality. Observes Juan Gómez Casas, former CNT general secretary, "We have seen according to the general census of organized groups conducted prior to the February 1937 plenum, that FAI then possessed some five thousand members, never more than seven thousand if we were to add the possibility that for various reasons some groups might not have been included" (*Historia de la FAI* [Bilbao: Zero, 1977], p. 256).

68. The Negrin-Prieto estrangement divided socialist moderates and nearly caused the PSOE to cease functioning as a party. See Jackson, *The Spanish Republic and the Civil War,* p. 410.

69. An account of the meeting between Prieto and the CNT delegation appears in Lorenzo, *Les anarchistes espagnols et le pouvoir* pp. 313–15. Lorenzo's father, Horacio Prieto, was a member of the CNT delegation.

70. "The reason for CNT participation in the Negrin government was the need to place limits on the intrigues of the C.P. and its expansion and to secure power by fighting it with the same weapon it employed. The time for ideological scruples had passed; no longer could anarchism avert its efface-ment, its being shunted aside, or its debilitation. It was now a matter simply of averting its destruction and saving the lives of its militants" (ibid., p. 319). See also José Peirats, *Los anarquistas en la guerra civil española* (Madrid: Jucar, 1976), p. 295.

71. Peirats, *Los anarquistas,* chap. 22. Leading spokesmen for the various points of view in the debate within the libertarian movement participated in a symposium that was published in several issues of *Timón* during 1938. The monthly review, which was edited by Abad de Santillan, served as an an-archist theoretical journal.

Index

Index 543

144, 194–95; on parliamentary system, 97; press of, 282; on Primo, 273, 283; in reform movements, 188, 357; repressed, 273; in Second Republic, 310–25; shattered, 355; v. socialism, 222; terrorism by followers of, 210, 229, 504–5 n. 41; in Valencia, 311; in Vizcaya, 280; in Zaragossa, 311
Ancien régime, 4, 147, 152–53
Andalusia: agricultural labor force in, 10, 12, 13, 15, 16, 17, 42–43, 86, 134, 201, 204, 329; anarchism in, 78–81, 85–88, 134, 166, 461 n. 25, 464 n. 45; anarcho-syndicalism in, 207, 311; Black Hand affair in, 61, 87, 88, 89, 150; Catholic unions in, 204; climate in, 18; CNT in, 143, 201, 202–3, 221, 311, 323; ethnic/regional loyalties in, 79; Faista uprising in, 322, 330; FNA in, 202; FNTT in, 336; FRE in, 78–81, 461 n. 25; FTRE in, 85; illiteracy in, 16; labor legislation in, 66; labor unrest/strikes in, 17–18, 79, 134, 202, 206, 244, 247, 291, 329, 336; land invasions in, 368; land tenure in, 10, 16, 17; mining in, 37, 48, 201; monarchism in, 521 n. 91; mortality rates in, 16; petty bourgeoisie in, 79; *pueblos* in, 12; socialism/PSOE/UGT in, 134, 203–4, 210, 221, 335, 488–89 n. 50, 489 n. 57; social unrest in, 79, 80, 86–87, 116, 132–34; sugar factories in, 47; wages in, 15. *See also* Cádiz, Córdoba; Jerez de la Frontera; Málaga; Seville
Andalusian Regional Labor Federation, 202
Anderson, R. D., 245–46
Anguiano, Daniel, 191–92, 193, 194, 195, 208, 209
Annual debacle in Morocco, 211, 232, 234, 263, 270
Anticlericalism, 139, 158, 285, 331, 477–78 n. 26
Anti-Fascist Militias Committee, 389
Antona, David, 342
Antonov-Ovsëenko, Vladimir, 403, 404
Aragon, 37, 78, 377; anarchism in, 143, 410; CNT in, 143, 291, 388, 393–94; collectivization in, 391, 393–94, 410; cooking oil made in, 47; labor conflicts in, 202, 291. *See also* Zaragossa
Aranda, Antonio, 376
Araquistáin, Luis, 125, 300, 306, 347, 373, 521 n. 95

Arbitration tribunals, 64, 66, 244–45, 273
Arboleya, Fr. Maximiliano, 111, 166, 168–70, 171, 286, 483 n. 45
Argentina, 282
Argentine Regional Labor Federation. *See* FORA
Arlegui, Col. Miguel, 233, 234, 235, 263, 265
Aróstegui, Julio, 535 n. 45
Arquer, Jordi, 129, 291
Artisans, 41, 42, 73, 285, 466 n. 8; in FRE, 78, 80–81, 461 n. 25; guilds for, 70; in Madrid, 39; as socialist, 96; in textile industry, 45
Artola, Miguel, 448 n. 39
Ascaso, Francisco, 236, 316, 371, 379
Asensio, Gen. José, 396, 397, 402
ASP (Popular Social Action), 161–62, 163, 167–68, 493 n. 90
Assassinations, 131, 229; anarchist, 311, 349; anarcho-syndicalist, 210; Cenetista, 383; Falangist, 366, 375; by Libres, 233; by Socialist Youth, 369. *See also* Terrorism
Assault Guards, 309, 317, 322, 375
Association, right of, 72, 239–40, 494 n. 8
Associations Law (1887), 239, 494 n. 8
Asturian coal mines, 32, 33, 37, 380; collective bargaining in, 110–11, 250, 255; communist influence in, 210; crisis/depression in, 253, 344, 354; financing of, 34; insurrection/rebellion in, 344, 354–55, 356, 358, 369; labor force of, 38–39, 108; labor organization in, 108, 109, 113, 253, 306, 353 (*see also* SMA); labor shortage in, 108–9, 113, 254; owners of, 169, 170, 176, 254, 255; socialist influence in, 108, 109–11, 112; strikes in, 31, 110, 111, 113, 121, 245, 255, 344, 353–55
Asturian Miners Union. *See* SMA
Asturias: agricultural disentailment in, 17; anarchism in, 109, 111; anarcho-syndicalism in, 262; *casas del pueblo* in, 111; Catholic social centers in, 169; CNT in, 353–54; coal mines in (*see* SMA); collectivization in, 391; communism in, 210; corporatism in, 344; emigration from, 9; food riots in, 116; illiteracy in, 473 n. 44; industrialization in, 7, 111; labor force in, 38–39, 57, 115; labor organization in, 105, 109, 110, 111, 112–13, 118, 119, 262 (*see also* SMA); labor un-

Viadiu, Josep, 184
Vicens Vives, Jaime, 19, 50, 258, 456
n. 55, 486 n. 20, 491–92 n. 79; on labor
force, 41, 44; on living conditions, 48,
116–17; on textile economy, 25–26; on
urban immigrants, 57–58
Vicent, Fr. Antonio, 150–51, 152, 154,
156, 171, 172
Vidarte, Juan Siméon, 359, 537 n. 55
Vidiella, Rafael, 466 n. 8, 515 n. 45
Vienna second and a half international,
209–10
Vignaux, Paul, 166
Vineyards, 116, 166–67, 178, 447–48
n. 32, 464 n. 45
Vizcaya: anarcho-syndicalism in, 280; Catholic unions in, 164; collective bargaining
in, 250; communism in, 280; emigration
to, 179; labor force in, 38, 42, 45, 115;
labor organization in, 118, 306, 459
n. 8, 469 n. 29; labor unrest in, 51, 113,
118, 207, 255, 418–19; metallurgy in,
33–36, 44–45, 122; mining in, 7, 32,
33–34, 51, 105, 106–7, 108, 114, 117,
121, 122, 144, 176, 242–43, 247, 250,
254, 344, 469 n. 24; PSOE/UGT/social-
ism in, 102, 103, 105–8, 118, 210,
221, 252, 280, 281, 488–89 n. 50; public works program in, 277; shipbuilding
in, 176–77, 344; SOV in, 165; strikes
in, 106–7, 108, 117, 144, 193, 194,
242–43, 245, 247, 353, 469 n. 24, 479
n. 35; terrorism in, 230; wages in, 56,
455–56 n. 47. *See also* Basque provinces;
Bilbao
Vizcayan Industry Center, 254
Vizcayan Metalworkers Federation, 122
Vizcayan Mineworkers Federation, 122
Voyard, André, 65–66

Wages: agricultural, 14, 15, 31, 305, 348,
447 n. 30; in Barcelona/Catalonia, 52,
55–56, 78; for children, 53–54, 91, 129,
260; CNT on, 366, 393; v. cost of living, 27, 54, 55, 56, 90, 117, 179–80,
182, 183–84, 189, 201, 211, 273; decline in, 276, 425; inflated, 305–6; in
Madrid, 51, 54, 55; for miners, 14, 31;
piecework v. day rate, 202; in Second
Republic, 305, 348, 523 n. 106; strikes
over, 118, 122, 127, 308; in textile industry, 24, 27, 91, 129; UGT on, 366,
393; in Valencia, 54; in Vizcaya, 55, 56,

455–56 n. 47; for women, 52, 53–54,
260, 276; in 1970s, 422
Welfare: role of Catholic organizations, 159,
164–65, 166–67, 173, 483 n. 40; state,
238–39
Wheat, 330
Winston, Colin M., 155, 161–62, 285,
502 n. 22, 506–7 n. 53
Women in labor force, 39, 67, 177; in agriculture, 42; in cottage industry, 45–46;
discriminated against, 53; as domestics,
43; illiteracy of, 53, 454–55 n. 38; infant
mortality affected by, 49; legislation for,
24, 27–28, 57, 60, 64, 66, 129, 156,
182, 239, 244, 276; rights of, 346, 455
n. 43; status of, 54, 55, 276; in textile
industry, 24, 27, 43, 52–53, 54, 91,
129, 199, 262; in unions, 182, 335;
wages for, 52, 53–54, 260, 276
Wool Textile Manufacturers Association,
179
Work Accident Law, 494–95 n. 11
Worker Patronages of St. Vincent de Paul,
164
Workers Alliance, 353–54
Workers and Peasants Bloc. *See* BOC
Workers Commissions. *See* CCOOs
Workers' Compensation Act, 65
Workers control, 300, 304, 363
Workers Federation of the Spanish Region.
See FTRE
Workers Marxist Unification party. *See*
POUM
Workers societies, 82, 83, 103, 131. *See
also* CADCI
Workers Solidarity. *See* SO
Working Class Atheneum, 82
Working conditions, 48–58, 453 n. 25,
455–56 n. 47; in Barcelona, 50–51, 57,
453–54 n. 28; in building construction
industry, 50, 68, 277; IRS on, 57; legislation for, 59, 64, 65, 68, 156, 239; in
Madrid, 57; of miners, 50, 57, 68, 106,
107, 251, 470 n. 31; strikes over, 67,
101–2, 111, 127, 130, 214, 215, 281;
in textile industry, 23–24, 57, 68; for
women and children, 57, 64, 65, 156,
182, 239; workday length and, 24, 57,
64, 65, 67, 68, 91–92, 101–2, 107,
111, 130, 156, 214, 215, 239, 250–51,
301; workweek and, 24, 57, 68, 92,
182, 301
Works councils, 304–5, 418, 419

ABOUT THE AUTHOR

Benjamin Martin is a writer and lecturer whose primary focus is contemporary Spanish political and labor developments. He has written for the *New Republic*, the *Nation*, and *Dissent*, as well as for other popular and academic publications. He is co-editor of *Labor Relations in Advanced Industrial Societies: Issues and Problems*.

Martin began his career as a factory worker and actively participated in the birth and early years of the Congress of Industrial Organizations. A founder in Chicago of the United Electrical, Radio and Machine Workers, he held a variety of posts with the union in the 1930s. He was a member of the national field staff of the International Union of Electrical, Radio and Machine Workers from 1949 to 1960 and an international representative of the United Steelworkers of America from 1960 to 1962. While on leave from his union post during the late 1950s to study Asian labor affairs under a Ford Foundation Fellowship grant, he served as labor columnist for the *Japan Times*. From 1966 to 1977, Martin was the senior labor specialist with the Department of State and, prior to that, he was a labor information officer with the U.S. Information Agency in Santiago, Chile. He directed the Spanish program as a senior associate with the Carnegie Endowment for International Peace from 1977 to 1979.